Developmentally Appropriate Practice

Curriculum and Development in Early Education

FOURTH EDITION

Carol Gestwicki

Central Piedmont Community College

WADSWORTH
CENGAGE Learning

Australia • Brazil • Japan • Korea • Mexico • Singapore • Spain • United Kingdom • United States

WADSWORTH
CENGAGE Learning™

Developmentally Appropriate Practice: Curriculum and Development in Early Education, 4e
Carol Gestwicki

Acquisition Editor: Christopher Shortt

Development Editor: Beth Kaufman

Assistant Editor: Caitlin Cox

Editorial Assistant: Linda Stewart

Associate Media Editor: Ashley Cronin

Marketing Manager: Kara Kindstrom Parsons

Marketing Communications Manager: Martha Pfeiffer

Art Director: Maria Epes

Print Buyer: Paula Vang

Permissions Editor: Mardell Glinski Schultz

Production Service: Pre-PressPMG

Photo Researcher: Pre-PressPMG

Cover Designer: Bartay Studio

Compositor: Pre-PressPMG

For product information and technology assistance, contact us at
Cengage Learning Customer & Sales Support, 1-800-354-9706

For permission to use material from this text or product,
submit all requests online at **cengage.com/permissions**
Further permissions questions can be emailed to
permissionrequest@cengage.com

Library of Congress Control Number: 2009934662

ISBN-13: 978-1-4283-5969-7

ISBN-10: 1-4283-5969-9

Wadsworth
10 Davis Drive, Belmont,
CA 94002
USA

Cengage Learning is a leading provider of customized learning solutions with office locations around the globe, including Singapore, the United Kingdom, Australia, Mexico, Brazil, and Japan. Locate your local office at:
international.cengage.com/region

Cengage Learning products are represented in Canada by Nelson Education, Ltd.

For your course and learning solutions, visit **academic.cengage.com**

Purchase any of our products at your local college store or at our preferred online store **www.ichapters.com**

Printed in the United States of America
1 2 3 4 5 6 7 11 10 09

CONTENTS

SECTION TWO

DEVELOPMENTALLY APPROPRIATE PHYSICAL ENVIRONMENTS / 125

CHAPTER 5

Developmentally Appropriate Physical Environments: For Infants / 126

CHAPTER 6

Developmentally Appropriate Physical Environments: For Toddlers / 144

CHAPTER 7

Developmentally Appropriate Physical Environments: For Preschoolers / 163

CHAPTER 8

Developmentally Appropriate Physical Environments: For Primary-Age Children / 192

SECTION FOUR

DEVELOPMENTALLY APPROPRIATE COGNITIVE/ LANGUAGE/LITERACY ENVIRONMENTS / 315

Guest Editorial by *John Holt* / 314

CHAPTER 13

Developmentally Appropriate Cognitive/ Language/Literacy Environments: For Infants / 316

CHAPTER 14

Developmentally Appropriate Cognitive/ Language/ Literacy Environments: For Toddlers / 337

CHAPTER 15

Developmentally Appropriate Cognitive/ Language/Literacy Environments: For Preschoolers / 357

CHAPTER 16

Developmentally Appropriate Cognitive/ Language/Literacy Environments: For Primary-Age Children / 394

PREFACE

THE GOALS OF THIS BOOK AND INTENDED AUDIENCE

Over the past several years, early childhood professionals have been enriched by a series of position statements on developmentally appropriate practice. These position statements have been issued by various professional early childhood organizations. In 1997, the National Association for the Education of Young Children (NAEYC) published a revised position statement on developmentally appropriate practice (Bredekamp and Copple, 1997). The most recent revision of the NAEYC position statement was published in November 2008 (Copple & Bredekamp, 2009).

Classroom teachers and pre-service students struggle to understand how the philosophy of developmentally appropriate practice translates into everyday decisions and actions in early childhood classrooms. This book is designed to help pre-service and in-service early childhood teachers as they try to implement the philosophy of developmentally appropriate practice every day—in their classrooms and with their students.

The ideas found in this book are practical and comprehensive, applicable to students and teachers within various early childhood courses such as developmentally appropriate practice, early childhood curriculum, best practices in early childhood education, and others. The book is also designed for those who do work or will work in a wide variety of private and public settings, and with diverse client populations. In sum, this book is intended for you, as a student, a new or experienced teacher, or any professional working with children in the schools, early childhood centers, family childcare homes, and Head Start, pre-kindergarten, kindergarten, or primary classrooms.

In addition, others are involved in the wider conversations about helpful practices in the early years. Administrators and decision-makers in the community also must gain clear understandings of positive learning environments for young children. Parents who are making choices for the care and education of their young children need to learn what good practice looks like, so they can make informed choices about classroom placement and also advocate for best practices in their children's schools.

A critical component of the philosophy of developmentally appropriate practice is the idea of *individual appropriateness*; that is, that no absolute standard can be set that precisely meets the needs of every individual. This principle also holds true for the particular teachers and programs that work to find their optimum functioning. So this book is intended as a guide for thoughtful consideration of classroom practices, not as an absolute prescription that would push every classroom mindlessly into the same mold. It is assumed and planned that the dialogue in the profession will continue, expanding our thought and our horizons. This book is offered in the hope that young children will be offered the best experiences that caring and knowledgeable adults can provide.

ORGANIZATION AND CONTENT

The fourth edition of *Developmentally Appropriate Practice* is organized into 16 chapters and four sections.

Each Section begins with Guest Editorials written by various luminaries in early childhood education, such as David Elkind and Caroline Pratt. These Editorials frame the discussion about the group of chapters in each Section.

In **Section One**, the concepts of developmentally appropriate practice are explored by introducing general principles that are made specific and concrete in subsequent chapters. Because play is at the heart of developmentally appropriate practice, this Section includes a chapter (2) that introduces the theory and research of play, and its contribution to development. Another introductory chapter (3) examines issues of curriculum and describes teacher roles in planning appropriate curriculum. Finally, this introductory section includes a chapter (4) that describes key curriculum approaches and considers how these models fit into the principles of developmentally appropriate practice.

After the general introduction, students are guided through **Sections Two, Three, and Four,** to examine developmentally appropriate physical environments, social/emotional environments, and cognitive/language/literacy environments. The idea of environments for developing creativity is included in considerations of physical environments, as well as throughout the social/emotional climate, and the kinds of learning experiences described in the cognitive/ language/literacy environments. "Environment" is used here to include comprehensively the materials, activities, arrangements, relationships, and interaction that adults provide in the classroom. In each of these sections, separate chapters are devoted to describing appropriate practice for infants, for toddlers, for preschoolers, and for primary-aged children. **Section Five** includes chapters that explore the process of making changes for teachers and for gaining support for these changes. In a change for this edition, this section is available only on the premium Web site, for advanced consideration.

For those instructors or students who prefer to use an age/stage rather than topic approach, the chapters on infancy can easily be designated for consecutive reading and discussion (e.g., Chapters 5, 9, and 13), then those on toddlers (Chapters 6, 10, and 14). Instructors also may prefer to discuss the various curriculum approaches after a thorough grounding in DAP. The author assumes that students who use this text have already been exposed to a child-development course, because the body of current child-development knowledge is beyond the scope of this book. However, both in the introductory chapters and where appropriate throughout, reference and/or summary of the necessary theoretical base is included. Whether students are at beginning levels or more advanced ones, the references and ideas for further study meet individual needs.

NEW TO THE FOURTH EDITION

The following is a list of key content revisions within the fourth edition. It is important to note that all chapters have been substantially revised to include the most current thinking about developmentally appropriate practices and practical issues.

- First and foremost, the text has been thoroughly revised and updated to reflect *the new NAEYC position statement on Developmentally Appropriate Practice (2009)*. Students will also find frequent references to other recent and important early childhood position statements.

- The text includes *a newly expanded chapter (4) on the most common educational models and curriculum used within early childhood education*, and how these models and curricula fit into the principles of developmentally appropriate practice. Waldorf education has been specially added to the chapter.

- Included in this fourth edition is a strong focus on *the continuing debate about the application of these DAP principles* for all children in all early childhood settings. Such debate enriches the dialogue, and will continue to enhance professional development and knowledge for those who follow the discussion.

- The fourth edition offers expanded coverage throughout on *cultural diversity issues related to developmentally appropriate practice*, such as cultural sensitivity to diverse child rearing practices.

- The new edition includes increased coverage of applying principles of developmentally appropriate practice to *working with children with special needs*.

- The new edition discusses *Early Learning Standards as developed by individual states*, as well as the implications of the *No Child Left Behind legislation*. These issues are discussed in several chapters. Professional standards are also referred to throughout.

- Information on the *most up-to-date brain research* is also included throughout the text.

- An *expanded discussion of play* has been added to Chapter 2. This coverage emphasizes the rich research that is being conducted on this subject, and the issues that surround the topic of play, including helping families understand its importance.

- The *chapter on planning for curriculum is substantially revised* to reflect current thinking about planning curriculum linked with assessment and learning standards.

- All *in-text bibliographies and references have been thoroughly updated* to demonstrate the most recent research and discussion within the early education field, as are the Suggestions for Further Reading and Study located on the premium Web site.

TEXT FEATURES

DEVELOPMENTALLY APPROPRIATE PRACTICE, Fourth Edition, offers students a rich collection of pedagogical tools for learning, study, and reflection:

Each chapter includes the following new and retained features:

1. **Chapter Opening Introductions** and **Learning Objectives**—These two features provide students with a brief overview of key chapter topics.

2. **Journal Reflection boxes (NEW)**—Recognizing the importance of teachers becoming reflective practitioners, these boxes provide opportunities for personal reflection throughout the text, in the hope that students will stop to consider their own experiences and ideas. These Journal Reflection boxes are also included on the premium Web site so they can be easily used by students and instructors.

3. **Cultural Considerations boxes (NEW)**—These boxes describe cultural issues or conflicts that may arise in typical classroom situations. Readers will have opportunities to consider ideas and circumstances from the others' viewpoint, and discover ways of finding common ground and compromise.

4. **Video Activity boxes (NEW)**—These video clip descriptions (actual clips housed on the text's premium Web site) with reflective questions will help students apply ideas and principles that they have read about within the text. The activities and questions may be used for individual assignments, or to stimulate class discussion.

5. **Real life photographs and vignettes**—Each chapter includes multiple photographs and vignettes about children and teachers within early childhood settings.

6. **What Would You Do When… boxes**—From questions and challenges from parents to requests from administrators, teachers are often placed in the position of having to interpret appropriate practices and responses to others. These very realistic situations and scenarios raise some of the everyday predicaments for teachers and help students learn how to solve problems and explain their work to others. These may often form the basis for important class discussion and individual reflection.

7. **Practical Applications boxes**—These handy boxes outline important teaching tips and best practices for early childhood educators.

8. **Chapter Summaries**—These brief reviews summarize the key concepts addressed within each chapter.

9. **Questions to Assess Learning of Chapter Objectives**—These questions at the end of each chapter help students and instructors assess that the key points of each chapter have been mastered.

10. **Think About It Activities**—The new edition offers these end of chapter activities for further study, which may be used for in-class or out-of-class assignments.

11. **Apply Your Knowledge Questions**—These questions at the end of each chapter help students apply and reflect on the principles in the chapter.

12. **Helpful Web sites**—This new feature recognizes the important role that technology plays in today's world in expanding resources for learning. Web addresses are included at the end of each chapter that will allow readers to further explore topics and organizations discussed in the text. The same links are also included on the premium Web site, chapter by chapter.

Note: The author and Cengage Learning affirm that the Web site URLs referenced herein are accurate at the time of printing. However, due to the fluid nature of the Internet, we cannot guarantee their accuracy for the life of this edition.

ANCILLARY MATERIALS TO ACCOMPANY DEVELOPMENTALLY APPROPRIATE PRACTICE

Premium Web site for students
www.cengage.com/login

The premium Web site includes two additional textbook chapters: one on the process of change (17) and the other about communication with families and communities about the principles of developmentally appropriate practice (18). The premium Web site also offers access to the TeachSource Videos, and other study tools and resources such as links to related sites for each chapter of the text, suggestions for further reading and study, tutorial quizzes, glossary/flashcards, reflection questions, reading lists, online journal activities, additional material not included in your text, and more. Go to www.cengage.com/login to register your student access code. If your textbook does not include an access code card, go to *www.ichapters .com* to obtain an access code.

ANCILLARIES FOR INSTRUCTORS

Instructor's Manual

The Instructor's Manual includes discussion topics and suggestions for classroom presentation and activities, ideas for assignments, multimedia resources, answers to review questions, and a test bank.

Premium Web site

The instructor area of the premium Web site offers access to password-protected resources such as an electronic version of the instructor's manual and PowerPoint® slides. Go to *www.cengage.com/login* to access the premium Web site.

PowerLecture w/ExamView

This one-stop digital library and presentation tool includes preassembled Microsoft® PowerPoint® lecture slides by Carol Gestwicki. In addition to a full Instructor's Manual and Test Bank, PowerLecture also includes ExamView® testing software with all the test items from the printed Test Bank in electronic format, enabling you to create customized tests in print or online, and all of your media resources in one place including an image library with graphics from the book itself and the TeachSource Videos.

WebTutor Toolbox for Blackboard and WebCT

With WebTutor™ Toolbox for WebCT™ or Blackboard®, jumpstart your course with customizable, rich, text-specific content within your Course Management System. Go to webtutor.cengage.com to learn more.

Professional Enhancement Text

This resource will help beginning early childhood professionals with resources that can be used in the classroom and for professional reference.

FEATURES GUIDE

Cultural Considerations

Practical Implications

Journal Reflection

Video Activity

ACKNOWLEDGMENTS

Many conversations and experiences contribute to a work such as this. More than 30 years of college classroom discussions with new and experienced teachers have shaped my questions and assumptions, and I am grateful to students who have pushed me to find better ways to explain. I have been fortunate to have had colleagues all along the way to support and stimulate my growth as an educator. In particular, I want to thank the late Betty High Rounds, a valued friend and colleague who first gave me the idea, then gave helpful feedback on chapters in an early draft, and who provided both the excitement and many materials on Reggio Emilia. I also appreciate the thoughtful comments of reviewers:

Reviewers of the Third Edition

Pamela Chibucos, MS
Owens Community College
Toledo, OH

Barbara Nilsen, Ed.D.
Broome Community College
Binghamton, NY

Karen Menke Paciorek, Ph.D.
Eastern Michigan University
Ypsilanti, MI

Karen Ray, M.Ed.
Wake Technical Community College
Raleigh, NC

Wenju Shen, Ed.D.
Valdosta State University Valdosta, GA

Reviewers of the Fourth Edition

Rose Weiss
Phylis J Green Early Childhood Center,
Director

Lindsey Russo
Teachers College, Columbia Univeristy

Bridget Murray
Henderson Community College

Karen Menke Paciorek
Eastern Michigan University

JoAnn Brager
West River Head Start, Vice President

Pamela Chibucos
Owens Community College

Susan Gilbert
National Univeristy

Radhika Viruru
Texas A&M University

Barbara Nilsen
Broome Community College

Wenju Shen
Valdosta State University

Karen Ray
Wake Technical Community College

And of course, much love and gratitude to my family—who have always been developmentally appropriate and willing to ignore the many shortcomings a work such as this produces. This edition also notes that my granddaughters, Lila and Rose, are now school-aged children—amazing!

I dedicate this edition again particularly to the memory of Betty High Rounds. It is when I am considering current issues in early childhood education that I most miss the chance to talk with her. *Note to the Reader:* I am well aware that a work of this kind could always be larger and more comprehensive; it is my assumption that a text such as this might be used in several courses, covering the age spans. It may well supplement development texts and courses. I have endeavored to convey the ongoingness of the discussion on developmental appropriateness. The reader is invited to contact the author through the publisher with questions, comments, and suggestions related to these materials.

ABOUT THE AUTHOR

Carol Gestwicki was an instructor in the early childhood education program at Central Piedmont Community College in Charlotte, North Carolina for more than 30 years. Her teaching responsibilities included supervising students in classroom situations as they attempted to put these principles into practice. Earlier in her career, she worked with children and families in a variety of community agencies and schools in Toronto, New York, New Jersey, and Namibia (South West Africa). She received her M.A. from Drew University. She has been an active member of NAEYC for many years, including making numerous presentations at state and national conferences. Other publications include more than two dozen articles on child development and family issues, and scripts and design of 14 audiovisual instructional programs. The author has three other books on topics in early education published by Thomson Delmar Learning: *The Essentials of Early Education* (1997); *Home, School, and Community Relations: A Guide to Working with Parents,* 7E (2010); and *Authentic Childhood: Exploring Reggio Emilia in the Classroom,* with Susan Fraser, (2002). Since her retirement from full time teaching, she continues to teach early childhood courses online at Central Piedmont Community College and writes a regular column titled "Grandma Says" for Growing Child Publications.

Developmentally Appropriate Practice

Curriculum and Development in Early Education

GUEST EDITORIAL

by David Elkind

Dr. David Elkind is Professor and Chair of the Department of Child Development at Tufts University. An expert on child and adolescent cognitive and social development, Dr. Elkind has written extensively about some of his concerns regarding healthy development in today's world. Some of his well-known works include The Hurried Child: Growing Up Too Fast, Too Soon *(2001, 3rd Edition);* Ties That Stress: The New Family Imbalance *(1995); and* Miseducation: Preschoolers at Risk *(1988), from which the below excerpt is taken.*

What is happening in the United States today is truly astonishing. In a society that prides itself on its preference for facts over hearsay, on its openness to research, and on its respect for "expert" opinion, parents, educators, administrators, and legislators are ignoring the facts, the research, and the expert opinion about how young children learn and how best to teach them.

All across the country, educational programs intended for school- aged children are being appropriated for the education of young children. . . . Many . . . kindergartens have introduced curricula, including work papers, once reserved for first-grade children. And, in books addressed to parents, a number of writers are encouraging parents to teach infants and young children reading, math, and science.

When we instruct children in academic subjects, or in swimming, gymnastics, or ballet, at too early an age, we miseducate them; we put them at risk for short-term stress and long-term personality damage for no useful purpose. There is no evidence that such early instruction has lasting benefits, and considerable evidence that it can do lasting harm.

Why, then, are we engaging in such unhealthy practices on so vast a scale? Like all social phenomena, the contemporary miseducation of large numbers of infants and young children derives from the coming together of multiple and complex social forces that both generate and justify these practices. One thing is sure: Miseducation does not grow out of established knowledge about what is good pedagogy for infants and young children. Rather, the reason must be sought in the changing values, size, structure, and style of American families; in the residue of the 1960s effort to ensure equality of education for all groups; and in the new status, competitive, and computer pressures experienced by parents and educators in the eighties.

While miseducation has always been with us—we have always had pushy parents—today it has become a social norm. If we do not wake up to the potential danger of these harmful practices, we may do serious damage to a large segment of the next generation. (Elkind, 1988, pp. 3–4)

Defining Developmentally Appropriate Practice

INTRODUCTION

In Chapter 1, we will explore what is meant by developmentally appropriate practice. The chapter examines the general history of the position statements, definitions, understandings, and implications of developmentally appropriate practice. We will then consider a theoretical understanding of play, because rich play experiences form the heart of programs using appropriate practices. And, because teachers create environments and construct experiences that enrich this play, we will consider teachers' roles in planning a curriculum. The final chapter in this section explores many commonly used curriculum approaches, considering developmentally appropriate practice. This introductory section will lay the foundation for later chapters when we translate principles into action.

Defining Developmentally Appropriate Practice

Seth Adams and Maria Jimenez are two of the nation's millions of preschoolers who will begin attending early childhood programs this year. Seth is entering the two-year-old class at Busy Learners Day Care Center, and Maria is enrolled in the half-day program at Happy Days Nursery School. Both sets of parents looked at several programs in their communities before making a choice.

Seth's parents chose his center because of its philosophy and the activities they saw during a visit. The center handbook states:

> *We believe young children are capable of serious learning, so our day is arranged to provide opportunities for your child to gain the important academic skills that will gain him/her entrance to the school of your choice. Our curriculum includes beginning reading skills, with emphasis on phonics, and introductory math activities. Before your child leaves our two-year-old class, he/she will be able to recite the alphabet and recognize many letter sounds, name the shapes and colors, and count to 20. Our Spanish teacher spends an hour a week with the two-year-old class. The children's day is spent in large- and small-group instruction by our competent staff. We believe that the learning potential of the preschool years is too great to waste on play.*

The Adams' visit to the classroom found young children sitting quietly at tables coloring a picture of a dog and a letter D. The work from the day before was hanging on the walls; the children had pasted the precut outline of a dog. The teachers seemed competent and completely in control as they gave instructions to the toddlers. This school matched Seth's parents' concept of what a school should be.

Maria's parents also chose their school based on its philosophy and their visit. The handbook states:

> *We believe that children should be actively involved in play to develop the whole child. Teachers prepare a variety of interesting choices for children each day, carefully designing an environment for active learning. Children make their own discoveries about the world, as they are able to explore materials and learn to play with other children, with the supervision and support of interested teachers.*

A visit to this classroom showed groups of children busy all around the room. One child painted at an easel. Three were building with blocks in an area where another was pushing a truck. Three children were talking as they dressed in grown-up finery. Another group was helping the teacher mix play dough at a table. There was a lot of conversation.

Both sets of parents were confident that they had made the best decision for their child's entry into the world of school. Yet it seems obvious to any observer that the children in these two programs will encounter very different experiences. The philosophies stated by the programs seem to claim very different methods of educating young children. How do we reconcile such differing views on how to appropriately educate and nurture the development of young children?

Programs as different as those of Seth and Maria exist everywhere. The differences extend downward into the nursery and upward into the elementary school classroom. In many centers and schools, the statements on developmentally appropriate practice appear to have had no impact or recognition at all. This may be due, in part, to the human tendency to avoid recognizing ideas or information that conflict with past experience or present comfort levels. This book is intended to help students, professionals, parents, and concerned community members consider the definitions and implications of the developmental appropriateness of programs for children from birth through age eight. Together we will consider ideas that can help translate theoretical statements into actions that are applicable in particular situations.

The debate is not new, nor is it finished, but it has entered a new stage since the publication in the 1980s and 1990s of several position statements about developmentally appropriate practice by several major educational organizations in this country, up to the most recent revised position statement of 2009. With the twenty-first-century national conversations about how best to ensure that "no child is left behind," early childhood educators and parents continue to try to find the best learning environments and practices for children from birth through age eight. In this book, many aspects of these conversations will continue.

First, let us consider what is meant by developmentally appropriate practice.

LEARNING OBJECTIVES

After completing this chapter, students should be able to

- define developmentally appropriate practice.
- describe the essential components of developmentally appropriate practice.
- identify twelve **developmental principles** relevant to understanding developmentally appropriate practice.
- discuss ten positive interpretations of misunderstandings related to developmentally appropriate practice.
- describe concerns regarding inappropriate educational experiences for young children.

BACKGROUND AND HISTORY OF THE GUIDELINES FOR DEVELOPMENTALLY APPROPRIATE PRACTICE

The first definitive position on developmentally appropriate practice was adopted by the National Association for the Education of Young Children (NAEYC) in 1987. With the development of NAEYC's **accreditation** system (the National Academy of Early Childhood Programs), it had become obvious that a more specific definition of developmentally appropriate practice was needed. Otherwise, statements like "using developmentally appropriate activities or materials" were too open to varieties of interpretation. That first publication was soon followed by a statement expanded to include specifics for programs serving children from birth through age eight and outlines of both appropriate and inappropriate practices (Bredekamp, 1987). The Association for Childhood Education International (ACEI) published an article corroborating the importance of play in 1988 (Isenberg & Quisenberry, 1988), and the National Association of Elementary School Principals (NAESP) elaborated its own standards for quality programs for young children in 1990 (NAESP, 1990). The National Association of State Boards of Education (NASBE) followed with statements as part of the report of the National Task Force on School Readiness (NASBE, 1991). NAEYC has since published jointly with the National Association of Early Childhood Specialists in State Departments of Education (NAECS/SDE) a position statement, "Guidelines for Appropriate Curriculum Content and Assessment in Programs Serving Children Ages 3 Through 8," Volume 1 (Bredekamp & Rosegrant, 1992) and Volume 2 (1995). A more recent statement on curriculum, assessment, and program evaluation was issued jointly by NAEYC and the NAECS/SDE in 2003. Other recent position statements include

"Learning to Read and Write: Developmentally Appropriate Practices for Young Children," by the International Reading Association (IRA) and NAEYC (1998), and "Early Childhood Mathematics: Promoting Good Beginnings," by NAEYC and the National Council of Teachers of Mathematics (NAEYC, 2002). Other specific position statements on early learning standards; school readiness; responding to linguistic and cultural diversity; unacceptable trends in kindergarten entry and placement; and technology and young children, ages three through eight, will be discussed in the relevant chapters later in the text and can all be read at the NAEYC Web site listed at the end of the chapter.

In the field of early intervention and early childhood special education, the Division for Early Childhood (DEC) of the Council for Exceptional Children recommended practices in a DEC document published in 1993 and more recently updated in a book in 2005 (Sandall, Hemmeter, Smith, &, McLean, 2005).

The conversations continued. In 1997, the first major revision of NAEYC's position statement and guidelines for developmentally appropriate practice appeared—"Developmentally Appropriate Practice in Early Childhood Programs, Revised Edition" (Bredekamp & Copple, 1997). The preface of that publication acknowledged that the changing knowledge base derived from both research and the continuing conversations among professionals would demand a review process and revised document every ten years or so. The most recent position statement was published in November 2008 (Copple & Bredekamp, 2009).

Many early childhood professionals, parents, and communities have been grateful for the guidelines as they endeavor to chart the path in ever-changing territory. New trends and concerns encountered in the early childhood field include

- the ever-increasing numbers of infants and toddlers being cared for in groups.
- the inclusion of children with special needs.
- the increasing numbers of linguistically and culturally diverse children and families to be served.
- the increasing emphasis on academic assessment and readiness requirements for kindergartens and even **prekindergartens**.
- the establishment of prekindergarten classrooms within many school systems.
- the establishment of **early learning standards** in most states, impelled by the Good Start/Grow Smart Initiative.
- the pressure to achieve in standardized tests in the primary years and the demands of *No Child Left Behind* legislation.

The third edition of the NAEYC position statement outlines the current context in which early childhood programs operate and in which the statement is made. The critical issues of the current context are defined as: the urgency to reduce learning gaps to enable all children to succeed; the necessity of bringing prekindergarten and elementary education together; and the importance of recognizing teacher decision making for educational effectiveness (Copple & Bredekamp, 2009).

Since the publication of the first position statement, early childhood professionals have continued to question and debate developmentally appropriate practice. Jipson suggested that developmentally appropriate practices ignore issues of cultural variation when determining what constitutes "appropriate" (Jipson, 1991). Delpit shared the concern that the statement does not address the specific needs of African-American children, citing Eurocentric bias (Delpit, 1988, 2006). Mallory and New further discussed the idea of cultural validity and questioned the principles when related to children with disabilities (Mallory & New, 1994). Kessler warned that professionals should be wary of prescriptions for practice based on the perspectives of a particular group of individuals and suggested the multiplicity of views of the purposes of education (Kessler, 1991). Walsh suggested the consensus about child development is more apparent than real and ignores important alternative perspectives on learning and development (Walsh, 1991). Wien suggested that recent critiques fall into two categories: those that see the dominant culture as projecting norms onto all children and are blind to other cultural values and norms, and those that see a lack of inclusion of a range of practices, such as direct instruction, that are considered necessary for all children (Wien, 1995). A series of published dialogues between two early childhood professionals exemplifies the nature of the debate over whether or not developmentally appropriate practice is for everyone (see Charlesworth, 1998a, 1998b; and Lubeck, 1998a, 1998b). The 1997 position statement recognized the need to clarify and address some of the concerns, as well as to "express NAEYC's position more clearly so that energy is not wasted in unproductive debate about apparent rather than real differences of opinion" (Bredekamp & Copple, 1997, p. 4). Yet the most recent position statement recognizes still more issues confronting the profession, and continues to encourage discussion and debate, noting the importance of such dialogue for the continuing growth of professional knowledge in the field.

One of the original purposes of the position statement was to have a clear understanding of appropriate practices that could be used by programs seeking accreditation by NAEYC. Certainly, the diversity of programs that have been accredited points to the broad principles of developmentally appropriate practice that can be applied in unique programs and situations.

All these issues raise concerns about how best to serve the needs of developing children. The position statements help us make judgments and inform our decisions. It is important for all students and professionals to be familiar with these position statements, especially the most recent NAEYC publication (Copple & Bredekamp, 2009), and they should be part of your reading and professional library. The NAEYC publications form the basis of the principles that lie behind this book (see Figure 1-1).

Figure 1-1
NAEYC position statements frame the dialogue about developmentally appropriate practice.

WHAT IS THE POSITION STATEMENT ON DEVELOPMENTALLY APPROPRIATE PRACTICE?

The NAEYC position statement on developmentally appropriate practice offers a rationale for the statement and a discussion of the critical issues and current context in early education.

NAEYC recognizes that every day, early childhood practitioners make many decisions, keeping in mind the identified goals for children's learning and development, and planning intentional strategies to help children achieve those outcomes (Copple & Bredekamp, 2009). "The core of developmentally appropriate practice lies in this intentionality, in the knowledge practitioners consider when they are making decisions, and in their always aiming for goals that are both challenging and achievable for children" (Copple & Bredekamp, 2009, p. 9).

The hallmark of developmentally appropriate practice is "not based on what we think might be true or what we want to believe about young children. Developmentally appropriate practice is informed by what we know from theory and literature about how children develop and learn" (Copple & Bredekamp, 2009, p. 10). In a later section of this chapter, we will consider the set of principles of child development and learning that inform decisions about developmentally appropriate practice.

The position statement goes on to present guidelines in five interrelated dimensions of early childhood program practice.

Figure 1-2

The position statement gives guidelines for five interrelated dimensions of early childhood program practice.

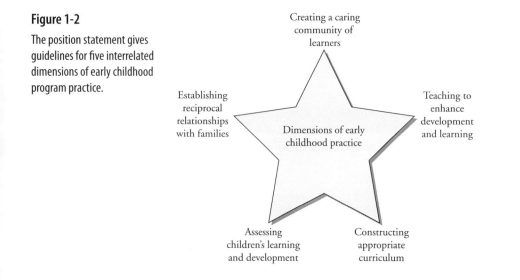

1. Creating a caring community of learners, within the context of relationships in the classroom
2. Teaching to enhance development and learning, with a consideration of teacher roles and strategies to support children's learning processes
3. Constructing appropriate curriculum, with attention to both content and strategies
4. Assessing children's learning and development
5. Establishing reciprocal relationships with families (see Figure 1-2)

Although not part of the position statement, examples of appropriate and contrasting practices and strategies for implementation in relation to each of these dimensions are given for infants and toddlers, for children ages three through five, for kindergarten children, and for children ages six through eight.

Additional comments in the position statement relate to the perception that the position statement was suggesting "either/or" **polarities** in thinking. Out of this criticism came the suggestion that our thinking should include the complex responses such as "both/and," because often two approaches are developmentally sound and work best in combination; thus teachers and parents need not choose one method over the other.

The last section delineates supportive policies and resources for implementing developmentally appropriate early childhood programs.

This most recent position statement reflects even further progress in the complex thinking and decision making that will inform practices for excellence in early education programs.

Developmentally Appropriate Practice—Further Definition

Developmentally appropriate practice refers to applying child development knowledge in making thoughtful and appropriate decisions about early childhood program practices—the understanding that "best practice is based on knowledge—not on assumptions—of how children learn and develop" (Copple & Bredekamp, 2009, p. xii). Everything that has been learned through research and formulated into theory about how children develop and learn at various ages and stages and in particular contexts is used to create learning environments that match their abilities and developmental tasks. This means that developmentally appropriate practice is based only on what is presently known and understood about children. It is not based on what adults wish children were like, hope they will be like, or even surmise they might be like. Nor is it based totally on future goals.

Developmentally appropriate practice is based on the accumulation of data and facts of what children are like. Developmentally appropriate practice "is not a curriculum; it is not a rigid set of standards that dictate practice. Rather, it is a framework, a philosophy, or an approach to working with young children" (Bredekamp & Rosegrant, 1992, p. 4). This is important to understand at the outset. Those concerned about narrowing the standards of good practice until all programs look the same and do the same things need to realize that no such intention exists. Rather, the intention is to focus philosophically on what we know about children and what we can learn about individual children and their families as a basis for decision making.

To translate knowledge of child development into the practical implications for nurturing and educating children, adults have to make many decisions. The deciding question when designing program curricula and formulating plans is, "How does this fit with what we know about children?" If our practice complements and accommodates our knowledge of children, then the decision is based on developmentally appropriate practice. If it is not compatible, then the practice should be questioned, examined, and likely changed.

The clear implication is for early childhood practitioners to be steeped in child development knowledge. Without that background, it is too easy for students, teachers, and caregivers to fall back on making decisions based only on vague notions that are part personal values, part memories, part expediency, and part images of desirable future behavior. If you have not completed basic child development courses and/or reading, that is an important place to start before attempting to plan and evaluate quality programs for young children. This book briefly reviews pertinent developmental knowledge to remind readers of the theoretical basis for the suggested actions in the classroom.

Obviously, child development knowledge alone will not give practitioners all the answers they need to plan programs and curricula for young children. Educational programs are products of decisions about curriculum content (what children will learn), learning processes (how children will learn), instructional strategies (how teachers will teach), and **assessment** methods (how to know what children have learned and how to plan for the future). Decisions are made on the basis of child development knowledge and also on the basis of family, community, and cultural values and priorities. Finding the correct balance between professionals' knowledge and parental and community expectations is an important component of the philosophy of developmental appropriateness.

As the NAEYC position statement reminds, three important kinds of information and knowledge form the basis of professional decision making.

1. What is known about child development and learning—knowledge of age-related human characteristics that permits general predictions about what experiences are likely to best promote children's learning and development. Understanding child development and learning allows teachers to know what children of a particular age group will typically be like, what they typically will and won't be capable of, and how they will best learn and develop. Such knowledge will allow teachers to make initial decisions about environment, materials, activities, and interactions. Child development knowledge is most useful for helping teachers understand how children learn so that the learning environment can present experiences that are both achievable and challenging.

2. What is known about each child as an individual, to help teachers be able to adapt for and be responsive to individual variation. By observing, interacting, considering children's work, and talking with families, teachers learn the individual uniqueness of each child within a group, with particular life experiences, strengths, interests, and approaches to learning. Individual children have followed their own patterns of development, and the position statement demands a definition of developmental appropriateness that is responsive to every child's individuality. That individuality is related to both **genetic** and **experiential** factors, including the culture and context in which the child lives. As teachers support the growth and development of all children, they must use everything they can learn about each child, including individual learning styles and preferences, interests, personality and **temperament**, abilities and disabilities, challenges, and difficulties. Such knowledge allows

teachers and programs to support the development of all children fully, including those with **disabilities** or **developmental delays**. The perspective of responding to individual children prevents viewing differences as deficits. Responding to children as individuals is fundamental to developmentally appropriate practice.

3. What is known about the social and cultural contexts in which children live, including the values, expectations, and behaviors of their homes and communities that must be understood to ensure that learning experiences are meaningful, relevant, and respectful to the participating children and their families (Copple & Bredekamp, 2009, pp. 9–10).

One of the major differences between the first position statement on developmentally appropriate practice and the 1997 and 2009 revisions is that the latter recognize the role of the cultural context in which development and learning occur. In the first statement, cultural differences were considered one of the dimensions of individual variation. But group cultural differences are now recognized as separate from individual differences; that is, at the same time individuals develop with personal histories, they also develop within a cultural context that influences behavioral expectations shared within a group. **Culture** consists of values, rules, and expectations for behavior that are passed on within families and communities, both explicitly and implicitly. Within contemporary society, children and their families form distinct cultural and linguistic groups that must be recognized with sensitivity and respect by classroom teachers. When the importance of culture in children's development is not recognized, problems can result for the children (see Figure 1-3).

One set of problems comes when incongruent demands are made on children by home and school. Other difficulties come when cultural or linguistic differences are treated as deficits in the context of the school, instead of being recognized as strengths or capabilities. In this instance, children's self-esteem may be seriously undermined and their competence underestimated. The position statement's addition of the cultural context as one of the important factors in making decisions about the care and education of young children is important.

Three dimensions—knowledge of age-related developmental information about how children learn; knowledge of each child's abilities, characteristics, and need for support; and knowledge of the cultural context from which each child comes—must be given attention when planning truly developmentally appropriate programs. As teachers make complex decisions for classrooms, they will find that the decisions they make one year may be quite different from those made the next year as a result of changing circumstances and people. Thus, the one fear expressed by those

Figure 1-3

Developmentally appropriate practice emphasizes the importance of recognizing the influence of culture and home experiences on each child's development.

whose understanding of developmentally appropriate practices is limited—the fear that the position statements will result in creating uniform programs that all look alike—could never be realized.

When making appropriate decisions for the care and education of young children, it is essential for adults to have an attitude of respect. This attitude allows adults to accept children's developmental behaviors and differences without wanting to change them or hurry them on to a later stage of maturity. Respect demands that teachers recognize and accept the diverse backgrounds from which children come and the contributions of their families. (Diverse backgrounds may include differences in family structure and experiences, racial or ethnic heritage, community lifestyles and traditions, socioeconomic background, special needs related to physical or mental conditions, and much more.) Respect demands that teachers and families continue a dialogue of negotiation in making decisions for the benefit of the children. Respect for the construction of knowledge allows adults to have faith in children's capacity to develop and change in their own ways, in their own time. Respect demands that adults search for developmentally compatible answers in each particular situation, not just move around solutions that have seemed to "work" with other groups. The attitude of respect for developmental knowledge allows early childhood professionals to feel unpressured in the face of questions about proving accountability. They know that curiosity, experience, support, and appropriate instruction ultimately move children on to increased knowledge and skills, given an environment that supports appropriately and does not thwart (see Figure 1-4).

Figure 1-4
Curiosity and experience help move children on to new skills and knowledge.

To summarize the discussion up to this point, developmentally appropriate practice is a philosophy of making decisions related to children's programs based on child development knowledge. Professionals base their knowledge of age appropriateness on research and recognized theory, and do their own research to learn what is also individually appropriate for each child in their care. The standards recognize that culture provides strong determinants of children's behavior and therefore requires decision making that is responsive to that dimension. Respect governs teachers' interactions with children and their families in searching for the best responses. An understanding of development and of the interrelated factors that influence growth and learning is critical to making developmentally appropriate decisions.

BASIC PRINCIPLES OF DEVELOPMENT

Developmentally appropriate practice is based on the knowledge of how children develop and learn. All early childhood teachers must understand what occurs in the first eight years of life and how best to support that growth and development. An ever-growing knowledge base comprises the foundation of child development courses. In its position statement, NAEYC offers twelve principles distilled from decades of research, study, theory, and practice. These principles are restated briefly here as we consider practice based on developmental knowledge. (All these principles are drawn from the third edition of the NAEYC position statement in Copple & Bredekamp, 2009, pp. 10–16);

1. **All the domains of development and learning—physical, social, emotional, and cognitive—are important, and they are closely interrelated. Children's development and learning in one domain influence and are influenced by what takes place in other domains.**

    What is occurring in development in one **domain** can both limit and facilitate development in other domains. A program that strives to nurture development optimally supports all domains as having equal importance. All learning experiences are recognized as integrated opportunities for growth, instead of separate skill or content entities. The emphasis on one domain only, such as the **cognitive,** is bound to upset the interrelationship among the various domains. Decisions about comprehensive curriculum content and teaching strategies must be made with this principle in mind.

2. **Many aspects of children's learning and development follow well-documented sequences, with later abilities, skills, and knowledge building on those already acquired.**

   Study of child development reveals fairly predictable patterns of growth and development during the first nine years, with individual variation in manifestation of changes and related cultural meaning. Understanding the behaviors and abilities associated with typical development provides a general framework for adults in recognizing usual growth patterns, as well as knowing how best to support children's optimum learning and challenge. Knowing the sequence of learning specific concepts and skills that build on prior knowledge and skills helps teachers make appropriate curriculum decisions. Knowing the value of early steps in the **sequence** also helps adults resist the pressure to provide less appropriate experiences before learning foundations have been laid. Development cannot continue well when children are pushed to skip or hurry through earlier stages. Children need the time to proceed through the sequence.

3. **Development and learning proceed at varying rates from child to child, as well as at uneven rates across different areas of a child's individual functioning.**

   Comparing the development of individuals of similar **chronological** ages is impossible and dangerous. Each child has a pattern and pace of development unique to the individual, with factors such as **heredity,** health, individual temperament and personality, learning style, experiences, and family and cultural backgrounds creating enormous differences. Rigid expectations for age-related group norms conflict with principles that demand individual support of particular strengths, needs, and interests (see Figure 1-5).

4. **Development and learning result from a dynamic and continuous interaction of biological maturation and experience.**

   Development is the result of the interaction between the growing child and the child's social and physical environments. Genetic potential for healthy growth may be impacted

Figure 1-5

Each child's rate of development is unique, based on factors of heredity, health, family experiences, learning style, and temperament.

by inadequate nutrition in the early years, for example. Inherited temperament shapes and is shaped by interactions with others. It is not nature versus nurture—it is nature *and* nurture.

5. **Early experiences have profound effects, both cumulative and delayed, on a child's development and learning; and optimal periods exist for certain types of development and learning to occur.**

   Both positive and negative effects result from repeated experiences early in the lives of young children, and these effects have implications for later development. For example, children given the opportunity to develop social skills through play with peers in the preschool years usually develop confidence and competence in their social relations with others. This allows them to enter confidently into later peer relationships as they begin primary school and to enter group learning situations with considerably more ease than children lacking those earlier social experiences. Times of readiness for optimal learning occur in the early years and need to be taken advantage of in planning curricular experiences; for example, growing **neurobiological** evidence indicates that the social and sensorimotor experiences of the first years affect brain development, with lasting implications for children's learning.

6. **Development proceeds toward greater complexity, self-regulation, and symbolic or representational capacities.**

   Children's functioning becomes increasingly complex, in language, physical movement, problem solving, social interaction, and every other domain. Learning in the early years proceeds from physical, **sensorimotor** understanding to **symbolic** knowledge. Programs recognizing this developmental principle provide firsthand experiences in which children may extend their behavioral knowledge and then provide media and materials that allow children to represent their symbolic knowledge and growing understanding of concepts.

7. **Children develop best when they have secure, consistent relationships with responsive adults and opportunities for positive relationships with peers.**

   Warm, nurturing relationships with responsive adults are necessary for many important areas of children's development. Attachment to parents and primary caregivers is positively correlated with aspects of development that include language and communication, self-regulation, cooperation, peer relationships, and positive identity. Social and emotional competence is a necessity for success in later school experiences.

8. **Development and learning occur in and are influenced by multiple social and cultural contexts.**

   Children's development is best understood within the context of their family, then their school community, and finally the larger community. These separate contexts are interrelated, and all influence the developing child. Children are capable of learning to function in more than one cultural or linguistic context when supported respectfully. Children should be able to add new cultural and language experiences without giving up on the contexts with which they began. Recent knowledge helps us understand what can be lost when children's home languages and culture are not respected and reinforced in the early education setting.

9. **Always mentally active in seeking to understand the world around them, children learn in a variety of ways; a wide range of teaching strategies and interactions are effective in supporting all these kinds of learning.**

   Key principles of developmentally appropriate practice are based on the work of theorists such as Piaget and Vygotsky and those who followed their work, about whom you will

Figure 1-6

Knowledge is constructed through interaction with people, materials, and experiences.

read later in this book. They view intellectual development as occurring by a process of **constructivism** through interaction with other people, materials, and experiences (see Figure 1-6). Young children learn about the world from family members, teachers, peers and older children, and the ever-present media.

As children form and test their own hypotheses about how the world works, their thought processes and mental structures undergo continual revision. Appropriate classrooms create environments that provide the materials and interaction needed for such constructions. Teaching strategies support children's active learning and rely less on direct transmission of knowledge that young children have not created themselves.

10. **Play is an important vehicle for developing self-regulation as well as promoting language, cognition, and social competence.**

Play is the optimum context in which children can actively construct their knowledge of the world. Play "allows children to stretch their boundaries to the fullest in their imagination, language, interaction, and self-regulation as well as to practice their newly acquired skills" (Copple & Bredekamp, 2009, p. 18). The position statement goes on to declare that research shows the links between play and foundational capacities such as memory, self-regulation, oral language abilities, social skills, and success in school.

Understanding fully what play is and how it supports development of the whole child is such an important aspect of developmentally appropriate practice that we will deal with it more fully in Chapter 2.

11. **Development and learning advance when children are challenged to achieve at a level just beyond their current mastery, and also when they have many opportunities to practice newly acquired skills.**

Children's images of themselves as successful learners result from experiences in which they can succeed most of the time. Thus, teachers have an important role in identifying children's growing competencies and interests and in matching curriculum accordingly, setting challenging, achievable goals for children. In addition, children can learn when experiences are just above their present abilities, especially when supportive adults and more competent peers collaborate to help children stretch to achieve more complex levels of skill and understanding. We will talk more about this process, known as **scaffolding**, later.

12. **Children's experiences shape their motivation and approaches to learning, such as persistence, initiative, and flexibility; in turn, these dispositions and behaviors affect their learning and development.**

"Approaches to learning" has been identified as one aspect of school readiness. The emphasis here is on the *how* instead of the *what* of learning, and involves children's feelings such as pleasure and motivation for learning, and their behavior while learning, with aspects such as persistence, flexibility, attention, and self-regulation. Children's experiences in their families and early education programs influence their approaches to learning. Early childhood staff in turn can influence these as they strengthen their relationships with children and work with their families, and as they select effective curriculum and teaching methods.

A careful study of these twelve principles will indicate **interrelationships** between them. These basic principles are the important ideas that influence adults as they make decisions about their practices. In practice, it is important to state that nothing is so clear-cut as to be either/or: either child-initiated or adult-directed; either process-oriented or product-oriented. The variables are not meant to be absolutes—the good versus the bad. Developmentally appropriate practice demands that a balance is found, including a balance that each teacher finds compatible with personal experience and values. Many programs include practices that are somewhere along a **continuum** between the two poles. Some include practices that are developmentally appropriate, along with others that are less appropriate. The goal of developmentally appropriate practice is to examine all aspects of programs for children to determine whether actions support healthy overall development. (See Figure 1-7.)

CULTURAL CONSIDERATION

The Importance of Cultural Awareness

"During this new century, children of traditionally underrepresented groups—often called minorities—will constitute a new majority within the United States. Currently African Americans, Latinos, Asian Americans, and Native Americans constitute one third of the U.S. population. It is projected that within 50 years, they will account for more than half! . . . As families become more diverse, child and family professionals must be prepared to meet their unique needs" (Trawick-Smith, 2006, p. 11).

Part of the preparation of every early childhood professional must be the attitudes and skills necessary to communicate and work effectively across cultures.

Figure 1-7

Developmentally appropriative programs support healthy overall development.

IS IT ALWAYS CLEAR WHEN PRACTICES ARE DEVELOPMENTALLY APPROPRIATE?

In an article included in the NAEYC (1997) publication on developmentally appropriate practice, Sue Bredekamp asks early childhood professionals to consider which of the following situations describe developmental appropriateness:

- an activity for three-year-olds that lasts for thirty minutes, during which the children mostly watch and listen to the teacher

- a teacher reading a picture book to a group of four-year-olds

- a one-hour period of free-choice time in a kindergarten, during which children may play with blocks, table toys, dress-up clothes, or other early childhood materials

- a whole-group math lesson for second-graders, conducted by a teacher standing at a blackboard (Bredekamp & Copple, 1997)

Many professionals are quick to define reading aloud out of a storybook and the free-choice time as developmentally appropriate, but question the appropriateness of the long listening activity for three-year-olds and the whole-group math lesson. The article then gives additional information that causes most professionals to completely reverse their initial opinions. It turns out that the long listening activity is for children living in a rural Native American community, being taught by a member of their community. In that culture, which values **interdependence** over independence and expects children to learn by observation and nonverbal communication, this experienced teacher is helping children develop valued skills; thus the activity is culturally, and therefore developmentally, appropriate. On the other hand, the background information in the story time episode reveals that most of the children's primary language is Spanish, and the teacher is reading an English alphabet book that is incomprehensible to them, particularly to one child who is hearing impaired and not supported by an interpreter. The teacher's response to their inattention is a time-out. Obviously, this scenario shows a lack of knowledge about how children learn second languages.

Similarly, the free-play activity provides only materials that have been unchanged for six months; the children either wander or engage in unchanging patterns of play. The teacher plays a passive role, only correcting children who misbehave and looking at yesterday's work sheets; this can now be seen as inappropriate practice because the teacher ignores the interactive learning style of young children. The whole-group math lesson has followed weeks of working on the concepts with math manipulatives and involves the children actively in collaborative problem solving; therefore, it is a developmentally appropriate way to help children learn math concepts. So it becomes clear that decisions about developmentally appropriate practice require making complex judgments involving many factors and sources of knowledge. Rather than making instant judgments, " the answer to 'How do I know if a given practice is developmentally appropriate?' always begins with 'It depends'" (Copple & Bredekamp, 2009, p. 47). Developmentally appropriate practice is not a narrow prescription for what to do (or not do), but a larger approach to determining appropriate actions in particular contexts for particular children. (See Figure 1-8.)

Many of the developmentally inappropriate practices noted by the examples included with the position statements relate to the early teaching of academic skills that focus purely on cognitive development, particularly in the preschool years. Bredekamp and Rosegrant (1992) note that the "goal [of the position statement] was to 'open up' the curriculum and teaching practices and move away from the narrow emphasis on isolated academic skills and the drill-and-practice approach to instruction" (Bredekamp & Rosegrant, 1992, p. 4). The crux of the "appropriate/inappropriate" discussions is probably in the differing answers to three questions.

- How do children most effectively learn at this age?

- What is most important for children to learn at this age, whether they are in a program of one sort or another or at home?

Principles of Appropriate and Inappropriate Practice
There is general agreement on these practices as:

Developmentally appropriate

❑ curriculum and experiences that actively engage children
❑ rich, teacher-supported play
❑ integrated curriculum
❑ scope for children's initiative and choice
❑ intentional decisions in the organization and timing of learning experiences
❑ adapting curriculum and teaching strategies to help individual children make optimal progress

Developmentally inappropriate

❑ highly linear instruction, especially following an inflexible timeline
❑ heavy reliance on whole-group instruction
❑ fragmented lessons without connections meaningful to children
❑ rigid adherence to packaged curriculum, without regard for children's responses
❑ narrow focus, such as only on literacy and math instruction
❑ highly prescriptive requirements, and rigid timelines for achieving them
❑ From Copple and Bredekamp (2008).

Figure 1-8

There is general agreement on these principles.

• What are the repercussions later in the child's school years, adolescence, and adult life of the academic preschool experience versus experience in a developmentally appropriate program? (Greenberg, 1990, p. 75)

The answers to the first two questions, what and how children of various ages should be learning, form the content of Sections 2, 3, and 4 of this book. At this point, we will consider this issue of the later repercussions of early learning experiences that are more heavily academic.

RESULTS OF DEVELOPMENTALLY APPROPRIATE VERSUS INAPPROPRIATE PRACTICE

Why do many early childhood educators believe it is crucial to delineate developmentally appropriate practices, so that more teachers can provide them for their young students? The answer lies primarily in four important areas of development: self-esteem, self-control, stress, and later academic patterns.

Self-Esteem

Self-esteem grows as children are able to master new experiences and challenges in their lives (see Figure 1-9).

A key concept here is *mastering*. As adults expect children to engage in learning activities beyond their developmental level, an unnecessary sense of failure is created. When children do not master a task, they have no way of judging that adults have in fact been mistaken in their

Figure 1-9

Self-esteem grows when children master meaningful challenges.

selection of the style or tasks of learning for children. Children simply know that the learning style is alien and difficult for them, and that they have not measured up to the adult standards. Continually getting disapproval because he can't sit still during teacher instruction hurts a child's self-esteem. Being directed over and over again to cut on the lines when she just can't do it hurts her self-esteem. Programs centered on academic learning stress mastery of narrowly defined cognitive skills and imply to children that mastery in other areas is of little value. "Another risk that may attend introducing young children to academic work prematurely is that those children who cannot relate to the content or tasks required are likely to feel incompetent" (Katz, 1988, p. 30). Such negative experiences have an impact on the development of self-esteem.

Self-Control

As children mature cognitively, they are increasingly able to govern their behavior according to the guidance they have received from adults. If children have been disciplined by adults who primarily use arbitrary, power-driven techniques, the children have little opportunity to learn and to slowly **internalize** the information they need to gradually take over more control of their lives. These children are so controlled by external power that they not only suffer in self-esteem ("Nothing I do seems to please my teacher or parents"), but suffer also in self-control ("I'll go as far as I can because I know sooner or later they'll stop me, and then I'll pay for it").

All early childhood teachers believe children need discipline and guidance in the form of limits on behavior and impulses. The difference between developmentally appropriate and inappropriate guidance techniques, or those likely to lead toward eventual self-control (as opposed to others that only temporarily stop misbehavior), is how well adults select teaching techniques

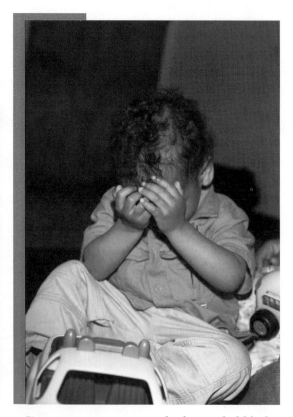

Figure 1-10

It would be inappropriate to expect this toddler to understand others' needs or control his impulses.

that match what is known of the young child's learning ability. Adults are more likely to use power disciplinary techniques when they do not understand the developmental capabilities and limitations of children in verbal expression, cognitive reasoning and judgment skills, or abilities to emphasize or decenter mentally. For example, when adults become annoyed with toddlers who cannot share and then ask them to sit in "time-out" to emphasize this point, they are paying no attention to the real nature of the toddler, who is truly unable to comprehend and internalize the notion of others' rights or to control his own impulses (see Figure 1-10).

More developmentally appropriate discipline would recognize the developmental limitations and redirect the child toward a positive substitution or alternative. Later, when the preschooler is able to recognize others' wishes as well as her own, she will be encouraged to find a solution for taking turns or cooperating on the use of the sought-after toy. Such disciplinary techniques put the adult in the position of **facilitator** and guide, rather than the adult who manages all behavior for the child. Self-control can grow only when children are able to understand and experience why it is desirable to behave in certain ways, rather than simply being stopped when the adult decides to stop them.

The impact of developmentally inappropriate disciplinary practices on future behavior is suggested by a study that indicated first-grade students from developmentally inappropriate kindergarten classrooms were perceived by their first-grade teachers as more hostile and aggressive, anxious and fearful, and hyperactive and distractible than children who had attended kindergartens using developmentally appropriate practices (Hart, 1991). Children in more appropriate classrooms view themselves as more cooperative than do children in less appropriate settings.

Learning to make good choices is an important component of self-discipline. Environments and interactions that inform and support choices are crucial to healthy self-control.

The impact of developmentally appropriate programs on both self-esteem and self-control has been highlighted by the **longitudinal studies** reported by David Weikart and his colleagues (Berreuta-Clement et al., 1984; Schweinhart, Weikart, & Larner, 1986; Schweinhart & Weikart, 1993, 1997; Schweinhart et al., 2005). The purpose of the study was to assess whether high-quality preschool programs could provide both short- and long-term benefits to children living in poverty and at high risk of school failure.

Children who had participated in three different models of preschool programs in Ypsilanti, Michigan, have been followed after they left their preschool until they reached age forty, so far. The three approaches used with the group of disadvantaged preschoolers were a direct-instruction program, in which "teachers followed a script to directly teach children academic skills, enforcing their attention and rewarding them for giving correct answers to the teachers' questions" (Schweinhart & Weikart, 1997, p. 9), now called DISTAR; a traditional nursery school program that encouraged children's active involvement in self-initiated play organized around themes, such as community helpers, seasons of the year, holidays, and so on, with teachers responding to children's expressed needs and interests in a socially supportive setting; and an "open-framework" approach, now called the High/Scope curriculum. In this approach, both teacher and child plan learning activities jointly with a variety of interest centers, the teachers interacting with an open-ended questioning style to facilitate active learning in **key experiences**, using a plan-do-review structure. Both of the latter programs included social and academic objectives and called for child-initiated activity (Schweinhart, 1988). Although the study involved relatively small numbers of children, the results are thought provoking.

When the Perry preschool study initially found that all children who had participated in any of the preschool programs showed dramatic gains in intelligence scores over children without preschool experience, and that these gains in achievement remained over time at a higher level through their tenth year, it was concluded that any preschool program of high quality could make a significant difference in a disadvantaged child's educational life. As the participants were contrasted with the control group at age nineteen, again at age twenty-seven, and most recently at age forty (Schweinhart & Weikart, 1993, 1997; Schweinhart et al., 2005), it was discovered that those who had participated in any preschool program were significantly more likely to graduate from high school, enroll in postsecondary education, and be employed. But by age fifteen, and even more significantly in later years, the participants in the two programs that had emphasized child initiation showed increasingly greater social skills and responsibility than did the direct-instruction group. The child-initiation group was significantly less likely to be assigned to special education classes, to commit crimes, to have children themselves during their teenage years, or to receive welfare assistance (Schweinhart & Weikart, 1997). At ages twenty-three and forty, the adults who had participated in the child-centered preschool programs had completed higher levels of schooling; earned significantly higher salaries; were more likely to own their own homes, own second cars, and be married; received significantly fewer social services; had fewer arrests; and were more likely to have participated in volunteer work in their communities. Those who had participated in the direct-instruction group showed greater dispositions toward antisocial behavior, including "felony arrests, property crimes, early teen misconduct, work suspensions, and need for treatment for emotional impairment and disturbance" (Schweinhart & Weikart, 1997, p. 9).

Such marked differences suggest the gains by the young children who had opportunities to make choices, build up their self-confidence as learners, and gradually develop self-control (Schweinhart et al., 1986) (see Figure 1-11).

Figure 1-11

In the Perry Preschool Project, children had opportunities to make choices and build their self-esteem as learners.

The essential process connecting early childhood experience to patterns of improved success in school and the community seemed to be the development of dispositions that allowed the child to interact positively with other people and with tasks. This process was based neither on permanently improved intellectual performance nor on academic knowledge. . . . It was the development of specific personal and social **dispositions** that enabled a high-quality early childhood program to significantly influence participants' adult performance. (Schweinhart & Weikart, 1993, pp. 11, 12)

In light of this finding, the researchers concluded that a high-quality preschool curriculum must have an abundance of child-initiated learning activities, as described in recommendations for developmentally appropriate practice, allowing them to develop the skills and dispositions of decision making, planning, and getting along with other children and adults. This thinking later became embodied in the High/Scope curriculum approach, which will be discussed in more detail in Chapter 4.

These results call into question the advisability of pushing formal academics on four-year-olds. In particular, such programs, focusing on teacher-directed activities, may not be the best way to improve a disadvantaged child's chance for a successful life. To overcome obstacles to success, disadvantaged children must have opportunities to chart their own course. To be self-directed, they must initiate their own learning, follow through with their plans, and evaluate the outcomes. (Schweinhart et al., 1986, p. 43)

The results of the study suggest that children in developmentally appropriate programs—who plan and have responsibility for their own activity, and who initiate their own work—develop dispositions toward lifelong learning, with "**initiative**, curiosity, trust, confidence, independence, responsibility, and **divergent** thinking" (Schweinhart & Weikart, 1993, p. 12). The implication is also that children who are taught directly what to do, working within adult-controlled limits and on objectives determined by adults, have no sense of investment in themselves, in the educational systems, or in the community (Schweinhart, 1988).

Stress

Some child psychologists today claim that our children are at risk because of the stresses involved in being hurried through childhood (Elkind, 1981, 1988). Hurrying can take many forms, including early entry into competitive sports and specialized lessons, early exposure to the problems and rapid changes in the adult world, or bearing increased emotional and physical responsibility in families that are themselves under stress, for example, with divorce and single parents. The earlier introduction of academics to educational programs for young children is one of the kinds of hurrying this book is most concerned with.

Stress is a common risk noted in children when excessive and inappropriate demands are made on them through formal instruction. When young children are asked to learn content with methods contrary to their natural learning style, they experience a natural conflict between their desires and the systems imposed and expected by adults. In denying their natural instincts in order to win adult approval, children must make enormous efforts to suppress and control their behavior. An example is the five-year-old boy who seems physically unable to sit and listen as the teacher has asked him to, or the eighteen-month-old who is driven to climb and is removed every time she does so. This is true stress (see Figure 1-12).

A number of studies corroborate the increased stress on children in developmentally inappropriate settings. Children in developmentally inappropriate practice kindergarten classrooms exhibited significantly more stress behaviors than children in developmentally appropriate practice classrooms. More stress was evident in boys in developmentally inappropriate practice classrooms than in developmentally appropriate practice ones. The activities found to be most stressful for kindergarten children were workbook and work sheet assignments, waiting, and

Figure 1-12

Premature academic expectations may cause stress in young children.

transition activities (Burts et al., 1992). Similar findings have been made about stress in developmentally inappropriate versus developmentally appropriate preschool classrooms (Durland et al., 1992). Children from racial minority or lower socioeconomic backgrounds exhibited more stress behaviors in both developmentally appropriate and developmentally inappropriate classrooms (Burts et al., 1992; Hart, Burts, & Charlesworth, 1997; Charlesworth, 1998a). However, when low-socioeconomic status African-American children were taught literacy using developmentally appropriate whole-language methods, they progressed rapidly, while simultaneously, stress behaviors were observed to decrease in frequency (Weems-Moon, 1991).

To see how developmentally inappropriate expectations of uniform learning styles or timing put children under unnecessary stress, consider the following scenes that occur in too many early childhood settings. Watch the acute frustration of the toddler who can't sit still for the teacher's instruction period when asked. Imagine the anxiety of the four-year-old who wants to, but can't, form the letters to copy the teacher's perfect example. Picture the six-year-old who just can't seem to distinguish the letters and stumbles through the reading page, shame-faced and shaking each time the teacher corrects her. The fear of failure can become overwhelming, and is an unnecessary hazard after adults learn what is developmentally appropriate.

Later Academic Patterns

Do the benefits in later academic situations justify the earlier stress caused by pushing academic learning prematurely onto young children? On the contrary, children who are asked to learn through methods unsuited to their stage of development may become turned off to education very early.

> Certainly young children can be successfully instructed in beginning reading skills; however, the risk of such early achievement is that in the process of instruction, given the amount of drill and practice required for success at an early age, children's dispositions to be readers will be undermined. . . . What is sad to see in kindergartens is children so willing to do so many things that are so irrelevant to them at that age and so frivolous, and by second grade find many of them turned off. It isn't either-or. You don't acquire dispositions or skills. The challenge for educators—at every level—is to help the learner with both the acquisition of skills and the strengthening of desirable dispositions. (Katz, 1988, p. 30)

There is a real risk that these children may learn helplessness; that is, they may become dependent on the kind of learning structured only by adults, rather than learning to take their own initiative, raise their own questions, and solve their own problems. Thus the child's natural motivation to learn may be seriously disrupted (Elkind, 1987b).

In fact, some evidence indicates that delaying rather than speeding up children's exposure to the learning of abstract academics has positive effects and certainly appears to have no handicapping effects. First-graders who attended developmentally inappropriate kindergarten classrooms received lower reading report card grades when compared with children from developmentally appropriate classrooms (Burts et al., 1992). Results on test scores do not indicate the differences that justify the stress on young children from being exposed to developmentally inappropriate instruction methods. Children in kindergarten classrooms using developmentally appropriate practices scored no differently than those in classrooms that used inappropriate practices (Burts, Charlesworth, & Fleege, 1991). At the end of the first and second grades, children who had experienced developmentally appropriate practice in kindergarten scored no differently on the test average than children who had spent kindergarten in developmentally inappropriate classrooms (Verma, 1992). Other studies corroborate the academic benefits to children in developmentally appropriate programs over the long run.

An implication worth considering may be that early exposure to academics has in fact jeopardized later success, and that delaying exposure has been beneficial. It may be worthwhile to heed the words of Lillian Katz: "While there is no compelling evidence to suggest that early introduction to academic work guarantees success in school in the long term, there are reasons to believe that it can be counterproductive" (Katz, 1988).

CONSIDERING SOME MISUNDERSTANDINGS ABOUT DEVELOPMENTALLY APPROPRIATE PRACTICE

We should realize that some of the resistance to instituting developmentally appropriate practice comes because certain misunderstandings about what it means have developed. Some of the misunderstandings result from a less than thorough grounding in child development knowledge; others come from trying to simplify and close a complex discussion that should remain open ended as early childhood professionals continue to puzzle through its implications. A danger certainly exists that standards of practice be interpreted as crystallized and fixed. Whatever their source, however, the misunderstandings cloud the acceptance of developmentally appropriate practice. The misunderstandings also often contribute to educational inequality. It is advantageous to consider these misunderstandings here as we try to understand the nature of developmental appropriateness. Students and teachers who want to advocate developmentally appropriate practice need to be comfortable explaining why these misunderstandings are not true.

Misunderstanding 1—There Is Only One Right Way to Carry Out Developmentally Appropriate Practice

This untrue characterization makes it seem as though developmentally appropriate practices add up to a single curriculum. Bredekamp and Rosegrant suggest that this misinterpretation resulted from the format of the 1987 position statement, contrasting appropriate and inappropriate practice as if they were two opposite poles instead of just differences on a continuum with gradations in between. Obviously the misinterpretation of only one right way contradicts precisely what is intended in terms of uniqueness and emphasis on molding teacher strategies and responses to the assessed needs and interests of individuals.

Some children will need more adult guidance, direct instruction, and classroom structure than others (see Figure 1-13).

Children whose experiences are limited, who bring less **foundational** knowledge and fewer skills to the classroom than others, and who come from different linguistic or cultural contexts, need teachers who can continually modify their teaching strategies, learning what works best at any particular time. If a program needs to match its practices to the unique population served,

Figure 1-13
Some children may need more support or direct instruction than others, depending on their experiences.

it will look very different from another program, even though both may be developmentally appropriate. A program that serves mostly Caucasian upper-middle-class children living in a big city will likely offer different curriculum experiences than one found in a rural desert community serving Hispanic children whose families are farmers and migrant workers. What any program looked like and did last year may be quite different as it tries to work with this year's children. Many of the children in a classroom will not be involved in the same activity at the same time, because of their unique learning styles and paces, abilities and interests, needs and experiences. Teachers who follow developmentally appropriate practices aren't looking only for one right answer, but for the best answers for these particular children at this particular time.

Misunderstanding 2—Developmentally Appropriate Classrooms Are Unstructured

When some people hear that teachers are not in direct control of all instruction and learning activities, they fear a chaotic environment will ensue. Every developmentally appropriate classroom is structured; however, the structure is just not as obvious as the structure in a completely teacher-directed classroom.

Structure refers to the teachers' formulations of instructional plans and their careful orchestration of space, time, materials, and interaction in the physical, social/emotional, and cognitive/language environments to achieve their instructional goals. As we will see in our discussion of these environments later in the book, developmentally appropriate classrooms are carefully balanced between child-initiated and teacher-led activities. Purposeful planning and intentional interaction support children's growth in all these areas. Children actively participate in and influence planning and have some choices, but teachers are definitely in control. Casual visitors may not perceive the organization—the planning, assessment, and evaluation that go on behind the scenes in classrooms in which children learn through active involvement. Although developmentally appropriate classrooms contain movement, diverse activity, conversation, and play, they are not chaotic or aimless.

Misunderstanding 3—Teachers Teach Minimally or Not at All in Developmentally Appropriate Classrooms

Once again, the misunderstanding relies on the limited view that teachers teach only by directing and controlling all learning in a classroom—instructing, assigning tasks, and correcting errors. The implication in this misinterpretation is that teachers are merely passive observers in developmentally appropriate classrooms, not really doing much to promote learning. Teachers in developmentally appropriate classrooms are in charge, but not dominating, and they use a variety of teaching strategies. Some of the strategies—the observing, planning, scheduling, arranging, and organizing—create an invisible structure that supports learning activity. Some of the strategies are embedded in personal interaction with children busy at play; teachers comment, ask, suggest, and provide information and additional materials. They model, demonstrate, challenge, and help children change direction (see Figure 1-14).

They collaborate with children involved in learning activities, scaffolding children's efforts to reach to greater heights. They help form small groups and partnerships in which children can support and extend each other's learning. They provide direct instruction and demonstration when these strategies are needed to advance children's learning. They plan small-group learning sessions, and also teach with large-group activities. Teachers recognize that learning doesn't happen only when their mouths are open. When they intervene in learning situations, it is because their observation and judgment have led them to conclude that their intervention will enhance learning. Teachers in developmentally appropriate classrooms teach by supporting children's active learning with a multitude of direct and indirect strategies.

Figure 1-14 (a & b)

Teachers may model, challenge, and help children change direction.

(a)

(b)

Misunderstanding 4—Developmentally Appropriate Programs Don't Include Academics, Generally Interpreted to Be the Formal Skills of Learning Reading, Writing, and Arithmetic

This misunderstanding stems from a passionate disagreement between those who feel that children not exposed to academics will be unable to achieve at expected levels in later education and those who feel young children are not yet ready for this style of learning. Each side ignores the real nature of how children's learning and interest in materials naturally brings them to literacy—and to mathematical-related activity and exploration: "Read it again!"; "What does that say?"; "I need two more places for the table!"; "Timmy's got too many—I've only got one!" Children's interests bring opportunities for academic content into the teaching day of any preschool and drive them to continue learning the skills they need in the primary years; thus, it is a simplification to say that academics are not developmentally appropriate. Rather, curriculum activities that focus on aspects of isolated skill development and teaching strategies such as whole-group teacher instruction and teacher-directed abstract work sheet drills are not appropriate methods of teaching young children. In a developmentally appropriate classroom, academic content is presented by integration with all other classroom experiences; many formal methods of traditional teacher-directed instruction used with older children are not used to any great extent.

A comment from David Elkind is pertinent here:

A developmental approach to education does not deny the importance of such knowledge. The difference between the two approaches is a matter of which acquisition comes first. . . . From a developmental perspective, the creation of curious, active learners must precede the acquisition of particular information. . . . To put the difference more succinctly, the developmental approach seeks to create students who want to know, whereas the psychometric approach seeks to produce students who know what we want. (Elkind, 1989, p. 115)

One of the voices in the debate on developmentally appropriate practice (Walsh, 1989) suggests that the issue is not that

such-and-such is bad because it is happening in preschool or kindergarten . . . but the reality that many of these practices are inappropriate for any child. . . . The problem is not that kindergarten looks like first grade; the problem is what kindergarten and first grade (and second and third), that is, what the elementary school is beginning to look like. (Walsh, 1989, p. 389)

The real irony is that, when children are judged "unready" for the rigors of academic kindergartens or first grades, they are often tracked into "developmental" kindergartens or "transitional classes" that emphasize active, hands-on learning experiences for young children. Developmentally appropriate practices are offered to these children who are "failing" in the less appropriate, traditional settings.

Misunderstanding 5—Developmentally Appropriate Programs Are Effective Only for Particular Populations, "Usually Assumed to Be Typically Developing, White, Middle-Class Children"

(Bredekamp & Rosegrant, 1992, p. 5). This implies that children of diverse racial, cultural, or socioeconomic backgrounds, or children with special needs, will not be well served in such programs. A number of experts planning intervention programs for children from lower socioeconomic backgrounds feel that a directly academic approach is essential to counteract the early lack of experiences and stimulation in the preschool years. The DISTAR method of working with preschoolers and kindergartners, developed by Bereiter and Engelmann, relies heavily on drill and **rote-learning** style of letter sounds and number skills in preplanned curriculum packages (Bereiter & Engelmann, 1966).

Others disagree, notably David Elkind and David Weikart, contending that the DISTAR approach is inappropriate for most young children of all socioeconomic backgrounds.

> DISTAR is even worse for young disadvantaged children, because it imprints them with a rote-learning style that could be damaging later on. As Piaget pointed out, children learn by manipulating their environment, and a healthy early education program structures the child's environment to make the most of that fact. DISTAR, on the other hand, structures the child and constrains his learning style. (Elkind, in Shell, 1989, p. 53)

> The Direct Instruction group did not fare as well in the long run as the other two curriculum groups in the study. . . . Direct Instruction focused on academic objectives, not on child-planning or social objectives, and this strategy does not appear to have been in the best interests of the children it served. (Schweinhart and Weikart, 1997, p. 10)

It is not only early childhood professionals who are unsure about the benefits of direct instruction versus developmentally appropriate.

> Many parents (of minority children) view the nondidactic and child-initiated activity characteristic of a developmentally appropriate classroom as inimical to their children's success; these parents believe that work sheets and other evidence of information and skills are more appropriate than the "messing around" characteristic of informal classrooms (Bowman, in Bredekamp & Rosegrant, 1992, p. 132).

Renata Cooper states one perspective coming out of the African-American community that is "rooted in our social and historical context in the United States. . . . Given the economic and social realities of our people, our children don't have time to play in school" (Lakin, 1996, p. 40).

Teachers of special education and parents of children with special needs voice similar concerns that their children need all the direct instruction they can get.

According to the basic principles of developmentally appropriate practice, modifications are made to curriculum experiences, environments, and strategies to respond to individual needs and abilities. This makes the developmentally appropriate classroom suited for every child, no matter what the experience or ability. Because there are no uniform standards of achievement for all children in the class, it is more likely that children with special needs or particular cultural backgrounds will grow comfortably and successfully without fear of failure. Everyone learns at their own rate and in their own way in a developmentally appropriate classroom (see Figure 1-15).

In addition, the position statement makes it clear that programs must respond to cultural variations in the children they serve. Programs must adapt themselves to all individual needs,

Figure 1-15

Everyone learns in his or her own way, at an individual rate, in a developmentally appropriate classroom.

interests, languages, and heritages. Those who criticize developmentally appropriate practice on the basis of failing to acknowledge variations in cultural values and experiences seem not to understand that an essential part of the curriculum is the relationship between children's personal and cultural histories and the classroom environments. If culture is taken seriously, if educators really include parents and other community members in decisions about how their children will be educated and cared for, programs will necessarily be very different in their philosophy and design.

It is vital, moreover, in the continuing dialogue about developmentally appropriate practices, that none of us fall into the trap of believing we can speak about what is best for other people's children (Delpit, 2006), or that those who speak from the perspective of the dominant culture not silence others without intending to or even being aware of it.

Teachers using developmentally appropriate practice must work to make their classrooms individually appropriate for every child and supported by every parent.

Misunderstanding 6—In Developmentally Appropriate Classrooms, There Is No Way to Tell If Children Are Learning

The misunderstanding here is that methods other than the traditional, easily applied techniques of testing children's retention of material are used. The pressure for accountability has brought standardized testing into classrooms for young children. Even the youngest children are frequently subjected to pop quizzes. (What color is this? How many balls do I have?) Children's learning in all domains cannot be so easily quantified and measured as these tests for achievement of cognitive concepts suggest. Children's constructed understanding of the world, its objects, and its people is indicated by their increasingly complex use of materials and by their style of interaction. Their language, questions, and concentration indicate development. The essence of teaching in a developmentally appropriate classroom lies in continual observation of children's play, language, interaction, and increasing abilities to use **literacy** skills and other media to communicate their learning. As teachers record specific observations, they identify patterns of growth and change in each child (see Figure 1-16).

These observations lead to creating the next challenges for children. The observations also answer adult questions about learning. Teachers who respect children's innate ability and desire to teach themselves have faith that children will develop and learn in a responsive environment, and their observations are a concrete way of justifying that faith.

Figure 1-16

Teachers observe children at play to learn how best to support their learning.

Misunderstanding 7—Developmentally Appropriate Practice Can Be Achieved Simply by Acquiring Certain Kinds of Toys and Materials

This statement is not only nonsense, but a gross simplification of important ideas. It is the same kind of gross misunderstanding evidenced when centers purchase selections of toys designed by Montessori and then call themselves Montessori programs. Without a thorough understanding and grounding in the educational philosophy, those toys are just additional materials in the class-room. The truth is that materials are important components in the active learning environment, and the standards for developmentally appropriate practice express concern with too much em-phasis on pencil-and-paper kinds of learning activities. Teachers in developmentally appropriate classrooms understand that children's actions and interactions with materials help them create their own sensorimotor understandings, preoperational learning, and concrete concepts. Thus, much time and effort goes into making thoughtful choices of toys and materials in children's learning environments. Because children need materials they can use with success regardless of their ability and skill, many of the resources in the developmentally appropriate classroom are open ended—that is, open for use in a multitude of ways. But beyond this, materials include both traditional toys of early childhood, such as blocks, books, and small items to manipulate, and materials from the real world, such as water, sand, grown-up clothes, kitchen utensils, and old clocks. The one criterion for including materials in a developmentally appropriate classroom is that they support a specific learning interest or goal.

Misunderstanding 8—Developmentally Appropriate Practice Uses No Goals or Objectives

(Bredekamp & Rosegrant, 1992). The belief that children alone decide what they will learn and how they will learn it in developmentally appropriate classrooms results from the misunderstand-ing of the phrase "child-centered," often interpreted to mean child-determined, child-dictated, or child-indulgent, when a more accurate understanding is "child-sensitive" (Bredekamp & Rosegrant, 1992). Although emphases on narrowly academic skills have been rejected by NAEYC as inappropriate practice for young children, developmentally appropriate practice does use goals and objectives. "All effective educational programs have clearly stated **objectives** (or outcomes) toward which the teacher plans and works with children to achieve" (Bredekamp & Rosegrant, 1992, p. 5). Paying attention to the early learning standards of individual states gives a framework for desirable outcomes. The difference in developmentally appropriate classrooms is that those goals are for all areas of development, based on knowledge of the children's age-level development and on individual needs in learning and development.

Children's needs, questions, and interests play a major role in influencing teacher planning in a child-centered curriculum; however, teachers also know how, why, and when to extend learn-ing possibilities in play and projects. They monitor a child's progression through the specific lessons needed to move toward acquiring literacy and numerical abilities, as well as social skills, emotional control, and physical competency, and other objectives of the learning standards.

Misunderstanding 9—In Developmentally Appropriate Practice, the Curriculum Is Child Development

(Bredekamp & Rosegrant, 1992). This misinterpretation loses sight of the fact that other knowl-edge must work together with child development to ensure that all children reach their individual potentials. Although child development knowledge is crucial to determine appropriate teaching practice, other considerations influence decisions about curriculum. Development is only one of three dimensions that influence classroom practices. The other dimensions include the cultural dimension (considering a society's values of what its members want their children to be like) and the knowledge dimension (what children need to know, according to enunciated standards). This implies a continuing need for conversations between educators and communities to make decisions about

- the skills and dispositions children will need as citizens of the twenty-first century.
- values of the family and community.
- identifying necessary knowledge and subject areas.
- areas of interest to the child/children.

Considering these dimensions does not conflict with concepts of developmental appropriateness; rather, this process of dialogue results in making decisions that are truly individually and culturally appropriate.

Misunderstanding 10—Developmental Appropriateness Is Just One in a Sequence of Changing Trends in Education

Obviously, there have been changes in what educators have been asked to do in the past, and teachers tend not to take too seriously that which they think may not last too long. However, if developmental appropriateness is conceived of as an evolving of professional thinking that will continue over the coming decades the philosophy is likely to be integrated into professional thinking and practice. The roots of developmental practice lie at the beginning of this century, with early childhood philosophers and educators such as John Dewey, Patty Smith Hill, and Caroline Pratt. So today's teachers are not being asked to begin something new and change everything they do; instead, they are being asked to consider their actions in the light of integrating their developmental knowledge of children. The abiding question will be, "Is what I do supported by what I know to be true about this child/children?" The strategies may change, but the knowledge and attitude will remain constant. Developmentally appropriate practice should remain the unifying value that draws early childhood professionals together. The subject is an ongoing conversation; NAEYC will lead the process of reviewing and revising the position statement for currency every ten years or so.

This book is intended to help students and practitioners and others interested in developmentally appropriate practice consider specific implications for action in their particular environments. Although it is not presented as a definitive statement or an absolute plan of action—the assumption is that no such statement would be developmentally appropriate for adults—it is intended to stimulate questions and examinations of current practice and to help early childhood practitioners create the most supportive learning environments for young children.

> Excellent teachers know:
>
> - It's *both* what you teach *and* how you teach.
> - It's *both* teacher-guided *and* child-guided experiences.
> - It's *both* joy *and* learning.
> - See these and more both/ands in Copple and Bredekamp (2009, p. 49).

SUMMARY

NAEYC and other professional educational organizations have published statements defining developmentally appropriate practice as actions based on developmental knowledge of age-level guidelines, individual interests and needs, and cultural responsiveness. Developmentally appropriate practice specifies the provision of active learning experiences, intentionally supported by knowledgeable and responsive teachers using a wide repertoire of teaching strategies. In NAEYC's publications, specifics are defined as appropriate and inappropriate for each age group from birth through age eight, and guidelines are given for curriculum and assessment. A number of misunderstandings have arisen among practitioners about the implications of developmentally appropriate practice. The most important component may be the respect of children and their characteristics. This respect leads adults to continually question whether their practices match what they know about child development. A thorough grounding in developmental knowledge and principles is essential. Inappropriate practices for young children create negative results.

THINK ABOUT IT ACTIVITIES

1. Talk with several early childhood teachers. Ask them what the term "developmentally appropriate practice" means to them. Ask them to give examples of ways their classroom practices are developmentally appropriate. Ask them to describe ways they meet individual needs in their classrooms. Discuss your thoughts about their responses later with your classmates.

2. Talk with parents of young children about their feelings and concerns about a play curriculum. Discuss with your classmates the implications of their responses as if you were teachers who were implementing developmentally appropriate practice.

3. Obtain and read through NAEYC's book titled *Developmentally Appropriate Practice* (Copple & Bredekamp, 2009) to note the major areas discussed. Also, try to get a copy of the earlier position statements (1988 and 1997) to note the changes and expansions in the most recent statement. These and other position statements are available online at http://www.naeyc.org. The complete 2009 position statement on DAP may be downloaded from this site.

QUESTIONS TO ASSESS LEARNING OF CHAPTER OBJECTIVES

1. Describe, as fully as you can, what is meant by developmentally appropriate practice.

2. Identify and describe the various essential components of developmentally appropriate practice.

3. List and discuss the implications of several principles of development.

4. Identify four possible negative results of inappropriate practices for young children.

5. Discuss several concepts related to developmentally appropriate practice that have been misunderstood. Discuss a more accurate interpretation for each.

APPLY YOUR KNOWLEDGE QUESTIONS

1. Describe a specific example from your experiences and observations of children that illustrates each of the twelve principles of development discussed in the chapter.

2. Prepare statements that could refute each of the misunderstandings held about developmentally appropriate practice. Analyze *why* people have these misunderstandings. As you consider the source of the misunderstanding, you may consider how to approach their viewpoints.

3. Consider the dialogues between Charlesworth and Lubeck, found in the references in this section. Reflect on the arguments that each makes for her position. Find examples that support and/or refute each position.

HELPFUL WEB SITES

http://www.naeyc.org

The Web site for the National Association for the Education of Young Children has all the position statements on developmentally appropriate practice referred to in this text.

http://www.ecewebguide.com

This Web site is an invaluable resource on many topics. Type in "developmentally appropriate practice" for the search, and you will find several dozen articles.

www.ceep.crc.uiuc.edu/
eecearchive/index.html

This Web site is the archive of ERIC/EECE Digests. Search here for several articles on developmentally appropriate practice.

Please visit the premium Web site for Developmentally Appropriate Practice, *4th edition, to access more chapter web links, suggestions for further research and study, additional book chapters, interactive quizzes, video exercises, online journal activities, flashcards, and much more! Go to www.cengage.com/login to register your access code.*

CHAPTER

2

Understanding Play: Its Importance in Developmentally Appropriate Practice

All over the world, children play. They play by themselves, with other children, and with adults. They play with toys specifically made for children that resemble toys made for centuries—like balls and hoops, dolls, and miniatures of objects used in daily life. They play with objects they find, which become transformed into whatever props the play demands. They play in ways adults and older children have taught them to play, so that peek-a-boo and hide-and-seek games are passed on to each succeeding generation. They play in ways that show they have been watching the adults in their world, soothing pretend babies or hunting with small bows and arrows. They play using words barely mumbled to themselves or using stylized dialogue in which they prompt one another. They play joyfully, spontaneously, and using elaborate rules easily recognized by the generations who played similar games before them. They begin playing when they're just babies, and they're still playing when they're supposed to be concentrating on schoolwork. Children's play is recognized as an inseparable part of childhood.

The universality of children's play has attracted the attention of countless researchers and theorists over the years. Although these researchers have differed in some of their basic assumptions about play, all have agreed that play is significant in the development of children physically, socially, emotionally, and cognitively. Montessori was the first to say "Play is the child's work." This solemn phrase is repeated frequently to describe play's importance. In this chapter, we will try to go beyond that cliché, to understand why play is considered the heart of developmentally appropriate practice.

LEARNING OBJECTIVES

After studying this chapter, students should be able to

- define play and describe its key elements.
- describe categories and social stages of play.
- describe major theories about how play affects development.
- identify reasons why play is the most developmentally appropriate curriculum method.
- discuss conditions that support play.
- discuss current issues regarding play, including violent play, cultural influences on play, play for children with special needs, play and early learning standards, and helping families understand and accept the power of play.

WHAT IS PLAY?

Play has been defined in a variety of ways, depending on the perspective of the researcher/theorist or the participant. When children are asked what constitutes play, they refer to it as pleasurable and self-selected (Monighan-Nourot, 2003). Characteristics noted by researchers in defining play include these.

- Play is **intrinsically motivated** and spontaneous; individuals want to play. While this statement may not apply to all children with special needs or developmental delays, generally the urge to play seems innate.

- Play involves nonliteral or symbolic activity; creativity and imagination are involved in play.

- Play actively engages children; children become lost in their own worlds of playful activity.

- The goals of play are flexible, self-imposed, and may change during the course of the play; children are not bound by rules in their play, which may take many directions.

- In play, attention is on the means rather than a particular end—**process-oriented rather than product-oriented**; the play is important in and of itself, no matter what results from the play (Monighan-Nourot, 1990; Trawick-Smith, 1994; Stone, 1995).

Fromberg (2002) adds the words *meaningful, episodic,* and *rule-governed* (more about rule-governed when we consider Vygotsky later in this chapter). An early theorist talked about a continuum between play and work with particular components necessary to define an activity as play (Dewey, 1916). An interesting additional idea about play is that it integrates and unifies "apparently paradoxical properties" (Monighan-Nourot, 2003, p. 130), which allows for the opposing ideas of play being both pleasurable and frustrating or difficult.

Thus, a definition of play includes the ideas of pleasure, self-imposed ideas and spontaneous activities, and activity not restricted by reality or instruction. Monighan-Nourot (2003) defines play as involving an integration of experience, symbolic meanings, and paradoxes.

This definition excludes some forms of activity frequently seen in early childhood classrooms. For example, when the teacher gives directions for activities to children using colored wooden cubes to place on patterns, this is certainly hands-on and active, with a particular goal in mind, but the activity is not self-selected or intrinsically motivated. Similarly, when children in Montessori classrooms are using materials in ways specifically taught by teachers, the children may experience pleasure, but the other characteristics of play are missing. Finally, when teachers assign children roles in dramatic play ("You can be the Big Billy Goat Gruff"), this is not true play. Alternatively, when children (or adults) elect to engage in activity that might seem like work, such as writing a story or working on a math problem, they may be engaging in play, because the activity is freely chosen, pleasurable, and process-oriented (Trawick-Smith, 1994). Think of other examples that could be defined as either play or work, depending on the circumstances.

Very young children play. Babies enjoy interaction first with their own bodies and then with the materials they are given by adults. They play with the people around them, loving the repetition, surprise, and joy of the interaction. The element of symbolism may be missing from their play, but we can recognize the aspects of freely chosen, pleasurable activity in their play.

As we continue to define play, it is important to note the different categories and stages of play.

CATEGORIES OF PLAY

Piaget's cognitive theory of intellectual development (1962) identified different categories of play based on observations of his own children, later adapted by Smilansky (1968). The three categories of play are

- functional,
- symbolic,
- games with rules.

These categories coincide with certain cognitive developmental stages, although they continue in some form throughout development. Piaget believed that children's play evolves through these stages as their mental structures change.

Functional Play

Functional play, also called sensorimotor or practice play, is most common in children in the first two years of life, although it is obvious in all later stages as well. Children repeatedly practice their mental schemes by interacting with objects, people, and language. Children derive great pleasure from the movement and sensory exploration involved in playing in their environment.

Functional play is seen when

- babies explore bead toys by moving the beads over and over. (See Figure 2-1.)
- toddlers climb on every available object.
- four-year-olds finish a puzzle and then immediately dump out the pieces to begin again.
- six-year-olds roller skate every waking minute.

Through such practice play, children acquire confidence in their physical skills. Again, this is the predominant form of play for infants and young toddlers.

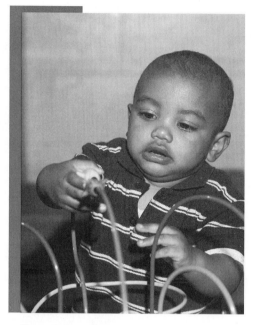

Figure 2-1

The baby who repeatedly moves the beads is engaged in functional play.

Symbolic Play

Symbolic play, or **representational play**, appears at about age two and continues in various forms into adulthood. Symbolic play includes constructive play and dramatic play.

Constructive Play. Children using materials or objects to make other things are engaging in **constructive play** (see Figure 2-2). Constructive play is a link between functional play and more sophisticated symbolic play. Children create and construct by using concrete materials to form representations of objects. Examples of constructive play include

- a two-year-old stacking three large blocks and saying, "My house."
- a three-year-old constructing a tall Lego tower.
- a five-year-old carefully selecting markers to illustrate his trip to the farm.
- a seven-year-old working for long hours to create a clay model of a spaceship.

Dramatic Play. Children creating imaginary roles in which they pretend to be someone or something else are engaging in **dramatic play**. The play often draws on first- or secondhand experience in various familiar situations. When two or more children are involved, such play is designated as **sociodramatic play**, (see Figure 2-3) and the play proceeds based on the interaction between the players acting out the roles and negotiating the pretend themes (Smilansky, 1990).

Dramatic play may also involve constructing pretend objects, although the representation may be far more abstract than in constructive play. For example, the child who puts detail into constructing a tower may then represent it by saying, "Pretend we're up really high in my tower here, okay?" gesturing as though he's having to maintain his balance carefully.

Learning to master symbolic play through both constructive and dramatic play is the major task of preschoolers; this is what clearly differentiates their play from toddler play. Symbolic play

Figure 2-2
This child is engaged in constructive play.

Figure 2-3
Sociodramatic play involves cooperating with others.

lays the foundations for literacy development and representational abstract thought, as we will discuss later in the chapter.

To become a master player is the height of developmental achievement for children ages 3 to 5. Master players are skilled at representing their experiences symbolically in self-initiated improvisational drama. Sometimes alone, sometimes in collaboration with others, they play out their fantasies and the events of their daily lives. Through pretend play, young children consolidate their understanding of the world, their language, and their social skills. (Jones & Reynolds, 1992, p. 1)

Dramatic play is seen when

- an older toddler holds a block to her ear and says, "Hello."

- a three-year-old carefully carries a pegboard filled with pegs over to the teacher, singing "Happy Birthday."

- a four-year-old manipulates small figures in and out of a house, talking for each character.

Sociodramatic play is seen when

- several five-year-olds play shoe shop, with one child playing the role of the store clerk and two others coming to try on shoes.

- one child says to another, "You can be the mother now, okay, and I'll be the big sister getting ready for my date."

Games with Rules

Games with rules become part of the play of school-age children and beyond. This play depends on children's understanding and agreement to use a set of prearranged rules. Logical thinking and social controls and skills are necessary for this stage of becoming "serious players" (Wasserman, 2000). Sometimes, the games are formally named and recognized; at other times, they involve simple play pacts between children, who establish their own informal sets of rules on the spot. In both cases, being able to play games with rules is contingent on concrete mental operations that enable children to reason logically and understand order in the world.

Ability to play games with rules is seen when

- a group of seven-year-olds chooses teams for a game of kickball.
- two six-year-olds play a game of checkers in which they have decided that each player may move twice in a row.
- the after-school program has abundant equipment to encourage various ball games.
- the neighborhood group using the bike ramp for jumps decides that those who jump the highest get to go first next turn.

SOCIAL STAGES OF PLAY

In a now-classic study of children's social participation in play, Parten (1932) described various stages in children's social behavior. These stages are described in the following sections.

Onlooker Behavior

The child who simply watches others at play is engaging in **onlooker** behavior. Onlookers may be children who are reluctant to join others or who are learning to play by watching others (Anderson, 2002).

Three children are digging a hole together in the sandbox. A fourth child sits nearby, watching.

Solitary Play

The child who plays alone, without any overt interaction with others, is engaging in **solitary play** (see Figure 2-4). This play is often typical of young and inexperienced players, although older children who undertake complex pretend play or remove themselves from the play of others also engage in it.

Two-year-old Renata sits on the floor, fitting together a collection of rings.

Five-year-old Pietra sits on the floor with an assortment of farm animals and figures arranged around her and small block buildings for each group.

Parallel Play

Figure 2-4

Solitary play allows children to explore their own interests.

Parallel play is seen when children share materials or play near each other without attempting to coordinate or connect their play. Children engaging in parallel play do not acknowledge the play of others. This kind of play may be a precursor to group play.

Two boys sit on the carpet pushing toy cars. Both make car sounds with their mouths, but neither looks at the other.

Two children are coloring with markers. When one puts down the red marker, the other picks it up. No words are spoken.

Associative Group Play

Associative group play is the first kind of group play differentiated by Parten. This type of play occurs when children are involved in similar activities near each other, perhaps sharing materials, but without committing to a joint focus in their play. Some interaction occurs between the children.

Two children digging in the sand agree that each can use one of the dump trucks, but each child continues digging her own hole.

Cooperative Play

Cooperative play is the second form of group play and represents real efforts to negotiate play themes and roles with peers. Conversation among the players establishes the roles and events of the play.

"Okay, but pretend that the baby got real sick, and you have to take her to the doctor real quick."

"Okay, then you better get the car." The players then resume their play roles of mother and father.

Understanding the terminology introduced in this section will help teachers and students identify the categories and stages of children's play, a necessary first step to understanding how best to support the play. Before considering teacher support, however, it is important to understand the theoretical basis of learning through play.

THEORIES OF PLAY AND DEVELOPMENT

Major perspectives influencing our understanding of play derive from well-known theorists. Piaget and Vygotsky, the two theorists whose ideas have dominated the field of research on play during the past sixty years or so, have different perspectives concerning how play influences cognitive development, but both find that play is the vehicle for children's construction of knowledge. First we will consider their separate perspectives on play and cognitive development.

Piaget and Play

Piaget believed that learning takes place through constructivist processes. This means that knowledge is not acquired by taking in information from the environment or imitating the actions of others, but by building knowledge and skills through a slow, continuous process of construction, modifying the understandings that children bring to each situation. Two processes, **assimilation** (taking in information and using it for one's own pleasure without adapting one's thinking to it) and **accommodation** (adapting current levels of thinking or **schema** to take new information into account), allow children to make changes in their mental models, that is, to intelligently adapt. As children play, Piaget believed, they encounter (assimilate) new things and ideas. When the new information or situation doesn't fit what they already know, children experience confusion (**disequilibrium**). They try to master the new idea by adjusting their current ideas (accommodating) to the new idea, thus learning something new and reaching a new level

Figure 2-5

This girl is deeply involved in exploring the physical properties of oobleck—cornstarch and water.

of understanding (**equilibrium**). Piaget believed that play is primarily an assimilatory activity (Berk & Winsler, 1995; Kagan, 1990), in which children can integrate the reality around them into their mental structures, practice newly formed representational ideas, and construct meaning from their experience. In the play, children "intuitively express elements of an experience or situation that do not fit neatly into already developed structures for interpreting and expressing meaning. In reflecting on their play . . . children formulate their inquiry" (Monighan-Nourot, 2003, p. 134). Even when children play with others, the play is primarily carried out as part of an individual child's developmental growth.

Piaget pointed out that young children need three basic kinds of knowledge: physical, logical-mathematical, and social. Children obtain **physical knowledge** from activities that allow them to observe and draw conclusions about the physical properties of objects (see Figure 2-5). For example, through play, children discover that cars roll quickly down an incline and that heavy objects sink in water. Children develop **logical-mathematical knowledge** as they discover relationships among objects, people, and ideas. A child playing with blocks discovers that placing a longer one on the bottom provides a sturdier base than a shorter one. Play offers children the experiences necessary to construct these kinds of knowledge. Other people teach **social knowledge** directly, as children learn cultural and societal customs and expected behavior. Nevertheless, play experiences with others allow children to apply the ideas they have learned in social situations. The preschool child develops the three kinds of knowledge by using spontaneous oral language, tools, and materials for creative expression and investigation.

Piaget noted that the development of symbolic or abstract thought is the major aspect of intellectual development in the early childhood years. The ability to transform objects, through pretend play, into a meaning different from the original reality denotes the beginning of **representational thought**. To think abstractly, children must be able to separate their actions in the here and now from the mental representations of those actions. Successively, through repeated rich play experiences, children grow in the stages of symbolic play. "Children's ability to enter 'as if' frames and to negotiate with others within those frames marks the human capacity to enter wholly mental realms of experience in the real world" (Monighan-Nourot, 2003, p. 134).

Piaget found another condition to promote cognitive restructuring in play in which children cooperate and interact with others. When children argue and disagree with peers, this conflict jars them into noticing that others hold different worldviews from their own (Berk & Winsler, 1995). Thus, in Piaget's view, contact with other children at play is important for a decline in the **egocentric thinking** that characterizes the preschool years (Piaget, [1923] 1926).

Vygotsky and Play

A Russian psychologist studying the relationship of social experience to children's learning about the same time as Piaget also had a constructivist approach, but with a difference. Rather than positing, as did Piaget, that children's increasing maturity and brain development allowed them to refigure their own mental processes, Vygotsky believed that the increasingly complex mental activities of the child were derived from social and cultural contexts. That is, social engagement and collaboration with others is the powerful force that transforms children's thinking. "According to Vygotsky ([1930–1935] 1978), through cooperative dialogues with more knowledgeable members of their society during challenging tasks, children learn to think and behave in ways that reflect their community's culture" (Berk & Winsler, 1995, p. 19). The key element in collaborating with more mature peers or adults is not conflict, as Piaget saw, but rather "the extent to which differences of opinion are resolved, responsibility is shared, and discourse reflects cooperation and mutual respect" (p. 20). This guided participation, or scaffolding (see Figure 2-6), will be discussed later in this chapter as we consider the roles of adults in supporting play.

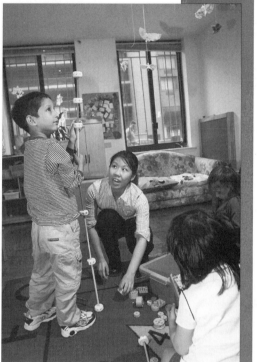

Vygotsky wrote only twelve pages on play (Vygotsky, [1930–1935] 1978), focusing on the importance of representational play during the preschool years. Fantasy play occupied an important place in his theory of cognitive development. In Vygotsky's words:

> Play creates a **zone of proximal development** in the child. In play, the child always behaves beyond his average age, above his daily behavior; in play it is as though he were a head taller than himself. As in the focus of a magnifying glass, play contains all developmental tendencies in a condensed form and is itself a major source of development. (Vygotsky, [1930–1935] 1978, p. 102)

The *zone of proximal development* cited by Vygotsky is the distance between the child's *actual* developmental level of independent problem solving and the *potential* developmental level of problem solving with adult guidance or working with more capable peers. (The zone of proximal development will be discussed more in later chapters.) Vygotsky believed education precedes development—that through guidance and support, children actively construct new cognitive abilities.

Figure 2-6

"Scaffolding" means supporting children to take steps they might not yet be able to take without adult assistance.

Vygotsky identified two critical features of play that indicate play's uniqueness and its role in development. (Interestingly, he differed from Piaget in highlighting play's symbolic features, noting that symbolism is not exclusive to play.) The first feature is that pretend play creates an imaginary situation that "permits the child to grapple with unrealizable desires" (Berk & Winsler, 1995, p. 53). Play first appears at the time when caregivers are insisting that toddlers postpone gratification of their desires and adopt socially desirable behaviors. Children see one situation, but act differently in relation to what they see; they rely on ideas to guide their behavior, not on the stimuli of the surrounding world. Their ability to use object substitutions in imaginative play is critical to this process. When a child uses a stick to represent a horse, the stick becomes a way to separate the meaning of the word (symbol) *horse* from a real horse. This use of a *pivot* object allows a separation of meaning that is critical to relying on abstract thought to guide behavior.

The second feature of symbolic play is that it contains rules for behavior that children must follow to successfully play the pretend scene. (This view is apart from that of researchers who define play as free of rules, although play rules are imposed by children based on their understanding of how things should be.) Imaginary situations are governed by the rules the child has learned in social contexts, as in rules or customary behaviors for playing house: "No, first you have go to work, and then you can have dinner." As children play together, they are working out meanings that relate to the needs of play, and many of these meanings are culturally constructed.

Although pretend play may be chosen spontaneously, children may not just act any way they please, but must follow the hidden or implicit rules of behavior. For Vygotsky, these two features of make-believe play support the development of two related capacities: the ability to separate thought from present objects and actions and the ability to restrict impulsive action and act in deliberately self-regulated ways.

One other difference between Vygotsky and Piaget relates to their understanding of the function of **private speech** in cognitive development. Private speech is often overheard as children play imaginatively or work their way through problem solving. Piaget believed that private speech is merely a characteristic of the mind of the preoperational child, egocentric and unable to take the perspectives of others, and having no positive function in development. However, Vygotsky interpreted private speech as used for a different purpose than for communicating with others. The goal of private speech, he felt, is to "communicate with the self for the purpose of self-regulation or guiding one's own thought processes and actions" (Berk & Winsler, 1995, p. 37). Gradually, private speech becomes covert, as inner speech or verbal thinking. This puts private speech in the important process of learning to think.

Cognitive Development and Play

Researchers following the theories of Piaget and Vygotsky discover relationships between various aspects of cognitive development and children's participation in imaginative play. Play gives children chances to practice divergent thinking, using objects in novel ways and increasing their ability to think flexibly and inventively as they solve the problems of play (Stone, 1995). "In the same way that adults 'talk through' processes and possible outcomes to problems they face, children 'play through' alternatives" (Monaghan-Nourot, 2003, p. 135). Children engaging in pretend play enhance creativity and imagination. Wasserman (2000) calls play the main source of our creativity, noting how many creative persons recall their play experiences as a beginning to their later creative expression.

Fantasy play strengthens memory for both narrative information and lists of objects. Language is embedded in play of all kinds (see Figure 2-7) and especially in sociodramatic play. Children have opportunities to hear others use speech correctly and to increase their vocabulary. In negotiating roles and disputes, children develop linguistic and conversational skills. Children continue to form and modify concepts through play. The capacity to reason theoretically also seems to be influenced by children experienced in entering the pretend mode. Make-believe play may even help children distinguish between appearance and reality. Thus, cognitive abilities are enhanced by children's participation in imaginative play.

Figure 2-7

Language is embedded in enjoyable play with others.

Bodrova and Leong (2004) point out that their research indicates that an emphasis on play does not detract from academic learning, but actually enables children to learn. "Play does not compete with foundational skills: Through mature play, children learn the foundational skills that will prepare them for academic challenges" (p. 10). They also report the research of Daniel Elkonin, a student of Vygotsky's. Elkonin identified four ways in which play influences cognitive development.

- Play affects children's motivation.
- Play facilitates cognitive **decentering**.
- Play supports the development of mental representations.
- Play fosters the development of deliberate behaviors.

Watch for more specifics on just how play influences foundational skills later in this chapter.

Emotional Development and Play

Erikson (1963) wrote of the role of play in children's ego development, seeing themselves as unique beings in relation to others. Through play, children become aware of their own and others' feelings and are able to take on the perspective of others. Observations show that play allows children to both release and reveal to others their feelings in a pretend world, where expression is not forbidden.

Children who play get opportunities to develop confidence and to master reality as they structure their own reality in a make-believe world. Vivian Paley's work with children in preschool and kindergarten classrooms describes children who write their own stories, and then act them out. Her guided play combines storytelling, writing, reading, and drama. The teacher helps children write their own scripts, as they take turns dictating stories that the teacher then reads aloud to the class. Then the children work together as a group to act out their stories. Paley says that children's questions and explanations are worked out dramatically every day. As she says, "There is no activity for which young children are better prepared than fantasy play. Nothing is more dependable and risk-free, and the dangers are only pretend" (Paley, 2004, p. 8). In play, she has observed children moving "from one strong emotion to the next, from pleasure to jealousy, from power to abandonment, to recovery," with almost every story beginning with, and returning to, a mother and child (Paley, 2004). Children use fantasy to calm their anxieties; Paley worries about the diminishing of play, particularly in children's school lives, saying, "When play is curtailed, how are they to confront their fantasy villains?"

Elkind (1981) suggests that play offers children a release from modern stress; actual physiological evidence links anxiety reduction to play (Stone, 1995). Bettelheim (1987) says play gives children a means of coping with past and present concerns, as well as a useful tool for preparing for future tasks.

> Play teaches the child, without his being aware of it, the habits most needed for intellectual growth, such as stick-to-it-iveness, which is so important in all learning. Perseverance is easily acquired around enjoyable activities such as chosen play. But if it has not become a habit through what is enjoyable, it is not likely to become one through an endeavor like schoolwork. (Bettelheim, 1987, p. 36)

The pleasure associated with play offers a positive emotional context for developing the disposition of perseverance. Play asks children to be involved only for the sake of the experience and as an end in itself, not for an external reward or the approval of others. Play encourages and empowers children to take risks; risk taking is necessary to extend learning and personal horizons. Play, says Wasserman (2000), strengthens children's feelings of personal power and helps them develop a "can-do" attitude. And for children with difficult life circumstances, emotional problems, or developmental delays, play may be even more critical (Golinkoff, Hirsh-Pasek, & Singer, 2006).

Figure 2-8

Play involves making compromises and cooperating with others.

Social Development and Play

Play encourages social interaction and, through this interaction, children acquire the social skills that can be learned only through experience. Thus, it is not surprising that teachers see preschoolers who spend more time in dramatic play as more socially competent. Play provides the context for learning to take another perspective. In play, children are presented with social problems to solve. Flexibility and the ability to consider multiple perspectives allow children to compromise or suggest alternatives in roles and scripts that prevent the play from breaking down. Children who are seen as *master players* (Reynolds & Jones, 1996) have this ability. Social popularity is related to the social abilities to resolve conflicts in friendly, nonaggressive ways (Trawick-Smith, 1994). The skills of learning to get along—taking turns, cooperating, sharing, compromising—are practiced in play (see Figure 2-8). Positive peer relationships and friendships are outcomes of repeated play experiences.

Play gives children the opportunity to learn and practice social conventions, as Vygotsky pointed out. In play, children also have opportunities to go beyond the social constraints of the real world; for example, children who are not generally encouraged to use particular materials or activities may move beyond such stereotypes in play. Play allows children to test concepts of socially acceptable and unacceptable behavior.

This separate discussion of social development should convey the complete interconnectedness of learning about the world within the social context. Vygotsky would state it strongly: There is no learning outside the social context (Berk & Winsler, 1995).

Physical Development and Play

JOURNAL REFLECTION

Memories of Childhood Play

Recall memories of your childhood play. Remember what you liked to play, favorite places to play, favorite playthings and playmates. Was much of your play indoors, or outdoors? Record these memories in your journal, as you consider the power and importance of play in the life of a child. Where possible, share your memories with a friend, and discover elements of play you shared. Reflect on what made your play rich and meaningful.

These memories are important, because teachers will not become real advocates for play until they convince themselves of the richness and power contained in play.

 Visit the premium Web site to complete this journal activity online and email it to your professor.

Physical development is nurtured primarily through play, as both gross and fine motor skills are practiced. Children at play develop control of their bodies as they run, climb, and skip. They judge distances as they turn cartwheels and jump. Their eye-hand coordination develops as they paint, cut, and construct. They enjoy testing out their bodies in motion. Play is a source of physical confidence, as children increase their skills and coordination. Playing is doing, which translates into physical development, mastery, and a positive self-concept.

In short, theorists and researchers alike find that play is the medium for learning that integrates all aspects of human development and helps children develop the skills and attitudes they need to adapt to future demands. No wonder an NAEYC position statement declares: "Child-initiated, teacher-supported play is an essential component of developmentally appropriate practice" (Bredekamp & Copple, 1997, p. 14).

PLAY AS DEVELOPMENTALLY APPROPRIATE CURRICULUM

Play is the medium best suited to preschool children's cognitive development. Early childhood educators a half century ago affirmed the importance of play in classrooms for young children. John Dewey, Patty Smith Hill, and Susan Isaacs all supported play as an opportunity for children to explore materials and develop concepts and problem-solving abilities, as well as enhancing social growth (Isenberg & Jalongo, 2000). Current thinking continues this emphasis. Statements from the major organizations for early childhood professionals (Association for Childhood Education International and the National Association for the Education of Young Children) affirm that play is the medium through which children most appropriately develop in all aspects (Bredekamp & Copple, 1997; Copple & Bredekamp, 2009; Isenberg & Quisenberry, 1988; ACEI, 2002). The developmental principle articulated in the most recent edition of the NAEYC Position Statement is # 10: **"Play is an important vehicle for developing self-regulation as well as promoting language, cognition, and social competence."** When we understand that children are not just empty pitchers to be filled with knowledge from someone else, but instead are active participants in constructing their own knowledge, we understand that play is the context for this active learning. It is through play that children literally teach themselves.

Play is being seriously challenged in many schools and programs, as parents and others pressure teachers to move to more controlled and specific curricula. Later in this chapter we will address the topic of how to help families appreciate the importance of play for laying foundations for academic success. Right now, it is vital for teachers to be able to articulate the important value of play. The following sections describe what play offers that makes it the most appropriate curriculum for young children.

1. Play Provides for All Areas of a Child's Development

Play provides for all areas of development in a simultaneous and integrated way; for example, when Thomas and Will work together on a large structure in the block area that they later call a space station, they are

- cooperating and sharing ideas and conversation.
- problem solving.
- developing eye-hand coordination and fine motor skills.
- working on an understanding of balance.
- representing a concept symbolically.
- extending attention span, task perseverance, and concentration.
- learning to listen and take into account the perspectives of others.
- expressing themselves in language.
- enjoying companionship and feelings of success.

Just consider other possible learning, and which of the domains is being developed in such a play scenario. What better curriculum could there be than one that supports the development of the whole child?

2. Play Emphasizes Learning as an Active/Interactive Process

The involvement of children in meaningful activities gives them a context for their learning. Vygotsky helped us understand that play leads development, that social engagement and collaboration with others is the powerful force that transforms children's thinking. Through cooperative dialogues and interactions with more knowledgeable peers or adults, children learn to think and behave in more mature ways. The following shows how the interchange between Thomas and Will began.

Will: "But we can't live there, because people don't live in space."

Thomas: "Well, but they live on space ships because I saw pictures. They were bouncing around."

Will (for whom this was obviously a new idea): "Okay, but there's no bouncing on the space station, because then it would fall to the water. Here, this can be the water," as he runs over to get a piece of paper from the art shelf across the room.

Figure 2-9

Children learn new ideas as they interact with other children.

Children who interact with other children are exposed to ideas they have to fit in with their own previous understandings. Mental growth results. (See Figure 2-9.)

3. Play Presents Highly Motivated Opportunities for Learning

Because children *choose* to participate in activities that are meaningful to them, play presents highly motivated opportunities for learning. They choose whether or not to play, their play partners and their tasks, their roles, and their involvement. The children accept the learning challenges because they are interested in and ready for the tasks they have selected.

Thomas: "Oh no, that part fell off." The two boys stare at each other and at the structure.

Will: "Here, I know. Put that big block on the corner. You hold it while I put the little one back on. See, that will do it."

A hundred lessons offered directly by a teacher on the concepts of size and balance could not have taught these two more than they taught themselves in their play.

Adults must be careful to distinguish between those kinds of adult-manipulated play that thinly disguise the adult's teaching/learning agenda and do not really allow children to freely choose what and how they will play. For example, Montessori's fine materials may be used only in a particular way, in a particular progression of skills, as presented by the teacher. This does not provide for children's choice, creativity, or true play.

4. Play Allows for Differences

Play allows for differences in developmental ability, interest, and learning style. Within the choices prepared by the teacher are opportunities for children to play alone or together; to play with simple or more complex materials; to construct, create, match, manipulate, explore, and pretend; and to succeed at their own level. "It is reasonable to assume that where a single teaching method is used for a diverse group of children, a significant proportion of these children are likely to fail" (Katz, 1987, p. 3). No such failure occurs in play where children are able to find the activities best suited to them, their needs, and their interests. Obviously, as children with special learning needs or disabilities are included in classrooms with more typically developing children, they can succeed at their level (whatever that level may be) in an environment designed for play (Sandall, 2004). (See Figure 2-10.)

In the center next to Thomas and Will, Julio is filling containers with red play dough. He pushes hard to see how much he can get in each container. Julio is challenged by his cerebral palsy and has difficulty using fingers separately. Beside him, Hilary and Anna chat about making pizza as they roll out and shape the play dough. Sam, at the end of the table, is making an "s" with his play dough and excitedly points it out to Julio: "See Julio, that says 's' for me!"

Children who play can set their own tasks and are likely to succeed at such self-assigned challenges. Self-confidence as learners grows.

5. Play Allows for Practice and Repetition of Newly Acquired Skills, Competencies, and Ideas

As the position statement reminds us, development and learning advance when children have many opportunities to practice newly acquired skills. Children need to be successful at learning much of the time in order to maintain their persistence and motivation. Practice in play and activity enhances that success.

This is why adults will often see children return to the same familiar puzzle or building activity, or to the same scripts for their play. Practice makes perfect, and again builds children's confidence as learners.

6. Play Promotes Self-Regulation

Children learn to regulate their behavior in dramatic play, as the explicit role they adopt limits their actions with its implicit rules. In play, children understand that they are imposing certain rules, ways that things are supposed to be done. One child grabs the phone to speak to the other, and the other child corrects him, "No, first you have to say 'Hello, this is the fire station, what is your emergency?'"—words they learned on a recent visit to the fire station. Or children plan together, knowing what the role behaviors and appropriate role speech will be: "Pretend you're the mean sister, okay?" Everybody knows how the "mean sister" behaves differently than the "good sister." Though pretend play is a spontaneous activity, children may not act just anyway they choose. Instead, in following the hidden rules of behavior learned from their environments, they learn to regulate their own behavior. Vygotsky said that only sustained, intentional make-believe play would foster deliberateness and **self-regulation**. How many elementary school teachers have you heard say that children in their classrooms don't seem to have self-discipline anymore?

7. Play Contributes to Brain Development

The preschool years are the fastest growth period for the frontal lobe networks, with play contributing to brain development. The speed of processing, memory, and problem solving increases as a result of this rapid growth. Because of the activity in the higher brain centers, preschool children increase in the levels of attention and their ability to inhibit impulses. Research shows that the synapses in the higher brain centers are activated by following scripts and taking roles that require self-regulation and problem solving (Bergen, 2004). Complex play experiences with other children enhance the development of the higher brain centers.

Moreover, play that links sensorimotor, cognitive, and social-emotional experiences provides an ideal setting for brain development. Optimal brain development occurs when the child interacts with the environment and the environment is responsive to that interaction. Play provides that kind of stimulation and integration (Johnson, Christie, & Wardle, 2005). Neuroscientists point out that the connections between brain cells that underlie new learning become hard-wired if they are used repeatedly, as happens in rich play experiences. "The more senses involved during learning,

Figure 2-10

When the environment is adapted for all children to play, children with special needs can succeed as well. Here a wide tray allows this girl to join the lotto game.

the more likely the brain will receive and process information" (Schiller & Willis, 2008, p. 54). Play activity uses multiple senses. Healthy brain development is essential for later academic success.

8. Play Promotes Acquisition of Foundational Skills

In today's climate of high concern about test results, a major interest of many parents and educators is making sure children will enter school ready to succeed in their academic future. This is where proponents of developmentally appropriate practice must be clear and specific in helping explain the link between play and foundation skills. There are literally dozens of studies that show the connections between play and many complex cognitive activities, such as memory, self-regulation, distancing and **decontextualization**, oral language abilities, symbolic generalization, successful school adjustment, and better social skills (Bodrova & Leong, 2004).

Children remember more when learned under play conditions. Given a list of ten words, children are better able to remember them in a play context. Children use more vocabulary in play, and more advanced oral speech patterns. Play allows children to advance in their mental representations. In their beginning pretend play, they use replicas to substitute for real objects—a toy telephone, for example. Then they move to using new objects that are different in appearance but can perform the same function—a block for the telephone. Finally, most of the substitution takes place in the child's speech, with no prop needed—the child who stares off into space, hand held to ear, and paces while carrying on an animated conversation with an invisible partner. This ability to make mental transformations contributes to the development of abstract thinking. Later, in school, when children learn the written symbols of language and mathematics, they use this ability, developed through play, to perform symbolic transformations. The ability to understand that H and K, cat, boy, 14 and 7 are combinations of lines that represent sounds, words, and numbers is similar to this capacity to use a block to represent a telephone.

In their spontaneous play activity, children show their knowing in the doing. In literacy-enriched play settings, they show us they understand the uses of literacy materials, as they take orders in a restaurant, write a prescription for a sick dog in the vet's office, or make highway signs for the roads built in the block area. Understanding what written language is for and how it works is an important part of emergent literacy. In studies that focus on the relationship between play and literacy, researchers find an increase in children's use of literacy materials and activities and gains in **phonological awareness** (Roskos & Christie, 2001). Thus, through play, children can learn in ways that the competent preschool mind can use to succeed, rather than in the deficiency models of the academic preschool that "demand premature practice of what one doesn't know how to do" (Jones & Reynolds, 1992, p. 5). The skills that children learn through purposeful, high-quality play experiences include skills in verbalization, language comprehension, vocabulary, problem solving, observation, empathy, imagination, taking on another's perspective, learning to cooperate with others, and using symbols. These are all foundational skills for all cognitive development and academic achievement.

But beyond foundational skills, there are other qualities of developing imagination and creativity in play that relate to the curriculum appropriate to prepare children for future success in this twenty-first century. Jerome Bruner put the dilemma of appropriate learning experiences this way: "How can school systems that prepare the young for entry into the society deal with a future that is increasingly difficult to predict within a single lifetime?" At least one answer to this question is to foster adaptive, flexible, creative thinking. Make-believe play is essential to the development of this capacity. "Let's pretend" is the foundation for the kinds of thinking that does not just lead to test results. (See Figure 2-11.)

Figure 2-11

High-quality play experiences lay important foundational skills.

And, when teachers are dealing with skeptics who believe that direct teaching of foundational skills is more important than play, they can report that a study that followed children from preschool through second grade, reported by David Elkind, found that children who had engaged in dramatic play as preschoolers demonstrated superior literacy and numerical skills. It doesn't have to be either/or. It's play *and* foundational skills.

9. Play Lays the Cornerstone for Social and Moral Development

As they create imaginary worlds together, children are presented with social problems to solve: What happens when two players both want to be the mommy? What if the pretend daddy refuses to help clean up the dishes? How can we include Suri, who doesn't speak any English but wants to play with us? And, perhaps the most urgent question of all, What do I do if they say I can't play?

Within the context of play, children learn to see things from another's viewpoint. (Wow, she really wants to be the mother too, or Suri looks like she wants to play, or even, they don't want me to play because they said I knocked down their house.) The ability to consider other perspectives enhances social flexibility and allows children to compromise or suggest alternatives in roles and scripts that allow the play to continue. (Okay Suri, you can be the kitty, as the child realizes that kitties have no need for English, or How about we both be mommies taking our babies to the park to play?) Children who are experienced players have the ability to resolve conflicts in friendly, nonaggressive ways. The skills of learning to get along—taking turns, cooperation, sharing, and compromising—are practiced in play. These skills, in fact, can be learned only through experience, not taught by adults. Positive peer relationships and friendships are outcomes of repeated play experiences. And the best outcome is acquiring the skills to treat others with respect and consideration, while feeling competent and accepted in the world of peers. Studies show that teachers evaluate preschoolers and primary children who spend more time in dramatic play as more socially competent. An important study by the National Institutes of Mental Health, published in 2000, was titled *A Good Beginning—Sending America's Children to School with the Social and Emotional Competence They Need to Succeed.* That social competence, achieved through the interaction of play, will have more lasting effects on early academic success than any pile of preschool work sheets.

10. Play Supports Children's Emotional Development

Daniel Goleman argues that emotional intelligence, or EQ, is a more influential factor determining a child's future than his IQ. Play provides simultaneously for intellectual and emotional development. Through play, children become aware of their own and others' feelings and are able to empathize and take on the perspective of others. Play allows children to both express and cope with their feelings in a world that is not real, so expression is safe and acceptable. For example, sometimes teachers see a child punish a baby doll harshly, and then comfort it, as she perhaps deals with her own feelings at receiving adult anger, or even being replaced by a new baby.

As children play, they can come to understand their feelings in an intuitive sense and deal with them in concrete yet imaginary ways. Real-world stress, pain, and fear can be decreased through play. Consider the child who had recently moved to a new apartment after Mom and Dad had split, spending playtime after playtime packing clothes and dishes in a box, transporting them, and then unpacking, as her play helped her cope with the new situation and changes in her life.

Three common themes in children's play have their roots in children's emotional realities and desires: the need for protection (I'll be the baby, okay, and you can be my mommy.); the need for power over things (I'm going to be the Superflyer and I'm faster than everybody.) and the need to attack and destroy (Did you know that Superflyers can wreck people's houses?). Play

Play Across Cultures

While it is true that all over the world children play, culture determines the kinds of play that are typical, and how adults interact with children as they play. "Culture helps determine whether play is seen more as something that children do on their own with little or no adult involvement or whether adult involvement is valuable" (Gonzalez-Mena, 2008, p. 103). Another cultural variation is the degree to which adults believe that children should play just because it is part of childhood, and the degree to which play is valued as the medium for children's learning. These ideas will influence how readily adults can accept the idea that play is essential for laying the foundation for all later learning. This understanding is vital, especially to teachers who are proponents of developmentally appropriate practice.

Consider also the reasons that dressing up for pretend play is not acceptable for children in some cultures, or is frowned on for just some children, such as boys—how do cultural values influence this attitude?

gives children opportunities to master these feelings and impulses and to struggle with the sense of good and bad. Play allows children to make sense of their relationships with their family and friends. Play allows kids to figure out who they are.

For years, David Elkind has written about the stress of modern children, and the release play offers them from this stress. Actual physiological evidence links anxiety reduction to play. Play makes children feel better.

These, then, are ten good reasons that play should be considered the most developmentally appropriate medium for young children. Use them as you discuss the question "Why play?" with parents and colleagues.

Children who are actively involved in activities they have chosen with materials they can use successfully show the correctness of considering play as the appropriate curriculum for them. They are filled with energy, enthusiasm, and curiosity. They are excited by their discoveries and confident in their abilities. Participation in the play is extending their ability to stay with a task, that is, to persevere. They do not have to be harangued or manipulated into staying with the task a little longer. Their self-esteem as learners and as people is nurtured.

In the light of such evidence of the importance of play, some contemporary authors are arguing for clear play policies to articulate and promote the importance of play for all children and to enable all children to have equal access to good quality play environments in their local communities (Hampshire Play Policy Forum, 2002).

In addition, research has shown that certain conditions support and enhance play optimally. We will now consider these conditions.

CONDITIONS THAT SUPPORT PLAY

Play occurs within particular contexts, and the context may provide certain conditions that support the quality of play. Read the examples that follow to identify some of the conditions that foster quality play.

This morning one of the classroom choices is the sensory table filled with sawdust. The teacher has added some small plastic dinosaurs and pieces of greenery to the table. Another choice is a small table that holds three mounds of play dough along with some small baking utensils. Still another choice is a box of small cars, placed on the floor near the cubbyhole behind the easel.

On the playground, a box of scarves and old ties stands ready for the children to find them, along with some plastic hoops and ropes. Yesterday, playground play was disrupted several times by children attempting to duplicate some superhero play they had seen on television. Knowing many of them had been to the circus the week before, the teacher is hoping the materials will suggest a change in the theme of the play.

The teacher sits cutting materials near the dramatic play area, where Heather, Rob, and Lia are playing with medical props, bandaging some of the stuffed animals. When a dispute over the stethoscope breaks out, the teacher asks, "Are any of the patients ready to go home yet?"

A teacher, noticing the store play again today in the dramatic play area, hands a pile of newly made money to a child standing nearby, and says "Looks like they'll need some more money for the change."

Examining these vignettes yields some ideas about the conditions adults can control when creating environments to support play. Bruner (1983) noted that play is improved when the following conditions exist: available playmates; appropriate play materials, especially those planned to encourage more combining experiences; and an adult nearby, not necessarily involved in the action, but as a source of stability in the play situation. When teachers stay close to the play, they can see where appropriate intervention could be helpful (see Figure 2-12).

Other researchers have noted that factors in the physical context, such as amounts and arrangements of space and materials for play, help children focus their attention on play. Sufficient unscheduled time is another physical variable that influences the duration and complexity of play that develops. Play is also affected by real-world experiences and the context of social and cultural relationships in the larger world. We will consider these aspects separately here.

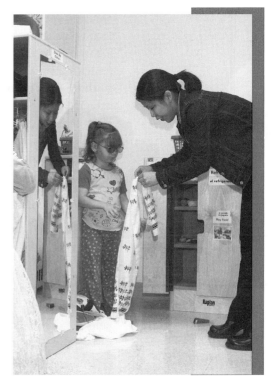

Figure 2-12

When teachers stay close to children's play, they see when intervention might be helpful.

Physical Environment for Play

The arrangements teachers make in the physical environment influence children's ability to make play choices, become involved and sustain play, and interact with others. Elizabeth Jones suggests that teachers consider themselves as stage managers, creating the settings that will promote play. As teachers create play spaces, with clear pathways and boundaries, children can readily identify play choices and materials, as well as find the privacy needed to create play scenarios. Flexibility about placement, movement, and use of furnishings and materials—"Hey, that little stool could be our campfire!"—can allow play to expand, as well as support creative representation. Space is important; aggression and less social play behaviors increase as the amount of space decreases (Ward, 1996). Providing spaces both large enough for several children to play together and small enough to support private fantasy play helps children at all stages of play. More sociodramatic play occurs in partitioned spaces than in large open areas (Ward, 1996). The teacher who set up the area that suggested individual play with cars and the play dough table that invited three to "bake" together created this kind of physical environment.

Providing a variety of materials influences play from both developmental and cultural viewpoints. Having realistic replications of real-life objects may help children who are not yet advanced in their symbolic representation, as well as children who identify items familiar from their home and cultural context. The little cars are an example of such realistic materials. Also, providing abundant **loose parts**—open materials that can be used and combined in any number of ways—allows children to create and extend their own ideas in play. The scarves, ties, ropes, and hoops mentioned earlier are examples of such loose parts. Play needs plenty of props.

Alert teachers also add, or provide an atmosphere in which children feel free to add or create their own props that extend play or encourage more children to join in, as did the teacher with the play money and the children with the stool. When children move with materials to other areas, teachers should not feel the need to make children put toys away as they move on—later at the end of play is fine, lest great ideas be interrupted. Time is another variable of the physical environment. When teachers allow large, uninterrupted blocks of time, complex play will more likely develop. In one study, a minimum of thirty minutes was required for children to become fully involved in quality play (Johnson, Christie, & Wardle, 2005). It takes time to produce an idea, select roles, find pretend props, negotiate, and communicate. Just as children vary in their social stages of play, temperament, and style, some may need more time to involve themselves in play. An onlooker may have to observe the play long enough to find a convenient entry place and method, and a parallel player may slowly warm up to group interaction. Enough time allows children to expand and develop play scripts; too little time may push them into merely repetitive or very simple play themes. Classrooms that support play provide unbroken periods of time, both indoors and out. Outdoors, dramatic play develops after physical exploration—usually taking more than forty-five minutes to get started. And, of course, time for play also means not interrupting children's play to achieve a teacher's goal, such as making a picture to take home to Mom, when the child is happily constructing in the block area.

Real-World Experiences

Opportunities for hands-on, real-world experiences provide children with the basis for imagination. Classroom teachers provide these experiences by planning field trips, inviting visitors from the surrounding community into the classroom, and carefully selecting children's literature. The teacher who hoped to stimulate a circus theme for play, for instance, provided props to help the children re-create and revisit their real experience. (The aggressive play that had disturbed the playground the day before was an imitation of a not-real experience from television that had not given as much richness for the children's imagination to explore.)

Teacher Intervention

Smilansky (1968) was the first to suggest that adult intervention in children's sociodramatic play might enrich the quality of the play. In her research on low-income immigrant children in Israel, she found that some children play in less social, imaginative, verbal, or organized ways than do others; in fact, some do not engage in pretend play at all. She hypothesized that children's inability to engage in sociodramatic play could correlate with later academic difficulties in school, and that specific adult strategies could teach children new play skills. In today's world, many educators are concerned that children's home and classroom experiences are not sufficient to produce the rich, imaginative play long considered to be a characteristic of early childhood. Reasons for this may include the fact that changes in the social context now place children for most of their playtime in the company of same-age peers who may not act as effective teachers of advanced play skills. In addition, toy manufacturers produce increasingly realistic playthings, which do not encourage the need for representational skills. So-called "educational toys," created for marketing to anxious parents, often do not stimulate pretend play. The present emphasis on increasing academic demands in preschool and kindergarten programs also contributes to children's lack of play opportunities (Bodrova & Leong, 2004).

Smilansky developed a system for assessing the quality of children's sociodramatic play that included being able to

- choose a role and maintain pretend behavior consistent with the role.
- use make-believe props, gestures, and words in pretend actions.
- expand pretend play into episodes, rather than simply imitating brief actions.
- sustain their pretend play over time (a minimum of five minutes for preschoolers).
- play with at least one other child.
- communicate verbally to coordinate and direct the action.

Heidemann and Hewitt (2010) have developed a Play Checklist for teachers to use in observing children's play, adapting some of Smilansky's ideas, and further expanding it to include social skills needed for play (see Figure 2-13).

Play Checklist

Child's Name: _____   Date: _____   Date of Birth: _____

Check the highest level skills you consistently observe:

*1. Pretending with Objects
❑ Does not use objects to pretend
❑ Uses real objects
❑ Substitutes objects for other objects
❑ Uses imaginary objects

*2. Role-Playing
❑ No role play
❑ Uses one sequence of play
❑ Combines sequences
❑ Uses verbal declaration (for example, "I'm a doctor")
❑ Imitates actions of role, including dress

*3. Verbalizations About the Play Scenario
❑ Does not use pretend words during play
❑ Uses words to describe substitute objects
❑ Uses words to describe imaginary objects and actions (for example, "I'm painting a house")
❑ Use words to create a play scenario (for example, "Let's say we're being taken by a monster")

*4. Verbal Communication During a Play Episode
❑ Does not verbally communicate during play
❑ Talks during play only to self
❑ Talks only to adults in play
❑ Talks with peers in play by stepping outside of role (for example, "That's not how mothers hold their babies")
❑ Talks with peer from within role (for example, "Eat your dinner before your dad comes home")

*5. Persistence in Play
❑ Less than five minutes
❑ Six to nine minutes
❑ Ten minutes or longer

*6. Interactions
❑ Plays alone
❑ Plays only with adults
❑ Plays with one child, always the same person
❑ Plays with one child, can be different partners
❑ Can play with two or three children together

**7. Entrance into a Play Group
❑ Does not attempt to enter play group
❑ Uses force to enter play group
❑ Stand near group and watches
❑ Imitates behavior of group
❑ Makes comments related to play theme
❑ Gets attention of another child before commenting

8. Problem Solving
❑ Gives in during conflict
❑ Uses force to solve problems
❑ Seeks adult assistance
❑ Imitates verbal solutions or strategies provided by adults
❑ Recalls words or strategies to use when reminded
❑ Initiates use of words or strategies
❑ Accepts reasonable compromises

9. Turn Taking
❑ Refuses to take turns
❑ Leaves toys, then protests when others pick them up
❑ Takes turns if arranged and directed by an adult
❑ Asks for turn, does not wait for a response
❑ Gives up toy easily if done with it
❑ Gives up toy if another child asks for it
❑ Proposes turn taking, will take and give turns

10. Support of Peers
❑ Shows no interest in peers
❑ Directs attention to distress of peers
❑ Shows empathy or offers help
❑ Offers and takes suggestions of pees at times
❑ Encourages or praises peers

Note: The developmental progression outlined in each segment of the Play Checklist can be used as a guideline when assessing most children's development. However, not all children will go through the same steps in development nor through the same developmental sequence.

* Smilansky, Sara. 1968. The effects of sociodramatic play on disadvantaged preschool children. New York: Wiley.

** Hazen, Nancy, Betty Black and Faye Fleming-Johnson. 1984. Social acceptance: Strategies children use and how teachers can help children learn them. Young Children, 39: 26–36.

Play by Sandra Heidemann and Deborah Hewitt, copyright © 2010. Redleaf Press grants permission to photocopy this page for classroom use.

You can download a copy of the Play Checklist from the Redleaf Press Web site, www.redleafpress.org. Enter "Play" into the search field and follow the links.

Figure 2-13

The checklist could help teachers assess children's social skills needed for play. Checklist from *Play: The pathway from theory to practice* by Sandra Heidemann and Deborah Hewitt, copyright © 2010 by Sandra Heidemann and Deborah Hewitt. Reprinted with permission of Redleaf Press, St. Paul, MN, www.redleafpress.org

The intervention techniques Smilansky identified include the following:

- providing real experiences for children to play out and then providing props that relate to those experiences
- observing children's play carefully to note those who don't pretend or who need adult assistance to extend their play
- intervening actively to help children develop their play abilities. Returning to the term used by Vygotsky's followers to describe helping children take the next steps in their understanding, this intervention, or play coaching, is a kind of scaffolding.

Teachers who are considering appropriate intervention in children's play must observe certain cautions (Smilansky & Shefatya, 1990). Teachers should intervene only if and when children need support. When play is proceeding well, a teacher's best role is observer, learning about the children through their play. When teachers do intervene, their methods should not disrupt the play, but instead preserve and continue it. Intervention should be brief, with teachers withdrawing as soon as possible. When children indicate that they would rather play alone, this should be respected.

When teachers decide that intervention would benefit play, they may take several approaches, including helping children plan and organize play, prompting to add new ideas, modeling to demonstrate play behaviors, and providing props.

Helping Children Plan and Organize Play. In mature play, children can describe to each other what the play scenario is, who is playing which role, and how the action will proceed. After the teacher observes the play, it may be appropriate to help the children define their focus and intentions. This might seem necessary when play is not developing into complex episodes, as when children are developing their play fragments independently or are not making their pretend intentions clear to other participants. The teacher then can enter play that has already started as a *co-player;* the adult influences the play by asking for instructions, and responding to the children's actions and comments (Heidemann & Hewitt, 2010). By asking a question, the teacher can help children organize their make-believe mentally and interact more verbally with other players, resulting in more complex play.

"Where are you going in your car?"

"What are you going to cook for supper?"

"Who are you going to be?"

Figure 2-14

Asking children questions may help them organize their pretend play.

Prompting to Add New Ideas. Teachers may extend play by asking questions, giving hints, or providing direct suggestions—cues, like a stage director (see Figure 2-14). This may encourage children to use objects for representation, involve other children in the play, or otherwise extend the play theme. This play tutoring may come from outside the play (outside intervention) as the teacher sits close by, making comments and suggestions to the children, or from within, as the teacher plays with the children (inside intervention), taking a role as an active participant (Ward, 1996). In this more direct intervention, the teacher suggests specific strategies to help play develop, and teaches new play behaviors within the episode.

"Maybe you could use a block for your notebook."

"We need somebody else for a patient—you could ask Darren."

"What could you use to keep your baby warm?"

By imaginatively entering play that is beginning to deteriorate, teachers can successfully extend it. They may model strategies from within the play.

"Well, I'm getting pretty hungry—is supper nearly ready?"

"Could I hold the baby for you while you cook our supper?"

Modeling to Demonstrate Play Behaviors. When teachers model, they actually demonstrate the pretend behaviors associated with playing roles. They may model as they play parallel with children, not interacting with children or directing the play, but doing what the children are doing in more sophisticated ways, and perhaps commenting on her own play. Teachers may model when invited to join play episodes, adding new ideas or information (see Figure 2-15).

They may also model how to start play episodes. You will read more about modeling in Chapter 15.

"I'm tired and hungry after our trip. I'll sit here and wait for you to serve supper."

"Mmm, this is delicious. How did you cook this chicken?"

"Uh-oh, I'm not feeling so good. Could you please drive me to the doctor's office?"

Providing Props. Children's pretend play can be supported when teachers add props related to the theme when appropriate. Adding props may extend the play or make it more complex. As teachers provide culturally relevant materials, they encourage children to play with familiar items.

  VIDEO ACTIVITY

Go to the premium Web site and watch the video clip for Chapter 2 entitled "The Importance of Play." Then answer the following questions:

REFLECTIVE QUESTIONS

1. As you watch this video, be sure you understand the distinct kinds of social play illustrated, as they were discussed in this chapter. Consider what the child gains from each kind of play.

2. As you watch the final scenario, consider the separate roles of a teacher, as discussed in this chapter, which support this play.

3. If the teacher felt she could extend this play, what would be a good way for her to enter the play?

Visit the premium Web site to complete these questions online and email them to your professor.

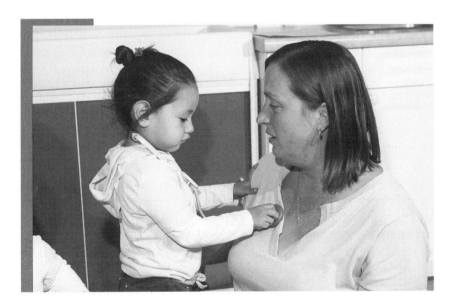

(a)

Figure 2-15 (a & b)

When teachers play with children, they may model behaviors and add new ideas.

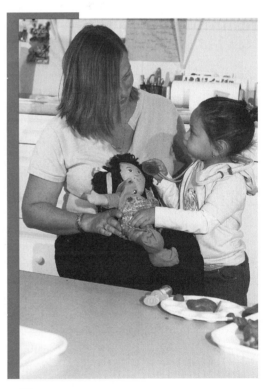

(b)

PRACTICAL IMPLICATIONS

Understanding the Importance of Play

Teachers who understand and value play as the optimum medium for development and learning can:

- articulate to others the reasons why play supports development, to gain support.
- identify kinds of play and classify social stages of play, so that they know when children need help.
  - set up environments that support play.
  - provide materials that enhance play.
  - schedule their time to allow play to develop fully.
  - provide play opportunities to match the abilities of all children.
  - display helpful interaction while avoiding interference.
  - let children play in productive situations that help achieve the goals and objectives of early learning standards.

"I see you're going on a bus. Here are some tickets."

"Here's a spoon if you need one to taste your soup."

"Would you like to use this wok to fix your dinner?"

Teachers should, however, be cautious regarding intervention. Some teacher intervention may actually interrupt the play. Sometimes when teachers enter the play, they are so dominant that the play begins to center around the adults. This is obviously disruptive.

Another temptation is to interrupt the play to teach concepts. When teachers do intervene, their methods should not disrupt the play, but instead preserve and continue it. As Elizabeth Jones has written,

> When in doubt, trust the play. It is the children's curriculum. Play that is scattered or potentially disruptive may require refocusing, but well-focused complex play requires no intervention. . . . Adults who interrupt play, whatever their reasons, are usually in so much of a hurry that they fail to pay attention to the children's purposes. SLOW DOWN is advice to keep in mind. . . . We learn most about

children, and help them learn most, when we pay attention to what is happening for them as they play. (Jones & Reynolds, 1992, pp 55–56)

ISSUES INVOLVING PLAY

There are many questions and concerns that arise regarding children's play. Discussion of these issues follows.

Violent Play

An ongoing question about intervention in children's play relates to the violent kinds of play teachers call "war and superhero play." Often stimulated by children's exposure to certain kinds of television programming, one concern has been that such play is merely repetitive, limited to the very narrow range of ideas introduced by a particular program, and painstakingly reenacted without development but with complete duplication of the violence. In addition, teachers worry that such play will cause children to feel out of control, frightened, or hurt, and will teach harmful lessons about violence. Certainly in recent times, children have been exposed to many violent world events. Many of today's best-selling toys are linked to violent media, drawing children into replicating the violent stories they see in the media.

There are opposing schools of thought about this kind of play. Some argue that it should be restricted completely or at least limited to particular times or places, such as outdoor playtime. Others limit it by prohibiting weapons, saying, "No guns/knives/and so on, allowed." Enforcing such a rule brings constant struggle. But some proponents argue that children's play based on television themes should not be restricted in these ways because developmental benefits may result from such play (Carlsson-Paige & Levin, 1987, 1990; Levin, 2004). For example, children may gain a feeling of power or explore the distinctions between reality and fantasy in such play. Unfortunately, though, superhero play may end abruptly when someone gets hurt. Levin reports that children who appear to be most obsessed with war and superhero play have the hardest time engaging in creative and imaginative play of their own scripts.

One way out of the dilemma is to permit the play but actively intervene to help children develop understandings about violence and war and alternative methods of solving problems (Carlsson-Paige & Levin, 1987). A teacher's questions can help children consider the consequences of violence and other options, broaden their roles, or encourage more imaginative, less stereotypical reenactments. Such teacher intervention may be appropriate for this kind of play. Teachers can encourage children to talk about media violence, correct children's misconceptions, and provide reassurance about safety. They can also help children convert the stereotyped behaviors into transformational play; for example, they could help children make up their own stories about their favorite characters from a TV program.

Such an important topic should be addressed with families, helping them learn more about protecting children from violence, including promoting play with open-ended toys, rather than those toys linked to violence. See the NAEYC position statement on media violence in children's lives (NAEYC, 1990).

Cultural and Technological Influences on Play

Although play is universal, the appearance of specific forms of play differs across different cultures. How play is expressed depends on a child's cultural context. Reasons for this likely depend on distinct cultural values regarding the value of play for children in general and expectations or limitations on activity for both genders. Adults in a culture determine the play environments and materials they will provide for children and the kinds of play they model and approve. The kinds of mother-child pretend play vary from culture to culture. As adults involve themselves in children's play, this intervention is indeed cultural, sometimes teaching lessons of facilitating play directly, leading to the thought that there is not necessarily one best way for children and adult to play.

Many observers have noted recently that the very ability to play is being affected in young children in contemporary America, because they are so influenced by developments in culture today. The popularity of technology and the availability of computer and video games may be having an effect on social play and on creative imaginative play. Screen time—time before television, DVDs, computer screens—takes an increasing amount of time in children's lives, time they once spent in play. This means that children are usually passive recipients of someone else's agenda. Two-thirds of children under two use some kind of screen media on a typical day for about two hours—this despite the fact that the American Academy of Pediatrics has recommended *no* television for children under age two, partly because of the lack of information about the prolonged effect of television viewing on the immature eye. Children under age six spend an average of two to three hours a day with screen media—at least three times longer than the time they spend being read to or reading. The deregulation of children's television programming in the late 1980s allowed toy manufacturers to both produce children's television programming and market toys during television shows. Such an influence obviously affects children's play. Moreover, prolonged time spent in passive communication with screen media reduces the time they are spending in interesting exploration, writing their own scripts, or acting out their own stories. Too often, when children play out the stories they have seen, the scripts of television stories become a limiting force, not something to use as a springboard for their own stories. And also not incidentally, children spending screen time are basically spending time alone, not interacting with siblings or neighborhood playmates. So much that could be learned about how to play with others is missed when children are denied such interaction with other children. They are indoors, inactive, and missing so many of the joys of being in the natural world. In the book *Last Child in the Woods* by Richard Louv (2008), the author asked some children where they most preferred to play. One boy replied, "Inside, because that's where the electrical outlets are." Those outlets and everything plugged into them are threatening children's ability to really play.

Screen time is not the only insidious contribution of the technological age. Toys containing embedded computer chips have also affected children's play. All kinds of toys are going high-tech—industry analysts estimate that at least 75 percent of toys debuting this year have a microchip that controls the action and dictates the play.

Another cultural influence on play is the loss of freedom for children to play freely outdoors, as parents react to dangers in neighborhoods. Today, adult supervision and protection is deemed necessary, and that diminishes real opportunities for play. In addition, some of the overprogramming of children's time in organized activities also takes away from their time and ability to play spontaneously. Classes and enrichment activities abound for even the youngest children, meaning that adults are organizing and controlling the activity. Once again, child-initiated play suffers.

Cultural values have impact on children's play. For example, one study compared populations of middle-class Korean-American and middle-class Anglo-American children in separate pre-schools. Influenced by Anglo-American values, that preschool encouraged independent thinking, problem solving, and active involvement in learning, with available choices from a wide range of activities. The Anglo-American preschool encouraged social interaction among the children and collaboration with the teacher. In the Korean-American preschool, in keeping with their traditional values, there was an emphasis on completing tasks and developing academic skills. The Korean-American preschool allowed children to talk and play only during outdoor playtime.

The observers found that Anglo-American children engaged in more social play, and that the Korean-American children engaged in more unoccupied or parallel play. The Korean-American children played more cooperatively, often offering toys to other children, likely a reflection of the cultural emphasis on group harmony. The Anglo-American children were more aggressive in their play, often responding negatively to other children's suggestions, perhaps showing the cultural value of competitiveness in American culture (Papalia, Olds, & Feldman, 2006). "Cultures that value verbal expression, fantasy, and imaginative play will encourage that kind of play, and cultures that value play, movement, and manipulation of real objects will place more value on functional and constructive play" (Johnson, Christie, & Wardle, 2005, p. 188).

Another observer noted that children in New Guinea play games in which neither side wins, and the game ends only when both sides achieve equality. This sounds quite different from games in America that typically stress competition. Play, then, reflects and expresses the cultural knowledge children have acquired.

Research shows that there is enormous variation across cultures in the content and style of children's play. Current research on culture and play centers on: investigations that describe play and related behaviors in specific cultures; comparisons of play of children in different countries; and study of the play of immigrant children attending preschools in a new culture (Johnson, Christie, & Wardle, 2005). Sociocultural approaches have begun to articulate a culturally sensitive theory of play, one that tries to understand how universal and cultural variable aspects of play interact in specific communities.

Principles from preschool programs around the world are worth considering by American early childhood educators. The entire issue of *Young Children* from September 2004 highlights similarities and unique perspectives from early childhood education in Malaysia, Japan, Cuba, Kenya, Iceland, Budapest, and Nordic countries, as well as an extensive bibliography of resources about play and early childhood education around the globe.

Play is a powerful way for young children to practice the roles and skills they will need as adults in their culture. Therefore, it follows that specific play behaviors and scripts will vary from culture to culture.

Researchers also find that boys and girls play differently in most cultures, perhaps attributable to cultural influence on their play, as well as to biological and brain differences (Gurian, 2001). Boys generally like rough-and-tumble play in groups. Girls generally play more quietly, with one playmate (see Figure 2-16). Moreover, across cultures, parents and teachers tend to treat boys and girls differently, encouraging boys in stereotypically masculine activities such as block play and rough-and-tumble play, and girls in doll and nurturing play (Johnson, Christie, & Wardle, 2005).

Figure 2-16
Girls generally prefer quieter kinds of play, often with just one other friend.

Even when boys and girls play with the same toys, they play more socially with others of the same gender. Boys play more boisterously and girls more cooperatively. In dramatic play, boys generally create scenarios that involve danger and fighting, whereas girls' plots generally focus on maintaining social relationships. Again, no doubt cultural values and expectations influence some of these differences. It is also worth noting that the majority of early childhood teachers are females who may or may not be able to appreciate rough-and-tumble play of male children.

It is important for teachers to be aware of the cultural values of all the families in a classroom, to become sensitive to their attitudes regarding play, and to understand the expectations they have for both girls and boys. Teachers should not expect that all parents will necessarily appreciate the value of play and should anticipate the need for clear, accepting, and ongoing dialogue. Indeed, concern about the academic achievement gap between many minority children and white and Asian children causes many of their parents to assume that they will benefit more from direct instruction, and that play is not the best path to later success. Many parents believe that learning important academic skills and concepts should not necessarily be pleasurable and certainly not child-initiated, as is good play. We shall address this issue later in the chapter.

Play for Children with Special Needs

Children who have particular disabilities are children first. Their families and teachers are challenged to provide environments that allow the children to participate as fully as possible in the play of childhood. As teachers understand the limitations and necessary adaptations for particular children, they can help all children participate in and learn from their play. There has been a bias toward direct instruction in special education, believing that the desired outcomes would not occur without intervention and explicit teaching. Recently the Council for Exceptional Children, Division for Early Childhood (DEC) has paid specific attention to the importance of play for children with disabilities. The DEC Recommended Practices specifically states: "Play routines are structured to promote interaction, communication, and learning by defining roles for dramatic play, prompting engagement, prompting group friendship activities, and using specialized props" (Sandall, Hemmeter, Smith, & McLean, 2005). It is recognized that direct instructional strategies may be needed to help children with disabilities initiate activity, use materials appropriately, and make choices. Many of the ideas for adaptations will come as teachers observe each child's play and learn to match the level of support with the child's specific need.

Modifications will depend on specific disabilities and may include changes to the physical environment. This might include clearly marked, traffic areas wide enough for wheelchairs and

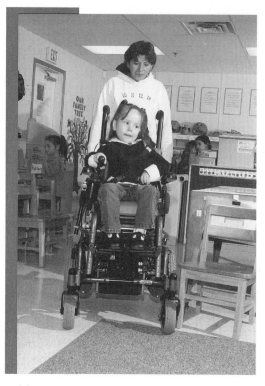

(a)

(b)

Figure 2-17 (a & b)

Wide traffic pathways and adaptive devices support the involvement of children with special needs.

walkers, specific quiet areas, additional light, and accessible playground surfacing (see Figures 2-17a & 2-17b). The environment should be highly ordered and predictable, so that children can learn where equipment and materials are located.

- large enough chunks of time to fully initiate play and engage in exploration.
- adaptations of materials. This might include using simple tabletop easels, using adaptive equipment to hold books, inserting crayons through tennis balls for easy gripping, attaching paint brushes to a child's hand with Velcro, making adaptations to dress-up clothing, adding knobs to puzzle pieces for easy handling, or providing realistic toys that give children cues of how to play with them.
- simplified activities. This might include breaking an activity into smaller parts or drawing pictures for the child to follow the steps.
- using child preferences. Teachers encourage children to play by using their preferred materials, activities, or people. An example of this would be creating an airplane theme in dramatic play for the child who is fascinated by planes.
- special equipment. Special or adaptive devices might facilitate children's participation in play, such as positioning a child in a beanbag chair rather than his wheelchair, to be more accessible to the action in the dramatic play area.
- adult support. Teachers or other adults join in children's play to encourage their involvement through modeling, verbal guidance, physical assistance, use of visual cues, and commenting.
- peer support. When teachers pair children with buddies, children with special needs receive support for their play (and other children learn prosocial ways of helping others).

It is vital that teachers realize their role in making adaptations so that all children can benefit from rich play experiences.

Play and Learning Standards

In recent years, particularly following the Good Start/Grow Smart initiative begun by the Child Care Bureau in 2002, all states and the District of Columbia have established early learning standards related to language, literacy, and math for three- to five-year-olds.

Defining Learning Standards. The Early Childhood Education Assessment Consortium of the Council of Chief State School Officers defines standards as: "statements that describe expectations for the learning and development of young children across the domains of health and physical well-being; social and emotional well-being; approaches to learning; language development and symbol systems; and general knowledge about the world around them" (Early Childhood Education Assessment Consortium, 2005).

The standards for young children focus on the primary tasks of young children of acquiring and refining foundational skills of listening, using language, working with others, and focusing attention on activity that they will later use to learn content matter in later grades. The idea for the early learning guidelines is that they should be aligned with state K–12 standards and describe what children need to know and be able to do to succeed in kindergarten.

There are positive aspects to defining early learning standards. As stated by the National Association for the Education of Young Children (NAEYC) and the National Association of Early Childhood Specialists in State Departments of Education (NAECS/SDE) in the position statement *Early Learning Standards: Creating the Conditions for Success,* "By defining the desired content and outcomes of young children's education, early learning standards can lead to greater opportunities for positive development and learning in the early years" (NAEYC & NAECS/SDE, 2002, p. 2). Several other positive aspects of early learning standards are noted by Gronlund (2006) and Seefeldt (2005). These include:

- matching standards to what we are already doing

- linking to primary standards to contribute to school readiness

- helping to identify next steps and transitions, providing for continuous curriculum

- providing higher expectations for children

- creating a commonality and clarity for communication

- providing a mechanism for accountability.

The NAEYC position statement (2009) notes that "to be beneficial, standards need to be comprehensive across the learning domains and disciplines, aligned across grade levels, and appropriate to children's development and learning" (Copple & Bredekamp, 2009, p. 4).

Unfortunately, the various state learning standards show unevenness in their attention to these aspects. As you examine your own state early learning standards, consider whether they give great attention to some areas of development while neglecting other domains. (If you don't already have a copy of your state learning standards, you can search for them at www.reasearch-connections.org.) Developed with little coordination, every state's standards address cognitive and academic skills such as language, literacy, and mathematics, but many pay less attention to social-emotional development, physical health and development, and "approaches to learning," such as curiosity, persistence, and flexible thinking.

Thus the negative possibilities of early learning standards cause concern among early educators. These include:

- teaching to the standards and loss of unique and appropriate curricula

- the risk of pushdown curricula and inappropriate expectations for young children

- reliance on direct instruction to ensure addressing the standards

- focus on superficial learning objectives

- use of testing and other inappropriate methods of assessing progress.

Connecting Play with Learning Standards. The biggest concern is how to connect children's play with learning standards. Many educators feared that they would just not have time to allow children to play, with all the "requirements" that would take so much class time. How can educators help children reach the guidelines in developmentally appropriate ways?

The good news is that it can be done. Learning standards and developmentally appropriate practices can indeed go together. What is required is to incorporate learning standards into play, into emergent curriculum and projects, and into small- and large-group times (Gronlund, 2008). Children's play becomes the vehicle for accomplishing the learning standards, and the medium for assessing their progress toward those standards.

As teachers provide rich, integrated learning experiences for children, they can see that children's engagement leads to genuine involvement in learning, helping them make connections and the strong memories that are created when the brain is emotionally involved. As teachers plan curriculum experiences, they use a variety of teaching strategies, including some that are teacher determined and directed, and others in which children's interests and curiosity play a role in determining the direction of learning. They keep as their goal children's active involvement in learning, and then they consider how to meet the standards. The sure knowledge of the importance of play and active learning for engagement is the starting point in planning appropriate experiences, not concern about planning narrow lessons to teach the content or skills outlined by the standards.

In order to integrate standards into play-based learning, it is first vital that teachers understand and know the knowledge, skills, and dispositions outlined by the standards (see Figure 2-18).

Teachers must make sure they understand the "*what* children need to learn, and then anticipate *how* they might learn these in the learning experience" (Helm, 2008). Making consolidated lists of the global standards, specific goals, and **benchmarks** helps teachers understand exactly what the standards indicate should be taught. These are the yardsticks against which children's progress and learning will be measured. Generally, the standards give enough flexibility that teachers are able to introduce skills or information when they are most meaningful to children in the course of their activity and explorations. This is why many educators now speak of "negotiating play-based curriculum," as teachers move back and forth mentally between the children's play and projects while ensuring that they are progressing, learning, and growing in their knowledge and skills. The early learning standards give teachers the framework of remembering where they want to go, being intentional about what they do. Standards show us where we want to go. They don't tell us how to get there. They don't lay out a linear process. How teachers get there will be guided by their understanding of the children's interests and questions. In Chapter 3,

Figure 2-18

Children's play becomes the vehicle for accomplishing the learning standards, and the medium for assessing their progress toward those standards.

we will explore more deeply the process by which teachers plan both to meet standards and to deepen and enrich children's play. For now, let us briefly consider how teachers integrate play and learning standards.

One thing that teachers can do is called **backtracking**, which means that they consider all the important play and learning experiences that have gone on in the classroom, and see which of the standards have been met by the activities. This process connects the play and standards after the fact. When teachers know, for example, that children should develop familiarity with sounds in words, by listening to, identifying, recognizing, and discriminating sounds, they note that the rhyming word books they have read and the games they have played with words have helped support this learning. Or, remembering the measuring activities in making the class height chart, the teacher notes that the math standard for perceiving differences was at work. A class project of making pizza, planned after the teacher noticed the children making pizzas in the sandbox and at the play dough table, engaged the children in literacy activities as they followed a recipe, math as they counted and measured, and science as they stirred, baked, and witnessed the transformation of the ingredients into a delicious lunch. As the teacher backtracked through the standards, she found how very many of the language and literacy, math, science, social, and approach-to-learning foundations had been met through the activity. Observing and note taking, as well as evaluating lesson plans, help teachers assess children's progress toward these goals, achieved through activity and engagement. Obviously, a first requirement for this kind of assessment is a thorough familiarity with the standards, and an understanding of their language that can be easily translated into the meaningful activity of the classroom.

Teachers also use the standards framework to plan intentionally. A teacher who plans to make water play with a variety of objects available is providing an enjoyable and appropriate experience for the children, and one that may spark their interest for further exploration. But she is also planning to observe how many of them grasp the concepts of sinking and floating, to see how much progress has been made toward the goal, under Scientific Thinking and Invention in the standards, of "identifying, discriminating, and making comparisons among objects by observing physical characteristics."

In integrating play with early learning standards, teachers engage in a cycle of observing, assessing, thinking about children's interests and questions, and deciding on materials and experiences that will help deepen children's play, as they move toward the goals and objectives defined by the state. The cycle answers the argument that teachers can't be sure their children are learning and progressing if young children "just play." It is *not* just play, and in the complexity of negotiating a curriculum that meets the standards, teachers play many roles. Skilled decision making accompanies well-grounded intentionality, with teachers understanding child development and learning in general, their individual children, and the sequences in which a domain's specific concepts and skills are learned, and employing a repertoire of teaching strategies (Copple & Bredekamp, 2009).

Helping Families Understand the Power of Play

In the competitive environment of modern America, families are often most concerned about how to give their children a superior start to their education. When preschools and primary classes emphasize active learning through play, these families are often confused and doubtful of just how this helps their children. Administrators and teachers have an important role in helping families understand how play lays the best foundations for later learning.

There are several steps educators can take to help families come to appreciate the value of play in their children's learning. First and foremost, teachers can make clear and tangible the real learning in play. Through pictures, videos, narratives, and displays or **documentation panels**, teachers can articulate the specific learning in block building, for example, or in a rich episode of dramatic play. Telling the story with enthusiasm helps parents see the development and learning that is taking place joyfully each day. (See Figure 2-19.)

Figure 2-19

Teachers prepare displays to illustrate the specific learning in play experiences.

Newsletters, bulletin boards, and traveling teacher journals can all be used to help parents keep up with the development and exploration of ideas through play. Parent workshops, where parents participate in play activities themselves, help families to experience the learning possibilities of play. Opportunities to observe in the classroom and then discuss their observations with teachers gives parents firsthand experiences that contribute to their growing understanding. Providing articles that describe some of the benefits of play defined by research offer a breadth of professional understanding that goes beyond the individual teacher or school. Sharing teacher methods of setting goals, planning appropriate play experiences, and monitoring progress reassures parents of teacher accountability.

As teachers themselves commit to the medium of play for optimum learning, they take every opportunity to share their knowledge and enthusiasm with families. Engaging in a continuous dialogue allows families to answer their questions and concerns, and to become proponents of best practices, as they in fact observe the results of rich play experiences. It is important for teachers to understand that the burden of family education lies with them, that families will not support or accept what they do not understand. An important teacher role is helping families come to respect and value the power of play.

For more about ways of achieving cooperation and communication with families, see Chapter 18, available only on the text Web site.

Later chapters will help deepen the basic ideas about other teacher roles in creating environments and providing appropriate intervention to support play. Teachers must realize the importance of appropriate play environments both indoors and outdoors (see Figure 2-16). What is most important at this point is to develop a respect for play as the most important thing children can do. Supporting and enhancing play is a teacher's best work in developmentally appropriate classrooms.

> The spontaneous play of young children is their highest achievement. In their play, children invent the world for themselves and create a place for themselves in it. They are re-creating their pasts and imagining their futures, while grounding themselves in the reality and fantasy of their lives here and now. Re-creating children's play in her own words, the teacher shows respect for its integrity, while building on it as one of the shared, recurrent experiences out of which the group's culture can grow. For this purpose, as well as for play's inherent value for children, teachers need to pay attention to play. (Jones & Reynolds, 1992, p. 129)

SUMMARY

Play is pleasurable, spontaneous, self-motivated, integrative activity that provides a medium for learning and development in all domains. Several categories and stages of play have been identified. Play supports development and learning in all domains. Both Piaget and Vygotsky found that play supports optimum cognitive development. There are numerous reasons why play is the best medium for learning. Teachers can support the development of quality play by designing the physical environment and intervening appropriately. Teachers should understand that there are several issues to explore involving play, including the issue of violent play, cultural influences on play, play for children with special needs, integrating play with early learning standards, and helping families understand the importance of play.

THINK ABOUT IT ACTIVITIES

1. Observe a classroom of young children and try to find examples of each category of play: functional, constructive, dramatic, and games with rules. See if you can also find examples of all the kinds of social participation described in this chapter: onlooker, solitary, parallel, associative, and cooperative. Discuss your examples with a small group in your class.

2. During your classroom visit, try to determine what the classroom teacher does to support play. Consider aspects of the physical environment, such as definition and size of play spaces, quantity and kind of available materials, and time scheduled for play. Observe the teacher's role during play. What kinds of interventions discussed in this chapter do you see?

3. Record several examples of children's conversations during sociodramatic play. What are you learning about their understanding of the world through these conversations?

QUESTIONS TO ASSESS LEARNING OF CHAPTER OBJECTIVES

1. Define play, describing the key components involved.

2. Name and describe the four categories of children's play. Give an example for each category. Name and describe the five stages of children's social play. Give an example to illustrate each stage.

3. a. Discuss the ideas of Piaget related to play and cognitive development.

   b. Discuss the ideas of Vygotsky related to play and cognitive development.

   c. Describe the contributions of play to development in all domains.

   d. Identify several characteristics of play that make it the most appropriate curriculum for young children.

4. a. Describe factors in the physical environment of play that support quality play.

   b. Identify specific behaviors identified by Smilansky as appropriate teacher intervention.

5. Discuss ideas related to violent play, to cultural influences on play, to play for children with special needs, to integrating play and learning standards, and to helping families understand the importance of play.

APPLY YOUR KNOWLEDGE QUESTIONS

1. An inexperienced teacher asks you why her three-year-olds can't follow the rules for traditional children's games and why they don't pick up on her suggestions for playing Chinese restaurant. What information would be helpful to her understanding?

2. The principal of the school where you teach kindergarten wants all play and free-choice time eliminated from your schedule, so you can concentrate on teaching academic skills. What documents and information might you share to explain your viewpoint that play is important in laying foundational skills?

HELPFUL WEB SITES

http://www.instituteforplay.com   The Importance of Play Web site has much information about play.

http://www.playingforkeeps.org	The Playing for Keeps Web site has information and the latest research on play for parents and professionals.
http://www.eduref.org	The Web site for the Educator's Reference Desk has much information on a variety of topics. Click Program Areas, and then Child Care and Development to find articles about play. Search for an article from the ERIC Digest titled "Pretend Play and Young Children's Development, 2001, PS029929."
http://www.ncsu.edu	The Web site for the International Association for the Child's Right to Play offers its *Declaration of the Child's Right to Play*.
http://www.naeyc.org	The Web site for the National Association for the Education of Young Children has a forum on Play, Policy, and Practice. Click on Members Only, and then on Interest Forums.
http://www.researchconnections.org	This Web site has much information, including about your state learning standards here.

Please visit the premium Web site for Developmentally Appropriate Practice, 4th edition, to access more chapter web links, suggestions for further research and study, additional book chapters, interactive quizzes, video exercises, online journal activities, flashcards, and much more! Go to www.cengage.com/login to register your access code.

Planning for Developmentally Appropriate Curriculum

Play and other quality learning experiences do not just happen. Enriched and meaningful play requires teachers to plan curriculum—so that children have environments and materials to stimulate curiosity, exploration, and creativity—and experiences and interactions to support their constructivist learning. Spontaneous play and teacher planning go together, although the concepts may sound contradictory. The planning is not the traditional kind, where a lesson plan is quickly filled in, based on narrowly defined objectives of what children will learn by engaging in tasks designed and controlled by teachers. That method lacks a full understanding of developmental appropriateness. Developmentally appropriate planning is based on understanding curriculum and how it evolves in the context of particular classrooms with particular children. Although teachers' general knowledge about development may help them identify learning tasks in the general sequence of development, the specific information about individual personalities, interests, learning styles, family values and backgrounds, and community connections and mandated standards must be the real source of information for planning. Teachers cannot plan just by using benchmarks of development or curriculum checklists, or by preparing lessons far in advance using only purchased resource books or textbook guides. They must genuinely understand how to mesh their general developmental knowledge and understanding of how children learn with their specific knowledge of what a particular group of individual children is ready to learn. In addition, in this time of state- and program-defined learning standards, teachers must understand how to meet those objectives by using integrated appropriate activities, rather than by planning an isolated lesson that merely satisfies the requirements. This chapter explores general ideas about planning for developmentally appropriate curriculum; these ideas are explored more specifically in the sections that follow.

LEARNING OBJECTIVES

After studying this chapter, students should be able to

- describe indicators of developmentally appropriate curricula, as defined by position statements.

- describe integrated curriculum.

- discuss the cycle of planning, describing each of the components.

- identify advantages and disadvantages of theme planning.

- define emergent curriculum and discuss sources of emergent curriculum.

- discuss strategies for planning emergent curriculum.

- describe the need for flexible planning forms.

- identify ideas for changing the planning process.

WHAT IS CURRICULUM?

Essentially, the task for early childhood teachers is to create curriculum for learning in the early years and develop their understanding of how that curriculum is created. Early childhood educators are challenged with finding a balance between "the early childhood error"—inadequate attention to the content of the curriculum in preschool programs with resulting trivialization or loss of learning opportunities—and the "elementary error"—overattention to specific, limited curriculum objectives and less attention to the specific needs and interests or the developmental characteristics of the children (Bredekamp & Rosegrant, 1995). That is, the curriculum strategies used with many children do not demand enough of the youngest children, whereas others ask for too much of the wrong thing for them and primary-age children. The guidelines of the NAEYC position statement related to planning curriculum begin the process of describing curriculum planning appropriate for children from birth through the primary grades:

a. Desired goals that are important in young children's learning and development have been identified and clearly articulated.

b. The program has a comprehensive, effective curriculum that targets the identified goals, including all those foundational for later learning and school success.

c. Teachers use the curriculum framework in their planning to ensure there is ample attention to important learning goals and to enhance the coherence of the classroom experience for the children.

d. Teachers make meaningful connections a priority in the learning experiences they provide children, to reflect that all learners, and certainly young children, learn best when the concepts, language, and skills they encounter are related to something they know and care about, and when the new learnings are themselves interconnected in meaningful, coherent ways.

e. Teachers collaborate with those teaching in the preceding and subsequent grade levels, sharing information about children and working to increase the continuity and coherence across ages/grades, while protecting the integrity and appropriateness of practices at each level.

f. In the care of infants and toddlers, practitioners plan curriculum (although they may not always call it that). They develop plans for the important routines and experiences that will promote children's learning and development and enable them to attain desired goals.

Reprinted from Copple, C., & Bredekamp, S. (Eds.). 2009. *Developmentally Appropriate Practice in Early Childhood Programs* (3rd ed., pp. 20–21). Washington, DC: NAEYC. Copyright © 2009 by the National Association for the Education of Young Children.

Curriculum involves making decisions about what will be taught (content) and how it will be taught (methods). Curriculum guidelines are meant to help young children achieve goals that are developmentally and educationally significant. Recommended methods include integrating curriculum to involve the whole child, building on prior skills and knowledge, and integrating methods with content.

A position statement on curriculum, assessment, and program evaluation was published jointly by NAEYC and the National Association of Early Childhood Specialists in State Departments of Education in 2003 (NAEYC/NAECS/SDE, 2003). Regarding curriculum, the recommendations are for teachers to implement curriculum that is "thoughtfully planned, challenging, engaging, developmentally appropriate, culturally and linguistically responsive, comprehensive, and likely to promote positive outcomes for all young children." The statement states that the goal is not to identify one "best" curriculum—in fact, it states, there is no such thing—but rather to identify the components of a curriculum that indicate effectiveness. An effective curriculum includes the following components.

- Children are active and engaged, cognitively, physically, socially, and artistically.

- Curriculum goals are clearly defined and shared by all stakeholders, including administrators, teachers, and families. Goals state the essential desired outcomes for children.

- Curriculum is based on evidence that is relevant for the children involved and organized around known child development and learning principles.

- Important content is learned through investigation, play, and focused, intentional teaching. Teaching strategies are matched to children's ages, developmental abilities or disabilities, language, and culture.

- Curriculum builds on prior learning and experiences. Both content and implementation of the curriculum build on children's prior individual and cultural learning, includes children with disabilities, and supports background knowledge learned at home and in the community.

- The curriculum is comprehensive, including important areas of development, as in physical well-being and motor skills, social and emotional development, language development, cognitive and thinking development, and dispositions to learning. In addition, subject matter areas such as science, mathematics, language, literacy, social studies, and the arts are part of a comprehensive curriculum.

- The curriculum's subject matter content is validated by **professional standards**. Standards of relevant professional organizations, such as the National Council of Teachers of Mathematics and the National Science Teachers Associations, are reviewed and implemented.

- The curriculum is likely to benefit children in a wide range of outcomes, according to research or plans to obtain such evidence.

These NAEYC position statements regarding curriculum make it clear that the guidelines are intended only for constructing appropriate curriculum; the specifics of "what" and "how" are left to individual teachers, programs, and school systems according to their philosophies and goals. See Figure 3-1 for examples of ways in which the recommendations can be implemented in programs for various age groups.

Head Start standards are currently being applied to many Title I preschool and pre-K programs around the country, as well as guiding the education for the hundreds of thousands of young children enrolled in Head Start programs. Regarding curriculum, the standards state that curricula should

- be adapted for each group.

- support each child's individual pattern of development and learning.

- provide for the development of cognitive skills by encouraging children to organize their experiences, to understand concepts, and to develop age-appropriate skills in literacy, **numeracy**, reasoning, problem solving, and decision making as a foundation for school success.

- integrate all educational aspects of health, nutrition, and mental health services into program activities.

- ensure that the program helps children develop emotional security and social relationships.

- enhance each child's understanding of self as an individual and as a member of a group.

- provide each child opportunities to succeed to help develop feelings of competence, self-esteem, and positive attitudes toward learning.

- provide individual, small-group, and large-group activities both indoors and outdoors.

CURRICULUM in programs for infants, toddlers, preschoolers, kindergartners, and primary-grade children

POSITION STATEMENT RECOMMENDATION:
Implement curriculum that is thoughtfully planned, challenging, engaging, developmentally appropriate, culturally and linguistically responsive, comprehensive, and likely to promote positive outcomes for all young children.

Infants/Toddlers	Preschoolers	Kindergarten/Primary
Curriculum that is thoughtfully planned: Whatever the children's ages, curriculum goals link with important developmental tasks and are comprehensive in scope. Teaching strategies are tailored to children's ages, developmental capacities, language and culture, and abilities or disabilities. A major shift as children move into kindergarten and the primary grades is toward greater focus on subject matter areas, without ignoring their developmental foundations.		
Goals focus on children's development as they learn about themselves and others, as well as ways to communicate, think, and use their muscles.	Goals focus on children's exploration, inquiry, and expanding vocabularies.	Goals focus on children's emergent knowledge and skills in all subject matter areas, including language and literacy, mathematics, science, social studies, health, physical education, and the visual and performing arts.
Goals for infants address security, responsive interactions with caregivers, and exploration.	Goals address children's physical well-being and motor development; social and emotional development; approaches to learning; language development; and cognition and general knowledge.	Goals continue to address all developmental areas including socioemotional development and approaches to learning ("habits of mind").
Goals for toddlers address independence, need for control, discovery, and beginning social interactions.	Experiences provide for knowledge and skill learning in literacy, mathematics, science, social studies, and the visual and performing arts.	
Curriculum that is challenging and engaging: For all ages the curriculum leads children from where they are to new accomplishments while maintaining their interest and active involvement. Content that is engaging for children of different ages changes with development and with new experiences, requiring careful observation and adaptation.		
Children can use their whole bodies and their senses as they manipulate toys and other safe objects and engage in play alone, with a primary caregiver, and at times with or near other infants.	Curriculum facilitates children's construction of knowledge through their interactions with materials, each other, and adults.	Curriculum promotes children's developing attitudes as "learners"—using their curiosity, creativity, and initiative.
Children's enthusiasm for exploring is supported by matching their interests with challenging curricula.	Curriculum promotes experiences in which children's thinking moves from the simple to the complex, from the concrete to the abstract.	Curriculum provides experiences in which children use oral and written language, mathematical and scientific thinking, and investigatory skills to build a knowledge base across disciplines and expand their skills repertoire.
For toddlers, curriculum also focuses on their emerging abilities to play with other children.	Curriculum provides opportunities for children to initiate activities, as well as for teacher initiation and scaffolding.	Curriculum leads to children's recognition of their own competence.
	Curriculum leads to children's recognition of their own achievements.	

(chart continued on page 69)

The information in this chart is based on the recommendations of the NAEYC-NAECS/SDE Position Statement on Curriculum, Assessment, and Program Evaluation (www.naeyc.org/resources/position_statements/pscape.pdf). The chart provides examples of ways in which the recommendations of the NAEYC/NAECS/SDE Position Statement on Curriculum, Assessment, and Program Evaluation can be implemented in programs for infants/toddlers, preschoolers, and kindergarten/primary age children. The examples can best be understood within the context of the full position statement.

CURRICULUM chart (cont'd)

Infants/Toddlers	Preschoolers	Kindergarten/Primary
Curriculum that is developmentally appropriate and culturally and linguistically responsive: Whatever the children's ages, curriculum fits well with their developmental levels, abilities and disabilities, individual characteristics, families and communities, and cultural contexts. Curriculum supports educational equity for children who are learning a second language. Curriculum for younger children makes cultural connections primarily through relationships, daily routines, and "rituals"; older children benefit from more explicit incorporation of culturally relevant materials and from topic-centered as well as integrated learning opportunities.		
Curriculum addresses the wide variations in infants' and toddlers' interests, temperaments, and patterns of growth and development.	Integration across subject matter areas is high, while some "focusing" is appropriate (e.g., experiences devoted to learning about print and numbers).	Curriculum focuses on a continuum of learning in topic areas and integration across disciplines. The curriculum also facilitates adaptation of instruction for children who are having difficulty and for those needing increasing challenges.
Curriculum planning and implementation emphasize understanding of and respect for home culture, efforts to incorporate home values and practices, and discussion with families about differences between their expectations and those of the program.	Curriculum planning and implementation—including the use of "props" for play and other representations—emphasize experiences that reflect the children's cultures and cultural values.	Children learn ways to develop constructive relationships with other people and respect for individual and cultural differences.
Curriculum that is comprehensive: Whatever the children's ages, the curriculum attends to a broad range of developmental and learning outcomes—across domains and subject matter areas and including experiences that promote children's nonviolent behavior and conflict resolution. For older children, the curriculum pays greater attention to specific content areas but without ever ignoring some domains in favor of a narrow set of other outcomes.		
Curriculum incorporates children's relationships with their caregivers and routines (e.g., sleeping, diapering/toileting) as opportunities for learning, as well as through experiences in which children play with objects, their caregivers, and (increasingly) each other.	Curriculum facilitates children's learning through individual and small and large group experiences that promote physical well-being and motor development; social and emotional development; approaches to learning; language development, including second-language development; and cognition and general knowledge.	Curriculum and related instruction are increasingly focused on helping children acquire deeper understanding of information and skills in subject areas (e.g., language and literacy, science, mathematics, social studies, and visual and performing arts) within a comprehensive set of developmental outcomes.
Curriculum provides a context in which teachers use their knowledge about each child to plan opportunities for learning across domains—physical well-being and motor development; social and emotional development; approaches to learning; language development; and cognition and general knowledge.	Curriculum provides a context in which children learn through meaningful everyday experiences, including play. Within this context, various academic disciplines are addressed—including mathematics, literacy, science, social studies, and the arts.	Curriculum helps children recognize the connections between and across disciplines and domains.
		Curriculum-based experiences encompass a variety of active strategies in which individuals or small groups explore, inquire, discover, demonstrate, and solve problems.

(chart continued on page 70)

CURRICULUM chart (cont'd)

Infants/Toddlers	Preschoolers	Kindergarten/Primary
	Curriculum that promotes positive outcomes: Whatever the children's ages, the curriculum is selected, adapted, and revised to promote positive outcomes for children. Outcomes include both immediate enjoyment and nurturance and longer-term benefits. Curriculum for younger children pays special attention to those key developmental outcomes shown to be essential to later success—not focusing simply on earlier versions of specific academic skills.	
Curriculum promotes experiences that lead to documented evidence that infants and toddlers are learning about themselves and others, communicating their needs to responsive adults, gaining understandings of basic concepts, and developing motor and coordination skills appropriate for their ages. Outcomes also include evidence that each child is developing a sense of trust, security, and, increasingly, independence.	Curriculum provides experiences that lead to documented evidence that preschoolers are acquiring and applying knowledge and skills in physical well-being and motor development; social and emotional development; approaches to learning; language development; and cognition and general knowledge—as well as more specific skills important for later school success. Children demonstrate positive attitudes toward learning and their increasing abilities to represent their experiences in a variety of ways (e.g., through drawing/painting, dictating/writing, and dramatic play).	Curriculum provides experiences that lead to documented evidence that children are acquiring important competencies in literacy, mathematics, science, visual and performing arts, and other subject matter areas—as well as continuing to develop cognitive, physical, and socioemotional competencies. These outcomes are appropriate for children's ages as well as their interests and the communities in which they live. Children demonstrate positive attitudes toward learning and their increasing understanding of key concepts, skills, and tools of inquiry of the subject matter areas; their application of these understandings to various situations; and their understanding of the connections across disciplines.

Figure 3-1

Examples of implementation of principles of curriculum for various ages.

From all these guidelines, it should be clear that a good curriculum is more than just a collection of activities or lesson plans. It is useful to consider curriculum as "a framework for developing a coherent set of learning experiences that enables children to reach the identified goals" (Copple & Bredekamp, 2009, p. 42). In some cases, programs or schools adopt a specific curriculum. The decision about adopting a curriculum should be made by considering how it fits with the goals, values, and program standards that have been developed, including the values and desires of the families served by the program, and how it meets the sociocultural, individual, and linguistic characteristics of the children to be educated. The quality of the curriculum is the major factor. Often scripted, or so-called "teacher-proof," curricula are adopted by administrators, believing this will solve the problem of having inexperienced or fewer well-qualified teachers. Elizabeth Jones, an early childhood expert who has written much on the subject of play and curriculum, has referred to these curricula as "canned," meaning that they have been mass-produced to try to fit the tastes of many consumers. Unfortunately, these curricula generally tend to be narrow and intellectually weak. It is far better to support staff development so that teachers are able to plan and implement effective curricula.

INTEGRATED CURRICULUM AND THE STANDARDS MOVEMENT

As discussed previously, play and active learning provide for learning in all domains of development—the "how" of the curriculum. But another aspect of considering curriculum is to consider the "what," which is the content that children should learn. Recent developments in early childhood education include standards that describe desired results, outcomes, or learning expectations for children before kindergarten. Head Start has developed a Child Outcomes Framework. All of the states have developed early learning outcomes standards, and NAEYC has issued a joint position statement with the National Association of Early Childhood Specialists in State Departments of Education with recommendations to guide the development and implementation of standards for young children (NAEYC &NAECS /SDE, 2003). National organizations have developed content standards in areas such as literacy and mathematics (NAEYC, 1998, 2002).

As described in Chapter 2, many early childhood educators are somewhat concerned about the early learning standards and their impact on appropriate practices. Many of the state standards minimally address social-emotional development and "approaches to learning." The documents pay little attention to adapting the standards for children with disabilities or for children who are culturally and linguistically diverse. The standards often seem to address content as if it were neatly compartmentalized into very separate subjects.

Experienced early childhood teachers recognize that they are in fact teaching important content from the various academic disciplines and have always done so, but that this content is integrated in curriculum activities. When they cook with young children in the classroom, for example, they are teaching math as they count out the cups of flour indicated on the recipe card, language and literacy as they read the recipe card and use the vocabulary of measurement and cooking, science as they point out the changes in the batter being stirred and the finished product they will eat, social skills of group participation, and many other things, all integrated into the single activity (see Figure 3-2). Teachers in the primary grades also recognize that projects and theme work allow children opportunities to use the skills they are being taught.

The concept of integrating curriculum comes in part from considering the integrated nature of development—what happens in one aspect of development, such as physical development, inevitably influences development in other domains, such as social or emotional (Bredekamp & Rosegrant, 1995). **Integrated curriculum** includes the various subject matter disciplines—such as science, mathematics, social studies, the arts, technology, and literacy—in common related activities or projects, rather than as separate branches of knowledge. Integrated curriculum allows children to form meaningful mental connections without artificial separations. Integrated

Figure 3-2

Cooking is an example of curriculum that integrates math, literacy, social skills, and science learning in a single activity.

curriculum allows the child to function fully using all domains while pursuing topics of interest and using knowledge and skills acquired within a meaningful context. The purpose of integrating curriculum is to make that curriculum more meaningful to young children. Integrated curriculum experiences allow for individual learning styles and multiple intelligences (Gardner, 2000; Campbell, Campbell, & Dickinson, 2003).

Various approaches are used for integrating curriculum in early childhood classrooms, but generally, curriculum is integrated by using a project approach (Katz & Chard, 2000; Chard, 1998a and 1998b; Helm & Katz, 2001; Helm & Beneke, 2003), or a theme approach, developed through the process of connection called webbing, as introduced later in this chapter. The Creative Curriculum for Preschool Children (2002) refers to *studies* as the meaningful way to integrate curriculum content. What all these approaches have in common is the emphasis on building from children's interests and experiences, offering a concrete context of activities to associate learning in a meaningful way, and offering opportunities to apply skills and knowledge on meaningful problems. Being able to study a topic in depth, over a period of time, allows children to develop a true understanding. Lilian Katz once said that we tend to underestimate children's intellectual abilities. In-depth projects recognize that children are indeed capable of complex learning, when it is meaningful and matched to their learning style. Integrated curriculum activities also offer a variety of related benefits to learning through integrated curriculum.

- Integrated curriculum provides coherence for children's experiences and permits optimum construction of meaning. They learn skills and knowledge through meaningful content, rather than concentrating on discrete and separate—and often meaningless to them—skills.

- The isolation of curriculum areas from one another does not allow children to understand how to apply the knowledge in broadly relevant ways. Learning principles of numeracy through math lessons only does not help children understand the uses of math in everyday life. Instead, understanding how many cards to make if we're inviting all of our parents for a picnic is a relevant math problem that allows children to apply knowledge in the context of their activity.

- Integrated curriculum allows children to learn through activities in large time blocks, rather than having to endure numerous fragmenting transitions as teachers shift from a lesson in one discipline to a lesson in another. (Now we'll finish our language lesson; next we'll work on our math.) Having to physically and mentally shift attention wastes time and disrupts attention.

- The time and opportunity for children to engage in the repeated activities needed for real learning and mastery is gained when teachers do not feel pressure to "cover the curriculum," which often leads to rushing children on to new topics and lessons before they have had enough time to become self-motivated and construct ever-expanding knowledge. Integrated curriculum often leads to deepening interest in and exploration of related ideas, allowing children opportunities to revisit and extend their learning. In the discussion of the Reggio Emilia approach found in Chapter 4, you will learn how that example of excellent early childhood programs relies on using projects that often extend over months, with children growing in understanding as the work continues.

- Internal motivation to learn is a result of involvement over time in projects and activities of interest.

When teachers separate knowledge and skills into the discipline areas that make sense to adults only, they often have to rely on external motivators (stickers, test grades) to motivate children for whom the subject matter seems less relevant (adapted from Bredekamp & Rosegrant, 1995).

Perhaps the most encouraging development is the expansion of integrated curriculum upwards beyond the preschool, to change the way subject matter is taught to older children (Hurless & Gittings, 2008). Curriculum from many subject areas can be achieved through integration around theme topics to children.

▶❙❙ **VIDEO ACTIVITY**

Go to the premium Web site and watch the video clip for Chapter 3 entitled "International Teaching." Then answer the following questions:

REFLECTIVE QUESTIONS

1. How does the concept of intentional teaching seen in the video clip relate to the ideas about standards and play discussed in the chapter?

2. How does teacher knowledge of the standards affect the ability to plan and enrich play?

3. How does teacher knowledge of child development and individual children allow teachers to plan effective curriculum?

Visit the premium Web site to complete these questions online and email them to your professor.

THE CYCLE OF PLANNING

How then do teachers learn to plan for curricula? Planning is not an activity separate from teaching that teachers engage in occasionally to meet the requirements of their directors or supervisors. For example, in some programs, lesson plans may need to be submitted by Thursday afternoon for the following week so that supervisors can be certain that the planning requirement is being met. This often means that many teachers are hurriedly filling in lesson plan blanks during Thursday naptime to meet the deadline. Plans made in this way are likely not made thoughtfully and purposefully. Frequently teachers fall back on ideas from the past or copy something from one of the available teacher resource books on their shelf. Such lesson plans are usually based on general knowledge of children and general goals for their learning. The chances of meeting all children's needs and program goals with such a system are rather haphazard.

Rather, developmentally appropriate planning is part of an ongoing cycle that occurs in the context of teachers' daily interactions with children in their classrooms. The cycle consists of

- learning about individual children and the whole group through a system of observation, regular note taking, and documentation.

- reflecting on observations, and assessing where each child is in relation to predetermined goals and objectives, including those that have been determined by others, such as families, state guidelines, and educational systems.

- learning about children's interests, experiences, and questions through focused attention.

- deciding on strategies, materials, and experiences that would move children toward meeting the goals and objectives in the context of meaningful activity.

- observing to discover the results and outcomes to evaluate the effectiveness of the plans, adding new ideas from these observations and assessments.

See what this cycle looks like in Figure 3-3. The cycle of planning thus allows teachers to use the three sources of knowledge to make developmentally appropriate decisions as discussed in

Figure 3-3

The cycle of planning.

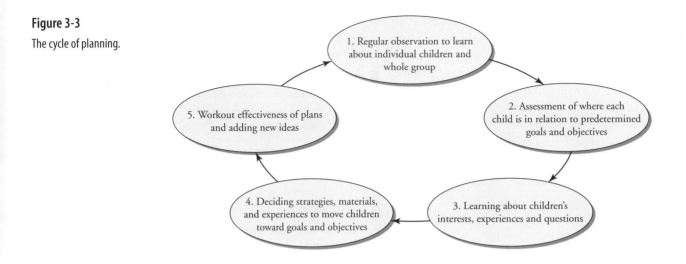

1. Regular observation to learn about individual children and whole group

2. Assessment of where each child is in relation to predetermined goals and objectives

3. Learning about children's interests, experiences and questions

4. Deciding strategies, materials, and experiences to move children toward goals and objectives

5. Workout effectiveness of plans and adding new ideas

JOURNAL REFLECTION

Curriculum Planning

Many teachers feel overwhelmed by the process of planning. What experiences have you already had with curriculum planning? What was helpful to you as you planned, and what challenges did you find? As you consider the concept that planning is embedded into both the daily life of the classroom and all interaction between teachers and children, does this help with some of the challenges?

 Visit the premium Web site to complete this journal activity online and email it to your professor.

Chapter 1: (1) knowledge of age-related characteristics; (2) knowledge of strengths, interests, and needs of individual children; and (3) knowledge of social and cultural contexts in which children live to ensure that learning experiences are both meaningful and relevant.

Planning is thus embedded into the daily life of the classroom and into all the interaction between teachers and children. Let's consider each component of the cycle separately, to see how teachers create the curriculum to support children's learning and development.

Systematic Observation and Note Taking

In the following chapters, you will find much discussion about creating appropriate learning environments for young children that nurture them in all developmental domains. The physical arrangements of the interest areas in the classroom, the time schedule, and the specific materials and activities that are made available are all factors that allow teachers to find the time and opportunity to observe children regularly while they are busy throughout the day. Some ways that the classroom arrangements and management can give teachers opportunities to observe are

- allowing children to get their own materials and initiate their own activities, which frees teachers to move about the room to watch and interact with individuals in various interest areas.

- providing **open-ended materials** for creativity, exploration, and construction, so that teachers do not have to have eyes and hands busy always providing assistance and direction.

- creating clear and separate work spaces for children—with systems that control numbers in various activities—to avoid being drawn into frequent conflict resolution.

- providing materials that allow children of various abilities to use them successfully, at their particular skill level.

- providing large time blocks for children to get engaged in activities, so that teachers do not get caught up in managing too many **transitions**.

- having clear cleanup systems and other opportunities for children to participate in classroom responsibilities so that teachers are not busy at every moment.

- planning a schedule that gives opportunities to interact with individuals and small groups, as well as the whole group.

As teachers recognize the priority of creating opportunities for observation, they understand that creating the classroom environment is the best way to free their eyes and ears for paying attention to children. Although by coordinating with coworkers or volunteers, teachers may be able to schedule formal observation times when they can focus exclusively on taking notes or using assessment tools, most teachers find that their best opportunities for observing come while they are busy interacting with children.

Let's consider just one example. When a teacher has structured a small-group time in the schedule, this allows him to watch and listen to just a few children at a time (see Figures 3-4a-e). Say that on a particular day, the teacher has planned a small-group activity of mixing play dough. During that time, he notices that Crystal is enormously curious about how things change and understands ideas about measurement; that LaPorche remembers that flour is also used in baking bread from the story *The Little Red Hen* that was read last week; that Rodney is able to focus his attention exclusively on this activity, as opposed to games during whole-group activity; and that Damon is still having a hard time with waiting for a turn. This, and more, information is important to note down, to get the current status of each child's abilities. Observation has begun because of the planned schedule and activity. Teachers watch how children use materials, their

(a)

(b)

(c)

(d)

Figure 3-4 (a-e)

When a teacher plans a small-group activity (a), he can quickly observe who needs his assistance (b), who has difficulty holding the scissors (c and d), and who has mastered the skill (e).

(e)

social interactions, and differences in complexity and change in children's play. See more about observation techniques and reminders for objectivity and description in Chapter 15.

Observation requires note taking. Interesting as all this information from the children in the small group is, it will not be useful (or even remembered) in the long run unless it is written down. Teachers must develop methods of making quick notes that can later be organized into a more comprehensive system. Even just recording one or two words will allow the teacher to flesh out the observation in later recording. Some ways that teachers find effective for quick note taking while children are busy are

- carrying a pencil and pad of sticky notes or file cards in a pocket for making a brief note.
- posting a clipboard and pen in every interest area for quick jottings.

- preparing labels with each child's name to carry on a clipboard and fill in as opportunities present. This has the advantage of making sure that all children will be noticed.
- taking a quick digital picture. Although this has not recorded any words, it may be enough to bring the incident back to mind for later documentation.

At the end of a day, a teacher will have numerous notes on different children. The key then is to have an efficient system for collecting and organizing this information. Many teachers find that it is useful to have an accordion file folder or loose leaf notebook with a section for each child. This allows for observations to be added throughout the year. This can be further subdivided into sections for physical skills, social and emotional development, cognitive and concept development, creativity, language and literacy development, and numeracy and math concept development. When the teacher sits down to organize the observations, she just has to make sure that the details are complete, including the date, and then place the sticky note or the file card in the appropriate place. A system that has pages or sections for each of the developmental domains allows a quick check to see which children need particular attention, as the teacher has not yet accumulated observations in that particular area.

Some observations will involve more than one child or more than one developmental domain. The teacher can quickly make copies of the observation to file accordingly. Observation goes on in this way on a daily, regular basis.

Observations may be noted in a shared journal used by all classroom teachers. Teachers may write notes in a large, conveniently placed notebook. When there are several teachers who work with the children in a classroom, this may become not only a form of communication, but also a source for reflection, dialogue, and shared thinking (Stacey, 2009).

In addition to observations, teachers may collect samples of work. Similar samples of drawings or writing samples, collected over a period of time, can be used to document growth and learning. Sometimes teachers have the children write their names or draw a self-portrait each month, to note progress. These can be added to the observations to make a complete portfolio for that child, used not only for assessment and planning, but also for sharing information with families.

As an example, from the play dough small group, the teacher added these notes to the children's folders (see Figure 3-5).

Assessment

Every month or two, the teacher can read through the observations accumulated to assess progress and particular needs. The objective observations collected over time add up to a picture that can be written as a summary of where the child is in each aspect of development and learning at this particular time. The specific goals and objectives that have previously been defined in the curriculum framework provide the vehicle for assessing learning. In other words, teachers summarize the child's abilities and skills, and then see how these measure up with the final goals.

This information then allows the teacher to individualize planning, with the particular goals for that child in

> 11/21 Crystal asking several "how" and "why" questions about how the flour and salt become the play dough.

> 11/21 Crystal said, "We already put in 1 cup of flour, so now we only need to fill up the cup half-way."

> 11/21 LaPorche said, "I remember flour from when the Little Red Hen made the bread, and nobody would help her." (book was read one week ago.)

> 11/21 Activity took 15 minutes. Rodney sat still, participated and watched, and talked appropriately through the whole experience—no restlessness or inattention noted.

> 11/21 Damon grabbed the spoon twice, and whined, "I want a turn," when it was Crystal's turn to stir, and then began to cry when told he would have to wait until after Rodney.

All of these notes are filed in the appropriate sections in each child's notebook.

Figure 3-5

Sample observation notes.

Effective curriculum planners:

- think through their actions.
- cultivate a mind-set of receptivity.
- seek the child's point of view.
- notice the details to discover more possibilities.
- share conversations following the children's lead.
- support children's connections with each other.
- take action to build on children's strengths.
- challenge children to go further in their pursuits.
- explore children's theories for deeper learning.
- invent new ways to meet requirements.
- expand possibilities for prescribed curriculum.
- take risks to try new things.

Read more about these, and other, ideas in *Learning Together with Young Children: A Curriculum Framework for Reflective Teachers,* by Deb Curtis and Margie Carter (2008), St. Paul, MN: Redleaf Press.

mind. Ideas for what content to teach and how to teach it are linked to these individual goals. Assessment is like the process of pausing along a journey to see what progress has been made in relation to what the final destination should be. Assessment involves reflection and interpretation. As one teacher put it, "If we don't know where we want to go, how will we know how to get there, or how close we are getting to the end?"

Some widely used curricula have clearly defined objectives and goals that teachers can use as a developmental assessment tool. The Work Sampling system includes ongoing observations, progress reports, and developmental checklists (Meisels & Atkins-Burnett, 2000; http://www.pearsonearlylearning.com). There is a Work Sampling System for Head Start; see the references at the end of the chapter. (This is different from the Head Start Outcomes Framework that lists primarily program content areas that should be assessed: language development, literacy, mathematics, science, creative arts, social/emotional development, physical health and development, and approaches to learning.) In some of these other tools, there is overlap with these domains. High/Scope has a Preschool Child Observation Record (COR) organized around the key experiences (Hohmann & Weikart, 2002). You will read more about these in Chapter 4. The Creative Curriculum Developmental Continuum Assessment (identifying fifty goals and objectives in social/emotional development, physical development, cognitive development, and language development) is available in print form, as well as on CD-PORT, a software program that allows early childhood programs to show progress on the group of children, as well as on the individual (Dodge, Colker, & Heroman, 2002). See sample pages from the Developmental Continuum Assessment in Chapter 4.

All these assessment tools use **performance-based** methods; that is, teachers watch children busy in the activities of daily life, rather than create artificial testing situations. They all involve strategies for collecting and recording information about children's progress in the various developmental domains. Many of the elements involve specific skills, as well as general approaches to learning.

Head Start teachers are now required to use the Head Start Outcomes Framework as a guide. The emphasis on outcomes should not be seen as preparing children for a "test," but as specific guidance to help all early childhood teachers collect information on children's progress and therefore be able to improve the quality of learning experiences for children. The information collected is used for program development purposes and for documenting children's learning (see Figure 3-6).

Figure 3-6

Teachers use notes to create assessment summaries and set goals.

Let's go back again to our play-dough example. For each of the children, the teacher has accumulated many examples in all the sections of his files, indicating abilities and progress in all developmental domains. During his planning period one day, he sits down to go through the specifics and make brief summaries. Among the notes he makes under cognitive development for Crystal, he writes: "Crystal shows great curiosity, asking specific questions. She understands one-to-one correspondence and how many parts are in a whole."

For Damon, part of his summary under social/emotional development reads: "Damon continues to have difficulty when having to wait for a turn and shows frustration with his classmates frequently."

The assessment summary sheets help identify current strengths and needs. From these assessment summaries, teachers can move toward planning appropriate experiences for each child in the group.

Planning Strategies to Move Children Forward

Because teachers are challenged with planning for individuals and the group as a whole, the next step in the planning cycle is to list all the needs identified on the individual summary sheets. In essence, this means identifying all the children who may need more help with fine motor experiences, for example, or with specific self-help skills, or with learning social skills. This list then helps teachers consider what kinds of experiences, materials, and activities can be planned to allow children to enhance specific knowledge and abilities. Thus, the teacher is planning curriculum that may appeal to all children because of what he understands about the characteristics of an age group in general; in addition, he has specific children in mind that may particularly benefit from the plan. Because children have choices of an array of experiences, he makes the plans particularly appealing to those he wants to encourage to participate, as part of his individualized plan. On the general weekly lesson plan, teachers often note the initials of the children they particularly want to support and encourage in an activity, to remind themselves of the planned focus for their interactions.

For example, remembering that Damon is listed on his class summary sheet as one of several children who particularly needs help with concepts of turn taking and cooperative social interaction, the teacher plans an art activity where children may work on a box construction with a partner. On the day in question, he encourages Damon to partner with Ricardo, who is an easygoing child. He interacts with the boys as they cooperate on their box construction, commenting on their joint efforts. Damon is pleased with the positive recognition and follows Ricardo's lead in waiting for the pot of red paint they want to use. Other children enjoyed the box construction activity as well, but the teacher noted on his summary sheet that he had carried out a plan to help Damon enhance his social skills.

With Crystal in mind, another plan was to make pizza, cutting up the whole pizza into enough slices so that each child could have one. The teacher wanted to nurture her interest in numbers and whole-part relationships and felt this activity would do so appropriately.

Individualizing plans helps teachers work in a coordinated way, linking their goals and objectives, their assessments of individual children, and their daily and weekly planning.

This same cycle of planning for individualization is used to build appropriate curriculum for infants and toddlers, as well as older children. Caregivers observe infants and toddlers to note where they are in acquiring the abilities that indicate developmental milestones in fine and large muscle control, and in sound and language production. They then assess the baby's progress in the continuum of developmental attainments. They observe the baby's preferences in sensory exploration and then provide appropriate materials and experiences that will help these youngest children strengthen and practice emerging skills and move toward their next accomplishments.

Children's Interests as a Basis for Meaningful Curriculum

For children to become truly engaged in their explorations and play, the planned materials and activities must be interesting to them. Thus an important component of the planning cycle is for teachers to learn about the questions and experiences that are particularly compelling for the individual children within the group. Generally, as teachers make lesson plans, they organize them around particular projects or themes. In this section, we will consider how teachers can use children's interests and life experiences to plan meaningful curriculum.

It should be stated at the outset that the approach of having an organizing theme for planning has some real advantages. Theme planning at its best offers an array of activities built around a central idea, so one advantage is that this related web of experiences allows children to make their own meaningful mental connections. When children find a common thread around much of their play and work, they are able to make linkages between individual experiences to construct concepts. Theme planning may offer a variety of means of exploring a concept via different methods and media; if a particular activity does not interest or fit the specific learning style of a child, other methods may be used to explore the same idea. Another advantage is that theme planning can allow for integrated learning experiences where children have the opportunity to learn and develop skills in several domains at once. This is why theme planning is usually a positive step in broadening the curriculum in primary classrooms. Themes also allow children to immerse themselves in topics that deeply interest them. Play and projects centered on a particular theme may last weeks, or even months, depending on sustained attention. Theme planning may allow families to become involved in the learning activities, as families share resources and reinforce learning activities at home. Still another advantage is that themes provide a method to support teacher organization and thinking around a particular topic. The best kinds of brainstorming and creative thinking can result when teachers are trying to web related ideas and activities to help children explore themes. Developmentally appropriate planning occurs as teachers identify and sustain children's themes.

On the other hand, theme planning at its worst can narrow the focus of children's learning in very inappropriate and restrictive ways that are to be avoided. Traditional theme planning revolves exclusively around adult decisions about what children need to learn and how they can learn it. Teachers predetermine what direction the curriculum will take and what learning will result from it. Adults decide what body of knowledge is appropriate for the children and when they will teach it. There is no question that adults have the "big picture" because of their knowledge about children in general and their understanding of what children need to learn and develop in curriculum areas; however, relying only on adult perspectives omits the important component of children's initiative and interests.

Traditional theme planning works from a defined time frame for each unit. Frequently, teachers plan the calendar year in advance, deciding on the theme for each week before the learning year even begins. Thus, teachers are commonly able to describe in September their unit themes for February (for example, Valentine's Day and Community Helpers, including a week each for police officers and considerations of safety, firefighters, and medical people). Similarly, April may bring theme units on Easter, planting seeds, flowers, and baby animals. There is no shortage of popular preschool topics and cultural holidays. When the time frame is decided so far in advance, teachers feel an urgency to stay on schedule, moving the children on as soon as the activities for the week have been completed. But such defined time frames fail to leave space for responding to children's blossoming interests and their need to revisit topics and move on to deeper levels of understanding. How could it be possible for teachers to always know in advance what topics would interest a particular group of children and for how long?

Another danger with narrowly sticking to specifically defined themes is that this can exclude other interests. It is not so much that teachers say arbitrarily that another subject introduced by the children cannot be followed at the time. Rather, they may exclude other topics because their own planning for the week tends to preclude openness to other contributions. Thus, children's ideas tend not to carry enough weight to justify deviating from the theme topic. Having put the effort into creating a theme plan, it is hard for teachers to let go of the plan and to include children's ideas or "teachable moments."

Having developed theme units, some teachers fall into the trap of recycling them on an annual basis, bringing out dusty boxes and lesson plans and going through them with the next group of children. This method of curriculum planning—called "embalmed" by Elizabeth Jones because it was once alive but is now quite dead—leads to teachers who go through the motions, bored with the repetition. The themes become merely topics to be "covered."

> In the tradition of using holidays and themes as the focus for planning, children are consumers of activities and images rather than inventors. [Teachers] offer preplanned, premade, and simplistic projects . . . overlook the opportunity to have the children explore their own understandings and underlying rationale for the project. There is no "real" connection to their lives as children; there is even less sensory exploration or active participation. (Curtis & Carter, 1996, p. 12)

Children are interested in the events occurring around them, and many of these are the cultural or religious holidays whose messages are boomed from the television and shopping mall and are alive in most homes and communities. Deciding how to use the best elements of holidays for genuine, child-centered curriculum versus merely echoing the popular culture is part of the thoughtful decision-making process for teachers.

Some teachers, recognizing the conflict between the constraints of teacher-dominated plans and children's desires to pursue particular interests, create lesson plans to post on the wall, but then ignore them in favor of child-initiated play. This is an essentially negative process, because the amount of teacher effort that goes into creating useless plans could be better spent puzzling over the next steps to support and deepen children's spontaneous interests and to link activities to assessment and goals. Still others believe they should give up planning and simply follow the lead of children—what Elizabeth Jones calls "accidental/unidentified curriculum." When things just happen and no one follows up, many starting points for **emergent curriculum** are missed. Unfortunately, this planning method, or lack of method, does not permit the deepening of questions and richness of experience that support constructivist learning. Neither of these alternative actions is helpful.

When teachers change their focus from deciding on themes arbitrarily, and instead move to observing the children's own deep interests, questions, and curiosity (see Figure 3-7), they do not make decisions long in advance about what will be the themes studied. Thus they free themselves

Figure 3-7

Teachers use children's deep interests and questions to plan activities, such as in this veterinary office.

Figure 3-8

There are varying degrees of child initiation and decision making as teachers choose different approaches to planning. Reprinted by permission of the publisher. From J. Helm & L. G. Katz, *Young Investigators: The Project Approach in the Early Years* (New York: Teachers College Press, 2001). Copyright © 2001 by Teachers College, Columbia University. All rights reserved.

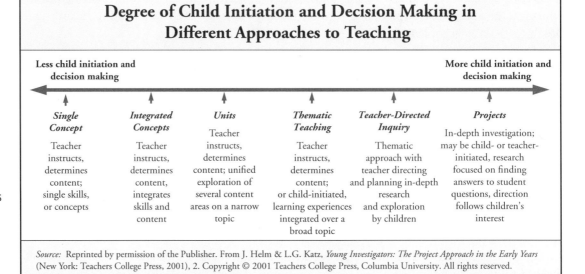

Degree of Child Initiation and Decision Making in Different Approaches to Teaching

Less child initiation and decision making ⟵──────────────────────────────⟶ More child initiation and decision making

Single Concept	*Integrated Concepts*	*Units*	*Thematic Teaching*	*Teacher-Directed Inquiry*	*Projects*
Teacher instructs, determines content; single skills, or concepts	Teacher instructs, determines content, integrates skills and content	Teacher instructs, determines content; unified exploration of several content areas on a narrow topic	Teacher instructs, determines content; or child-initiated, learning experiences integrated over a broad topic	Thematic approach with teacher directing and planning in-depth research and exploration by children	In-depth investigation; may be child- or teacher-initiated, research focused on finding answers to student questions, direction follows children's interest

Source: Reprinted by permission of the Publisher. From J. Helm & L.G. Katz, *Young Investigators: The Project Approach in the Early Years* (New York: Teachers College Press, 2001), 2. Copyright © 2001 Teachers College Press, Columbia University. All rights reserved.

and the children to follow *authentic* topics of interest, exploring them as deeply as the children's developmental abilities allow. This matches with what we know about how children learn best. Children learn when they are self-motivated to explore questions that are deeply meaningful to them—when they find things to be "uncovered." Note in Figure 3-8 the varying degrees of child initiation and decision making in different approaches to planning. This brings us to a consideration of emergent curriculum.

WHAT IS EMERGENT CURRICULUM?

In early education today, you may hear the term "emergent curriculum." Emergent curriculum describes the kind of curriculum that develops when exploring what is "socially relevant, intellectually engaging, and personally meaningful to children." The basic idea is that organic, whole learning evolves from the interaction of the classroom participants, both children and adults. "As caring adults, we make choices for children that reflect our values; at the same time, we need to keep our plans open-ended and responsive to children" (Jones & Nimmo, 1994, p. 3). In emergent curricula, both adults and children have initiative and make decisions. This power to impact curriculum decisions and directions means that sometimes authentic curriculum is also negotiated between what interests children and what adults know is necessary for children's education and development. In other words, children's interests and questions can become the organizing theme for planning, and within that framework, teachers are able to plan the activities that embed the early learning standards and curriculum requirements (Gronlund, 2006).

With emergent curriculum, ideas for curriculum emerge from responding to the interests, questions, and concerns generated within a particular environment, by a particular group of people, at a particular time (Cassady & Lancaster, 1993). Emergent curriculum is never built on children's interests alone; teachers and parents also have interests worth bringing into the curriculum. The values and concerns of all the adults involved help the classroom culture evolve. The curriculum is called emergent because it evolves, diverging along new paths as choices and connections are made, and it is always open to new possibilities that were not thought of during the initial planning process (Jones & Reynolds, 1992).

The basis, and ongoing process, of emergent curriculum is observation of children's interests, experiences, and activities. By carefully observing and listening to children, teachers get cues about their questions, knowledge, skills, and interests. Planning after observation is focused on finding activities and materials that will lead children to sustain deeper interests and construct new understandings. Children collaborate with teachers in discussing and planning the next steps for investigation. Teachers, continually involved in watching children's responses to their experiences, puzzle through additional learnings that might be found in new ideas or materials. The best planning for emergent curriculum comes after the fact, as teachers consider children's responses and anticipate the next directions. One teacher describes the challenges of planning in emergent ways as "responding and anticipating, following and initiating" (Pelo, 1996, p. 102). Teachers follow the children's lead and then introduce new activities to sustain their interests and deepen their explorations—a subtle balancing act that requires genuine responsiveness and attention to more than just the teacher's goals.

Where do ideas for emergent curriculum come from? Jones and Nimmo (1994) identify a number of sources.

> Emergent curriculum is:
>
> • framed by the teacher, allowing for collaborations between children and teachers, giving everyone a voice.
> • responsive to children, allowing teachers to build upon children's interests.
> • flexible, because curriculum planning is constantly developing, instead of being done well in advance.
> • facilitated by the teacher, who takes what is seen and heard, and provides opportunities for children to dig deeper and construct further knowledge.
> • represented by various forms of documentation, enabling children's learning and teachers' thinking to be made visible.
> • theoretically supported by the work of Dewey, Piaget, and Vygotsky.
>
> (Adapted from Stacey, 2009).

- Children's play, comments, and questions. Different children have different interests. For example, a child is playing out going on a camping trip after summer vacation; another keeps talking about his baby brother's lack of teeth.

- Adult interests and passions. For example, a parent wants to introduce the children to composting; a teacher enjoys finding bird nests.

- Things, events, and people in the environment (see Figure 3-9). For example, the hill at the bottom of the playground leads to exploring the force of gravity. A visit to a neighbor's garden becomes an experiment in watching the growth of vegetables over time or leads to exploring what earthworms do in the soil.

- Developmental tasks. The tasks to be mastered at each developmental stage require a lot of practice for skills and social-emotional issues (see Figures 3-10a & 3-10b). For example, a lot of opportunities to use scissors; plenty of space to jump; a curriculum that helps children explore friendship.

Figure 3-9

Curriculum may come from opportunities to explore things in the environments.

Figure 3-10 (a & b)
Curriculum may come from children's own developmental interests, such as stringing beads or working puzzles.

(a)

(b)

Figure 3-11
Curriculum may be found in learning to live together, such as finding ways to assign classroom chores.

- Family and cultural influences. For example, a Jewish family offers to introduce the children to Chanukah traditions; a visiting grandmother tells stories of her childhood.

- Issues that arise in the course of living together day to day (see Figure 3-11). For example, discussions about fair ways to use the new computer; finding ways to assign classroom chores.

- Serendipity or what just happens. For example, a heavy rainstorm creates new gullies in the playground; caterpillars arrive in the spring.

- Curriculum resource materials. Although these are not teachers' primary sources of curriculum, they often give ideas that can be adapted to the setting, the children's interests, or the teacher's style. For example, a teacher may find activities related to firefighters, after she has discovered her children's interest in this topic.

- Values held for children's learning in school and the community. For example, a class visits the nursing home on the corner; children discuss making holiday gifts for others.

These are just some beginning points to pursue in depth to find children's themes. This is a redefinition of theme planning (Curtis & Carter, 1996). In child-centered theme planning, teachers identify the themes emerging from the children's play and life experiences and then translate those ideas into materials and activities to provoke curiosity in and exploration of the new ideas and questions that children keep generating. Good planning allows for well-prepared starting points for children's play and exploration. Good planning then requires teachers to stand back and ask what they have learned as they watch children's playful interactions with materials and activities. In uncovering the child's developmental goals and objectives, teachers have a specific direction to plan for. This thoughtful consideration inevitably leads to the next plans.

As teachers thoughtfully supply a variety of experiences and media for children to explore, the sustained activities may develop into long-term projects (Katz & Chard, 2000; Chard, 1998a and 1998b; Helm & Katz, 2001; Helm & Beneke, 2003). These are called "studies" in the Creative Curriculum (Dodge et al., 2002). In this growing curriculum, teachers and children together concentrate on exploring subjects deeply. Good projects provide opportunities to work in many curriculum areas, such as science, math, social studies, communication, and the arts. Projects, then, are the vehicle for truly integrating curriculum and allowing many kinds of knowledge and skills to develop. As such, projects are especially meaningful for creating appropriate curriculum in the primary grades, although also occasions for deepening learning in the preschool, and even with toddlers (LeeKeenan & Edwards, 1992). Every piece of emergent curriculum doesn't necessarily develop into such projects; teachers carefully follow the direction of children's interests and help them move on to new ideas when the time seems right. "Through this process, the curriculum keeps emerging and the teacher, together with the children, keeps learning" (Jones & Reynolds, 1992, p. 105).

Emergent curriculum is dynamic, always developing, never completely predictable. Its very organic process, growing from real actions and interactions, keeps both children and teachers highly motivated and learning. It is important to realize, however, that emergent curriculum is not just "whatever happens, happens." Rather, it is as highly structured as a teacher-directed approach. The difference is that its structure does not come from preset curriculum plans, but from knowledgeable teacher responses to children.

The question asked by many teachers today is how they can use the concept of planning emergent curriculum, while reconciling it with the demands to meet specific state standards.

As discussed in Chapter 2, rather than give up on the approach, teachers are using the concept of *backtracking* to demonstrate how the standards have been met when using emergent curriculum. That is, they are mindful of the standards as they guide the children through their projects and studies. As the children's work is finished, teachers can then identify the specific skills, knowledge, and abilities that were used during the experience. This allows teachers to be accountable for the required curriculum while supporting children to learn in very appropriate activities. Teachers also plan specific activities that they know will offer opportunities to enhance children's knowledge and skills to meet the standards.

It should be noted that families have important roles to play in helping teachers with developing and carrying out curriculum. The first role is to understand and support the teacher's efforts in developing curriculum that may not appear established, and therefore comfortable to families concerned about their children's learning. As teachers communicate their goals for children and their enthusiasm for the active learning process, families will come to understand that specific objectives will still be met, though perhaps in a less scripted way.

Another role is for families to become active in the dialogues about their children's interests and learning style. Families have firsthand knowledge that can be shared with teachers in collaborative partnerships.

Still another role is for families to help identify and supply resources for project work. With their community connections, families may provide important ideas to add to the planning process. They may themselves become resources, as well as adding materials from home. As teachers document the children's work, parents will catch the enthusiasm of the explorations, and themselves become involved, strengthening all learning possibilities.

STRATEGIES FOR PLANNING FOR EMERGENT CURRICULUM

As teachers begin to understand the appropriateness of emergent curriculum, some key activities can aid the planning process. Observation of children busy at play and work is the heart of uncovering the questions and interests of children's learning and the skills and knowledge they already have. We have already discussed the importance of observation for assessing where children are in relation to predetermined goals and objectives. Note that recording descriptive data about children at play guides teachers in responsive planning.

In reflecting on observations, teachers should ask: What did I see and hear, specifically? What would I call this experience for the child? What does this child know and know how to do? What does this child find frustrating or puzzling, meaningful or challenging? How does this child feel about herself or himself? What is the child trying to do, in play or exploration? What experiences, knowledge, or skills are present to build in? What questions, inventions, or problems are being encountered? What might help next, from me or from peers? (Curtis & Carter, 1996). Answers to these questions help teachers define children's self-chosen themes and "recognize the curriculum that is actually happening" (Washington & Baker, 1996, p. 155). Finding the answers to questions about children's play also helps teachers identify the learning activities that might best sustain the children's explorations. Observation is an ongoing process that continues as teachers plan and provide for the next steps (see Figure 3-12).

The following sample observation illustrates the teacher's process of identifying themes and issues to plan for:

> From the teacher's notebook: Jenny and Ramon are playing in the sand. Ramon pats the sand firmly into the pail and turns the pail over. The sand falls out. He seems disappointed, then refills the pail, pushing even harder this time. Again he turns the pail over. The sand falls out again. Next he grabs Jenny's bucket and begins to fill it. Jenny says, "No, Ramon" and grabs it back. Ramon struggles to get it again, saying "I want to use this bucket so the sand won't fall. This is the one I had yesterday."

> Interpretation: The sand in the sandbox was wet yesterday following a rain, and the children were able to create molds when they filled their pails and upended them. Ramon thinks the ability for the sand to hold its shape is connected with a particular pail, rather than the consistency of the sand. He plans to test out this idea, but is frustrated because someone else has the pail. He grabs rather than asks. Jenny knows how to assert herself against Ramon.

Figure 3-12

Teachers integrate knowledge of child development, individual children, and standards as they create, evaluate, document, and communicate curriculum. No strand can be missing.

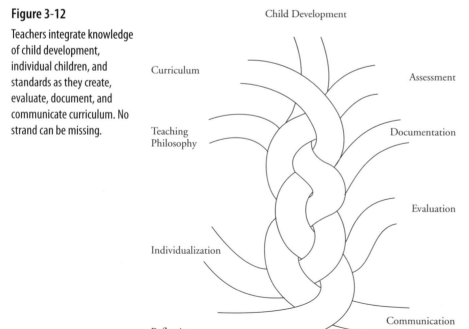

Child Development

Curriculum

Assessment

Teaching Philosophy

Documentation

Evaluation

Individualization

Reflection

Communication

After observing Ramon's interest and question, the teacher can plan subsequent experiences to help Ramon explore the properties of wet and dry sand, other substances that allow molds and imprints, and so on. By thinking about individual children's interests, questions, and needs, teachers can plan activities to specifically target individual children (Buell & Sutton, 2008). Thinking about the possible experiences that might support further related exploration is often accomplished by a process known as *webbing*.

Creating a web involves brainstorming about where a particular exploration might go and listing the potential related connections that could be made. One thing leads to another, one idea to the next, like a big spider web. A web always includes more possibilities than can be followed before other interests move the curriculum into other directions, as well as ideas that are ruled out due to lack of interest, lack of appropriateness for a particular group, or lack of appropriate resources or experiences. A web is also open to other additions as children and families become involved in discussion and activities, and new ideas occur along the way. The web helps teachers remain open to possibilities and begin preparing materials and planning for activities that might give opportunities for learning. A web is a tentative plan, a starting place to begin trying ideas, paying attention to what happens, evaluating, and moving on with further activities (Jones & Nimmo, 1994). The function of the web is not to create an elaborate set of teacher-planned activities—the "curriculum plan for the month"; rather, it serves as a starting place for teachers to focus their thinking. As one teacher said, "I see this initial web more as a guidebook for traveling, with reminders to 'Be ready for . . . ,' 'Be sure to spend some time at . . . ,' and 'Bring along. . . .' This web would not be a map marked in red to be followed unwaveringly" (Pelo, 1996, p. 102). Webbing allows teachers to be creative and playful in their planning, rather than just logical and linear. For example, a web to show the teacher's thinking about learning related to Ramon's ideas in the sandbox might look like Figure 3-13.

These webs represent the teacher's thinking about possible developmental learnings or concepts as well as the potential activities and materials listed on the web. This is an important way for teachers to negotiate between following the children's interests while ensuring that they are supporting their progress toward the defined learning goals and objectives of the standards.

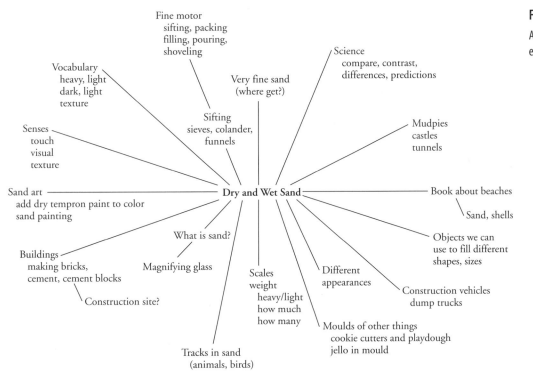

Figure 3-13

A teacher's web to consider exploring dry and wet sand.

Sometimes teachers find it useful to separate these two parts into *activity webs* (the what, when, and how of potential plans) and *concept webs* (the why or possible outcomes), so that they can check that all aspects of development and required knowledge or skills are being covered. This thinking process is also important when teachers are trying to document children's progress for parents. Figure 3-14 shows an activity web for the sand and water explorations, while Figure 3-15 shows a content web. (A similar web could be used after the fact, to identify the goals achieved, as discussed previously with the concept of backtracking in Chapter 2.)

After some preliminary thinking with the webs, the teacher continues to plan. The first step in planning to carry out a child-centered curriculum is to *provision the environment.* (These four

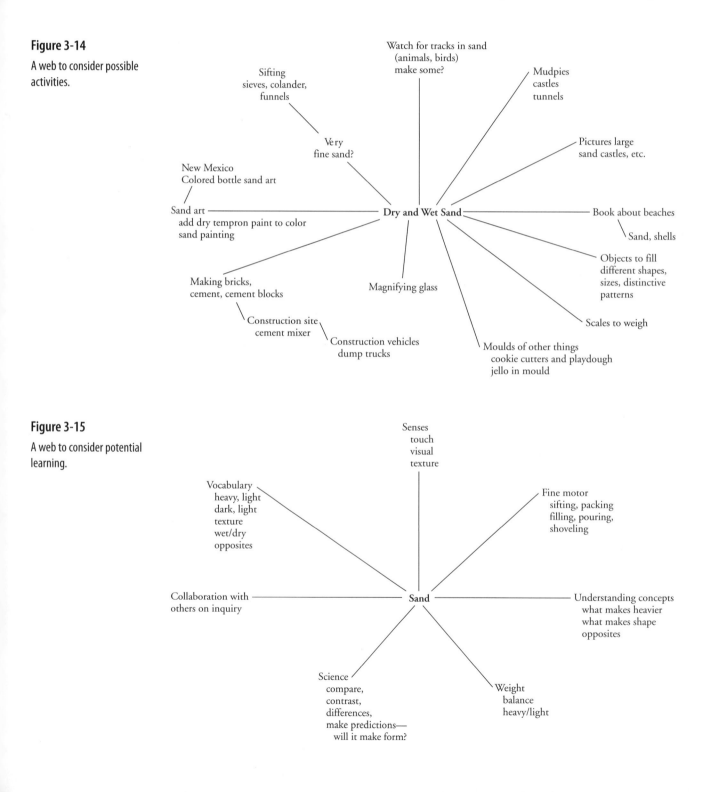

Figure 3-14

A web to consider possible activities.

Figure 3-15

A web to consider potential learning.

stages of planning are described in Curtis & Carter, 1996, and Stacey, 2009.) Selecting a focus from the activity web, teachers carefully set up the environment with materials and activities chosen to help children explore a given theme. Teachers may create a *provocation,* which is an event or experience designed to spark interest. Teachers then observe carefully to see what the children do with the materials provided, what themes and experiences they talk about and represent in their play, and what they seem to question or understand. In this way, teachers get ideas for additional props and materials. The next step is planning to *sustain the play theme.* Further observations will help teachers realize the new ideas, solutions, and answers that children are coming up with, or other materials that could extend the experience. The third step is planning to *enrich the play* by adding still more new materials that suggest or support new ideas. As a final step, teachers plan materials and opportunities for children and teachers to *represent the learning experience.* As children are given varieties of media and encouraged to represent their thinking and experiences, they expand their symbolic thinking and representation skills. This is planning for the literacy component within the classroom. Teachers also plan for ways to represent the children's learning to others, including the children themselves and their parents This documentation may include: samples of children's work at various stages of the project; photographs telling the story of the work in progress; comments written by the teacher; transcriptions of children's discussion and explanations about the activity (Seitz, 2008).

Documenting learning experiences helps teachers understand where they have been in the collaborative learning and planning and gives them ideas for where they might go next. It also helps children remember and understand the process of their learning and gives parents concrete representations of their children's growth in learning (see Figure 3-16). The better the documentation, the more visible the evidence of the teacher's thinking and planning, which forestalls the complaint that developmentally appropriate curriculum is spontaneous, left up to the children's desires. Documentation, then, shows accountability, extends the learning, and makes the learning visible (Seitz, 2008).

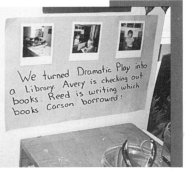

Figure 3-16

Documentation informs families of the curriculum, and allows children to revisit their experiences.

These four steps in planning to create a developmentally appropriate, child-centered curriculum are well illustrated in the teachers' planning in the Reggio Emilia schools in Northern Italy and those who follow their approach (see Chapter 4).

An example of these planning steps in action is a teacher who provisioned the dramatic play area in her preschool classroom with several baby dolls and related baby paraphernalia, such as diapers, powder, and baby bottles. This provisioning was in response to a number of conversations and experiences with children in the class whose mothers were pregnant or had small babies. The teacher observed the children playing parenting roles and listened carefully to their conversations. As she heard the young players discuss the need to bathe their babies before putting them to bed, she added a baby bathtub and some plastic bath toys. Learning expanded with carefully planned activities, such as looking at the children's baby photos, clothes, and baby books their parents had made; reading books about babies; visiting one of the newborns at home; and visiting the infant room in the child care center. Thus the interest in this play was sustained for another period. Other conversations led to ideas for adding other materials to further enrich the play. One child had accompanied her mother to the pediatrician when the baby was given a checkup; subsequently, some of the young mothers began to play taking their babies to the doctor for their shots. The teacher then added doctor's office props. A later addition was a small potty-chair; the teacher heard one of the children commenting that the doctor always had to check the baby's pee. Other medical equipment was added to expand on ideas about what doctors do. Throughout this experience, children were busy talking about their ideas and feelings about small babies, others' roles in caring for them, what was needed for growth and development, and a multitude of other deepening understandings, including gender roles (yes, fathers could look after little babies!). The teacher planned and created a web after the completion of the learning cycle to illustrate its full complexity for the parents.

Although all children in the classroom were involved in some of the activities planned for the whole group, such as visiting the infant room and reading the books about babies, some children were also interested in pursuing other questions. During this time, perhaps as a result of seeing the baby books, several children began making books of their own. They spent several mornings in the writing center, using the book-making materials provided there. Meanwhile, other children, less interested in the baby theme, continued constructing elaborate block cities. By planning and preparing the entire environment with items designed to attract interest, teachers find that children generate their own diverse ideas. While watching all the children at play, teachers may be planning for several separate strands of interest at the same time. In the classroom just described, the teacher kept the writing center richly provisioned, brought in some old books that children could take apart to examine the bindings, and established an author's corner. The block cities were enhanced with the addition of real building materials and picture books of city skyscrapers. The environment should be designed so that children can discover what interests them, rather than having to study what everyone else is working on.

Teachers planning appropriate curriculum for primary-age children understand that through concrete experiences with real objects and materials and through interaction with people in the environment, children construct concepts about the world and begin to use symbols to represent their thinking. Scoy (1995) describes a curriculum model titled 4 E's: Experience, Extension, Expression, and Evaluation. Harris and Fuqua (1996) describe a curriculum-planning strategy that begins with impression or intake activities in which children have real firsthand experiences with situations, things, and people to provide raw materials for thinking. This is followed by extension activities, which promote greater understanding by involving children with related reading and listening experiences, and then by expression opportunities, in which children express their learning through a variety of media and methods. These frameworks are expansions of the planning approach to include the subject matter of the primary classroom in an integrated curriculum approach (Hart, Burts, & Charlesworth, 1997).

WHAT ABOUT PLANNING FORMS?

Following this discussion of planning for emergent curriculum, it is probably evident that the traditional, Monday-to-Friday fill-in-the-time-slot planning form usually is not very useful. These forms are usually required to demonstrate to principals, supervisors, and licensing inspectors that teachers are thinking about the activities they provide for children. Every bit as much, if not more, thought is required of teachers who plan in response to children's issues and interests. But as teachers write notes to plan that type of curriculum, they are generally writing after observation of play and adding new ideas as they go along. Therefore, they need to create forms that allow for more open-ended exploration, more tentativeness, and addition of ideas as they become appropriate. Such a lesson-planning form allows for the additional ideas the children provide, as well as the materials their parents might contribute as they become aware of interests. It also allows for evolving ideas and interests rather than limiting children and teachers to preplanned activities. A flexible planning form might look like the one in Figure 3-17.

A flexible planning form documents emerging interests and the additions made to the environment to support those interests. Rather than spending hours trying to make artificial connections between themes before the fact, this plan offers a starting place, with additions to follow as the play develops. The burden for planning is still on the teacher, but the interaction with children in

Figure 3-17
A flexible planning form allows teachers to respond to all interests and needs.

the classroom informs every aspect of the work. It is authentic, joyful work, involving all those who read it—parents, supervisors, other teachers, and licensing consultants alike—in the organic life of the classroom. This kind of planning form allows teachers to enjoy planning again, rather than dreading the need to fill in all the blanks before the Thursday deadline.

Many teachers who want to move to more developmentally appropriate methods of planning often hesitate because the old form suggests a particular planning mode. They fear their supervisors will not accept changes that reflect different approaches. When a class of college students approached local licensing consultants to ask if change in the form was acceptable, they were surprised to receive encouragement rather than a negative response. The supervisors were pleased to see that so much thought was going into work with children. These supervisors' main interests were evidence of a knowledgeable concern for developing the children's understanding and skills and the presence of a rationale for classroom plans. Thus, teachers should not let the fear of change limit the flexibility of their planning methods.

CHANGING THE PLANNING PROCESS

For teachers who have been involved with traditional, teacher-dominated planning, changing to more child-centered methods may start best with small steps. Often when new teachers, educated in ideas of developmentally appropriate practice, begin working in schools, they are dismayed to find that what they have been taught is not being practiced. These ideas might provide beginning places for change.

In the entire planning cycle, observation is the beginning, middle, and end of the process: observation to learn about children's abilities, skills, and interests; observation to determine progress toward defined goals and objectives; observation to learn about children's ideas and questions; and observation to evaluate how well the teacher's plans have moved children toward greater learning and richer play experiences. Making regular opportunities to observe is crucial to changing the planning process.

1. A first step is to begin really listening to children, trying to find out their questions and interests. Tape-recording children at play could be useful to play back later. Vivian Paley has given early childhood educators an important model of what adults learn when they listen to children and then reflect on what they have heard (Wiltz & Fein, 1996). Planning just one material or activity that would support the interest is a beginning. An example of this is a teacher who adds more markers when she notices the children's engaged activity with them.

   Sometimes really listening to children means reflecting not only on what they are saying, but on what they are doing, trying to figure out why. Their play may indicate nonverbal interests in exploring certain questions.

2. Teachers accustomed to traditional theme-based planning may try to find themes from events in the children's lives rather than a preplanned schedule for the year. The teacher who planned the activities involving babies after the birth of small siblings was finding the topic for the theme in such an event.

3. Try leaving the end of a theme open in terms of time frame. When the time frame is open, teachers do not feel pressure to move children on to the next topic too quickly before their exploration and learning has been satisfied. By not planning to end a theme unit on a Friday, but continuing the materials and activities over to the following week, teachers may find children using the materials in more complex ways. Time is given to revisit and make play, and learning, more complex.

4. Notice how children use materials in various areas of the room. Adding more materials can enhance involvement and stimulate further exploration. Planning for the environment opens up teachers' thinking, rather than planning to teach isolated concepts. For example, a teacher who is planning to add additional sensory materials to the creative area is not as focused on a concept as on children's open-ended use of the materials. The teacher who plans to enrich the block area with real building materials and pictures of their use is stimulating additional forms of construction, not worrying so much about teaching the concept of "tallest."

5. Watch what developmental tasks children are practicing. Focusing on the separate domains, and children's progress within each, allows teachers to consider the activities and materials that can support growth. For example, the teacher who notices the children's developing fine motor skills plans to offer several new implements to the writing center, such as hole-punchers and stencils. The teacher who watches burgeoning cooperative play adds props to the dramatic play center that support several related roles.

6. The direction of children's interest may be extended in new directions. For example, the children playing at taking their babies to the doctor were supported in a new direction when the teacher added medical props. Children who have been exploring planting seeds and their growth may get very interested in the cooking experiences the teacher plans as a natural outgrowth of their watching foodstuffs grow.

7. Teachers working in classrooms burdened by prescriptions of state curricula and learning objectives may find the idea of moving from teacher-dominated planning difficult to contemplate. So much material must be covered that they feel all the planning must go toward meeting objectives. However, the integrating method of planning for curriculum areas and objectives under the umbrella of long-term projects or theme studies may make it possible to satisfy the requirements while still exploring topics of interest to children and teachers. You

may read examples of such projects in Harris and Fuqua (1996); Helm and Beneke (2003); and Booth (1997).

As previously discussed, teachers may use the technique of backtracking to identify the objectives for the standards that were met while children have been involved in long-term projects that integrate curriculum. This means that, after the project is complete, teachers can go back over what children actually did in their project work, isolating the individual skills and knowledge acquired in appropriate studies.

8. Brainstorming and collaborating with another teacher may support changing the planning process. The richness of ideas that come through thinking with another person may help teachers widen their focus and move from narrow theme planning. Emergent curriculum grows from reflection and dialogue.

The process of change has emotional significance as well as complex problems to overcome that need planning and support. Read more about the process of change in Chapter 17, available only on the Web site.

These small steps toward planning for more developmentally appropriate curriculum may move teachers in important directions. Learning to plan a child-centered curriculum is a growth process. In her excellent article describing a classroom project that allowed the children to collaborate with the teacher on emergent curriculum, Booth (1997) describes the steps she took and what she learned to do differently the next time. For example, she learned to include more consultation with the children at the beginning of projects and in the planning webs, to slow down to involve the children in all steps of the project, to allow children's curiosity to open up whole new areas of investigation, and to observe "more deeply what children are trying to understand or accomplish and planning in terms of challenges I can provide to further their efforts" (Booth, 1997, p. 82). Beginning the process of planning for developmentally appropriate curriculum allows teachers to grow and experience their own creativity as well.

This kind of planning for curriculum is not an easy process, but it is exciting, offering dynamic opportunities for learning and growth for teachers as well as children. Curtis and Carter (1996) compare it to learning to swim in the ocean—"understanding the nature of waves by spending quite a bit of time with your body immersed in the experience."

> There's not really a way to control it; you can only watch closely and respond accordingly. You have to anticipate what might happen, try to stay one step ahead of them, and follow their lead as events unfold. And you have to do this while staying focused with them in the moment. (Curtis & Carter, 1996)

Responding is what planning for developmentally appropriate curriculum is all about.

SUMMARY

Planning developmentally appropriate curriculum involves a cycle of teacher activity that includes

- observation and note taking.
- reflecting and assessing children's progress toward specific developmental goals and objectives.
- observing and reflecting to learn themes of children's interests.
- identifying strategies, materials, and experiences that will support children's progress.
- observing to evaluate the effectiveness of plans.
- starting the entire cycle over again.

Professional organizations have published position statements on curriculum that emphasize whole-child development and active learning, with teachers employing a variety of strategies to help children progress.

Theme planning for long-term projects may be useful for children and teachers. This focus allows both children and teachers to organize their thinking and to experience the repetition needed for learning. Teachers must be mindful of not getting bound too closely to the plans or of not using children's interests as the focus for the themes.

Emergent curriculum refers to the curriculum on themes that are meaningful in children's lives, that is, negotiated by children and adults in a particular environment. Webbing refers to the brainstorming process that identifies potential related activities for learning. Teachers plan through observation, provisioning the environment to sustain and enrich learning activities and to provide opportunities to represent learning cycles. Teachers may have to develop new planning forms that provide for flexibility in following the children's lead. Taking small steps away from teacher-dominated planning may make the planning process more developmentally appropriate.

THINK ABOUT IT ACTIVITIES

1. Obtain several lesson-planning forms from teachers in your community. As you and your classmates analyze them, see if the forms support developing curriculum to follow children's themes.

2. Working with a partner, brainstorm and develop beginning planning webs, both activity and concept, for the topic of babies, similar to the theme developed by the teacher in this chapter. Think of as many possible materials, activities, and experiences as you can that could support preschool children's learning about the topic. On your concept web, see how much learning would be possible in the activities you thought of. Are you finding learning in all domains of development?

3. Walk with a partner around the building in which your class meets. List all the things you see in the environment that might intrigue a group of young children enough that a teacher could plan related materials and activities to extend their interest.

4. Generate a list of all the activities you enjoyed as a child. Share this list with a small group. Create a master list on chart paper and post it. Now generate a list of all the things you enjoy doing and/or are interested in as an adult; compile a master list. Do you find activities that could form the basis for planning some experiences for children?

QUESTIONS TO ASSESS LEARNING OF CHAPTER OBJECTIVES

1. Describe several key indicators of developmentally appropriate curricula, as defined by the various position statements.

2. Describe the planning cycle, identifying the various components.

3. Discuss what is meant by emergent curriculum. Identify sources of ideas for emergent curriculum.

4. What is meant by webbing as a planning method?

5. Discuss considerations in adopting a planning form.

6. Identify several first steps teachers could take in moving from teacher-dominated planning to more child-centered approaches.

APPLY YOUR KNOWLEDGE QUESTIONS

1. Discuss some of the classroom arrangements that would support teacher availability for observing and recording information on individual children.

2. Compare and contrast the earlier and the later NAEYC position statements on curriculum. What differences do you see? What might be some of the reasons for these differences?

3. Watch children working and at play for a period of time. Then use the concept of backtracking to identify specifics from your state's early learning standards.

HELPFUL WEB SITES

http://www.projectapproach.org	This Web site, under the direction of Sylvia Chard, professor emeritus of early childhood education at the University of Alberta, contains information, project examples, and resources.
www.naeyc.org	Read the position statement on curriculum and assessment at this Web site. Click on Publications, and then scroll down to click on Read NAEYC Position Statements.
http://www.pearsonearlylearning.com	At this Web site, read more about the Work Sampling Assessment System.
http://Illinoisearlylearning.org/ project-approach.htm	The Illinois Early Learning Project offers information on the project approach, including project examples and links to various resources.
http://www.mothergooseprograms.org	This Web site has reading lists and book programs for teachers to integrate reading with explorations of math, science, and other topics.

Please visit the premium Web site for Developmentally Appropriate Practice, 4th edition, to access more chapter web links, suggestions for further research and study, additional book chapters, interactive quizzes, video exercises, online journal activities, flashcards, and much more! Go to www.cengage.com/login to register your access code.

A Consideration of Various Curriculum Models

One concept stressed throughout this book is that the standards for developmental appropriateness are not intended as an exact prescription, but rather as philosophical guidelines to inform decisions and provide questions to reflect upon. As teachers, administrators, and parents make decisions for individual children and specific educational programs, they create their own developmentally appropriate environments and curricula. The knowledge of age-related characteristics that make certain activities, materials, interactions, and experiences interesting and appropriate for children will provide elements in common with other developmentally appropriate programs. However, thoughtful responses to individual variations in interests and capabilities and respectful attention to the social and cultural contexts in which children live ensure that appropriate programs bear a distinctive stamp that reflects the efforts of individual decision making.

As students and teachers encounter various curricula that have been adopted in schools and early childhood programs across the country, they will hear many different names and identify specific curricula approaches. Sometimes curricula are adopted without teacher input or approval. It is important to understand what each separate curriculum model offers and to see how each curriculum's ideas may fit into the larger framework of principles of developmentally appropriate practice. With the exception of the Montessori, Waldorf, and Reggio approaches, many programs use a rather eclectic mix of ideas found in some of the curriculum models.

This chapter briefly introduces several of the more widely known and practiced curriculum approaches. Students and class discussions should focus on discovering how closely each curriculum adheres to the principles of developmentally appropriate practices. The curricula are discussed in the order of their inception. Their descriptions are provided for informational purposes and not as specific recommendations of the author. The links to video clips provided give a glimpse of each approach in action. The various packaged curricula that are marketed ready-made are not discussed here, as it should be obvious from all earlier discussion that most do not meet the standards of individualization necessary for developmentally appropriate practice.

LEARNING OBJECTIVES

After completing this chapter, students should be able to

- describe several different curricula approaches and philosophies common in early childhood education.
- discuss how each curriculum model follows the principles of developmentally appropriate practice.

THE MONTESSORI APPROACH

History and Philosophy

Maria Montessori (1870–1952) was the first Italian woman to earn a medical degree. From her observations of children, Montessori recognized the uniqueness of each child, and she observed particular periods she called **sensitive periods**, when children are particularly sensitive to particular kinds of stimuli for their learning (Montessori, 1995). She described four planes of development, with each stage having its own developmental characteristics and challenges. The period from birth through age six was the time for sensorial exploration, when children created their own intelligence. The time from age six through age twelve was the time of conceptual exploration, when children were developing their powers of abstraction and imagination. From ages twelve through age eighteen was the stage for humanistic exploration, when children understood their place in society and how to make a contribution to that world. And from eighteen through twenty-four, young adults were doing more specialized exploration, seeking their niche in the world. Montessori believed each person has a need to find meaningful work (see Figure 4-1).

Figure 4-1

Montessori's ideas are embodied in Montessori schools worldwide.

Another term from Montessori's philosophy is the **absorbent mind,** by which she meant the ease with which young children learn unconsciously from the environment. Montessori was fascinated with the power of learning within each child, and an important part of her belief is that children deserve respect for their capabilities, their individual pace, and their rhythm of learning. She believed that children are capable of developing concentration and self-discipline, and need an environment that can support these characteristics. She also believed that children in the first developmental plane do not benefit from imagination, but rather are focused on the realities of sensory experience (see Figure 4-2).

After working with children in the slums of Rome, she created a school that incorporated her philosophy and methods in 1907 (Casa dei Bambini), and since that time, Montessori schools have proliferated in the United States and elsewhere. Most Montessori schools are for children ages two through six, although in some communities, Montessori education may continue through the elementary grades and beyond. Today in our country, we find Montessori schools that strictly follow the original techniques (Association Montessori International, AMI), and others that follow practices adapted to American culture and current thinking (American Montessori Society, AMS). Montessori's ideas have also had an influence on early childhood education in general.

Key Components of Montessori Applications

Montessori schools use unique methods, materials, and specially trained teachers to follow Montessori's directions. Essential elements of Montessori education include

- teachers specifically educated in Montessori philosophy and methods.
- partnerships with families.
- multiaged, heterogeneous groups of children.
- diverse Montessori materials and experiences, carefully presented and sequenced to children's needs.
- schedules that allow large blocks of time to problem solve and become deeply involved in learning.
- a classroom atmosphere that encourages social interaction for cooperative learning.

Figure 4-2

Montessori believed that young children are focused on realities of sensory experience rather than imagination.

Figure 4-3

A Montessori teacher may present an activity to an individual child, using a carefully prescribed sequence.

Teacher Education. Montessori teachers have received specialized training in an institution accredited for Montessori teacher education. Listings of accredited Montessori teacher training schools are available at the Web sites listed at the end of the chapter. The training emphasizes learning how to observe children to know what activities they are ready for, and learning when and how much to intervene. Teachers also study specific materials and activities that can move children toward goals. Part of the study includes the sequences of prescribed tasks—using precisely designed didactic Montessori materials—to be presented to children in a designated order. For examples of these tasks and the procedures for presenting them to children, see the Montessori Albums made available at the home page of Shu-Chen Jenny Yen (Web site listed at the end of the chapter).

Teachers, formerly called "directresses," have the ultimate objective of helping children learn independently, and thus the teachers function most often as facilitators. With the younger children, teachers are most active, demonstrating the use of materials and presenting activities based on their assessment of children's need and developmental level. Often they present their lessons to an individual or to a small group of children in a sequence of tasks that will help children learn specific skills and concepts (see Figure 4-3). Teachers are given instruction in presenting directions in sequential steps for the activities. In most Montessori programs, teachers work with groups of children in three-year age spans, from three to six years, from six to nine years, and so on.

Teacher Practice A major teacher responsibility is creating the *prepared environment*. Recognizing the importance of stimulating curiosity and interest for learning, Montessori environments place a great deal of attention on order and beautiful materials that appeal to the senses. A Montessori classroom is divided into learning areas with carefully arranged materials on open shelves. Many of the areas are different from those in typical classrooms for young children. We will identify these areas in the next section on components of the curriculum, but here we note the emphasis on preparing the environment as a teacher role.

Montessori teachers also create an atmosphere of calm and order. There are specific customs for speaking to others in the Montessori classroom, again emphasizing respect. Because children are frequently busy with individual work, there is an atmosphere of purposeful busyness, in a mostly quiet room. When teachers speak to children, they do so in a low voice, and often privately. Children often work on individual mats, and teachers circulate among them to comment and question. Collaboration for learning is certainly encouraged. Montessori believed that the younger children in a group would learn from the older, and the older would learn by teaching the younger. Montessori emphasized the important teacher role of keeper of the environment, to support such opportunities within a peaceful classroom.

As children are introduced to tasks, teachers again take on the role of observers, noting where children need further support and opportunities for practice.

Figure 4-4

This series of wooden cylinders with knobs, with increasing diameters, is a Montessori didactic material.

Curriculum Materials and Activities Montessori is most known for specific **didactic** materials, often beautifully made from wood. *Didactic* materials are those that teach children directly by making any errors in their use obvious to the child for self-correction. Examples of this include the famous Montessori Pink Tower, which consists of a collection of pink cubes, seriated in size from the smallest (1 cubic centimeter) to the largest (10 cubic centimeters). When children select the correct cube in order of size, they are able to complete the entire tower successfully. Another example is a series of wooden cylinders (with knobs) in a series of increasing diameters to insert into the hole of the correct size (see Figure 4-4).

Other components of the curriculum are *sensorial* materials and activities and *conceptual* materials.

Sensorial materials and activities include any that allow children to order and classify by impression, to help them broaden and refine their sensory perceptions. The use of these materials helps children develop concepts of size, shape, color, texture, weight, smell, and sound. They might include collections of fabric to match similar textures, sound or sniff bottles, or collections of cubes.

Conceptual materials are concrete academic materials used to introduce children to reading, writing, mathematics, and social studies. In a Montessori classroom for children ages three through six, one might see puzzles that are maps of the world or the United States; math counting boards with golden beads grouped in tens to represent the decimal system, and other concrete materials for learning math concepts; or collections of sandpaper letters (see Figure 4-5). Within the classroom, one can usually distinguish a language area, a math area, and a sensory area.

Montessori's philosophy included introducing children to varieties of *practical life skills*, such as washing dishes, sweeping floors, and watering plants. Thus, in a Montessori classroom, another area for practical life skills includes real tools and utensils and real work to undertake, such as polishing a mirror, peeling vegetables, or preparing their own snacks and drinks (see Figure 4-6). This contrasts with the "pretend" house play in a dramatic play area with toy plastic utensils. Dramatic play areas and dress-up clothes are not included in Montessori classrooms for young children, as Montessori believed that fantasy did not have a place in curriculum for young children. Another area that is not in a traditional Montessori classroom (although it may be found in American adaptations) is a creative art area. Art materials may be used to help children develop the fine motor skills needed for writing development, but are not used for creative expression with young children.

Figure 4-5

This child, working on her own mat, is using math materials.

Figure 4-6

This child in a Montessori classroom is cutting her apple for snack.

Children may not have free choice of materials to use until they have been appropriately presented to them. Then they may select the activity materials that they would like to use and must use it in the way they have been instructed. Teachers may ask children if they want to try a task, if they need help doing it, or if they feel they aren't yet ready.

Impact of Montessori Ideas

The Montessori philosophy has made lasting contributions that impact the discussion of developmentally appropriate practice in this book. One important idea is that children are worthy of respect, developing uniquely. Another idea that resonates is that children are essentially self-didactic, learning through their own activities and adaptations. The prepared, attractive environment, furnished so that children can be independent within the classroom, is something that we continue to see emphasized in developmentally appropriate environments. The importance of high-quality materials for hands-on experiences is an idea that is emphasized in good early childhood programs everywhere.

 VIDEO ACTIVITY

Go to the book's premium Web site and link to the Chapter 4 video clip titled "Planting the Seeds of Learning." As you watch this video clip about Montessori, consider the specific components that suggest how this approach meets the guidelines for developmentally appropriate practice.

REFLECTIVE QUESTIONS

1. What do you notice about the children's roles and activities?

2. What do you notice about the teachers' roles and interactions?

3. What do you notice about the physical environments, materials, and activities?

4. How do you see the philosophies described in the chapter demonstrated in action?

 Visit the premium Web site to complete these questions online and email them to your professor.

Montessori's Model and Developmentally Appropriate Practice

In the light of some commonly accepted assumptions of good practice, there are also contemporary questions about Montessori practice. In traditional Montessori education, classrooms for young children emphasize work and an absence of fantasy, at least under the age of six. This seems incompatible with our understanding of the importance of play at the heart of developmentally appropriate practice. Because children do not have the freedom to experiment with materials but must use them in the manner demonstrated by the teacher, some question how this develops the independent problem-solving and thinking abilities valued by most American educators. The strictly sequenced series of activities and tight teacher control of how space, time, and materials are also questioned in the light of current developmentally appropriate practice discussions. And while the individual working on a specific task on his or her own mat may present an image of order and responsibility, others are concerned about limited opportunities for social interaction. Because Montessori philosophy and training have been maintained separately from other institutions within early education, Montessori and her schools maintain a separate and unique place in our history.

THE BANK STREET APPROACH

History and Philosophy

One of the important names in the history of early childhood education in America is Lucy Sprague Mitchell (1878–1967). Mitchell joined with Caroline Pratt and Harriet Johnson to establish the Play School, which has been called "one of the first nursery schools in the United States of the kind we now define as 'developmentally appropriate,' learning through play schools for 2s,

3s, and 4s" (Greenberg, 1987, p. 77). Then, together with Harriet Johnson, in 1916 she founded the Bureau of Educational Experiments, in New York City. "The name reflected the idea that educational practice should be based on studying children to better understand their development" (Shapiro & Mitchell, 1992, p. 15). The unique idea of the plan for the Bureau of Educational Experiments was to combine an experimental school and research organization in a functional organization. Three years later, a nursery school was established as part of the Bureau, and joined with Pratt's play school, with a class for eight-year-olds added. This was what later became the Bank Street School. Mitchell, heavily influenced by her studies with John Dewey, believed in the power of education to affect and improve society. She coined the term "the whole child" and wanted to create opportunities for teachers to foster development of children's physical, emotional, social, and cognitive development.

Sometimes also called the "developmental-interaction approach," the ideas behind the Bank Street approach are that children are active learners, experimenters, explorers, and artists. The belief is that learning takes place in a social context. Children learn in interaction with their environment. The developmental-interaction approach also refers to the understanding that cognitive and affective development are not seen as separate, but as interconnected.

> It is a basic tenet of the developmental-interaction approach that the growth of cognitive functions—acquiring and ordering information, judging, reasoning, problem solving, using systems of symbols—cannot be separated from the growth of personal and interpersonal processes—the development of self-esteem and a sense of identity, internalization of impulse control, capacity for autonomous response, relatedness to other people. (Biber, Shapiro, & Wickens, 1971, in Cuffaro, 1977, p. 77)

Development is not something that happens to children, but rather results from children's interactions in the social and physical world.

In their view of the child, attention is given to the development of

- competence, seen as how the individual uses skills and knowledge, involving resourcefulness and resilience.

- individuality, with an emphasis on autonomous functioning, ability to make choices, take initiative, risk failure, and accept help without giving up independence.

- socialization, on two levels. The first level involves control and rechanneling of impulses, and adaptation and internalization of behavior; the second level refers to developing relations with others that are characterized by caring, fairness, responsibility, and cooperation.

Thus, the educational goals of the Bank Street approach include fostering whole-child development; sharing responsibility with children's families and communities; developing competence and motivation to use one's abilities; developing a sense of autonomy and individuality; developing a sense of social connection, as in caring about others and caring in an ecological context; fostering creativity; and promoting a sense of integration and connection.

Shapiro and Mitchell (1992) say that Bank Street's approach is not unique to Bank Street, but has six general principles of development that are important.

1. Development involves changes in the way individuals understand the world, moving from simpler to more complex.

2. Individuals operate within a range of possibilities and are never at a fixed point on a continuum of development.

3. Progress in development involves both stability and less stability, needing both old and familiar along with new challenges.

4. Children have innate motivation to engage actively with their environments. Developing a sense of a unique self is vital.

5. Children's sense of self is constructed from experience with other people and objects, and testing that self in interaction.

6. Growth and development involve conflict, within the individual and with others.

Bank Street focuses on child-centered education, noting that children learn at different rates, in different ways. An abiding concept of the Bank Street approach is the belief that learning should encompass several subjects at once—what we have earlier called "integrated" curriculum—and that learning occurs best in collaborative groups.

Structure of a Bank Street Program

The classroom curriculum is based on the idea that if children can learn about and study the human world, they can make sense of what they encounter. Bank Street focuses on themes of great interest to children—the "how," "what," and "why" explorations of the physical and social worlds and the question of origins (Cuffaro, 1977). Five key social studies subjects—cultural anthropology, history, political science, economics, and geography—are integrated into classroom activities. Thus, the community is the educational environment. The arts and sciences are woven in with the social studies–centered experiences and activities that help children find meaning in the world around them.

In the classroom, children play with materials that are predominantly open ended: blocks, water, wood, paper and art materials, and clay. Children can choose freely what they want to play with, working by themselves or in groups. Children are encouraged to learn in their own way (see Figure 4-7).

There are also common group activities, such as cooking, taking trips, spending time outdoors, listening to music, and having group discussions.

Play is at the heart of the developmental-interaction approach. Play is "seen as one of the most profound means available to children for constructing and reconstructing, formulating and reformulating knowledge" (Cuffaro, 1977 p. 52).

Teacher Roles

In the Bank Street approach, the teacher is a central and important figure, functioning to create the physical and psychological learning environment. An essential element of this environment is trust, so that teachers must establish a mutuality of trust.

Teachers are required to have not only a base of child development understanding, but also a fundamental knowledge of the potential of each material, and the opportunities for learning that

Figure 4-7

Water is one of the usual choices in a classroom using the Bank Street approach.

Figure 4-8
The teacher functions as facilitator, treating each child with respect.

each may offer. Teachers choose and arrange materials so that initiative and independence are promoted. The teachers must know children as individuals, so that careful observation is a key role of the teacher. And another essential role is that of facilitator, responding to each child with respect (see Figure 4-8).

Teachers concerned with the social interactions and atmosphere of the classroom function to develop a connection between home and school, to understand children's experiences, and to interpret the educational program and goals. The cooperation and trust developed among all the adults in children's lives create a model of community behavior and expectation for the children.

The Bank Street approach is taught at the Bank Street Graduate School in New York. Information about the teacher curriculum can be found at the Web site listed at the end of the chapter. The original Credo for Bank Street, written by its founder Lucy Sprague Mitchell, indicates the large ideas that govern education for both children and teachers (see Figure 4-9 for the Credo.)

Figure 4-9
The Bank Street Credo.

A Credo for Bank Street

What potentialities in human beings—children, teachers, and ourselves—do we want to see develop?

- **A zest for living that comes from taking in the world with all five senses alert.**
- **Lively intellectual curiosities that turn the world into an exciting laboratory and keep one ever a learner.**
- **Flexibility when confronted with change and the ability to relinquish patterns that no longer fit the present.**
- **The courage to work, unafraid and efficiently, in a world of new needs, new problems, and new ideas.**
- **Gentleness combined with justice in passing judgment on other human beings.**
- **Sensitivity, not only to the external formal rights of the "other fellow" but to him as another human being seeing a good life through his own studies.**
- **A striving to live democratically, in and out of schools, as the best way to advance our concept of democracy.**

Our credo demands ethical standards as well as scientific attitudes. Our work is based on the faith that human beings can improve the society they have created.

—from http://www.bankstreet.edu

VIDEO ACTIVITY

Go to the text's premium Web site and link to the Chapter 4 video clip titled "Empowering New Teachers: Bank Street College of Education." As you watch this video clip, consider the specific components that suggest how this approach meets the guidelines for developmentally appropriate practice.

REFLECTIVE QUESTIONS

1. What do you notice about the children's roles and activities?

2. What do you notice about the teachers' roles and interactions?

3. What do you notice about the physical environments, materials, and activities?

4. How do you see the philosophies described in the chapter demonstrated in action?

Visit the premium Web site to complete these questions online and email them to your professor.

Bank Street and Developmentally Appropriate Practice

Many educators see a direct historical link between the principles and practices of the first Bank Street nursery school and the ideas espoused in today's position statements. Certainly there are visible elements of commonality, such as

*   the emphasis on play.

*   the concept of children's active roles in constructing their understanding of the world, through interaction with materials and others in the environment.

*   the consideration of the whole child.

*   the recognition of the importance of family involvement and communication.

*   the teacher's role as observer and facilitator of learning.

THE WALDORF APPROACH

History and Philosophy

Waldorf education is the **pedagogy** based on the educational philosophy of Rudolf Steiner, an Austrian philosopher (1861–1925) who had developed anthroposophical philosophy, a sort of "spiritual science" that allowed the individual to do research into the spiritual world. One of his key understandings was the human as the integration of body, soul, and spirit. Troubled by the overly academic emphasis of schools, Steiner felt that the aesthetic side was being overlooked, and should be developed along with the intellectual side. He used the phrase "head, heart, and hands" to describe the three elements. He wrote his first book on education, *The Education of the Child,* in 1907. The first school based on his principles opened in 1919, in response to a request from the owner of the Waldorf-Astoria Cigarette Company in Stuttgart, Germany. The company's name became the source of the name Waldorf, which is now trademarked for use with this educational method. As the Stuttgart school grew, schools inspired by the pedagogical method opened in the United States, Britain, Switzerland, the Netherlands, Norway, Austria, and Hungary, as well as other towns in Germany. As the Nazis grew to power, most Waldorf schools in Europe were closed, reopening after World War II. As of May 2008, there were nearly 1,000 independent Waldorf Schools in sixty countries throughout the world, of which more than 250 are in the United States. In America, some Waldorf charter schools are supported with public money. The coordinating body in America is the Association of Waldorf Schools of North America (see Web site at the end of the chapter).

In Waldorf schools, learning is interdisciplinary, integrating practical, **aesthetic**, and intellectual elements, and is coordinated with the natural rhythms of life. The goal is to educate the whole human being, so that thinking, feeling, and doing are integrated. Steiner felt that developing a balance of all capacities would make individuals so strong, free, and healthy that they would renew society. Waldorf education places an emphasis on the role of imagination in learning. Creativity is emphasized in all aspects of the children's work. Schools and teachers are given considerable freedom to define curriculum.

Steiner divided childhood into seven-year developmental stages, each with its own learning requirements; in fact, the stages are similar to those described by Piaget.

From birth through age seven, learning is largely experiential, imitative, and sensory-based. Learning through practical activities is an emphasis in the Waldorf kindergarten. Learning primarily through doing is the "hands" part of Steiner's philosophy.

In the elementary years, from ages seven to fourteen, learning is artistic and imaginative. The Waldorf approach emphasizes developing children's feeling life and artistic expression—the "heart" part, as feelings are engaged. Because reading instruction does not begin until age seven, most children are not reading fully until third grade.

In adolescence, as children are developing the capacity for abstract thought and conceptual judgment, learning is through intellectual understanding and ethical thinking (the "head" part), including an emphasis on taking social responsibility.

The stated goal of Waldorf education is to graduate balanced individuals who have heads to think for themselves, the heart to serve others, and the courage to take action for the common good.

Curriculum in the Waldorf Approach

Schools and teachers are given considerable freedom to define their curriculum. In the early childhood years, extensive time is given for guided free play in an environment that is homelike in design, function, and atmosphere, including natural materials, and offers examples of productive work in which children can take part, such as baking, gardening, and cooking. Oral language is emphasized, with daily story times, where teachers often tell stories by heart, as well as puppetry, games, singing, and fingerplays, in addition to movement games (eurythmy). **_Eurythmy_** is unique to Waldorf schools; this is a movement art that usually accompanies spoken texts or music and includes elements of role-play, again emphasizing integration. Other early childhood activities include painting, drawing, and making wax models.

The early childhood curriculum emphasizes early experiences of daily and annual rhythms. Daily rhythms include times to come together for daily chores, stories, for puppetry, for art, and so on. Annual rhythms include celebration of seasonal and religious festivals drawn from a variety of cultures. Throughout the curriculum, Waldorf schools are infused with spirituality, so a wide range of religious traditions are included without being oriented in favor of any one tradition. The faculty of each school decides which festivals and celebrations best meet the needs and traditions in a particular school. The goal is to support children's basic reverence for the world as an interesting and a good place to live in. The goal of the early childhood curriculum is to develop physical coordination, finger dexterity, listening skills, the ability to relate socially in a group, and initiative. Play is one very important way by which children develop a sense of community.

In the early childhood years, in fact up until fourth grade, the Waldorf approach discourages exposure to media influences such as television, computers, and recorded music.

In the elementary years, the schools present a multidisciplinary arts-based curriculum that includes visual arts such as painting and sculpture, drama, artistic movement, vocal and instrumental music, and crafts such as knitting, weaving, and woodworking. In addition, there are activities such as physical education and gardening. The purpose of the artistic forms is not as a means of self-expression, but as a means to learn, to understand and relate to the world, building an understanding for different subjects out of what is beautiful in the world. Studies focus on a single theme over the course of about a month, integrating all subjects. Concepts are first introduced through stories and images, so that academic instruction is integrated with the arts. So, for example, English is based on world literature, myths, and legends; history includes study of the world's great civilizations; math includes arithmetic, algebra, and geometry; science includes geography, astronomy, meteorology, and physical and life sciences. Throughout, children study two foreign languages, usually German and French or Spanish.

There is little reliance on standardized textbooks. Instead, each child creates his or her own illustrated summary of the coursework in a book form. There is an emphasis on social education, with students taught to work in groups. Waldorf classrooms typically have twenty-five or more students.

Teacher Roles and Training

The central focus of Waldorf teachers is to develop the essence of each child, instilling an understanding of and appreciation for their background and place in the world, as members of humanity and as world citizens. In most Waldorf schools, the teacher loops with the class throughout their elementary school years, teaching at least the principal academic subjects for eight grades. This allows for relationship building, and for in-depth understanding of individual children, permitting teachers to support individual variations in the pace of learning, as they expect each child to achieve a skill when ready, trusting in the innate human will of the individual to develop capacities and talents. Waldorf teachers are trained to observe each child carefully, and have regular conferences with parents to gain complete understanding of the child. Learning is noncompetitive. There are no grades. Teachers write a detailed evaluation of each child at the end of the year.

Another role is the teacher as authority. Steiner posited the idea that the teacher had the task of being the unquestioned authority in the classroom, because he felt children longed for a show of authority. The role is the loving guidance of respected authority. Thus, the teacher functions not as a facilitator, but as the authority that leads the class in a variety of teacher-directed activities. Steiner felt that this was the way to achieve balance, because children would be exposed to ideas and activities that they might not choose for themselves. Yet the teacher, whose job is not to fill the students with information, does not play an all-knowing role, but rather helps children find their answers to the world.

Central to the teacher role is fostering particular teacher-student relationships that are essential to learning. To quote Steiner himself, "The science of spirit teaches how to stimulate a particular part of the soul that brings about a certain relationship between the educator and the child, which allows something to flow from the teacher directly to the innermost feeling-life of the child's soul" (Steiner, 1970). He felt that the task of helping children learn is inseparable from the path of the teacher's own learning and self-development. The development of the child's ethical and moral character is as important as anything else in the curriculum. Again, recall that Steiner's worldview required that teachers accept certain anthroposophic principles, but they do not directly teach those beliefs in the schools. In the United States, questions have been raised about the appropriateness of spending state money to support the Waldorf approach, because it is based on a particular religious worldview.

One Waldorf principle is that all schools should be self-governing, so individual teachers have a high degree of creative autonomy within a school. Most Waldorf schools are not administered by a principal or head teacher but by the college of teachers, who decide on the pedagogy. (A board of trustees decides on matters of governance, such as finances and legal issues.) Teachers also work closely with parents, who are encouraged to take an active part in the noncurriculum aspects of the schools.

Teachers for Waldorf schools must have completed a college degree and then undertake specialized education in one of the fifteen Waldorf education centers in the United States that offer certification. The program is a two-year process for full-time students, or three or four years if done in summer intensive sessions. The first year includes foundation studies in basic anthroposophy and Waldorf pedagogy. There are also courses in practical curriculum applications, and in artistic activities. Classroom observations and practice teaching in Waldorf schools are part of the training.

 VIDEO ACTIVITY

Go to the premium Web site and link to the Chapter 4 video clip titled "The Waldorf Experience, Part 1." As you watch this video clip, consider the specific components that suggest how this approach meets the guidelines for developmentally appropriate practice.

REFLECTIVE QUESTIONS

1. What do you notice about the children's roles and activities?

2. What do you notice about the teachers' roles and interactions?

3. What do you notice about the physical environments, materials, and activities?

4. How do you see the philosophies described in the chapter demonstrated in action?

 Visit the premium Web site to complete these questions online and email them to your professor.

Figure 4-10
Waldorf education includes many celebrations of festivals and holidays.

Used by permission of Photographer Jon Sevison and San Diego Waldorf School

Waldorf and Developmentally Appropriate Practice

Some components of the Waldorf approach clearly echo ideas from developmentally appropriate practice. These include

- the emphasis on play and activity in the early years
- integrated curricula and learning through theme study
- less pressure on early academics
- highly individualized attention
  - understanding of developmental stages
  - emphasis on the whole child

Areas that seem less closely aligned include

- teacher direction excluding facilitation
- an emphasis on celebration of festivals and holidays (see Figure 4-10)
- remaining questions regarding the philosophical emphasis of the founder

THE REGGIO EMILIA APPROACH

History and Philosophy

Immediately after the end of World War II, under the leadership of some committed parents, preschools opened in the northern Italian town of Reggio Emilia. Since then, the programs have expanded to include centers for infants and toddlers, all now supported by the municipal government.

Several features of these schools have captured the attention of the education community worldwide, attracting more than fifteen thousand visitors on study tours since 1981. Leading the list of important ideas is the philosophy of children's active collaboration with adults to construct their expanding understandings of their world. Also noteworthy is the children's use of many kinds of symbolic language to express this understanding and their involvement with the world around them. An exhibit titled "The Hundred Languages of Children" has toured Europe since

1984 and in North America beginning in 1987 and up to the present. The images presented by the children's exploration and expression are truly astounding, provoking deep questions about young children's capabilities, and making many wonder if our traditional practices have underestimated and undervalued children's capacity to work, to maintain attention over extended periods, and to develop and express their understandings of the world.

Beyond the beauty and creative expression, components of the programs deserve closer scrutiny in a consideration of educational excellence. An article in *Newsweek* named the Diana School in Reggio Emilia as one of the ten best schools in the world, with much for us to learn from it ("The Ten Best Schools in the World, 1991). But it is necessary to caution, as do those who have been immersed in the work and philosophy of the Reggio schools for many years, that the programs should not be viewed as a model or curriculum to be copied in other contexts or countries. "Rather, their work should be considered as an educational experience that consists of reflection, practice, and further careful reflection in a program that is continuously renewed and readjusted" (Gandini, 1997, p. 163). The educators in Reggio Emilia support others in using the Reggio approach as a stimulus for reflecting about teaching and as a challenge to our own ideas and practices. Carlina Rinaldi, the pedagogical director of the infant-toddler centers and preschools, has said: "The Reggio approach is not a method that can be taught, but a way of thinking about children, schools, education, and life."

Key Concepts of the Reggio Approach

Some of the concepts of the approach include the following:

*   *The image of the child*—The cornerstone of Reggio Emilia experiences conceptualizes an image of the child as competent, strong, inventive, and full of ideas, with rights instead of needs.

*   *The environment as a third teacher*—Preparing an environment that is carefully designed to facilitate the social constructions of understanding and to document the life within the space, as well as to nurture aesthetics (see Figure 4-11).

*   *Relationships*—The importance of relationships among children, teachers, and parents is a vital component of functioning in the Reggio approach.

*   *Collaboration*—Working together at every level through collaboration among teachers, children and teachers, children and children, children and parents, and the larger community.

Figure 4-11

The physical beauty and attention to detail in the environment at Reggio Emilia is noteworthy.

- *Documentation*—Providing a verbal and visual trace of the children's experiences and work, and opportunities to revisit, reflect, and interpret.

- **Progettazione**—This difficult-to-translate Italian word means making flexible plans for the further investigation of ideas and devising the means for carrying them out in long-term projects through collaboration with the children, parents, and, at times, the larger community.

- *Provocation*—Listening closely to the children's interests and devising a means for provoking further thought and action.

- *One hundred languages of children*—Encouraging children to make symbolic representations of their ideas and providing them with may different kinds of media for representing those ideas.

This is by no means a finite list of the principles fundamental to the Reggio Emilia approach, but a selection of some of the important ones. For more in-depth discussion of the ideas and practices of Reggio Emilia schools, see the author's book *Authentic Childhood: Exploring Reggio Emilia in the Classroom* (Fraser & Gestwicki, 2002) and other references listed at the end of the chapter.

Structure of the Programs

Children are not all expected to do the same thing, and their originality is valued. They may work in small groups, alone, inside or outside, or in any room in the center, as well as in the central piazza and **atelier**, or art studio (described later). Activities may go on for hours, days, or months.

In the preschools, children are assigned to classes of twenty-five with two coteachers. This group of children, teachers, and families remain together for the three school years, moving to a different space each year as their needs and interests change, but maintaining the continuity of relationships over the three-year period. Similarly, the slightly smaller groups and three classroom teachers in the infant-toddler centers remain together for three years, although changing space to provide new scope and challenges.

When project work develops, the teachers are careful to create small groups—usually no more than five preschoolers. They believe that working in the small group allows children to understand the rhythm and styles of communication. The conflict that occurs within the peer relationships—the opposition, negotiation, reconstruction of ideas and hypotheses—is seen not just as social learning, but as an essential part of the cognitive process.

Environment as Third Teacher

The space is recognized as having a powerful capacity to convey messages, including to welcome, to invite attention, and to convey a history of culture, identity, and interest of the adults and children who use the space.

Every space and everything in every space contribute to the educational experience. The rooms are beautiful, with an attention to aesthetic detail in color, light, plants, reflections, and arrangements of objects in such often-overlooked areas as bathrooms, kitchens, hallways, and entrances. Obvious care and thought go into not only arranging furniture and areas but also into displaying even the smallest items.

Each center and school has a central piazza area, echoing the cultural center of the town, where people gather and communicate. There are comfortable chairs to invite parents to sit, areas for dress-up clothes, and other interesting things to do and look at. Children from different classrooms can join here to play and work on projects.

The emphasis on expression using a variety of media is seen in a central atelier, or art studio, with an abundance of art supplies, natural materials, and recycled materials, where an **atelierista** (a teacher trained in individual arts) works with the children. In addition, each classroom has a mini-atelier, with supplies and space for children to work on long-term projects. Materials are meticulously organized and stored in transparent containers. Parents and children help accumulate and organize the materials.

Children's Interests as Curriculum

At the core of Reggio Emilia's curriculum are projects devised as outcomes of children's initial interests. A project might grow from an initial experience planned by the teachers to help children explore their cultural heritage or physical surroundings, or might result from a spontaneous happening such as a child's idea or question responded to by the teachers. Almost any experience that intrigues children can become the basis of the project. The projects are undertaken in great depth and detail, using varieties of investigative methods and a selection of visual and graphic forms. Integral to this process of investigation through long-term projects is the creative use of materials by children to represent and communicate their learning, using the "hundred languages."

The best way to illustrate the Reggio Emilia approach is by telling the story of the investigation of the lion, made fairly well known now by the videotape made in Reggio in 1987, *To Make a Portrait of a Lion.*

The teachers planned a trip to the historic center of Reggio Emilia, the busy market square presided over by a group of old stone lions. Their actual intent had been to introduce the children to the phenomenon of the market, but the video captured the children's instant fascination with the lion statues, as they touched them, climbed on them, and explored them from all angles. The teachers had brought along sketch pads for recording the children's perceptions. On a later visit they brought cameras. Back at the school, the children had opportunities to talk about the lions and to explore the photographic images made by the teachers and projected on walls. As the project continued over time, children worked with clay, paints, puppet props, and costumes, and with shadow-play to continue to re-create their experiences. The lion became the basis for a rich and extended project.

At each step of the activities, teachers observe, discuss, and interpret together their observations, making further choices to offer to the children. By discussing in the group and revisiting ideas and experiences, children grow in their understanding. (Note that many things are going on in the classroom and center besides work on projects, as project work alone takes up only a part of each day. Other time is spent in traditional preschool activities, such as dramatic play in very realistic home centers, block play, time with books, writing, vigorous play, responsibilities in the school, and just talking with friends.)

Teacher Roles

The Reggio belief in the dominant role that children play in constructing their knowledge and understanding demands that learning be considered more important than teaching. This is not to say that teaching is not present, but rather that the aim of the teaching is to provide appropriate conditions for learning to occur.

> The role of the adult is above all one of listening, observing, and understanding the strategy that children use in a learning situation. . . . We must be able to catch the ball that the children throw us and toss it back to them in a way that makes children want to continue the game with us, developing, perhaps, other games as we go along. (Filippini, in Edwards, 1998, p. 134)

Teachers are listeners and observers in any good developmentally appropriate program, asking questions and reflecting on the responses to know what materials and ideas children can use to expand their understanding. But teachers at Reggio create incredible depth to their listening and observing. They routinely take notes and photographs and make tape recordings of children's play, discussion, and work (see Figure 4-12).

These records are the basis for hours of discussion with other teachers each week. The documentation allows them to focus on children's flow of ideas and questions, as well as to help them illustrate to children and parents what is being learned and how. The documentation helps teachers find the ideas and form the hypotheses that may be the basis for future group experiences.

Figure 4-12

Teachers in Reggio take careful notes on children's work and thinking, and create documentation panels for further reflection.

A fundamental Reggio principle is that a team of at least two teachers is essential for the development of complex dialogue about children. Each week several teachers review the documentation, communicate their own perspectives about the children, and arrive at a shared interpretation. Of the thirty-six hours that staff are paid for each week, six hours are available for discussing the documentation and other planning and for professional-development activities. The pairs of teachers are coteachers, providing a model to children and parents of cooperating with a peer. Other adults may also be involved in the discussions; at times the atelierista helps the teachers pull together the documentation and think about a project, as well as possible modes of expression. Other discussion may include the **pedagogista**. The role of the pedagogista is difficult to describe with an English word or in terms of American educational structure; neither coordinator nor educational advisor is quite right. Each pedagogista works with several preschools and infant-toddler centers, having responsibility for staff development and for working with teachers on educational issues and relationships with children and families. Out of this constant dialogue grows the rela-

tionships and thinking on which the rich emergent curriculum depends. The task of these resource people is not simply to satisfy or answer questions, but instead to help children discover answers and, more importantly still, to help themselves ask good questions. Interaction between teachers and children gives importance to the role of each in the learning process. Teachers see themselves as partners in the process of learning, continually involved in research and learning, constructing knowledge, and enjoying experiences with the children.

Kennedy (1996) suggests that the difference in the Reggio preschools has as much to do with "their construct of the teacher as of the child" (p. 25). The Reggio understanding of the early childhood teacher is of someone extremely cognizant of the extent to which she constructs childhood and developmentally appropriate practice, recognizing that this construction is continually in progress. Thus, the ongoing, collaborative inquiry into childhood and best practices is seen as a fundamental dimension of her work. The emphasis in this dialogue is on "ongoing, deepening inquiry" (p. 25), rather than coming to any immediate resolution or conclusion.

▶❚❚ **VIDEO ACTIVITY**

Go to the text's premium Web site and link to the Chapter 4 video clip titled "Early Years: From Reggio Emilia to the West Midlands." As you watch this video clip, consider the specific components that suggest how this approach meets the guidelines for developmentally appropriate practice.

REFLECTIVE QUESTIONS

1. What do you notice about the children's roles and activities?

2. What do you notice about the teachers' roles and interactions?

3. What do you notice about the physical environments, materials, and activities?

4. How do you see the philosophies described in the chapter demonstrated in action?

 Visit the premium Web site to complete these questions online and email them to your professor.

The Reggio Approach and Developmentally Appropriate Practice

What do we learn from examining the Reggio approach? The thoughts and lessons continue to attract the attention of those interested in excellent early education. Questions are raised by some American early childhood thinkers about whether the Reggio Emilia approach is adaptable here (Katz, 1994), or even suitable to be adapted here, given differences in practice that may reflect cultural beliefs about, and expectations for, children in our society (New, 1993). The question has been raised whether "childhood is at least partially a historical and cultural invention" (Kennedy, 1996, p. 94), and whether there is, in fact, a scientific, objective way to describe young children, leaving us to consider again our own cultural and historical perspective.

Sue Bredekamp, on considering the power of the schools at Reggio, reflects that their practices "have gone beyond DAP, at least in its current incarnation, especially in their emphasis on the social construction of knowledge and their articulation of the teacher's role as co-constructor with children and documenter of the learning process" (Bredekamp, 1993, p. 13). She describes challenges for early childhood educators in America to

- reclaim the image of the competent child (see Figures 4-13a & 4-13b).

- promote conceptual integrity in programs and experiences for children and adults.

- refine our definition of developmental appropriateness.

- balance standard setting with questioning.

- reflect on professional development.

- expand our understanding of the roles of the teacher.

Katz, in considering where to start in attempting the Reggio approach, hypothesizes that a beginning would be to "focus our collective and individual energies on the quality of our day-to-day interactions with children so that those interactions become as rich, interesting, engaging, satisfying, and meaningful as those we observe in Reggio Emilia" (Katz, 1997, p. 110). She also suggests that one important effect of looking at the Reggio experience is to see what is possible

Figure 4-13

The long-term projects and detailed creative work raise questions about children's abilities.

(a)

(b)

when a whole community is deeply committed to its children (Katz, 1997). Perhaps the greatest influence of the schools at Reggio Emilia on early childhood education in North America is to stimulate thinking and discussion among early childhood professionals concerning the most appropriate and excellent practices.

Teachers and schools in many areas in America have already begun to examine their practices and attempt to implement some changes based on the Reggio approach. (For specific descriptions of some of these, see Hendricks, 1997, 2003; Fraser & Gestwicki, 2002.)

CULTURAL CONSIDERATIONS

Cultural Influences on Learning Experiences

It is interesting to note that these first curricula approaches evolved as a result of the particular philosophy of the founding adults, at a particular time and in a particular place. Consider how the social and historical cultures that were present at the time influenced the kinds of learning experiences that were considered important for children. Note also that two of these approaches were developed in Italy, though in different time periods. What similarities and differences can be noted?

HIGH/SCOPE APPROACH

History and Philosophy

This curriculum was developed under the leadership of David Weikart, whose earlier work was in the Perry Project, one of the best-known intervention programs of the 1960s. In Chapter 1, you read of the results of the three experimental preschool programs that worked with children in Ypsilanti, Michigan. High/Scope in fact was developed as Weikart and his associates recognized the effectiveness of the "open-framework" program that supported children's active involvement in self-selected learning activities. The High/Scope approach has been used since 1962. You will recall that the longitudinal studies conducted on the children from the original High/Scope program have continued up to age forty (High/Scope Foundation, 2005). These studies have shown that the children from that program have developed into adults with positive social and emotional outcomes in their lives. Today the High/Scope approach is used widely, in both public and private, half- and full-day programs for young children, and in many Head Start settings. The curriculum has been expanded to include infants and toddlers. The High/Scope Foundation has the functions of providing training in the High/Scope philosophy, conducting research projects, publishing books and videos to support those who would learn more of the curriculum, and operating a Demonstration Preschool in Ypsilanti, Michigan.

The High/Scope curriculum is based on Jean Piaget's constructivist theories of child development. "The curriculum rests on the fundamental premise that children are active learners, who learn best from activities that they themselves plan, carry out, and reflect on" (Epstein, 1993, p. 30). The philosophy is that children need active involvement with people, materials, ideas, and events in order to learn.

Key components of the High/Scope approach include

- children as active learners, spending much of their time in a variety of learning centers.
- **plan-do-review**, in which teachers assist children to choose what they will do each day, carry out their plan during work time, and then review with the teacher what they have done.
- **key experiences**, which include concepts based on Piaget's ideas of the cognitive characteristics and learning potential of preschoolers. These are used as a focus for teacher planning of teacher-led small-group experiences.
- using anecdotal notes to chart individual children's progress on a High/Scope tool, the Child Observation Record.

The High/Scope curriculum identifies five ingredients for active learning for young children.

- materials for the child to explore
- manipulation of materials by the child
- choices by the child about what to do with the materials

- language from the child
- support from the adult (Epstein, 1993)

High/Scope describes fifty-eight key experiences to guide activities, organized into ten categories: creative representation, language and literacy, initiative and social relations, movement, music, classification, seriation, number, space, and time. (See Figure 4-14 for an outline of the key experiences.)

Materials and Activities

Most High/Scope classrooms look like typical good preschool settings, with interest areas for a variety of explorations. High/Scope recommends areas for blocks, art, house play, small toys, computers, books and writing materials, and sand and water. The curriculum offers general guidelines for selecting materials, but does not require specific materials. Materials are organized in the centers for visibility and for independent access by children. Art and music are part of daily activities.

A consistent routine is followed each day so that children are aware of the sequence of classroom activities. The daily sequence is presented in pictorial form on the wall as reminders of the routine. The schedule offers time for both small and large groups, for outdoor play, and for work time. Planning is a regular part of the program day. Teachers plan with children in small groups or individually, allowing each child to express his or her intentions. As Epstein (2003) points out, planning is "choice with intention," where children identify their goals and decide on actions to achieve them. At the end of the opportunity to work, there is also a time to reflect on how their plan worked out. This deliberate planning and reflection has been found to develop children's thinking skills (Epstein, 2003).

In keeping with current practice, the High/Scope approach targets literacy and math skills, but is careful to point out that they use no sequenced activities, drills, or work sheets. Rather, the classrooms provide experiences and materials that help children develop and broaden their language and logic abilities. A High/Scope classroom emphasizes a print-rich environment, with plenty of stories, books, and writing tools, as well as opportunities for counting, comparing numbers, and practicing one-to-one correspondence. One component of High/Scope literacy is having young children begin to identify and interpret symbols before they identify letters and words. Thus, children's work and belongings may all be identified with unique symbols, such as a star for Joey and a triangle for Sam.

Teacher Roles

Teachers may learn High/Scope methods through training sessions and workshops, as well as by reading the publications from the High/Scope Research Foundation. The basic construct of the teacher is as a participating partner in activities, rather than as a manager or a supervisor. High/Scope training emphasizes

- formulating positive interaction strategies.
- focusing on children's strengths.
- forming authentic relationships with children.
- supporting children's play ideas.

▶ II VIDEO ACTIVITY

Go to the text's premium Web site and link to the Chapter 4 video clip titled "High Scope: Who We Are, What We Do." As you watch this video clip, consider the specific components that suggest how this approach meets the guidelines for developmentally appropriate practice.

REFLECTIVE QUESTIONS

1. What do you notice about the children's roles and activities?

2. What do you notice about the teachers' roles and interactions?

3. What do you notice about the physical environments, materials, and activities?

4. How do you see the philosophies described in the chapter demonstrated in action?

 Visit the premium Web site to complete these questions online and email them to your professor.

High/Scope Preschool Key Experiences

Creative Representation

- Recognizing objects by sight, sound, touch, taste, and smell
- Imitating actions and sounds
- Relating models, pictures, and photographs to real places and things
- Pretending and role playing
- Making models out of clay, blocks, and other materials
- Drawing and painting

Language and Literacy

- Talking with others about personally meaningful experiences
- Describing objects, events, and relations
- Having fun with language: listening to stories and poems, making up stories and rhymes
- Writing in various ways: drawing, scribbling, letterlike forms, invented spelling, conventional forms
- Reading in various ways: reading storybooks, signs and symbols, one's own writing
- Dictating stories

Initiative and Social Relations

- Making and expressing choices, plans, and decisions
- Solving problems encountered in play
- Taking care of one's own needs
- Expressing feelings in words
- Participating in group routines
- Being sensitive to the feelings, interests, and needs of others
- Building relationships with children and adults
- Creating and experiencing collaborative play
- Dealing with social conflict

Movement

- Moving in nonlocomotor ways (anchored movement: bending, twisting, rocking, swinging one's arms)
- Moving in locomotor ways (nonanchored movement: running, jumping, hopping, skipping, marching, climbing)
- Moving with objects
- Expressing creativity in movement
- Describing movement
- Acting upon movement directions
- Feeling and expressing steady beat
- Moving in sequences to a common beat

Music

- Moving to music
- Exploring and identifying sounds
- Exploring the singing voice
- Developing melody
- Singing songs
- Playing simple musical instruments

Classification

- Exploring and describing similarities, differences, and the attributes of things
- Distinguishing and describing shapes
- Sorting and matching
- Using and describing something in several ways
- Holding more than one attribute in mind at a time
- Distinguishing between "some" and "all"
- Describing characteristics something does not possess or what class it does not belong to

Seriation

- Comparing attributes (longer/shorter, bigger/smaller)
- Arranging several things one after another in a series or pattern and describing the relationships (big/bigger/biggest, red/blue/red/blue)
- Fitting one ordered set of objects to another through trial and error (small cup–small saucer/medium cup–medium saucer/big cup–big saucer)

Number

- Comparing the number of things in two sets to determine "more," "fewer," "same number"
- Arranging two sets of objects in one-to-one correspondence
- Counting objects

Space

- Filling and emptying
- Fitting things together and taking them apart
- Changing the shape and arrangement of objects (wrapping, twisting, stretching, stacking, enclosing)
- Observing people, places, and things from different spatial viewpoints
- Experiencing and describing positions, directions, and distances in the play space, building, and neighborhood
- Interpreting spatial relations in drawings, pictures, and photographs

Time

- Starting and stopping an action on signal
- Experiencing and describing rates of movement
- Experiencing and comparing time intervals
- Anticipating, remembering, and describing sequences of events

© High/Scope Educational Research Foundation

HIGH/SCOPE PRESS
600 North River Street, Ypsilanti, Michigan 48198-2898
Phone: 734-485-2000   Fax: 734-485-0704

Figure 4-14

High/Scope Preschool Key Experiences. Reprinted with permission from High/Scope Preschool Key Experience Card, ISBN 0-929826-98-6, Ypsilanti, MI: High/Scope Press. Copyright © 1995, High/Scope. Educational Research Foundation.

Considering the Various Approaches

As you are reading about these various educational approaches, which have you already heard of or experienced? What were your responses to the ideas and practices of these systems? What ideas from the approaches will you take into your own classroom? As a decision was made about adopting a curriculum, what questions would you ask an administrator to ensure that developmentally appropriate practice is being followed?

 Visit the premium Web site to complete this journal activity online and email it to your professor.

- developing skill in asking questions to promote learning, reflection, and communication.
- adopting a problem-solving approach to helping children learn to deal with social conflict.

An important part of the teacher role is observing children. High/Scope teachers take daily anecdotal notes on significant behaviors during children's normal activities. A High/Scope tool is the Preschool Child Observation Record (COR), which provides a framework for organizing information about children's development and understanding of key experiences.

The daily observations are used in team planning sessions, so that the curriculum can support the observations and needs revealed by the COR. High/Scope emphasizes team observation and communication to meet goals for children. The High/Scope curriculum provides teachers with a framework to make appropriate decisions (see Figure 4-15).

High/Scope and Developmentally Appropriate Practice

As observers consider principles of developmentally appropriate practice and the High/Scope approach, it is clear that these basic principles are recognized:

- based on work of theorist—Piaget
- central role of active learning
- importance of manipulating materials
- adult's role in focusing children's attention and language on learning
- choices and activity centers emphasized
- importance of observation and assessment

Figure 4-15

High/Scope Preschool "Wheel of Learning." Reprinted with permission from High/Scope Preschool Wheel Card, ISBN 0-929826-98-6, Y psilanti, MI: High/Scope Press. Copyright © 1995, High/Scope Educational Research Foundation.

High/Scope Preschool "Wheel of Learning"

Assessment
- Teamwork
- Daily anecdotal notes
- Daily planning
- Child assessment

Adult-child interaction
- Interaction strategies
- Encouragement
- Problem-solving approach to conflict

Active learning
Initiative
Key Experiences

Daily routine
- Plan-do-review
- Small-group times
- Large-group times

Learning environment
- Areas
- Materials
- Storage

THE CREATIVE CURRICULUM

History and Philosophy

Diane Trister Dodge is the creator of the Creative Curriculum and founder of Teaching Strategies, Inc., the organization that produces and distributes Creative Curriculum materials and provides staff-development training. Her experiences in child care programs led her to see the need of developing a curriculum model as a framework to guide teacher involvement and decision making. The first (1978) and second (1988) editions of the Creative Curriculum were based on the idea that the first step toward implementing a curriculum is to help teachers organize their rooms into interest areas for effective learning. The Creative Curriculum evolved as more consensus developed in the early childhood field about how to define curriculum and how to use concepts about curriculum to implement developmentally appropriate practice. The third edition of Creative Curriculum, published in 1992, presented a framework with the philosophy, goals, and objectives for children's learning, and guidelines for teaching and working with families. There was also a first tool for tracking children's progress: the Child Development and Learning Checklist.

Additional research and reports on how children learn have been the impetus for further development of the curriculum. In addition, increasing demands for accountability in demonstrating positive outcomes for children have necessitated a focus on systematic assessment that allows teachers to learn about and plan for each child and the group. The fourth edition of *The Creative Curriculum for Preschool,* published in 2002, offers a further expansion of teacher roles in supporting children's active learning (Dodge, Colker, & Heroman, 2002).

The basic philosophy of the Creative Curriculum is that teachers must use a variety of strategies to meet children's social, emotional, physical, cognitive, and language developmental needs. A vital strategy is to become good observers of children. This allows teachers to assess children's needs, interests, and abilities in relation to specific developmental goals, and to plan meaningful learning experiences that build on children's interests and knowledge. Teachers then integrate the learning of skills, concepts, and knowledge in literacy, math, science, social studies, the arts, and technology that have been set in national and state standards into daily classroom learning experiences in the interest areas. The Creative Curriculum is a comprehensive curriculum linked to an assessment system.

Figure 4-16 shows the framework and the relationship between the various components of the Creative Curriculum.

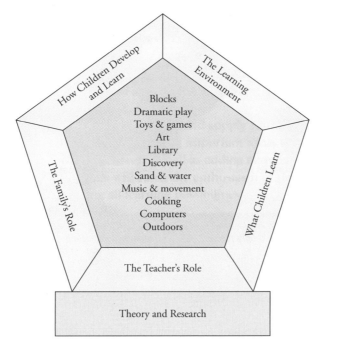

Figure 4-16

The Framework for the Creative Curriculum For Preschool. From The Creative Curriculum® for Preschool (p. xiv), by D. T. Dodge, L. J. Colker, and C. Heroman, 2002, Washington, DC: Teaching Strategies Inc. Copyright © 2002 by Teaching Strategies, Inc. Reprinted with permission.

The essential elements of the Curriculum include

- a foundation of research and theory of child development, including the ideas of Maslow, Erikson, Piaget, Vygotsky, Smilansky, and Gardner, as well as recent information on brain research and resiliency research.

- an understanding of how children develop and learn. This also includes goals and objectives for children, and the Developmental Continuum, a tool for observing children's development and tracking their progress in relation to Curriculum objectives. The Developmental Continuum includes fifty specific objectives, divided into social/emotional development, physical development, cognitive development, and language development. For a sample of continuum objectives, see Figure 4-17.

- an emphasis on setting up the structure of the learning environment, including setting up and maintaining interest areas, establishing schedules and routines, organizing choice times and small- and large-group times, and creating a classroom community where children learn how to get along with others and solve problems.

Cognitive Development
Logical Thinking

Developmental Continuum for Ages 3–5

Curriculum Objectives		I	II	III
27. Classifies objects	**Forerunners** **Finds two objects that are the same and comments or puts them together** **Groups similar kinds of toys together such as cars, blocks, or dolls**	**Sorts objects by one property such as size, shape, color, or use** e.g., sorts pebbles into three buckets by color; puts square block with other square blocks	**Sorts a group of objects by one property and then by another** e.g., collects leaves and sorts by size and then by color; puts self in group wearing shoes that tie and then in group with blue shoes	**Sorts objects into groups/subgroups and can state reason** e.g., sorts stickers into four piles ("Here are the stars that are silver and gold, and here are circles, silver and gold"); piles animals and then divides them into zoo and farm animals
28. Compares/ measures	**Forerunners** **Notices something new or different** e.g., a new classmate or a new toy on the shelf **Notices similarities of objects** e.g., "We have the same shoes"	**Notices similarities and differences** e.g., states, "The rose is the only flower in our garden that smells"; "I can run fast in my new shoes"	**Use comparative words related to number, size, shape, texture, weight, color, speed, volume** e.g., "This bucket is heavier than that one"; "Now the music is going faster"	**Understands/uses measurement words and some standard measurement tools** e.g., uses unit blocks to measure length of rug; "We need 2 cups of flour and 1 cup of salt to make dough"
29. Arranges objects in a series	**Forerunners** **Uses self-correcting toys such as form boards and graduated stacking rings** **Sorts by one attribute** e.g., big blocks and little blocks	**Notices when one object in a series is out of place** e.g., removes the one measuring spoon out of place in a line and tries to put it in right place	**Figures out a logical order for a group of objects** e.g., makes necklace of graduated wooden beads; arranges magazine pictures of faces from nicest expression to meanest	**Through trial and error, arranges objects along a continuum according to two or more physical features** e.g., lines up bottle caps by height and width; sorts playdough cookies by size, color, and shape

Figure 4-17

Examples from the Developmental Continuum, for Logical Thinking and Language Development. From The Creative Curriculum® for Preschool (pp. 52, 56), by D. T. Dodge, L. J. Colker, and C. Heroman, 2002, Washington, DC: Teaching Strategies, Inc. Copyright © 2002 by Teaching Strategies, Inc. Reprinted with permission.

Language Development
Listening and Speaking

Developmental Continuum for Ages 3–5

Curriculum Objectives	Forerunners	I	II	III
30. Recognizes patterns and can repeat them	**Forerunners** Completes a sentence that repeats in a familiar story / Hums, sings, or responds to a chorus that repeats in a familiar song / Completes a simple form board	**Notices and recreates simple patterns with objects** *e.g., makes a row of blocks alternating in size (big-small-big-small); strings beads in repeating patterns of 2 colors*	**Extends patterns or creates simple patterns of own design** *e.g., makes necklace of beads in which a sequence of 2 or more colors is repeated; continues block pattern of 2 colors*	**Creates complex patterns of own design or by copying** *e.g., imitates hand-clapping pattern (long clap followed by 3 short claps); designs a 3-color pattern using colored inch cubes and repeats it across the table*
41. Answers questions	**Forerunners** Answers yes/no questions with words, gestures, or signs *e.g., points to purple paint when asked what color she wants*	**Answers simple questions with one or two words** *e.g., when asked for name says, "Curtis"; says, "Purple and blue" when asked the colors of paint*	**Answers questions with a complete thought** *e.g., responds, "I took a bus to school"; "I want purple and blue paint"*	**Answers questions with details** *e.g., describes a family trip when asked about weekend; says; "I want purple and blue like my new shoes so I can make lots of flowers"*
42. Asks questions	**Forerunners** Uses facial expressions/ gestures to ask a question / Uses rising intonation to ask questions *e.g., "Mama comes back?"* / Uses some "wh" words (what and where) to ask questions *e.g., "What that?"*	**Asks simple questions** *e.g., "What's for lunch?" "Can we play outside today?"*	**Asks questions to further understanding** *e.g., "Where did the snow go when it melted?" "Why does that man wear a uniform?"*	**Asks increasingly complex questions to further own understanding** *e.g., "What happened to the water in the fish tank? Did the fish drink it?"*
43. Actively participates in conversations	**Forerunners** Initiates communication by smiling and/or eye contact / Responds to social greetings *e.g., waves in response to "hello" or "bye-bye"*	**Responds to comments and questions from others** *e.g., when one child says, "I have new shoes," shows own shoes and says, "Look at my new shoes"*	**Responds to others' comments in a series of exchanges** *e.g., makes relevant comments during a group discussion; provides more information when message is not understood*	**Initiates and/or extends conversations for at least four exchanges** *e.g., while talking with a friend, asks questions about what happened, what friend did, and shares own ideas*

Figure 4-17

(Continued)

- a consideration of the body of knowledge discussed in national and state standards and research reports in six content areas: literacy, math, science, social studies, the arts, and technology.

- a range of instructional strategies for teachers to use in large- and small-group times, and long-term studies.

- a construction of the teacher's role that includes becoming a careful observer and using a variety of instructional strategies and interactions with children to guide their learning. A system for ongoing, authentic assessment—based on observations made during everyday classroom activities—enables teachers to plan for each child as well as the group.
- an acknowledgment of the importance of creating partnerships with families, with emphasis on communicating ways families can support children's learning at school and at home.

The Creative Curriculum has also been developed to extend the philosophy into programs for infants and toddlers, into ideas for working with primary- and school-age children, and into family child care homes.

Classroom Environment

The framework indicates the eleven interest areas considered important for a Creative Curriculum preschool classroom: blocks, dramatic play, toys and games, art, library, discovery, sand and water, music and movement, cooking, computers, and outdoors. Both the various materials that should be included and their organization, to meet the developmental needs of young children and enhance learning and teaching in each of these interest areas, are presented in the Creative Curriculum books and in the staff training available from a network of trainers through Teaching Strategies. Children are encouraged to actively make their choices from the abundance of appropriate materials. The classroom is designed to offer inclusive messages of welcome to diverse families, to provide opportunities for children to function independently, and to support children's individual interests and abilities.

In a classroom that uses the Creative Curriculum approach, children are active and engaged. Content is learned through investigation and play, as well as focused, intentional teaching to build on prior learning experiences (see Figure 4-18).

Accountability and the Creative Curriculum

As noted earlier, teachers are now being asked to meet Early Learning Objectives in every state. Creative Curriculum has developed correlations with the Head Start Outcomes Framework and with the early learning standards of the states, using the goals and objectives of the Creative Curriculum Developmental Continuum for children ages three to five (see Figure 4-17). The correlations can be found on the Teaching Strategies Web site, under Curriculum and Assessment. In addition, curricula being used today are being asked to provide documentation that learning outcomes are being met. Especially since the No Child Left Behind Act, there is

Figure 4-18

Technology is one of the content areas of the Creative Curriculum.

a mandate to use "scientifically based" models. Whether this means that the curriculum is based on scientific research, or that the curriculum model works when tested with scientific methods, the Creative Curriculum answers that it meets both these criteria (J. Park-Jadotte, http://www.teachingstrategies.com). The philosophy of the curriculum is based on the theories and research recognized in the early childhood field.

The most notable research citing successes of children in Creative Curriculum classrooms is findings from FACES 2000, a national longitudinal study of Head Start that examined children's development. Researchers found that children in Creative Curriculum classrooms had greater improvement across a number of measures than children in classrooms that did not use an integrated-learning approach, most notably in language scores. Ongoing studies in Head Start programs in Georgia, North Carolina, Tennessee, and Oklahoma continue to research the outcomes. Most recently, in 2004, research on programs in Hartford, Connecticut, showed significant improvements across five major developmental areas associated with school readiness, following intensive teacher training in the Creative Curriculum.

The Creative Curriculum is being used in many Head Start programs and in armed services child care programs throughout the world. National standards of the various professional organizations are used for the content of the curriculum.

> ## ▶❚❚ VIDEO ACTIVITY
>
> Go to the premium Web site and link to the Chapter 4 video clip titled "The Creative Curriculum in Action." As you watch this video clip, consider the specific components you see that suggest how this approach meets the guidelines for developmentally appropriate practice.
>
> ### REFLECTIVE QUESTIONS
>
> 1. What do you notice about the children's roles and activities?
> 2. What do you notice about the teachers' roles and interactions?
> 3. What do you notice about the physical environments, materials, and activities?
> 4. How do you see the philosophies described in the chapter demonstrated in action?
>
> *Visit the premium Web site to complete these questions online and email them to your professor.*

Creative Curriculum and Developmentally Appropriate Practice

As the developmentally appropriate practice principles are considered in relation to the Creative Curriculum, the following components are present:

- concepts based on background of research and theory
- active roles of children busy at play and exploration
- emphasis on quality of materials and environmental arrangements
- focus on observation and assessment, related to supporting children in meeting developmental goals for the whole child
- importance placed on relationships with family and between teachers and children

In addition to the curricula models discussed in this chapter, there are many other approaches and others that combine elements of several. The direct-instruction approach discussed in Chapter 1, now called Distar, offers a model that seems removed from the principles of developmentally appropriate practice.

SUMMARY

As students and teachers encounter curricula models, it is important to understand their philosophies and practices to see how they fit into our understanding of developmentally appropriate practices and one's own personal ideas, interests, and teaching style. At this time in America, students are likely to encounter any of these following approaches, or influences of them: Montessori; Bank Street; Waldorf; Reggio Emilia, High/Scope, and the Creative Curriculum. Take time now to compare and contrast the approaches and to consider which elements of each program fit your own educational philosophy.

THINK ABOUT IT ACTIVITIES

1. Create a chart that compares the six approaches discussed under these headings: Major Ideas of Philosophy; Environment and Materials; Teacher Roles; Components Related to Developmentally Appropriate Practice. Discuss your charts with a small group of classmates.

2. Interview, and if possible visit, teachers from several of these approaches. Share your findings with your class.

QUESTIONS TO ASSESS LEARNING OF CHAPTER OBJECTIVES

1. Identify key elements in the Montessori model.

2. Identify key elements of the Bank Street approach. Contrast these with those from Montessori.

3. Identify key elements of the Waldorf approach.

4. Identify key elements of the Reggio Emilia approach.

5. Identify key elements of the High/Scope approach.

6. Identify key elements of the Creative Curriculum approach.

7. For each program, discuss aspects that seem to fit with principles of developmentally appropriate practice, and any that seem less compatible with the principles.

APPLY YOUR KNOWLEDGE QUESTIONS

1. Montessori and Reggio Emilia approaches were both developed in Italy. Describe the similarities and differences between the two approaches. Which seems closest to ideas about developmentally appropriate practice that you have read in this text? The Waldorf approach also comes from Europe. Do you see similarities and differences?

2. Consider the differences and similarities you see between the High/Scope, Bank Street, and Creative Curriculum approaches, all created in America.

HELPFUL WEB SITES

Montessori

http://www.montessori-ami.org	The Web site of the Association Montessori International, the organization that follows traditional Montessori practice, has information about the philosophy and locations of Montessori training.
http://www.amshq.org	The Web site of the American Montessori Society has much information, including FAQs and listings of training institutions.
http://www.montessori.org	Montessori Online, the Web site of the Montessori Foundation and International Montessori Committee, has much information on contemporary Montessori.
http://www.ux1.eiu.edu	The home page of Shu-Chen Jenny Yen gives links to her Montessori Albums, with comprehensive listings of materials and activities, and directions that teachers follow in their presentation.

Bank Street

http://www.bankstreetcorner.com   Information for teachers about a number of ideas from the Bank Street approach.

http://www.bankstreet.edu   The Web site of the Bank Street Graduate School has information about the approach.

Waldorf

http://www.whywaldorfworks.org   The Web site of the Association of Waldorf Schools of North America is comprehensive, with articles, research, and answers to questions about teacher education.

Reggio

http://www.reggioalliance.org   The Web site of the North American Reggio Emilia alliance (NAREA) has much information about what educators are doing in their explorations of the Reggio approach.

http://www.cdacouncil.org   Reggio Children USA is found at the Web site of the Council for Professional Recognition. Click on Council Programs, then on Reggio Children USA. Information is available about opportunities to learn more about Reggio and related publications.

http://www.mpi.wayne.edu   On the home page for the Merrill Palmer Institute, click on Early Childhood Education for the Reggio Approach, and get information about the *Innovations* periodical.

http://www.reggiochildren.it   This is the official Web site for Reggio children, with information in both English and Italian.

High/Scope

http://www.highscope.org   The Web site for the High/Scope Educational Research Foundation has much information about the philosophy and resources for learning more about the High/Scope Curriculum.

Creative Curriculum

http://www.teachingstrategies.com   The Web site for Creative Curriculum has much information about all aspects of the curriculum and resources.

Comparison of Models

http://parentcenter.babycenter.com   Click on topics and then on the Preschoolers category to find an article by S. Robledo titled "The Top Preschool Programs and How They Differ."

Please visit the premium Web site for Developmentally Appropriate Practice, *4th edition, to access more chapter web links, additional book chapters, suggestions for further reading and study, interactive quizzes, video exercises, online journal activities, flashcards, and much more! Go to www.cengage.com/login to register your access code.*

GUEST EDITORIAL

by James Greenman

Jim Greenman has been actively involved in the early childhood field for more than thirty-five years as a childcare administrator, facility designer, educator, teacher, director, and consultant. He is currently a senior vice president at Corporate Family Solutions, a leading provider of employer-sponsored childcare. One of his best-known books is Caring Spaces, Learning Places: Children's Environments That Work. *This excerpt is from the most recent edition of that book.*

An environment is a living, changing system. More than the physical space, it includes the way time is structured and the roles we are expected to play. It conditions how we feel, think, and behave; and it dramatically affects the quality of our lives. The environment either works for us or against us as we conduct our lives. (p. 1)

Space speaks to each of us. Long corridors whisper "run" to a child; picket fences invite us to trail our hands along the slats. Physical objects have emotional messages of warmth, pleasure, solemnity, fear; action messages of "come close," "touch me," "stay away," "I'm strong," "I'm fragile." (p. 13)

Space speaks to our emotions. We build images of places, meaningful spaces, out of fragments of experiences, experiences significant to us for reasons of our own. Our memories, imaginings, hopes, and dreams transform places and things. (p. 14)

Children and adults inhabit different sensory worlds. Imagine a young infant's world of touch and taste—a world where you see and hear more than you look and listen—where you, in effect, think with your body and actions, and your whole body is your only means of reacting. Consider the way that young children run from place to place. Children respond to the sensory and motor messages of space, while adults are more utilitarian: "Adults notice whether an environment is clean or attractive to an adult eye" (Prescott, 1984, cited in Greenman, 2005, p. 45).

What we often don't notice are the elements that a child will zoom in on: the right place with the right shape, like a tight angular corner between the wall and a couch or the excitement of a perch; the right sight and sound, like a vantage point from which to watch and hear the torrential rain pouring out of the gutter and splashing to the ground below; or the right feel. We, who don't inhabit the floor, undervalue the hot, sunny spot on the floor that draws cats and babies. We are not drawn to the pile of dirt or the hole, to the puddle or dew, or to the rough spot where the plaster is chipping away that beckons small fingers. Our cold, utilitarian eyes assess for order and function, cleanliness and safety. We assess how the space will bend to our will (Greenman, 2005, pp. 21–22).

Good space for children (and adults) is the result of asking the right questions to establish goals and thinking through the important feelings and behaviors that are to be supported. Good space doesn't force behavior contrary to goals, such as dependency, or overemphasize unimportant goals, such as tolerance for waiting (Greenman, 2005, p. 25).

Developmentally Appropriate Physical Environments

INTRODUCTION

In this section, we will examine the nature of the physical environments that set the stage for developmentally appropriate practice. The discussion of physical environments will include the arrangement of space into areas created for learning, the kinds of materials and equipment available for children, and the structuring of time. Recognizing the particular developmental tasks of various stages, the section is divided into four chapters: infants, covering the first year of life; toddlers, including children from about one to three years; preschoolers, from age three through five; and primary-age children, from ages six through eight.

Developmentally Appropriate Physical Environments: For Infants

In the past couple of decades, the number of infants entering childcare settings has grown faster than any other group. Although many families try to replicate home care by finding substitute care in a family childcare home, many have no choice but to look for care in a more traditional early childhood center. Nationwide, programs are faced with the dilemma of trying to adapt physical settings and schedules to the needs of ever-growing numbers of babies. The care of babies in groups brings out some unique questions and problems that require a thorough rethinking of long-held assumptions and practices for programs that are more accustomed to dealing with older children. (This may also lead us to discover more developmentally appropriate practice for those older children!) Infant programs can rely on what they know about settings for older children and preschoolers and move those ideas down by merely adding cribs, or instead they can create environments that more closely resemble home-rearing practice. Decisions need to be based on knowledge about development during the first year.

LEARNING OBJECTIVES

After completing this chapter, students should be able to

- identify several developmental needs of infants that must be considered when planning physical environments, including the establishment of trust and attachment.
- identify several ways the environment can meet each of those developmental needs.
- discuss considerations in outdoor environments for infants.
- list several practices in providing for health and safety in infant rooms.
- identify several appropriate materials for infant rooms.
- discuss appropriate schedules for infant rooms.
- identify inappropriate components in infant rooms.

THE NATURE OF BABIES

Babies are very different from people at all later stages of development. In the first rapidly changing year of their lives, they move from helpless dependence to mobile independence; from communicating with cries and coos, to understanding quite a vocabulary and using some words of their own; from demands for physical needs being met quickly by anyone, to very particular demands for social responses from very specific people. As they progress through these changes, babies spend a good deal of time being cared for by adults.

To plan an environment for babies, the starting point is to ask what babies do and what they need. Babies sleep, eat, cry, and are bathed and changed frequently. They use all their senses and their unfolding motor and manipulative abilities to explore their immediate world. They become attached to a few very special people in their worlds. Behind these objective statements lies a world of small but important steps and actions, which need to be recognized in planning environments for babies.

According to Greenman (2005, pp. 131–132), among other things, young babies are sensory-motor scientists, performing all the actions listed next.

see	hold	lift his or her head up
watch	squeeze	sit up
look	pince	pull up
inspect	drop	crawl to, in, out, over
hear	transfer hand to hand	creep around, in, and
listen	shake	under
smell	bang	swing
taste	tear	rock
feel	clap together	coo
touch	put in	babble
mouth	take out	imitate sounds
eat	find	react to others
reach out	look for	accommodate to others
reach for	kick	solicit from others
knock away	turn	experiment endlessly
grasp	roll	

Add to this list later infancy accomplishments, which may include cruising, holding on, walking, holding a bottle, drinking with a cup, taking apart, stacking, knocking over, transporting, splashing, sliding, climbing, maneuvering a spoon, playing peek-a-boo, and making a loud raspberry sound. (There are a lot more left off this list—what else can you add?)

Another point needs to be stated here: Each baby is unique, with her own temperament, his own activity level, and her own particular need for sleep. Each baby has been nurtured in a unique cultural milieu, with caregiving patterns that shape his behavior. No two six-month-old infants will be ready for, or interested in, the same kind of exploring.

WHAT DO BABIES NEED?

Now that we know what babies do, the next question is, what do they need to grow well? The previous list suggests some components. Babies need intimate relationships with key adults who respond to them promptly, consistently, and warmly. They need adults who interact with them, giving them face-to-face language so they can begin to understand the process of human communication. They need space and opportunity to move at their current capabilities. They need a place rich with objects to explore with every sense and using all of the actions listed previously

Figure 5-1

Babies need a place rich with objects to explore.

(see Figure 5-1). They need a place that is safe for them to be in, but one that does not restrict free movement and active curiosity.

Look back at those statements again. In fact, they are applicable to children at any stage throughout the early years. Clues about how to make these general statements more specific in the design of an infant room come when we watch babies in action and consider what they like, how they move, what attracts their attention, how far they can look, how far they can reach, what they do when they encounter a new object, what disturbs or frustrates their activity and exploration, what comforts them, and how they seek attention (Greenman, 2004).

A reconsideration of child development theory related to infancy is also necessary in this preliminary phase of considering what environments need to offer infants. Erikson (1963) describes the central task of infancy as the need to form a sense of trust against a negative component of mistrust. During the first year, as infants find that their needs are met consistently and warmly, they come to believe that the world and the people in it are good. This basic sense of trust forms a component of personality—an orientation toward positive outlooks and interactions. Ainsworth (1992) refers to forming primary and secondary attachments during the first year, through patterns of repeated, mutually responsive behaviors between baby and adult. **Attachment** refers to a deep, long-lasting emotional tie between people who feel most secure in each other's company. Brazelton and Greenspan underline the importance of consistent, caring relationships in the early years (2000). Thus, issues of security and responsiveness become paramount when making decisions about infant environments.

Piaget (1963) described the first stage of cognitive development during the first two years as the **sensorimotor** stage. During this period, the infant increasingly coordinates information from the senses, the movements, and the manipulation of the body to move toward a practical understanding of the surrounding world. The sensorimotor stage involves this practical, physical intelligence. Thus, environments for infants must provide opportunities to move and to manipulate, and materials to stimulate the senses.

In recalling what babies do, what they need, and these theories, we get our first clues about environmental planning. Adults planning developmentally appropriate physical environments for infants need to consider environments that nurture these developmental tasks: formation of trust, development of attachment, mobility, sensory learning, and language.

ENVIRONMENT TO NURTURE TRUST

An environment of trust for babies includes the ability to provide a consistent response as infants express their needs. In physical environments, this means allowing for differences in babies' schedules for feeding, sleeping, and playing. Babies must not be required to fit into an arbitrarily drawn schedule; each child's daily schedule will be based on particular needs, temperament, and natural rhythms. Thus, in an infant room, some children will need to sleep, while others are being fed or exploring their bodies and surroundings. Separating crib areas from play areas as far as possible is helpful; a quiet, dark alcove adjoining the activity area is preferable, because it allows caregivers to observe the sleeping baby in the crib while interacting with the other babies (see Figure 5-2).

An environment of trust includes consistent responsiveness by the same adults. This assumes a stable staff, often difficult in the realities of today's childcare system. Responsiveness is given when infant caregivers are trained about the crucial importance to later development of the relationships of the first year. The very best teachers need to be given the important responsibility of infant care, not the least trained, who will be most likely to leave the position or be unable to see the value in prompt attention to infant needs.

Centers that understand the need for consistent responsiveness are likely to institute **primary-caregiving** patterns in the room; this means that each adult is primarily responsible for the care of her own small group of babies. For example, Mary is the primary caregiver for Seth, Sarah, and Kenyetta. LaTonya is the primary caregiver for Jon, Jose, and Anna-Li. Much, but not all, of the care, nurturing, and parent communication is provided by the primary caregiver. When their babies need diaper changes, feeding, comfort, or playtime—the prime times of the infant's day—the caregivers respond as their primary contact. Of course, when one of the caregivers is occupied with a baby already, her coworker may step in to assist if one of the other babies needs something. Not only are there fewer babies for a caregiver to interact with and respond to, but this system also allows her to get to know the individual babies and their families intimately and to individualize care accordingly. The purpose of primary-caregiving systems is to give each infant and family an opportunity to develop a special relationship of mutual trust and respect (Bernhardt, 2000). Parents feel more confident leaving their infants with someone who has become close to the family and reports directly to them at the end of the day the details they want to hear. Parents feel included and supported in the first important year of their babies' lives. Relationship-based approaches to infant/toddler care and education de-sign their programs around attachment principles. Some programs also allow for continuity of care, so that an infant stays with the same primary caregiver over many months, or even years. Program decisions are considered through a relationship lens, so that practices support relation-ships among children, their parents, and their caregivers (Edwards & Raikes, 2002; Butterfield, Martin, & Prairie, 2004). Parent-child attachment is thus enhanced by primary-caregiving sys-tems and continuity of care. Infants benefit by this consistent closeness with a particular person.

Staff members continue to advocate the small adult-child ratios that allow for true respon-siveness. Recommended practices that support responsiveness include limiting the group size and the adult-to-child ratio to allow caregivers one-on-one interactions with individual babies. Check the **ratio** in your community.

Consistent responsiveness and meeting individual needs are facilitated by regular communi-cation between caregivers, including staff members and parents. Systems are needed to ensure a regular exchange of information that will help plan appropriate responses. Notebooks in each baby's cubby for caregivers and parents to jot down items regarding daily routines and devel-opmental changes are one example of such a system. Each baby comes from his or her own family and unique culture. Caregivers must learn, respect, and accept the variation in caregiving practices that come with each culture, such as keeping infants in constant physical contact with an adult.

An environment of trust considers size and perspec-tive from the infant's point of view of comfort and se-curity, recognizing that the smaller the baby, the smaller the group size and space around the infant should be. It is preferable to create small groups rather than doubling the size, even with double the adult caregivers; larger groups are noisier and have more of a sense of chaos. Newborns like confined space, such as a bassinet; older infants who are mobile are ready to move beyond fur-niture that restricts movement. Arranging the furniture and layout of an infant room to provide smaller nooks creates this sense of enclosure.

Figure 5-2
When play and caregiving areas are separate from sleeping areas, infants can be on individual schedules.

JOURNAL REFLECTION

Your Earliest Memories

Go back as far as you can in your memory. What do you remember about the home you lived in as a little child? Search for memories about things you saw, touched, smelled, felt in that home. Continue to reflect on the importance of place in creating an environment of comfort and security.

 Visit the premium Web site to complete this journal activity online and email it to your professor.

WHAT would you DO when...

"One of my parents has a mother who has terrified her daughter by telling her that if she responds to the baby's every need, he'll be spoiled." How do the infant room staff respond to this family who wants them to follow the practice of not responding to the baby's cries unless it is to meet a physical need? What would you do, if you were this caregiver?

This is difficult, because people have such deeply felt opinions about how children ought to be raised, and mothers who have raised children may be closed in their opinion, in the face of research or theoretical beliefs. No one wants to be around children who have become nuisances because of their insistence on demanding their own way; we can certainly sympathize with that.

It may be useful to help those parents to state what their goals actually are for the infant; no doubt they really want him to care for others, to be a happy, learning child—perhaps even self-sufficient, although this may depend very much on their cultural orientation toward independence versus interdependence. These are probably goals that caregiver, parent, and grandmother can agree upon. What may need to be discussed is the means by which developmentalists tell us these goals are reached.

The prompt responsiveness to young babies slowly, over repeated experiences, adds up to an impression that the world is a good place, that people in it care for him, and that he will be cared for. Because he simply doesn't have the mental capacity until he's nearly eight months old or so to connect cause and effect, he simply can't do the devious plotting that grandmother fears might be going on in the baby's head. To lie in his crib and plan to cry to get someone to come to him because he recalls that the last time that's what happened is simply beyond the baby who hasn't yet achieved object permanence (see Chapter 12) and can thus call back an earlier mental image to make adults do what he wants the next time. Knowing something about the baby's abilities allows adults to respond more appropriately to him, instead of being afraid that he can learn to manipulate them in ways not yet possible.

As certainty builds, babies actually cry less and less toward the end of their first year, confident that they will be cared for. (In certain cultures where babies are continually carried by caregivers, infants tend to cry less, because they communicate their needs in different ways.) They also come to feel so comfortable in the world that they are able to move away from adults and concentrate on learning by firsthand exploration. What a good first lesson about love and about respecting others' needs, which infants learn just by example! The responsiveness of the infant room staff can be seen as a very developmentally appropriate component of the physical environment.

PRACTICAL IMPLICATIONS

Appropriate Environments for Infants

Make sure your trustworthy environment for infants includes:

- separate sleeping, caregiving, and active play areas.
- well-trained adults who are committed to nurturing infants' development.
- primary-caregiving systems.
- small adult-child ratios and small groups.
- systems for frequent and regular oral and written communication between families and caregivers.
- space suited to the perspective of babies.
- a familiar place, through environmental organization for easy restoration, and predictable patterns to accompany routines.
- an environment in which verbal prohibitions are avoided by a carefully prepared space for free exploration.

An environment of trust is a safe, familiar place. The patterns of things, people, and events are predictable; the infant can feel "at home." Caregivers provide this predictability by ensuring a place for everything, easily restorable from the clutter of infants' active exploration. Clearly marked storage bins, trays, baskets, and boxes help return things to the same places for babies to find again.

Rituals of repeated experiences form the predictable sequence that even babies can comprehend: always a song before being tucked in the crib for a nap; the few minutes to make funny noises and laugh that accompany a diaper change.

Emotional safety is also included in a physical environment in which the prohibitions and restrictions are built in by thoughtful caregivers, instead of becoming verbal contests of will. When the fragile ornament is removed or a gate added to prevent access to a forbidden area, infants are safe from having to contend with a barrage of "Nos." The environment is positive and trustworthy because adults recognize babies' inability to limit themselves.

Environment to Nurture Attachment

Obviously, the consistent responsiveness and stability of caregivers we've discussed are components of attachment. However, there are other considerations as well.

Assume that the most important times for the child are those one-to-one moments of real nurturing and communication, where the baby has the caregiver's full human presence. These are the times that need to be relaxed and even extended *prime times* (see Figure 5-3).

> The term **prime times** signifies the critical importance of care in the child's life in the program. Caring times are prime times . . . these times occupy a large part of both the child's and the caregiver's day in care. With a relaxed pace and gentle one-to-one contact between caregiver and child full of language, interactions, and real give and take, these are prime times for developing a strong sense of personal worth and power, language, and a basic trust in the world as a good place. (Greenman & Stonehouse, & Schweikart, 2007, p. 107)

The environment needs to provide for adult comfort for such encounters; rocking chairs (preferably gliders for safety), hammocks, overstuffed chairs, big cushions, or couches allow adults to sit and hold a child while feeding or talking to her, and soft, cushioned areas on the floor invite staff to interact with babies as they play. Staff also need to consider their role in nurturing parent-infant attachment. The environment needs to convey a clear sense of welcome for parents who have time to visit the center to nurse or play with their babies. Having a quiet corner chair labeled for parents who might like a private time with the baby encourages such interaction.

The arrangement of areas for routine care, such as diaper changing or feeding, may help caregivers avoid the sense of having to rush through the routine without time for interaction. If the work areas are positioned so the adult can still see the rest of the room while providing care to one baby, the routine is less likely to be hurried. If all materials the adult may need are conveniently stored together, time for interaction is gained, and attention can be given to the infant.

When adults are interacting with babies, they will want to screen out as many distractions as possible, so that the human interaction is the focus. This means removing the distracting toys or mobiles from over the changing table;

PRACTICAL IMPLICATIONS

Physical Environments That Foster Attachment

Be sure your environment for attachment contains:

- comfortable chairs and floor areas for adults to relax and enjoy one-to-one interaction with babies.

- a designated parent space for private parent-infant interaction.

- work areas that are located to allow the caregiver to supervise the room, care for an individual baby, and access all necessary materials.

- no toys and other stimulation in the areas of caregiving, such as the feeding and diapering area, so babies can focus on the adult and their shared activity.

Figure 5-3

Prime times together nurture attachment.

Figure 5-4

Immobile babies need protection from older, mobile infants.

the adult's face and words are the only stimulation necessary. This is the opposite of what many caregivers do when they hand the baby a toy to occupy him during the diaper-changing routine. Toys are used then to distract the baby so the adult can efficiently complete the caregiving task. Such efficiency prevents the eye contact and sheer enjoyment of each other that are important components for attachment. Magda Gerber's philosophy describes using such caregiving times as opportunities for respectful interaction and suggests that handing the baby toys to distract trivializes the baby's role in active participation. Read more about this in Gonzalez-Mena and Eyer (2008) and Gerber (1991).

Environment to Nurture Mobility

The unfolding physical abilities of the first year are inextricably tied to the development of sensorimotor intelligence. Therefore, babies need all the space and opportunity to use their bodies that they can safely use. There are several key implications here.

When babies are awake, they need to be removed from the confines of a crib and the soft mattress that gives entirely different support for their muscles than does the firm floor. This may be a practice that parents of particular cultural backgrounds do not understand or support (Gonzalez-Mena & Eyer, 2008), and so it will need careful explanation and dialogue from the staff. Next, methods need to be created to protect immobile babies from older mobile ones (see Figure 5-4). Too often, the little ones are left in the crib "for their own protection" or are confined out of reach of the older ones in devices such as infant seats, swings, walkers, or jumpers. The biggest problem with such items is that they hold young babies in positions the babies often cannot assume for themselves, which is certainly physically stressful, and they do not permit the freedom to practice whatever skill the baby is currently ready for. In addition, infants are at risk of injury from such devices. A better solution needs to be created for separating infants who are able to move about from those who are less mobile—a solution in which no one's needs suffer. A pile of large boxes, a sturdy shelf arrangement, a gate, movable low dividers, a pile of sofa cushions—all might serve as easily portable barriers at various stages. Allowing very little ones opportunities to lie in empty plastic swimming pools, foam circles, or playpens gives them a protected play space, suitable until they begin to need the space to roll over (see Figure 5-4). This may be the only age at which a playpen is suitable, because the older babies who need to creep or walk around become justifiably frustrated by its limitation. It must be emphasized, however, that overuse of a playpen is not recommended. Infants are at risk of retarding motor development, or possible injury, from playpens that are used too much.

All the freedom a baby can safely use is a necessary part of the environment for **mobility**. This requires that adults lie on the floor regularly to see from the perspective of babies. This way, potential hazards can be removed before they become tempting or before there is a need for verbal restrictions, and the environment becomes an inviting place, rather than one where babies continually have to be removed or restricted. See more about safe environments later in this chapter.

Environmental planners need to remember that space is relative to size; quite a small space offers freedom to a small infant. Large room areas need to be broken up for a feeling of security for babies. A new walker can be quite frightening to see a huge space to traverse before getting to the comfort of the shelf he plans to grab on to.

PRACTICAL IMPLICATIONS

Environments That Foster Mobility

Provide an environment for mobility by

- allowing babies to play freely on the floor when awake.
- protecting less mobile babies by creating barriers.
- removing devices that restrict the free movement of infants.
- safety-proofing the environment completely and regularly.
- creating smaller movement zones within the larger space available.

Environment for the Senses

Consider the sensory stimulation offered to infants by a typical home. An ever-changing variety of interesting things to look at is available close by: the pattern of light and shadow as the sun comes through the curtains; the movement of the leaves on a plant near an open window; the colors of furnishings, kitchen dishes, clothing on people who move in and out of rooms. There are smells of flowers; coffee perking; clean, wet laundry; and onions frying. Babies can hear the thump of the clothes drier, the chiming of the clock, the soft hum of radio music, the rhythm of voices, or the birds in the yard. They feel the soft carpet, the cool kitchen linoleum, the prickly grass in the backyard, and the warm breeze. They taste everything from the rubber of the pacifier to the sweetness of applesauce.

Babies in a childcare center need to have an environment just as rich in sensory stimulation and variety. Adults need to beware of providing so clinical a setting that this myriad of sensations is not available. Consider the questions in Figure 5-5.

Environment planners should realize that everything in the life of infants goes on below the height of 24 inches or so and even lower for babies who are rolling, sitting, or crawling. Certainly there are times when adults hold or carry babies to look at mobiles or out of windows, but the majority of time, babies should be able to make their own discoveries and explore freely without adult assistance.

The area under 24 inches, therefore, needs to offer babies a rich variety of materials to stimulate all the senses. There should be interesting things to look at: unbreakable stainless steel mirrors attached along the baseboards; large, colorful photos firmly attached under clear Contac paper to baseboards, linoleum, low on doors and cabinets, on the ends and undersides of cribs and chairs; goldfish swimming in an aquarium; prisms hung at windows to reflect rainbow colors around the room; low windows or gates at the door that allow babies to look at the passing world; streamers attached to catch the breeze. (When attaching objects with Contac paper, be sure to use circles rather than leaving tempting corners for exploring fingers to pick at.)

What will the babies touch? Plastic toys are so limited in the sensations they yield. Wooden toys and baskets of scarves and other interesting objects offer far more interest for sensory exploration. Squares of various kinds of carpet can be firmly attached at intervals on the floor, lower walls, and pieces of furniture—be sure to include the surprise of a rope mat or grass indoor-outdoor carpeting. Balls of yarn scraps, velvet, or chore-girl can hang down from the ceiling within grasping reach. Different surfaces in the room—soft carpet, hard linoleum, cushioned pad—offer challenges in traction as well as variety in sensation. Imagine the surprise of a young crawler who discovers a square of clear Contac paper positioned sticky side up.

Elizabeth Prescott defines the importance of softness in the environment, found in the "presence of objects which are responsive to one's touch—which provide a variety of tactile sensory

---

Examine the infant space when all the children and adults are gone. Ask yourself:

Does this seem like a great place to be a baby?
Does it seem like a great place to be with a baby?

This will include:

- a comfortable place, in which adults can relax while feeding, soothing, changing, and nurturing babies. It is warm, comfortable, and homelike, with lots of available softness.

- lots of different places to be, to avoid the clumping that jangles nerves—places to be under, behind, semisecluded, alone while protected.

- attention to beauty and aesthetics that shows attention to color, light, texture, and pattern, as well as to order.

- **tactile** impressions of soft and responsive materials, in the furnishings and materials, in the protection from overwhelming noise.

Figure 5-5

What is your first impression of an infant environment? (Ideas adapted from Greenman & Stonehouse, 1996).

CULTURAL CONSIDERATIONS

Floor Freedom for Infants

Floor freedom for infants is a concept that is not accepted in some cultural environments. Consider some of the likely reasons that this is not valued. Counter these ideas with reasons that could be presented by a proponent of developmentally appropriate infant care. Now try to find ways that both of these opposing views could be reconciled, so that it is a win-win situation for families and caregivers.

stimuli" (Prescott, 1994). Objects such as couches, large pillows, rugs, swings, grass, sand, and water are included in her list, as well as laps to sit on. Quilts, thick vinyl mats, and soft carpeting are appropriate places for babies to lie on backs or stomachs.

Don't forget the smells. Leave the windows open when the grass is being cut, as well as the door when the cook is preparing lunch for the older children or when the cleaning staff is working with wax and cleansers, although caregivers should be mindful of babies who have allergies. Prepare snack foods for adults and older babies in the room, so the natural odors of hot chocolate and apple pieces linger in the air.

Particularly when stimulating the sense of sound, adults must be sensitive to the natural sounds in the environment—the murmurs of soft language and the louder sounds of adult conversations, the hum of the lawn mower, and the roar of a plane passing by. It is tempting to surround babies with more artificial sounds such as nursery rhyme songs on the CD player or the radio playing music for the adults to enjoy as they work. Although some of this is certainly appropriate stimulation, too much can provide a sound overlay that masks the important sounds of human speech or creates an unnecessarily chaotic atmosphere. Let the infants focus frequently on the real sounds in their environment, occasionally supplementing them with deliberate variety: the banging of a couple of aluminum pie plates hanging on yarn (also fun visually), an occasional wind chime, or the fun of an old-fashioned metronome set on the shelf.

Varieties of tastes are provided by adding new foods at regular intervals. The usual array of infant toys—rattles, chime balls, bells, soft blocks and animals, teethers, and mobiles—also provide sensory stimulation. Sturdy homemade toys can be replaced more easily than expensive commercial ones when babies get bored. Examples include dried beans or a mixture of colored water, oil, and glitter in a plastic soft drink container (be sure the cap is attached tightly with a super glue); texture blocks; or a clear plastic mailing cylinder with an assortment of items inside that make sounds when rolled. Simple, open-ended materials, such as Mylar paper to crumple or a silk scarf for handling, offer varied sensory experiences. At all times, caregivers must recall that babies get most of their sensory information by mouthing objects, so realize that everything will go into babies' mouths—please don't try to stop them! Instead, simply ensure that absolutely everything is safe, in sizes too large for swallowing or choking, with no pieces that can come off and decorated with no substances that can harm.

When planning the sensory environment, sensory overload must be considered. The walls and floor must not be filled or cluttered with so much that the infant becomes distracted and overstimulated. It is better to remove the things babies just don't comprehend that are included only for adult amusement, such as a mural of Big Bird or Mickey Mouse, which would have no meaning to infants (and probably have no place in a child-centered classroom for any age). As materials seem to attract less and less of the babies' attention, replace them and find newer objects of interest.

The only place where sensory stimulation should not be provided is in the infant's crib. Many manufacturers deliberately market toys for cribs, and too many caregivers get tricked into thinking the baby's bed should be a mini-playground. However, the baby's bed should be kept for sleeping. When infants are awake, they need to be removed from their cribs to play elsewhere, so the bed

PRACTICAL IMPLICATIONS

Providing an Appropriate Sensory Environment for Infants

Provide an appropriate sensory environment by:

- using the areas and furniture 24 inches above the floor on which to place materials that infants can explore independently.
- considering all the senses when preparing the environment.
- providing homemade toys that have sensory appeal, as well as commercial toys, and continually checking all toys for safety.
- avoiding sensory overload by removing things beyond infants' direct understanding.
- removing sensory stimulation from cribs.

needs to be quietly and soothingly dull, to encourage only sleep when babies are tucked in.

Environment for Language

Much of what has already been said contributes to an environment that nurtures infant language development. Two important factors are opportunities for one-to-one interaction during caregiving and playtimes, and a room that is not too noisy from the sounds of too many babies and adults or from constant artificial sound. In addition, talk is encouraged by a variety of interesting objects, views, experiences, and pictures.

Caregivers sing and play rhyming and simple action games with infants. Appropriate books are available, some of them homemade picture books, as well as books that adults can read to infants; reading is done regularly with infants. Read more about specifics in the language environment in Chapter 13.

 VIDEO ACTIVITY

Go to the premium Web site and watch the video clip for Chapter 5 titled "Environments for Infants." Then consider the following questions:

REFLECTIVE QUESTIONS

Consider aspects of the environment shown that relate to concepts from the chapter, such as an environment to nurture trust and attachment; an environment to encourage mobility; an environment for the senses. How do you see that this environment can respond to individual needs as well as caregiving needs?

Visit the premium Web site to complete these questions online and email them to your professor.

RETHINK THE TRADITIONAL

Babies are different in most respects from the older children in the childcare center, so their physical environment should also look very different. For example, it may be beneficial to use items that might be seen in homes more frequently than in classrooms, such as a couch. Besides the obvious comfort for adults, a couch offers versatility. A perfect spot for caregivers and parents to sit with babies—several at a time when necessary—the couch can also be moved out from the wall to create a new pathway when babies become crawlers. For those ready to pull up and cruise along holding on, the couch is a perfect height and provides casual support (Greenman, 2004). Also rethink the traditional when it comes to the décor of the classroom. See things from the perspective of infants—then you will discover that the bottoms of things like chairs and cribs, or the ceiling for babies who spend much time gazing upward, need something interesting on them (see Figure 5-6).

Figure 5-6

Rethink the traditional! This bright art on the wall under a window is just right for infant viewing.

(a)

Figure 5-7 (a & b)

Appropriate centers in an infant room include a cozy corner and an exercise mat.

(b)

Babies play alone, and when they are crowded together, unintentional hurting is more likely. The traditional classroom arrangement that has learning centers with space for several children is less appropriate for infants. More appropriate individual infant learning centers are created when caregivers observe what babies are ready for. For example, when an infant is ready to reach and grasp, a small area on the floor at one protected end of a couch might be made into a reaching center, with a changing array of materials suspended from a dowel. The space under a table or in the lowest cabinets (with the door removed) might be the spot for a sitting baby to explore the box of different textured materials—a curly wig, a piece of sandpaper, a large end of packing Styrofoam. A baby ready to "fingerpaint" with flour and water mixture can sit in his high chair and use the tray. A small packing box with pillows makes a cozy spot for an infant who is looking at some cardboard-paged books. Individual playing spots are most appropriate for infants who will be at their own developmental level, for solitary play and for interaction with a caregiver.

Separate areas appropriate for an infant room might include a rattle corner; a reaching/grasping/kicking area, with objects hanging on rope or elastic; a peek-a-boo/object permanence area, such as a divider or large box with holes in it; a play pit or plastic wading pool, for sitting play with a variety of soft objects; a climbing area, with futon, cubes, and mattresses; a mirror area, with mirrors attached to walls or divider backs; a stacking block area, with large foam blocks and sturdy boxes; a discovery corner, with scent boxes, baskets of textures, colored plastic, shakers, and chimes; an action area, with busy boxes, switches, locks and latches, and things to take apart; a book corner; and a cozy corner with all kinds of cushions (Greenman, 2005) (see Figures 5-7a & 5-7b).

OUTDOORS FOR INFANTS

Babies need to be taken outdoors regularly—how else can they experience the unique sensory and mobility environments of the larger world around? "Infants and toddlers deserve natural outdoor spaces that challenge their emerging sensory and physical skills and are *good places to* be for babies and to be *with* babies" (Greenman, 2005, p. 300). Many of the same principles apply to the infant's outdoor environment as apply indoors. The primary component of the environment is an alert, available adult who enjoys being outdoors and doesn't feel babies have to be protected totally from the world around. To be sure, adults must be watchful for items dangerous to mouth: small rocks, acorns and berries, and discarded wrappers. Daily monitoring for hazardous materials and maintenance of all surfaces is an important adult responsibility. The surface for babies needs to be both soft and level. All vegetation should be checked for toxicity, in case a curious baby takes a taste. It is best for babies to be separated from toddlers outdoors however possible. Much of the time outdoors for babies will be spent in gross motor play—"tummy time," crawling, cruising, and perhaps climbing (see Figure 5-8). Clean blankets can provide a safe surface for the youngest children, who will also occasionally enjoy watching from the adult's lap. This may be the best time to use infant seats or swings to give less-mobile babies a vantage point. Crawlers will enjoy ramps, tunnels, or cardboard boxes to crawl in, under, and through. Smooth round boulders and logs allow places for babies to crawl over safely. Being close to a fence allows the young "cruisers" a natural support, or low rails can be built (see Figure 4-7). Tiny ramps and low steps may add variety for these children. Partially filled inner tubes are useful for infants at several stages. (See more ideas about design in Greenman, 2005.)

Shade is important for tender skin, even if created from a canopy, umbrella, awning, or pop-up tent. Parents can also bring hats and sunscreen to protect their babies. Large strollers or baby buggies will allow caregivers to transport the babies outdoors, as well as take walks into the neighborhood (see Figure 5-9). The outdoors offers many natural kinds of sensory stimulation,

Figure 5-8

Much of the time outdoors is for gross motor play on appropriate surfaces.

Figure 5-9

Baby buggies help caregivers take infants outdoors regularly to enjoy safe walks in the neighborhood.

such as bird sounds; varied textures of grass, trees, and bark; and the play of sun and shadow. Interesting additions to the outdoor play area can include hanging colored Plexiglas, aluminum pie plates, and wind chimes on the fence, and providing buckets for collecting interesting found materials. (For additional ideas, see Dodge, Rudick, & Berke, 2006.)

HEALTH AND SAFETY

Surely an extremely important component of the physical environment for infants is the consideration of health and safety. Babies depend on alert adults to keep them safe at all times and to prevent the spread of infection. Statistics indicate that accidents are leading causes of death in infants, and that babies cared for in groups are at greater risk for many kinds of infections and diseases than babies cared for at home. This indicates the seriousness of the caregiver's responsibilities in this area, both indoors and outdoors. Caregivers must understand the need to continually monitor and evaluate the environment for safety.

Dangers to be monitored as babies explore the world with their bodies and mouths include ingestion of small or poisonous objects; falls from furniture or stairs; falling objects, pulled over by exploring infants; cuts from sharp objects or projections; pinches in hinges, doors, or under furniture; and burns from hot objects or electricity.

Detailed plans for sanitizing and safe-proofing environments for infants can be found in the guidelines developed by the American Academy of Pediatrics, the American Public Health Association, and the National Resource Center for Health and Safety in Child Care (2002).

Safe environments for infants include

- shatterproof mirrors and protection from windows that could break, as well as from windows open at the bottom.

- covered electrical outlets and no electrical cords that could trip or be chewed on.

- protection from radiators, hot-water taps, light bulbs, heaters, or other potential sources of burns and scalds.

- only nonpoisonous plants.

- all medicines, purses, cleaning substances, and other hazardous chemicals kept locked away from infants.

- no broken or damaged toys, no toys with easily removable small parts, and no toys painted with lead or other toxic materials.

- completely stable furniture that cannot be pulled over by, or fall onto, babies; be sure cribs and other furniture follow consumer protection standards, so babies cannot get their heads stuck.

- covering/padding of sharp edges that could be dangerous if fallen on or bumped into.

- staff knowledgeable regarding emergency procedures, including infant CPR and first aid, location of emergency equipment and emergency numbers, and evacuation procedures.

- constant supervision so that babies are not left unattended even for a moment; safety restraints used in high chairs, strollers, and changing tables.

- placement of cribs and use of baby monitors, so that caregivers can supervise infants at sleep.

- following safe sleeping practices, such as back position, firm mattresses, and appropriate bedclothes as recognized prevention for SIDS (sudden infant death syndrome).

- supervision of babies as they eat and drink; no leaving them with bottles propped; finger/solid foods cut into appropriate-size pieces.

- outdoor play areas that are enclosed by fences or natural barriers.

- outdoor play equipment that conforms to height standards for the age of the child and surrounded by resilient surface materials to absorb shock.
- no overprotection of babies; staff that work on finding ways of safely allowing babies to practice a challenging skill, such as putting pillows by the step the baby is drawn to climb on, rather than continually removing the baby.

Healthy environments for infants include

- scrupulous standards of adult hand washing after coughing, sneezing, wiping an individual's nose, or changing diapers, and before handling food or bottles; adults use paper towels to touch faucets or waste containers after washing.
- staff members who follow licensing standards for the changing area, providing a cleansed and covered surface for each diaper change.
- refrigeration of food and bottles until time of use.
- staff members who wash babies' hands frequently, with individual washcloths.
- staff members who sanitize toys and surfaces daily, even more often when they are aware that children are sharing and mouthing toys.
- staff members and parents who remove street shoes before walking on floors where babies lie.
- cleanliness of individual cribs.
- good record-keeping, confirming up-to-date immunizations for all babies.
- exclusion of babies with signs of illness, according to standards and symptoms defined by the program.
- administration of medicine to babies only from prescribed medications with written permission and instructions from parents. (For more about healthy infant environments, see Dodge, Rudick, & Berke, 2006.)

Care for health and safety is an important part of the physical environment.

MATERIALS FOR INFANT ROOMS

Every infant room should contain

- mats or rugs for playtime.
- cribs for sleeping.
- infant seats to be primarily used for feeding before the baby sits alone or to provide an occasional change of scene or position.
- high chairs, or a substitute that takes less room, such as seats that snap on low tables for babies who sit.
- grasping toys, such as soft balls, stuffed animals, and blocks; rattles; large bristle blocks; plastic keys and beads; and squeeze toys.
- toys for skill development, such as stacking cones, nesting materials, simple busy boxes and gadget boards for manipulation, and containers to be filled and emptied.
- cloth and cardboard books, and books of familiar pictures, as well as additional books for adults to read (see Figure 5-10).
- unbreakable mirrors.
- mobiles.
- reaching gyms.
- simple dolls.

Figure 5-10

Board or washable books allow babies to begin their first literacy experiences.

- a variety of balls, including some with special effects.
- one-piece push toys.
- collections of objects with diameters from 2 to 5 inches to hold and explore.

Most of these items are the toys traditionally seen in homes and centers. Caregivers will know which items babies are ready for as they watch their individual motor and cognitive development (more about this in Section 3). Remember that well-constructed toys made from ordinary discards allow caregivers to ensure novelty for babies.

An NAEYC publication—*The Right Stuff: Selecting Play Materials to Support Development* (Bronson, 1995)—discusses appropriate play materials for both young infants through six months and older infants from seven through twelve months. You will also find good ideas in White (1995) and Dodge, Rudick, and Berke (2006).

SCHEDULE CONSIDERATIONS FOR INFANTS

A schedule, if defined as an unchanging, predictable sequence of daily events for the children in a group, does not exist in an infant room, because each infant has individual daily patterns for rest, feeding, changes, and playtime that need sensitive responses.

When five-month-old Andrea arrives one morning at eight o'clock, her mother tells the caregiver that the baby did not sleep well the previous night, and she is put directly into her crib to see if she needs more sleep. When she awakens, she is very hungry. After an immediate feeding, she is relaxed and ready to play with some rattles, lying on her back on the carpet and rolling from side to side. The next day, she arrives rested, but ravenous, so the caregiver immediately prepares some cereal for her. After a bottle, she wants to lie drowsily on her caregiver's lap for a while before being placed on the carpet to play. It would be impossible to post a schedule that would meet Andrea's needs, as well as those of eleven-month-old Ben, who is trying to change his napping schedule to a short morning nap and a much longer afternoon one.

Caregivers do not attempt to move babies to fit into a predetermined schedule. Instead, they communicate daily with parents to learn what current needs might be and then watch the baby's reactions to determine what is needed next. This has been called a **self-demand schedule**, meaning that infants communicate their own needs, and adults respond appropriately. This rhythmic responsiveness slowly builds a baby's inner sense of certainty that needs will be met by trustworthy people. A self-demand schedule builds healthy social/emotional development.

WHAT would you DO when...

Mary Cassidy is a single mother of a five-month-old in your childcare center. She asks you to keep Sam on a by-the-clock schedule so she can feed him his evening meal as soon as she gets home from work and put him right to bed, leaving her free to do the household chores. You find it difficult to keep to the schedule, because sometimes it means waking him from a nap to feed him, and other times it means he's hungry before the prescribed hour. How would you respond?

When parental needs seem to interfere with the self-demand schedule that is considered developmentally appropriate by the caregiver, both caregiver and parent may be frustrated. A continuing dialogue focused on infant needs is necessary. The caregiver may help the parent realize that infants become much more amenable to a more regulated schedule in the latter months of their first year, as they move more naturally to two long naps and a three-meal-a-day pattern. Perhaps Mom will be able to defer her needs for a few more weeks. It is important to help parents of infants realize that developmental needs are specific and different at each age, and appropriate responses help infants build the developmental base for later stages.

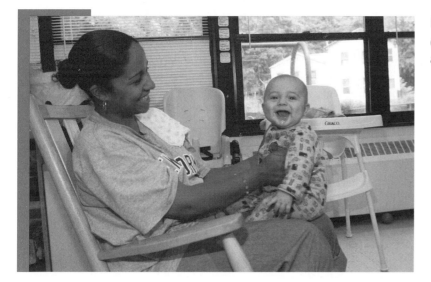

Figure 5-11

Caregivers use every opportunity for interaction and communication.

Much of the daily time frame is spent on routine caregiving. Caregivers who regard these times as important for interaction and communication—in fact, the heart of the curriculum—do not rush through them, but allow for a relaxed and responsive pacing (see Figure 5-11).

THINGS NOT SEEN IN A DEVELOPMENTALLY APPROPRIATE ENVIRONMENT FOR INFANTS

Note that conspicuously missing from the list of materials for the infant room are the large pieces of equipment such as traditional playpens, swings, walkers, jumpers, and so on. (If these items are recommended by a child's Individualized Family Service Plan, or **IFSP**, their use would be appropriate in those circumstances only.) Although there is some limited use for all of these items at various stages, they are too space consuming and expensive to justify their value. Besides, when they are present, it is too tempting for caregivers to overuse them, to the detriment of optimum development. Although it may be an exaggeration to say they are never present in a developmentally appropriate environment, they are certainly not a dominant feature and may well be done without.

Another component not seen in a developmentally appropriate environment for infants is a by-the-clock sequence of scheduled events for all infants. As mentioned in the previous section, each infant needs individual responses that a set schedule does not permit. Infants' needs must take precedence over those of adults.

Also not seen in a developmentally appropriate environment is the chaos of a large group of infants and several caregivers, perhaps with ratios as high as one adult caring for five to seven babies and group sizes of around twenty together in one room. Such large groups simply do not allow for developmentally appropriate interaction, mobility, or individualization. Be sure to know what your state licensing requirements mandate for caregiving ratios and work to change ratios too high for developmentally appropriate practice.

Television is not part of the appropriate environment for infants. The American Academy of Pediatrics recommends that television not be part of children's lives under the age of two. Face-to-face language and singing are much more appropriate sources of language than is a television, which does not provide for responsive interaction.

SUMMARY

The physical environment for infants provides for meeting developmental needs of trust, attachment, mobility, sensory exploration, and language in a world that provides for safety and health considerations. Individual needs dictate daily schedules as well as the kind of materials that caregivers provide for babies at various stages. This environment serves as the framework for the interaction that will form the basis for the social/emotional environment and the cognitive-language environment, as we will discuss in Sections 3 and 4.

THINK ABOUT IT ACTIVITIES

1. Visit a center that has an infant room. Identify and note down
   - health and safety practices.
   - components to nurture trust and attachment, mobility, sensory exploration, and language.
   - communication methods between parents and staff.
   - an outdoor play area for infants.
   - materials and arrangement of furniture in the room.

   Compare your findings with the ideas discussed in this chapter. Share your findings with those of classmates who visited other centers.

2. Write a brief report that could (but won't) be presented to the staff of the center of the infant room you visited, suggesting some changes you feel would improve the quality of the physical environment provided for infants. Be sure your writing includes the reasons you recommend these changes. Share these ideas with other students.

3. Write a rationale for the board of why the most highly trained teachers should be assigned to the infant room.

4. Discuss what is lost for optimum development when infant rooms have higher ratios.

QUESTIONS TO ASSESS LEARNING OF CHAPTER OBJECTIVES

1. What are several of the developmental needs of infants that must be considered when planning the physical environment?

2. For each of the developmental needs listed in question 1, describe several things that can be done in the environment to meet each need.

3. Discuss factors to be considered when planning outdoor environments for babies.

4. List as many things as you can that provide safe and healthy environments for infants.

5. What are several appropriate materials for infant rooms?

6. What is an appropriate schedule for infants?

7. What conditions are unlikely to be found in a developmentally appropriate environment for infants?

APPLY YOUR KNOWLEDGE QUESTIONS

1. Describe all the reasons to provide primary caregiving systems in the infant room that you would present to your director and families in asking for such a change.

2. One of the families in your group is shocked to find that the infants spend much of their awake time playing on the floor. What are the points you would like to make in your discussion of this matter with them? What do you need to hear from them regarding their ideas? In the event of a cultural difference that does not appear likely to be reconciled, what possible suggestions could you offer?

HELPFUL WEB SITES

http://www.teachingstrategies.com	On the Web site for Creative Curriculum, click on Infant/Toddler, and then click on Articles. Browse through to find articles on health, safety, and infant learning through routines.
http://www.zerotothree.org	On the Web site for Zero to Three, there is a great deal of information about the care and education of infants and toddlers.
http://www.eichild.com	On the Web site for Environment materials, find the interactive planning guides for infant environments.
http://www.clas.uiuc.edu	On this Web site, search for an article by J. R. Lally and Jay Stewart titled "Infant/Toddler Caregiving: A Guide to Setting Up Environments."
http://www.educarer.org	The World of Infants Web site has much helpful information about caring for infants.

 Please visit the premium Web site for Developmentally Appropriate Practice, 4th edition, to access more chapter web links, additional book chapters, suggestions for further reading and study, interactive quizzes, video exercises, online journal activities, flashcards, and much more! Go to www.cengage.com/login to register your access code.

Developmentally Appropriate Physical Environments: For Toddlers

Near the end of their first year, when babies begin to move around freely, we begin to call them toddlers, and do so until they are thirty to thirty-six months old. In only about a year, toddlers have made dramatic gains in physical mobility and dexterity, in language understanding and sound production, and in their ability to explore actively the world around them. With their need for sleep decreasing, they spend many hours each day engaging in physical activity.

Toddlers are definitely not "group" creatures; they are centered on exploring their concept of self and everything that means. An impartial observer can note that they care little about the rights or needs of other toddlers, although they are as intrigued by exploring other children in their environment as they are by exploring any other interesting object they come upon.

All these characteristics have implications for planning appropriate physical environments that will match toddler development and nurture understanding of the tasks of toddlerhood.

LEARNING OBJECTIVES

After completing this chapter, students should be able to

- identify several developmental characteristics and needs of toddlers, particularly a sense of autonomy.
- identify several ways the environment can meet each of these developmental needs.
- identify several appropriate materials for toddler rooms.
- discuss schedule and transition considerations for toddlers.
- identify inappropriate components in physical environments for toddlers.

WHAT ARE TODDLERS LIKE?

Imagine the reaction of a bright young explorer from another planet who first stepped foot on planet Earth! Every waking moment would be spent busily attempting to figure out this strange new place, its inhabitants, and everything else encountered. Not knowing any of the rules or customs of the place, the newcomer would undoubtedly make some errors along the way, breaking either physical objects or social norms. Not being very familiar with the language, attempts to teach or explain might be frustrating for both the visitor and those trying to enlighten him.

It is not very different for the toddler, who is suddenly able to move about the world and come to a firsthand understanding of it. Full of a sense of this new power, the toddler is at a peak of curiosity and frustrated (but undaunted) by any sense of limitation. The toddler has a drive to use the body to explore everything and everybody with whom she comes in contact and the tireless energy to keep exploring even when others make it difficult. However, the toddler does not yet have much language for self-expression, much of the self-control that goes along with understanding concepts and language, or much concern about the needs, wishes, or rights of others in the world. The contrast between what toddlers have and what they do not have makes them such interesting and challenging individuals to care for in groups.

This may be one of the places where a picture is worth many thousands of descriptive words. In Figure 6-1, you see an approximation of the movements of an eighteen-month-old around a typical preschool classroom, set up with a variety of interest centers and activities. The movements were recorded over a period of seven minutes. From the lines, you can see the nearly ceaseless movement from one area to another, retracing pathways, obviously not staying with one activity for longer than seconds. The need for physical movement, the endless curiosity, the short attention span, the sense of autonomy and personal will—all can be seen as the lines on paper trace ceaseless toddler exploration. Incidentally, this drawing does not show what would happen if a group of equally busy toddlers were moving about the same space; undoubtedly numerous physical clashes and conflicts of will would occur as each independent explorer, intent on personal goals, encountered another. It might be comforting for caregivers to share this drawing with parents of toddlers who despair of their frenetic children! Look at the much more controlled behaviors of the older twos, let alone the supremely confident four-year-olds who can

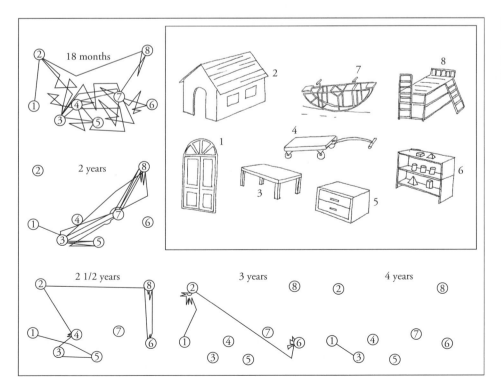

Figure 6-1

As the drawing illustrates, toddlers are almost constantly on the move. Adapted from a drawing in the September 1986 issue of *Child Care Center*.

focus on one interest, without change, for the full period. **Maturation** and development will soon change some things that no amount of teaching or adult guidance can.

This, then, is the nature of toddlers: exuberant physical energy, boundless intellectual curiosity, a strong sense of self, and a wish for independence.

> Toddlers learn with their whole bodies—not just their heads. They learn more through their hands than they do through their ears. They learn by doing, not only by thinking. . . . Toddlers solve problems on a physical level. "Me—mine!" indicates toddlers are beginning to see themselves as individuals with possessions. And, of course, the "NO!" toddlers are so famous for is a further clue to their push for separateness and independence. (Gonzalez-Mena, 1986, pp. 47–48)

WHAT DO TODDLERS DO?

Toddlers walk, run, and move during all their waking hours—and frequently protest loudly when an adult suggests that it is time to stop moving and time to sleep. They have an insatiable desire to climb as high as they can manage. They rarely sit still for long, and when they do, it is because some interesting thing to handle or manipulate has caught their attention. They use their full repertoire of manipulative abilities to discover the properties of anything they touch. They enjoy dumping, dropping, banging, poking fingers in things, and trying to pull things apart—all in the interest of pure research. They repeat and practice activities. They do a lot more undoing than doing, being able to pull socks and shoes off, pull diapers off, dump puzzle pieces out, or throw objects, long before they are interested in putting things back. And, as active as they are, toddlers also spend a good deal of time staring at things and people and doing nothing much. Evidently, this is yet another form of exploration (White, 1995). Remember, however, that this generalization does not describe the unique temperaments and cultural environments of individual toddlers, which are forces that create their own style of approaching life.

Toddlers want to do most everything "Myself!" even if tasks are beyond their capability. They manipulate spoons and cups to feed themselves, albeit a messy process. (See Figure 6-2.) They prefer to wash their own faces and hands. They try to dress themselves. They often jerk away from well-meaning adults who are trying to assist them.

Toddlers spend only about 16 percent of their time in social activities (White, 1995), alternating between seeking physical contact and attention from adults and resisting them. Yet, ambivalent as their social responses to loved adults are, toddlers resist and protest separation. Toddlers may show brief and transitory interest in peers, but they mainly use other toddlers as vehicles for asserting self or conducting research. For example, when Yolanda pulled at Petra's hair, she seemed at first to be just exploring the long blond curls. After receiving a loud shriek in response, she seemed to pull again quite deliberately, as if to see what the second reaction would be. Toddlers may respond aggressively to others—biting, grabbing, hitting. Although they are not yet very verbal, they manage to express strong emotions both physically and loudly.

Figure 6-2

Toddlers struggle to "do it myself"—although this is undeniably a messy process.

> Neither infants nor preschoolers, toddlers are furiously becoming: increasingly mobile, autonomous, social, thoughtful creatures with language and insatiable urges to test and experiment. They embody contradictions: anarchist with an instinct to herd and cluster, assertive and independent now, passive and completely dependent moments later. These restless mobile characters have a drive to take apart the existing order and rearrange it, by force if necessary, to suit their own whimsically logical view of the universe. (Greenman, 2005, p. 137)

WHAT DO TODDLERS NEED?

Knowing what toddlers do allows us to consider what they need to encourage their development. Probably what toddlers need most is to be accepted for who they are. They suffer badly in comparison with older children, for they are by no means as capable of understanding or reasoning, self-control, or social learning as children a year or so older. They are accused of being clumsy, destructive, selfish, stubborn, and just plain "mean." None of this is fair or true.

Just because they can walk and talk, many adults feel that it is now appropriate to begin teaching lessons of self-control and are visibly frustrated when toddlers do not respond. Using methods of teaching that are traditional with older preschoolers just doesn't work with toddlers, who are likely to wander out of circle time or resist adult-directed activities. Inappropriate expectations usually lead to a battle of wills between adults and toddlers, with the unhealthy possibility that toddlers end up feeling they have failed to live up to the standards set by their adults.

More than anything else, toddlers need adults who can enjoy the exuberance and striving of the toddler to move to a sense of self. They thrive when adults can find ways to nurture a sense of autonomy (a sense of self as an independent being) as defined by Erikson, while recognizing the need to protect the toddler from the negative sense of shame and doubt that comes when the toddler is continually stopped or punished for normal physical or social testing. They need adults who can help them with separation (being apart from those to whom the toddler is attached). They need adults who can nourish a sense of the individual, while maintaining safety and rights for all toddlers as members of a group. They need adults who can protect them from their immaturity and impulsiveness, yet safeguard their right to explore and learn while still in Piaget's sensorimotor stage (recall from Chapter 5 that this is the time of practical, physical intelligence, slowly constructed by taking in information from sensory and manipulative exploration), and slowly move into the symbolic stage of the early preoperational years. (Preoperational cognitive functioning—basically a prelogical, intuitive approach—is described in detail in Chapter 15.)

Above all, toddlers need adults who can appreciate them for who they are, right now, with all their exuberance and delight in the world and their own abilities (see Figure 6-3).

As you note what toddlers are like, what they can do, and what they need to accomplish their developmental tasks, you can create a physical environment to enhance optimum development during toddlerhood. This environment should be unique, not one that is more appropriate for babies, nor a diluted preschool classroom.

How do you develop an environment that allows collecting, hauling, dumping, and painting (with the requisite tasting of the paint and experimenting with the logical primary canvas—themselves)? How do you allow the necessary robust, explosive, and occasionally motor learning with a group of amoral beings who are largely oblivious to the safety of others . . .

Figure 6-3

Toddlers need adults who can enjoy their exuberance.

how do you accommodate to and support the wonderful, albeit erratic, *do it myself* desire and the equally developmentally important but often less wonderful assertion of "No!" and still accomplish anything in a reasonable time frame? . . . "Mission impossible" may in fact understate the situation. (Greenman, 2005, p. 138)

In designing physical environments for toddlers, it is important first to consider several key components that must be present. There is a need for safety, so that mobile, curious toddlers are free to explore independently, protected from their own impulsiveness and immaturity, yet without being frustrated by unnecessary restrictions. There is a need for flexibility, so that the environment keeps in step with children's changing needs and provides spaces that must be used for several purposes, such as play as well as routine caregiving, practicing skills of new walkers, and activities of relentless climbers. There is a need for variety, to provide for different toddlers doing different things and individual exploring with appropriate challenges for all. Providing a variety of experiences will also take children and adults into the world beyond the confines of the four walls of a toddler room. There is a need for easily restorable order, because exploration is an untidy process; yet toddlers need the security of familiar objects being in familiar places. There is a need also for organization in the areas of toileting and dressing, so adults can help toddlers succeed at self-help and minimize frustrating waits. There is a need for challenge, as bored toddlers are more likely to get involved in undesirable behaviors. Adults need to keep these elements in mind as they evaluate the worlds they create for toddlers. In addition, adults need to consider the toddler developmental tasks they want to support, including autonomy, separateness, movement ability, **self-help skills**, and sensorimotor exploration.

Environment to Support Autonomy

An environment for autonomy includes components that allow toddlers to achieve a measure of independence and a sense of doing things for themselves (see Figure 6-4). Furniture and fittings need to be toddler-size, so toddlers can sit comfortably with their feet touching the floor and climb up to use sinks and toilets unaided. Sturdy chairs and low stools allow toddlers to safely seat themselves and wash their hands. Coat hooks and cubbies are within toddler reach, as are hooks for washcloths, and so on. A mirror at toddler height encourages face washing. A strategically placed paper towel rack allows toddlers to help themselves, although, of course, supervision is always necessary. Feeling some control over the environment increases the toddler's sense of competence. For toddlers who have physical limitations and special needs, efforts to provide for autonomy need to be increased, so that lack of mobility or ability does not mean lack of opportunities to develop autonomy. Adequate space must be created, for example, for a toddler to move using a walker, if necessary.

Toy shelves are low, open, and accessible, and toys and materials are stored in the same places each day, so toddlers can find their favorites confidently. If everything has a place, clearly indicated with pictures, photos, or other markers, it is easier to restore order (see Figure 6-5). Toddlers are encouraged to participate in meaningful responsibilities such as picking up toys if the items are stored in basins or on trays, where toddlers can return them. Some toddler teachers have found that cleanup time goes easier if each child uses a personal bucket to pick up small toys and carry them to the shelves. Nearby sponges help toddlers mop up their own spills.

When toddlers can use materials without adult assistance, they can enjoy their own accomplishment. Open-ended materials that can be used in whatever way the toddler chooses nurture a sense of autonomy. (Read more about specific materials in Chapter 14.)

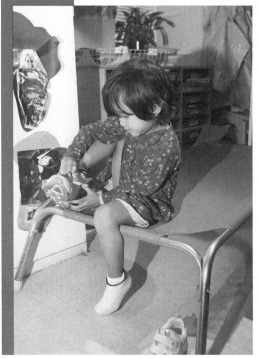

Figure 6-4

Putting on shoes after naptime is one thing this toddler can do for herself.

Figure 6-5
When toys are stored in clear spaces, it is easier for toddlers to find and put back favorite toys.

An environment for autonomy allows toddlers to have some space that is just theirs and does not have to be shared with others at the time. Toddlers love to have small nooks and crannies, hiding places into which they can retreat, especially when the demands of group life get to be too much—"a place to pause for a while, to watch, regroup, decide what she wants to do next" (Zeavin, 1997, p. 74). Removing the doors of low cupboards, throwing a blanket over a table, cutting a door into a large packing box—however it is done, toddlers enjoy a hiding place or time for quiet, solitary play. It is important for toddler caregivers to understand their need for time alone.

When the environment allows for toddler choice, autonomy is encouraged. A variety of materials and activities allows children the freedom to choose according to their interests and needs. Toddlers who do not have every movement controlled by the adult are more likely to accept those times when adults do take the lead.

An environment for autonomy during toddlerhood includes the possibility to be free of most overt restrictions. Toddlers definitely need limits, but they respond less negatively if the limits are built into the environment, nonverbally showing them where they can go and what they can do. Burton White (1995) described the adult's role in providing a safe, interesting environment for toddlers as designer of the child's world. There are several parts to this "design."

Physical safety is an important factor to monitor if the toddler is to explore and move about freely. Verbal prohibitions mean little to a curious toddler, and memory is shaky at best. Toddlers do not have the ability to look ahead to consider consequences or see the whole picture, so they have absolutely no judgment about what is potentially dangerous to them physically. This is borne out by the number of accidental poisonings and accidents that involve toddlers. Thus, if the toddler is to explore without frustrating restrictions, adults need to make the home or center safe for the child by

- covering electrical outlets with safety plugs and removing cords from reach.
- keeping poisonous liquids, soaps, art materials, plants, and medicines in locked cupboards or far beyond toddlers' climbing capacity—which is often far greater than imagined.
- locking drawers and cabinets that contain sharp utensils.

JOURNAL REFLECTION

Encouraging Autonomy

Consider something you learned to do for yourself when you were younger. How did you learn it? Describe the feelings of accomplishment as you continue to think about how to provide for autonomy for toddlers.

 Visit the premium Web site to complete this journal activity online and email it to your professor.

Figure 6-6

Toddlers must always have supervision, inside or out.

- disposing of small objects or toy pieces—such as any item less than $1\frac{1}{4}$ inches, those with detachable parts, marbles, Styrofoam packing materials—that inquisitive toddlers might swallow or choke on.

- removing unsteady pieces of furniture that children could climb on or pull over.

- using gates and locks to prevent access to stairs, doors, and other dangerous areas, such as bathrooms and cooking areas.

Adults must assume that toddlers have no sense about what could harm them, and thus do all the protecting for them. Toddlers must never be left without supervision for any period of time, whether inside or out, whether the child is quiet or active, or even if adults assume the child is asleep. (See Figure 6-6.)

The environment must not only be made safe *for* toddlers, but also safe *from* toddlers. Toddlers' overwhelming curiosity impels them to explore everything, and because they have no concept of property rights, everything in the environment is fair game. Anything adults value and want to keep intact needs to be removed during the toddler period, so the objects do not invite verbal battles of will. (Read more about what Burton White meant about this role of the designer of the child's world later in this chapter in the "Environments for Sensorimotor Exploration" section.)

By making the environment physically safe for toddler activity, adults also make the environment emotionally safe, as a place where autonomy and good feelings about self can flourish rather than be diminished by adult disapproval, prohibition, and frustration with toddler curiosity.

PRACTICAL IMPLICATIONS

Environments That Foster Autonomy

Make sure your environment for autonomy includes

- toddler-size furniture and access to areas that encourage self-help skills.

- an easily recognizable arrangement for toddlers to get their own materials.

- clues for toddlers to participate in responsibilities, such as helping restore order.

- opportunities for toddlers to make some choices.

- hiding places where toddlers may choose to play alone.

- childproof environments, so exploring need not be restricted.

Environment for Separateness

One of the true challenges in caring for toddlers in a group situation is that autonomy, a sense of self, is best nurtured by being able to concentrate on and test out the abilities of the individual. Only after toddlers have formed a basic self-concept are they ready to learn how to care about and interact with peers. Only after they have truly learned what it is to possess things are they able to understand the concept of sharing. When several children are testing out the nature of self at the same time, the adults who care for them are obligated to find ways to encourage separate activity while slowly helping children recognize the rights of others.

An environment that allows for separateness gives toddlers a variety of choices that suit particular moods or activity levels. Toddlers are not all expected to do the same thing at the same time; when toddlers clump, there will inevitably be infringements on one child's space or activity. It is helpful to partition the room off to define areas for many individual explorations, rather than a large, undefined space that encourages toddlers to bunch up too closely to one another. Small work spaces that fit individuals, or at most two or three children, can encourage parallel kinds of play alongside another child, yet still allow space for separateness (see Figure 6-7).

Rethinking the traditional preschool classroom furnishings is a good idea. Rather than big tables that put too many toddlers together, use small, easy-to-stack-and-move plastic Parson-type tables or plastic cubes that allow enough space for one toddler. Individual spaces can also be

Figure 6-7
When there are many choices and play spaces for toddlers, they can be separate from each other.

created by using a rug on the floor that defines the space to play with the animals or a hula hoop where the toddler sits with a stacking toy. Other ideas for creating small play spaces include small plastic wading pools, trays, boxes, large inner tubes, circles of hosing, and changes in the flooring such as a carpet area, a mattress area, a pile of cushions, a sheet of plastic, or small raised platforms. Separation allows toddlers to have a clearer understanding of what is "mine" and what is "yours."

Using every available space for interest or activity helps a classroom teacher "divide and conquer." Window ledges, spaces under tables, corners, in cupboards—all are places in the room that may offer flexibility and variety. Pictures or sensory materials on the ends or backs of shelves make a place for talking or patting; a sheet of paper with crayons attached to the side of the changing table makes a drawing nook; a sheet of Contac paper, sticky side out, taped to the wall, with a basket of collage stuff on the floor beside it provides a work area for a creative toddler. Such mini-centers help increase the number of available spaces for separate play.

One morning a toddler teacher set up the small slide; some foam blocks in the block corner; cars and trucks with a ramp on the floor; some pots and dishes; two baby dolls in a bed; a collection of hats and shoes for toddlers to try on; some fat crayons and paper on one small table; and a basin of beans and cups on another table. The permanent quiet corner in a tent big enough for one was also available, as was a big pillow located near the book shelf. The teacher looked around in delight to see all eight of his toddlers busy, involved, and exploring separately, except for the two who sat together using the crayons on a mural-size paper taped to the table. Planning enough different materials and activities in areas clearly separated by the arrangement of furniture allows for separateness.

When group activities are limited to a short informal singing or story time that children are not absolutely required to sit through, or are limited to coming together for eating, toddlers can slowly experience being part of a group while being free to be separate most of the time.

When duplicates, triplicates, or quadruplicates of toys or equipment are available, toddlers are able to play separately while encouraging interest in similar kinds of play.

PRACTICAL IMPLICATIONS

Environments That Foster Separateness

Make sure a toddler environment for separateness includes

- clearly separated individual areas for play and exploration, created by rethinking traditional interest-center design.
- varieties of materials for separate choices.
- brief periods of group interaction for singing, listening to a story, or eating.
- several similar toys to allow for separate yet parallel play.
- pictures of family, home, and self to encourage toddlers to feel comfortable with separation and feelings of self.
- cozy places for adults and toddlers to cuddle.

A task related to separateness is learning to cope with separation from parents. Moving from dependence to independence involves some scariness and sadness. Toddlers experience a good deal of ambivalence between wanting to be separate and wanting to stay close to the adult as a source of security. In classroom environments, teachers can help by providing a toddler-eye-level display of each child's family photos and other pictures of home for toddler reassurance. Some toddler teachers have found that a plastic picture cube allows toddlers to carry around their own personal collection of family photos—very comforting indeed! Pictures of the toddler facilitate the growing awareness of self; pictures on the cubby, for example, help toddlers identify their own separate space. Personal objects from home, including comfort objects and things that Mom or Dad may leave with the toddler as a reassuring symbol of promised return, may be kept in that private, separate space.

Although toddlers are interested in solitary exploration and independence, they also love moments for cuddling with their loved adults. Toddler environments should provide stuffed chairs, couches, or rocking chairs for such times.

Environment for Movement

An environment for toddlers recognizes that these small people are on the move. They move around the classroom, stopping when something interests them. Often they do not stop long enough to sit and settle in, as do older children. Toddlers much prefer to stand as they manipulate objects on the table, finger paint, or pour sand from one bucket to another. They also squat to explore something interesting in their path, and then they move on. To accommodate this active style, you can streamline the environment for movement, removing chairs from the tables, placing basins with interesting sensory objects about the room to capture attention as the toddler travels. (Wallpaper water troughs or small basins work well for solitary explorers.)

Clear travel patterns winding around furniture and play areas help avoid collisions between other toddlers on the move (see Figure 6-8). When toddlers have special physical needs that require the use of walkers, braces, or wheelchairs, even more attention to travel patterns is necessary, both indoors and outdoors.

When toddlers are on the move, inevitably they will carry toys or equipment from one area to another—lugging objects about with them seems to be a pleasure. Restricting this carrying behavior only leads to frustration for both child and adult. Creating systems to easily restore order when playtime is finished is a better idea. Adding baskets, little wagons, shopping carts, or buckets can support moving things about.

Gross motor practice—movement—needs to be at the heart of curriculum for toddlers, both indoors and out. They will climb, so safe space and equipment must be provided for them to do so. Adults who realize this need and support this movement will nurture feelings of confidence as well. Climbers, step arrangements, low, soft, climbing platforms, ramps, boxes to push and pull, riding and other wheel toys, push and pull toys, tunnels, and wide balance beams all need to have ample space in toddler classroom design (see Figure 6-9).

It is a real mistake to believe that toddler curriculum requires asking these active little ones to sit down or to think that brief periods of outdoor exercise will satisfy their need to move.

Figure 6-8

Toddler classrooms need clear traffic patterns for toddlers constantly on the move.

Figure 6-9

Toddlers love push toys like shopping carts for outdoor play.

In fact, teachers will probably want to include some purchased equipment for large muscle play in their classroom requests. Items such as

- climber/slide combinations.
- low, sturdy riding toys for foot propulsion.
- toys for pushing and pulling.
- tunnels.
- wheelbarrows and wagons.
- Other additions can probably be found, including
- large cardboard cartons to climb into or fill and push.
- inner tubes.
- balls.
- tree trunk sections to climb and pound on.
- old mattresses.
- piles of cushions to climb or jump on.
- things for throwing indoors—Nerf balls, crumpled newspaper balls, and yarn pom-poms.
- things for throwing outdoors—whiffle balls, bean bags and containers to throw them into, such as old laundry baskets.

Toddlers who are on the go wear themselves out long before they are ready to admit it, so an environment that provides an inviting cozy corner where a toddler may flop down on a large beanbag chair or pillow with a stuffed animal will indirectly guide children to alternate active and quiet periods.

Outdoor areas for toddlers provide additional possibilities for movement under the watchful eyes of adult supervisors. The equipment needs to reflect the development of toddlers: gently sloping ramps to provide challenge; broad steps with sturdy low handrails; low climbing structures; sling swings or low-hung tire swings for toddlers to lean over and maneuver themselves through; various elevations; rocking and riding toys that children can propel with their feet; gently graded sliding boards on which toddlers can go down head-first; and open spaces for running and playing ball. Opportunities for fine motor play and sensory exploration are met by providing sand and water in warmer months, along with a lot of things to fill and dump.

Areas designed specifically for toddler abilities and challenges and separated from older children and their equipment will allow for motor practice, as well as the freedom and good feelings of autonomy.

As toddlers become increasingly mobile, the issue of their safety concerns adults. A specific danger to autonomy is conveying the sense that the toddlers need protection, that they are not competent to do things for themselves. Adults must guard against the tendency to overprotect; this is particularly an issue when children with special needs are part of the group. Adults must consider creating a healthy balance between toddlers' needs to explore and their safety. Adults can be more relaxed when they prepare an appropriate toddler environment that allows for a balance of safety and challenge, so that toddlers can take risks without danger of serious injury. Emphasizing practice of large motor skills to promote balance and coordination so children can manage their own environments gives adults something to consider besides simple overprotection.

PRACTICAL IMPLICATIONS

Environments That Foster Movement

Provide an environment for movement by

- streamlining the classroom furnishings and arrangement to provide for movement paths and the toddlers' learning-on-the-move exploration style.
- providing space and equipment within the classroom for gross motor practice.
- incorporating a cozy corner into the classroom arrangement to suggest quiet periods for toddlers.
- designing outdoor play spaces suitable for toddler skills.
- avoiding the tendency to overprotect by creating an environment where toddlers can safely develop physical skills.

ENVIRONMENT FOR SELF-HELP SKILLS

Perhaps one of the best ways to nurture good feelings about self is to encourage toddlers' already strong interest in doing things for themselves. Rather than seeing toddlers' desire to help as something to support, some caregivers impatiently rush through routine care, believing they can complete the tasks more efficiently and quickly. When participation in self-care is considered important in toddler curriculum, however, the environment can support this.

Self-feeding is well within the ability of toddlers, especially when appropriate dishes and utensils are used. Short-handled spoons and forks allow for less spilling between dish and mouth. Broad-based bowls and cups, sometimes with lids, allow toddlers to do the job without adult hands involved.

Bibs or complete cover-ups minimize the need to change clothes afterward (see Figure 6-10). The eating area should be on a washable floor or a floor protected with a sheet of plastic. Enough space needs to be provided between toddlers to allow each child free movement. Seating arrangements that put feet directly on the floor increase toddlers' ability to sit. Still, the inevitable spills and messes need to be responded to in a matter-of-fact way. All these suggestions allow toddlers to enjoy doing it for themselves at mealtime and adults to be able to restore order fairly quickly afterward.

When toddler washcloths are available on hooks near the mirror so that toddlers can help themselves and then watch their own efforts, there is less resistance to cleaning faces and hands. Toddlers undoubtedly need help with dressing, caring for their hair, and brushing their teeth; they can still participate when adults allow both opportunities and time for practice. Toddler participation is fostered when adults start a zipper on the track, for example, for a toddler to finish pulling up. Generations of two-year-olds have learned to put on their jackets "the magic way" after an adult has demonstrated how to place the jacket on the floor and flip it over the head. Recognizing the importance of "doing it myself" for toddler autonomy encourages adults to find ways to allow toddlers to participate in their own care.

Toddlers can more easily learn to dress themselves when their clothing allows them to put them on easily, such as shoes with Velcro and pants with elastic waists.

One of the major self-help tasks of toddlerhood is learning toilet control. Besides learning to recognize physical cues for retention and release, toilet learning involves being able to remove clothing, gain access to the toilet facility, and carry out cleanliness routines following elimination. Toddlers need easily removable clothing with elastic waists; cumbersome belts, snaps, and so on should be avoided. Often caregivers need to talk with families to help them understand how important it is for toddlers to have easy-to-manage clothing that contributes to self-help skills. Some experts feel that using a child-size potty chair is not a good sanitation practice. Instead, it is recommended that using a child-size toilet or pulling a stool up to the larger-size commode (fitted with a smaller seat) allows toddlers to get to the toilet when needed and feel confident in its use, with their feet comfortably on a solid base. Removing doors from the bathroom area allows toddlers quick, independent access to the area, while allowing adults to keep an

VIDEO ACTIVITY

Go to the premium Web site and watch the video clip for Chapter 6 titled **"An Environment to Support Toddler Self-Help and Self-Esteem."** Then consider the following questions:

REFLECTIVE QUESTIONS

1. What does this scenario indicate about toddlers' need to do things for themselves? How does the caregiver support this need?

2. Consider what the caregiver does to help without taking over the task, and how she describes her actions. Notice the toddler's response. Would you evaluate this as helpful to developing self-esteem as well as self-help skills, or not?

Visit the premium Web site to complete these questions online and email them to your professor.

Figure 6-10

Mealtime for toddlers may be easier when cover-ups and cups with lids are used.

eye out for when assistance is needed (see Figure 6-11). (Read more about toilet learning in Chapter 10.)

An important component in the self-help environment is the adult's attitude that, even if messy or inefficient, it is worth it to allow children time to practice developing these abilities. The schedule should allow plenty of time for toddlers to try to do as much as they can; toddlers who are rushed become frustrated, uncooperative, and less able to function.

Environment for Sensorimotor Exploration

Still very much sensorimotor creatures, toddlers learn most by muscle skill mastery and manipulative exploration. When they are allowed free access to a classroom or home that is filled with interesting things to handle, their needs for novelty and intellectual stimulation are met naturally and are

PRACTICAL IMPLICATIONS

Environments That Facilitate Self-Help Skills

To ensure that your environment facilitates the development of toddler self-help skills, consider having the following:

- sturdy, child-size eating utensils and an easily cleaned area.
- stools to help with access to toilets, sinks, and mirrors.
- clothing that is easy for toddlers to manage independently.
- time to allow toddlers to participate as fully as they want or are able.
- a positive, supportive adult attitude.

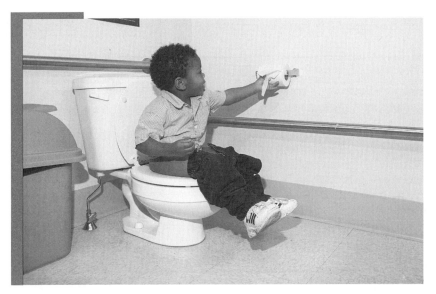

Figure 6-11
A child-size toilet contributes to toddler success in toilet learning.

CULTURAL CONSIDERATIONS

Different Perspectives on Independence

Allowing and encouraging young children to do things for themselves is not necessarily valued in some cultural environments. A family's culture may give greater priority to developing interdependence rather than independence. Consider some of the reasons that adults could think it better to continue to feed, dress, wash, and so on—doing things for toddlers instead of supporting the development of these skills to do it for themselves. What are some of the cultural values that might influence this thinking? Parents with these cultural ideas might actually think teachers are being neglectful if they leave children to attempt tasks for themselves. Sometimes teachers consider that parents are being overprotective or are creating a dependent child, when actually parental goals are to develop mutual dependence (Copple & Bredekamp, 2009). If you were working with families with these practices, consider some of the ways that you could find common ground to benefit the toddler.

propelled by their deep curiosity. As Burton White put it, "The child spends a good deal of the time examining the various qualities of as many objects as he can get to in the course of a day" (1995, p. 171).

Much of the natural learning style at this stage is experimental; that is, toddlers try out a variety of manipulative abilities on each object, evidently trying to see just what its limits are. They might drop and throw objects; strike them against various surfaces; look at, feel, and more importantly mouth each object; stand objects up, then knock them down, and replace them; put objects through openings; pour materials into and out of containers; hoard objects in pockets or containers, and drag them around the room; spin objects; or see if any part of the object can be made to move or come apart. Watch a toddler for a while to see what can be added to this exploratory manipulative repertoire.

Toddlers can become bored when their desire for novelty goes unmet. A bored toddler is naturally going to create his or her own interesting experiment, even if it is to see if the child who screamed when her hair was pulled the other day will scream just as loudly today! Part of designing the child's world is to ensure an interesting, unending supply of things to encounter and explore. Most of these will probably not be commercially bought toys, because the investment in toys means they are kept around far past the toddler's interest level, long after every attribute has been learned and figured out; these toys actually end up contributing to toddler boredom. Commercial toys that have most value for toddler exploration include balls of any size or shape (because they hold endless possibilities for unpredictable results and the delightful repetition of retrieval); push and pull toys; some of the better busy boxes and busy bath toys (for use with water) that allow manipulation of various levers, knobs, latches, and buttons; small wagons or carriages for filling and pulling; and large foam and cardboard blocks for stacking and knocking down, lugging about, and climbing on. Some manipulative materials that intrigue toddlers bent on mastery and repetition and that are uniquely suited for the toddler style of grasp include pegboards with large pegs; stacking rings and nesting cups; snap/zipper/button boards; shape/sorting boxes; simple puzzles with knobs; and bristle blocks and large-size Legos. Most of these are open-ended materials that suit any level of construction ability.

Many simple household objects and throwaways hold as much interest as commercial toys, and are easily replaced when their appeal is gone, such as all sizes of boxes or cartons; plastic

WHAT would you DO when…

"But what about my toddlers who insist on climbing? They climb on chairs, on tables, on the counter. The other day I found one trying to climb up on the toy shelf." If you were this toddler's teacher, what would you do?

Yes, toddlers will, and in fact must, climb. Unless you recognize this and provide safe places to redirect their climbing, you and they will be extremely frustrated. You just can't stop it, so figuring out how you can provide climbing opportunities in your environment is far better. One creative teacher, frustrated by continually having to remove toddlers from the toy shelves, took the toys off the shelves and turned the shelves on their back so toddlers could safely climb. Remember, you don't need a commercially designed climber; alternatives (depending on the toddlers' ages) may be piles of sofa cushions, arrangements of truck inner tubes, wooden boxes and cubes, and stools. You can't lick them, so join them!

bottles and containers of all sizes, sometimes filled with intriguing substances and tightly fastened tops, and sometimes just with tops to try to fit; funnels, tubes, sponges, and strainers for water/sand play; locks, keys, fasteners, switches, hinges, chains, doorknobs, slide bolts, and so on; cigar boxes, metal adhesive bandage containers, castors, and anything else that can be made to move; baskets filled with scraps of intriguing textures, such as fine sandpaper, fur, satin, net dish scrubbers, wigs, burlap, yarn, and so on. Adults must examine everything with an eye for safe exploration and look for creative exploration possibilities everywhere. White suggests giving toddlers a small suitcase or bucket filled with thirty or forty small objects of different sizes and shapes to handle.

Some toddlers with limited ability to grasp may need adaptations to their toys. Adaptations may include handles or built up knobs on puzzles; activity frames to anchor toys, attached to tables or wheelchairs; grasping aids, such as Velcro stick holders or Velcro palm holders and mitts; or playboards that attach toys to firm surfaces.

Natural objects also have great appeal. Large rocks, pine cones, big shells, gourds, large bones, leaves, and other objects will intrigue toddlers (see Figure 6-12). Basins of water, sand, rice, dry oatmeal, grits, beans, macaroni, cornstarch, or ice chips, with spoons, shovels, and varieties of containers allow for endless sensory and manipulative exploration. Of course, all these materials must be used with careful supervision, so that exploring toddlers don't try unsafe experiments with them.

In addition to sensorimotor exploration, older toddlers are moving on to the first stages of symbolic play. Interested in observing the world around them, they imitate the people and actions they have seen. Some simple **props** encourage imitative and beginning pretend play: recognizable household furniture such as a stove or bed; realistic household utensils, such as small brooms and dustpans or vacuum cleaners (see Figure 6-13); realistic-looking baby dolls representing the gender and racial diversity of the classroom and community; simple dress-up items

Figure 6-12

Natural objects, such as leaves and sand, have great appeal for toddlers.

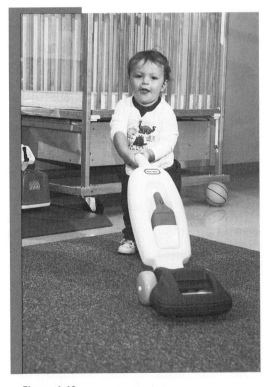

Figure 6-13

Simple and realistic props encourage beginning pretend play.

Figure 6-14
Giant sidewalk chalk is fun for toddlers to use.

easily used by toddlers such as scarves, ties, hats, purses, and shoes; pots and dishes; and empty food containers. Realistic-looking small cars, trucks, or small figures will also stimulate imitative play. We'll talk more about appropriate materials in Chapter 14.

Because of the movement and sensorimotor nature of toddlers, the classroom environment for learning will likely not include the typical furniture and interest centers found in classrooms for older preschoolers. Although it is important for toddlers' sense of order and confidence to separate the room into predictable areas for particular activities, these areas will be simplified beyond the traditional "art center" or "block center" orientation. It may be more useful to think of a place for climbing, a place for pretending, a place for relaxing, a place for toys, a place for interesting textures, and so on. Places for books, messy exploration, and manipulatives are other necessary areas for toddlers. Dodge, Rudick, and Berke (2006) talk about creating an area for creating with art, an area for imitating and pretending, for sand and water, for playing with toys, for playing with blocks, and an area for stories and books. (See Figure 6-14.)

Most of the materials mentioned for sensorimotor and imitative play allow for child-initiated, autonomous play and learning in an environment carefully prepared by an adult. The adult's role as consultant (White, 1995) in learning is discussed in Chapter 14.

It is important to realize that the toddler's learning environment includes the whole world around him or her, not just the toys and materials added to a classroom. Toddlers thrive on watching real people do real things and experiencing the way the world works. A toddler at home gets an opportunity to be in the kitchen while a parent cooks or in the backyard while the parent gardens. Toddlers in centers need the same opportunity to watch the world go by. Access to the view out the window or door may be given by placing a hollow block for a step up to a window or a folding gate to look past out the door. A walk down the hall may help a toddler figure out the noise coming from those machines in the office or watch the delivery man wheeling in the cases of food from his truck.

PRACTICAL IMPLICATIONS

Environments That Foster Learning

Plan an environment for learning that

- provides a changing variety of open-ended materials for sensorimotor exploration.
- provides realistic toys and props for beginning imitative play.
- simplifies the typical preschool environment, while dividing the space into appropriate areas for active learning.
- offers real experiences with people and things to observe.

SCHEDULE AND TRANSITION CONSIDERATIONS

One thing toddlers depend on as they struggle with their own autonomy is a sense of predictability in the world around them—a base for security. Having a dependable pattern for the way the day progresses gives the toddler security and prevents struggles between adults and children because the built-in rhythm becomes habit that is not open to challenge.

The schedule in the toddler room may still allow for wide individual variations in the need for rest. Carlos, a young toddler, still needs a morning nap, whereas a short rest or quiet period may be enough for Antoine and Michelle, now eighteen months old. Toddlers who are giving up their morning nap may need lunch moved up earlier so they can fall asleep in the late morning instead of the traditional after lunch naptime. After two days of trying to keep Jonathan from falling asleep as he sat at the table, his caregiver arranged for lunch to be served at 11:00 a.m. For the sense of predictability, however, the major events of the day still occurred in reliable sequence: playtime, snack time, outdoor play, cleanup for quiet activities before lunch, and so on. The adult may know she has shifted things forward an hour, but the toddler's sense of order has not been affected.

Because all toddlers would likely keep moving until they dropped from exhaustion (if no one stopped them first), providing periods of relative quiet and inactivity is a necessary part of the built-in schedule. After a busy hour outdoors, a teacher puts on a record of nursery rhymes, sits on the floor near the big cushions, and begins to sing. All the toddlers come and sit for a while with her. Later she'll put out some small cars and figures for them to play with while sitting on the carpet (see Figure 6-15).

Providing nonverbal cues about what comes next helps toddlers feel they are in control. When her teacher begins to sing the familiar cleanup song, Jessica recognizes it and importantly tells another toddler, "Cleanup time!" Another caregiver always puts on the same quiet classical music recording to signal the quiet period to lie on pillows while lunch is put on the table. Toddlers are creatures of habit and ritual, and this repetition provides soothing structure to their day. Because of their propensity to resist adult suggestions, nonverbal rituals help toddlers make the transitions.

Transitions also go more smoothly when toddlers are given plenty of warning that change is coming. Toddlers definitely do not like to be interrupted, so they need plenty of preparation to get ready to give up their activity. When their important assistance is invited during transitions, they are more likely to go along with the caregiver. When Dana announces cleanup time, he gives the toddlers something each can do to help. Concentrating on their responsibilities, the toddlers eagerly begin to assist.

As discussed in the section on self-help, toddler eating, dressing, and bathroom routines/hygiene take a lot of time for practicing new skills and allowing toddlers to participate as fully as they can (see Figure 6-16). Toddlers react with frustration to being hurried, so the schedule must allow ample time for satisfactory completion. If caregivers believe this is truly an important part of the day, they will feel less compelled to rush toddlers on to other activities.

PRACTICAL IMPLICATIONS

Creating Schedules for Toddlers

Schedule considerations for toddlers include

- a need for a predictable order to the day that is combined with a need for flexibility to accommodate individual physical needs.

- built-in periods of quieter activities.

- nonverbal clues that help toddlers recognize the schedule.

- ample time for full toddler participation in routines and transitions.

- transition times planned to warn toddlers about change and to minimize the need for them to wait.

Figure 6-15

Periods of relative quiet and inactivity are a necessary part of the toddler's built-in schedule.

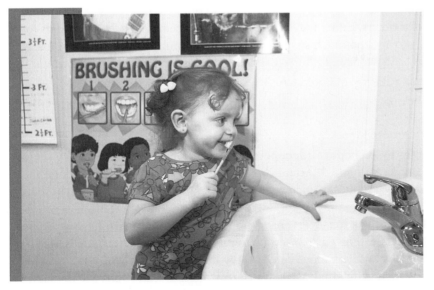

Figure 6-16

It takes time to allow toddlers to participate as fully as they'd like during routines.

When possible, transition times go more smoothly if toddlers are helped to move to a new activity individually, thus minimizing waiting time and allowing interaction with the adult, which encourages cooperation. Toddlers find it nearly impossible to wait, so they should not be put in situations where they have to. If one caregiver is busy changing diapers, another can be singing songs with the children as she sets the table, so there is no empty waiting time for hungry toddlers before lunch. Adult planning ahead will avoid waits during transition times.

THINGS NOT SEEN IN A DEVELOPMENTALLY APPROPRIATE ENVIRONMENT FOR TODDLERS

The environments least helpful for toddlers' development of autonomy are those that are most restrictive. The presence of playpens or small play areas, where it is obvious from the ratio of table and chair space to open space that toddlers are not permitted much movement, are evidence that an environment is not suited to toddler needs. In inappropriate environments, items that should be forbidden from toddler exploration—such as teacher books, paint supplies, or materials to use only with adult supervision—have not been removed and become sources of repeated contention.

A large group area will not be present in an appropriate environment for toddlers. Toddlers are not able to sustain attention for much formal group activity. Moreover, a large area permits too many toddlers to congregate in one area, with likely friction resulting from physical contact that is too close.

Also missing from a developmentally appropriate environment for toddlers is a large concentration of fine motor manipulative materials suited for older preschoolers. Knowing that toddlers are unable to sit for the periods of concentration required and knowing that their finger dexterity lags behind their motor skill, adults omit these items from the environment. Safety is a factor too, as small pieces present a hazard to toddlers who explore all items orally. The natural toddler tendency to dump makes small pieces a frustrating item for caregivers.

A "time out" chair is never found in a toddler environment. Expecting toddlers to think about their behavior is not recognizing their limitations in cognitive development and self-control. Appropriate guidance will help when toddlers' interests conflict with those of others. We will discuss more about appropriate toddler guidance in Chapter 10.

Finally, a rigid schedule is not found in an appropriate toddler environment. When sleepy toddlers are literally kept walking to avoid their falling asleep before the scheduled lunch or naptime, they get the feeling that their needs are not important.

Inappropriate toddler physical environments do not recognize the unique developmental characteristics and needs of toddlers. Either they are structured to resemble the environments for older preschoolers or they provide too much space and too little stimulation for the enormously curious and mobile toddler.

SUMMARY

The physical environment for toddlers provides opportunities to develop autonomy and a sense of self as a separate and unique individual. Attention to physical safety allows toddlers all the freedom they can safely use. Physical arrangements and time to encourage toddler self-help skills contribute to the sense of self. Teachers provide for the toddlers' desire for robust physical movement and practice of skills, as well as for their sensorimotor and imitative learning styles. The best environments allow toddlers within a group setting to move and explore individually.

A predictable schedule helps toddlers move comfortably through the day while allowing for the flexibility demanded by their individual needs for food and rest. Transitions are managed without long waiting times. Within such a positive physical environment, toddlers can develop a positive sense of self.

THINK ABOUT IT ACTIVITIES

1. Examine the room in which you are presently sitting. How would it have to be modified to allow toddlers to explore freely? What ordinary objects would toddlers be able to explore? Which ones would have to be removed? If you had three or four toddlers in this same room, what changes would you make to encourage their freedom of movement?

2. Observe a toddler in any public place—a house of worship, restaurant, bus, or park. What does the toddler do? What draws the toddler's interest? What restrictions are made on the toddler? How does the toddler respond to the restrictions? What modifications could have been made in the environment to improve the situation from the toddler's point of view?

3. Be an observer in a toddler classroom in a childcare center. See what evidence you can find that the environment nurtures (or does not nurture):
   - a sense of autonomy.
   - a sense of separateness.
   - a curriculum of movement.
   - a curriculum of self-help skills.

4. In the toddler classroom in question 3, what materials are available for sensorimotor exploration and for imitative play? Visit the playground at the center. What modifications have been made for toddler outdoor play? Are there any children with physical disabilities present? If so, what modifications do you see in the physical environment and materials? Discuss your observations with a small group of classmates who have also visited toddler classrooms and playgrounds.

5. If you could make changes in the physical environment you visited, what would they be, and why? Explain how your changes would improve the environment for toddlers. Share these ideas with students who have visited other centers.

QUESTIONS TO ASSESS LEARNING OF CHAPTER OBJECTIVES

1. What are several developmental needs of toddlers that must be considered when planning the physical environment?

2. For each of the developmental needs you listed in your answer to question 1, describe several things that can be done in the environment to meet each need.

3. List the appropriate materials to include in the toddler learning environment.

4. Discuss several considerations in planning appropriate schedules and transitions for toddlers.

5. Identify several components that would be omitted from a developmentally appropriate toddler physical environment.

APPLY YOUR KNOWLEDGE QUESTIONS

1. Your coworker feels it is far easier to pick up after toddlers and streamline their washing and dressing routines by doing it herself. Describe several of the points you would plan to make as you prepare to have a conversation with her about this subject.

2. You are planning a parent meeting for the families in your toddler group. What important toddler developmental tasks will you plan to discuss, and how will you get their help in continuing some of your ideas in their homes?

HELPFUL WEB SITES

http://www.headstartinfo.org	On the Web site for Head Start information, search for an article on infant/toddler transitions.
http://www.communityplaythings.com	On the Web site for Environment materials, use the interactive model for planning toddler environments.
http://www.eichild.com	On the Web site for Community Playthings, click on Resources to find sample activity areas, room planning, and an archive of articles on infants and toddlers.

Please visit the premium Web site for Developmentally Appropriate Practice, *4th edition, to access more chapter web links, additional book chapters, suggestions for further reading and study, interactive quizzes, video exercises, online journal activities, flashcards, and much more! Go to www.cengage.com/login to register your access code.*

Developmentally Appropriate Physical Environments: For Preschoolers

By around age three, the toddler evolves into the young child. If fortunate enough to have had positive life experiences in infancy and toddlerhood, preschoolers approach the world confidently and with a genuine desire to become part of it, to learn how it works and how they can function within it. Now that they have a rudimentary self-concept, they are ready to learn to interact with others; it is amazing to see three-year-olds eager to conform, after the resistance and "me-ness" of toddlerhood. Although still egocentric, preschoolers move toward experiences with peers. Learning to play with other children is not a skill that can be taught by words alone; through day-to-day real experiences, young children discover firsthand how to modify their behavior to become more acceptable in childhood play groups. The issues of friendship preoccupy preschoolers; the greatest threat of all is the warning, "You're not my friend."

Preschoolers are talkers, excited to convey to others their perspective on experiences. Talk is powerful, and preschoolers slowly move toward self-control as they increase their understanding of reasons for behavior and alternate ways of behaving. Still gaining mastery over their large motor skills, they are challenged to also refine fine motor skills. And above all, play dominates the life and learning of children aged three through five years.

LEARNING OBJECTIVES

After completing this chapter, students should be able to

- describe the nature of children ages three through five, and what they do.
- identify needs of **preschoolers** to be supported by the physical environment.
- discuss components of an environment for initiative.
- discuss components of an environment for play, including outdoors.
- discuss components of an environment for self-control.
- identify characteristics of good schedules for preschoolers.
- discuss components of good transitions.
- describe issues regarding kindergartens today.
- identify components not found in developmentally appropriate physical environments for preschoolers.

WHAT ARE PRESCHOOLERS LIKE?

By the time they have lived three or four years, children have experienced such widely varying environments and experiences that the differences between individual children have become ever greater. It becomes difficult to generalize with much certainty about children; for every statement made, you can find several examples of children who do not fit the characterization. Nevertheless, certain truths seem evident for most three-, four-, and five-year-olds—at least much of the time.

The number of changes that occur during the much longer period of the early childhood years also becomes evident. Three-year-olds play, communicate, and understand the world very differently than do four-year-olds, who are qualitatively different from most five-year-olds. This stage encompasses a longer period than the first two stages discussed, so it is understandable that development creates differences over a period of three years or so.

Note that this chapter discusses children three through five years, following the model of the NAEYC publication on developmentally appropriate practice (Copple & Bredekamp, 2009). The age group is referred to as "preschoolers," although this word does not connote its importance as a stage of development in itself, not simply as a period before real learning begins. "Although most 5-year-olds are developmentally more like preschoolers than like older children, kindergartens are usually housed institutionally with elementary schools" (Tomlinson, 2009, p. 188). Because many prekindergarten and kindergarten programs are located within school systems, they are influenced by decisions that are being made for the instruction and evaluation of older children. School systems often lump four- and five-year-olds together with older children in their planning and offerings. Instead, the real characteristics and needs of the children must be recognized if their programs are to match their developmental status. Following the model of the most recent DAP position statement (Copple & Bredekamp, 2009), special mention is made of kindergarten children, who are not quite preschoolers and not quite primary-age children.

With these cautions in mind, let's consider how to describe preschoolers. Preschoolers are physically active creatures. By the end of toddlerhood, they have mastered most of the **large motor** physical abilities they will have. However, they have not yet achieved the **coordination** and **agility** that will be evident by the end of the preschool period. Coordination improves with each year. For example, two-year-olds can run and throw balls, but the quality of these movements is markedly different from the smooth skill of the five-year-old. The need for activity to increase coordination keeps preschoolers on the move, while lengthening attention spans allow them to stick with activities without the ceaseless movement of toddlers.

Preschoolers gradually depend less on attention and constant assistance from adults, although they are still bound to them by affection and a desire to please and be like them. This affectionate bond motivates preschoolers to adopt adult standards of appropriate or inappropriate behaviors. Developing a **conscience** and becoming more self-controlled, however, is a long, slow process only begun during the preschool years. While they are learning to become members of a group, children in these years struggle with egocentric perspectives.

As preschoolers move from dependence on adults, other children become increasingly important to them. Children of this age are searching for friends and learning lessons about how one behaves as a friend.

The nonstop buzz of talk that is part of good early childhood classrooms is a clear indication of the preoccupation of threes, fours, and fives with speech, in the form of monologues, dual monologues (when it looks like children are talking together, but in reality they are talking about what each wants to talk about), questions, comments, arguments, stories, and play discussion. Talk is the stuff of preschool learning about the world, self, and others. There are, therefore, special challenges for children who enter classrooms speaking a home language different from that of the classroom.

What truly distinguishes preschoolers from younger children, however, is their ability to enter into increasingly complex forms of play. Preschoolers imagine and pretend, with wonderful fluency and fantasy, and gradually in cooperation with other children. Their play is focused, serious, and involves the whole child, nurturing physical, cognitive, social, emotional, and language development.

Play enables children to create understandings of their world from their own experiences and exerts a strong influence on all aspects of their growth and development. Children become empowered in play to do things for themselves, to feel in control, to test and practice their skills, and to affirm confidence in themselves. Play is important for children's developing sense of competence (Isenberg & Jalongo, 2000, p. 32).

Preschool children play. They play alone, with others, inside, outside, and whenever they can (see Figure 7-1).

The tragedy is that factors in the contemporary world of education have led to the devaluing of play for preschool children. In many kindergartens and even prekindergarten programs, there is far more emphasis on narrow curriculum goals of skill development and far less attention to designing environments that support rich and productive play.

What are preschoolers like? They are beautifully confident creatures who have tested themselves out in toddlerhood and are now filled with enthusiasm to explore the world around them and the people in it. Hungry to learn how to live in this world, their awareness is moving from a strictly egocentric (that is, centered only on self) perspective to an outward perspective. They are like adventuring explorers who have an insatiable need to know and do more in the larger world around them.

Developmentally Appropriate

This place looks lived-in
There were children here
I can tell by the markings
They are fresh and clear.
Walls covered in artifacts
And tables with books
The shelves somewhat misarranged
Like jackets on hooks.
The neatness is almost fragile
In its cluttered array
Anticipating the first student
Who'll return this day.
To this place of opportunities
Where a teacher seems to know
That there is much to be learned
As children continue to grow.
So she's harnessed their power
And captured the intensity of their play
By structuring intriguing possibilities
That they will meet along the way.
This place does look lived-in
There were excited children here
I can tell by the learned markings
They are fresh, intense, and clear.
The markings of hard work and delighted struggle,
The powerful learning comes through.
This is a place for children
Where no child needs to be dragged to.

Figure 7-1

A developmentally appropriate classroom for preschoolers is designed to meet their needs and interests. Permission for use granted by the author, Sigmund A. Boloz.

WHAT DO PRESCHOOLERS DO?

If you have recently been in a room full of three-, four-, or five-year-old children, images probably crowd your mind when you read this question: what *don't* they do?

They hold up paintings for adults to view after working painstakingly on them for fifteen minutes, busily talking with a friend about what they are creating on paper, and arguing about their ideas. They yell, they giggle, and they talk back to their friends and to adults. They build, they knock down, and they argue over whose building was the tallest. In their discussion, they show their diverse experiences that create their understanding of the world. "This is the Empire State Building; it's the biggest in the world." "No, it's not anymore. My dad showed me a picture of one that is bigger." They tease, they tattle, and they exclude others from playing in housekeeping. They beg to help, they find reasons why they shouldn't have to clean up, and they brag about their achievements. They defy adult restrictions, they smilingly agree to share, and they demand turns. They wobble across the room in high heels, they work thirty-five-piece puzzles, and they tell long, complex stories about their vacation trip to Grandma's. They insist on an extra kiss good-bye, they leave their dad without a backward glance, and they tell you everything their family did on the weekend. They lead a game of Simon Says without really "getting it," they insist it's their turn in Candyland, and they invent a word to describe the bubbles floating in the wind: a "Bubblefly." They hit back at another child, they look guilty when they get caught, and they go off to a corner to play for a while. They beg you to read the story again, they print their name carefully on their art paper (often with letters backwards), and they demand that you watch them print. They find their own place at the table, they try determinedly to use the scissors again, and they show you proudly that they can button all the little buttons. They shriek with laughter at a good book, they ask question after question, and they insist on being the baby when they play house. They hang upside down, they run down the hall, and they tell you that you can (or can't) come to their birthday party.

You can add to this list. What they do and can do goes on and on. They are competent and confident about what their legs, fingers, and minds can do, although these skills are still developing. Those preschoolers who are limited physically or mentally—by special needs or learning a new language—find their own ways of impacting the world with their initiative. They burst with ideas, energy, and enthusiasm. Their excitement overflows on a daily basis, and often they get out of bounds and test the limits. The difference is, however, that they now know there are limits, understand why there are limits, and sometimes even conform to the limits.

WHAT DO PRESCHOOLERS NEED?

Considering what preschoolers do is the first step in thinking about what preschoolers need for their development to be nurtured. They need an environment that can support all that active energy and challenge with experiences that introduce ever more of the world. A reminder of what some theorists have said about these childhood years before formal school is also helpful. The psychosocial issue defined by Erikson for the preschool years is forming a **sense of initiative**, as opposed to a sense of guilt. Initiative refers to a sense of self as a doer—competent, full of ideas, energy, and enthusiasm to explore the larger world. With the energy and ability of these years, children learn to initiate their own activities, enjoy their accomplishments, and become purposeful. If they are not allowed to follow their own initiative, they feel guilty for attempting to become independent and competent. The curious preschooler needs a sense that he or she can do, can make, and has good ideas (see Figure 7-2).

Piaget helps explain something of the young child's thinking and learning processes in his description of preoperational thought. As we will discuss more fully in Chapter 15, this cognitive perspective is mental activity that is not yet logical but is more intuitive, based on limited perceptions; concrete, egocentric in being able to understand only one's own perspective; and limited

Figure 7-2

A sense of initiative comes from preschoolers feeling that they have good ideas.

in ability to focus and generalize logically. Thus, learning experiences for preschoolers need to match these characteristics. Piaget defined play as the appropriate medium for learning by pre-operational children.

Vygotsky helps explain how others in the environment—both peers and adults—support learning for young children. In the context of social interaction, preschool children refine old ideas and add new ones. Scaffolding by more experienced playmates or helpful adults helps children achieve a level of action, thought, or problem solving that would not be possible without the assistance of the other. Three- through five-year-olds learn through such interaction with others.

Developmental tasks for this period include becoming **socialized** to **norms** of behavior, forming a sense of identity within the social context, beginning to form a conscience and develop self-control, and coming to understand one's position in the world. Continuing competency with language is critical to all these tasks. Adults must plan developmentally appropriate environments that encourage this learning, appropriate to the development of all preschoolers.

Environments encourage different kinds of experiences, depending on the physical arrangements of space and materials, of time, and of varying degrees of access to other people. Specific program goals may be affected by the behind-the-scenes decisions adults make that influence behavior. For example, in a classroom where cooperation and problem-solving skills are a major goal, a teacher might decide to deliberately put out limited numbers of materials to stimulate dialogue and interaction about turn taking and discussion among the children. In a program that emphasizes nurturing emerging literacy skills, a teacher might place many picture and word labels for common items at children's eye level. In programs that include many children with special needs, adaptations to the environment and to activities will be made (individualized plans and therapists help children develop optimally). The educational goals of any program will be reflected in the physical environment.

In addition, as teachers develop individual goals for individual children in the classroom, they use their environmental decisions to work toward these goals. A teacher who wants to promote lunch-table conversation in a quiet child or a child learning English might place that child beside a more talkative one at the table. Another teacher, realizing that a particular child needs special help with screening out distractions, might create several small, protected work spaces stocked with materials of particular interest to the child and encourage him to choose a friend to explore the area. The scissors and magazines are provided to promote fine muscle skills for the two children who need particular practice in this area, and two pairs of scissors with built-up handles are provided for children whose disabilities require adaptations.

Thus, the physical environment may encourage goals both for the developmental stage and for individuals, as well as specific program goals. In addition to creating an environment to

Figure 7-3

Dimensions of an environment. Elizabeth Prescott, 1994.

Prescott's Dimensions of an Environment

1. Softness/Hardness
2. Open/Closed
3. Simple/Complex
4. Intrusion/Seclusion
5. High Mobility/Low Mobility
6. Risk/Safety
7. Large Group/Individual

promote specific goals, physical environments may also work to solve or prevent typical problem behaviors associated with individual or age-span development. Adults have much to consider as they plan physical environments for preschoolers.

Dimensions of Environments

Elizabeth Prescott states that children's memories of childcare settings seem to be stored "primarily as tactile impressions" (Prescott, 1994, p. 9). This suggests the importance of paying attention to the physical surroundings in early childhood programs. In her classic discussion on physical environments, Prescott describes seven components—dimensions, to use her word—to consider in physical environments, as shown in Figure 7-3. As adults plan environments, they should consider where on the continuum their particular environment falls, and whether modifications might benefit children.

Prescott advocates a balance of the dimensions for an optimum environment to encourage the kinds of play that enhance development.

Objects that are soft, malleable, and responsive to touch create softness in an environment and provide a variety of tactile sensory stimulation (finger paints, play dough/clay, couches, pillows, rugs, grass, water, sand, dirt, animals that can be held, swings, laps). Hardness (tiled floors, wooden furniture, asphalt playgrounds) gives a more unyielding environmental message, one that encourages children to shape themselves to the environment, which is inevitably tiring and stressful for both children and adults. Hardness might also refer to harshness of artificial light, especially the fluorescent lighting used in so many childcare centers. Alternative forms of lighting may contribute to a softer, more homelike atmosphere. (A balance means the environment is both responsive and resistant.)

Openness in an environment is perceived by the presence of open equipment and materials—those that can be used in a variety of ways, with no one correct way of using them and no arbitrary stopping point. Sand, blocks, collage, and other art materials are all open (see Figure 7-4). Activity formats may also be open, based primarily on children choosing from a selection of activities planned and prepared by the teacher. The issue of openness is related to choices.

Closed materials can be used in only one way to come out right; puzzles and various Montessori materials are closed. Although such materials are useful in building a sense of competence, they may also become boring once mastered, or be frustrating if children are unable yet to master them. Program styles that use mostly teacher-directed group and individual activities are called closed, as are experiences that have a clear ending. Although there are advantages to both open and closed materials and experiences, Prescott

Figure 7-4

A board to stretch rubber bands on is an example of an open material.

Figure 7-5

Play dough becomes supercomplex with the addition of rollers and other tools.

believes open materials and experiences are especially important for preschool children to experience success and a sense of initiative.

As children interact with materials, it becomes obvious that some materials have greater holding power than others. The simplest play unit has only one aspect and one obvious use with nothing to improvise, for example, a swing or tricycle. More complex units combine two different kinds of materials; supercomplex units combine three different kinds of materials. Examples of complexity include adding shovels to a sand pile or rolling pins to lumps of play dough (see Figure 7-5); supercomplex units would add water or molds to the sand pile or decorative elements to the play dough and rollers. A supercomplex dramatic play area adds cookbooks, pads and paper for grocery lists, a shopping cart, food containers and boxes, and brown paper shopping bags to the usual household furnishings and utensils. Simplest arrangements usually do not hold attention as long as complex arrangements, which increase the number of things that can be done in an area or activity and the kinds of interaction that can take place.

An environment introduces the dimensions of intrusion and seclusion as it defines boundaries and provides opportunities for privacy and control over personal territory. Defining areas allows children to work without becoming easily distracted. Every classroom will have areas that must be shared by the group of children, but it is also important to provide areas where children may withdraw to be alone or apart from the total group, and to safeguard their personal property and interests. Small, quiet areas allow children to play with just another child, rather than a larger group. Desirable intrusion also comes when the classroom makes connections with the outside world, such as by windows or by visitors to the classroom (Gonzalez-Mena, 2008).

Mobility is the dimension of the environment that concerns the freedom children have to move around. With high mobility, space and equipment are used to encourage gross motor, active movement, such as running, climbing, and tricycle riding. Traffic patterns are created

---

▶❙❙ **VIDEO ACTIVITY**

Go to the premium Web site and watch the video clip for Chapter 7 titled "Preschool Environments for Play." Then consider the following questions:

REFLECTIVE QUESTIONS

1. What do you notice about this block area related to physical arrangements of the environment that supports good block play? Be sure you consider components such as space, protection, materials, and so on.

2. What potential do you see provided to support complex play in the dramatic play environment? Can you suggest any improvements to this environment?

 Visit the premium Web site to complete these questions online and email them to your professor.

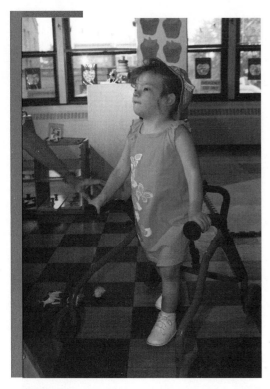

Figure 7-6

Wide pathways help all children move comfortably, including those using walkers.

within the classroom for all children to move comfortably, including those who need walkers or wheelchairs (see Figure 7-6). With low mobility, children are required to sit still for activities such as story time, working puzzles, and other fine motor experiences. Too little mobility creates problems for active preschool children. A balanced environment provides space and materials for both.

Curtis and Carter (2003) refer to the needs for both risk and safety within the environment. Although children need to be protected from obvious dangers and taught safe practices, such as fire precautions and using utensils carefully, the environment must not overlook important opportunities for risk taking, such as experimenting with bodies in space: swinging, climbing, jumping off. There is a difference between teaching children how to do interesting and challenging things with care and forbidding any kind of risk or innovation because it is unsafe.

Again, with large versus small groups, balance is needed in the social structure within the classroom, without an overbalance or omission of either dimension. A large-group experience is listening to a story at group time; small group work may involve illustrating the story; an individual experience is being read to one on one. All these kinds of experiences are necessary and valuable.

The key to using these dimensions in considering the physical environment is not an either/or approach. Most appropriate environments include selections from both ends of the spectrum. The important task is to evaluate the environment for appropriate balances of experiences, matching the developmental levels and needs of individuals and programs. Attention to the dimensions is useful for problem solving. Prescott (1994) points out, for example, that common problems such as children not sharing, not becoming involved, or coming unglued at the end of the morning can be dealt with environmentally.

As children and adults enter a classroom, the arrangements of furniture and materials convey messages about expected activities and ways of behaving. For example, if most of the classroom space is filled with tables and chairs, it is evident that the teacher expects the children to spend most of their time seated doing quiet activities, implying a good deal of teacher direction. If, on the other hand, a number of different learning centers are arranged throughout the room, it seems likely that the children will be more actively involved with materials of their own choosing. The way physical space is arranged implies an underlying philosophy that will have a definite impact on what children can and will do in learning activities.

JOURNAL REFLECTION

Your Favorite Place

In your mind, visit the place where you feel most comfortable. Consider which of Prescott's elements are present in this favorite place. What can you do to bring these aspects into your classroom space?

Visit the premium Web site to complete this journal activity online and email it to your professor.

Environment for Initiative

Because developing a sense of initiative is an important task of the preschool years, an environment that encourages making choices and plans enhances children's active participation as decision makers. Much of their time will be spent in active play of their choosing, rather than in teacher-directed lessons.

Teachers can help children choose a particular play area by making the available choices clear. Each activity needs to be set up in its own clearly defined zone, separated from other activities by space, furniture, and other distinct dividers. This means the room is divided into many small play areas, appearing as a number of obvious choices, not one large area (see Figure 7-7). Arrangement of shelves, cubbies, tables, carpet pieces, masking tape markers, and other creative

Figure 7-7

Children see clear choices in a learning environment arranged with clearly defined centers and carefully labeled shelves.

kinds of dividers (for example, hanging shoe bags; lattice or pegboards with feet; rows of low-hanging plants; walls of tree stumps; crates, cartons, or ice cream containers wired together; hanging curtains, sheets, or bamboo blinds) act to create visual boundaries, while still allowing for adult supervision. (See Greenman, 2005, and Curtis & Carter, 2003, for more suggestions on dividers.) Teachers planning environments to include children with special mobility needs must modify the open floor space in centers to allow room for maneuvering wheelchairs or walkers. Traffic patterns between interest centers must be widened. Tables may need adjustments to fit wheelchairs underneath. (See very specific ideas in Gould & Sullivan, 1998.)

Teachers decide what interest centers are appropriate for their particular group. Typical centers may include a creative art area, a block area, a house area for pretend play, a book or library area, a music and movement area, a manipulative or table toys area, a science or discovery area, a gross motor area, a writing area, a woodworking area, a water/sand area, and a computer area. An extensive discussion of the rationale for arranging the environment in learning centers is included in Chapter 15. Centers are labeled so children can "read" the choices. Labels are at child eye level and include both a picture representation and print in English and the children's home languages. When the label includes a sample of the object, such as a bristle block or marker, it is helpful for children with visual impairments or those learning English as a second language (Dodge, Colker, & Heroman, 2002).

To further encourage child choice, teachers should make sure that materials are stored near the location where they will be used, displayed on low, open shelves where children can reach what they need. When classrooms include children with limited mobility, duplicate materials may be stored in several areas of the classroom, placing materials at two different heights. Storing materials at table level and floor level reduces the need for bending or overreaching, which can cause children to lose their balance. Containers are open or clear for visibility or distinctly marked with labels children can interpret, or feel in the case of children with visual limitation. The arrangement of the materials on shelves highlights the separate choices by surrounding each material with space. Teachers create picture or shape markers on shelves to make it obvious where materials should be

Good storage gives children opportunities to:

- feel a sense of control and competence.
- learn about the relations between things.
- develop more complex play and creations.
- take responsibility.
- respect materials and their own work.
- feel the environment is their own.

(Adapted from Greenman, 2005)

WHAT would you DO when…

A young teacher argues with a more experienced preschool teacher. The young teacher insists that they should have computers available as a choice for the young children in their classroom. The other teacher believes that children need to be involved in active play, not sitting looking at a computer screen. In fact, she believes that young children's use of computers is potentially harmful and unnecessary. "Technology is changing so fast, children might as well wait until they are older to use computers." The younger teacher argues that children will not be prepared for their future if they do not begin learning about technology in the early years. What about this difference of opinion about appropriate learning experiences? What would you do in this situation?

Although some early childhood educators still take the position that computers have no place in the early childhood classroom, this seems to ignore or misinterpret most of the research on technology in early education (Clements & Sarama, 2003). Computers often serve as catalysts for positive social interaction and emotional growth. Good computer software encourages children to talk about their work and engage in more advanced cognitive types of play than they do in other centers. Computers can help creativity blossom. Computer work can support new kinds of collaborative work and can increase social interaction between children with disabilities and their typically developing peers.

Wise use of computers in the early childhood classroom requires careful planning. High-quality software must be chosen. Journals from organizations such as the National Council of Teachers of Mathematics (http://www.nctm.org) and the International Society for Technology in Education (http://www.iste.org) publish reviews that rate quality.

The classroom setting should have two child seats in front of the computer and one at the side for adults, and computers placed close to each other to facilitate interaction and sharing of ideas among children. Use of computers is offered as a choice, not as a scheduled computer lab time. And, as with everything else, respect children's choices to participate in this activity or not, and use computers in the classroom only when they contribute to children's development. In addition, total time in front of television or computer screens should be limited.

PRACTICAL IMPLICATIONS

What Message Does Your Classroom Convey?

The Creative Curriculum for Preschool Children (Dodge, Colker, & Heroman, 2002) suggests that teachers evaluate their environments for the messages they intend to convey. These messages include the following:

- "This is a good place to be."
- "You belong here."
- "This is a place you can trust."
- "There are places where you can be by yourself when you want to."
- "You can do many things on your own here."
- "This is a safe place to explore and try out your ideas."

Consider what aspects of the environment convey each of these messages.

returned to. As materials are readily available in predictable places, children learn to take responsibility for their environment and develop a sense of initiative as learners.

> We also found that organized storage seems to produce more complex and longer lasting play. It seems that storage can help children to visualize relations and to plan future actions. Thus organized storage would appear to support initiative and imagination. (Prescott, 1994, p. 48)

The environment subtly supports children's idea development. Centers that might logically be combined in children's play are positioned near one another; for example, the book center and the writing center are side by side, as are the house play and block areas. Having an area where children may display personal work conveys value for their ideas. This area may be a clothesline on which art may be pinned near their name tag; a designated shelf space for completed items, such as a puzzle or manipulative creation to show parents; an area for works in progress and projects to be protected over the time period of creation; and a poster for each child's use on the backs of shelves. Most of the classroom decor is created and designed by children and displayed at children's eye level. Children with initiative will want to see that they can impact their environment, that it is not purely the creation of adults. Many teachers feel that a key question in the preschool classroom is, Do the children feel a sense of ownership of the environment?

Figure 7-8
These necklace hooks are methods to help children make conscious choices for their activity.

Open-ended materials support and encourage creativity, decision making, and original thinking in all interest areas. Initiative and self-esteem as a learner are encouraged when many of the materials offered have no right or wrong uses and are process oriented rather than product oriented. Open-ended materials provide for the variation in individual abilities because children may use such materials as they are able. We'll talk more about specific open-ended materials later.

Initiative is encouraged when children are able to decide which activity to participate in and when to terminate it. To encourage preschoolers' thoughtful choices about self-selected activities, some teachers find it helpful to institute systems for "signing up" for activities. Such systems may include planning or choice boards with hooks or library pockets for adding a child's name tag to indicate a choice to work in the art area, for example. Simpler choice methods might include the use of color-coded clothespins, wrist bands, or necklaces hanging by an interest center to indicate whether space is available to play there; putting on and removing the name tag or necklace helps children make conscious decisions, as well as indirectly control the number of children that can productively play in an area (see Figure 7-8). Part of the High/Scope structure in preschool classrooms is based on a plan-do-review sequence, with children supported to think through their plans for the work period first, then carry out their plan, and later summarize their activities and learnings with an adult. See more about the High/Scope philosophy and curriculum in Chapter 4.

An environment designed to maximize independence encourages feelings of initiative. Teachers use placement and **pictograph** sequences as clues to guide preschoolers through the steps of using an area without direct teacher instruction. For example, in the art area, easily managed cover-ups hang nearby. A stack of fresh easel paper is right beside the easel. There are easily managed clips to fasten the paper to the easel and a drying line with clothespins right behind it. The pictograph for the children in charge of cleaning the area after its use shows hanging painting to dry, washing hands, and returning the smock to its hook. An important sense of accomplishment results when children can move independently through their chosen activities.

PRACTICAL IMPLICATIONS

Environments That Foster Initiative

Be sure to provide preschoolers with an environment that develops initiative by

- encouraging child choice of play opportunities in clearly defined and labeled activity centers.

- displaying materials that children may get for themselves.

- allowing children opportunities to display their work in the classroom.

- offering open-ended materials that encourage creativity and use at varying levels of individual ability.

- establishing systems that help children make conscious choices for play.

- providing opportunities for independence and responsible participation in the classroom.

Figure 7-9

Classroom responsibilities help children develop a sense of community.

Figure 7-10

Children develop creativity as they learn to express themselves using many media.

Initiative is encouraged when children are enabled to play meaningful and responsible roles in their classrooms. Preschool children thrive on doing important, real work. Teachers can capitalize on this desire by offering regular opportunities to contribute to classroom routines and maintenance. Taking care of the classroom is a shared responsibility. A helper or job chart allows children to rotate responsibilities and to recognize the importance of participating in the tasks needed for successful communal living, such as watering plants or feeding fish (see Figure 7-9). Thus children begin to form an idea of themselves and others as contributing group members.

Environment for Creativity

Creative development is intrinsically linked with children's cognitive development, with their physical development, with their expressive language development, and with their development of self. As such, it is a part of the overall environment that nurtures in children a sense of freedom to express their thoughts and feelings, a sense of aesthetic beauty and appreciation, and both materials and time for creative activity (see Figure 7-10). Creative development is part of the environment that, rather than providing models for children that inhibit their thinking and intimidate their efforts, encourages each child's process as well as unique products.

While teachers plan separate areas for creative art and music, they should be mindful that creativity will appear in every area of the classroom in children's play—in the block area with unique and thoughtful constructions, in the discovery/science area as they explore and formulate questions, in the writing area as they find new ways to express themselves. It is not really possible to designate components for creativity that are distinct from other elements to enhance the quality of play, but teachers must be continually mindful of factors that support creativity. Some of these factors for creativity include the following:

- attitudes of acceptance and interest conveyed to children, as they make individual choices for play and expression, and genuine appreciation for their creative work

- open-ended materials readily accessible to children in all areas of the room, displayed beautifully and logically

- experiences that allow children to enjoy many forms of creative expression

- attention to aesthetics and beauty, in the way the classroom is arranged and designed, in the way materials are stored, and in the way children's work is displayed

- an emphasis on the beauty of the natural world and natural materials, rather than creating a classroom that looks as though it has been ordered from a catalog

- information for families about the development of creativity in children

Environment for Learning Through Play

A teacher's belief in and support of learning through play is conveyed by the careful preparation of the physical environment. In a classroom where teachers believe that children learn best through active involvement with materials, other children, and adults, the physical design of the classroom will offer well-designed places to play and materials to play with. The placement of centers and the design of the classroom contribute to meaningful play experiences for children.

Most teachers do not have the luxury of designing a preschool classroom; some architect or builder has already done so. (For those fortunate enough to be involved in preliminary designs, the issues and questions raised in Greenman [2005], Curtis & Carter [2003], and Ceppi & Zeni [1998] are excellent.) When teachers are assigned to a particular classroom, however, they can begin the process of visualizing the learning environment, forgetting what they know about how the room has been used, and starting fresh. The room arrangement, as Greenman says, grows out of "fixed space, inhabitants, program goals and philosophy, and resources" (Greenman, 2005, p. 217). Setting up the traditional classroom that emphasizes teacher instruction and individual study is relatively easy; but in the developmentally appropriate classroom for three- through five-year-olds emphasizing "active, individualized learning, autonomy, and social interchange" (Greenman, 2005, p. 217), teachers are challenged to create a dynamic, inviting atmosphere. When programs last for a full day, the quality of living experiences that include eating, sleeping, privacy, and adult ease and comfort must also be examined.

When deciding how to set up the room, Greenman suggests beginning with the fixed space: doors, windows, sinks, bathrooms, and electrical outlets. Think about the flow patterns of air and light, of people and supplies. List every activity that will take place in the room, big and small, from play to snack time and from dressing for outdoor play to teacher-parent conversations. Think about special physical accommodations needed by children with special needs. Decide what activity centers will be part of the classroom learning and which areas will be used for more than one purpose—eating and table toys or art, for example.

The placement of centers determines how well children can become involved in meaningful play. Teachers should separate messy and neat activities, noisy and quiet ones, spread-out activities and contained activities, and table activities and those that happen on the floor or in other nooks. See Figure 7-11 for a preliminary placement sketch.

Check out your environment:

Is the setting a place of beauty?

Does the setting promote strong families?

Does the environment encourage community?

Are there places for listening and conversation?

Does the environment challenge children to explore and learn?

Is the environment a great place for the staff to learn and work?

—Ideas adapted from *Places for Childhood in the Twenty-First Century: A Conceptual Framework* by Jim Greenman, 2005.

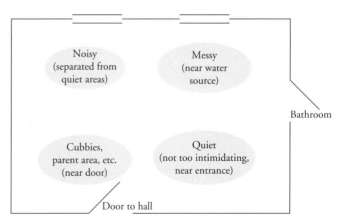

Figure 7-11

Preliminary placement sketch.

CULTURAL CONSIDERATIONS

"Messy" Activities

Often teachers are faced with family members who complain about the messy activities children are involved in, such as getting clothing wet or dirty, finding paint on pants, and so on. Consider some of the cultural reasons that parents might dislike these activities and the messiness associated with them. Now, frame the reasons that teachers might give for including messy activities and materials in their classrooms. Can you find common ground, so that parents' feelings can be respected, and children can still participate in exploration and creative play? See Janet Gonzalez-Mena's comments about reconciling cultural differences in the article "Bridging Cultural Differences" in Copple & Bredekamp (2009).

As the designing continues, teachers need to consider pathways throughout the room, recognizing that straight, unbroken pathways encourage running, as do large, empty spaces that spend most of the day waiting for something, like group time, to happen. Pathways recognize the need to prevent intrusion on play; some activity centers, such as books and blocks, need to be protected from through traffic to cubbies and bathrooms, for instance. The dividers for defining areas discussed earlier in the chapter are also important for screening out distraction for children trying to concentrate on their own play, yet they must allow teachers to supervise the entire room from every location. See Figure 7-12 for a sample diagram of a preschool classroom. Notice the grouping of noisy areas for play (dramatic play, blocks, gross motor center). Notice also that the areas most likely to need frequent access to water are strategically placed, and appropriate floor coverings are considered. There is no dead space. Areas where children write or draw or care for plants are positioned near natural light. Children's entrance into the classroom is inviting without overwhelming them with too many choices and too much activity. The Environmental Rating Scale (Harms & Clifford, 1998) is a useful tool for teachers wanting to analyze and improve the effectiveness of their learning environments.

Figure 7-12

This drawing shows the interest areas, with wide pathways and accessibility for all. From *The Creative Curriculum for Preschool* (p. 63), by D. T. Dodge, L. J. Colker, and C. Heroman (2002). Washington, DC: Teaching Strategies, Inc. Illustration by Jennifer Barrett O'Connell. Copyright © 2002 by Teaching Strategies, Inc. Reprinted with permission.

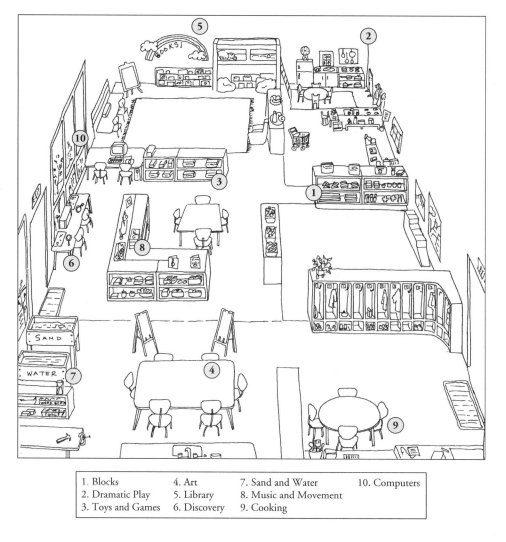

1. Blocks	4. Art	7. Sand and Water	10. Computers
2. Dramatic Play	5. Library	8. Music and Movement	
3. Toys and Games	6. Discovery	9. Cooking	

As preschool children with special needs are included in the classroom setting, teachers will consciously modify arrangements so that children of all abilities are able to play. Wide pathways and entrances to interest centers, architectural modifications, and materials organized for accessibility and avoiding visual or physical clutter will improve the classroom for all children.

It is important for teachers to analyze their tentative classroom sketches for areas carefully balanced to provide learning opportunities for all domains (gross motor, fine motor, self-help, language, cognitive, emotional, and social experiences) and for a variety of curriculum subject areas (art, reading, construction, manipulation, science, math, music, dramatic play, movement). It is equally important for teachers not to be drawn into thinking that learning is as clearly divided as the interest center areas suggest. Boundaries are defined so children can think of their play opportunities and have meaningful play protected and sustained. Boundaries are not meant to suggest that only a particular kind of learning goes on in that one center, or that learning is one dimensional. In other words, creativity and pretend play go on all over the room, and the art area involves creative expression, scientific discovery, manipulative skills, cognitive concepts and planning, and a good deal of socialization and language content areas. Nor are boundaries meant to be inflexible ("The blocks need to stay in the block area," when a child takes one to housekeeping to use as a camera). One of the recommendations of emerging literacy approaches is to incorporate books and writing materials into every activity center, encouraging children to look at books about science and to write signs on their block constructions, for instance; such practices may help teachers move to less compartmentalization philosophically, while still keeping the room organized to encourage productive play. The room arrangement is not meant to be permanent; as children's interests and play behavior expand, the need for new or expanded centers may emerge.

Arrangement into separate interest centers is not the only consideration for physical environments to encourage play. The thoughtful selection and display of materials invite children's use. The scales and a box of rocks on a science table suggest an activity; the notepad and pencil arranged beside the telephone in the house corner suggest a beginning plot line. Today, the play dough table, with a dish of bright beads, invites sculpting, when last week the same table had a set of tiny dishes to suggest producing a tea party with the play dough. Careful arrangement of materials helps children begin their play without needing teachers to tell them what "we are going to do today."

Play is often interactive. The physical environment supports social encounters by providing spaces designed for small groups, varying from two to five or six children. For children who are beginning social interaction, activity areas for just two support early social skills, with parallel kinds of play and chances for face-to-face conversation. A small table and two chairs may be the setting for play dough, writing, table toys, and for a good talk with a friend. Other centers may accommodate larger numbers of children, each with their own place. Groups of four or five work well for preschoolers. Teachers are careful to provide cues about how many children may use the area at one time; four chairs surround the art table, and three smocks hang by the water table. Block builders find three large masking tape squares on the carpet to indicate building space for three, and two pads at the writing table limit participation to two children (see Figure 7-13).

PRACTICAL IMPLICATIONS

Welcoming Children with Special Needs

Teachers can transform their rooms so that they meet the needs of children with diverse abilities by

- including pictures of people with disabilities in the classroom displays. Show people with different disabilities participating in work, playing instruments, taking part in recreational activities, and so on.

- including dolls with "disabilities" in the dramatic play area. Items such as eyeglasses, hearing aids, and leg braces added to the dolls will lead to questions and opportunities for direct answers.

- inviting adults with disabilities to visit. They may come to read stories, play musical instruments, or work with wood.

- placing all supplies in appealing and accessible arrangements.

- allowing all children to try special tools, such as extra-wide paintbrushes or double-holed scissors, and then point out why the child with a disability gets first choice for these tools during activity times.

- using multisensory materials for activities. Ideas include adding fabrics of varying textures in dramatic play, and fragrant and tactile ingredients in cooking and science projects.

- encouraging independence for all.

Figure 7-13

When the teacher places four pieces of paper on the art table, this is a cue that four children may work there.

Figure 7-14

Individual carpets used in Montessori classrooms define play spaces for children.

The systems that support conscious choice also limit the numbers in areas to facilitate social play and interaction.

All play is not social, however; there are times when children need and want to play alone, to read a book, or to concentrate on some challenging task. A room should have some small play spaces and an atmosphere that allows children to withdraw or define a space of separateness for play (Curtis & Carter, 2005). If a child chooses to build alone, for example, he should be able to put a tape strip across the carpet to indicate his personal area for building. The individual carpets used in Montessori classrooms allow for such individual involvement (see Figure 7-14).

Involvement in play takes time. Teachers should support the environment for play by providing blocks of time long enough for play to become established and embellished, without unnecessary intrusion. We'll talk more about this later in the chapter.

Adults are also an important part of the environment for play. Play that is not facilitated often goes undeveloped. The adult's role as facilitator will be discussed fully in Chapter 15. Perhaps most importantly, adults who believe in the way play functions to develop the whole child in the preschool years can indicate their support and approval in ways that benefit young children. Adult attitudes about the importance of play will permeate the atmosphere.

Outdoor Play

Outdoor experiences are considered a vital component of the environment for play. Developmentally appropriate preschool programs value play and learning experiences for children both indoors and out, and consider both equally essential (DeBord, Hestenes, Moore, Cosco, & McGinnis, 2002). Outdoor play is not thought of as just a time for children (and adults) to blow off steam, a sort of recess before going back indoors to get down to the serious business of learning. Rather, qualitatively different kinds of play experiences can be had outdoors, different in scale, scope, and decibels.

Children need opportunities for physical challenge and risk on playgrounds. They need places for swinging, sliding and rolling, climbing and jumping, running, throwing, kicking, riding, and transporting. For all these active pursuits, they need space, suitable equipment, and adults who supervise with encouragement and without excessive caution and restriction.

In addition to the physical challenges, outdoor environments for play must also support more contemplative pursuits: making discoveries in the environment by digging, planting, exploring with water and sand, finding a quiet spot to sit, or maybe reading a book. Creative opportunities exist with outdoor art and construction materials, and props for dramatic play—the curriculum simply goes outdoors. Many programs emphasize nature by designing playgrounds that foster children's appreciation of the natural environment, and planning activities such as gardening and bird-watching.

Planning the materials and activity areas for outdoor play is essential. See Figure 7-15 for an appropriate outdoor design for three- through five-year-olds.

Part of the planning is providing for safety, so that children may be permitted to play freely. Poor playground design and equipment selection, and lack of maintenance contribute to most playground accidents. Adequate pathways and space around equipment are essential to avoid crowding. Appropriate installation of fixed equipment and continual monitoring

Figure 7-15
Appropriate outdoor design
for three- to five-year-olds.

1. Garden	6. Storage house	8. Balance beam	11. Paved bike trail
2. Water table	with utensils, costumes,	9. Play house	12. Climbing structure
3. Shade trees	pots, pans, and other	10. Large outdoor	13. Ball court
4. Art easels	loose parts	building materials,	
5. Sandpit	7. Tent	crates, tires, etc.	

are important adult responsibilities (see Figure 7-16), as is teaching children responsibility for safety.

Children with special needs must be actively supported with both environmental adaptations and specific teacher strategies to be involved in outdoor play. Teachers help when they reflect on the quality and quantity of multisensory activities available to children, and when they promote independence for all children. Adaptations may range from extremely simple to complex and must be specific to individual needs. For a complete list of possible adaptations, see Flynn and Kieff (2002).

Environment for Self-Control

Preschoolers who are learning to control their own behavior benefit when the environment provides a sense of stability, order, and predictability.

The arrangement of **interest centers** to convey clear guidelines about the activity expected in each area, places to use materials, and numbers of children in each

PRACTICAL IMPLICATIONS

Environments That Foster Play

Environments for play are provided when adults

- arrange the classroom to suggest that active play is the main vehicle for learning.

- design the classroom with interest centers arranged to protect play and screen out distractions.

- arrange materials to invite active participation.

- plan area size to facilitate small-group interactive play, as well as spaces for secluded play.

- provide long time blocks for play.

- function as facilitators of play.

- plan outdoor play areas and materials as carefully as indoor play areas.

Figure 7-16

A checklist for daily monitoring of the outdoor environment. Adapted from L. Marotz, M. Z. Cross, and J. M. Rush (2005), *Health, Safety, and Nutrition for the Young Child,* sixth Edition, Clifton Park, NY: Thomson Delmar Learning.

Safety Outdoors

Outdoor safety includes:

- **area enclosed by fence and locked gate**
- **assurance that all plantings are nonpoisonous**
- **a well-drained play area**
- **protection from sun for hot days**
- **soft ground cover under climbing and sliding equipment, at least one-foot deep**
- **play equipment that is inspected daily for missing or broken parts, splinters, sharp edges, rust, flaking paint, frayed ropes**
- **play area that is inspected daily for trash, sharp debris, animal waste**
- **large pieces of equipment anchored firmly in the ground and sturdily constructed**
- **railings protect from falls on high equipment (slides and climbers)**
- **equipment spaced for safe movement between pieces and adequate supervision**
- **swings that are separate from riding or running areas**
- **groundskeeping and maintenance chemicals and tools that are locked away from play area**
- **equipment that is appropriate and stimulating for children's developmental abilities (infant, toddler, preschool, schoolage)**

Figure 7-17

A chart reminds children of the classroom rules.

area provides **indirect guidance** to make appropriate behavior become habitual. As children know what is defined as appropriate behavior, they are more able to behave in acceptable ways without constant direct instruction or control by adults.

Other teacher decisions that indirectly influence behavior include the kind of materials available for use, including materials that are neither too simple (boring) nor too difficult (frustrating); the quantities of materials available for use to avoid squabbles or boredom; the predictability and balance of the time schedule to yield a sense of security; and the presence and availability of adults to support learning. Behind-the-scenes management of such factors can prevent problems that often lead to classroom conflict: overcrowding, disputes over rights to use materials, distraction, boredom, overstimulation and too much noise, too little supervision, and fatigue. Attention to the physical environment contributes to a positive social atmosphere.

Posters or signs that pictorially remind children of classroom behavior expectations are useful reminders for self-control. The chart on the wall behind the teacher at group time reminds: "We listen; we keep our hands to ourselves; we sit on our bottoms." (See Figure 7-17.) Other clues for self-control may be added to the classroom. A child's name on the carpet helps him find his place for story time in a place the teacher knows he is least distracted, away from a talkative friend and close to the teacher. Outlines of two feet on the floor remind a child where to stand while waiting his turn to brush teeth, and thus prevent crowding and water play in the bathroom. Preschoolers want to behave well, and such clues are helpful reminders.

Within a group situation, the demanding rules of social interaction may be exhausting for young children. Adults need to provide **private spaces** where children can retreat when they feel a little tired, unhappy, or out of control. A small, quiet, soft area should be available, and its purpose clearly explained to children, so they learn that withdrawal is approved and may even be necessary as children learn to control their feelings. Tentlike spaces may be created with arrangements of sheets or blankets, crates and barrels, or spaces behind or under furniture. Private spaces do not take much room and are important components of an environment for self-control.

Preschoolers are helped to respect the rules of social interaction as they perceive that they personally are treated with respect. The physical environment conveys respect for each individual child by recognizing his or her need for a sense of belonging. Each child needs a personal space in the classroom, a place to keep items of personal value such as a toy from home, a note a child wrote for Mom, a rock found on the playground. This space, whether provided by a cubby or a small basket, needs to be labeled and accessible for the child, and declared off-limits to everyone else. Respect for individuals is also conveyed by the presence in the classroom of materials with which children personally identify. Pictures, books, dolls, housekeeping props, and clothing need to represent the ethnic and cultural diversity of the families of the classroom, including the various family structures children live in and the neighborhoods and work experiences they recognize. Chapter 11 includes a more detailed discussion of classroom materials that encourage self-acceptance and development of **antibiased** attitudes toward differences.

An environment for self-control may also offer materials and activities that can be used as outlets for the physical release of emotion. Classrooms that have punching bags, pounding boards, tearing corners, closets designated for yelling, or outdoor space for stomping give tangible evidence that it is acceptable to do something physically to express strong feelings. When a child comes to the teacher to say, "I need to tear some papers to stuff in the pillow case," it means this child has learned to control impulses to hurt when angry and to divert that strong energy into socially acceptable outlets.

Classrooms that promote peace and negotiation provide "a peace place" in classrooms: a quiet out-of-the-way place where children can choose to go to solve their problems (Lamm, Grouix, Hansen, Patton, & Slaton, 2006), as children are encouraged to actively discuss problems and look for mutual solutions. After teaching, modeling, and reminders from adults, children learn to move to their own negotiation when the chairs and attitude are part of the physical environment for self-control. Note: this is not a time-out place, but a place where children can go to negotiate problems with peers.

PRACTICAL IMPLICATIONS

Environments That Foster Self-Control

Environments for self-control are available when adults

- plan physical environments that prevent problems caused by boredom, frustration, overcrowding, and fatigue.
- plan physical environments that clearly convey positive expectations for appropriate behavior.
- use posters and other visual clues to remind children of appropriate classroom behavior.
- provide private spaces for withdrawal.
- use classroom materials that demonstrate respect for individual rights and differences.
- offer materials for vigorous use as outlets for expressing emotion.
- model opportunities for children to meet for problem solving.

SCHEDULES FOR PRESCHOOLERS

In an environment in which initiative and self-control are important goals and active play is the dominant activity, a good schedule gives children large blocks of uninterrupted time and the security of knowing what comes next. It is important that schedules not work against these goals. When schedules function not as predictable sequences, but as rigid timetables, they intrude and disrupt, ignoring children's needs. (See Figure 7-18.)

How is a schedule for preschoolers designed for developmental appropriateness? Every program must adapt its own schedule based on program goals, required sharing of space and facilities, length of the program day, and staffing patterns. Whatever the variations, certain features will be found in schedules that meet children's needs.

Figure 7-18

A poster with pictures reminds children of their predictable schedule.

1. A good schedule is predictable. No matter what event comes first, second, and third, these events always follow each other. Children function with confidence when they recognize a pattern to the structure of each day. They do not have to guess what their next action will be. An understood order and rhythm to the day is comforting to children and helpful to adults (see Figure 7-19).

2. A good schedule is flexible. At first glance, this principle might seem to argue directly with the preceding one. But the two components can be held simultaneously by understanding **time blocks** (Hildebrand & Hearron, 2008). Rather than a strict by-the-clock system for deciding when an activity is over, teachers gauge children's involvement or restlessness to

Figure 7-19

A sample preschool schedule shows flexible time blocks.

Activities	Flexibility
Arrival and Selection of Child-Chosen Activities Indoors	*Shortened when:* • **Children are not involved in play** • **Field trips/visitors planned for later** *Lengthened when:* • **Children are deeply involved in play** • **Bad weather**
Teacher-Guided Activities Indoors such as clean-up, snacks, group time	*Shortened when:* • **Children are unusually active** • **More time needed for play in or out** *Lengthened when:* • **Special visitors/activities** • **Issues to be discussed**
Child-Selected Choices Outdoors	*Shortened when:* • **Weather is inclement (gross motor activity indoors is substituted)** • **Other time blocks have been lengthened** *Lengthened when:* • **Time is needed to go to particular outdoor environment** • **Projects on playground bring extra interest**

decide whether to shorten or lengthen a time block. Thinking about blocks of time, rather than specific points on the clock, allows teachers to give children the time needed to get deeply involved in their play, without the interruptions necessary to keep on a strict timetable.

On Monday, Felicia's preschool class seemed unusually active. A number of the children looked tired and wandered from activity to activity during free choice period. She decided to give the signal for picking up toys after about forty-five minutes, and they then moved to the carpeted group area. She played some quiet music for them to move like butterflies for a while and then shared two quiet stories. After snack time, they moved outdoors. Felicia added art materials and water play to the playground activities. The beautiful spring weather allowed the children to enjoy more than an hour of outdoor play. The next day, such complex block building and dramatic play interaction were going on that she extended free play to about seventy-five minutes, making group time and outdoor play a little shorter.

Flexible time blocks also permit special events or adaptation for weather, without disturbing children's sense of the predictable sequence.

Wednesday's group time included a visit from B.J.'s dad, who plays guitar in a band and enjoys singing with the children. The event extended group time to almost forty minutes; interest was high. On Thursday, Felicia planned a spring walk through the neighborhood to talk to a couple of gardeners. She knew that the walk would take quite a bit of time, so after a song with the group, she used a few minutes to explain what they would do on their walk and remind the children of safety rules. After five minutes, they were ready to leave.

3. A good schedule balances **child-initiated** time blocks with those that are **teacher-initiated**. For children to become truly involved in their play, they need unbroken periods when they may choose and carry out their plans. Teachers direct children's activities during the briefer periods when they need children to follow directions, such as cleanup time, or to participate in a teacher-initiated large group activity, such as mealtime, small group instruction, or story time. Much of the day in a developmentally appropriate program for preschoolers is spent in blocks of child-initiated free choice activity, indoors and outdoors.

4. A good schedule balances active and quiet, and indoor and outdoor, learning experiences. Children need a variety of learning experiences, so alternating active and quiet experiences in the schedule prevents excessive fatigue, boredom, and loss of control. Activities that require concentration, such as large group time, should be scheduled early in the day before children become too fatigued. Shorter, quieting group stories or music may be scheduled to help children relax before lunch after a period of active outdoor play.

5. A good schedule provides a reasonable pace for children's participation. Nothing diminishes self-confidence more than to be rushed through the day. The general feeling of being hurried destroys a positive learning environment, and filling the day with times of "hurry up to wait" leads to boredom and social friction. A helpful schedule leaves enough time for children to complete tasks in a satisfying way and allows for individual differences in ways that avoid empty waiting times. For example, children who have already finished with bathroom routines may gather for finger plays on the carpet with one of the teachers while waiting for the rest to finish. The younger the children, the more time they need for self-help transitions; more time is also needed for children with special needs.

6. A good schedule recognizes developmental differences in attention span. Although most two-year-olds can benefit from only very brief large group experiences and need considerable choice and variety during free-play periods to keep them occupied, preschoolers generally have a longer attention span. Many three-year-olds are able to sustain interest in self-initiated activities for forty-five minutes or longer, and fours and fives may remain productively involved for longer than that. Group times for three-year-olds, or at the beginning of the year, might last ten to fifteen minutes, extending to twenty minutes or so for older or more experienced preschoolers.

WHAT would you DO when...

"The worst time of the day for me is getting the children ready to go out to the playground. My director insists that children walk quietly in straight lines, and it's agony for all of us to try to get them to wait for the line to be straight and quiet. What do I do?" What would you do, if this were your situation?

Most likely the director is concerned that the children be safe while walking down the hall. For a long time we've confused our desire for order and control with a perception that the only way to achieve it is for children to adopt semimilitary procedures of lining up and achieving perfect control under the adult's direction. Although it is certainly desirable to keep children from mad dashes that would likely lead to someone getting hurt, there are more developmentally appropriate ways to keep children together, focused on safe behavior, and quiet in a way that respects the rights of others in the building. Some teachers who want to avoid the lines they feel are inappropriate for young children try more creative approaches, capitalizing on preschoolers' imagination and willingness for group participation.

They might play a quiet follow-the-leader down the hall, first patting their head, then crouching down, then raising their hands in the air, then waving first one hand, then the other. By the time they have reached this point, they have likely arrived at the door to the playground, without once having to remind the children to walk, so intent were they on the game.

Suggest that the children pretend to be a quiet thing, often creating a "mental bridge" from an earlier experience. After reading a story about the first snowfall, Deidre suggested they each be a quiet snowflake going down the hall: "Careful! Don't let anyone touch you or you'll melt!" Annie suggested her four-year-olds look for something red to tell her about when they got outside. Having a mental focus helps children maintain their control.

Use a "magic rope." A rope with a bead knotted at strategic intervals along the rope helps keep children together, yet spaced a bit to avoid crowding. A teacher whose director felt very strongly about "lines" found this to be a less directive way of keeping the children together.

The other reason some adults insist that preschool children learn to walk in lines is that they will need this skill for later schooling. This is truly inappropriate, emphasizing what will happen in children's future more than their current well-being. Spending early childhood preparing for future stages of growth ignores the understanding that childhood is a meaningful time for development in its own right. A child who has developed self-confidence through respectful, appropriate responses and expectations is better able to conform to later guidelines than one who has failed to fit adults' inappropriate expectations and is thus less self-confident.

Transitions

The times in the schedule that require the most thoughtful adult planning are the transitions, the times when children move from one activity to the next. These may include arriving in the classroom, moving from large group meeting to centers, cleaning up after center time to get ready for snack, going outdoors to play, and the like. To prevent chaos, children need adult attention and guidance during these times. Some children may have a particularly difficult time with transitions due to disabilities, or limited communication, social-emotional, or social skills (Hemmeter, Ostrosky, Artman, & Kinder, 2008). Unfortunately, in too many transitions, much of the adult attention focuses on unpleasant interaction meant to keep children under control. It is important to recognize that many of these problems are related to developmentally inappropriate practices, such as having children wait for everyone to line up quietly before they walk out to the playground or trying to control their behavior with nothing to occupy their attention.

Developmentally appropriate transitions for preschoolers incorporate the following principles:

- Advance notice is given that change will be forthcoming. Interrupting children abruptly and arbitrarily from their play suggests the unimportance of that play and encourages resistance. Before it is time to clean up, the teacher moves to each interest area, announcing, "It's five minutes until cleanup time. Think about finishing up what you are doing."

- Familiar cues, such as cleanup songs, notes played on a piano, or a particular music tape, emphasize the repetition of a familiar pattern, encouraging children to notice and behave according to habitual experience. This also ensures getting children's attention. Clues may be environmental, such as darkening the room before naptime. Following consistent routines helps children know what to expect from day to day.

- Understanding what to do next is improved when teachers are clear and specific in their directions. "Time to put toys back on their shelves" helps children more than "Time to clean up." (Clean up what? Hands, tables, toys—what?) Adults establish eye contact or touch children gently to be sure they have their attention. Teachers use names to be sure children realize the instructions are meant for them personally. It is also age-appropriate for teachers to limit the number of instructions given at one time to avoid confusion. After most of the toys are picked up, teachers may come back to remind children to use the bathroom before snack.

- Using an adult to begin the next activity avoids empty waiting time. While one teacher is encouraging those still picking up toys and keeping an eye on the bathroom, another is having a conversation or leading a finger play with those already seated for snack. While one adult accompanies the children who already have their coats on to the playground, the other assists those who need more help and time with zippers. When the next activity doesn't have to wait until everyone is ready, it provides incentive to children to move on and does not penalize children who are either quicker or slower paced in their abilities. Teachers develop a repertoire of transition songs or games children can enjoy as they prepare to change activities.

- When there is only one adult in the classroom, as in many pre-K classrooms and family childcare home settings, teachers plan activities that children can do by themselves when they have finished the tasks of a transition, such as read a book before circle time begins while other children are using the bathroom, or playing a tape to sing along with as children wait at the table. Keeping children busy and focused is the key to successful transitions.

- Chaos is minimized when everyone doesn't move at once and when children move purposefully because there is no doubt where they are going. For example, when group time is over, the teacher sings a song that dismisses three children at a time to go to their cots and the books waiting for them there.

- Giving children classroom responsibilities and specific tasks, or opportunities to assist peers, provides purposeful experiences during transition times, as well as freeing teachers to give encouragement or instruction to children who need more assistance during transition. Sarah has put her shoes on after naptime and is ready to go outdoors to play. As she waits, she helps Maria and Keisha with theirs (see Figure 7-20).

- As teachers recognize the importance of planning to manage transitions smoothly, they may also ask themselves whether any transitions can be eliminated. By reviewing the schedule, teachers might be able to omit any unnecessary transitions. It is always useful to count the number of times that children are being asked to transition during the day. Also, as teachers discover that individual children still have problems during transitions that are well planned and managed, they may need to consider particular attention and responses to help children cope with the transitions (Hemmeter, Ostrosky, Artman, & Kinder, 2008).

PRACTICAL IMPLICATIONS

Developmentally Appropriate Schedules

Developmentally appropriate preschool schedules incorporate

- predictability.
- flexible time blocks.
- balance of child-initiated and teacher-directed activity.
- balance of active/quiet and indoor/outdoor experiences.
- reasonable pace of participation.
- recognition of developmental differences in attention span.

Well-planned transitions support smooth changes throughout the day by

- giving advance notice.
- providing familiar cues.
- giving clear, simple, personal directions.
- having adults beginning the next activity or providing an activity children can do when finished.
- minimizing chaos by not moving whole groups at one time.
- giving children responsibility during transitions.

Figure 7-20

Children can help each other during transition times.

THE KINDERGARTEN DILEMMA

Time was when **kindergarten** was a five-year-old's gentle introduction into the world of school. "As originally conceived, kindergarten was a preparation year, designed principally to support children's social and emotional adjustment to group learning" (Tomlinson, 2009, p. 187). Children spent a half-day playing with other children, using blocks, dress-ups, art materials, and games to learn how to get along with others. Brief group gatherings exposed children to stories and songs and developed their ability to focus attention and follow directions. Most kindergartens today, however, offer markedly different experiences, with practices that narrow the curriculum to developing abilities linked to a tightly sequenced list of skills in separate content areas. Kindergarten children in most communities are more likely to be found spending much of their time using paper and pencil to work on learning rather abstract material, probably in full-day programs. "More than a preparatory year—about 95 percent of kindergarten age children in America are enrolled in some type of kindergarten program—kindergarten is now generally considered the first year of school" (Tomlinson, 2009, p. 187). Many kindergarten teachers report being asked to remove blocks and housekeeping corners from their classrooms. "Choice" time is limited to rotating among a series of tasks designed to focus on literacy and numeracy, with no opportunities for creative, child-initiated play. The radical change in focus of the curriculum in kindergarten makes it difficult to distinguish the kindergarten curriculum from the curriculum and methods used with older children.

Why have kindergarten experiences changed so drastically for most children? One reason is that the research about the capabilities of young children has been misrepresented and misunderstood. Understanding about the importance of the early years in brain development has led many to believe it appropriate to introduce academic content and methods earlier and earlier. The popular view is that today's children are smarter, having been raised with the stimulation of television and preschools. Parents are often demanding that their children be "taught" more, expecting them to learn to read in kindergarten. Classroom teachers continue to report that they have little or no part in decisions that determine curriculum and instructional methodology. Instead, decisions are made by administrators who are influenced by the public demand for more stringent educational standards and by the increased reliance on standardized testing for decision making. Additional pressure comes from primary teachers who face requirements for higher pupil achievement and argue that the kindergarten program should do more.

A number of questionable practices have appeared, resulting from the trend to demand more of kindergarten children. These include an increase in the inappropriate use of **screening** and

readiness tests; discouraging or denying entrance; developing segregated **transitional classes**; and an increased use of **retention**. See discussions of some of these alternatives in Marshall (2003) and Taylor (2003). As kindergarten curricula have changed, a growing number of states have raised the age for kindergarten eligibility, offering further evidence of the changed expectations for kindergarten education and kindergarten children.

Two predominant considerations underlie these changed practices. One idea is that schools will achieve homogeneity in instructional groupings. Despite evidence that children learn better in mixed-ability groupings and have more positive social-emotional responses, many school systems are doing what they can to create instructional groupings in which teaching does not have to be adapted to the needs of the individual. A second idea is the well-meaning notion that children need to be protected from inappropriately high demands on their intellectual abilities and emotional maturity. Schools are asking that children be made ready for the demands of the program, inappropriate as those demands may be, instead of tailoring programs to respond to the strengths and needs of individual children. (See Figure 7-21.)

Responding to the current issues in kindergarten curricula and instruction, the National Association of Early Childhood Specialists in State Departments of Education (NAECS/SDE) has issued a statement of principles (2001). The statement recommends the following:

- Kindergarten teachers and administrators guard the integrity of effective, developmentally appropriate programs for young children, not yielding to pressure for acceleration of narrowly

Ready for Kindergarten

I don't understand the focus,
Somehow it seems misplaced and wrong,
As when the melody being played
Does not match the song.
I thought schools were for children,
Not children for schools,
Perhaps we have dropped the pieces
Confused the rules.
Wasn't kindergarten envisioned
As a supportive place to learn,
Not a sweathouse for young children
With intricate competencies to learn?
Look at the advice given to parents,
At what young children need to know,
So that children will be ready for kindergarten,
Ready before they go.
Assessment-taking tips
The eventual entrance test.
Of physical adeptness, social skills
And academic readiness.
I don't understand the focus,
Somehow it seems misplaced and wrong,
As when the melody being played
Does not match the song.
A sweathouse for young children
The notion seems absurdly wild
But I don't hear many voices asking,
Is kindergarten ready for your child?

Figure 7-21

What does it mean to be "ready for kindergarten"? Used with permission of the author, Sigmund. A. Boloz. Copyrighted.

focused skill-based curricula or enforcement of academic standards determined without regard for what is known about young children's development and learning.

- Children should be enrolled in kindergarten based on their legal right to enter, rather than pressuring families to delay the entrance of their young children.

- Kindergarten teachers and administrators should be informed regarding assessment strategies and techniques, and they should be involved responsibly in their use.

- Retention should be rejected as a viable option for young children.

- Tests used at kindergarten entrance should be valid, reliable, and helpful in initial planning and information sharing with families, rather than used as gatekeeping devices.

- All children should be welcomed into heterogeneous kindergarten settings.

In the third edition of *Developmentally Appropriate Practice in Early Childhood Programs* (2009), for the first time there is a section on practice for kindergartners, illustrating the idea that the kindergarten year is "worthy of special focus in its own right, not merely as the last year of preschool or the first of elementary school" (Copple & Bredekamp, 2009, xi). The NAEYC has reminded early childhood practitioners that, although kindergarten marks an important transition from preschool to the primary grades, getting kindergarteners ready for elementary school does not mean substituting academics for playtime, forcing children to master first-grade skills, or relying on standardized tests to evaluate children's success. The Association for Childhood Education International has a similar position paper, titled "The Child-Centered Kindergarten" (Moyer, 2001).

The dilemma continues, however. In a recent *Young Children* article, one kindergarten teacher noted that kindergarten children had no recess, because so much of their time was spent on literacy activities that there was no time left for snack and recess (DeVault, 2003).

But ideally, kindergarten experiences promote positive approaches to learning and prepare children for more stringent academic expectations and activities of the primary grades. Recommended practices for developmentally appropriate kindergartens include:

- indoor and outdoor physical activity areas with adequate space for free and safe movement

- opportunities for daily high-quality movement instruction with lots of time for practice, in addition to outdoor play time

- appropriate equipment for physical development

- a warm, responsive emotional climate in the classroom with enjoyable daily routines

- teacher monitoring of children's interactions in the classroom, and coaching appropriate skills and attitudes for problem solving

- space, materials, and encouragement for dramatic play, cooperative work, and problem-solving opportunities, conversations, and group discussions (see Figure 7-22).

- inviting, well-organized classrooms with opportunities to make choices

- high-quality curriculum and teaching strategies that include asking thought-provoking questions, encouraging children to use various representational methods, and designing experiences that encourage children to interact and collaborate with peers.

- language- and literacy-rich environments, with opportunities to learn and practice listening and speaking skills

- differentiated instruction that allows children at different levels to gain new knowledge and skills within the same activity or lesson.

(Read more about this in Tomlinson, 2009.)

Achieving such goals presents enormous challenges for teachers torn between administrative and parental demands and knowledge of what is good for young children. All developmentally appropriate kindergartens have one thing in common: the focus is on the development of the child as a whole. Although a rising tide of academic expectations is occurring in kindergartens

Figure 7-22

Appropriate kindergarten curriculum lays foundations for literacy and math learning.

nationwide, those concerned with developmentally appropriate kindergarten experiences for young children can

- acknowledge what is right about the new expectations, recognizing the importance of the end goals, even though other teaching strategies to meet the goals may be preferable.

- promote appropriate practices by demonstrating to others what good literacy instruction looks like in kindergarten and documenting children's progress.

- stay informed about current methodologies and policies.

- become advocates and join with others, while choosing issues wisely (DeVault, 2003).

THINGS NOT SEEN IN A DEVELOPMENTALLY APPROPRIATE PHYSICAL ENVIRONMENT FOR PRESCHOOLERS

In a developmentally appropriate physical environment for preschoolers, you won't find

- **physical arrangements that suggest mostly direct teacher instruction.**

    For play to have the central place in the curriculum of a preschool classroom, physical arrangements must support movement, interaction, and activity. When the physical space and furnishings allow only sitting, and when the teacher arranges tables or desks so they focus on his or her position in the classroom, the physical environment dictates passive learning experiences for children.

- **a schedule dominated by teacher lesson time.**

    When the teacher's talk and structured lessons are valued more highly than child-initiated play experiences, the schedule reflects only short free-play periods, both inside and outside. Play is used here to "let the children be children" for brief breaks from the "real learning" that the teacher directs.

- **work sheets, ditto sheets, flashcards, and other abstract materials.**

    The predominance of these materials in a preschool classroom suggests a lack of recognition of preschoolers' concrete style of learning and thinking. The emphasis on developing particular skills represented by such structured materials reflects a narrow cognitive focus on learning in the classroom, rather than nurturing holistic child development.

- **a time-out chair.**

     The central position of a chair labeled for "time-out" in the physical environment suggests adult reliance on teacher power and punishing techniques to control behavior. In Chapter 11, we will discuss appropriate guidance for preschoolers; at this point, we will merely note that it is inappropriate to include "an unhappy place" in the preschool classroom.

- **models for artwork.**

     When a classroom emphasizes creativity, children have ready access to a variety of open-ended materials that can be used for creative efforts all around the room. Their creativity is not stifled by having to follow the teacher's pattern and not being encouraged to invent their own ways of expressing themselves.

SUMMARY

Developmentally appropriate physical environments for preschoolers include well-defined separate interest centers for a variety of active play experiences; spaces large enough to encourage social interaction, as well as some spaces small enough to encourage solitary or pair play; private space to withdraw to, and personal space to feel a sense of belonging; carefully selected, open-ended materials arranged to invite exploration; a decor that reflects children's interests, identity, participation, and planning; an outdoor play area that provides for gross motor challenges as well as space and materials for other choices; a predictable schedule that allows for adjusting to children's needs and interests; and transitions planned to avoid chaos, confusion, and empty waiting. Kindergarten children are more like preschoolers than older children in the primary grades, and need developmentally responsive environments and curricula.

THINK ABOUT IT ACTIVITIES

1. Visit a preschool classroom. Consider each of Prescott's seven components for the physical environment. List specifics that you find for each of the components. Mark the places on the continuum of this classroom for each of the components and then discuss your findings with classmates.

2. Sketch the arrangement of interest centers, indicating storage space, work areas, other dividers, pathways, and traffic patterns. Indicate the number of play spaces shown in each center.

     Evaluate the room arrangement for

     - separation of noisy and quiet areas, clean and messy areas.

     - clear messages about where to use and store materials.

     - protection of play areas from traffic.

     - clear pathways and entrances to centers.

     - no empty dead space.

     - centers large enough for group play and small enough for pairs and singles.

     - attention to aesthetics, and materials for creativity.

     - Are there obvious ways this arrangement could be improved? If so, redesign it on paper.

3. List the cues you see that would help children know

     - where to return toys and where to clean up.

     - how to plan their play.

     - how many children may play in an area.

- where their personal spaces are.
- how to behave during particular activities.

4. Evaluate the schedule for
   - flexibility allowed by time blocks.
   - alternating active and quieter periods.
   - most of time spent in child-initiated time blocks.
   - alternation with teacher-directed periods.

5. Observe several transitions. Note evidence of
   - giving advance warning.
   - using familiar songs and other clues.
   - ensuring that children understand what to do.
   - avoiding empty waiting time.
   - giving children real responsibility during transitions.

6. Did you see children with special needs in the environment? What adaptations did you see in the physical environment to promote their participation?

7. Visit a local public school kindergarten. Which of the principles of appropriate physical environments described in this chapter are present in the classroom? Which are absent? Where possible, speak with the teacher about the mandates from the school district that influence the planning of schedules, planned activities, and the physical environment.

QUESTIONS TO ASSESS LEARNING OF CHAPTER OBJECTIVES

1. Describe what preschool children are like, what they do, and what they need.
2. Identify some of the considerations in creating an environment for initiative.
3. Identify some of the considerations in planning an environment for play.
4. Identify some of the considerations in planning an environment for self-control.
5. Discuss some of the characteristics of a good schedule for preschool classrooms.
6. Describe things teachers can do to create smooth transitions in preschool classrooms.
7. Identify several things seen in a developmentally appropriate kindergarten classroom, as well as questionable practices related to kindergarten.
8. List several things not seen in the physical environment of developmentally appropriate preschool classrooms.

APPLY YOUR KNOWLEDGE QUESTIONS

1. Describe the explanations you will give to parents of the four- and five-year-old children who wonder why you allow so many opportunities for children to make choices in your classroom.
2. Plan a schedule for a half-day program for a class of three- and four-year-olds that follows the principles discussed in this chapter.
3. Assume you have two adults and two dozen five-year-olds in your kindergarten classroom. Make a detailed transition plan for the end of choice time, cleanup, and using the bathroom before sitting at the tables for snack time. Be sure you plan for each adult's actions, and use the principles of good transitions discussed in this chapter.

HELPFUL WEB SITES

http://www.naeyc.org

The Web site for the National Association for the Education of Young Children. Search for an article titled "Early Years Are Learning Years: The Value of School Recess and Outdoor Play" (1998), and for the position statement titled *Still Unacceptable Trends in Kindergarten Entry and Placement* (2000).

http://www.gsa.gov

This U.S. General Services Administration Web site includes the *GSA Child Care Design Guide,* with comprehensive childcare design guidelines.

http://www.brighthorizons.com

The Bright Horizons Family Solutions Resource Room has information on the design and adaptation of children's environments.

http://www.kidsource.com

The Kid Source Web site. Search for an article titled "Top 10 Signs of a Good Kindergarten Classroom."

Please visit the premium Web site for Developmentally Appropriate Practice, *4th edition, to access more chapter web links, additional book chapters, suggestions for further reading and study, interactive quizzes, video exercises, online journal activities, flashcards, and much more! Go to www.cengage.com/login to register your access code.*

Developmentally Appropriate Physical Environments: For Primary-Aged Children

Our society has created an arbitrarily chosen milestone in young children's lives: the entry into "big" school at age six. Although many children today have likely been attending educational care programs before this time, traditional thinking links the entrance to "big" school with the beginning of the learning needed to equip children for their future lives. Although children are aware of the importance adults place on this symbolic event, no decisive change in the children themselves has precipitated it. Six-, seven-, and eight-year-olds are not so very different in their learning styles and abilities from children a year or so younger. They are more comfortable away from their parents than younger children, but are still very eager for recognition and relationships with other important adults. They enjoy being with other children, and are still learning the skills that allow them to function as group members. They are still active creatures, gaining control over their bodies, practicing both gross and fine motor skills. Their understandings of the world around them are still related to their concrete experiences; the errors in their judgments and logic are still governed by their preoperational mode of thinking. Much in the world around them is still very new and interesting to them. The one thing that has changed is that adults are expecting them to accomplish skills the culture has deemed necessary. So the transition to school is likely to be accompanied by excitement and anticipation of a new experience, as well as anxiety and apprehension about succeeding in it.

This is a whole new environment for six or seven hours a day in most cases. And for children whose working parents must find supplemental care for them before and after school and during school vacation times, it often means still another environment for more hours each day. With the pressures that have come to school systems with the No Child Left Behind legislation, in which end-of-grade high-stakes testing has now become a way of life, life for most primary-age children has become more standardized and anxiety-fraught, as their teachers and administrators focus on end results, leaving many developmentally appropriate practices behind. It is unfortunately true that many beginning teachers who enter primary classrooms will find too few of the appropriate practices discussed in this text. That is no reason, however, to abandon these ideas, but rather even more reason for early childhood professionals to become knowledgeable about what is appropriate. Only then can they keep advocating with decision makers and administrators to allow some room for professional input for more appropriate decision making.

In this chapter, we will consider the physical environments of both the primary school classrooms and the after-school care classrooms that are best suited to the developmental tasks of primary-age children.

LEARNING OBJECTIVES

After completing this chapter, students should be able to

- describe what primary-age children are like.
- describe what primary-age children need for optimum development.

- describe the elements of an environment that nurture a sense of industry.
- describe the elements of an environment that are designed to foster early literacy.
- identify the elements of an environment that promote relationships.
- discuss considerations in developmentally appropriate schedules for primary children, including recess.
- identify components of appropriate after-school environments.
- describe elements not found in developmentally appropriate primary classrooms.

WHAT ARE PRIMARY-AGED CHILDREN LIKE?

So much has already happened to children by the time they begin formal schooling at age six or so that millions of unique histories and developmental patterns exist. Within every first-grade classroom, there are likely to be children whose lives have been blessed with secure love and attention from their parents and families since birth and others who have been abused, neglected, or ignored by adults unable to cope with the responsibilities of parenthood or overwhelmed by their own lives. Some children shout with glee when a funny story is read to them, and others are puzzled by the very words and are unused to handling books. Some move comfortably into the new challenges and relationships in the classroom, and others hang back, timid, fearful, and mistrusting. Some can read and print their names and are eager for more challenges, and others struggle with learning English as their second language and seem to expect not to succeed in this new world. Some climb, swing, run, and jump with zest, and others are unable to because of physical limitations or lack of experience. Some children work along with their parents in fields,

Figure 8-1

The desire for competence is a driving force in primary-age children.

Jose Luis Pelaez Inc/Blend Images/Corb.

and others never do a chore. Some children have lost their first teeth and put them hopefully under their pillows for the tooth fairy, and others have already lost teeth due to poor nutrition and health, lack of dental care, or accidents. Some children's out-of-school lives involve busy rounds of lessons, visits at friends' homes, and family activities, whereas other children spend much of their time watching mostly unsuitable television. There are differences influenced by the culture, neighborhood, and social and economic circumstances of their families, as well as by temperament and individual rates of development. Although enormous differences exist among the children, they all have some things in common.

What primary-age children have in common is their entrance into a period of their lives when they are in enough control of their bodies, minds, emotions, and communication abilities that they have the potential to do just about anything they want to do, things that have not before been possible. Perhaps the most outstanding characteristic of many primary-age children is their thirst to know and to understand. A desire for competence is their driving force, and they are willing to spend time and energy at becoming competent at the things that interest them and that seem important to adults (see Figure 8-1). This is the age of creation, when children want to make things, to make them well, to be good at doing things. They are capable of becoming totally absorbed in passionate interests.

What primary-age children do with friends is one of those passionate interests. The friendships of the early school years tend to be somewhat longer lasting than the tempestuous first efforts of preschoolers. There are still episodes of pain and hurt feelings, but these friendships give primary-age children important opportunities to explore social relationships and become less egocentric. Interaction with **peers** gives children important feedback to incorporate into their personal identities.

Physical competence and skill is also an important component of self-concept for primary-age children. Physical abilities often form the basis for common activity and entrance into games with others. Primary-age children are great game players. The traditional games of childhood have been passed virtually unchanged from one generation to the next. Because the children's growth rate has slowed, their bodies change more slowly, giving them more time to "feel at home" inside their "skins." Their joy and skill with large muscle activity is reflected in their boundless energy and activity. Primary-age children are still creatures who find it difficult to remain still for very long.

Time is still a rather vague concept for primary-age children. They tell somewhat disjointed stories about experiences that happened at some time in the past or will happen in the future. They are instead creatures of the moment, enjoying the present to the fullest.

What Do Primary-Age Children Do?

The most obvious answer to the question of what primary-age children do is that they spend long hours away from home and families in formal, organized schooling and in less formal, but often equally organized, recreational and after-school activities. In these settings, they spend a lot of time listening, sitting, following instructions, and working at new skills. Depending on the classroom practices, they may spend a lot of time with pencils in hand, working on paper assignments. They may spend time waiting until their reading group is called, either working industriously at the list of assignments on the board or trying to catch the eye of a friend and talk with him until the teacher asks them to be quiet. They may spend time waiting for everyone to line up to walk to the gym, the cafeteria, or the playground. They may spend time sitting in time-out because they were unable to wait quietly.

In other classrooms, children may spend their school day deeply involved in reading with a friend, writing a story about a trip to the bakery, enjoying the big book read by their teacher, and then constructing a bakery in the block center. So the experiences of primary-age children can be very different, based on the decisions made by teachers, administrators, and their individual communities.

After school, children may be among those who go home to play in their yards or streets, enjoying the increased freedom parents allow at this age: freedom to talk, to play games, to just hang around with friends. Or they may be among the children who are dropped off by bus or van at an after-school program or a family childcare home arrangement to wait several more hours until their parents pick them up. There they may engage in planned recreational activities, supervised homework sessions, or television viewing. When they do go home, they will likely watch even more television—many primary-age children spend more hours watching television each week than they spend in school. They likely also spend less time with their parents than they did as younger children.

Whatever their after-school arrangement and no matter what the classroom practices are, primary-age children actively seek to be with friends (see Figure 8-2). They want to talk with them, play with them, and do things together. Friends are the big new influence in their lives. What their friends do and say is what is important to them. Primary-age children create separate worlds with their friends, worlds entered only by other children. Primary-age children spend a lot of time measuring themselves physically, emotionally, cognitively, and socially against one another as an important contribution to their self-concept.

In addition, their families and individual cultures shape what these children do. They may spend time helping care for younger siblings, talking with grandparents, or helping a parent prepare tortillas or spring rolls for a family celebration. They may help with chores on the farm, go to dance class, or accompany a parent to the Laundromat. They may spend time in classes learning about the family's religious or cultural traditions, spend time watching the older boys in the neighborhood fight on the corner, or spend time receiving individualized evaluation and therapy for special needs. Saturday mornings may be spent playing in organized sport programs, watching cartoons, and getting ready for Dad to pick them up for a weekend visit.

Figure 8-2

Whatever their after-school arrangement and whatever they choose to do, primary-age children most want to spend time with their friends.

All these different primary-age children are becoming members of their society, learning its ways, its customs, and its knowledge. More is expected of these children, and they are ready to participate more fully in the world around them. They are ready to become competent and ready to be seen as competent.

WHAT DO PRIMARY-AGE CHILDREN NEED?

Primary-age children need a world in which they can experience competence. Erikson designated the psychosocial conflict for this period as balancing a **sense of industry with** a sense of inferiority. By this he meant that children need to feel a measure of success in accomplishing the tasks that adults feel are important for participation in the culture. They need to see themselves as succeeding as a worker in the culture, rather than feeling a sense of failure in measuring up to the expected standards. The environment, then, must nurture those feelings of competence by selecting tasks that are attainable and by supporting children in their accomplishments. **Competence** refers not only to academic tasks, such as reading and writing, but also to other achievements that are deemed valuable. These may be as varied as learning to play a sport well, learning to play a musical instrument (see Figure 8-3), sweeping leaves from the driveway, caring for siblings, or being able to make others laugh. An environment that promotes competence gives children time, space, materials, and opportunity to practice the skills they are learning. The environment also conveys acceptance and recognition of the diverse abilities, skills, and interests that are obvious in children's differing capacities, and the diverse cultural backgrounds that have shaped the individuality of each child.

Figure 8-3

Learning to play a musical instrument is another way of proving competence.

Primary-age children need an environment that allows them to proceed at their own pace in developing skills without being compared with the pace or ability of someone else. An environment that recognizes differences in development and readiness for learning is critical. Children are helped when practices support their development within an atmosphere of cooperation, rather than a spirit of competition.

Becoming socially accepted is an area in which primary-age children set their own tasks of accomplishment and in which it is important that they do not feel inferior. An environment that supports group participation and peer interaction nurtures both the skills and the satisfaction of group membership. Primary-age children need opportunities to select their peers, to spend time with them, and to have their friendships accepted as important and valuable.

Primary-age children also need opportunities to communicate and to develop their communication skills. This means they need an environment that supports talk as well as listening, and that links speech with the other methods of communication demanded by the culture. An environment that supports literacy communicates the practical uses of reading and writing and the pleasures involved (see Figure 8-4).

As Piaget described the preoperational stage of children's thinking, he noted that the stage extends to age seven or so. This means that most primary-age children still retain the learning style and limitations of thought associated with preoperational mental activity. The environment must recognize this fact and support learning through **concrete** methods, related to real experiences, allowing children to construct their own understandings of concepts. The active learning style of preschoolers does not change in primary-age children because their mental abilities have not changed. Environments for preoperational thinkers use materials that teach children through active learning experiences. Where the environment for primary-age children does look different from that for younger children, it does so because of their intense curiosity and passionate interests in particular topics and their developing skills related to literacy. The environment for primary-age children offers time and space to pursue their expanded interests and to experience the world.

Figure 8-4

Learning the pleasure of reading is part of literacy development.

These eager entrants into their larger culture need an environment that supports the development of a sense of industry; of learning about the world around them, including literacy skills as acquired by a mostly preoperational child; and of relationships, primarily with the peer group.

DIFFERENCES IN PHYSICAL ENVIRONMENTS FOR PRIMARY-AGE CHILDREN

Contrast the situations for these two six-year-olds. Joel is a first-grader at Elm Heights Elementary School, and LaToya attends the Parkwood School first grade.

When Joel enters his classroom, he goes immediately to his desk. It is the third desk in the row by the door. He waves to his friend Rodney, who sits in the front desk of the row by the windows. Joel would like to go over to talk, but Mr. Jordan looks up from his desk to remind them to get out their reading books. This is the time to read silently the books they have brought back from the library. Joel found out yesterday that his is too hard, but he has it for the week, so he sits looking at it until the bell goes. None of his good friends sit near him anyway; Mr. Jordan moved their seats all around after the first month of school, so nobody would be near their friends and tempted to talk.

The bell is the signal for everyone to put away his or her books. Mr. Jordan calls for a child to go to the front of the classroom to lead the pledge of allegiance. The flag hangs at the front of the classroom, along with a large calendar and pictures of several early presidents. The teacher's desk, file cabinets, and storage shelves are at the front of the classroom. At the back of the room are shelves for the children to store lunch boxes and hooks for their coats. A bulletin board by the door has the schedule for the week posted. It doesn't change.

There are the usual questions about the day of the week, the month, and the year to complete the calendar discussion, and a discussion about the weather to fill in the weather chart. Then Mr. Jordan writes their assignments on the board, to work on while he supervises the reading groups. Joel is usually in the third reading group to be called, so he settles in to do his seat work. Turning to page 17 in his reading workbook, he answers some questions about yesterday's lesson that involved a small dog. He underlines the correct answers to the questions, but there is a word in the fourth question he can't figure out. He raises his hand, but Mr. Jordan says, "Just go on with your work. I'll help you later." He turns to the next of the board assignments, which is to complete Section 2 on pages 34 and 35 in his math workbook. He discovers these are the same kind of subtraction problems Mr. Jordan showed them on the board yesterday. They were pretty easy for him, so he finishes them quickly. The third assignment was to read the next story for his reading group and write ten words for his spelling lesson.

Mr. Jordan is only calling the second reading group, and Joel is getting tired of sitting. He goes to the pencil sharpener although his pencil really doesn't need sharpening. On the way back to his seat, he takes the long way so he can talk to Rodney about the ball game last night. When they start giggling, Mr. Jordan looks up from the reading group and warns, "If you don't get your work done now, you can stay in at recess and finish it then." Joel goes back to his seat and writes some of his spelling words.

When his reading group is called, Mr. Jordan asks Joel to read first. He stumbles over a word in the second sentence. Mr. Jordan says, "That's 'thing,' Joel. Sound it out. You should have been paying more attention to reading than talking with Rodney. How do you think you will do well on the end-of-grade tests if you don't work hard every day?" Joel repeats "thing," then has trouble with "light." Mr. Jordan interrupts the reading to speak to the others working in their seats, who are getting restless and a bit noisy. When all the children have had a turn to read, Mr. Jordan tells them to read through the story again quietly at their seats, and then finish their seat work. Joel can hardly wait for lunchtime. After the short recess, they come back to their desks to listen to Mr. Jordan's math lesson.

Now switch to Parkwood School. When LaToya enters her classroom, she looks around to see where her best friend Joy is sitting. She spots her over on the carpet near the bookshelves. She goes over and joins her. Together the two girls look at the book Joy has chosen, a favorite of theirs. In the book area are large posters and pictures from some of the books on display, as well as a collection of hand puppets and a small stage. Other children select books from the shelves and go to various places to read—some in the loft, a couple in the individual nooks, some sitting together at a low table, some on the steps by the window. The teacher, Mrs. Guerrera, moves around to greet them. When everyone has arrived, she plays a chord on her autoharp, and the children move over to the large meeting area where the teacher is seated beside a big book on an easel. She reads the book, and the children join in, for it is a favorite—*Curious George at the Zoo*. After the book, the class discusses some of the words that reminded the children of their visit to the zoo the week before. Mrs. Guerrera removes the book and places an easel pad on which to print the children's responses on the list. There is a lot of laughing and talking. When she finishes the list, she posts it on the wall.

Then it is writing time. LaToya gets her notebook and pencil from her box and moves to one of the tables grouped together near the writing center (see Figure 8-5). Posted on the walls nearby are several of the group stories the children have written recently with the teacher, as well as several individual stories children have posted to share.

There are several posters with words and one with alphabet letters on it. Several other children join LaToya, and others take their work to the carpet area. Several more children choose the individual tables placed at the sides of the room. LaToya started her story yesterday. She is writing a story about a little girl going to the zoo. She decides to add a monkey to the things the little girl sees. She goes back to the reading area to find the big book so she can see how to spell "monkey." She looks through the book until she thinks she has found it. She carries the book to Joy, and they decide together that the word she found is really "mischief." They keep looking till they find "monkey," and LaToya writes it in her story. Mrs. Guerrera comes around to talk with the children about their stories and admires the new sentence LaToya has written. She asks LaToya if she wants to be on the list of children who will read their stories to some other

Figure 8-5

Children work at tables, not at individual desks.

children. Mrs. Guerrera writes her name on a list taped to the wall. LaToya is pleased. She goes and gets Joy so Joy can hear it too.

After the story reading, Mrs. Guerrera announces it is time for children to choose their activity centers. LaToya takes her turn to go to the planning board on the wall in the meeting area and moves her name tag to one of the five spaces under the heading Block Area. A glance around the room shows other children busy in a number of other centers. Three children are working on a large papier-mâché dinosaur in the art area. Several children are wearing earphones at a listening center, turning the pages of books and making comments to one another. Several others are constructing with a variety of small manipulative toys, and another group is playing a game. Three children are working on a plan for a visit to the nature museum, listing the questions they want to have answered for their project. A group in another area of the room is setting up an elaborate store, complete with marking prices on groceries.

LaToya wants to build a cage for the monkey. She signals Joy and another friend to come to the blocks also. When they finish, they make a sign for their construction: "CAJ. Dont tuch." After lunch, they plan to play monkeys on the playground. They ask their teacher what they can use for cages. She suggests taking some of the large boxes out of the storage shed.

The profound differences in these physical environments for primary-age children reflect deep variations in educational philosophies. The arrangements of time and space dictate the kinds of learning opportunities available for children, as well as the specifics about curriculum, the teacher's style of interaction, and the children's role as learners. In this discussion of developmentally appropriate physical environments for primary-age children, it is obvious that we must question how well the traditional sit-in-rows-of-desks-and-work style of classroom matches the learning style and developmental needs of the children.

Unfortunately, the recognition that primary-age children learn best through their active involvement and play has frequently been lost in elementary schools as educators strive to reach prescribed academic goals that match narrow cognitive specifics for each grade level.

The NAEYC position statement and examples of developmentally appropriate practice for primary children remind us that we must all become open advocates for play and active learning in the primary grades.

There has been abundant criticism of the quality of education provided in elementary schools. The Report of the Carnegie Task Force on Learning in the Primary Grades summarizes the key reasons for schools' lack of success:

- low expectations held out for many students

- heavy reliance on outmoded or ineffective curricula and teaching methods

- poorly prepared or insufficiently supported teachers
- weak home/school linkages
- lack of accountability systems
- ineffective use of resources by schools and school systems (Carnegie Task Force, 1996)

The No Child Left Behind Act of 2001 was passed to rectify some of these problems. Major components of the law call for

- accountability for results, with specific requirements for children's test results and schools.
- emphasis for doing what works based on scientific research.
- expanded parental options, notably removing their children from underperforming schools.
- expanded local control and flexibility. (The entire law can be seen at http://www.ed. gov/nclb.)

Many educators, however, are dismayed by some of the strategies that are being used to achieve these desirable goals. "Mandatory proficiency testing in language arts and mathematics, begins in the third grade in the United States and has led to roughly one-third less instructional time spent on learning in other disciplines" (Tomlinson in Copple & Bredekamp, 2009, p. 258). Instead of learning to apply academic skills to problems and real situations, the focus is on acquiring the skills alone to achieve the desired testing results that have become the focus of many school systems. Complex thinking skills are being sacrificed for the short-term results. Early childhood professionals need to become advocates for more appropriate learning situations for primary-age children.

Environment for a Sense of Industry

As primary-age children begin their formal school learning experiences in the early grades, they need an environment that conveys a message about their active roles as learners. Classrooms need to be designed for children to learn in the ways that are natural to them, so that they experience feelings of success and competence. The traditional arrangement of children sitting in rows facing the teacher's desk and blackboard at the front of the room is designed to make the teacher the focus of attention and to discourage any interaction among children. In such physical arrangements, children quickly learn to let the teacher be in charge of all their learning, becoming dependent on teacher ideas and assessment for their personal evaluations of their success. When children who find such inactive and confined learning arrangements difficult receive negative feedback from teachers about their classroom failures, their self-esteem as learners is doubly threatened.

An environment that expects children to make some of the decisions about what work they will do and how and where they will do it allows children to develop positive feelings about their learning. For this reason, developmentally appropriate primary classrooms offer children a range of choices throughout their day. One choice will be what their learning activities will be during a significant portion of the school day. This means the classroom will offer a variety of learning centers so that children may select from assorted materials and media that teachers have made available to them. Children with different interests, learning styles, and abilities may find work that is personally meaningful in learning center arrangements (Stuber, 2007).

These learning centers will likely bear some similarity to learning centers in preschool classrooms, but the individual stamp of primary-age children's environments will be found in the size and complexity of the centers. For example, although blocks may be found in both preschool and primary classrooms, the block center for the older children will more than likely be larger

WHAT would you DO when…

Every other first grade in your school has desks neatly arranged in rows, and "that's the way it has always been done." As a new first-grade teacher, you want to implement some of the ideas you learned in college about active learning and integrated curriculum projects. You want to start somewhere, and think the best place might be to change the room arrangement. But you're afraid of the criticism of the more experienced teachers. What do you do?

First of all, prepare. Think through carefully what you want to do and why. Be sure you can explain it clearly to other teachers and administrators. Prepare a handout for parents who will also want to understand how learning is taking place. And be sure you have considered carefully the whole picture of your goals, learning requirements, and children's needs.

Then begin with one thing. Perhaps the environment is the easiest thing to change, and a change that will certainly support the active kinds of learning you visualize. As the children become comfortable within the flexible seating arrangements, observe their interactions and ways of supporting each other in their work. Find time to listen to them talk, and you will likely soon get ideas for a topic to explore more deeply in a project. Go slowly, and document the changes with photos and journals, so that you can share the progress with others. And keep reflecting on what learning is taking place, and how the environment is affecting it.

and contain more blocks, recognizing their need for planning grander structures and working with a group on a common plan. Teachers may incorporate reading and writing in creating challenges for the builders. Challenge cards may invite: "Build something that reminds you of our trip last Monday" or "Find a friend or two to help you build a building with six sides." Some books displayed nearby may include *Mike Mulligan and His Steam Shovel* and a book showing buildings from countries around the world. Teachers will also likely include writing materials nearby so that builders can design, label, or describe their efforts. Extra space may be provided where ongoing projects can remain until completion.

In addition to complexity, other differences in the primary classroom include degrees of responsibility. Primary-age children will be asked to assume complete responsibility under limited adult supervision, helping to prepare materials for centers, caring for them, and working independently (Scully, Barbour, & Seefeldt, 2003). Space and materials are arranged to require increasing degrees of skill.

In addition to blocks, primary classrooms often include centers for creative reading and writing, for math/manipulatives/games, for creative art, for science, for dramatic play, and for listening, as well as for computer use. Occasional options may be cooking, woodworking, and playing with sand and water.

One of the benefits to the learning center approach is that it allows for the kind of integrated curriculum suggested for developmentally appropriate practice.

Whatever they are studying, children at this age learn best through concrete experiences; they need to see connections, and they seek coherence and relevance across domains. When teachers encourage children to build connections across disciplines, they simultaneously foster intellectual growth, social connection, and a joy in learning, making progress deeper and more extensive. An integrated curriculum taps children's interests and senses while enhancing learning across all domains. The purpose of integrating content is not only to make school more enjoyable and interesting, which promotes enthusiasm and a love of learning; it also is to support children's ability to connect new learning to prior knowledge, which has the effect of expanding children's memory and reasoning capacity. (Tomlinson, in Copple & Bredekamp, 2009)

Rather than chopping the day into separate periods for separate subjects such as science, social studies, math, reading, and so on, with a fixed amount of time allotted for each, children busy in learning centers or theme study are actively incorporating various subjects within single activities. Learning centers allow teachers to use intentional experiences, strategies, and materials

Figure 8-6

Teachers design the environment so that children can make choices and work without distraction.

to further curricular goals. The children's learning is hands-on, experience-based, and individualized to meet particular needs, interests, styles, and abilities. When a considerable portion of program time is spent in learning centers, teachers are free to observe and interact with individual children to assess their instructional needs and plan future strategies (see Figure 8-6).

There are decisions for teachers to make as they move to planning curriculum through learning centers and cooperative projects. They need to decide on mechanisms for encouraging children to carefully plan their activities within the parameters of weekly requirements. They need to decide whether all learning centers will be available each day and whether time will be devoted to the centers each day.

Other decisions are whether each child must use each center during a specified time frame and whether they are free to leave a center when they choose or only when the teacher guides. Some teachers want to ensure that children get a balanced selection of learning opportunities, so they ask children to participate in a certain minimum number of activities each day or week. See Figure 8-7 for an example of a planning contract that allows children to see the requirements for center participation. Additional ideas for monitoring children's use of centers include giving children a certain number of colored tickets with their names on to deposit for admission to a particular center (Kostelnik, Soderman, & Whiren, 2003) or asking children to stamp a color-coded card to leave in the teacher's basket. Others feel such a system inhibits children from learning to make independent choices and may keep them from becoming involved in long-term projects and learning activities. They believe that any center can incorporate a wide variety of different learning opportunities. As mentioned earlier, teachers must make such decisions based on what they know of children's development, experiences, and needs, also taking into account other variables such as school system guidelines, parent and community preferences, and teacher comfort.

Figure 8-7

Sample planning contract.

Sample Planning Contract

Put a ✔ in the appropriate box each time you use this subject in a week. You should have at least ten check marks by Friday, including at least 5 for reading, 3 for math and 3 for writing.

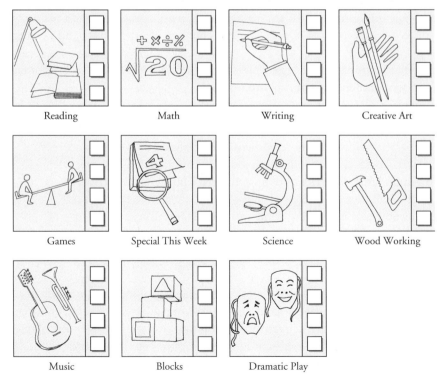

| Reading | Math | Writing | Creative Art |

| Games | Special This Week | Science | Wood Working |

| Music | Blocks | Dramatic Play |

Teachers also differ in deciding whether all learning centers should offer children unrestricted opportunities to direct their learning or should suggest particular activities to be done in prescribed ways. There are three kinds of learning centers: self-directing/self-correcting, self-directing/open-ended, and teacher-instructed/exploratory. The first type allows teachers to set up activities for particular purposes, with the materials telling children whether they have been used correctly. An example is a puzzle in which children match numerals with numbers of objects or pairs of picture cards with common beginning-letter sounds. Self-directing/open-ended centers, on the other hand, offer materials that may produce varieties of learning, depending on individual children's abilities and interests. Blocks offered with no instruction or specific challenge suggestion is an example of this. The third type of center offers opportunities for children to explore concepts that have previously been introduced by teachers. An example might be using eyedroppers to mix colors or working with salt and other ingredients to explore melting ice, after teachers have led lessons on these subjects. Teachers may use different proportions of these kinds of centers at different times, depending on children's curriculum needs.

> ## CULTURAL CONSIDERATIONS
>
> ### Different Perspectives on Teaching and Learning
>
> Teachers must recognize that a family's cultural background includes expectations for what teaching and learning look like. Some cultural assumptions may be that the teacher must direct all learning, and children must simply follow the teacher's directions. In that case, parents may be confused or disturbed by a developmentally appropriate emphasis on children as active learners. In addition, culture determines family attitudes toward the teacher's profession and authority, which may make them more or less willing to engage in dialogue about classroom goals, methods, and assumptions. Clearly these attitudes will influence communication, and should be understood by teachers, who will find themselves needing to clarify their expectations for family participation and involvement.

Teachers who use learning centers as a primary instructional approach will organize learning experiences for the children around common themes of interest to the children, structuring in-depth projects that allow children to pursue topics of interest that also relate to learning goals. Projects that may take "days, weeks, or even an entire program year" (Bredekamp & Rosegrant, 1995, p. 171) allow children to become immersed in lengthy explorations, observations, and investigations that provide opportunities to explore meaningful content across discipline areas. Projects may include "periods of focused instruction as well as child-selected activity" (Tomlinson, 2009, p. 259). Thus, the active and interactive play of primary-age children becomes the way of teaching curriculum, not just something that is seen as extra or enrichment. For example, children living near the ocean may be very interested in exploring this topic; teachers use such a project to work on language and literacy, math, science, social studies, and artistic and music skills. (See more about this in Chapter 16).

The thoughtful selection of materials that will challenge curiosity and sustain complex investigation of topics is an important component of the physical environment. Teachers provide a variety of materials that are concrete, real, and relevant to their children's lives. These may include objects for children to manipulate and explore, such as construction materials, art media, scientific equipment, games, collections of interesting objects and artifacts, and computers. Teachers work diligently to create inviting displays of materials that are available for use and manipulation. The physically attractive classroom conveys the teacher's recognition that children need to be joyfully involved in their learning. As discussed later in this book, teachers are careful to select all materials to indicate their respect for the diversity of race and culture, physical ability, gender, and socioeconomic backgrounds represented in the classroom and in the community, as well as choosing materials that are aesthetically pleasing and inoffensive.

An advantage to providing a number of separate learning centers is that the arrangement allows children to choose where to work during other periods. There simply is not enough space in a classroom for both the traditional arrangement and the tables, shelves, and other furniture needed to create separate interest zones. The small tables and the separate work areas for individuals and small groups allow children to select the places that seem most comfortable for them to work, whether by themselves or with others; even the floor is not excluded. Pillows and carpet make relaxing areas to work in. "Teachers arrange tables or flexible groupings of desks to enable children to work alone or in small groups. A variety of spaces are provided in the classroom, including comfortable work areas where children can interact and work together and also places for silent or shared reading, working on construction projects, writing, playing math or language games, and exploring science" (Copple & Bredekamp, 2009, p. 293). Display tables allow children to continue thinking about their work and that of others. There is no explicit or implicit prohibition on movement, conversation, or assistance from others. In such a room, there is no particular "front" to the classroom; something is happening everywhere, and both teacher and children are mobile rather than occupying a fixed position.

Children may feel that the school classroom is an alien environment when their physical comfort and natural inclinations are less important than the teacher's insistence that they remain seated in order to be recognized as working (see Figure 8-8). In the learning center atmosphere, children are likely to sense success or industry rather than a feeling of inferiority at not being able to learn the narrowly prescribed curriculum in the specifically defined ways and places.

Planning Boards. A sense of industry is also nurtured when children feel they are making important decisions related to their learning. Many primary teachers use various forms of planning boards to help children make conscious choices about their learning activities. A central planning board is suitable for six- through eight-year-olds to allow them to decide among all the possibilities, possibly in conjunction with the decisions of peers. The children have individual name tags to slip into pockets or place on hooks or places where they can write their own names.

The ability to plan and organize individual activity to accomplish goals is an important skill for primary-age children to develop. Moving beyond the basic decision about where to play, children may need help formulating goals and thinking through the steps of complicated projects. Conversations with teachers and peers and writing ideas down may be helpful (see Figure 8-9). Talking about the successes and problems that occur in completing planned activities also helps children learn how to control their progress. The High/Scope method refers to this technique as plan-do-review. Selma Wasserman, in her excellent book about primary-age children as "serious players" (2000), refers to the sequence of "play-debrief-replay," meaning that after the initial active learning experience, children are helped by explaining what they have done and discovered, and by reflecting on their discoveries, problems, and learnings. This is then followed by an opportunity to "replay"—to gain additional practice with the concepts or skills, and perhaps to extend into new areas, taking their concepts one step further. By such reflection about actions, children learn to evaluate their own work and that of others, to offer each other suggestions, and to collaborate on complex projects.

Portfolios and Work Samples. A sense of industry is also achieved as children are able to see the progress they make in their self-assigned learning tasks. Teachers may devise systems that help

Figure 8-8

Children may choose places to work that are most comfortable for them.

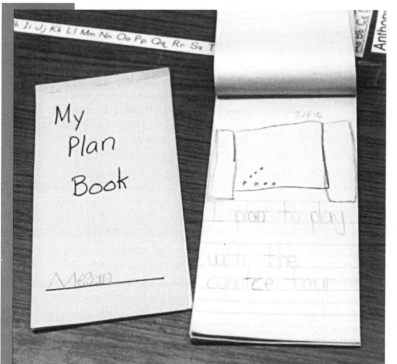

Figure 8-9

Planning books help primary-age children manage their activities and time.

Figure 8-10

Children develop a sense of industry by reviewing drawings, projects, stories, or other samples of work retained in their own individual portfolios.

children keep track of their development. One such system is the development of a **portfolio**. Each child has individual file folders in which to keep various papers, such as drawings, stories they have written, words they have learned to read, photos or sketches of their projects and constructions, and other samples (see Figure 8-10). Portfolios benefit the children, their parents, and their teachers, as they show how the work being done relates to the learning standards developed by the state and school system. In Chapter 16, we'll talk about using portfolios for assessment; here it is important to note their uses for children in following their own progress. Other variations on the portfolio idea are designed to give children tangible evidence of their learning. One example is envelopes to hold the letters and numbers recognized by younger children or the envelopes described by Sylvia Ashton-Warner and Sydney Clemens in which children may keep their words that they have chosen to read (Ashton-Warner, 1964; Clemens, 1983). Another example is a list of books that children have finished reading.

Figure 8-11

A sample list of materials for a working portfolio. Used with permission of Beth Bellemere, Scarborough School Department.

The Working Portfolio

The **working portfolio** is kept in the classroom and is meant to be a compilation of the child's growth over time. Some work may be sent home at the end of the quarter or at the end of the year. Some may accumulate for the length of time the child stays in the classroom. These decisions will be made as the faculty refines the portfolio process. While we experience this process firsthand, some changes will certainly be made as we gain knowledge and experience. The following lists are suggestions of what will be considered for inclusion in a child's working portfolio:

Writing: journals, writing folders, weekend news, published books, computer stories, handwriting samples, shared writing, directed writing, notes, letters, thank you notes, science reactions, theme or subject-related journals (farm, math, etc.), labeling examples, spelling work, center record sheets, center recording sheets, lists.

Science, Social Studies, Health: observational drawings, sorting work and recordings, journals, center recording sheets, recipes, classification work, brainstorming lists, field experience records.

Art: drawings (observational, free, teacher directed, child choice), sewing, 3-D work, paintings, prints, self portraits, puppets, story boards and aprons, prints, weavings, cut and paste activities.

Math: center recording sheets, sorting, seriating, patterning tasks, graphs (individual, group, child generated, teacher directed), game boards, geoboard work, classifying, problem-solving strategies.

Reading: book lists, word lists, literary passages, Marie Clay checklist, book reaction sheets, attitude inventory, word and letter recognition sheets, book projects, reports, poems, word families, word search, published books, tape of the child reading or retelling a story, phonics work, a copy of a page of text the child reads comfortably.

PRACTICAL IMPLICATIONS

Fostering a Sense of Industry

In primary classrooms, teachers help nurture a sense of industry by:

- creating learning centers for children's active learning at their individual level of interest and ability.

- using the thoughtful selection and display of concrete materials to stimulate curiosity and productivity.

- designing an informal and flexible physical arrangement that allows children to work alone or in small groups.

- using planning systems to help children learn to plan and reflect on their activities.

- using portfolios and other methods to help children measure their own progress and to have a personal storage area (see Figure 8-11).

A central and accessible place in the classroom is created for portfolios, so that children may make additions when they are ready (see Figure 8-11). The traditional primary classroom gives each child a desk in which to store individual work. The active learning –center–based classroom gives children individual storage areas of some kind, in addition to the general portfolio storage area.

Evidence of children's work and progress is also everywhere in the room. Teachers create a sense of common ownership, so that children can feel comfortable displaying the things that are important to them. Lists of accomplishments and posters that celebrate achievements of all kinds attest to children's industry. Group accounts of projects may be written or created.

Environment for Literacy

The development of literacy and numeration skills is an important objective in classrooms for primary-age children. Current thinking about the emergence of literacy as development of a number of related skills has implications for the physical environment.

The physical environment should be print-rich. Children need to see reading and writing skills practiced in their environment daily. Everything in the environment is labeled (boxes for "scissors" and "scrap paper"; hooks for "hats"; "Bathroom—3 at a time"). Lists (songs we like, favorite foods, things we saw on the bus ride, things we need to make vegetable soup, words that sound funny) are made and displayed. Notes and schedules are posted. Signs and stories are everywhere (Morning News; Our Trip on the Bus). There are sign-up sheets for turns at the computer or for adding something to the agenda for the class meeting. Books and posters are in every area of the classroom. Children see adults write things down and read them back. When the environment is print-rich, children discover the usefulness of reading and writing and are highly motivated to do these activities themselves.

Two large and important learning centers related to literacy—the reading center and the writing center—are located close to each other to suggest their linked function. The reading center may include pillows and beanbag chairs to encourage comfort; open-face shelves to display books (face out) and shelves to store books; many types of books, including stories, information and concept books, poetry, alphabet and counting books, wordless picture books, books made by individual children; duplicates of favorite books to encourage children to read the same book at the same time as their friend does; puppets, props, and flannel boards to encourage children to retell stories they've read; posters and pictures about books; the teacher's stock of big books for the whole group to read aloud; perhaps a library system for checking books out for classroom and/or home use. This center may also include several sets of headphones and books on cassette so that children can follow along with the words as they listen to the story.

The writing center should contain small tables and chairs, and shelves to store an abundance of writing supplies: paper of various sizes, unlined and lined; pencils, pens, markers, and crayons; pencil sharpeners; file cards, pads, notebooks, and tablets; stationery and envelopes; chalkboard and chalk; magnetic letters; sand or salt trays for writing letters; a primary or regular typewriter. Computers may be here or elsewhere. Some teachers add personal mailboxes for each child as well as personal journals for drawing or writing. Posters on the wall that include letters and print are appropriate. Children's portfolios for writing work may be kept in this center. As children progress in their literacy experiences, both of these centers will expand to accommodate changing needs; for example, construction paper, staplers, and other fasteners may be added as children begin creating their own books.

Materials for creative art may also be included in this center, as children may be more interested in writing if they can add their own creative touches.

Literacy materials should not be confined to these two centers, but added to all the other learning centers as well. The creative center may have books of famous artworks or books with beautiful pictures that may inspire; the block center may have books showing buildings and construction. Cookbooks, catalogs, and magazines may be added to pretend play (see Figure 8-12);

Figure 8-12

Literacy materials and print are included in this dramatic play area in a K–1 classroom.

books related to the theme may enhance science; math has counting books; and so on. Providing writing materials in each area also extends learning possibilities.

When children spend their school lives in classrooms filled with materials they see used regularly for reading and writing, they begin to use them. Early literacy depends a great deal on the availability of materials in the physical environment and on regular opportunities to use these materials and see them used.

The schedule includes times for personal reading, as well as whole-group and small-group reading. Specific time blocks are also created for writing in personal journals and whole-group writing, as well as instruction in specific skills.

Another component of a literacy environment is providing opportunities for oral communication. We will discuss methods of using physical space to encourage oral communication in general in the next section.

Environment for Relationships

The growing importance of peers and friends in the six- through eight-year age groups means that teachers need to plan for environments and practices that nurture a sense of group membership and cooperation. Current concerns about increases in aggressive behavior among young children, as well as the recognition that well-developed social skills and healthy emotional development are crucial to children's success in every aspect of school, make it important for teachers to support character development and the ability to work collaboratively with peers and function responsibly with others. Although both explicit discussion and implicit example are important here, as is teacher planning to create group work situations, the physical environment plays a role as well. Several aspects of the physical environment can be used to nurture friendship and peer relationships.

In the traditional classroom, teachers who were trying to minimize conversations to concentrate attention on their instruction were likely to deliberately separate friends. Children were also put into groups arbitrarily, based on common skill levels. In developmentally appropriate classrooms, teachers recognize that social and communication development are as valid as cognitive skills and are inextricably linked with cognitive development. They realize also that insights, help, and ideas do not come only from the teacher, but from other children as well. For these reasons, they often allow children to choose where they will work and with whom. The flexibility in physical arrangements allows children to select the location and group size that feels comfortable to them personally and to move furniture when necessary to accommodate the needs of the group.

When children's choices interfere with their concentration and productivity, teachers help them learn the natural and logical consequences of those choices for future self-control. For example, Shawn and Rodney spent more time today talking about their baseball team than they did writing their stories. The teacher reminds them that the group will be reading their stories aloud the next day, so she suggests they think about where they can best work to complete their stories. The following day they again sit together, but concentrate on their writing. Specific assignments of physical placement usually are not made, although teachers may encourage isolated children in social skill development by occasionally creating paired situations.

The arrangement of tables or desks to allow for the formation of small groups encourages interaction and group work. Physical arrangements that permit children to converse face-to-face are important. Children in such arrangements learn to ask peers for help. There should also be spaces small enough to allow for individual children or pairs to work alone (see Figure 8-13). When children are able to move freely about the classroom, they may form new groupings or

Figure 8-13

Primary-age children often work in small groups.

work in different areas as they choose. The composition of small groups may be flexible and temporary, changing with different learning experiences. They may work in several different groups during the day, for particular reasons. During the morning, they may choose to sit near particular friends to write their stories. Later, a child may choose to join another group that is working on constructing an airplane model. Still later, the teacher may ask a child to join a group of children who have shown a common interest in a particular science experience. Both time and ideas encourage children to work together in groups.

Most of the day is spent in small-group or individual activity. Primary-age children are still shy enough that large groups are often intimidating. When children do come together for large-group meetings, they feel more comfortable making their own choices about where they will sit.

Primary-age children need to be able to regulate their own needs for food and rest and to make these decisions along with their friends. Teachers can provide a small snack area that children may use during specified times, forming their own small snack groups. During specified quiet periods, children may find a common activity with friends.

The other important relationships in the primary classroom are those between children and the teacher. Time and personal contact are key ingredients in nurturing these connections. The physical environment allows opportunities for children and teacher to converse and interact meaningfully. Informal arrangements of work areas and learning centers encourage conversation. The teacher functions sometimes as facilitator and observer as well as instructor, putting him or her in immediate contact with children involved in their work and ideas. As teachers get to know each child well, they can plan learning experiences and work individually in ways that take into account individual differences in ability and

---

JOURNAL REFLECTION

Working with Other Children

Do you remember working with other children in primary grades, or were you frequently told to do your own work? What were your feelings in either of these situations? How would that influence the arrangements you would make in an elementary classroom?

 Visit the premium Web site to complete this journal activity online and email it to your professor.

PRACTICAL IMPLICATIONS

Fostering Peer and Teacher-Child Relationships

Encourage peer and teacher-child relationships by

- allowing children to choose where and with whom they work and sit at large-group meetings.
- using flexible arrangements of tables and chairs to accommodate group needs.
- providing spaces small enough for one or two children to work in, as well as for small groups.
- providing spaces for children to have snack or rest with a small group.

interests. Opportunities for individual interaction are definitely enhanced when primary class-rooms are arranged into less formal work areas. Space here sends the message that children have active roles to play, including communicating in partnership with teachers.

SCHEDULE

The traditional school day schedule is divided and subdivided into short time segments, with teachers directing the separate lessons. For example, after taking out their notebooks for a fifteen-minute exercise in handwriting, Miss Stewart's first-graders are directed to put those notebooks away and get out their social studies books to read and discuss the lesson on bridges. Not only is the day broken up into individual lessons, but other interruptions are frequent—time to go to the gym with the physical education teacher, to the library, and to music and art classes. Usually the children are unable to keep up with the frequent changes in their day, so they follow the teacher's directions. ("Time to put your social studies book away. We'll have to finish that later. It's time for us to go to the library now.") Often children are asked to follow a schedule that makes sense only from the point of view of the adult keeping order. ("Sit quietly at your desk until everyone has finished their math pages, and then we'll begin our spelling lesson.") Because of the emphasis on whole-group instruction, the traditional schedule is filled with such meaningless periods.

The result of these fragmented primary classroom schedules is that children's attention spans for task orientation actually decrease after spending a year in such classrooms. When they are frequently shifted from one activity to another, children become dependent on having an adult direct their learning and less able to concentrate on and establish their own meaningful activities.

In the developmentally appropriate primary classroom, teachers attempt to give children uninterrupted blocks of time to involve themselves fully in activities that demand their concentration. Blocks of time are essential when the curriculum is accomplished in an integrated way, so that children have opportunities to think, reflect, and make connections. As children work together on long-term projects, time is needed for communicating, planning, and carrying out the plan. With blocks of time, both teachers and children concentrate on the tasks to be planned and accomplished, rather than letting the clock dictate what learning should be occurring at any given time. Children need blocks of time to experience learning to manage their own time.

An appropriate schedule allows children to proceed at their own unique pace. Individual needs are well served by the large-block approach to scheduling; children who work faster or slower or whose learning style requires particular modifications or the help of instructional specialists, are not rushed, hindered, or segregated. Within the blocks of time, children may be involved in individual or small-group activities, either independent or teacher-guided. Large-group activities alternate between the longer blocks for child-initiated activity. A large proportion of the day is spent on child-planned and child-initiated activity. The time blocks are organized to allow for alternating periods of physical activity with quiet times.

Teachers minimize interruptions, allowing children to direct their own productivity within the time block. For example, if a snack table is made available for children from 9:30 to 10:30, children may choose the time when they want to take a break from their work or chat with a friend, or are hungry (see Figure 8-14) without the teacher interrupting everyone from their work at the same time to announce they must clear the tables for the whole group to have a snack.

Figure 8-14

With flexible snack times, children may choose to eat when they are hungry.

As far as is practical, teachers schedule necessary breaks for times when children need a change of pace, such as later in the day or between large work time blocks. For example, the visit to the music teacher might be scheduled for midmorning, after the children have spent an hour on their reading/writing projects and before their learning center time. The standards of the National Association of Elementary School Principals (1990) suggest that programs or activities that pull children out of the classroom should be "minimal or nonexistent." This does not, of course, refer to field trips into the community that may be an important part of integrated theme study. It does mean the interruptions for specialized instruction that is routine in some schools. With an integrated curriculum, creative experiences are part of the classroom day.

Teachers establish reasonable routines that make sense to the children, so they can manage their day without having to wait for teacher instruction. For example, the children know that after the teacher has read to them in the morning, they will select their own reading books and read independently before they decide they are ready to begin writing their own stories. Transitions flow smoothly and are kept to a minimum when meaningful routines have been developed.

An appropriate schedule for a primary classroom is based on allowing children to become involved in their individual learning activities early in the day when their interest and energy levels are high (see Figure 8-15). Later in the day, whole-group activities that are likely to interest

Figure 8-15

Sample daily schedule for primary classroom. Used with permission of Beth Bellemere, Scarborough School Department.

Nongraded Primary Program—Sample Daily Schedule*

8:45 a.m.	Greetings, attendance, lunch count, opening
8:50 a.m.	**MORNING MEETING**
	WHOLE GROUP: (child and teacher directed)
	Includes morning message
	Date and number of days
	Whole language (chart, story, poem, or song)
	Review plans for day's activities
	SMALL GROUP/INDIVIDUAL ACTIVITIES (teacher directed)
	Letter work/phonics skill work
	Content work related to theme topic being studied
	Introduction of literature related to theme topic
9:30 a.m.	**CENTERS**
	Examples:
	Mathematics problem solving with manipulatives
	Creative writing
	Construction
	Listening
	Water
	Science
	Art
	Handwriting
10:15 a.m.	**OUTDOOR PLAY**
10:30 a.m.	**FORMAL MATH**
	Skills groups
11:30 a.m.	**LUNCH AND RECESS**
12:15 p.m.	**AFTERNOON MEETING**
	Story starter
	Teacher introduction related to theme topic
	Children share
12:30 p.m.	**PERSONAL READING**
	Teachers hold individual reading conferences
1:00 p.m.	**SHARED READING/SHARED WRITING**
	Teachers continue reading conferences
1:30 p.m.	**MEETING (ON MONDAYS ONLY) TO INTRODUCE CENTERS**
	Centers (continuation of a.m.)
	Students sharing of center work
	Students share books and creative writing
2:25 p.m.	**END OF DAY JOURNALS**
	Students write about their day's activities
2:45 p.m.	**BUS TIME**

*Components used by all teachers, but there may be variations in order depending upon individual teacher's interests and needs.

most children can be scheduled. For example, most of the morning is spent in reading/writing activities and in learning center projects. After lunch, the teacher plans a whole-group activity to introduce a new science experience to the children.

WHAT ABOUT RECESS?

In recent years, more and more elementary schools are abolishing recess. Although safety and liability are frequently offered as reasons for this, by far the most prevalent reason is to have more instructional time. The pressure to keep children learning on task has meant that recess times are seen as nonessential. However, a body of research indicates that recess offers important learning conditions and opportunities (Jarrett, 2002).

In almost all forms of work, breaks are considered essential for satisfaction and alertness. Studies of brain function indicate that attention requires periodic rest periods. The brain actually needs some "down time" to recycle the chemicals that are crucial for long-term memory formation. Several studies find positive effects of time spent in physical activity, including improved attitudes and improvement in test scores.

In addition to cognitive functioning, recess needs to be considered in relation to other aspects of the whole child. Recess may be the only opportunity many children have to engage in social interaction with other children, particularly when the rest of the day is spent in highly structured classrooms or after-school activities. Much of what goes on during recess time—sharing folk culture, making choices of who and what to play, and developing rules for play—involves developing social skills. Adults who are observing children during such free play outdoors can observe the social interaction and intervene in situations that involve aggression or social isolation.

In addition, child health and physical abilities are affected by the physical activity. Statistics indicate alarming trends in children's levels of activity and attendant obesity. Many children have few opportunities for physical activity, being involved in more sedentary pursuits such as playing computer games and watching television. The research indicates that children who have been physically active during recess periods are more likely to engage in physical activity after school as well. In its position statement on the need for recess in elementary schools, the National Association for Sport and Physical Education makes the point that physical education classes are no substitute for recess (Council for Physical Education and Children, 2001). Recess is a necessary time for practicing and using the skills that

---

 VIDEO ACTIVITY

Go to the premium Web site and watch the video clip for Chapter 8 titled "Physical Development in the Primary Years." Then consider the following questions:

REFLECTIVE QUESTIONS

1. As teachers note children's varying physical abilities, what plans and support would help all children develop physical skills and abilities?

2. What are the connections between physical development and development in the other domains?

3. How do these ideas relate to the chapter discussion about recess?

 Visit the premium Web site to complete these questions online and email them to your professor.

PRACTICAL IMPLICATIONS

Appropriate Classroom Schedules

An appropriate schedule for primary classrooms includes

- providing uninterrupted large blocks of time for children's learning, alternating quiet periods with times of physical activity.

- providing for individual learning styles and paces.

- minimizing interruptions.

- scheduling necessary breaks.

- establishing meaningful routines for children's self-direction.

- scheduling whole-group activities later in the day.

- recess times, for active play.

are developed in physical education classes, without too much structure (see Figure 8-16).

The research suggests that recess can play an important role in the learning, social development, and health of elementary school children. Perhaps as more research is done on this topic, teachers and principals will have stronger support for retaining recess, if only to improve test scores, attitudes, and behavior (Jarrett, 2002).

AFTER-SCHOOL CHILDCARE

When the school day is over, many children still spend several hours in other care arrangements until their parents are finished working. This is important time. Assuming school ends about 3 p.m., and parents pick children up after work about 6 p.m., this is about 20 percent of the time that a primary-age child is awake. These are hours that can be filled with enriching experiences, new interests, socialization, and time just being a child.

Children need opportunities for physical activities, for socialization with peers, and for creative expression through arts and crafts. After six or seven hours already spent in an academic environment likely heavy on teacher-directed emphasis, the setting of after-school care probably needs to have more of the flavor of a neighborhood than yet another school (see Figure 8-17).

What components might add to this neighborhood feeling? One is the creation of **mixed-age groupings**. An age range of three or four years is similar to the natural play groupings that develop at home. Mixed-age groupings allow older children to develop initiative and responsibility, to demonstrate nurturing and cooperation. Younger children learn by imitating older ones. Read more about mixed-age groupings in Chapter 12.

Another component is a variety of choices. Out of the school environment, children need freedom to select the activities for after school, even the freedom to choose to do nothing at all. Many choices should be available: outdoor play, arts and crafts, games, cooking, woodworking, and other self-help and creative skills, exploring hobbies, or dramatic play.

The environment must include *challenge*. Greenman (2005) comments that it is not uncommon to see five- to twelve-year-olds in after-school settings that are primarily designed for preschoolers bored because the planners don't pay enough "attention to the developmental differences between school-age children and preschoolers" (Greenman, 2005, p. 279). They need an environment that acknowledges they are bigger and more capable, with interests in doing real things in the world. By age seven, play is different from reality. Rules and roles become important elements, and games, plays, and clubs reflect the school-age child's interest in the world of people (Greenman, 2005). These children need physical challenge, such as using real tools, and intellectual challenge, such as complex jigsaw puzzles and projects that can last over a period of time. Greenman suggests real-world challenge in the world of machines—seeing how things work and are put together; in the world of commerce—producing, buying, and selling; and in the world of communication—producing newsletters and

Deborah Jaffe/Corbis.

Figure 8-16

Recess can play an important role in academic learning, social development, and physical skills.

JOURNAL REFLECTION

Your After-School Experience

Think about what you did after school—where did you do it, and with whom did you do it? What did you gain from these after-school experiences? How could an after-school childcare program allow children to have similar experiences?

Visit the premium Web site to complete this journal activity online and email it to your professor.

Figure 8-17

After-school programs need the flavor of a neighborhood instead of seeming like an extension of school.

plays. Challenge may also be derived from fulfilling the responsibilities of maintaining the environment for the program—real adult chores, assisting one another and the adults, always in reasonable doses, so that the responsibility is fun and not just more work. Care must be taken to promote a nonsexist approach to challenge and responsibility; both boys and girls should feel comfortable and included in all possible activities.

The environment must provide for *privacy*. Having been in group situations all day long, children may want to play alone or with one or two friends. Privacy should be an option. Older primary-age children often create their own clubs and secret societies; they need space and privacy for this activity.

Gross motor activity is essential after the physical confinement of the typical school day. Primary-age after-school care programs need to offer time and space for children to run, jump, climb, yell, and generally have physical and emotional release from the restriction of the day. Cooperative games may be part of this gross motor activity; leaving behind the competition of the school environment is a good idea.

For children who need to do homework or study, the after-school program should offer a *quiet work place*. After-school programs must support differing parent and child needs, but be careful not to simply extend the academic day for more hours. If children need to spend a part of their time doing homework, they should first have opportunities to relax and refresh themselves after the day's work.

Television and video games or not is an issue to be resolved by any after-school program. Those who argue for it point out that children would more than likely be

PRACTICAL IMPLICATIONS

Appropriate After-School Care Environments

Developmentally appropriate after-school care environments include

- mixed-age groupings.
- choices of many activities, with the option of doing nothing.
- challenges in both the planned materials and activities, with projects that can be extended over time.
- responsibilities in the program.
- privacy for individuals and support for clubs.
- time and space for gross motor activity.
- a quiet study area.
- television under supervision, if at all.
- a schedule that balances needs for rest and activity with attention to the beginning transition.

Figure 8-18

Sample schedule for an after-school program.

Sample Schedule for After-School Child-Care Program

2:30–3:00	Children arrive from various schools. Snacks, often prepared by children, and conversation.
3:00–4:00	Vigorous outdoor play, with free choices, and occasional organized group games (weather permitting). Indoor alternatives are balls, hula hoops, and cooperative games in gym. Special visitors, such as a dance teacher, may be scheduled during this time.
4:00–5:00	Choices of indoor activity centers, such as art, music, computers, cooking, or construction. Sometimes this period is used for work on long-term group projects.
5:00–6:00	Homework and/or reading time, until parents pick up.

watching it if they were at home and that they like it and learn from it. Opponents point out that violent content is not helpful to children trying to sort out prosocial behaviors, and passive viewing robs children of more constructive experiences. When programs do decide to include television viewing as part of the planned activities, teacher supervision and limits are necessary.

Schedule considerations are different for an after-school program. Only a few hours are spent there, so fewer transitions are needed than during the school day. The key transition, however, is the beginning period as children arrive from their full-day school program. They are liable to be tired and hungry and in need of relaxation after the day's work. Providing for these needs is important. It is often useful to have a period for snack and relaxed conversation, followed by opportunities for vigorous physical exercise, before the children are ready for the projects and activities of the later afternoon. Many families also benefit by providing a quiet period just before going home, when both children and parents are weary (see Figure 8-18).

THINGS NOT FOUND IN DEVELOPMENTALLY APPROPRIATE PRIMARY CLASSROOMS

The issues of developmental appropriateness can be seen perhaps most graphically when examining the variety of physical environments offered to primary-age children. School system traditions are undergoing scrutiny and change in many parts of the country, and many classrooms are currently in transition. In some cases, the speed of transition is dictated by school system budgets for purchase of new furnishings and materials. Some classrooms in transition are likely to exhibit mixtures of inappropriate and more appropriate components. Nevertheless, some elements related to space, physical arrangements, and time that are not considered appropriate for an optimum learning situation include the following:

- Curriculum is divided into separate subjects, primarily reading and math, with others covered if time permits.
- Teacher-directed reading groups take up most of the morning, while children spend most of their time doing paper-and-pencil practice exercises.
- Special learning projects, centers, and outdoor play are either absent or used as rewards for good learning behavior or occasional treats.
- Children work silently and alone most of the time in assigned desks that are not moved.
- Instruction is given mostly to the large group.
- Children have few choices in planning their activities or workday, which is broken up into short periods for different instruction. Find more specifics that contrast with developmentally appropriate practice in Copple and Bredekamp (2009).

Similar comments can be made about restrictions in after-school programs. See how closely these descriptions match primary programs in your community.

SUMMARY

Primary-age children are interested in becoming competent. They need physical environments that help assist them develop a sense of industry by succeeding at learning tasks that match their mostly preoperational learning style. They need environments that allow them to assume active roles in planning and directing their learning. They need environments in which plenty of well-chosen materials are available for exploration, investigation, and creativity. They need environments that allow them to interact and work with peers. They need environments that help their emerging interest and skills in literacy. The arrangements of space and time need to convey messages of children's active roles in their own learning. Both regular school day programs and after-school programs must recognize the developmental needs of primary-age children.

THINK ABOUT IT ACTIVITIES

1. Sketch your memories of what one or more of your primary classrooms looked like. Ask your classmates to share their memories of the physical environments they experienced in the early grades. Where did their friends sit? What did the teacher's desk look like? How did they spend their time? What do they recall about transitions? What provision was there for individual pace or style of learning?

   After this class discussion, list elements that seem appropriate from your reading in this chapter and elements that seem less appropriate.

2. Where possible, visit primary classrooms in your community. (Visit in pairs where practical, to compile and compare your observations.) Sketch out and describe the physical arrangements you see. Identify elements that contribute to an environment to form a sense of industry, an environment to promote early literacy, and an environment to promote peer and teacher relationships.

3. If after-school childcare programs are available in your community, find out about their programs and schedules. Compare your findings with the discussion in this chapter.

QUESTIONS TO ASSESS LEARNING OF CHAPTER OBJECTIVES

1. Describe what primary-age children are like and what they do.
2. Identify the developmental needs of primary-age children to which the physical environment must respond.
3. Discuss considerations in creating an environment to nurture a sense of industry.
4. Discuss elements present in an environment that promotes early literacy.
5. Describe environmental considerations for promoting the development of peer relationships.
6. Identify aspects of appropriate schedules.
7. Discuss issues related to recess.
8. Discuss considerations for appropriate after-school programs.
9. Identify elements not present in developmentally appropriate primary classrooms.

APPLY YOUR KNOWLEDGE QUESTIONS

1. Design a schedule for an after-school program that meets all the needs of primary-age children described in this chapter. Include a rationale for all activities offered and how they will be offered.

2. Write the description of your first-grade classroom environment and schedule that you would send to parents. Include explanations for questions that might arise regarding children's ability to make some choices in the classroom and how you plan to meet individual instructional needs.

HELPFUL WEB SITES

http://www.ed.gov	Go to this Web site to read the entire text of the No Child Left Behind legislation.
http://www.niost.org	The Web site for the National Institute on Out-of-School Time, sponsored by Wellesley College, has much information about curriculum and environments for after-school programs. Search here to find an article by D. Alexander (2000): "The Learning That Lies between Play and Academics in After-School Programs."
http://www.afterschool.gov	This Web site has resources for after-school programs.
http://www.schoolagenotes.com	This Web site has much information on setting up appropriate environments and schedules in after-school programs.
http://www.naesp.org	The Web site of the National Association of Elementary School Principals has much information. Click on Research a Topic, and then on After-School to find articles on after-school programs and curriculum, and many others.

 Please visit the premium Web site for Developmentally Appropriate Practice, 4th edition, to access more chapter web links, suggestions for further research and study, additional book chapters, interactive quizzes, video exercises, online journal activities, flashcards, and much more! Go to www.cengage.com/login to register your access code.

GUEST EDITORIAL

by Caroline Pratt

Caroline Pratt was the founder of the City and Country School in New York City, one of the oldest progressive elementary schools in the country, opened in 1914. The school was created out of Pratt's frustration and disillusionment with what she called "the repression of formal education." Pratt's school later became part of the first Bank Street School. (Read about Bank Street philosophy in Chapter 4.) The wooden unit blocks she designed are a basic material used in preschools all over the country. Pratt described her experiences in the book I Learn From Children (1948), from which this excerpt is taken. It still seems to have relevance today, as we think of children's growing abilities to live with others.

One can almost predict, from the impact of a baby's first cry, whether his social relations are to be happy ones. How his mother receives his first vocal demand is an omen of his future. If his mother loves him, if she offers him the simple respect which one human being owes to another human being, he is a lucky child. For him the world will have a friendly face, because the one on whom he first depended has tried to understand him.

But no child has gone far who has merely come to terms with his mother; there are many other relationships with which he must deal. Unlike his mother, (other children) are utterly uninterested in finding out what he wants; they care only about what they want, and how to get it. This first step from home is enormously important in the pre-school years. If he already has healthy relationships at home, and is allowed to make his way with his own kind outside the home, he is well on his way to becoming a happy citizen of the community.

Now comes school where an entirely different kind of behavior is expected of him. He cannot make friends with his teacher, who has thirty or forty other children to look after. Whatever else he may learn in a formal school, he will not learn to live with others, for the system enjoins him strictly to go his own way and mind his own business. Fortunately he spends only six hours of his day in this confinement. Though he is free to play, there is no one to help him and his friends to get the most out of their play together, to show them ways of planning together for the good of the whole group, of settling disagreements, of understanding each other.

I don't think I overstate the failure of traditional schools in ignoring this part of a child's learning. Some of them are beginning to realize this responsibility, and to make tentative efforts toward a "socialized curriculum." With standardized systems and, above all, classes and schools that are always too large, it is uphill work. (Pratt, 1948, pp. 165–167)

Developmentally Appropriate Social/Emotional Environments

INTRODUCTION

In this section, we will examine the nature of the social and emotional environments that nurture development in the most appropriate ways. The discussion of social/emotional environments will include practices and interaction that encourage healthy emotional growth and relationships; appropriate guidance to move children toward self-esteem and self-control; adult behaviors that encourage development of prosocial awareness and socialization skills; and classroom planning considerations for teachers who want to encourage cooperation and group participation skills.

When speaking of the social/emotional environments for children, we are talking about the people and relationships made available in the environment. Who the adults are and how they respond to the children they care for determine the quality of the social/emotional environment.

This section is also divided into four chapters focusing on social/emotional environments for infants, toddlers, preschoolers, and primary-age children. Certain aspects of the social/emotional domain are distinct to each of these periods of development (for example, toddler biting in Chapter 10), whereas others are continuous, begun in one stage and continuing on into the next, such as helping children with emotional development. Some topics, such as an antibias respect for diversity, discipline, and mixed-age groupings, are relevant to all stages; however, for the sake of brevity, they will only be discussed at length in only one of the chapters (antibias and discipline in Chapter 11, mixed-age groupings in Chapter 12).

Developmentally Appropriate Social/Emotional Environments: For Infants

Babies are born with a predisposition to notice, interact with, and attract the attention of the people around them. Even in the first hours of life, babies react to their social world, gazing into eyes and seriously staring at faces, responding to verbal sounds, and molding their bodies to fit into arms waiting to hold them. And this is important, because babies are totally dependent on others to provide the necessities for physical survival and to nurture development of all domains. From newborns who vary between states of peaceful calm and passionate generalized upset, the first year of life finds babies developing particular specific emotions. In addition, infants become adept at communicating with those about them, entering into a world of social relationships. A crucial developmental task of infancy is to form an attachment with one, or more likely several, key persons in the environment in which each baby lives. Becoming attached during the first months of life is vitally important to healthy development in infancy and to optimum development in later periods.

Every infant has a unique environment, depending on family structure and roles played by the adults, cultural and community custom, and supplemental care. Those who respond to the baby's needs may be related by birth or by profession. But whatever adults share the care of the infant, certain behaviors and characteristics will contribute to a healthy social and emotional environment.

LEARNING OBJECTIVES

Upon completion of this chapter, students should be able to

- discuss several social/emotional issues of infancy.
- describe characteristics of developmentally appropriate interaction.
- discuss positive implications for caregivers.
- list practices to avoid.

SOCIAL/EMOTIONAL ISSUES IN INFANCY

In this chapter, we will first consider the issues raised by various theorists and the social/emotional tasks of infancy before going on to a more detailed discussion of adult behaviors.

Attachment

There have long been debates about how babies become attached to their mothers. ("Mothers" is used to indicate primary caregivers, noting that today babies are increasingly cared for by other important adults to whom strong attachments are formed, including fathers, childcare center staff, and other surrogates.) When Harry Harlow discovered that his baby monkeys clung to the terry cloth "mother," even when the wire "mother" held the feeding bottle, it seemed to indicate that feeding or satisfying physical needs alone was not the source of attachment (1958). The later work of Bowlby and Ainsworth focused on specific styles of parenting and quality parent-child relationships as most important in promoting secure and mutual attachments and everything such attachments mean in terms of security, personality, future relationships, and approach to life. Specifically, secure attachments seemed to result when mothers responded with sensitivity to what their babies communicated they needed and were warmly and physically responsive to their babies' signals for socialization. Mothers of anxiously attached infants had been observed as inconsistent, unresponsive, or rejecting (Bowlby, 1988; Ainsworth et al., 1978, 1982). A good discussion of the influence of both Bowlby and Ainsworth on current attachment theory is found in *Becoming Attached* (Karen, 1998).

Studies also indicate the importance of recognizing differing temperaments in children (and in parents) and the influence on attachment (Chess & Thomas, 1977, 1982). The concept of "goodness of fit" refers to how adults are able to adapt to and accept the temperamental responses of their infant, and how the infant can adapt to the responses received from the environment. Obviously, problems for attachment can develop when the behavior of either partner does not mesh well with the expectations and responses of the other. Later studies have found correlations between preschoolers' approaches to problem-solving situations, peers, curiosity, persistence, and self-reliance, and the earlier formation of a secure attachment between parent and child. Given the strong evidence that attachment is so globally important to optimum development, attachment theory has implications as we consider developmentally appropriate social/emotional environments for infants.

Note that attachment theory, influencing the direction of much of the research about infants in childcare, was built on studies done with "nonworking, middle-class mothers" (Leavitt, 1994, p. 6). Leavitt states her concern about the exclusive focus in attachment theory on the mother as the primary attachment figure and the contribution this makes to the "underlying ideology in the day-care research that directs the political debate over day care" (Leavitt, 1994, p. 11).

Trust

As Erik Erikson described the stages of psychosocial development, he emphasized the first, the stage of infancy, in which the infant has the potential of forming a basic **sense of trust** or a sense of mistrust, as a result of how the social environment (caregivers) responds to the communication of infant needs. When needs are met consistently, with appropriate messages of caring, babies come to feel that the world is a good place to be, and by extension, that the people in it are good, interesting, and caring (see Figure 9-1). With less positive experiences, babies may find the world less friendly and people less helpful and available; such an attitude truly shadows and influences later relationships with others (Erikson, 1963).

An obvious connection exists between the development of primary attachments and the baby's capacity to trust. In a loving relationship with adults who respond warmly and positively to the baby as he or she communicates need, the baby learns these people are dependable and trustworthy.

The responses of others allow the baby to first learn trust.

Figure 9-1

A sense of trust is built when babies' needs are met consistently and with tender care.

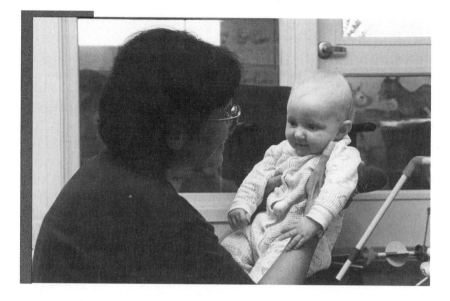

Separation and Stranger Anxiety

Sometime in the latter months of the first year, infant behavior indicates that milestones in the attachment process have been reached. After even a few months, the baby indicates a clear recognition and preference for the mother or primary caregiver, saving the biggest smiles, most emphatic gurgling sounds, and most insistent attempts to attract attention from that special person. At around eight months or so, babies begin to protest desperately when mother leaves for even a brief absence. This first **separation anxiety** indicates that true attachment has occurred, and the baby feels anxiety about losing mother's presence. At about the same time, many babies become very wary of people who are not familiar to them. Often misinterpreted by adults as the baby suddenly becoming "shy," **stranger anxiety** is another positive indication that the baby absolutely recognizes the special, trustworthy people in the social environment. Child psychiatrist Margaret Mahler refers to the process of separation individuation as a kind of psychological birth occurring as children emerge from a **symbiotic** relationship with their mothers (1979). Both of these social responses should be recognized and accepted as part of the attachment process, and babies need to be supported as they slowly learn to trust that loved ones will reliably return and that new faces can also be accepted. Cultural variations influence what separation and care by others means to individual families. Recognizing that separation reactions can be expected in infants, and understanding how to support babies and their families through this is an important role for an infant caregiver (Balaban, 2006).

Obvious practical implications exist for timing separation and/or new experiences with caregivers, if parents have the luxury of choice. Entry into a childcare situation either before or after the acute period of separation anxiety might help both baby and parent avoid some of that early pain (see Figure 9-2). Maintaining staff stability in infant rooms seems critical in helping babies develop comfort with familiar faces.

Emotional Responsiveness

The fear of strangers and anxiety when out of the comforting presence of a loved adult are examples of the developing emotional repertoire of infancy. Very young infants have vaguely defined emotional responses, seeming to feel either relatively calm or in an uproar. By the end of infancy, however, it is possible to differentiate the various feelings of fear, anger, frustration, pleasure, love, pride, or jealousy. Cognitive capacities of memory and increased understanding have a role in this differentiation. Emotional responsiveness is also a factor of culture. The critical factor in the appearance of emotion seems to be the first experience of love. Babies who have not been involved in that close, secure attachment seem to remain emotionally flat, indifferent to what

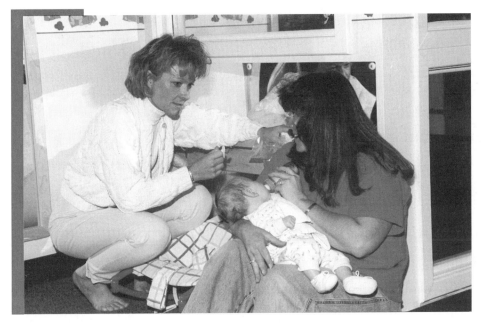

Figure 9-2

Parents may experience their own separation anxiety when leaving their infants in the care of others.

goes on in their lives. It is important that adults who care for babies recognize that infant feelings are real and strong. Appropriate adult responses include respecting the feeling, neither teasing nor distracting the child away from the feeling, and helping deal with the cause of the feeling.

Stanley Greenspan has charted milestones in infants' emotional growth. During infancy, he describes (1) self-regulation and interest in the world, from birth; (2) falling in love, as they move into relationships, from four months; (3) developing intentional communication, from eight months; and (4) the emergence of an organized sense of self, from ten months (Greenspan & Greenspan, 1989.)

Spoiling

Although no theorist has formally dealt with the topic of "spoiling" babies, every parent and caregiver has opinions on the subject, thus making it a social/emotional issue of infancy.

What most adults mean by spoiling is teaching babies to believe that they can get what they want by crying or other methods of voicing demands. Such teaching, so goes the argument, is done when adults pick up babies when they cry. **Behavioral theory** asserts that this practice reinforces the crying, thus producing a child who has learned to cry to get what is wanted (Skinner, 1938).

Actually, the attachment studies seem to refute this notion, as do findings that babies who have received prompt responses during the first six months of infancy actually cry less and are more self-sufficient in later infancy (Ainsworth et al., 1982; Copple & Bredekamp, 2009).

> Some people worry that if we make life too easy for babies they will be spoiled. A secure start, being given to, having needs met quickly and sensitively nourishes a much later capacity in the child to give, to wait, to share. In other words, it ensures against what is commonly termed "the spoiled child." (Stonehouse, 1986, p. 41)

Nevertheless, popular thinking about spoiling, rather than developmental research, influences the practice and interaction of many parents and infant caregivers who have strong feelings about the way babies are supposed to be taken care of. Adults in particular cultures and communities have beliefs about what is good for babies, and these beliefs reflect their varying value systems

JOURNAL REFLECTION

Can Infants Be Spoiled?

Before you read any further, find a sheet of paper and write down a brief response to these questions: Do you believe babies under the age of six or seven months can be spoiled? What is the evidence for your belief? Why do you believe this? Keep this response handy to refer to at later points in the chapters on infants.

 Visit the premium Web site to complete this journal activity online and email it to your professor.

(Gonzalez-Mena, 2007). Gonzalez-Mena quotes Edward T. Hall's book *Beyond Culture:* "The world is divided into those cultures who cut the apron strings and those who do not" (Hall, cited in Gonzalez-Mena, 2007, p. 90). Adult responses to babies are based on larger cultural goals and themes, thus generating very strong feelings about correct responses. Our consideration recognizes these strong feelings, while focusing on the critical need for responding to babies' signals.

Childcare for Infants

Today, fully one-third of American women who give birth have returned to work by the time the baby is two –months old, and about half are back to work by the baby's first birthday. Thus, it is obvious that many families have had to include caregivers outside the family in the baby's social/emotional environment (see Figure 9-3).

Although many families have always had others to supplement parenting efforts, the numbers of babies cared for full-time by nonfamily members today raise questions about its effects on attachment and relationships.

Certainly no clear agreement exists among researchers about whether infant childcare is harmful or not. Jay Belsky was one of the first researchers who pointed to a finding that increased numbers of insecurely attached infants are found among children enrolled in childcare during the first year of life for more than twenty hours each week (Belsky, 1988). Although other researchers raised questions about how the quality of care and family characteristics might influence such negative conclusions (Phillips, 1987; Clarke-Stewart, 1989; Hoffman, 1989), the controversy continues. As recently as 2001, Jay Belsky, one of the more than thirty researchers conducting the National Institute of Child Health and Human Development (NICHD) Study of Early Child Care (NICHD, 1997), stated that there was a relationship between time in childcare and problem behaviors, especially those involving aggression and behavior. But subsequent comments from other researchers involved in the study (Caldwell, 2001) pointed out that the researchers have been concerned with family variables, childcare variables, and child characteristics, and that the study is ongoing. Regarding attachment, the general finding is that "not one of the major childcare variables—age of entry, type of care, amount of care—*in and of itself* is associated with lack of secure attachment. The most powerful predictor was *maternal sensitivity*" (Caldwell, 2001). Nevertheless, the discussion about the effects of early childcare has continued with an article published in 2007 by Belsky and other researchers reporting that the more time children spent in center-based care before kindergarten, the more likely their sixth-grade teachers were to report such problem behaviors as "gets in fights," "disobedient at school," and "argues a lot." On

Figure 9-3

Child care is a common occurrence for many infants and their families.

Figure 9-4
The quality of interaction between caregiver adult and infant is most important.

the other hand, the study also reported that children who had received higher-quality childcare before entering kindergarten had better vocabulary scores in fifth grade than did children who received lower-quality care (Belsky et al., 2007).

Such questions being raised about the effects of childcare are even more alarming when the results of the Cost, Quality, and Child Outcomes Study of childcare quality in four states indicated that most childcare for infants—92 percent, in fact—was either poor or mediocre (Heburn, 1995). Leavitt's work (1994) raises questions about how the powerlessness of childcare workers translates into power struggles that impact on care experiences for infants and their families. (For a good overview of the opinions of many recognized child development specialists, see Chapter 3 in Greenberg, 1991.) Clearly this issue will continue to be researched and discussed in light of developmentally appropriate practices for the social/emotional health of infants. The one obvious fact is that the quality of interaction either at home or in a childcare center is very important (see Figure 9-4).

Another important issue related to childcare for infants is the cultural differences in values and practices that determine how babies are cared for. "The most basic acts of daily care— feeding, toilet training, comforting, playing—reflect the cultural values of both the parent and the caregiver, but these expectations may not necessarily match" (Chang, 1993, p. 10). Smiling, touch, and eye contact, as well as physical and sensory stimulation as communication that accompanies the caregiving, are all communication that is specific to each culture (Gonzalez-Mena, 2007). Differences are inevitable; what is not inevitable is that one cultural view remains dominant over the other. Infant caregivers must openly explore cultural beliefs and practices with parents, finding solutions that do not ignore either the views of the parents or optimum environments for infants.

DEVELOPMENTALLY APPROPRIATE INTERACTION PRACTICES

Developmentally appropriate interaction behaviors match what is known about the issues of social and emotional development just discussed. Warm responsive attention from adults is necessary for babies to form the first important relationships from which so much healthy development follows. We need to consider the various components of warm responsiveness that lead to the development of trust, attachment, and emotional responsiveness in infants. In their work, *The Seven Irreducible Needs of Children,* Brazelton and Greenspan state that the most important need for healthy development is ongoing, nurturing relationships (2000).

Warm responsiveness comes with respect, sensitive responses, close physical contact, repetition, and consistency in patterns of caregiving, and recognition of infant limitations in social relationships.

Respect

Caregivers must respect infants' needs as real and important. Babies are treated with an appropriate degree of seriousness. Despite their inability to talk and their real dependence on adults, babies are not simply helpless dolls, ready to have things done to them at the whim of adults. When this respect is present, adults will try harder to discover what infants are trying to convey.

A lack of respect is shown when Candace shrugs to her coworker, "I just changed her, and her bottle's not due for more than an hour, so she's crying for no reason at all." A more respectful approach occurs when Robin comments, "Well, she's dry and fed, so that can't be it, so I'll have to figure out what else she's trying to tell me."

Respect is the key word in Magda Gerber's philosophy of caring for infants. (Read more about this in Gerber, 1991.) Respect implies that infants are not treated as passive recipients of whatever adults decide to do for them, but can actively participate and communicate in a care partnership.

Babies need an active voice in decisions about their lives as described in the following paragraphs and examples.

- Follow babies' self-demand schedules for feeding, sleeping, playing. Have an attitude of respect that does not assume that adults know what is best for babies and should attempt to make them conform to adult timetables. Each baby is cared for as physical and social needs are interpreted, without any preconceived adult ideas about what the appropriate timing should be. Needs and decisions of individual families are also respected.

CULTURAL CONSIDERATIONS

Approaches to Infant Care

Culture is the strongest influence in determining child-rearing behaviors. Parents learn most of what they know about parenting from watching their own family members and hearing discussions in their communities about what constitutes "good parenting." Therefore, many families will have views that oppose the idea of self-demand schedules for eating and sleeping, believing it is best for infants to learn to inhibit their needs and adapt to family schedules and expectations. When adults believe that establishing a predictable schedule is the goal in their infant care, they obviously respond to infants in very different ways than when they believe that natural rhythms should be respected. Obviously such opposing viewpoints can create conflict between families and caregivers outside the family. It is important for caregivers to sort out whether the issues are important enough for the child's well-being, or if there is merely a difference of opinion. Looking at issues from parents' perspectives and understanding their point of view and reasons for their assumptions are important first steps in resolving cultural conflicts about infant care issues. Caregivers must be aware that assuming their way is the "right" or "normal" way to care for babies can create conflicts, and instead be responsive to, as well as responsible for, initiating dialogue.

Jill is ready for her bottle at about 9 a.m. Ebonee has been sleeping for an hour and will likely sleep until about 10 a.m. Jasmine finished her nap at about 8:30 a.m. and is on the floor playing with foam blocks. Their caregiver respects their varying needs and responds accordingly.

- Assume that crying babies have real needs, and respond promptly to let babies know their message is heard. Responding does not necessarily always mean, as some misinterpret, picking the baby up, but may mean speaking, making eye contact, changing the baby's position or viewpoint, or offering a new activity. Responding means letting the infant know the message has been received.

  Michelle talks softly as she begins to warm Angel's bottle. "I hear you, I know you're hungry. It will take just a minute." Angel quiets as she hears the gentle voice.

- Allow babies to take the lead and try to interpret their communication. Respectful adults assume that babies will have their own nonverbal methods of communicating.

  "I think you want to get moved over by the window. I see you watching the curtains move."

- Wait to see if infants can solve a problem, soothe themselves, or find something interesting to do before adults step in. This is known as practicing "selective intervention" (Gerber, 1991). There are times to help and times not to, and only waiting to give the baby the first chance will help adults decide which time this is.

> Charlotte watches Alexandro, whining softly, crawl around the floor toward the musical ball. She continues to watch as he stops whining and sits to grab at the ball. Problem solved—and by Alexandro.

- Give babies cues and watch for their readiness to respond before proceeding with care. Respectful interaction assumes that babies are active participants in the routines that involve them; adults talk and explain coming events as if babies could comprehend.

> Stephan is dressing Myra and tells her it's time to put her shirt on. He waits patiently for Myra to stretch out her arm.

- Respect infant preferences for certain people and obvious discomfort in contact with others. Particularly when babies have reached the landmark of stranger anxiety, caregivers allow infants to withdraw from those people they object to. They support babies positively as they encounter new situations and allow them to set the pace in becoming accustomed to new people and places (see Figure 9-5).

> Charlotte holds Alexandro and allows him to bury his face in her shoulder when a visitor comes too close. She explains, "No, he's not shy, he just doesn't know you yet. If you sit over there and let him get used to you, he'll probably get comfortable soon. Let him come to you, instead of you going to him."

- Treat infants' emotions seriously as they begin to demonstrate specific feelings. Adults support the child to find methods of coping and to acknowledge feelings.

> "You're pretty unhappy this morning aren't you? There you go—good idea. I think your blankie will help you feel better."

- Respect parents' culturally derived feelings about what is appropriate care for their infants. Although there may be real differences between caregivers' usual practices and parents' requests, each difference deserves to be explored, to understand parents' thinking and parenting decisions. Through careful communication, parents and teachers may be able to compromise or at least to accept the other's viewpoint as valid. Caregivers must not assume that culturally different practices reflect poor parenting.

> Charlotte talks with Alexandro's parents, learning their reasons for allowing him to sleep in their bed. She explains that licensing regulations require him to sleep in his own bed in the center and agrees to move his bed closer to the heart of activity in the room.

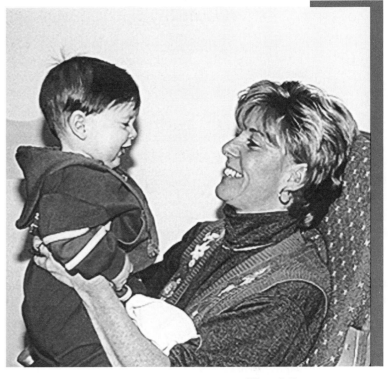

Figure 9-5

Infants need the support of familiar caregivers as they encounter new situations.

PRACTICAL IMPLICATIONS

Respecting Infants

Caregivers do not:

- ignore babies' crying, responses, or initiatives.
- interrupt their play without words when adults want to do routine caregiving tasks.
- force the attention of strangers on unwilling babies.
- dismiss the feeling, distract the baby from the feeling, or ignore the feeling.
- ignore culturally different views on infant care.
- treat babies as cute objects, such as putting play hats on them and laughing at how "cute" they look.

Sensitivity of Responsiveness

Relationships grow as individuals learn to interpret the messages from others. Even very young babies have their own temperamental style and tempo, their own moods and feelings. Attachment is a two-way mutual process between adult and infant. Each partner must attend to the individual signals and style of the other, leading to "goodness of fit." Such discriminating sensitivity is linked to secure or insecure attachments.

> Ainsworth showed that mothers of babies who later are avoidant hold their babies as much as mothers of babies who later are secure. So if you just measure frequency of holding, you get no difference. But there's one circumstance in which mothers of babies who are later avoidant do not hold them, and that's when the baby signals that it wants to be held. (Karen, 1998)

As adults learn to read the messages from individual babies, they are able to modify their behaviors to match the real differences in need and temperament. Responsiveness refers to both how well the caregiver understands the infant's cues and how sensitively and accurately the adult responds. Responsiveness is a result of being tuned-in to the baby and showing sensitivity and care in the response (Petersen & Wittmer, 2008).

> Jacob, a slow-to-warm-up infant, may need an adult who stays close by, silently indicating her interest in his exploration; the same caregiver responds with loud, delighted laughter when Olivia, an extremely active baby, takes the initiative in patty-cake.

Sensitive responsiveness comes when adults

- take time to observe and tune into individual real differences and tolerances for sound, change, and activity, and do not simply respond to their own concept of what the baby might like or be like (see Figure 9-6). "Caregivers learn and watch for each infant's cues, so they are able to judge when the baby

 VIDEO ACTIVITY

Go to the premium Web site and watch the video clip for Chapter 9 titled "Interaction with Infants." Then consider the following questions:

REFLECTIVE QUESTIONS

1. In this interaction between adult and baby, what components of forming a relationship do you see?

2. Notice the pacing of the interaction, and the infant's response. How does such interaction support the development of attachment and trust?

 Visit the premium Web site to complete these questions online and email them to your professor.

Figure 9-6

Getting to know each baby helps caregivers respond to individual differences of temperament.

needs to eat, is uncomfortable, or would like to be held. Every infant gets responsive care" (Copple & Bredekamp, 2009, p. 77).

"It's been interesting what I've learned in the three months since the twins were born," says Allison. "Sam fits right in with what I expected my baby to be like—sociable, easy to please, ready to cuddle. But Will—he's another story. He can't stand loud noises, and gets downright irritable when anybody talks to him too loudly. I've really had to learn when he wants to play and when he just wants to be left alone."

• learn from others in babies' lives about infant style and experiences. Communication between parents and caregivers is important to enhance overall awareness of individual infants' personalities.

The twins' mother, who has cared for her babies for the past three months, has already learned much about the babies that the caregiver in the infant room can tap into. She passes on her learnings about Will's need for a calmer environment.

• realize that responsiveness implies reciprocal interaction. Caregivers have to practice turn-taking behavior, taking time in play and caregiving interaction to pause and allow the baby to participate and respond. A pause also allows a sensitive caregiver to learn how the baby is reacting and to pace or adapt accordingly (see Figure 9-7).

Tabitha places the rings in front of the baby's hands and waits to see if the baby wants to reach out for them. She does not just shake the rings to entertain the baby or just put them into the baby's hand. Her turn is to offer the toy; the baby's turn is to decide what to do with the toy.

Figure 9-7

A sensitive caregiver paces her responses by the baby's reaction.

Close Physical Contact

Touching, fondling, and skin contact are all necessary for attachment to take place. Alice Honig (1993) once expressed it as the infant "having absolute dominion over an adult's body," meaning being able to be in physical contact on demand. (She also said this means that a ratio of four infants to one adult is the maximum, with two arms and two legs able to supply that holding closeness!) The holding, nuzzling, and belly kisses that are a part of warm caregiving interaction are as crucial as the physical elements of food and sleep to healthy growth. Another important component is the eye-to-eye gaze that connects adult and baby, with a face filled with delight focused on the baby. Adults who care for babies must be able to freely demonstrate physical tenderness (see Figure 9-8).

> **PRACTICAL IMPLICATIONS**
>
> ### Sensitivity of Repsonsiveness
>
> Helpful caregivers avoid:
>
> • imposing adult ideas of play and interaction on babies.
> • frightening babies with a style that does not match theirs.
> • overwhelming babies by not giving them opportunities to "take turns" in interaction.
> • neglecting to form supportive and informative partnerships with parents.

Babies are born with attributes that promote physical closeness: the helpless cry designed to attract attention; the soft skin, and the way they grasp onto the fingers of the person holding them; the way they look right back into eyes; and of course, those first wide, toothless grins of social delight. Selma Fraiberg wrote that babies have the rudiments of a love language: "There is the language of the smile, the language of vocal sound-making, the language of the embrace. It's the essential vocabulary of love before we can yet speak of love" (Fraiberg, 1977, p. 29). Some babies are less responsive temperamentally, and with them caregivers have to reach out to promote attachment, knowing how critical it is to find ways to reach babies who seem to be passive or indifferent to physical contact.

Figure 9-8

Adults who care for infants must be able to demonstrate physical tenderness.

Figure 9-9

A couch in the infant room helps adults and babies spend quality time together.

Opportunities for close physical contact are a crucial part of good practices for infants. Such opportunities are found by

- employing only adults who can be freely physically demonstrative with babies, and who can reach out to those babies who do not participate as actively as others in responsive physical contact.

    The director at Alice's center observed her interaction with the babies for a morning before she was convinced that Alice was the right person for the position. Alice obviously was comfortable holding, touching, and nuzzling babies with genuine pleasure. Alice noticed right away that Joseph squirmed when she held him closely, so she put him in an infant seat beside her and continued to talk gently with him, looking into his eyes.

- allowing time, space, and opportunity for relaxed caregiving interaction, as described in Chapter 5.

    The director recently included a comfortable couch as part of the infant room furnishings (see Figure 9-9). She schedules a part-time caregiver to work for several hours in the late mornings so that the two full-time staff members do not have to rush through routines with the babies.

- including warm physical interaction in every encounter. Routines are seen not just as tasks to be completed, but as opportunities for physical closeness. With this philosophy, babies are always held closely as they are fed, and stroked as they are bathed and changed.

    When Lee feeds Kayla in the infant room, he holds her closely, uses his free hand to stroke her face and forearm gently, looks directly into her eyes as she stares at him, and smiles. He murmurs quietly to her and generally appears to be completely enjoying this close time with her.

Repetition and Consistency

No one has yet discovered how many hundreds or thousands of contacts between adult and infant are needed before attachment takes place. The stages of attachment indicate that it takes much of the first year spent in intimate, repeated, mutually satisfying experiences before attachment is evident. Studies of prolonged separation and disrupted relationships during this period show that attachments become anxious and difficult. Even without the drastic disruption of a mother's prolonged hospitalization or a series of different caregiving arrangements, however, there can be patterns of inconsistent responses. Imagine the dilemma of the mother who is torn between conflicting advice about spoiling from her mother and her doctor, or one who is exhausted by the demands of returning to full-time work outside the home and caring for other children, and feels she must get the baby to fit the family schedule. In both of these cases, parents may not respond consistently to babies each time they make their needs known.

Continuity of care is an important concept to be considered in appropriate infant programs. Having one caregiver over an extended period of time, instead of switching rooms and caregivers every six to nine months, is so important to a child's development. Just consider what is lost when babies have to learn a new way that the world and people work. Babies are in confusion and stress when they have to find new ways of communication. Many changes may make them reluctant to form new relationships. Continuity of care is also important for caregivers and families. Caregivers grieve when the children to whom they are attached move on, not allowing caregivers to experience the fruition of their efforts. Family members also grieve when they lose the relationships they have come to trust. Continuity of care supports trust and allows relationships that enhance development.

Practices that allow babies to develop a sense of predictability in their care are critical. Consistency is helped by

- communication between all adults involved in a baby's care to coordinate responses as much as possible.

    Both Alice and the twins' parents regularly write notes to one another in the log book on top of the twins' cubbies. This afternoon Alice wrote that Will had appeared quite relaxed today, and had not resisted being rocked before sleeping. His mother decided she would try rocking that night also.

- education of parents and caregivers about infant development, needs, and the importance of attachment practices, to dispel myths about babies learning to manipulate others and "spoiling." Using information to help adults become less fearful about responding to babies is one way to ensure predictable responses.

    When the twins' mother worried out loud regarding her own mother's advice about too much attention for the babies, Alice reassured her with some information about attachment formation.

- employing only those who are committed to being stable figures in infants' lives in childcare settings. The smallest possible adult-child ratios and practices, such as primary caregiving (see Chapter 5), all support consistency and ongoing, nurturing relationships (see Figure 9-10).

    In the infant room, Alice cares for Sam, Will, Julio, and MeiMei. Her coworker is the primary caregiver for Alexandro, Sandra, Vincent, and Olivia. All the children have

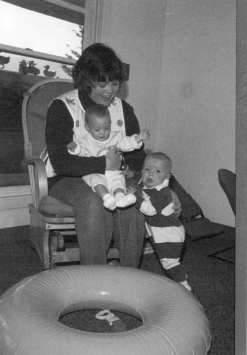

PRACTICAL IMPLICATIONS

Developing Close Physical Contact

Helpful caregivers avoid:

- leaving babies for long periods without adult attention or contact.
- accomplishing routines quickly without interaction with or involvement of the infant.
- treating babies with cold indifference or impersonal, brusque handling.

Figure 9-10

Warm, repeated interaction with caregivers helps infants build attachment.

PRACTICAL IMPLICATIONS

Consistency of Care

Unsupportive practices related to consistency of care include:

- ignoring babies' signals, trying instead to teach them to behave or schedule themselves as adults wish.

- responding unpredictably.

- "viewing work with infants as a chore and custodial in nature" (Bredekamp & Copple, 1997, p. 80).

---

formed close bonds with their primary caregiver, although they are contented to accept the care of the other consistent adult when their primary caregiver is on her break. All the families are happy to have one key adult for comfortable communication.

- the support of business, government, and community initiatives to assist families in the first months of babies' lives, thus enabling families to provide the majority of caregiving contact and eliminating some of the stresses that interfere with their ability to respond to babies.

Three of the local businesses have begun to offer part-time employment to mothers returning from maternity leave. This means the twins' mother is able to pick them up in the early afternoon most days.

Recognition of Limitations

As delightful and engaging as infants are in their first social relationships, it is important for the adults who care for them to recognize their limitations both socially and emotionally. These limitations are actually part of their developmental status regarding cognitive abilities and language. Caught up in the circle of attachment relationships, babies do not yet have a clear sense of themselves as individuals or even of a clear delineation between themselves and others. The idea that others have needs, feelings, or rights is developmentally far beyond them. Babies are beginning to understand language, but they are not yet controlled by it. In fact, control over feelings or behavior is still far from infants' abilities.

A caregiver who didn't recognize babies' limitations reacted with anger when Randy pulled Samantha's hair after he crawled over to where she was playing on the floor. She bent down and looked into his eyes with an angry look and said, "Bad boy." SunLi, who realized this was the innocent exploration of a curious baby, patted both Randy and Samantha's heads gently, saying, "Gently, gently, Randy." Then she took Randy's own hand to help him pat gently.

These limitations on understanding and control of behavior have clear implications for guidance and discipline. Adults are most helpful to babies in first social/emotional situations when they

- accept that infants do not intentionally hurt other babies and that they have no sense of property rights. They help babies learn to touch others gently and provide plenty of space and toys for each child. They recognize that preventing problems is more appropriate than trying to teach different behaviors (see Figure 9-11).

  "Gently, Will, gently," says Alice, as she pats Will's head gently and his brother's too. "Here, I think it is better if you play over here a bit," moving him toward more free floor space and away from his brother's head.

- expect that babies can't control their behavior by verbal direction, so rely on distraction, redirection, and removal of temptation to change the situation, rather than trying to change infant behavior directly. It is the adult's responsibility to provide the control; expecting babies to stop themselves is very inappropriate developmentally.

  "Here, Will, I think you might like this rattle to shake," as the caregiver quickly removes Will from the hair he seems drawn to pull.

Figure 9-11
Caregivers keep a watchful eye on situations like this, when infants get close to each other, recognizing that infants will explore one another.

• avoid frustration for babies as much as possible by planning to shorten waiting times and restrictions. Recognizing that babies cannot wait and cannot control their emotional outbursts when frustrated is important.

> When Alice hears the kitchen cart coming down the hall, she tells Andrea it's time for lunch now and gets her bib ready. She has learned that if she puts the bib on before the lunch is imminent, Andrea quickly loses patience with waiting.

WHAT would you DO when...

"Some of the parents seem horrified when I show them our discipline philosophy in the infant room, as we are required to do. One of my mothers said, "But aren't they much too young for discipline?" What should I say?" How would you respond, in this situation?

Here the problem is probably based on semantics, on different understandings of the word *discipline*. The center has no doubt formulated its philosophy to help parents understand their view on guidance suited to infant development. The parent is likely interpreting discipline to mean punishment, perhaps even physical punishment. Use of the word *guidance* may help parents understand the difference.

A developmentally appropriate guidance philosophy in the infant room stresses demonstrating respect for infant needs and abilities. There is an understanding that babies need to have their needs respected and responded to in an atmosphere of sincere caring before they will be able to recognize and respect the needs of others later in childhood. The atmosphere of loving care lays the base for good feelings about the world and the people in it, and eventually about self. A positive self-concept will help children want to behave in positive ways and to please those who care for them (see Figure 9-12).

Babies do not see dangers or problems in their behavior and need an adult to help direct their attention to positive actions. They are not guided effectively by words alone, but by the actions of patient adults who remove them from certain situations and direct their attention elsewhere. Recognizing their limitations, caregivers keep the atmosphere as positive as possible, preventing stressful situations such as overcrowding or waiting.

When this view of discipline is explained to parents as a preliminary to later teaching when children are able to understand words and limits, parents may broaden their definitions of "discipline" from a narrower, more negative focus. Guidance toward self-control is a long and gradual process extending throughout childhood, and positive social interaction in infancy lays a solid foundation.

Figure 9-12

The roots for discipline lie in an atmosphere of loving care, leading to good feelings about self.

- recognize that the basis for later teaching about others' needs and rights is laid in infancy as babies are treated with tender respect. "The basis for learning to control one's own behavior is feeling secure that one's own needs will be met. . . . That, in fact, lays the basis for a capacity that will come later to wait, give, trust, love, and care for others" (Greenman, Stonehouse, & Schweikart, 2008, p. 149). This is the true beginning of discipline, although not the kinds of discipline most adults associate with the term. (See Figure 9-12)

When Alice explains the discipline philosophy to parents in the infant room, some of them express initial surprise, commenting that they assumed their babies were too young for discipline. As she discusses how tender respect for infants lays the foundation for later learning to wait and care for others, they understand this positive approach.

SUMMARY

Developmentally appropriate social/emotional environments for infants offer

- adults who engage in warm, reciprocal interaction, tuning into individual infants' temperaments and developmental levels.
- opportunities for one-to-one communication and play, along with lots of physical cuddling with primary caregivers.
- primary caregiving systems that offer consistent care.
- prompt attention when babies indicate needs.
- recognition that babies need adult help in distraction and redirection in situations of conflict or frustration.
- childcare practices in staffing, and so on, that support these essential social encounters and emotional predictability.

THINK ABOUT IT ACTIVITIES

1. Discuss with several of your classmates your statement about "spoiling." How would your opinions affect practices appropriate for infant social/emotional development?

2. Watch an infant with his or her primary caregiver at home or at a center. What signs of attachment do you see? What interaction and communication suggests developmentally appropriate practice?

3. With a small group, devise an educational plan to introduce a group of new parents who are considering childcare options to what to look for in developmentally appropriate social/emotional environments for infants.

QUESTIONS TO ASSESS LEARNING OF CHAPTER OBJECTIVES

1. What are several of the social/emotional issues of infancy? Discuss each of them briefly, including how each issue affects decisions about practices that are developmentally appropriate.

2. Identify five characteristics of appropriate adult interaction with infants.

3. Discuss as many as you can recall of the practical, concrete things adults do and say to infants that are part of appropriate interaction.

4. List several of the practices identified in this chapter that are unsupportive for nurturing healthy social/emotional development in infants.

APPLY YOUR KNOWLEDGE QUESTIONS

1. Describe the rationale you would present to your director in proposing a new system of primary caregiving to be instituted in the infant room.

2. Write the paragraph that you would provide for parents to describe the ways you will nurture healthy social and emotional development while their babies are in your care.

HELPFUL WEB SITES

http://www.nichd.nih.gov	Go to this Web site to search for the summary of the SECC study on the effects of early childcare on infants.
http://www.babytalk.org	On this Web site, search for an essay on "Parent Infant Attachment."
http://www.scholastic.com	On this Web site, search for a number of articles on infant social and emotional development, including "Soothing Stranger Anxiety" by Alice Honig, as well as "How a Baby Learns to Love" and "How a Baby Makes Friends."
http://www.zerotothree.org	Browse the Web site of Zero to Three for much information regarding healthy emotional development in infancy.

Please visit the premium Web site for Developmentally Appropriate Practice, *4th edition, to access more chapter web links, suggestions for further research and study, additional book chapters, interactive quizzes, video exercises, online journal activities, flashcards, and much more! Go to www.cengage.com/login to register your access code.*

CHAPTER 10

Developmentally Appropriate Social/Emotional Environments: For Toddlers

A surprising transformation occurs about the end of the first year of life. From a generally docile, agreeable creature, the infant evolves into an individual with strong opinions about what she or he would like to do, much of which is contrary to what others want. It seems as if the new power of control that comes with mobility causes the child to see a new independent self, and most of life thereafter is devoted to a new, single-minded testing of this idea. Forming a sense of self dominates much of personality development and social interaction during toddlerhood. Being one's own person is somewhat frightening, however, so toddlers vacillate between independence and dependence, maturity and immaturity. Adults who care for them are never sure which swing of the pendulum will show itself on any given day. (In dealing with the child about ten years later, adults will face similar unpredictability due to the later thrust for independence in early adolescence.) Together with a lack of self-control, limited ability to communicate and understand, and only the most rudimentary social skills, happy coexistence with toddlers is a challenge for both adults and other children. However, developing a positive sense of self is a critical task of toddlerhood that is dependent on a social/emotional environment of appropriate guidance and interaction.

LEARNING OBJECTIVES

After completing this chapter, students should be able to

- discuss several social/emotional issues of toddlerhood.
- describe helpful adult behaviors for each of these social/emotional issues.
- discuss appropriate guidance techniques for toddlers.
- identify unsupportive adult responses to toddler social/emotional behavior.

SOCIAL/EMOTIONAL ISSUES OF TODDLERHOOD

Having lived only a dozen or so months, toddlers are just emerging from the insulated cocoon of parent-child attachment and discovering what it means to live independently and with others. Toddlers need to be respected for who they are at this moment, not compared unfavorably to later phases of development. After a brief discussion of social/emotional issues and developmental tasks, we will return to the practical implications of each issue.

Autonomy

When Erik Erikson (1963) talks about the second stage of psychosocial development, he describes the importance of forming a sense of autonomy versus the negative components of shame and doubt. Autonomy means seeing oneself as a separate, capable individual, able to function independently. Autonomy implies a belief in one's competence. Less positive responses from individuals in the toddler's environment lead the child to conclude that he or she is incapable of functioning independently in ways that adults approve.

Toddlers seem to have a built-in desire to test out their own abilities, so it is important that the adults who care for them demonstrate their approval and support of these first steps toward independence. An optimum social/emotional environment supports the development of a positive sense of self.

Note that the importance of autonomy is a cultural concept. Some cultures and subcultures within our world do not value autonomy to the extent that others do. In many cultures, depending on one another and functioning within the group are valued more than individuality. Caregivers need to initiate dialogue with families to learn their attitudes regarding nurturing their children's autonomy.

Negativism and Resistance

One of the ways toddlers prove autonomy is by resisting and testing the adults around them. Defining differences from others shows separateness, and toddlers are quite sure that they are on the opposite side of the hypothetical fence on every conceivable issue. If it is another person's idea, it's definitely not a good idea. Toddlers are sometimes so bent on resistance for the sake of resistance that they will loudly proclaim "NO" even when it's an issue they actually approve, as in "Do you want a cookie?" "NO," with hand outstretched.

It is often disconcerting for adults to find such vehement resistance in one so small, not to mention one who so recently gave wholehearted approval to literally everything this same adult did. Resistance touches adult feelings about being in control. If caregivers do not understand the positive developmental purpose that drives the negativism, they may try to nip it in the bud. Instead, they must accept the inevitability and importance of these behaviors. Adults who want to nurture positive feelings about self, use their skills to avoid head-on confrontations and find opportunities for toddlers to win some battles. This is not to be interpreted as letting toddlers take over and rule the world, however, as when adults find themselves begging the child to agree to particular behaviors. Toddlers absolutely need limits and adults who are confident in setting those limits. Neither group needs continual power struggles.

Separation

As paradoxical as it may sound after discussing resistance and negativism, one of the most difficult things for toddlers is separation from the adults who are important to them. Still in the attachment process (which lasts about two years), toddlers feel most secure when their adults are nearby, and they protest heartily when left behind. Learning that loved adults will return, and that one can cope in their absence, is a crucial task of toddlerhood (Mahler, 1979). How

Toddler's Creed

If I want it, it's mine.
If I give it to you and change
my mind later, it's mine.
If I can take it away from you,
it's mine.
If I had it a little while ago,
it's mine.
If it's mine, it will never
belong to anybody else,
no matter what.
If we are building
something together,
all the pieces are mine.
If it looks just like mine,
it's mine.

Figure 10-1

A toddler's creed.

adults help children handle separation is extremely important and will have implications for future social relationships and emotional well-being.

As toddlers focus on testing out concepts of self, the idea that other people have their own needs and wants is not yet an understandable concept. Although toddlers have fleeting interest in others, this seems no deeper than their interest in other objects in the world around them, whose properties can be explored before moving on to something else. The Toddler's Creed (see Figure 10-1) states succinctly how toddlers view the world—through the perspective of their needs and wants only. Again, it should be noted that no amount of talking, teaching, or scolding could change this toddler perspective. Only after a sense of self is formed can a child begin to care about others; only when objects have been truly possessed is there a possibility for sharing those objects. In a group of equally egocentric toddlers, the potential for social/emotional friction is enormous; only alert and creative caregivers can protect the rights of all.

Egocentric Behavior with Peers

Burton White states that "a child's social style seems to have become very well established by the time she is two years of age" (White, 1995, p. 167). White identifies the list of social abilities developing between ages fourteen and twenty-four months as

- getting and holding the attention of adults in socially acceptable ways.
- using adults as resources after first determining that a job is too difficult.
- expressing affection to adults.
- expressing mild annoyance to adults.
- leading peers.
- following peers.
- expressing affection to peers.
- expressing mild annoyance to peers.
- competing with peers.
- showing pride in personal accomplishment.
- engaging in role playing or make-believe activities.

The socially complicated toddler—trying to balance her interests in the world around her, in her primary caregivers, and in her own independence—is developing abilities that will become habitual patterns of behaving through "working out an unspoken social contract with the people with whom she interacts regularly. . . . In it is contained what the child has learned through thousands of interchanges with her caretakers" (White, 1995, p. 168).

Emotional Responsiveness

Toddlers who have been involved in caring relationships with others exhibit a wide range of feelings, from pleasure, joy, satisfaction, love, and affection to anger, frustration, jealousy, and fear. On close inspection, this list appears to nearly represent the spectrum of human emotions, but one or two are conspicuously missing.

Because of the cognitive inability to mentally put themselves in another's place, most toddlers are not yet likely to evidence much sympathy, **empathy**, or compassion for others. Occasionally, particularly sensitive toddlers may briefly appear upset when someone else is upset, although this may come from the unfamiliar tone of the other's voice or expression, which is more a cause for alarm to the toddler than an occasion for empathy. Sometimes adults cite examples of toddlers comforting others who are hurt as evidence of sympathy, but some experts believe that this may just be learned behavior, imitated from adults in similar situations and deferred. For example, a toddler may pat a child who is crying when her doll has been taken away, but then promptly take another toy away from the same child—certainly not seeming to truly care about the other's feelings.

Ideas about emotional intelligence (Goleman, 1995) may offer a different perspective here. This theory suggests that some children may be especially ready to be nurtured into developing an emotional awareness of other's feelings and needs. Gardner (1983, 1999) names an interpersonal intelligence, suggesting that some children may be particularly sensitive to nuances of relationships with other. Obviously, emotional responses vary from one child to another, depending largely on what responses their emotions have received and their cultural milieu, but the immature cognitive processes of the toddler make it more likely that these emotions are not yet strongly present.

One emotion that is not unique to toddlers, but does appear in some unusual ways, is fear. Toddlers learn to fear some things by associating them with something unpleasant, such as the toddler who has learned to fear the doctor's office because of the pain experienced there, or to fear a neighbor's yard because of the large barking dog that suddenly appears there. Other toddler fears appear to be unconnected with real unpleasantness but are rather based on the illogical assumption that the object threatens his or her person. An example is the bathtub drain. Many toddlers who have been quite happy sitting and playing in the bathtub during infancy suddenly scream at the thought of a bath. It seems that the sight of water disappearing down the hole suggests possible danger to the toddler. (Toilets and vacuums present similar frightening possibilities.) Although some toddler fears do not seem understandable to adults, they are nevertheless real and need respectful responses.

What toddlers have, then, are most emotions, strong and real (see Figure 10-2). What they do not have is control of immediate expression of these feelings and methods to express feelings other than purely physical. The result, in its most notorious form, is the classic toddler temper tantrum. A healthy social/emotional environment for toddlers avoids exacerbating negative emotional responses and guides children in these earliest stages while conveying acceptance of emotionality.

Figure 10-2
What toddlers have are most emotions, strong and real.

Positive Guidance for Toddlers

Immature and impulsive as they are, there is no question that toddlers need limits. Burton White (1995) defines one of the roles for toddler caregivers as authority. Toddlers, so frequently out of control themselves, need to know they can depend on the adults around them for limits. The authority issues concern what kind of limits and how to convey those limits. Developmentally appropriate guidance takes into account the toddler's limited language, understanding, and worldview, as well as the all-important developing sense of self.

DEVELOPMENTALLY APPROPRIATE INTERACTION WITH TODDLERS

Having looked at the important social/emotional issues of toddlerhood, it is time to consider developmentally appropriate interaction.

Fostering Autonomy

Adults foster a sense of autonomy in toddlers when they

- provide necessary support for toddlers to complete their self-defined tasks, allowing children to do everything they are capable of, and assisting gently with tasks beyond their abilities. Sometimes this means patiently allowing the longer time needed for the toddler "to do it myself"; other times it means unobtrusively offering a helping hand or a start on the task for toddlers to complete. Example:

    LaToya sits beside Roberto, who is struggling to put on his shoes. She busies herself with folding some laundry, occasionally smiling at him or commenting on his hard work. Across the room, Greg realizes that SooHa is not yet able to put her coat on by herself, so he steps in to help put her arms in, saying he'll need her help to zip up.

- recognize and appreciate children's accomplishments with genuine admiration and specific comments.

    "You put your dishes back in the tray all by yourself, Joey. Thanks for helping."

    "Look at you ready to slide down, Nadia. You climbed up all those steps!"

- offer real choices in areas toddlers can control. Adults can make decisions on big issues related to what needs to be done, but allow toddlers to feel they have some control over *how* it is done.

    "Lunchtime, Zoe. Do you want the blue cup or the red one today?" "Do you want to sing a song after we wash hands or before?" "Bananas for snack today, Isabella. Do you want a whole big one or two pieces?"

- encourage independent play requiring exploration and mastery (see Figure 10-3). As children feel they are allowed to do much on their own, autonomy grows.

    Vanessa sets up a fill-and-dump center for her toddlers with sturdy big boxes and a lot of smaller objects they can put into and get out of the boxes. As they push the boxes around, she smiles in approval and comments on how hard they work to push the big boxes.

- help children develop their concepts of self by using names frequently. Adults also play body awareness games with toddlers ("Where's your neck? Show me your knee") and use mirrors, photographs, and songs to help toddlers increase their self-identification.

    Luis added a self-identity corner to his toddler room recently. He included a full-length mirror and several small, unbreakable hand mirrors. On the walls are photos of every toddler, along with pictures of family and home. When he gathers the toddlers for singing, he sings each child's name. They don't sing much, but they beam when they hear their name.

Figure 10-3

Encouraging exploration and mastery allows toddlers to feel independent.

- provide all the freedom toddlers can safely use. Adults who avoid being overprotective by hovering or restricting encourage self-confidence. Does the toddler in Figure 10-4 look as if he needs help? He has squirmed inside the narrow hole to try to get the ball and is getting himself out just fine. An alert caregiver stands by and lets him do his own problem solving and confident learning. Moving in too quickly would foster his continued dependence on the adult, as well as make him feel inadequate.

    Annie has arranged the toddler play area so there is literally nothing she has to say "no" to. Parent volunteers made a sturdy, 6-inch-high climbing shelf so she doesn't have to warn the toddlers to be careful.

- make available materials, utensils, and equipment that toddlers can use with little or no assistance.

    Zaida's toddlers have smaller chairs than those in the preschool classroom, so the children can seat themselves without having to climb awkwardly into them. She also asked the kitchen staff to substitute special, short-handled utensils for the usual forks and spoons. The result has been toddlers who really can confidently look after themselves at mealtime.

- observe toddlers for signs of readiness for learning toilet control and then gently and without pressure introduce them to toilet use. Assume that time will be spent in the process and positively reinforce toddler attempts.

    Maria-Theresa smiles when Gabriel climbs off the toilet and proudly displays the results. This was the first day that he told her before the fact.

- examine adults' own attitudes to the changing relationship with toddlers. Adults need to respond to the push for autonomy with genuine delight at the emergence of unique personhood, rather than to thwart attempts at independence because of their own needs. Sometimes toddlers push on faster than their adults, who need to consciously modify their style of interaction. Toddlers no longer need adults who actively fill all their needs, but rather those who stand back to support new challenges.

    Susan grins and shakes her head, smiling at her toddler son, eager to try to comb his own hair. "It felt so strange at first," she admits. "I kind of liked being the one he always turned to. But I've gotten used to the idea that it's best to give him some freedom to move out on his own a bit. He still needs me—just in a different way."

Figure 10-4

Autonomy grows when caregivers do not over-protect toddlers, and allow them to solve some of their problems on their own.

CULTURAL CONSIDERATIONS

Interdependence or Independence?

As early childhood expert Janet Gonzalez-Mena reminds us, there are cultures that cut apron strings and others that keep them tightly tied. Caregivers should be aware that many cultures prefer to foster interdependence rather than independence. Within such cultures, parents will continue to feed and do other things for their toddlers long after independence-minded folk would. Rather than be frustrated when parents continue to do things at home that caregivers encourage toddlers to do in childcare situations, dialogue about goals for children is important. Understanding family desires for their children helps caregivers find ways to support those goals, while still allowing the little ones to develop confidence and skills (Gonzalez-Mena, 2007).

Responding to Resistance and Negativism

When resistance and negativism are recognized as steps toward autonomy, adults can be more effective in working with these toddler behaviors. Adults find it helps when they

- realize that toddlers need control and determine the few important issues regarding health or safety that need absolute adult authority.

    Rick says, "The one 'no' I have to stick to is him holding my hand when we walk in the parking lot. He squirms and clearly doesn't like it, but I just can't trust his judgment or control around sudden cars."

Figure 10-5

Adults understand toddler resistance, and work around or ignore what they can.

- understand toddler resistance for what it is—another method of testing self—and accept the concept of the child's need to say "no," without feeling threatened about losing control. (See Figure10-5)

  Another toddler parent: "I used to feel I had to tell him he couldn't tell me 'no.' I was afraid that if I let this slip past, in no time he'd take over the whole show. But I've learned that some of those 'no's' I can ignore, and some I can change by giving him a bit of control. It's not that big a deal—I still know I'm in charge, and he needs to find out he is somebody with a bit of power too."

- avoid power struggles that produce winners and losers. It is not emotionally healthy for toddlers to discover that they have manipulated adults into a losing position; they need to know somebody is in charge. Nor is it possible for a healthy sense of an autonomous self to develop when toddlers always lose.

  "I'm trying more to find a way to let him save face, so he doesn't feel he has to resist me quite so hard to prove he is somebody."

- give toddlers choices within absolutes to allow them to avoid resistance. Adults make the big choices, toddlers make the small ones.

  Alondra knows naptime is inevitable, but says, "A song or a story, Kenyetta—tell me which one you want before it's time to sleep." It is harder for Kenyetta to resist totally when she still retains a measure of control. She'll be so busy deciding that she'll forget to resist the main issue—at least, most of the time!

- use statements rather than questions that give the toddler the opportunity to resist when things need to be done.

  "Let's pick up toys" rather than "Are you ready to clean up now?" "Time to get in our chairs" rather than "Would you like to come to the table?"

- follow predictable patterns for the day and give clues of predictability during transitions with songs, and so on. Toddlers are less likely to resist when life follows a secure rhythm.

  "This is the way we pick up our toys," sings Emma, and the toddlers fall comfortably in to help.

- help toddlers develop rituals for those times of day that often meet resistance. (A word of caution here: Know that toddlers become quite rigid and unchanging, so don't start anything you don't want to repeat several thousand times!)

  If Joshua knows that Mommy always gives Bear a kiss on each cheek, then gives Joshua the same, and then says, "Goodnight snugglebunny," he can "control" her ("Kiss Bear first!") to do this, and forget the resistance.

- allow toddlers to do as much for themselves as they can. "No's" decrease when toddlers have already experienced a measure of autonomy.

  "Here Aaron, you can carry the wastebasket over to the table for the kids to throw in their trash."

PRACTICAL IMPLICATIONS

Creating Autonomy

Caregivers should avoid practices that produce shame and doubt instead of a sense of autonomy such as:

- overprotecting toddlers, making them feel inadequate.

- expecting toddlers to comply with all adult demands, offering them no choice in their daily lives.

- expecting too much or too little of toddlers.

- doing things for toddlers that they could do for themselves, given time, appropriate equipment, and support.

- imposing toilet learning, ready or not, and punishing or shaming children for toileting accidents.

- appearing clearly impatient with toddler exuberance, movement, learning style, or limitations.

- accept the fact that toddlers can resist physically if biological matters become matters of adult pressure and toddler resistance. Allow toddlers to indicate the amounts of food they can handle or their readiness for toilet learning and realize that sometimes it might be appropriate to back off and wait.

> Carolyn quietly removes Abduh's plate when it becomes obvious he isn't interested in eating any more. She has discovered that pressure from her to eat more only seems to make him more determined not to do so, and she certainly doesn't want to turn mealtime into the kind of battle where she pushes food into his closed mouth or bribes him into eating more with a game of "here comes the train—open wide!"

- avoid the use of the word *no* as much as possible, saving it only for important occasions where safety is involved. Toddlers are likely to imitate much of the negativism from the adults around them, so adults should word requests positively.

"Climb on the slide, Gadi" instead of "No climbing on the chair."

- keep a sense of humor ("This too shall pass!") and work around resistance by involving the toddler in interesting things that distract from the negativism. Adults are bigger and supposedly smarter, so use creativity instead of anger and power.

> Gabriela, responding with a resounding "no" to getting her face washed, laughs and starts singing along when her caregiver makes a funny face and sings "NO, I don't want to get my face washed, NO, NO, NO," getting quieter with each NO, all the while moving into the bathroom.

Helping with Separation

It is painful for toddlers and parents to give up what T. Berry Brazelton once called the love affair of the first year.

> With the realization of independence and the ability to "leave" comes an overwhelming feeling of dependence. The trusting sense that the mother is available gives him the necessary capacity to make such a choice for independence. Ambivalence is at the root of this choice, and the experience of it, the mastery of it, are at the base of the child's ability to become a really independent person. (Brazelton, 1974, pp. 14–15)

The experience of dealing with separation and increasing independence has lifelong impact. Adults can help toddlers most by

- accepting the evidence of fear, sadness, or anger that toddlers may show when experiencing separation (see Figure 10-6). This is a time that toddlers (and their parents) need sensitivity and support.

PRACTICAL IMPLICATIONS

Dealing with Resistance and Negativity

Unsupportive practices regarding toddler resistance and negativity include:

- rejecting toddlers' assertions of self, responding with either anger or mockery.
- punishing children for resistance or saying "no" ("No child of mine is going to say no to me!").
- fearing loss of power and involving themselves in power struggles over matters large and small.
- making all choices themselves.
- losing patience with the toddler's need for repetition and ritual.
- turning mealtimes and bathroom times into times of pressure and conflict in which adults have decided the amount of food to be eaten or the timing of toilet control.

▶❚❚ VIDEO ACTIVITY

Go to the premium Web site and watch the video clip for Chapter 10 titled "Separation in Toddlerhood." Then consider the following questions:

REFLECTIVE QUESTIONS

1. How do you see that these teachers are supporting the toddlers as they experience separation anxiety? What helpful strategies discussed in this chapter do you see illustrated?

2. Consider also what less helpful adult responses would be, and what would be their result on toddler emotional development?

 Visit the premium Web site to complete these questions online and email them to your professor.

Figure 10-6
Adults help toddlers deal with separation by accepting their feelings.

Laverne, holding a sobbing Alexis after her dad has just left, murmurs, "You wish your daddy didn't have to go to work, don't you? It makes you sad to see him go. I'll take care of you till he comes back."

- allowing time to prepare toddlers for new situations with simple words, visits, and chances to meet caregivers before the separation.

    Alexis came by with her parents for two short visits in the toddler classroom before her first day. She got to talk to her teacher, and at home her mom talked about going soon to play in Laverne's room.

- recognizing that toddlers use their parents as a secure base from which to venture out as they become comfortable. Caregivers help parents understand the necessity (whenever possible) for parents remaining in the room as the toddler explores new people and surroundings.

    After Laverne explained how it would help Alexis for one of her family to stay with her as she got used to the room, her mom took time off to stay the first day.

- creating separation policies in centers and classrooms that allow for gradual easing in and becoming familiar in a new situation. It is a good idea to shorten the time toddlers are expected to be separate from parents during the initial adjustment phase.

    Alexis's dad arranged time from his job to pick her up before lunch every day for the first week.

- helping parents and toddlers say good-bye to one another, even when crying, and helping toddlers watch their parents leave. Trust slowly comes as toddlers experience both the leaving and the returning.

    "I'll hold her while she says good-bye to you, Mr. Phillips. She'll cry, but we'll handle it. We'll see you after snack time."

- greeting toddlers and their parents warmly and helping toddlers get involved with a good deal of attention at the beginning of the day.

    "Hi Alexis. I'm glad you've come to play today. Look at the big boxes we've got to fill up. Mr. Phillips, it looks like we're all getting used to this morning routine, doesn't it?"

- staying physically close to toddlers so they can hold or touch adults when they want to or at least know adults are available to them (see Figure 10-7). Adults who move gradually, slowly, and gently convey a nonverbal impression of calm. When they speak, they talk quietly with toddlers, using both tone and words to convey understanding and acceptance of feelings.

    Laverne speaks quietly and stoops to be near Alexis as she talks. "It's hard, I know," she says. "Daddy will come back."

- recognizing that mealtimes and naptimes may be particularly difficult for toddlers having troubles with separation and paying extra attention during these periods.

    "Alexis, I've got a place for you right here beside me."

PRACTICAL IMPLICATIONS

Facilitating Separation

When helping toddlers separate from parents, caregivers should avoid:

- showing impatience and no understanding of the effort separation involves.

- proving untrustworthy at times of separation. Parents sneak out or do not appear after snack time, as they promised; caregivers ignore pain and are not available to help toddlers in parents' absence.

- trying to stop the tears with shame: "You're too big to cry"; with bribes: "Don't cry and Mommy will take you for ice cream"; or with impatient anger: "Now stop that! I'm tired of all this crying."

- treating the feelings with cold indifference. Toddler feelings are valid and need recognition and support.

Figure 10-7
Staying physically close and available may help toddlers deal with separation feelings.

- ignoring as many of the behaviors that may accompany the pain of separation as they can. Toddlers may test, withdraw, become aggressive, cling, or revert to earlier behaviors. The more accepting adults can be, the sooner toddlers will trust the environment as caring for them.

    Laverne and Alexis's parents have decided not to discuss her increased thumb sucking, assuming it will drop away as she becomes more comfortable.

- encouraging toddlers to bring favorite toys, blankets, other security objects, or something that belongs to their parents and not removing these objects from them. When toddlers feel ready to play, adults can encourage them to keep their precious bit of home safe in their cubbies, available for later retrieval when the children need it.

    Alexis brings her blankie that she likes to hold most of the day.

- surrounding toddlers with pictures and taped messages of parents, giving them the chance to talk about them and hear them as often as they need comfort.

    Alexis frequently walks over to the wall to pat the pictures of her mom and dad.

- encouraging parents and toddlers to develop plans and rituals for leaving one another (Gestwicki, 2010). This book was published in January, with 2010 date.

    Every day now Alexis's dad comes in and reads her one story over in the book corner, and then brings her to Laverne to help her say good-bye.

- expecting that each toddler will have an individual timetable for developing trust and coming to accept separation.

    Being at the center seems to be getting a bit easier for Alexis now after about four weeks.

Working with Egocentric Behavior with Peers

When toddlers are cared for in group situations, caregivers spend much of their time safeguarding the rights and safety of each child. Helpful adult interaction includes:

- recognizing that toddlers first have to be autonomous individuals before they can learn group membership rules and accepting the role of gently guiding social behavior, in recognition of toddlers' lack of self-control.

Figure 10-8

Having a lot of materials prevents toddler squabbles.

Figure 10-9

Close supervision allows the toddlers to enjoy the play dough experience together.

- preventing aggressive interaction by carefully preparing the environment to allow for separate play spaces and sufficient numbers and kinds of materials to avoid possession squabbles (see Figure 10-8).

- providing materials that toddlers can share easily, which usually means big, stationary things too large to be dragged away by one child and large enough so both children can act on the material at the same time. Examples are large boxes with two openings, climbing structures, and stairs.

- planning for brief cooperative experiences. Close supervision of the toddlers' play dough exploration allows the children to enjoy the activity together (see Figure 10-9).

   "Sarah, DeJuan needs a friend to help hold the side of the blanket so we can bounce the ball. Oh, isn't this fun?"

- helping toddlers become aware of each other positively.

   "Rachel, you and Ethan are both swinging high, aren't you?"

- playing with toddlers to model social behaviors of cooperation.

  "I'm going to play with my blocks right here beside you. Would you like some of my blocks?"

- playing with toddlers, which gives adults the opportunity to model verbal communication of needs.

  "DeJuan, I think Sarah wants to tell you she doesn't want you to take her truck. Sarah, you can tell DeJuan 'no.' Say 'I want it now.'"

- reinforcing any progress toward prosocial behavior.

  "Good words, Sarah. You told DeJuan 'no.' DeJuan, listen to Sarah please. She's telling you something important."

  "You waited till he was finished, Dakota. You were very patient."

- redirecting toddlers before frustration levels grow into aggressive outbursts.

  "DeJuan, Sarah is really busy with that truck now. Let's go find you the big dump truck to load until she's finished."

- pausing briefly before intervening in confrontations between toddlers. This may allow the toddlers experience in settling the matter themselves or allow the adult to see whether the interaction is really aggressive or just incidental exploration.

  Patrice watched as Antonio bumped into Derrick as they climbed the slide. Derrick pushed him back, but both toddlers proceeded with their activity, apparently not bothered.

- firmly protecting children and preventing physical aggression. Where necessary, firmly and gently hold a child's hands, feet, or jaws before hurting can occur. Children need a clear message that adults will protect and control.

  "DeJuan, I can't let you hit Sarah. Hitting hurts. No hitting."

- disapproving with strong and controlled emotion when toddlers have hurt others (see Figure 10-10).

  Say, "No! DeJuan, no biting! Biting hurts!" with a facial expression that matches the firm words, but does not convey a frightening loss of adult control.

- eliminating references to sharing that are beyond toddler comprehension. Adults should wait for this important teaching until it is developmentally appropriate. Meanwhile, they are responsible for safeguarding individual rights.

  "DeJuan needs a turn when you're finished with that, Sarah."

Biting

Biting is such a common occurrence in toddler group situations that it earns particular mention here. Because biting toddlers are in groups, this otherwise "natural phenomenon that has virtually no lasting developmental significance" (Greenman & Stonehouse, 1996, p. 154) does become significant. Biting is not something to be blamed on the child who bites or on the caregiver in whose room it occurs. Aggression because of frustration with others is not the only reason that biting occurs by any means. Other reasons include teething discomfort; stage of oral exploration (Ramming et al., 2006); imitative behavior; cause-and-effect exploration; overcrowding, excitement, and overstimulation; impulsiveness; or a need for attention. Several issues in toddlers' lives can cause tension that may be manifested in biting; these include learning to separate from those to whom toddlers

Figure 10-10

Adults must set clear limits on toddlers who hurt others.

are attached. Another frequent cause of tension for toddlers is the whole toilet-learning process. As caregivers try to puzzle out the cause for an episode of biting, they are more able to respond appropriately.

Chewing on a teething ring or a clean, soft towel that has been placed in the freezer might help a child who bites for teething discomfort. Frozen bread sticks or hard biscuits might also relieve teething pain. Rubbing the toddler's gums with clean hands might help, and some doctors recommend medications that numb the gums.

A child who bites as part of oral exploration may need a variety of clean, soft objects that can redirect for chewing experiences. Plastic rings, soft toys, celery sticks—all can be used when adults want to say, "You can't bite Sarah, that hurts her. Here's a ring you can bite on if you want to bite."

Toddlers who bite to investigate cause and effect ("What will happen when I push the book off the table? What about when I bite Suzie?") need toys and experiences to nurture the drive to find things that respond to children's actions. Cause-and-effect toys—such as busy boxes, jack-in-the-boxes, and open-ended materials, such as sand, water, or blocks, that can do lots of different things—give positive opportunities to explore.

Toddlers who bite when they get physically crowded need adults who can manage the available space to protect an area for each child and assurance that he and his possessions are safe. Environment, routines, or activities may need changing.

Toddlers who bite when they are trying to approach or play with another child need adults close by to monitor and guide their interactions. It is important to pay special attention to their positive interactions.

Toddlers who bite from frustration may need help with simple words to express themselves, or a recognition for what they seem to feel, if language is impossible. "You can tell him 'no,' Joel," or "I think Joel wants to tell you he doesn't want you to touch his bear right now."

Toddlers who bite from a strong need for control and independence may be helped when they are offered choices throughout the day.

A child who bites in imitation of another toddler who has been observed biting needs to discover that this is not the way to get attention. Any child who seems to be biting for attention needs to receive positive attention, a lot of it, when she or he is involved in busy, appropriate behaviors. Adult response when biting does occur must pay most attention to the child who has been bitten and only brief, disapproving attention to the biter.

If caregivers observe when biting occurs and try to explore the reason for biting, they are more likely to find the most appropriate solution (NAEYC, 1996).

It should be noted that biting is not limited to toddlers. Preschoolers and even kindergarten-age children sometimes bite. It is more likely that biting at these ages indicates a response that has been reinforced by attention or getting results at an earlier age. While some of these same responses may be helpful in situations with older children, particular consideration should be given to the social and emotional reasons for biting, and to reinforcing concepts of communicating needs with words.

When biting has occurred, adult reaction needs to be swift and clear. Turning to the victim, the adult gives her appropriate attention, including washing the area and holding ice on it. The biter needs to be quickly removed from the victim, while the adult shows with voice and facial expression that it is absolutely unacceptable to bite. Speaking very firmly, looking into the child's eyes, holding him firmly, the caregiver says, "I don't like it when you bite people. Look at her. She's crying. You hurt her." When possible, the biter can help the adult hold the ice on the hurt child, since this brings him face-to-face with the consequences of his actions. However, if the biter resists, it's inappropriate to give him more attention at this point. (The child who has been bitten also may not want the other child close at this time.) When order has been quickly restored or while comforting the hurt child, the adult can state alternative behaviors to the biter: "If you want something, you can tell her," or "If you want to bite something, you can use the plastic ring."

If a child bites frequently, it is worth the staff time for one caregiver to shadow this child closely, watching for potentially frustrating situations and being available to redirect the child before complete loss of control occurs.

Communication with parents is vital to coordinate responses to biting and to learn of possible stresses on the toddler. All parents of toddlers in a toddler room need information about biting: that it is developmental and normal, why it occurs, and what caregivers are doing to protect and help children. If this information is given as a matter of course before an incident occurs, parents may be less alarmed. It is important for caregivers to realize that angry parents will often demand to know who was attacking their child. The Code of Ethics reminds teachers that they have a responsibility to protect confidentiality regarding children, so this is not information that can be shared, but it is certainly important for caregivers to convey their concern with protecting all children, and their plan for avoiding future biting. (See Code of Ethical Conduct, Rev. 2005, NAEYC.) Communication is also important so all adults involved with the toddler can behave in similar ways when biting occurs. In most cases, toddler biting will not last a long time, especially if dealt with consistently using a logical consequence solution. When biting does persist, adults involved in the child's care may need to discuss other care alternatives, with fewer children or more one-on-one adult attention. There is a good book on issues regarding biting in toddler programs by Kinnell (2002); see more information at the end of the chapter.

> ## PRACTICAL IMPLICATIONS
>
> ### Supporting Social Relations with Peers
>
> In order to support appropriate social relations with peers, caregivers should avoid:
>
> - expecting toddlers to learn to share or take turns, and punish when they fail to do so.
> - showing no understanding of the modeling and prevention value of their play involvement with toddlers and thinking it silly or boring to play with them.
> - punishing or controlling aggressive toddlers in ways that "escalate the hostility"(Copple & Bredekamp, 2009, p. 95).
> - attempting to teach toddlers "how it feels to bite" (or hit or pull hair, or anything else the toddler has done), by doing it back to the child. This negative model should never be used.

FOSTERING EMOTIONAL DEVELOPMENT

The kinds of gentle guidance toward **prosocial** awareness that we have just discussed are appropriate to help toddlers toward the eventual capacity for sympathy and compassion. Adults who respond sensitively to toddler feelings of separation help toddlers master those feelings eventually, while learning that feelings of sadness and fear are valid and can be expressed.

A developmentally appropriate social/emotional environment helps toddlers learn that their feelings are respected and that there are ways feelings may be expressed and dealt with. Adults foster emotional development when they

- invest themselves emotionally in the children. Rich relationships permit toddlers to experience the power of a warm emotional climate firsthand (see Figure. 10-11).

- are authentic in their own expression of emotion and modeling of coping skills. Toddlers learn most by watching and listening to those around them. When adults accept their own feelings and express them constructively, toddlers have a positive model.

  "I'm so glad to see you today, Yvette," conveys love that a young child can perceive.

  "I really don't like it when you hurt Antoine. It makes me angry."

- accept both the feelings people enjoy and those that are more painful.

- recognize that although toddlers have strong feelings, they lack both the language to express emotions verbally and the ability to delay immediate expression of those feelings. Together, these facts mean that toddlers express emotion largely through nonverbal, physical means.

  Next, let's consider a common emotional issue of toddlerhood.

Figure 10-11

A warm emotional climate helps toddlers feel acceptance.

Temper Tantrums

Along with resistance and negativism, toddler temper tantrums have given the toddler period the cliché characterization of "terrible." Given the strong feelings, the lack of other than physical means of expression, and the amount of frustration met by many toddlers as they try to investigate their world, it is nearly inevitable that some emotional outbursts will occur.

> Tantrums spring from inner forces in the child over which he is seeking control . . . a reflection of the inner turmoil of decision-making that one is faced with when decisions become one's own, and are no longer made by a parent. In all likelihood, the tantrums are necessary and are private expressions of such turmoil. They are appropriate at this age. (Brazelton, 1974, pp. 20–21)

Although tantrums may be appropriate in toddlerhood, given the child's limitations, they are certainly not at later stages when other methods of expression and coping can be developed. The frequently strong responses of adults to toddler temper tantrums probably result from a fear that this undesirable behavior might linger on if not quelled permanently. It is more appropriate, however, for adults to focus on what is most helpful right at the present.

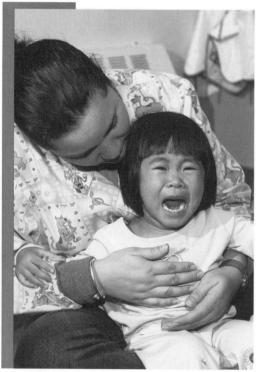

Figure 10-12

It helps out-of-control toddlers when adults respond calmly.

- Realize that ensuring that toddlers do not get too tired or hungry can prevent many outbursts. Managing the toddler's schedule to allow for sufficient rest and food can help increase toddler tolerance.

- Avoid frustrating incidents by keeping expectations and situations appropriate for immature toddlers. For example, a wait at a restaurant, doctor's office, snack table, and so on when there is nothing to occupy toddler attention asks for more tolerance than children can accomplish; this is extremely frustrating for toddlers and should be avoided. Although prevention is not the only answer for temper tantrums, it certainly deserves thoughtful consideration as the one component under adult control.

- Respond to toddler temper tantrums with calm control. When children have lost control, it is important that they can count on adults for secure boundaries (see Figure 10-12).

- Prevent toddlers from hurting themselves or others when they are out of control. Sometimes removing the child from the scene of the frustration is helpful. The toddler throwing herself on the floor in the supermarket will benefit from being taken outside or to the car. The purpose is not isolation, but removal from the stimulus.

- Verbalize quiet understanding of the toddler's frustration to let the toddler know his feeling is understood, to model other methods of expression, and to calm with gentle sounds, as in "It really made you mad when the puzzle pieces didn't fit."

PRACTICAL IMPLICATIONS

Responding to Tantrums

Unsupportive practices in responding to toddler temper tantrums include attempting to suppress the tantrum or responding in ways that actually reinforce and strengthen the behavior. Sometimes adults try to suppress the behavior by

- punishing the tantrum, with isolation or with angry outbursts of their own: "Now stop that, do you hear me? I don't want to hear any more of that screaming. I'll give you something to really scream about!" There is something incongruous about an adult having a temper tantrum of her own, while trying to stop that of a toddler.

- ignoring the child and his emotion altogether. Because this is the only method of expression available to the toddler, the implicit message is that the feeling is not valid or important. Toddlers are unable to understand that adults are disapproving of the *method* of expressing anger rather than the feeling itself, and they simply learn that if they want to retain adult approval, they'd better hide any evidence of feeling. Suppressed feelings are both unhealthy and dangerous.

- laughing at or mocking the toddler's outburst. This reaction also trivializes the feelings, to say nothing of compounding the emotional response by adding anger or more frustration. It certainly shows lack of respect for toddlers (as well as a lack of understanding of their cognitive ability) to see an adult down on the floor pretending to cry loudly, then saying, "Now doesn't that look silly?"

Sometimes adults actually reinforce the likelihood of temper tantrums recurring and lingering on long after developmental abilities to express in other ways appear. Tantrums are reinforced when adults

- give in to the tantrum. Rather than to be embarrassed or confronted with an out-of-control child, adults who want peace at any price are frequently willing to pay the short-term price, not weighing the long-term cost. This is the caregiver who gives the toy to the toddler flinging herself on the floor after the adult had already told her she couldn't have it, or the parent who buys the candy in the supermarket after the screams have gotten so loud they're attracting attention. After adults have set the boundaries, they need to stick to them, or toddlers learn that tantrums are a powerful tool to get what they can't get otherwise.

- pay attention that is beyond acknowledging the feeling and ensuring the child will not cause harm. Attention can be just as rewarding as the concrete object the child was fussing over in the first place. As Brazelton says, the "ultimate goal will be for him to incorporate his own limit" (Brazelton, 1974, p. 20). This means that children need to feel they are supported as they try to regain their own control. Too much adult attention may prevent the child from learning how to stop herself. Brazelton's words help us sort out the appropriate response from the inappropriate:

  > I feel that a parent's role at this time is to comfort and sort out the sides of the struggle. Certainly, retreating completely for fear of setting them off, or getting so involved that one ends up having a tantrum too, is no help to the baby. Picking him up to love and comfort him afterward, and realizing the fact that boundaries are necessary whether the baby must respond with a tantrum or not, may be the best roles a parent can play. (Brazelton, 1974, p. 21)

- Discuss the tantrums with other adults in the child's presence.

- Suggest alternative ways to express their anger. Adults tell toddlers, "If you're mad, you can tell us. Say 'I'm mad,' and then I'll know how to help you."
- Pick the child up to love and comfort after the tantrum has subsided and to help change the subject. Now is the time for diversion. (Diversion during the tantrum is futile and sends the negative message of ignoring the strength of the feelings.)
- Avoid any behaviors that reinforce temper tantrums as a method of getting something.

Developmentally Appropriate Guidance

There is so much for toddlers to learn as they grow. Learning what pleases and displeases adults and how to control impulses are some of the most challenging tasks for toddlers, and it is equally challenging for the adults to help toddlers in this process.

Burton White defines the third necessary role for adults (after designer of the child's world and consultant) as *authority*. He states that from his studies, when toddlers develop well, it is critical that they learn adults have the ultimate authority in the relationship.

> He needs to understand that no matter how much he is loved, whenever you say "no" firmly, he won't get his way, no matter what he does. Interestingly, babies who are raised this way become the happiest two-year-olds you will ever see. . . .

> By setting limits firmly and effectively, you teach your toddler the terms of the social contract. He will learn that most of the time he will get what he wants, and quickly, but whenever you make it clear that he won't, nothing he does will make any difference. (White, 1995, p. 195)

It stands to reason that, as the bewildered new visitors to the planet, it helps toddlers to believe that somebody knows what should be going on, because they themselves are so unsure.

But firmness should not be confused with adults' winning over toddlers' losing. Rather, the adult should keep two goals in mind: (1) helping the child learn from the experience, and (2) allowing the child to "save face," and get out of the situation without feeling stupid, ashamed, or embarrassed.

Building toward a positive self-concept is the important goal of toddlerhood, and methods of discipline should build up rather than tear down good feelings in children.

Developmentally appropriate guidance focuses on

- having age-appropriate expectations for behavior and control.
- changing the environment where possible instead of trying to get the child to change behavior. Examples include adding duplicate toys to prevent fighting; removing objects rather than having to verbally restrict their use; moving up the lunch schedule so tired toddlers do not have to wait (see Figure 10-13).
- using both actions and words to guide toddlers. It is frustrating for adults to observe that toddlers seem to recognize words, yet are not controlled by them. Toddlers need someone to help them physically stop or leave the situation.

  "Climb over here," says Debbie as she lifts Patrick down from the table.

  "That's Akwanza's, he needs it back," says Nicholas, as he helps Elizabeth hand back a toy, and then leads her to find another.

- redirecting children positively to desirable behavior.

  "Climb over here" tells Patrick what he may do, rather than just stopping him with "Don't climb" or "Stop climbing on the table."

- changing the child's direction of thinking is less frustrating for both toddler and adult than attempting to stop him altogether. Positive guidance feels less restrictive and contributes more to a toddler's sense of what is acceptable.

Figure 10-13
Moving up the lunch schedule may help, instead of dealing with tired toddlers.

- recognizing and accepting reasons children are doing things, while still pointing out the "buts." Slowly toddlers need to recognize that others have needs too.

   "You want to play with the doll, but Lindsay is using it now."

   "You like to climb, but this is not a safe place."

- offering solutions. For every "no," offer two acceptable choices (Greenberg, 1991).

   "You could play with the bear while you wait or come with me while I set the table."

   "You could climb on the pillows or jump off the step."

- relying heavily on techniques such as **distraction, substitution**, and **redirection** allows adults to set limits while avoiding having toddlers "lose." Burton White found that most of the effective caregivers of children from a year to a year and a half relied heavily on distraction and physical removal of either the child or the object; after one and a half, they used distraction, physical distance, and firm words.

   When Leah is grabbing the doll from Jonathan, Cindy tells her that's Jonathan's right now, and says, "Here's a doll for you to hold, Leah. Now you and Jonathan both have your babies."

   "Sand in the table," reminds Darlene when Hope throws sand on the floor.

   Such guidance helps children keep within the limits of acceptable behavior.

- following through consistently on a very few limits to help toddlers come to understand what is expected of them. Limits are selected for toddler protection, and the reasons are explained briefly, even as adults realize that toddlers are not likely to understand fully, and children will need adult help to follow the rules.

   "Crayon on the paper" is consistently maintained, so that toddlers no longer test the limit.

- displaying a calm, authoritative approach, recognizing the necessity for adults to provide secure limits because toddlers cannot yet control themselves.

Unsupportive practices do not help toddlers with positive guidance (see Figure 10-14). Most of the developmentally inappropriate guidance of toddlers results from assuming that toddlers can understand and control themselves much better than they actually can. As a result, adults become impatient and angry about what they interpret as toddlers being "mean," "stubborn," or "bad," and punish them accordingly.

Figure 10-14

Consider how to avoid discipline problems for toddlers.

What Creates Discipline Problems for Toddlers?

- too high expectations for self-control
- too little space or too much open space
- too few materials or too little equipment
- materials or equipment that are too challenging or too simple
- too much waiting time
- inflexible routines, spaces, schedules, and people
- too much change
- too many temptations, that is, objects and places that are forbidden
- too much noise
- excessive requirements for sharing
- long or frequent periods of sitting still
- too many times when children are expected to just look or listen instead of getting directly involved

From *Prime Times: A Handbook for Excellence in Infant and Toddler Programs* by Jim Greenman and Anne Stonehouse, St. Paul, MN: Redleaf Press, 1996, p. 139.

For example, when a toddler is told repeatedly not to touch others' belongings and she continues to do so, the adult may respond angrily with "I've told you three times to stay away from that. Now you go in time-out until you decide you're going to listen to me." Several things about this response do not match what we know about toddler development. First, words alone will not control the toddler, and the adult has not helped her comprehend and control actions by giving physical assistance with follow-through. Second, the concept of time-out as a time to think about one's actions and change according to one's recognition of what is right or wrong is beyond toddler mental capability. Third, the situation has been framed as a power struggle that the adult must win by having the toddler realize she is the wrong one and must give in to the powerful adult—certainly not helpful for the development of a positive self-concept.

Does this mean that time-out is generally a developmentally inappropriate guidance method to use with toddlers? Based on what we know about developmental abilities and understanding, the answer is *yes*. Generally time-out is inappropriate. If you have seen or used time-out frequently with toddlers, this is the time to rethink it. It may, however, be appropriate to have a "cool-down time" with older toddlers. The adult will likely have to help an upset toddler calm down, remaining with the toddler or nearby during the calming process. After she is calm, the adult can talk with her about the problem, and help refocus her energies.

Developmentally inappropriate guidance sometimes neglects to consider that toddlers learn much about behavior from imitating the actions of those around them; when adults behave in ways opposite to what they want toddlers to do, their actions speak much louder than the words they thought explained their actions. "I told you not to touch that," shouts the adult, popping the toddler's hand to underline the prohibition. The same adult is angry a little later when that toddler hits at a friend to try to emphasize her point. Many adults say they must use physical contact to "get through" to toddlers who "just don't understand words," by which the adult means the toddler's actions are not controlled by words. Realizing the negative lesson taught by aggressive physical contact may help some adults rethink using physical force for toddler guidance.

In general, developmentally inappropriate guidance does not recognize the limitations on toddler understanding and control, nor does it model the respect for needs and feelings of others that is necessary for true prosocial development.

Fostering Positive Self-Esteem

The critical formation of **self-concept** and **self-esteem** during toddler-hood means that caregivers must view their actions and interactions with toddlers through the filter of their effect on self-esteem. Self-esteem has several sources: feeling we can positively affect others; feeling lovable; feeling capable; and feeling listened to and accepted (Greenberg, 1991).

Adults foster positive toddler self-esteem when they

- are promptly responsive to toddler needs, requests, and communication.
- ask toddler opinions and take their advice ("Do you think we should make our play dough blue or green today?").
- snuggle, stroke, play with toddlers briefly.
- structure situations so toddlers can succeed.
- call attention to toddler success ("Look what Jamal can do. He flipped his coat on the magic way!").
- offer just the right amount of help for success (see Figure 10-15).
- pay close attention and make every effort to understand toddler communication.

From such daily occurrences, positive self-esteem grows.

Figure 10-15

When adults offer just the amount of help needed for toddler success, they foster positive self-esteem.

SUMMARY

Toddlers thrive in relationships with adults who recognize their need for proving autonomy and support their attempts at independence. They gain self-confidence as they function separately from their important adults and learn to master their sadness. They grow as adults protect them from their lack of impulse control with peers, slowly helping them become aware of the needs and rights of others in the environment. They need adults who can accept their expressions of strong emotions until they develop other capabilities for expressing them. They respond to respectful, firm, positive guidance based on knowledge of their inability to stop themselves.

Unfortunately, the most inappropriate social/emotional environments are likely to be found in the toddler room. It is vital that adults who care for toddlers realize their limitations and their struggles for independence, and learn how best to strengthen self-esteem during this time that is trying for child and adult alike. The formation of a healthy sense of self is too critical to later development to risk inappropriate interaction during toddlerhood.

THINK ABOUT IT ACTIVITIES

1. Talk to several parents and/or caregivers of toddlers. Ask them to describe some of the most difficult times they've had with their toddlers recently. Share these with your classmates. Try to identify which toddler social/emotional issues discussed in this chapter are at work in the situations.

2. Watch a toddler in a home or center. What evidence do you see of self-assertion? Of resistance?

3. Where possible, observe a toddler classroom in a childcare center. Note examples of guidance you feel are appropriate for toddlers and any examples you see that are less appropriate. Discuss them with your classmates. What principles of learning are at work in each example?

4. Try to imagine a day from the perspective of a toddler. What experiences might have a positive or a negative impact on the development of a sense of self?

QUESTIONS TO ASSESS LEARNING OF CHAPTER OBJECTIVES

1. Describe the major social/emotional issues of toddlerhood.

2. For each of these issues, discuss several kinds of adult interaction that contribute positively to its outcome. Give examples to illustrate.

3. For each of the issues, discuss several kinds of adult interaction that contribute negatively to its outcome. Give examples to illustrate.

APPLY YOUR KNOWLEDGE QUESTIONS

1. Create a handout to distribute to parents in a toddler room, discussing the issue of biting. Be sure you include possible causes, and appropriate responses.

2. Write a page for a newsletter about life from the toddler's viewpoint, focusing on the restrictions, frustrations, and ways that alert adults could prevent some of these.

HELPFUL WEB SITES

http://www.nncc.org	The Web site for the National Network for Child Care has a number of helpful articles. Search under Guidance and Discipline for articles on temper tantrums and biting.
http://www.kidshealth.org	The Kids Health Web site has a number of helpful articles on toddler issues.
http://www.aacap.org	The Web site for the American Academy of Child and Adolescent Psychiatry has information on toddler issues. Access this information by clicking on Facts for Families and Other Resources.

 Please visit the premium Web site for Developmentally Appropriate Practice, *4th edition, to access more chapter web links, suggestions for further research and study, additional book chapters, interactive quizzes, video exercises, online journal activities, flashcards, and much more! Go to www.cengage.com/login to register your access code.*

Developmentally Appropriate Social/ Emotional Environments: For Preschoolers

As the preschooler emerges from the isolated cocoon of the attachment relationship and the insistent separateness of autonomy, interest in the world of people blossoms. For many children, this also means moving beyond the confines of home and parents to begin spending time in groups with other preschoolers and other adults. Parents and teachers have new expectations about children's abilities to conform to social standards and limits. Although new social situations offer opportunities for developing new interpersonal skills, this learning is complex, and much time in the preschool years is devoted to understanding just how to fit into the larger world of people. Preschoolers must learn rules and develop controls. They must modify behaviors in order to earn acceptance as a friend in the play of childhood. Preschoolers must incorporate messages and teachings from the surrounding culture into their personal understanding of identity.

Along with the social experiences and learning, young children are coping with their emotions and learning just what constitutes acceptable expression of feelings. None of this learning comes without the guidance of caring adults, who demonstrate, explain, and teach alternative behaviors within the context of their teaching and/or parenting relationships.

Social and emotional competence is seen as a necessary foundation for children's later school success. "A number of factors in the emotional and social domain, such as independence, responsibility, self-regulation, and cooperation predict how well children make the transition to school and how they fare in the early grades" (Copple & Bredekamp, 2009, p. 7). Emphasis on developing these skills is an important part of the teacher's role in" "creating a caring community of learners."

LEARNING OBJECTIVES

After completing this chapter, students should be able to

- identify several social/emotional issues of the preschool years.
- identify ten components of emotional environments that encourage developmentally appropriate learning about feelings.
- discuss implications for teachers for nurturing positive identity.
- identify classroom practices that foster gender identity.
- identify classroom practices that foster racial/cultural identity.
- describe ways teachers can promote social skills for friendship.
- identify ways to nurture prosocial awareness.
- discuss ten positive guidance techniques to move preschoolers toward self-control.

SOCIAL/EMOTIONAL ISSUES OF THE PRESCHOOL YEARS

As children move beyond the infant and toddler years during which attachment is the key issue in social/emotional development, they enter a time when the process of **identification** plays a key role in their relationships and social development. From wanting to be near, children move to wanting to be like the important adults in their lives. Through the psychological process of identification, children seek to look, act, feel, and be like significant people in their social environments. Thus identification is a key force in personality and social development in the early childhood years. Theoretical perspectives vary on how identifications form, but the possibilities include observation and imitation, general conceptual and cognitive growth, and affectionate affiliation. Much of the identification process is on an individual and personal basis, although the larger culture certainly influences messages about valuing certain identifications.

The identification process is related to issues of acquiring a gender- or sex-role identity, acquiring a cultural or racial identity, internalizing adult standards for behavior, and developing feelings of self-confidence and personal competence, which are all important concerns of early childhood. Developmentally appropriate social/emotional environments recognize the importance of identification for personality and social learning.

Gender Identity

Gender identity consists of two components. One is the **sexual identity**, determined by biology; the other is **sex-role behavior**, determined by culture. Preschool children actively seek gender identity. By questions and observations, they go beyond their first knowledge of themselves as a boy or girl, to trying to figure out what makes them a boy or a girl.

> Children's comfortable acceptance of their gender anatomy is the cornerstone of constructing a healthy sexual identity and frees children to go beyond stereotypic gender-role constraints (Derman-Sparks, 1989, p. 50).

Beyond biology, preschool children are clearly developing a conceptual grasp of sex-role behavior defined by the culture. In the beginning of the preschool period, boys and girls play house in about the same way; costumes and behaviors representing male and female roles are casually exchanged (Paley, 1984), and children pay little attention to the gender of their play companions. But by age four, boys are less comfortable playing in the housekeeping corner, and by age five, girls have taken over the domestic calm, while boys occasionally raid, disguised as superheroes or "bad guys" (Paley, 1984). Four- and five-year-olds actively look for friends like themselves and emphatically exclude (almost, but not always) children of a different gender. **Gender-specific** forms of play are common, moving boys and girls into such different directions in their fantasy play that they simply do not know the script in order to join each other at play. Also by age four, children clearly distinguish between "boy toys" and "girl toys." Naturalistic studies tell us this happens, but do not explain why. Some experimental studies indicate that parental behaviors shape children's concepts and behaviors; in addition, social norms may override children's first-hand experience at home or in the classroom, as children struggle with powerful cultural messages. In addition, research indicates real differences in the brain and nervous system structure and functioning of boys and girls.

Cultural and Racial Identity

In addition to personal identification, preschool children identify themselves as members of families and their larger culture. Over time, children not only conceptualize their membership in a particular group through experience with their bodies and their social environments, but

WHAT would you DO when...

In your preschool classroom, you overhear children using negative racial terms to refer to another child. Although the other child did not hear them, you want to take action. What would you do?

Helping children learn about racial differences is an important part of helping them achieve a positive self-identity without feeling a sense of superiority or inferiority in comparison with others. When children have absorbed negative words or attitudes about race from others, these ideas should be challenged and discussed. As a teacher it is important to raise the subject with the children who used the terms with comments such as "The words I heard you use are words that some people who don't know any better use when they talk about people with dark skin. Those words hurt other people's feelings, so we don't use them in our classroom."

Then it is appropriate for children to engage in activities that acknowledge their interest in exploring differences in things such as skin color, hair texture, eye color, and so on. Doing self-portraits with flesh-colored paint, doing mirror games, making classroom graphs that depict the differences, as well as reading and discussing children's books on the topic are all useful classroom activities to help children become comfortable and accepting of differences.

In addition, teachers may want to develop bulletin board depictions of these explorations, and have handouts available for parents to follow up at home with helpful conversation.

It is in the best interest of all in a diverse community to become comfortable with discussing topics of acceptance and respect for all.

also show signs of being influenced by societal norms and attitudes toward the group of which they are members. Research indicates that children are aware of their **racial/cultural identity** by the age of four and have also absorbed attitudes toward their own and others' racial identity. Early studies were interpreted as evidence that young African-American children expressed negative feelings about their identification with their racial group (Clark & Clark, 1939); more recent studies indicate that their attitude toward their own and other people's ethnicity depends on the attitudes of adult caregivers, and on the perceptions of the power and wealth of their own group in relation to others (Derman-Sparks & Phillips, 1997). In a society with as much cultural diversity as ours, children learn about their cultural identity in an environment of diversity.

The NAEYC statement on developmentally appropriate practice emphasizes that it is important for programs to respond to cultural and linguistic diversity. In addition, NAEYC has published a position statement, "Responding to Linguistic and Cultural Diversity" (1996), in which the importance of respect and acceptance of children's cultural backgrounds is emphasized as one of the requirements for effective early childhood education. Clearly this is a social/ emotional issue that deserves attention (see Figure 11-1).

Initiative

A component of a healthy sense of self in the preschool years, as defined by Erikson's (1968) psychosocial theory of personality development, is a sense of initiative. Having developed a strong sense of autonomy during toddlerhood, preschoolers now want to assert themselves through initiative involving pretending, inventing, creating, taking risks, and playing with others. As children initiate their own activities, enjoy their accomplishments, and feel valued for their purposeful actions, they become confident in their own actions and abilities. If they are not allowed to follow their own initiative, they feel guilty for their attempts to do so that seem wrong to others. Certainly there is a close connection here with identification; just as children

Figure 11-1

Responding to linguistic diversity may mean providing books in children's home languages.

want to be like significant adults in their lives, they want also to please them. When they perceive that parents and teachers support their ideas and accomplishments, both initiative and identity are strengthened.

Play is the medium through which children test out their ideas about initiative. It is an unfortunate recent development that opportunities for play have been limited in prekindergarten and kindergarten classrooms. The sense of initiative may suffer, as a consequence of these policies.

Friendship

Nothing I say or do arouses the same intense interest Mollie has in her classmates. After many years of teaching, I must admit that mine is not the primary voice in the classroom. (Paley, 1986, p. 107)

Preschoolers are distinguished from younger children by their interest in spending time with peers. The questions "Are you my friend?" and "Who will I play with?" loom large in the awareness of three-, four-, and five-year-olds. Children at this stage are likely to define "best friends," individuals particularly selected for companionship, although the friendships may not be lasting and may be characterized by much friction.

Research has identified behavior patterns of popular and rejected or neglected children. Popular children are well liked by peers and have many friends. Generally, they are active socially, initiating contact with peers, and take a leadership role in directing play activities (Trawick-Smith, 2006), although rarely being bossy or aggressive. On the other hand, rejected children are frequently and often unpredictably aggressive. They seem unable to understand the feelings of their peers. Some choose to play alone and react aggressively when others approach them. Neglected children are frequently overlooked by both peers and adults. They remain isolated and often withdraw from social overtures, seeming to lack social skills to respond appropriately. It has been noted, however, that many of the desirable social skills can be taught and/or modeled by helpful teachers. Friendship and learning the skills of friendship are important social/emotional issues of early childhood, issues that need support in developmentally appropriate classrooms. In Chapter 2, we examined reasons for defining play as the appropriate curriculum for both cognitive development and social development. Through play, children can develop skills for friendship and cooperation.

Prosocial Behavior versus Aggression

The increased aggressiveness that was associated with the distinctive sense of self during toddlerhood is one of the behaviors that adults expect preschool children to begin to control. New verbal abilities allow children to learn to defend their rights with methods other than physical aggression. Preschoolers can be helped to move slowly beyond totally encompassing egocentrism to some awareness of the needs, feelings, and rights of others (see Figure 11-2). Here again the process of identification is an important teaching mechanism, combined with modeling, direct instruction, and experience. Positive discipline methods help promote prosocial behaviors and lessen aggression. Appropriate adult interaction is essential in helping preschoolers with these new abilities and understandings.

An issue related to aggression and prosocial behavior is emotional control and appropriate, constructive expression of feelings. Adult acknowledgment of feelings and help in learning to express them is also necessary here.

Self-Control

The long, slow process of developing the ability to regulate one's own behavior becomes a social/emotional issue of early childhood. The preschool child's expanded abilities for language and understanding enable them to comprehend standards of conduct taught by adults. The process of forming a conscience—"an inner voice of self-observation, self-guidance, and self-punishment" (Erikson, 1968, p. 119)—is the goal of appropriate guidance for preschoolers. (Selma Fraiberg's discussion of conscience formation is classic. See Fraiberg, 1959.) A discussion of positive guidance versus punishment is part of this social/emotional issue of helping children move toward self-control.

Developmentally Appropriate Social/Emotional Interaction

With so many important social/emotional issues to consider, it is vital that teachers of preschoolers realize that curriculum in their classrooms involves far more than narrowly defined skills such as learning colors, numbers, or how to cut with scissors. Curriculum very appropriately grows

Figure 11-2

Children exhibit prosocial behaviors when they become aware of the need to help others.

out of relationships and experiences that are important to children. Learning how to fit into the world around them is at the heart of the concerns of three-, four-, and five-year-olds. Also, nurturing individual children's needs gives them the strength to accept the difficult challenges of adapting to group demands.

Forming personal relationships with young children is the necessary first step in the process of identification; children only want to be like adults they care for and who they sense care for them. The interaction that comes from warm adult-child relationships is the vehicle for the crucial social/emotional guidance from adults. The positive, caring relationship also offers children an example of responsive social relationships. Research has shown that children whose first relationships with adults were positive played in more harmonious ways with others.

HELPING PRESCHOOLERS WITH EMOTIONAL CONTROL

The topic of emotions is inextricably linked with concepts of self and socialization. Learning to adapt one's behavior to social expectation can be stressful for children and frustrating for those guiding them. Developmentally, preschool children have the capacity to learn the vocabulary to express their range of emotions and some of the cognitive capacity needed to identify particular feelings. However, the limitations of preoperational thought restrict them to recognizing only one emotion at a time and to have trouble recognizing another's feelings, relying primarily on facial clues. They need support in learning to channel their emotional expressions into constructive verbal formulations.

A healthy emotional environment offers the security, example, and teaching necessary to nurture emotional control. The following discussion gives ten components of emotional environments that encourage developmentally appropriate learning about feelings for preschoolers.

Security

Classroom environments provide security in the predictability of unchanging sequences and repeated routines. Security is nurtured by meeting the physical and emotional needs expressed by children. Teachers create security when they encourage a sense of belonging to a community that supports individual growth, as well as when they value individual variations in temperament and ability. Children also feel secure when materials provide the experience of successful mastery and activities do not invite comparisons and competition. Teachers and parents create security when they communicate with mutual respect for one another's contribution, sharing information that will ensure continuity for children's care. In emotionally secure environments, children feel comfortable revealing their feelings and trust that adults will help them in gaining control (see Figure 11-3).

Warm Relationships

A responsive, affectionate environment contributes to children's emotional health by promoting positive relationships as the major means of teaching reciprocal caring and emotional responsiveness. When the teacher actively demonstrates genuine concern for others, the classroom climate is positive and based on warm relationships. Children can learn only in the context of warm, positive relationships. Teachers recognize that creating such a classroom atmosphere is an important part of their role. They do not become so busy with details of routine or organization that they fail to take the time for individual responsiveness. They comfort children when they cry and reassure them when they are fearful. Generally, they provide emotional bolstering.

Figure 11-3

Children thrive in emotionally secure environments.

Figure 11-4

Activities to help children identify feelings indicate acceptance of all feelings.

Acceptance

When adults recognize and accept children's emotional responses as normal parts of their being, children's self-awareness of feelings is positive. Feelings are recognized and respected when teachers talk about feelings, giving them names and concreteness. Regular classroom discussion about feelings, as well as activities and books can help children recognize the breadth of emotional experience and the commonality of the feelings they experience with others (see Figure 11-4). Thus, acceptance is conveyed. No limitation is placed on feelings; every feeling is respected as valid and important. No one is told what he or she does or doesn't feel ("That doesn't hurt, it's only a scratch." "You don't hate her, she's your friend.") No one is told what he or she should or should not feel ("You shouldn't feel jealous of her." "You should love your sister.") The only restrictions are on the methods of expressing the feelings. Adults are extremely careful to make this distinction clear to children, always first expressing recognition of the feeling without any judgment on whether the feeling is good or bad, or legitimate, in their opinion. Children are not shamed or made to feel guilty for having the feeling. The adult's attitude conveys the firm message that feelings are real and are accepted as an indivisible part of the person.

To honestly accept the feelings of others, teachers must examine their own attitudes toward emotions. Usually this means recalling how their own feelings were dealt with as children, because such examples often have long-lasting significance. Adults who are unable to accept their own range of emotional responses are unlikely to be able to convey acceptance to children.

> "You seem very angry with me because you think I let Carlos have a longer turn than you."

> "When you're angry, I can't let you hit me. You can tell me in words just how mad you are."

> These examples convey calm and nonjudgmental acceptance of the feeling, while defining a limit on expression and suggesting a more productive method of expression.

Active Listening

The previous example showed the adult reflecting back to the child a perception of what the child was experiencing. This **active listening** (Briggs, 1975; Gordon, 2000) technique identifies feelings that are expressed verbally and/or nonverbally and reflects that understanding back to the individual. In identifying the feeling, adults often make "educated guesses," using all the clues from the individual child as well as all the information they have about particular situations, to become sensitive to what the emotion might be. When the adults reflect the feeling back, they restate the child's feeling tentatively, for confirmation: "It seems to me that you . . ."or "Sounds to me like you feel. . . ." By labeling the feeling, the young child may realize just how to refer to this emotion, or may need to correct the adult's misperception: "No, I feel. . . ." In either case, the way has been indicated to discuss the emotional experience, releasing the feeling in words, and leading to possible problem solving.

The following examples illustrate the steps to helping children become aware of their feelings, aware of ways they can talk about them, and aware of steps they can take in dealing with feelings.

Example 1. The teacher has watched Sabrina playing listlessly by herself since her grandmother left her at the center this morning. Her grandfather had a heart attack last week and has been hospitalized. Although the doctor is optimistic, it has been a stressful week. Sabrina lives with her grandparents.

Teacher: "Sabrina, you seem pretty sad today. Would you like to talk about it?"

Sabrina: "Yeah, I want to see my Paw-Paw."

Teacher: "Sounds like you're missing him."

Sabrina: "Yeah, they won't let kids into the hospital."

Teacher: "You'd really like to see him—it's kind of scary when you know he's sick and you can't see him."

Sabrina: "My Grandma cried last night."

Teacher: "I guess that made you feel sad? And maybe worried too?"

Sabrina: (with a sigh, but relaxing) "Yeah."

Teacher: "We do worry when the people we love are sick and away from us. I wonder if there's something that would help you feel better about this? What about writing a note to your Paw-Paw? Then he'd know you were close by, even if you couldn't come to see him. And maybe a special picture would help Grandma not feel so sad?"

Sabrina: "Yeah. Will you write the words for me?"

Figure 11-5

It is reassuring for children to know that adults understand and accept the way they feel.

It is enormously reassuring to know that someone understands and accepts the way we feel, and emotionally healthful to release some of those feelings and feel control over them (see Figure 11-5).

Imagine the opposite effect if the teacher had dealt with the situation by ignoring the feeling.

Teacher: "Sabrina, it's time you got busy and found something to do this morning."

Another frequent response of adults who do not recognize the importance of helping preschoolers learn to express feelings is to deny the child's feeling.

Teacher: "Your grandma says your grandpa is going to be just fine, and she certainly doesn't need to see you walking around with a long face."

Sabrina would not sense that her feelings had importance or validity with such responses.

Example 2. The teacher watches a conflict between two boys on the playground, and notices Jesse sitting by himself afterward. She approaches and sees that he's crying.

Teacher: "Jesse, I'm sorry to see you're sad."

Jesse: (He says nothing and continues to cry.)

Teacher: "It looks to me like you'd like to figure out a way to play with Seth."

Jesse: (angrily) "I don't want to play with that stupid-head. He's not my friend."

Teacher: "Oh, I misunderstood. You sound pretty mad at him."

Jesse: "I am mad. He said I couldn't ride the tricycle with him anymore."

Teacher: "And that hurt your feelings?"

Jesse: "No, it's not fair, it was my idea to be policemen, and now he's just policemen with Kenny."

Teacher: "You're angry because it was your idea in the first place?"

Jesse: "Yeah."

Teacher: "Well, is there a way you could tell Seth how you feel about that? Maybe there's something you two could work out."

Jesse goes off to talk to Seth. The opportunity to talk about feelings has helped him to clarify his experience and to approach Seth with more control and focus.

A teacher who did not use active listening skills might try to handle the situation with a logical solution that does not touch the feeling:

Teacher: "Well, you could play with somebody else until they're tired of being silly."

Other teachers are tempted to deliver lectures on behavior, again ignoring the feeling at the heart of the matter.

Teacher: "All the children in the class are our friends, and you need to learn to play nicely together."

Active listening allows adults to facilitate children's expression of feelings so that they understand more of their own emotions and more about expressing them to others. Complete acceptance of feelings is part of active listening.

Limits on Expression

Although adults are emphatic in expressing acceptance of children's rights to feel, they are equally emphatic in setting limits on methods of expression. The same limits discussed earlier are the guidelines: children may not hurt themselves or others; they may not destroy property; and they may not infringe on others' rights in expressing their emotions. This means children may not throw toys when they are angry about having to share; they may not attack others aggressively when experiencing frustration; and they may not scream or yell hurtful things. These limits need to be firmly maintained, and the reasons given repeatedly. It is not a safe feeling for children to perceive that no caring adult is strong enough to help them control their own impulses.

> "I won't let you hit David when you're upset with him. You can be mad at him, but you have to let him know some other way than with your hands. Hitting hurts."

Providing Outlets

Recognizing that strong feelings often need strong release, and that just putting the feeling in words may not be enough for complete relief, adults suggest outlets for emotional release and calming effects. They explain carefully to children just how and why to use the outlet, so that children may internalize these concepts for future self-control. The goal is to help children learn methods of coping with and channeling their feelings. Emotionally healthy classrooms have materials available for such **outlets**. Materials might include clay or play dough for pounding; pillows or a punching bag for pounding; paper for tearing; a ball for kicking; and a place for yelling or running. Some children benefit from a quiet retreat: a soft pile of pillows to lie on, a basin of water to play in, or a lap to sit on.

> "You can come and pound on the clay to let all those angry feelings out. When you're feeling calmer, we can talk about your problem with David."

> "Playing in the water may help your sad feelings."

Modeling Behavior

Teachers know their example will help children learn many important lessons about feelings, such as accepting one's own feelings as an integral part of the self, verbally expressing feelings, and using self-control. They are honest about their feelings and don't try to hide them from children. Adults seldom succeed in disguising feelings, and attempts to do so send children confusing messages, like the teacher saying they will have fun today and looking anything but! Many teachers mistakenly believe they should always be above emotional responses in the classroom, but this robs children of important opportunities to experience what it means to be fully human and to respond to others' emotions. Besides, a teacher who has struggled to hold emotion in through a stressful day is somewhat like a smoldering volcano; an eruption is imminent, and no one knows exactly when or how it will occur. This is not a secure place for children to be! Although teachers should permit themselves to express emotion in the classroom, the importance of a positive adult example must be recalled. Adults should not behave in destructive ways. Nothing is more alarming than to see an adult having an uncontrolled temper tantrum! Following are a couple of positive examples.

> "I'm sad today because children in my classroom have destroyed the sand structure the three-year-olds built on the playground," says Diane to her group of four-year-olds. "I'm not feeling much like playing with you right now. I think I'll sit over here for a while and you can decide what you might do to help them."

> "I'm getting annoyed by so many children coming to me with complaints about other children. I'm going to go wash the paint brushes and maybe then I'll feel more like talking with you."

Such expressions allow children to understand how their behavior affects others' feelings.

Materials for Expression

Healthy emotional environments recognize that children express and deal with feelings and stressful situations through play. Providing materials that are meaningful for young children encourages playing out many feelings. Dolls and other house-corner props and puppets may encourage children to dramatize their emotions. Alert teachers may provide specific props based on what they know of children's immediate situations. A teacher who knew that several of her preschoolers were coming to terms with emotions following the birth of siblings added a lot of baby paraphernalia such as diapers, bottles, and pacifiers. When one of the young "mothers" reacted with anger to that "darn baby crying again," she was able to help the child express some of her very mixed feelings about the new baby at home. Another teacher, aware of the stress in a particular family that included a job change and moving to a new residence, added suitcases and packing boxes to allow the child to deal with the fearful unknowns of moving. Various art media may help other children express feelings through creative expression (see Figure 11-6). Supporting children's meaningful play is a very developmentally appropriate way to help preschoolers deal with feelings.

Learning about Feelings

Preschoolers need help understanding some of the cognitive concepts related to feelings. Teachers plan activities that help introduce children to common emotional responses, situations, and behaviors that may trigger feelings, and discuss possible courses of action in response to feelings.

CULTURAL CONSIDERATIONS

Expressing Emotions

Good early childhood practice expects teachers and parents to accept all feelings as valid, and to teach children to express feelings in appropriate ways. In many cultures, particularly Asian cultures, the expectations are different. In the words of one early childhood expert on cross-cultural differences, "The importance of maintaining social relationships, and of adopting a posture of respect for the feelings of elders and of authority, demands that each person not only suppress anger but, in addition, be ready to withhold complete honesty about personal feelings in order to avoid hurting another" (Kagan, cited in Gonzalez-Mena, 2007, p. 133). It is important for teachers to recognize that emotional expression may not be something that others are comfortable with, given their particular cultural orientation.

Figure 11-6

Art media help children express feelings through creative expression.

Classroom Teaching Strategies To Support Children's Emotional and Social Development

- **Modeling:** Teachers demonstrate the skill and explain what they are doing.
- **Modeling with puppets:** Puppets model the skill while interacting with children, adults, or other puppets.
- **Arranging peer partners:** More skilled children can help demonstrate the skill.
- **Songs and fingerplays:** Introduce new skills with activities.
- **Using a flannelboard:** Flannelboard stories can introduce new skills.
- **Playing games:** Games can teach problem solving, identification of others' feelings, friendship skills, and so on.
- **Discussing children's literature:** Books can introduce concepts about feelings, friendship, and the like.
- **Teaching during experiences:** Guide the children to use skills during interactions with others.
- **Giving encouraging reinforcement:** Feedback is important when children are using the skill.

For more on these and other ideas, look at the Web site for the Center on the Social and Emotional Foundations for Early Learning, listed at the end of the chapter.

Both planned group activities and informal discussions allow children to sort out more of the information they need for emotional control and expression. Direct instruction can help children learn the following social and emotional skills:

- identifying feelings in oneself and others
- controlling anger and impulses
- problem solving
- giving compliments
- understanding how and when to apologize
- expressing empathy with others' feelings
- recognizing that anger can interfere with problem solving
- learning how to recognize anger in oneself and others
- understanding appropriate ways to express anger
- learning how to calm down
- following rules, routines, and directions
- suggesting play themes and activities to peers
- sharing toys and other materials
- taking turns
- helping adults and peers (Fox & Lentini, 2006).

> "Look at this picture. What do you think is happening here? How do you think the girl feels? Why do you think she feels that way? What could she do to let her friend know about how she feels?"

> "Can you find the picture where someone looks worried? Show me how you look when you're worried. When have you felt worried?"

A list of books for preschoolers that encourage conversation about particular feelings appears in Figure 11-7.

 VIDEO ACTIVITY

Go to the premium Web site and watch the video clip for Chapter 11 titled "Helping Preschoolers with Feelings." Then consider the following questions:

REFLECTIVE QUESTION

1. What do you believe is the teacher's goal in this scenario?

2. Specifically, what social and emotional skills is she helping with, and what strategies is she using?

3. Do you find anything that you might do differently, in the light of ideas from this chapter?

 Visit the premium Web site to complete these questions online and email them to your professor.

BOOKS THAT HELP YOUNG CHILDREN KNOW IT'S ALL RIGHT TO FEEL . . .

Feelings, **Richard Allington & Kathleen Krull**
I Have Feelings, **Terry Berger**
Faces, Faces, Faces, **Barbara Brenner**
Happy, Sad, Silly, Mad, **Barbara Hazen**
Feelings Alphabet, **Judy Lalli**
*Feeling Mad, Feeling Sad, Feeling Bad,
    Feeling Glad,* **Ann McGovern**
How Do I Feel? **Norma Simon**
Things I Hate! **Harriet Wittels & Joan Greisman**
Make A Face, **Lynn Yudell**

Angry
*And My Mean Old Mother Will Be Sorry,
    Blackboard Bear,* **Martha Alexander**
Bear Party, William **Pene du Bois**
I Was So Mad, **Karen Erickson & Maureen
    Roffey**
Martha's Mad Day, **Miranda Hapgood**
I'm Not Oscar's Friend Any More, **Marjorie
    Sharmat**
*Alexander and the Terrible, Horrible, No Good,
    Very Bad Day,* **Judith Viorst**
Sometimes I Get Angry, **Jane Watson**
The Quarreling Book, **Charlotte Zolotow**

Jealous
Nobody Asked Me if I Wanted a Baby Sister,
    Martha Alexander
Bear's Bargain, **Frank Asch**
A Baby Sister for Frances; A Birthday for Frances,
    Russell Hoban
Big Brother, **Robert Kraus**
One Frog Too Many, **Mercer Mayer**
Lyle and the Birthday Party, **Bernard Waber**
It's Not Fair, **Charlotte Zolotow**

Embarrassed
Loudmouth George and the Big Race,
    Nancy Carlson
Donald Says Thumbs Down, **Nancy Cooney**

I Should Have Stayed in Bed, **Joan Lexau**
Felix, the Bald-Headed Lion, **Kenneth Townsend**

Afraid
Maybe a Monster, **Martha Alexander**
Harriet's Recital, **Nancy Carlson**
Jim Meets the Thing, **Miriam Cohen**
Noel the Coward, **Robert Kraus, Jose Aruego
    & Ariane Dewey**
There's a Nightmare in My Closet, **Mercer Mayer**
It's Only Arnold, **Brinton Turkle**
*My Mama Says There Aren't Any Zombies, Ghosts,
    Vampires, Creatures, Demons, Monsters,
    Fiends, Goblins, or Things,* **Judith Viorst**

Lonely
One to Teeter-Totter, **Edith Battles**
The Quiet House, **Otto Coontz**
Shags Finds a Kitten, **Gyo Fujikawa**
Nothing at All, **Wanda Gag**
The Trip, **Ezra Jack Keats**
The Bear Who Had No Place to Go, **James
    Stevenson**
Helena, the Unhappy Hippopotamus, **Yutaka
    Sugita**
Crow Boy, **Taro Yashima**

Sadness
Little Hippo, **Frances Allen**
Rat Is Dead and Ant Is Sad, **Betty Baker**
Everett Anderson's Goodbye, **Lucille Clifton**
Nana Upstairs and Nana Downstairs, **Tomie
    dePaolo**
Goodbye Rune, **Marit Kaldhol**
The Christmas Grump, **Joseph Low**
The Tenth Good Thing About Barney, **Judith Viorst**
Janey, **Charlotte Zolotow**

Figure 11-7

Books that help young children know it's all right to feel.

Vocabulary to Express Feelings

Not only do children need acceptance of their feelings and support for expressing them, they also need direct coaching on ways of expressing them to others. An over-used cliché in classrooms for young children is, "Use your words!" Although the intention is commendable, it is not so simple for young children to use language unless an adult has helped them learn just what words can be effective. Adults ask children to describe how they feel. They can then suggest words that children can use with others. Depending on the child's cognitive and verbal skills, they may suggest alternative approaches and longer sentences.

PRACTICAL IMPLICATIONS

Teaching Emotional Control

Unsupportive teaching practices that hinder healthy emotional development include:

- ignoring, distracting, mocking, shaming, or "cheering children up."

- showing anger with children's lack of emotional control.

- forcing children to express feelings they do not feel, as in a very unintended "I'm sorry."

After children have had some experience with using adults' words to describe their feelings to others, teachers may encourage children to think of their own.

"How did you feel when Sarah called you that name? Well, you could tell her, 'Sarah, I don't like it when you call me names.' She doesn't know that's how you're feeling."

"You're upset with Sarah. How could you let her know that?"

Learning to express feelings in language is a gradual developmental process. Children need encouragement and reminders to do so and reinforcement when they do.

"I like the words you used to tell David you needed a turn. Good talking."

Helping preschoolers learn to control and express emotional reactions is a very important role for the teacher, one that is integrated into each classroom day and every encounter.

NURTURING INDIVIDUAL IDENTITY

One of the most developmentally inappropriate aspects of any preschool environment is the tendency to treat children as if they were only members of a group, restricting attention only to group identity ("our friends"), whole-group activities ("you need to come and do this with everybody"), and group standards for behavior ("our rules"). Although teachers do work to help "create a sense of the group as a cohesive community" (Copple & Bredekamp, 2009, p. 151), developmental appropriateness involves considering the unique characteristics and needs of each child and trying to convey acceptance of that uniqueness.

In this section, we will consider implications for nurturing individual identity, looking specifically at nurturing positive gender and racial/cultural identity.

Implications for Teachers

Positive individual identity is nurtured when teachers do the following.

- Use words and nonverbal actions to show affection for children and sincere interest in them. Teachers greet children individually on arrival and help each child become involved in activities of personal interest. Their personal comments throughout the day indicate they are aware of what each child has done or cares about.

  "You look ready to play today, Dominique. We've got the clay out again—I remember how much you liked that last week."

  "Waldo, you've been working really hard on that puzzle. I see you like the ones with lots of pieces."

- Spend time talking individually with each child each day (see Figure 11-8). Routine times—such as bathroom time, getting coats on, walking to the playground, waiting for other children to gather for group time—are used as occasions for adult-child conversation. As teachers move among children busy at self-selected activities throughout the day, they are free to initiate conversation. They listen attentively to what each child has to say and are courteous in their interaction.

  "Tell me more about your visit with your grandparents, LaPorcha. It sounds like you had lots of fun."

  "I liked watching you climb on the bars, Rickie. I was remembering when you were too little to do that. Do you remember how you learned?"

- Create a classroom atmosphere that encourages and values individuality. Teachers call children's attention to each other's accomplishments, not to foster a spirit of competition, but to show children they value their competence. They recognize differences and strengths in all

Figure 11-8
Teachers make opportunities to talk individually with each child.

domains of development. Giving children real examples of past successes is a way to build their feelings of confidence. Important for all children, this respect for individual strength and accomplishment is especially important for children with disabilities who need to feel truly included and competent in their own right. As a component of an antibias classroom, typically developing children are helped to interact comfortably and knowledgeably with those who have special needs, as their real accomplishments are pointed out.

"Look, Jasmine, Anna had a good idea about using the funnel. Anna likes to figure out her own way of doing things."

"Christopher likes to make pictures of airplanes, have you noticed, Jeremy? I can always tell when it's a picture Christopher made." (Christopher is in a wheelchair.)

"I'm making a list of what we're all good at to put on the wall. Would you like to help me? I already got Susannah for tying her shoes and Jason for running fast. Oh, you're right—Christopher can go really fast! What about Leah for remembering things? She was good at that last week when we wrote our story about our trip to the farm." (Leah is hearing impaired.)

• Respond with sensitivity to children's individuality. Adults support and encourage individual styles of making decisions and choices for certain activities, people, and interactions. They try to learn each child's characteristics, rather than viewing evidence of individuality as interfering with adults' plans, or as problem behavior or weakness in personality.

"Sally would rather watch you sing than take a turn to sing by herself. Sally, do you want to sit with me while we watch them?"

"Enrico finds it hard to relax with a book at naptime, so I let him take his favorite little cars on the cot."

As expressed by Clemens (1983, p. 25):

Good teaching implies being comfortable making exceptions for people when they need them. It is the opposite of that killer phrase my teachers used to use: "If I do it for you, I'll have to do it for everybody." This was untrue and unfair.

• Convey respect also for individual parents' styles and needs and use parents' knowledge of their children as a primary source for getting to know individuality.

"Jeremy's mom is a single parent with three children, so I realize she doesn't have much time to spend in the classroom. I call her every now and then to let her know what we've been doing, and to have a chance for her to tell me how he's doing at home."

Figure 11-9

Children enjoy having mirrors in the environment as they explore personal identity.

"Rosa's mother is helping me get her to interact in the classroom more by telling me the things and people she mentions at home. Then I can plan activities that seem to have been her favorites."

- Provide opportunities, materials, and encouragement for children to initiate activities that have meaning and interest for them personally. As children experience a reasonable number of successful, positive play experiences in their classroom life, they will continue to take initiative. The child-centered curriculum of choice contributes to positive self-identity.

"Hey, look what I did," exclaims Victor as he displays his carefully balanced box construction.

"I thought you could walk that balance beam," comments the teacher, smiling; Jeremy grins broadly, agreeing. "It's pretty hard, and I can do it."

- Continually incorporate concepts related to personal identity into learning activities and conversations (see Figure 11-9). In some classrooms, teachers plan a one-week unit on the theme "I'm Me, I'm Special." Rather than paying cursory attention once a year to this theme, in developmentally appropriate classrooms teachers plan curriculum that is meaningful to children's experiences and lives and regularly help children see connections with their own experiences.

"There's a big grocery truck like the one Danny's daddy drives," notes the teacher as they walk down the street.

"You were just as little as LaPorcha's baby sister a long time ago, and your mommy gave you a bottle when you were hungry, just like that. Your mommy took good care of you." Alondra is curious about the visiting baby.

Gender Identity

In developmentally appropriate classrooms, teachers recognize that forming a healthy gender identity is a developmental task of preschool children. They help children by enabling them to clarify answers to biological questions and by promoting activities that encourage equality of participation by both genders. Teachers facilitate healthy gender identity when they

- accept children's right to be curious about their bodies and the need for simple, factual responses when they demonstrate that curiosity. Where needed, teachers find resources that help explain answers to preschoolers' questions in ways matching their cognitive abilities. *What Is a Girl? What Is a Boy?* by Stephanie Waxman (1976) is helpful.

"Roberto stands up when he uses the toilet because he is a boy. Boys' and girls' bodies are made differently. It's more convenient for girls to sit on the toilet seat."

"Some girls prefer to wear pants, but wearing pants doesn't make you a boy. The difference between girls and boys is not what they wear, but the way their bodies are made. Boys have a penis; girls have a vagina."

- offer experiences that challenge narrow, stereotypical views of gender behavior. Use parents and others in the community to help children understand the breadth of choices available to both genders. It is important for children to see males and females respecting one another as individuals.

"Roberto's father is visiting us today. He works as a nurse at the hospital."

"Yes, that's right. We did see two women firefighters when we visited the fire station, Jade. Firefighters can be men or women; they have to be strong and trained in how to fight fires."

- reorganize the play environment to encourage more cross-gender play choices. Studies show some differences in the activity level and play choices of boys and girls; boys tend to be more active in their play, whereas girls tend to play more quietly, choosing activities such as art or puzzles. Boys appear more interested in outdoor play than girls, and often select adventuresome activities. Differences in dramatic-play themes find girls generally choosing home and family themes and boys playing adventure or superhero roles. Because all these kinds of play are useful, teacher intervention may help children broaden their repertoire if children indicate their limited choices are based on ideas of gender appropriateness. Suggestions include expanding the dramatic-play area to include props from other rooms in the house: woodworking and tools; materials for a "study"; lawn and garden tools; or dress-up props related to work (tool chest, lunch box, hard hat, barber tools) that suggest male participation (Derman-Sparks, 1989; Gurian & Ballew, 2003). Mix it up by adding a dollhouse to the block area and tools to housekeeping.

- use art and photos to broaden children's view of what jobs men and women, young and old, and disabled or not, can do. Examples could be a worker in a wheelchair, women laying bricks, women repairing phone wires, men cooking dinner, and men holding babies. Images displayed without comment can help influence children's thinking.

- examine pictures and language in books in the classroom to make sure diversity in work and home roles is portrayed. Make anatomically correct dolls available for children to play with. Replace stereotypical books with those meant to open minds and eyes, for example, *Heather Hits Her First Home Run* by Phyllis Johnson (Lollipop Power Books) and *The Boy Toy* by Ted Plantos (Black Moss). See a list of good books to challenge traditional stereotypes in Wellhousen (1996).

- involve children in new activities. Derman-Sparks (1989) suggests teachers consider occasional teacher-initiated activities to counteract the limited choices children may make for play based on their perceptions of gender appropriateness. Having an "everybody plays with blocks day" or "group mural" art day may encourage children to experience new choices until they become comfortable enough to select them on

PRACTICAL IMPLICATIONS

Nurturing Positive Identities

Teachers do not contribute to positive feelings of identity when they:

- are too busy or involved with their own agendas to acknowledge and enjoy children's presence.

- use names as synonyms for "no," "don't," or "stop," as in "Tony!"

- fail to maintain eye contact or be available physically for conversation.

- pay superficial attention to what children have to say or actively discourage children from talking, preferring to maintain a quiet environment.

- speak to the whole group most of the time, speaking to individual children only to admonish or discipline them.

- create an atmosphere that fosters competition to meet the adult standard of behavior and evaluate children by narrowly defined standards that are focused on children's intellectual development.

- criticize or belittle typical childlike behaviors, as in "Why can't you sit still and do something quiet for a change?"

- use judgmental comments (often within children's hearing) to describe individual children's behavior, style, or interests, as in "He's the shyest child I've ever met."

- judge parents by their own standards of what "good" parents do.

- fail to communicate with parents respectfully as a necessary source of information to understand children's individuality.

- use highly structured, teacher-directed lessons without many opportunities for children to initiate their own ideas, make choices, or make connections with their own lives.

CULTURAL CONSIDERATIONS

Gender Identity

Issues of gender identity, gender roles, and gender exploration vary from culture to culture. Teachers will encounter many parents who are simply uncomfortable with or strongly oppose children's exploration of this topic through play. (Given the unique cultural backgrounds of teachers, many teachers may also be uncomfortable with these ideas.) Once again, understanding others' perspectives and working together to figure out what to do about discrepancies in these practices requires constant communication with families, with the goal of seeing a perspective other than the teacher's own.

Figure 11-10

Teachers and families may differ in their acceptance of children's role pretend play and gender-identified toys.

their own initiative. Boys particularly seem reluctant to choose activities that they identify as "girl" play; girls seem more easily interested in using "boy toys." This may justify planning to use particular activities or materials in art, for example, that boys might find interesting, such as cars, to create paint designs.

"We need some help preparing the vegetables for our soup. Will you help us, Pedro?"

"I'm wondering if you'd like to drive the baby to the doctor, Rachel. Jacob could hold her for you while you drive."

- communicate with parents about goals and classroom practices to support healthy gender identity. Teachers need to recognize that educational, ethnic, and cultural backgrounds influence parents' feelings about nontraditional gender behavior or responses to children's interest in sexuality. There may be tension about differences between home and classroom approaches (see Figure 11-10). Communication that conveys respect for different opinions is essential as parents and teachers resolve areas of difference. Read comments in Gonzalez-Mena (2007) as you think about this important topic. Derman-Sparks (1989) also addresses this issue.

- actively challenge children's gender stereotypical actions or comments, intervening whenever they see gender bias. Even in antisexist classroom or home environments, children often stubbornly maintain the stereotypes they have absorbed from the larger culture. Challenging them to compare their real experiences with their beliefs may eventually cause children to shift their thinking.

"But remember when Roberto's father came to visit us? Men can be nurses as well as women."

"I remember you told me that your daddy cooks you breakfast in the morning, so you could cook for the babies too. Not just mommies have to do the cooking."

- examine personal feelings about gender-free activities, comments, and attitudes.

A reading list for adults on the topic of healthy gender identity practices is included in Figure 11-11.

PRACTICAL IMPLICATIONS

Facilitating Healthy Gender Identity

In order to facilitate healthy gender identity, teachers should not:

- respond differently to boys and girls.
- reinforce gender stereotypes by their comments or expectations.
- use "boys" and "girls" as a way to separate the group for activities.
- ask boys only to help with big jobs, and ask girls to clean up.
- shame or punish children's curiosity about biological differences.

BOOKS FOR TEACHERS AND FAMILIES ON THE TOPIC OF GENDER IDENTITY

Racism, Gender Identities and Young Children: Social Relations in a Multi-Ethnic, Inner-City Primary School, **Paul Connolly**

Girls, Boys, Books, Toys: Gender in Children's Literature and Culture, **Beverly Lyon Clark & Margaret R. Higgonet**

Gender in Early Childhood, **Nicole Yelland**

Great Books for Boys Ages 2–14, **Kathleen Odean**

Great Books for Girls Ages 3–14, **Kathleen Odean**

Beyond Guns and Dolls: 101 Ways to Help Children Avoid Gender Bias, **Susan Hoy Crawford**

Boys and Girls: Superheroes in the Doll Corner, **Vivian Gussin Paley**

Figure 11-11

Books for teachers and families on the topic of gender identity.

Cultural and Racial Identity

Teachers can promote positive attitudes toward racial and cultural identity for all children when they create an antibias environment that conveys a true respect for diversity in all its forms. It is important that teachers become personally aware of prejudices that have influenced their own development and ways that messages of bias are passed on to children. Reading the NAEYC publication by Derman-Sparks, *Anti-Bias Curriculum: Tools for Empowering Young Children* (1989), is a good place to start. See additional suggestions in the list for adults in Figure 11-12.

An atmosphere of antibias enables all children "to construct a knowledgeable, confident self-identity; to develop comfortable, empathetic, and just interaction with diversity; and to develop

---

BOOKS FOR TEACHERS AND PARENTS ON THE TOPIC OF RACIAL/ CULTURAL IDENTITY

Common Bonds: Anti-Bias Teaching in a Diverse Society, **Deborah A. Byrnes & Gary Kiger, (Eds.)**

Anti-Bias Curriculum: Tools for Empowering Young Children, **Louise Derman-Sparks & the A.B.C. Task Force**

Starting Small: Teaching Tolerance in Preschool and the Early Grades, **Teaching Tolerance Project**

Affective Curriculum: Teaching the Anti-Bias Approach to Young Children, **Nadia Saderman Hall & Valerie Romberg**

Creative Resources for the Anti-Bias Classroom, **Nadia Saderman Hall**

Nobody Else Like Me: Activities to Celebrate Diversity, **Sally Moomaw**

Diversity in the Classroom: New Approaches to the Education of Young Children, **Frances E. Kendall**

Roots & Wings: Affirming Culture in Early Childhood Settings, **Stacey York**

Big as Life: The Everyday Inclusive Curriculum, **Stacey York**

Skilled Dialogue: Strategies for Responding to Cultural Diversity in Early Childhood, **Isaura Barrera, Robert M. Corso, Dianne Macpherson**

Connecting Kids: Exploring Diversity Together, **Linda Hill**

Celebrating Our Diversity: Using Multicultural Literature to Promote Cultural Awareness, **Marti Abbott & Betty Jane Polk**

One Child, Many Worlds: Early Learning in a Multicultural Community, **Eve Gregory**

"Opening the Culture Door," **Barbara Kaiser & Judy Sklar Rasminsky**

Young Bilingual Learners in Nursery School, **Linda Thompson**

Figure 11-12

Books for teachers and families on the topic of racial/ cultural diversity.

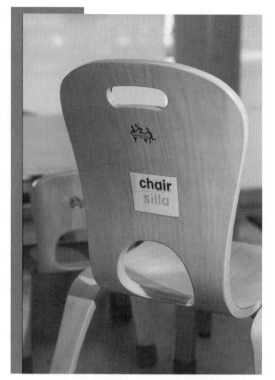

Figure 11-13

Visible signs of the home language throughout the learning environment help bilingual children.

critical thinking and the skills for standing up for oneself and others in the face of injustice" (Derman-Sparks, 1989, p. ix). As teachers are mindful of incorporating ideas about cultural diversity and respect, in daily interactions they examine all interactions, materials, and experiences to ensure that they convey attitudes of respect for all people. Teachers are aware that what is included or excluded in the classroom environment speaks plainly about what is valued by educational institutions and by teachers. In their own classrooms, teachers can do the following:

- Examine all pictures and books to ensure that they realistically portray the diversity of the individual classroom, community, and the total North American population, with respect to racial composition, nonstereotypical gender representations, different abilities, ages, classes, family structures, and lifestyles (see Figure 11-13). Such diversity is important whether the classroom population is primarily homogeneous or diverse (Hall, 2008). The Council on Interracial Books for Children analyzes children's books and other learning materials for racism and sexism. They also offer a checklist on how to analyze children's books for racism and sexism, about which you can find more information in the "Helpful Web Sites" section at the end of this chapter.

  Also locate other resources for finding culturally appropriate children's literature on the Web sites of the American Library Association and the International Reading Association.

- Read, read, read. There are wonderful books that help children appreciate the diversity of the world; see a very good annotated listing in Roberts and Hill (2003) and Derman-Sparks (1989).

- Provide toys, materials, and activities in every interest center that children can identify with and that represent both the families in the classroom and the major groups in the community and the nation. Art materials, manipulative objects, music, dolls and dramatic-play props, and circle-time activities should regularly celebrate diversity. See ideas in Derman-Sparks (1989) and Derman-Sparks and Phillips (1997).

The teacher must become an active **pluralist**, who will imbue every aspect of the classroom with cultural and racial diversity. The classroom should become a microcosm of the pluralistic society the children do and will continue to live in, always emphasizing the similarities among people more than the differences.

Ten Quick Ways to Analyze Children's Books for Racism And Sexism

1. Check the illustrations, looking for stereotypes, tokenism, and who is doing what.
2. Check the story line to note the standards for success, how problems are resolved, and the role of women.
3. Look at lifestyles, to see if white middle class seems to be the only norm.
4. Weigh the relationships between people, to see if white characters take all the leadership roles and how family relationships are depicted.
5. Note the heroes.
6. Consider the effect on a child's self-image.
7. Consider the author or illustrator's background.
8. Consider the author's perspective.
9. Watch for loaded words.
10. Look at the copyright date.

(Adapted from an article by the Council on Interracial Books for Children. More details can be found in the full article at the Web site http://childrensbooksabout.com.)

The teacher helps by focusing on the people in the child's world of today, not a historical world. The goal with preschoolers is not to teach history, but to help them stand against racism.

Teachers who actively create an antibias environment are helping children of all racial and cultural backgrounds form healthy identity and attitudes.

- Involve all parents in classroom activities, visits, and opportunities to share family stories, songs, drawings, and traditions of their cultural and linguistic background. This helps parents perceive the inclusion of respect and attention to their child's heritage, as well as enlisting their support in helping all children understand and appreciate differences.

- Work with families to support and maintain children's home language skills, while supporting children to learn English within the context of their play activities. It is helpful to give parents information on how preserving the home language learning contributes to the child's sense of identity, family socialization of beliefs and value systems, and natural relationships with parents, as well as the assets of **bilingualism**. Teachers who are multilingual will be invaluable in this support, but teachers who do not speak children's home language can still make efforts to "provide visible signs of the home language throughout the learning environment" (NAEYC, 1996, p. 11) through books, tapes, parent bulletin boards, visitors, and occasional grouping of children who speak the same home language. See Figure 11-13.

This sensitivity to representing each child's home culture and language follows the appropriate practices defined by NAEYC to help each child feel accepted in the classroom community, where "children hear and see their home language and culture reflected in the daily interactions and activities of the classroom" (Copple & Bredekamp, 2009, p. 17). Inappropriate practices ignore cultural and other differences, effectively excluding children who do not feel part of the group. Inappropriate practices also include creating what Derman-Sparks refers to as "tourist curriculum," such as having a Chinese week in which children create dragon masks and eat with chopsticks. Inappropriate practices also include emphasizing the exotic differences between cultures, creating a greater sense of separation, rather than helping children appreciate similarities and differences.

- Become sensitive to opportunities to help children move from discomfort or prejudice to what is new or unfamiliar to them, knowing how to gently challenge ideas that could lead to bias development. Aware of children's growing cultural identity, teachers identify nonverbal explorations as questions. Teachers intervene immediately with explanations that are appropriate to children's developmental levels, not ignoring either questions or discriminatory behaviors. They comfort and support children who are the center of questions, assuring them of their distinctiveness and worth.

> Three-year-old Chloe rubs thoughtfully at her brown skin, then touches the pink skin of the teacher. The teacher quickly says, "You have

JOURNAL REFLECTION

Your Experiences with Non-English Speakers

Consider what experiences you have had in working with others whose first language is not English. What emotions would you use to describe the experience? For example, did you feel frustration, anxiety, annoyance, or something else? How do these emotions affect your ability to work effectively with others?

Visit the premium Web site to complete this journal activity online and email it to your professor.

PRACTICAL IMPLICATIONS

Supporting Healthy Cultural/Racial/Linguistic Identities

Unsupportive practices related to cultural/racial/linguistic identity include:

- responding with discomfort to children and families whose racial/cultural backgrounds or family structure are different from their own.

- failing to challenge, and failing to help children to challenge, biased remarks or actions in the classroom.

- providing stereotypical materials that do not convey respect for diversity.

- offering a "tourist approach" (Derman-Sparks, 1989) that treats other cultural groups as if they were exotic and actually emphasizes differences.

- ignoring children's cultural and linguistic backgrounds and other individual differences or treating them as "deficits to be overcome" (NAEYC, 1996, p. 131).

beautiful brown skin, Chloe, just like your mother. My skin is pink, because that's the color of my mother."

When the teacher overhears a child tell another that her grandpa said she shouldn't play with black people, she tells the child that being black is no reason for not playing with someone, even if that is some people's way of thinking. She emphasizes that in this school they realize that leaving people out hurts their feelings.

Friendship

Preschoolers are exploring the beginnings of friendship. Through language ("I'll be your friend"; "Are you my friend?") and action, they are experimenting with the social skills that lead to friendship. Some children, through temperament or helpful life experiences, seem to move into friendship more easily than others. But all children can benefit as adults assist them in identifying effective ways to communicate with peers. Adults foster beginning friendships when they

- offer space and time for the face-to-face conversations that are essential for developing social understandings. Small-group areas such as the water table, play dough table, dramatic-play area, or block center, encourage social interaction (see Figure 11-14). Unstructured, uninterrupted time is necessary for conversation.

- pair particular children occasionally for a common activity, especially in the case of shy or neglected children.

    "Alberto, would you choose a friend to help you be our block area cleanup crew?"

    "Jennifer and Jasmine, our baby dolls need washing this morning. Here's a washcloth for each of you."

- help children clarify their needs by asking them what they would like to play or with whom. Preschoolers are so preoccupied with their own needs that they mistakenly assume others want what they want.

    "Would you like to play in the grocery store this morning? Or did you want to play with Alberto? He's in the block area this morning."

- help children develop effective skills for entering play. Young children sometimes alienate others by focusing on their own needs in the play ("Can I play?") or by the use of bizarre methods not easily recognized by other children as overtures (knocking down the block

Figure 11-14

Small groups encourage the interaction that is important in developing friendships.

structure as a way of saying "I'd like to play too"). Teachers can model or cue language to get another child's attention.

> "If you want to play with Jennifer go over and say 'Jennifer, do you want to play blocks? We can make a bed for the dolls.'"

> "You could ask Erika if you can go to the store with her."

- help children practice effective communication skills such as using names, talking directly to others, and maintaining eye contact. Teachers reinforce this by their own example as well as through specific coaching.

> "I don't think Jeremy knew you were talking to him, Sam. Look at him, and say his name when you're talking with him."

> "Nancy didn't look like she heard you when you asked for a turn. Say it again, and louder."

- give children information to help them recognize friendly overtures of others (Kostelnik, Phipps-Wirren, Soderman, Stein, & Gregory, 2006). Preschoolers generally have a difficult time grasping others' intentions. Examples:

> "I hear Sam asking you to play with him, Jeremy. You could have two steam shovel drivers."

> "It looks to me as if Jennifer would like to go to the store with you, Erika. You can get more groceries with two people to carry them."

- help children understand how their behavior affects the response of others. Some children do not see connections between their actions and others' feelings or responses. Teachers can help them understand the connection in order to modify their behavior for the desired response.

> "When you knocked down the blocks, it made the other boys angry, so that's why they said they didn't want you to play. If you want to play blocks with them, you need to ask what you can do to help."

> "Jasmine really enjoyed working on washing the dolls with you. You gave her turns, and that was a friendly thing to do."

- model play entry skills with children to help less-skilled children learn ways of entering the play, while supporting them emotionally. When teachers help children become participants in play, they supply a suggested role and demonstrate how to do it.

> "Catherine and I are going to be the passengers buying a ticket for your train. How much is the ticket? Where do we sit?"

> "It looks like they're cooking dinner. Let's go over and you can ask Michelle if dinner is ready yet."

- recognize that preschool friendships may be short-lived, and support children as they experience feelings of frustration or anger or a desire to withdraw temporarily from social interaction.

> "It upset you when Jeremy said he didn't want to be your friend. Maybe he'll feel differently later on."

> "I think Jennifer would rather play by herself for a while. You could ask her again later."

PRACTICAL IMPLICATIONS

Forming Early Friendships

Adults who want to nurture beginning friendships for preschool children should not:

- insist that everyone in the class are "friends," rather than help children learn to distinguish friendly behaviors.

- insist that everyone in the class like one another, rather than accepting children's real preferences in playmates.

- dictate children's play partners constantly.

- require children to do activities together or share toys.

- intervene too quickly or too constantly to manage social situations, preventing children from getting direct experience in managing interaction with peers.

Figure 11-15

Good books for preschoolers about friendship.

BOOKS ABOUT FRIENDSHIP FOR PRESCHOOLERS

Pajama Walking, **Vicki Kimmel Artis & Emily Arnold McCully**

Do You Want to Be My Friend? **Eric Carle**

Loudmouth George and the New Neighbors, **Nancy Carlson**

Jim Meets the Thing, **Miriam Cohen**

New Girl at School, **Lillian Hoban & Judy Delton**

Play with Me, **Marie Hall Ets**

Me and Neesie, **Eloise Greenfield & Jan Spivey Gilchrist**

Best Friends for Frances, **Russell Hoban**

Frog and Toad Are Friends, **Arnold Lobel**

Where Is My Friend? **Betsy Maestro**

George and Martha, **James Marshall**

Ernest and Celestine's Picnic, **Gabrielle Vincent**

Rosie and Michael, **Judith Viorst & Lorna Tomei**

Timothy Goes to School, **Rosemary Wells & Michael Koesch**

Hold My Hand; My Friend John, **Charlotte Zolotow**

JOURNAL REFLECTION

Your First Friendships

What do you remember about your first friendships? Who were your close childhood friends? What did you do together? Can you remember squabbles with them, times you were concerned because they said you couldn't play with them or they weren't your friend? How can remembering these experiences help you support the friendships of young children?

 Visit the premium Web site to complete this journal activity online and email it to your professor.

• explore ideas of friendship and social skills with children. Teachers may read books, talk about pictures, or use puppets to demonstrate skills.

A list of good books for preschoolers on friendship appears in Figure 11-15.

Teaching Prosocial Behavior

Beyond the social skills that encourage preschoolers to develop friendships, teachers recognize that preschoolers are developmentally ready for encouraging prosocial behaviors. These behaviors are the opposite of antisocial, aggressive behaviors, and include helping, giving, cooperating with others, empathizing, comforting, sharing, and displaying friendly and generous behavior in group situations. Most prosocial behaviors are established well into the school years, but the preschool years are the time to be aware of early opportunities for learning and teaching. Teachers can do several things to nurture prosocial behaviors.

Providing Materials. Materials that encourage playing together and cooperation on a task are helpful in giving preschoolers opportunities to share or support one another. Wagons, vehicles with two seats, simple board games, parachute play, and mural art are all examples of things that just don't work without the assistance of other children (see Figure 11-16). Timers can be introduced to help children regulate their own turn taking. Some teachers have found that by not providing an abundance of toys, they create the need and likelihood of sharing.

Providing Activities. When teachers plan activities to be done in pairs, such as creative movements or imitative games, they encourage children to learn to support and enjoy participating with one another. Providing partner activities that elicit teamwork, such as making sandwiches

Figure 11-16
Mural painting elicits cooperation.

with a partner, helping to fill the water table with two children carrying the bucket, and sweeping with one holding the dustpan, build a sense of togetherness and social participation (Jones, 2008). Planning group activities, such as writing group stories or making cards to send to the sick sister of one child, encourages both turn taking and opportunities to experience the positive results of cooperation. Assigning responsibilities in pairs also encourages mutual cooperation.

"Rosario, you and Luther are our table setters for today."

"We're making cards to tell Danielle we hope she's better soon."

Encouraging Assistance. In every group, there will be children who have different abilities or unique talents. Encourage children to ask one another for assistance.

"Thomas can tie shoes very well now. You could ask him to please help you with yours."

"You are being very friendly to the new child in our room who needs some friends."

Considering Prosocial Actions. Teachers actively guide children toward awareness of others' needs and feelings. Such guidance is necessary for the egocentric preschooler, who needs help in recognizing signals from others.

"Darius is looking very unhappy because he has had to wait so long for a turn. What could we do to help him feel better?"

"Anna hurt herself on the slide and she doesn't feel like playing now. What could we do to help her feel like joining us?"

Sometimes role playing, stories, or puppet play can help children take the perspective of other characters and become aware of how they feel in particular circumstances. Showing pictures of children being helpful or kind for the children to make up stories ("What do you think is happening here?") encourages thinking about prosocial thinking and actions.

Help Children Recognize Prosocial Behavior. Sometimes children are so caught up with their own interests that they fail to recognize the positive motivations of others. Teachers can point out when other children are attempting to show concern or helpfulness.

"Rob was worried that you were hurt, Anna. He wanted you not to feel all alone, sitting over here. That was a friendly thing for him to do, to come to stay by you."

"Tony got off the tricycle to give you a turn, Shaunda. That was kind of him, wasn't it?"

Reinforcing Prosocial Behavior. Teachers pay attention to instances when children play together cooperatively, share, and help one another. They make sure these occasions do not go unnoticed. They reward such behaviors nonverbally by smiles, touch, and attention. They also specifically point out the prosocial behavior and its positive results.

> "It's good to see you helping Kayla with her shoes, Thomas. Now she'll be ready to play with you."

> "Thanks for sharing your play dough with Tina, Lila. Now you'll each be able to work together."

Modeling Prosocial Behavior. Once again, teachers' actions speak louder than demands for caring behaviors. When teachers demonstrate and verbally explain helpfulness and cooperation, they show children the importance of behaving in prosocial ways.

> "Tina's mom is coming to help us on our field trip today. I appreciate her taking the time, so we can have a special time."

> "Let me share some of our new books with you," spoken to the teacher in the next room.

Limiting Aggression and Antisocial Behavior. Vivian Paley suggested one cardinal rule in her classroom: "You can't say you can't play" (Paley, 1992). Although she recognizes that rejection is one way children have always dealt with the difficulties of learning to be friends, this new rule protects everyone from being excluded.

> Paley believes that school should be a child's first experience of life in a democratic society. She likens the child's right to play to the adult's right to participate in society. (Heller, 1993, p. 27)

> Is it fair for children in school to keep another child out of play? After all, this classroom belongs to all of us. It is not a private place, like our homes. (Paley, 1992, p. 16)

> In general, the approach has been to help the outsiders develop the characteristics that will make them more acceptable to the insiders. I am suggesting something different: The group must change its attitudes and expectations toward those who, for whatever reason, are not yet part of the system. (Paley, 1992, p. 33)

It is worth considering further this notion of creating an absolute model of prosocial behavior for children. Certainly as teachers limit aggression as a method of social interaction, they direct children to more positive forms of contact.

Help Develop Empathy. When teachers verbalize others' feelings and their concern for them, children are gradually led toward understanding how others feel and what responses are appropriate to those feelings. This ability to "put yourself in another's place" comes more easily with school-age children, but teachers can certainly begin the awareness now.

> "I'll bet Emily is feeling pretty sad today, because her dad has left for a long trip. I think I'll see if she would like to sit with me to read a story."

> "He's feeling upset because the boys said his building wasn't as good as theirs. That hurt his feelings, didn't it?"

Opportunities for Kindness. Teachers help promote prosocial awareness and learning when they deliberately devise opportunities for children to participate in situations that foster kindness. Older children are encouraged to help and protect younger children, and those in the community who are less fortunate could receive assistance in ways children can understand, such as collecting mittens for children who don't have any.

Children's special needs are pointed out, and there is discussion about how to meet those special needs.

"Thank you for watching out for the little ones when you were riding your tricycle fast. We need to keep them safe."

"Sarah, since Hannah can't hear our words, could you show her the pictures carefully, so she'll know what we're talking about and not feel left out?"

Create a Caring Community. One of the dimensions of early childhood professional practice described in the position statement on developmentally appropriate practice is "creating a caring community of learners" (Copple & Bredekamp, 2009, p. 16). Teachers encourage children to consider and contribute to each other's well-being. Children are given opportunities to acknowledge and respect the different talents and abilities that are seen in each individual. One concrete method of building community is holding class meetings to discuss issues and problems that arise in the course of daily life in the classroom. Communicating together in these meetings allows teachers to help guide children in problem solving real situations. A useful resource for preschool teachers, available from NAEYC and written by two classroom teachers, is *Class Meetings: Young Children Solving Problems Together.*

> **PRACTICAL IMPLICATIONS**
>
> **Encouraging Prosocial Behavior**
>
> Adults do not support prosocial behavior when they:
>
> - expect too much in the area of sharing and cooperation.
> - insist on children exhibiting insincere prosocial behavior.
> - force adult solutions for conflict.
> - threaten to withdraw friendship or affection in response to negative behaviors.

GUIDANCE TOWARD SELF-CONTROL

Preschool children are developmentally ready to begin learning to control their impulses and behavior to conform to the demands of adult teaching and limits. They have the language to understand basic explanations and to express their needs and wants to others. They have the interest in interacting with others and in being socially accepted in their world. However, their judgment about what is right or wrong is still limited by preoperational thought processes, which center on just one aspect of a situation rather than the whole situation. They perceive behavior as "good" or "bad," based arbitrarily on rewards and punishments. Preoperational thought also limits preschoolers' abilities to take another's perspective and to accurately reason out cause and effect. Preoperational thought is concrete, based on understanding real experiences. Abstractions such as requests for "nice" behavior are too far from their reality. Adults who guide preschool children must take these developmental characteristics into account as they choose techniques to teach appropriate behavior.

In general, developmentally appropriate guidance is

- positive, focusing on helping children learn what they should do, rather than emphasizing what they did wrong.

- teaching-oriented, focusing on thoughtful selection of techniques that help children experience the sense of acting in more appropriate ways. As Katz said, "A trained teacher would ask: 'What can I be teaching the children in this situation?'" (Katz, 1984, p. 5). Copple and Bredekamp (2009) put it another way: "Guidance is effective when teachers help children learn how to make better decisions the next time" (p. 35). (See Figure 11-17.)

- collaborative, with adults and children working together to correct situations.

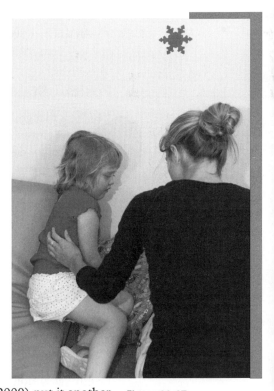

Figure 11-17

Effective guidance helps children learn to make better decisions the next time.

Practices that do not support guidance

- emphasize **coercion** and adult power to enforce rules or resolve disputes.
- rely on punishing unacceptable behavior.
- focus on **retaliation**.
- stop behavior without teaching alternatives.
- involve displaying adult anger with children's limitations in self-control.

Ten positive guidance techniques that are developmentally appropriate include modeling; positive statements; reinforcement, noticing, and strokes; redirection; setting limits; choices for control; natural and logical consequences; discussion for problem solving; "I"-messages; and renewal time.

Modeling

Adults teach very important lessons by living the behaviors they want children to adopt. Through the process of identification, children want to be like their beloved adults and to do things that will please them. Actions truly do speak louder than any number of words. The children's book *Miss Tizzy,* by Libba Moore Gray, is perhaps one of the best illustrations of how children learn helpful and appropriate behavior when the adults around them demonstrate such behaviors.

"I'm very sorry your feelings got hurt," says the teacher to an upset child.

"I can see that bothered you a lot. What could I do to help you feel better?" Her face echoes her compassion. None of this is lost on the children watching nearby.

"Hmm, let's see, we both want to take our classes to the gym. What can we do about that? How would it be if we went after snack time for a half hour, and let you know when we get back? Would that give you time to go after your story time?"

As teachers work out problems aloud, children get a chance to see the process of negotiation and problem solving that demonstrates respect for others' needs.

Positive Statements

Teachers recognize that preschoolers have much to learn about how to behave in the world, so they don't clutter the learning process by telling them what not to do. Instead, they focus on letting children know clearly, specifically, and briefly what is acceptable behavior. Some of the positive statements are mostly informational, and some are brief reminders. Cherry (2002) suggests using action verbs formed as gerunds (sitting, whispering, remembering) as respectful, quick, positive reminders. With such brief and positive statements, adults convey confidence that children will control their behavior in the light of the information, instead of having to be harangued. When adults imply that children will want to do right, children rise to the expectation.

"Puzzles stay on the table."

"Keep hands away from other people's work, please."

"Walking!"

Reinforcement, Noticing, Strokes

Positive attention is a powerful reinforcer; these terms—reinforcement, noticing, and strokes—are used by Reynolds (2006) to suggest the ways of letting children know their positive actions are noted. Teachers discover that time is well spent when children are "caught being good" and given appropriate and authentic notice for that desirable behavior. When adults give specific positive feedback, children will come to understand exactly what behavior earns them positive recognition. As adults dwell minimally on mistaken behaviors, ignoring them when possible, and focus instead on the behaviors they would like to see, both self-esteem and self-control in children are enhanced. When teachers pay attention to desirable behaviors, children quickly learn they don't have to misbehave to get the teacher's attention.

> "I liked hearing you tell Mario he could have a turn on the swing, DeJuan. Those are friendly words."

> "I like those walking feet, Ethan. Thanks for remembering."

Redirection

When teachers step in with suggestions of more acceptable activities, children are able to change direction before their behavior gets out of bounds. Suggestions related to children's interest and/ or activity level are most likely to be effective. Redirection helps avoid negative situations, and hence, negative feedback, which damages self-esteem.

Redirection requires that teachers be alert to situations that could deteriorate into conflict or rule breaking. It is much less effective to wait until a problem has occurred and then move in, because then time and attention have to go toward restoring order and discussing the problem, before redirection is used to change the mood. Effective teacher interaction when redirecting behavior is to escort children to the area of redirection and then sit down and play a little, in order to help children establish the momentum and an interest in the new activity.

> "Let's see how deep a hole you can dig with that shovel," to a child who looked dangerously as if he were about to throw the sand.

> "Blocks are for building with, Abigail. How about using the Nerf ball for throwing? See if you can get it in the box."

Setting Limits

When children understand that certain behaviors are not permitted, they are relieved of much of the need to test the parameters of behavior. Effective adults stop behaviors that are unsafe for the child or others, that are destructive, or that infringe on others' rights. They know that for limits to be incorporated into children's systems of self-control, those limits must be understood and make sense to children. This means that reasons are part of every limit. Reasons must be stated in words that children can understand from their personal experiences and in ways that suggest large principles of behavior that children may apply themselves in subsequent situations. In addition to reasons, children are reminded of more desirable behavior.

> "When you talk at story time, your friends who want to hear the story get interrupted. Please wait until later."

> "Hitting hurts, and people are sad when they get hurt. Please talk to him instead."

Choices for Control

Authoritative adults help children follow through on expected behavior, but in doing so they want children to retain as much control of their behavior as they can, as well as preserve their self-esteem. By letting children choose how (not whether) they will respond to a limit, adults share power with children. The adult has the power of deciding and defining the limit; the child has the power of controlling individual participation within the limit.

> "It's cleanup time now. You may pick up the blocks by yourself or ask a friend to help you."

> "It's cleanup time now. You may pick up the small blocks or the large ones—which would you prefer?"

> "It's cleanup time now. You can work when we do or you can work when we're starting our music."

In any case, the child is expected to do his share of picking up blocks, but a "face-saving" choice is his to make.

A contrasting and confusing situation occurs when adults make it sound as if children have choices when in fact they do not.

"Would you like to help pick up blocks now?" sounds as if the child has the option of refusing. This is not likely the adult's true intention.

Natural and Logical Consequences

Recognizing that preschoolers learn best from concrete experience and not so well from abstract words, teachers use consequences to help young children experience the reality of their behavior. With **natural consequences**, teachers have to do little more than help children see the connection between their actions and the results. With **logical consequences**, teachers have to select an obvious follow-up action to help children experience the effect of their behavior. Consequences help children understand and accept responsibility for their actions.

"When you forgot to put the paint smock on, you got paint on your shirt."—Natural

"Running in the hall made you slip."—Natural

"Tavarius wanted to play with you because you gave him a turn on the swing."—Natural

"Please get the mop to dry the floor where you splashed the water. Someone could fall."—Logical

"Look at Keisha's face. She is very sad because you took her truck. What can you do to make her feel better?"—Logical

"Please go back and walk down the hall, to remember our rule about keeping ourselves safe."—Logical

Discussion for Problem Solving

Children need a lot of help learning to resolve conflicts with one another. Teachers want to encourage the development of negotiation skills, so that children become increasingly able to work out interpersonal differences themselves and less likely to involve adults in solving their problems with peers. In encouraging negotiation, adults function best as facilitators and coaches, drawing children into direct discussion with one another while keeping themselves from taking over active solution of the problem or refereeing (see Figure 11-18).

Adults help children define the problem: "Hey, what's going on here? What seems to be the difficulty?" "Looks to me like two people both want to use the doll buggy."

They encourage children to talk directly with one another, and to listen to what others have to say: "This is something for you and Danny to work out. Please talk with him." "Danny, Sophia's saying something important you need to hear."

They make sure that children have opportunities to suggest their own solutions, knowing that their decisions will be respected. They check with children, to be sure they have understood and agreed to a solution: "I think we should park the buggy until you two have a chance to talk about how you can agree to use it. When you've decided, let me know."

"You've decided Danny can have a turn first for six minutes. Is that okay with you, Sophia?"

Moving beyond one's own egocentric perspective to take someone else's needs and wants into account is a slow and difficult process. Efforts at discussing differences rather than

Figure 11-18
Teachers facilitate discussion among children to solve conflicts in play.

fighting about them need to be supported and applauded: "I thought you two could come up with a good idea. Shall I tell you when six minutes is up, Danny?"

Although it is much quicker for adults to solve the problem themselves ("You'll each have to take a turn; who had it first? I'll just put it away if there is going to be fighting about it"), children need adults who can help mediate or encourage problem solving on their own. This is the only way to build skills and confidence in a child's ability to communicate with others. There is a helpful resource for teachers on helping children with conflict resolution, by Evans (2001); it can be found in the references at the end of the chapter.

Supporting children to solve problems for themselves sometimes means outlining a script for them to give them specific ideas on how they may assert their ideas positively with peers.

To Jamie, who has complained to the teacher that a playmate pushed him, "It doesn't sound as if you liked it when Sabrina pushed you. You could go and tell her 'I don't want to be pushed.'" Or, to a child more experienced in communicating assertion, "How could you tell her you don't like that?"

"I"-Messages. Adults give children powerful motivation to change undesirable behaviors when they express their personal emotional response to children's actions. An "I"-message is basically an expression of the adult's feeling and the behavior that caused this feeling, along with the reason for the reaction. Because of the affectionate relationship and the desire to please the adult, a child pays attention and responds when an adult lets him or her know the effects of behavior on the adult. The expression is straightforward and honest, not manipulative, and does not directly attack the child with judgment or shame. Instead, the child is helped to understand the reason for the adult's feeling. The burden is on the child to modify behaviors in response to the adult's message.

"When you hit your brother, I get angry, because I know hitting hurts him."

"I'm disappointed that we had to stop our music time because some children were too noisy to hear the record."

Renewal Time. As Cherry (2002) points out, there are times in every child's life when the demands of group life and the need to keep social rules become overwhelming. Whatever the reason—perhaps stress from changes at home, fatigue, personality conflict, frustration with developmental abilities—a child needs a chance to withdraw from the situation, calm down, and prepare to reenter the usual routine. It may mean leaving the area or the room where an upset has occurred; it may also mean participating in a solitary, quiet activity that allows time and opportunity to recover equilibrium. It may mean the presence of an adult to comfort or quiet. When considered this way, **renewal time** is a positive technique to help children control their feelings and behavior, not the negative, punishing "time-out" that is so frequently used. Helping children learn that withdrawing from a situation allows them to come back with a different frame of mind or renewed energies is teaching them self-control for the future.

"I think you need to do something quiet over there for a while. When you're feeling better, you can go back to your playing."

"It seems like things are bothering you a lot today. I'd like you to play by yourself until you feel more relaxed."

Developmentally appropriate practice recognizes children's limitations on impulse control and the need for firm, positive guidance that protects their self-esteem while moving them gradually toward self-control.

SUMMARY

The complexity of learning patterns of social behavior and rules and of achieving control over emotional expression and behaviors necessitates much positive adult guidance. Adults recognize that the learning begun during the preschool years will continue into later periods of development, so they maintain realistic developmental expectations. They recognize that positive issues of identity formation and positive relationships with adults help children learn acceptable behavior. Strong social-emotional development relates to later social and academic success (Bowman & Moore, 2006).

THINK ABOUT IT ACTIVITIES

1. Bring a selection of picture books for preschoolers. In small groups, students should analyze the books for positive or negative messages about acceptance of diversity in gender behavior, racial/cultural identity, family structures, and so on. Are there messages about friendship, prosocial behavior, and emotions?

2. Share examples of guidance techniques students have observed, used, or experienced in adult-child relations. How do they compare with the examples of positive guidance techniques discussed in this chapter?

3. Visit a preschool classroom that you have not visited before. After observing for an hour, write a report that includes specifics you noticed about

   • provisions to encourage a personal sense of identity.

   • overt acceptance of diversity.

   • active adult guidance for self-control, for developing friendship skills and prosocial awareness, and for emotional control and constructive expression of feelings.

   • the overall social/emotional climate, and your sense of how it was created.

4. For the following situations, role-play the responses of a teacher who is trying to guide children in developmentally appropriate ways to positive emotional and social behavior.

   • A child comes to you crying to complain that another child has taken her tricycle.

   • A child hits another child who called him a name.

   • A child tells another he can't play in the block area.

- A child cries quietly in the corner after her mother leaves.
- A child won't play in the block area, saying that's for boys.
- For additional suggestions, brainstorm other social/emotional situations you've encountered with preschool children.

QUESTIONS TO ASSESS LEARNING OF CHAPTER OBJECTIVES

1. Describe some of the important social/emotional developmental tasks of the preschool years.
2. Identify several of the ten positive components of an emotionally appropriate environment for preschoolers.
3. Discuss ways that adults can nurture positive feelings about identity.
4. Identify classroom practices that nurture positive gender identity.
5. Identify classroom practices that nurture positive racial/cultural identity.
6. Describe ways teachers can help children develop social skills for friendship.
7. Discuss methods of nurturing prosocial development in the classroom.
8. Identify several of the ten positive guidance techniques discussed in this chapter.

APPLY YOUR KNOWLEDGE QUESTIONS

1. Describe the components that you would add to a preschool classroom to support formation of positive gender, racial, and individual identity. Be detailed and specific.
2. Explain to parents your ideas about supporting young children who are just developing friendships.
3. Create a role play that illustrates some of your ideas about healthy emotional development for preschool children.

HELPFUL WEB SITES

http://www.tolerance.org	The Web site for Teaching Tolerance has much information and resources for teachers who want to implement antibias practices in their classrooms.
http://www.csefel.uiuc.edu	The Web site of the Center on the Social and Emotional Foundations for Early Learning has ideas for classroom practices to support children's emotional development. Under Resources, click on Practical Strategies.
http://www.nncc.org	The Web site for the National Network for Child Care has many articles, which can be accessed by clicking on Articles & Resources and then on Guidance and Discipline.
http://www.rootsforchange.net	The Web site for the Early Childhood Equity Alliance has information on racial and social justice education for young children and their families.

http://childrensbooks.about.com

This Web site has much information about children's books. Search under Tolerance/Racism/Prejudice for the article by the Council for Interracial Children's Books about evaluating children's books for racism.

http://www.ala.org

The Web site for the American Library Association has book reviews and multiple links to information on award-winning books by and about people of color.

 Please visit the premium Web site for Developmentally Appropriate Practice, *4th edition, to access more chapter web links, additional book chapters, suggestions for further reading and study, interactive quizzes, video exercises, online journal activities, flashcards, and much more! Go to www.cengage.com/login to register your access code.*

Developmentally Appropriate Social/Emotional Environments: For Primary-Age Children

Leah is spending the night with her best friend Joanna, who is also six.

Jabari plays on a team that practices twice a week and plays games on Saturday mornings.

Eddie and his friend will have recently begun a collection of rocks. They spend hours every week talking about it.

Danny and Hannah spend time each day playing video games.

Marty had a bad dream after he watched a scary television program last week, but he didn't call out for his parents, because he didn't want them to know he was scared.

Jamar watches the children on the playground, but doesn't join in the chase game.

Michelle draws a picture with a face covered with tears, and tells her mother, "This is how I feel when Daddy brings me home after the weekend."

A sign on the backyard gate proclaims "Secret Club—No girls get in—this means you, Rosa."

The expanding world of the primary-aged child includes increasing skill in interpersonal relationships, as evidenced by the preceding list. Peers become a major force in shaping children's behavior and adding new information to their self-concepts. Increasing control and communication abilities allow six- through eight-year-olds to deal with their emotions in more mature ways. Moving slowly to less egocentric perspectives, they become increasingly able to take another's viewpoint.

Yet they have much to learn. Learning group skills, developing a sense of moral judgment, discovering how to resolve conflicts without adult intervention, and maintaining friendships are important tasks for this age group. This chapter will examine the social/emotional issues for primary-aged children and consider the most helpful social/emotional environments for them.

LEARNING OBJECTIVES

After completing this chapter, students should be able to

- identify social/emotional issues of the primary years.
- discuss the implications of teacher responses for developing peer group participation skills.
- discuss the implications of teacher responses for self-esteem and a sense of industry.
- describe considerations about cooperation versus competition.
- describe the benefits of mixed-age groupings.
- identify strategies to nurture moral development.
- discuss teacher behaviors for optimum emotional development.

SOCIAL/EMOTIONAL ISSUES FOR THE PRIMARY YEARS

The development of self-esteem in the primary years is closely bound to the development of a sense of industry, defined by Erikson as the **core conflict** of the school years. This sense is influenced by both cognitive and social accomplishments. As children learn the cognitive skills expected in their early schooling, they either see themselves as capable learners or not. Socially, as children spend more time away from family members, the sense of self they acquired in their families is challenged; they add new information to their self-concepts, based on their perceptions of peer response to them. Moving outside the protection of home and family, primary-age children get new opportunities to see how they measure up to the standards of others. The school has its standards of accomplishment, as do other adults: Cub Scout leaders, religious school teachers, neighbors, coaches, dance teachers. The process of social comparison gives children new information to incorporate into their developing self-concepts: Am I as fast a runner? Do I learn as quickly? Do I have as many friends? Success is defined in relation to the child's social group.

Relationships with other adults and within the peer group are not the only influences on self-esteem during this period. Self-esteem has also been linked with patterns of child rearing and interaction with parents. Parental responses that convey acceptance of their children, respect for their individuality, and clearly defined limits are linked with high self-esteem in school-age children. Appropriate guidance for the primary years is crucial for the continuing development of self-control as well as positive self-esteem.

Peer Relationships and Group Skills

Increasingly, the lives of primary-age children become bound with spending time with friends at school and at home. It is estimated that from the age of six, most American children spend more than 40 percent of their waking hours in the company of peers. They play together, they talk together, and they do "nothing" together. Much of the time they spend with peers is unstructured, although the increasing numbers of organized recreational or alternate childcare arrangements affect the amount of adult supervision over peer activities.

> The increased time that children spend among their peers is both a cause and an effect of their development during middle childhood. Adults begin to allow their children to spend extensive time with friends because they recognize the children's greater ability to think and act for themselves. At the same time, the new experiences with peers challenge children to master new cognitive and social skills. (Cole, Cole, & Lightfoot, 2008, p. 593)

There are several basic developmental functions of friendships.

- Friendships are the source of learning basic social skills such as communication, cooperation, and the ability to enter an existing group.
- Friendships help children learn about themselves, others, and the larger world.
- Friendships offer fun, emotional support, and relief from stress.
- Friendships help children begin to learn about intimate relationships.
- Friendships seem to help children feel good about themselves.

Learning the skills to fit into a peer group is an important task for the primary years (see Figure 12-1).

Teachers who have narrowly constrained views of both curriculum and teaching strategies appropriate for five- through eight-year-olds often overlook their crucial roles in helping these children develop the social skills necessary for group membership. But recent research indicates that children who do not develop the skills to maintain friendships in childhood are at risk for poor achievement in school, a greater likelihood of dropping out of school, higher incidences of juvenile delinquency, and poor mental health as adults (Schickedanz, Schickedanz,

Figure 12-1
Friendships help children learn about themselves.

Forsyth, & Forsyth, 2000). Research also indicates that adult intervention and coaching can help children develop better peer relationships This underlines the importance of teachers in developmentally appropriate primary classrooms recognizing their function to support development in the social/emotional domain.

In many communities today, children no longer attend neighborhood schools, but instead are transported to other parts of town. What this means is that children no longer have easy access to school friends outside of school hours. This seems to heighten the need for teachers to recognize the importance of finding ways to support friendships during the school day.

As children learn more about social interaction through friendship during the school years, aggression generally declines. However, some children do not learn to control aggression. Bullying is increasingly discussed as an issue in primary school environments. Bullying is deliberate aggression, persistently directed against a particular target. Bullies generally get satisfaction from using physical or psychological intimidation over weaker peers, often timid, anxious children with low self-esteem. Patterns of bullying and victimization may become established as early as kindergarten. Aggressors quickly recognize those children who become the easiest victims (Papalia, Olds, & Feldman, 2005). Research indicates that bullying decreases when adults provide appropriate supervision and intervention, not tolerating the behaviors. When schools create a climate where all are protected as valuable members of the community, they help children not to become either victims or oppressors (Davis, 2004; Olweus, 1993). Many schools have adopted antibullying statements. Search the Web sites at the end of the chapter for more information on stopping bullying.

Moral Development

Primary-age children are becoming increasingly able to judge the rightness or wrongness of actions, based on what they understand about the intentions. Younger primary-age children, according to Piaget, are in the stage of **moral realism** in which rules are regarded as unchangeable, absolute, and imposed by an external authority (Piaget, 1965). Kohlberg refers to this same moral period as the **preconventional level** of morality in which moral reasoning is influenced by a concern for obedience and punishment and for satisfying personal needs (Kohlberg, 1976). Slowly, school-age children shift into the **conventional level** of moral reasoning, where they become more concerned with appearing "good" and "fair" and look to others to approve their moral acts. Primary-age children need opportunities to consider the basis for socially responsible actions and guidance from adults as they move toward regulating their moral behavior.

Emotional Development and Stress

The image of carefree children at play may be true of some school-age children, at least some of the time. But for many children, the early school years and the recognition of some of the realities of their lives bring stress. Creating less stressful situations for primary-age children is important, as is helping them learn to deal with their own stress. Learning how to cope with feelings continues to be a developmental task of primary-age children to be considered when planning social/ emotional environments.

Having considered the major social/emotional issues of the early school years, it is time to think about appropriate implications and responses.

IMPLICATIONS FOR TEACHERS PLANNING SOCIAL/EMOTIONAL ENVIRONMENTS

Teachers can arrange their classrooms and activities to have a profound influence on the social and emotional development of primary-age children. The attitudes of the teacher are extremely important in creating a learning community for the whole child, as are the plans for participating in the group.

Skills for Group Participation

Teachers trying to help children develop peer group skills will

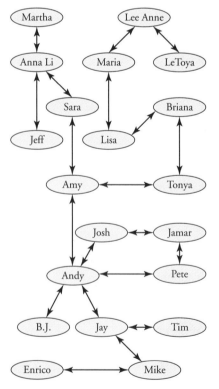

Figure 12-2

A sociogram shows teachers patterns of social interaction and isolation in a classroom.

- become aware, through careful, ongoing observation and note taking, of children's style of interaction, preferences in companions, and ease or difficulty in communicating with others. Understanding children's individual styles helps teachers plan appropriate groupings or pairings that may facilitate successful social experiences. Many teachers use their observations to create sociograms, which help them identify socially isolated children or others whose abundant social skills make them popular. See Figure 12-2 for an example of a sociogram, diagramming children's initiations of efforts to work with or sit near particular children in their primary classroom.

- create informal physical arrangements that allow children to work with particular people and allow for small-group interaction and conversation. Timid children tend to get lost in larger groups, but may be able to find their own place of comfort in smaller groupings. When the physical environment supports children's working and talking together, they gain opportunities for firsthand social experience, rather than simply having adults tell them what they "should" do or say in theoretical situations. As discussed in Chapter 8, the physical arrangements that allow for group interaction include work tables and other small, informal areas rather than traditional rows of desks; blocks of time in which children plan and carry out joint projects; and interest centers and group projects for common activity.

    Miss Hoban has a variety of work areas in her first-grade classroom; one area is big enough for five children, one for four, four areas for three children, three areas for two, and five areas for individual work.

- create specific pairings to work on particular projects, using what teachers know of children's interests and communication styles. Children become friends when they can do things together. As teachers design common activities, they help children experience a sense of cooperation for mutual benefit. Such plans "connect learning for real purposes with the social nature of the learning process" (Mecca, 1995/1996, p. 73) (see Figure 12-3).

Figure 12-3
Teachers may create work groups based on knowledge of children's interests and communication styles.

Miss Hoban arranged for the children to work in pairs as they planned their project on "Houses Around the World." She paired Stephen and Antonio, counting on Stephen's communication and social skills to help him respond to Antonio's quieter style.

- teach social skills directly. Less popular children tend to be unable to initiate contact successfully with other children and, in fact, alienate others with unprovoked hostility, whining, silliness, and other unattractive or disruptive behaviors. Such patterns of social style tend to become stable in the early primary years, so direct and early adult intervention is necessary to prevent lack of skills from becoming a permanent handicap (Plummer, Wright, & Serrurier, 2008). Teachers can help by calling attention to behaviors that work and those that don't, and by encouraging children to recognize and identify their own behaviors.

The following social skills can be taught directly.

1. Giving attention to others
2. Becoming aware of others' perspectives and wishes
3. Learning to take turns
4. Initiating conversation
5. Listening and talking appropriately
6. Being assertive rather than aggressive
7. Looking at and being supportive of other children
8. Learning to enjoy being with others

Miss Hoban said to Antonio: "You could ask Stephen what his ideas for the project would be. Be sure you look at him as he tells you."

Later she said, "Did you tell Stephen what you would like to build for your house? He needs to hear your good ideas too."

- coach children by encouraging them to consider the most appropriate behaviors with peers and provide feedback on their attempts at socialization and group work.

Miss Hoban asked Antonio, "What do you think would be the best way to let Stephen know you want to try your idea for building the house with wood? If you just say 'No, my idea,' it will likely make him mad."

JOURNAL REFLECTION

Remembering Less Popular Children

Do you remember less popular children from your elementary school days? What were their characteristics and behavior? Did adults try to intervene to help those children become more acceptable? What are your feelings about those situations now?

 Visit the premium Web site to complete this journal activity online and email it to your professor.

Later she said, "You know, Stephen really listened to you when you explained your idea clearly to him. Nobody can know what is in your mind until you tell them."

- mediate and teach children negotiation skills. Skills of conflict resolution are vital learning for primary-age children, who spend so much more time without adults available to them. Teachers help children learn to express their views and needs with appropriate assertion instead of aggression, and then to keep talking until they come up with a solution all participants can live with. Teachers help children see the importance of keeping calm so they can listen to others and work on generating alternative solutions when there are differences of opinion. "Children begin learning that strong feelings, including anger and frustration, are normal and okay, but acting violently is never okay, no matter how they are feeling" (Slaby, Roedell, Arezzo, & Hendrix, 1995, p. 105). Helping children become aware of their own abilities to solve difficulties without resorting to violence is important for children who have been exposed to so much media and real-life violence (Levine, 1998, 2003).

> There seems to be an impasse. Antonio and Stephen look genuinely disturbed, and angry words are flying. Miss Hoban takes them aside. "I see that you have a problem. Let's talk about it. Stephen, please listen while Antonio tells you what he wants, and then he'll listen to you."

- support children as they learn to take a social perspective. Teachers may plan classroom activities and discussions to help children understand others' feelings and viewpoints. Books that present particular responses and feelings in certain situations may be read and discussed. Skits presented at large-group meeting time may help children see social skills and others' feelings enacted. An experienced teacher introduces the children in her class to "Talking the Problem" (Fisher, 1994). Here, meeting time becomes a time for working through the steps she posts on a chart.

> What is the problem?
>
> What do we want to have happen?
>
> What are some ways to solve it?
>
> What way shall we try?
>
> Try our solution for two days.
>
> Was the solution a good one?
>
> Do we need to talk about the problem some more?

Such meetings teach skills and build a sense of classroom community.

> Miss Hoban noticed that several of the pairings were having difficulty with arguments and disagreements. At the morning group meeting, she asked two children to pretend to be partners disagreeing about how to build their house. Then she asked the whole group to brainstorm what would be better ways to handle the differences so they could handle it better the next time a problem occurred.

- plan group activities, so that curriculum and daily time are designed for cooperative learning experiences (see Figure 12-4). As children discover how much pleasure and benefit can be derived from working with others as a team, they are motivated to develop group participation skills. Children with socialization problems have many more opportunities to practice when classroom plans and structure stimulate interaction than when

Figure 12-4

Cooperative learning experiences help children learn how to work with others.

programs require isolated, seated silence. Teachers encourage children to support one another's efforts and to use one another's strengths. Positive group work experiences do not just happen. Teachers must carefully lay the foundations for positive interdependence. They help children define mutual goals and perceive their responsibility for one another's

Figure 12-5
Teachers help children learn the social skills needed to succeed in group work.

learning and success, while stressing the individual's accountability to the group (Kumar, 2009). Teachers stress a focus on social as well as academic goals for group activities, giving the direct instruction in social skills necessary for performing successfully in groups. Some of these skills include the ability to take turns, to share, to speak effectively and listen carefully, to be polite and respectful, and to assume responsibility for materials and cleanup. In addition, teachers must convey their confidence in children to have productive group experiences and the teachers' own enthusiasm for group process (Wasserman, 2000) (see Figure 12-5).

Miss Hoban plans regular times each day when the teams work together on their theme projects. Now that the teams have completed their brainstorming, they are proceeding to do the background reading for their buildings. Stephen discovers that Antonio is a good reader as Antonio helps Stephen understand some words he couldn't figure out for himself.

• create a classroom atmosphere that will not tolerate exclusion or unkindness to its members. Primary-age children can be cruel to one another, and they need teachers who convey respect for diverse races and cultures, gender-role behaviors, or physical abilities, and who challenge all exclusionary behaviors. Teachers regularly help children see that each member of the classroom community has a different and valuable contribution to make.

Look for daily and weekly opportunities for each individual to contribute appropriately and significantly to the group. Who has super humor—the class comedian? . . . Who has special abilities, such as the ability to get around in a wheelchair, the ability to speak sign language, the ability to dance, the ability to teach others? . . . Who enjoys working cooperatively? . . . Who is musically, aesthetically, artistically, athletically, theatrically, etc. talented? (Greenberg, 1992, p. 11)

Miss Hoban asked Antonio to teach the other children some words in Spanish, because he knew two languages. Now the other children occasionally ask him to tell them what a word is in Spanish.

Teachers should realize, however, that the problem with teaching children to continue to object to teasing or provocative peer behavior is that such responses could escalate into aggressive behavior (Slaby et al., 1995, p. 142). Teachers also empower children when they teach them that refusing to react to provocative behavior—simply walking away without showing signs of intimidation or distress—may be considered an assertive behavior that in fact requires considerable self-control.

Figure 12-6

Children are encouraged to ask their peers and teachers for help.

PRACTICAL IMPLICATIONS

Developing Group Participation Skills

Teaching practices that do not encourage peer group participation skills include:

- maintaining classrooms in which children learn mostly through silent, individual work, or in large, teacher-directed groups.

- avoiding using social issues as direct teaching opportunities by either ignoring problems or intervening to solve disputes directly without using discussion and problem solving.

- allowing unfair practices to occur without challenge and discussion.

- concentrating on narrow definitions of curriculum as cognitive skills and facts, rather than seeing the development of social skills as an ongoing, integrated, and important part of the curriculum.

- functioning as referees when conflict occurs, rather than as coaches who teach new skills and encourage the children to use the skills they learn.

- using competition as a motivation for learning.

- create a sense of a "caring community of learners that supports *all* children to develop and learn" (Copple & Bredekamp, 2009, p. 16). As children are helped to engage in empathetic activities and consider others' perspectives, they develop prosocial skills of consideration, concern, and kindness. They learn to balance their own needs with those of others. They are encouraged to ask others for help and to help others (see Figure 12-6).

Recently, when the teacher heard some boys teasing Antonio about his accent, she called a class meeting to talk about differences and about comments that hurt feelings. She wants the children to feel comfortable enough to defend themselves against unfair comments and treatment, so she encourages assertiveness.

Self-Esteem

Primary-age children continue to grow in self-esteem when teachers create environments in which

- children are able to succeed because the adults have chosen learning tasks and methods appropriate to their developmental level. School-age children are powerfully motivated to become competent at the knowledge and skills recognized by our culture as important. Teachers who individualize plans and materials allow children to learn at their own level without fear of failing or being embarrassed.

Mr. Rodriguez encourages his first-graders to select books that are simple, repetitive, and predictable. He teaches strategies such as reading to get context clues about what happens next and then rereading difficult parts, or substituting one or more words to get the basic idea. He encourages the children to collaborate on their figuring-out techniques (see Figure 12-7). His first-graders love to read.

Figure 12-7
Children collaborate on figuring out solutions in reading and math.

• primary-age children begin to use **social comparison** as a method of defining themselves. Aware of this, teachers attempt to broaden the scope of activities in which children see themselves involved with others, beyond just the acquisition of cognitive skills. They recognize achievement in interpersonal relations and communication, in athletic and artistic abilities, and in mechanical and constructive talents. They make sure every child can recognize his or her own areas of strength, as well as areas to work on.

Mr. Rodriguez keeps charts in the classroom that recognize many fields of accomplishment, including Jamar as the big-fish catcher—Jamar wears a leg brace and knows he cannot keep up with other boys in running games at recess.

WHAT would you DO when...

"What about a child who prefers to play alone? A boy in my after-school program never wants to join in games or play with other children. Should I be doing something about this?" What do you think your reaction would be?

As with so many situations, it is impossible to give a definitive answer to this. The answer begins with, "It depends." You will need to observe this child carefully and to find out other information from parents and teachers at school. For example, does this child seem contented playing by himself or frustrated and unhappy at being left out? Does the child make overtures to other children that are rejected, reject the overtures of others, or simply find his own independent entertainments? How does he spend his playtime? Is he deeply engrossed in his own activity or simply watching the other children? What does the child like to do, and are these interests different from others? Has the child had the opportunity to develop the skills used by the other children in their play? Are his language skills comparable to those of the other children? Is any physical impairment interfering with his ability to relate to other children? Most importantly, have adults given the child the opportunity to talk about his reasons for playing alone and his feelings about doing so?

Family information that might be helpful includes the family's cultural and ethnic background, living conditions and neighborhood experiences, factors in the family that might cause the child to prefer solitary play, typical past responses in group situations, and the child's temperament and patterns in relationships.

Putting together this kind of information should help you decide whether this situation would benefit by intervention or whether this child's temperament and interests make him contented in solitary play. Individual temperament must be respected; every child does not need to be the popular center of a group of friends. But every child does deserve the opportunity to develop the social skills that will help him or her ease into group situations. Teachers can ensure that children are not totally isolated from group situations by providing activities to do in pairs and some fun group activities to encourage everyone to join in for short periods. One goal is to ensure that everyone has the opportunity to benefit from social interaction, without forcing children to change their temperamental style.

VIDEO ACTIVITY

Go to the premium Web site and watch the video clip for Chapter 12 titled "Social Relationships in the Primary Years." Then consider the following questions:

REFLECTIVE QUESTIONS

1. Considering what these children are saying about popular children, what are some strategies, as discussed in this chapter that teachers can use in their classrooms to help all children be accepted?

2. What physical arrangements and activities can support peer acceptance?

3. What are helpful teacher behaviors when children are being excluded?

Visit the premium Web site to complete these questions online and email them to your professor.

PRACTICAL IMPLICATIONS

Growing Positive Self-Esteem

Teachers who want students to develop positive self esteem should not:

- select learning tasks that are too difficult for children and teaching methods that ignore their natural learning style.

- consistently hold up talented and gifted students as the exemplars for all—using comparison and competition as motivators.

- expect too much or too little of children and convey an attitude of differential responsiveness—for example, by having reading groups for the poorest readers, which imply that these children are less capable and which children clearly identify as the "smart group" and the "dumb group."

- ignore cultural and other differences or treat some children, such as English-language learners, as if they are expected to learn less.

- rely heavily on reward and punishment systems of discipline in the classroom, assuming a position of powerful judge and rule enforcer.

- children perceive that teachers expect and believe they are capable of learning, no matter what their social class, ethnic background, or gender. Children are treated with equal and positive respect and responsiveness. The classroom mirrors this concept of respect with multicultural and nonsexist materials carefully chosen to enhance individual self-esteem by conveying acceptance of the diversity represented in the classroom, the community, and the nation. Teachers remember that the way others respond to children helps form their self-concept; children will behave according to the image of themselves they perceive that others hold.

> Mr. Rodriguez's class is working on the theme of "Work." Every parent in the classroom has been asked to come to talk about his or her work. Two parents are disabled and do not work away from home, two parents have been recently laid off from their jobs, and a single mother is taking job-training classes. These parents came to talk about their work at home and school. The children understand that there are all kinds of important work, both inside and outside of the home.

> Miss Hoban recently attended a workshop on increasing awareness of gender-free responses to children, aimed at decreasing teacher differentiation in their responses and expectations of girls and boys.

- children are encouraged to be independent and self-reliant, to rely on their own thinking, answers, choices, and solutions. Teachers intervene, demonstrate, and suggest solutions only enough for children to succeed. Children are given meaningful responsibilities within the classroom community and are recognized for their contributions.

> Mr. Rodriguez frequently says, "You decide!" or "Why not ask a friend what he thinks about that?" or "I'll bet you'll have a good idea about that." The job list has twenty-five tasks on it, one for each child to do; the responsibilities rotate each week. One of the jobs is to remind anyone who has forgotten to do their job!

- teachers plan games and classroom activities designed to enhance self-esteem and self-awareness.

- children participate in **democratic discipline** (Rightmyer, 2003). They are encouraged to take an active role in classroom regulation, including participating with the teacher in developing positive classroom rules and in problem solving. Beginning principles of participation in a democratic society are taught in this way (Greenberg, 1992). Teachers are positive in

Figure 12-8

Teachers encourage primary-aged children to find their own solutions to conflicts.

their expectations and treat children with respect. When self-control slips, they redirect children or take them aside for individual discussion and problem solving (see Figure 12-8).

Mr. Rodriguez has planned a meeting to discuss the rough play on the playground that concerns him. The meeting leader (a designated weekly job) asks for solutions. Mr. Rodriguez makes sure children have opportunities to discuss the situation fully, so they understand the problem and know what is expected. He believes that children who know and understand the limits want to do what's right.

Games with Rules and Competition versus Cooperation in Developmentally Appropriate Classrooms

One of the ways primary-age children attempt to regulate their own social relations is by basing their play in games with explicit rules. Rules determine what roles children play and what they can and cannot do in their play together. Not only is the ability to engage in rule-based games related to cognitive development, but the games themselves are also a vehicle for developing skills of negotiating, settling disagreements, and learning to cooperate. Games with rules offer children standards for conduct that enable them to measure up to the criteria set by others. Rules allow primary-age children to play together for longer periods and in more complex ways. However, for young primary-age children, rules tend to be treated inflexibly; listening to primary-age children at play, one hears many references to "being fair" and "not cheating." Developing skills of communication and conflict resolution are important social tasks of the primary years.

One of the social/emotional issues to be resolved in developmentally appropriate environments for primary-age children is the extent to which competition among children is healthy or stressful and the need for a balance with learning cooperation as a skill of group membership. Critics of organized sports, like Little League, point out that the pressure to win from parents and coaches may put unhealthy stress on children and rob them of opportunities to engage in spontaneous activity with their peers. Classroom practices often pit children against one another ("Let's see who can finish their math problems first!" "Who got the most A's?") rather than encouraging them to support and help one another. An atmosphere of cooperation and support of one another results when curriculum is based around group projects and other modes that emphasize the community of learners. This has the effect of "creating and nurturing a morality of caring" (Mecca, 1995/1996, p. 72). The "relational virtues" nurtured by a cooperative classroom climate and learning activities planned to support connected, not competitive, relationships include sharing, supporting, cooperating, showing concern, and demonstrating empathy (Mecca, 1995/1996). The traditional atmosphere of competition in the classroom environment needs

Figure 12-9

Children should be able to make up their own games, instead of being pushed to compete.

reconsideration. "If competition is a factor at all, it should be at an individual level; adults can encourage children to compete with their own earlier performances or to meet their own goals" (Tomlinson, 2009, p. 263).

Teachers help by supporting children in their games with rules and helping children balance cooperative skills with competitive attitudes. Many early childhood educators feel that organized games are developmentally appropriate only when adults recognize and "positively confront the competitive element" (Isenberg & Jalongo, 2000, p. 236). Some helpful practices include the following:

- Providing materials, games, and time for children to organize their own games. The skills of leadership, communication, problem solving, and cooperation develop through games, so this is time well spent.

- Teaching children skills necessary to succeed at playing games. Children who are neglected or rejected by their peers are often those who cannot properly join in the games. Helping children develop gross motor skills such as throwing, catching, hitting, running, jumping, and so on, as well as giving them practice with the turn taking and reasoning needed for board games, may help them be included in the game playing. Varieties of games and materials are necessary to include all children, no matter what their physical or cognitive limitations.

- Letting children manage their games and rules without adult interference. Valuable learning may be lost when adults intervene too frequently with admonitions about playing properly or advice (or pressure) on how to win. If children choose to modify the rules for their games during play, their creative thinking should be encouraged and allowed. Children's competitive standards will be high enough, without adding adult standards. Children's games should be left to children (see Figure 12-9).

- Planning cooperative games for classroom and after-school programs. These games should emphasize pure enjoyment, rather than being first or winners versus losers. Although the American philosophy emphasizes individual achievement and a competitive spirit, young children probably don't need this overemphasized. For examples of cooperative games that can be used with primary children, see Orlick (2006), Luvmour and Luvmour (2007), LeFevre (2007), and Figure 12-10.

- Taking competition out of the classroom. Children's motivation for learning should come from the intrinsic satisfaction of making sense out of the world and acquiring competence. This kind of motivation is subverted when too much emphasis is placed on success and competition. When children chronically experience failure in competitive learning situations, they lose self-esteem. They also become primarily oriented toward avoiding more failure, thus inhibiting them from attempting tasks on which they will be evaluated competitively.

Figure 12-10

In games that encourage cooperation,—everybody wins!

Feathers Up
The object of this game is to keep the feathers in the air by blowing.

Lips Are Sealed
Children play whatever they like best in silence—no talking. Just watch the other ways they find to communicate.

Pretzels
Give the children directions to get into an odd position, holding it as they try a second move. Like, "Put your finger on someone's back. Now put your elbow on the floor." Keep it up until you run out of ideas—or they fall over.

Bang Bang!
The first player gives a nail a bang into a board with a hammer. Each player hits the nail once until it's all the way into the board. See how many hits it takes, then start over again.

Competitive practices such as acquiring stickers, letter grades, gold stars, candy, or extra privileges, or singling children out for extraordinary praise or humiliation, are not only contrary to the idea of setting personal challenges for achievement, but are also divisive in peer relations and frequently damaging to the self-esteem of children who receive fewer rewards. Research shows that competition and cooperation are partly a factor of the socialization patterns in a culture, but can also be heavily influenced by the social organization of the environment. Teachers need to examine the social/emotional environments of their classrooms with this in mind.

> ## JOURNAL REFLECTION
>
> ### How Do Abilities Influence Choices?
>
> What games did you love in elementary school? What games did you dread? How do you see that your skills and abilities influenced these choices? What about classroom subjects—what did you like and what did you hate? Did these preferences relate to your abilities and strengths? How can these memories influence your approach to competition with primary-age children?
>
> *Visit the premium Web site to complete this journal activity online and email it to your professor.*

Mixed-Age Groupings

One of the ways some schools and programs have dealt with the issues of competition versus co-operation is to create mixed-age groupings in classrooms and care settings. When it is very obvious that real differences exist among children who are grouped together over a two- or three-year span, it is easier to treat children as individuals who cannot benefit from comparison or competition with others. Because there is a wide range of abilities, the multiage class lends itself to a cooperative spirit. Students are more accepting of the uniqueness of themselves and others. Add to this the concept of "looping" when a teacher is promoted with the students to the next grade level and stays with the same group of children for two or three years (Hitz, Somers, & Jenlink, 2007), and there are clear benefits for children, families, and teachers.

In addition to social and emotional benefits, children in mixed-age groupings thrive in the supportive "family" environment that grows through contact with peers and teachers over an extended period of time. Teachers have the opportunity to learn intimately the social style and skills of each child to support individual social progress over a period of time. Although the benefits of mixed-age groupings are being discussed in relation to the social development of primary-age children, these same benefits are seen when preschoolers are similarly grouped. The benefits of mixed-age groupings need to be considered in positive social/emotional environments (see Figure 12-11).

A multiage classroom is multidimensional, legitimizing and extending the wide variations in ability and activity to be found in any classroom. Mixed-age groupings have been used successfully with young children both in the United States and abroad (for example, England, Sweden, and Italy). This is certainly not a new idea in education, but it merits rethinking as developmentally appropriate practice asks teachers to concentrate on individual appropriateness.

Following are the benefits to mixed-age classroom groupings in the preschool and primary years.

- Family and neighborhood settings have always offered mixed-age environments for children's socialization and education. In times when children now spend little time in either family or neighborhood settings, they do not benefit from those kinds of interage contact. It has been said humans are not usually born in litters, but we now educate them in litters, keeping them strictly with age-mates. Thus, younger children lose opportunities to observe and imitate the more mature social and linguistic competence of older children, and older children lose opportunities to provide assistance and leadership to younger children. Creation of mixed-age groupings allows children to experience the natural variations that occur in life.

- In mixed-aged groupings, social development is enhanced as leadership and prosocial behaviors increase. Mixed-age groupings give all children the chance to be the oldest and most mature at some point in their school experiences. Aggression is more likely to occur in same-age groups than in mixed-age groups, perhaps because a natural hierarchy exists in mixed-age groups.

Figure 12-11

Benefits of multi-age grouping.

MULTI-AGE GROUPING

Features	Benefits
Two- or three-year age range of students	Access to wide range of interests, thinking skills, and modeling
Heterogeneous grouping	Positive self-image; natural interactions; receptive to special needs
More than one year with classmates	Supportive "family" environment
Multiple years with same teacher possible	Secure stable child/family/teacher relationship
Two- or three-year skills continuum	Flexibility for children to progress at own rate
Individualized expectations	Develop independent learners; match curriculum with children's needs
Extended time for learning	Teacher-student familiarity allows teaching from first school day

---

• Research on cooperative learning and peer tutoring suggests that interaction between children with greater and lesser abilities benefits all, both academically and socially. When Vygotsky discussed the idea of a zone of proximal development (see more about this in Chapters 14 and 15), he hypothesized that help from those with greater cognitive competence could increase children's understanding, including more mature peers. Children whose knowledge is similar but different stimulate each other's mental growth and thinking.

• Rigid curricula with age-graded expectations must be relaxed in a mixed-age grouping. Children are taught as a class, and regrouped as necessary for different activities based on interests and/or ability levels (Hitz et al., 2007). This benefits all children, shielding them from the dangers of competition and failure and allowing for children's uneven development. Mixed-age groupings also permit children with special needs to be "included socially and intellectually as well as physically" (Copple & Bredekamp, 2009, p. 290). Their different abilities will not be as remarkable when included with children of widely varying abilities.

Teachers who work with mixed-age groupings are enthusiastic, recognizing that deeper relationships among teachers and children can develop when they are together for more than one year. Changing to mixed-age grouping involves work and adjustment for teachers, but the benefits may outweigh the initial disadvantages. Parents are often also concerned about the effects of mixed-age groupings on their children, fearing that older ones will be held back by the presence of the younger ones, or that the younger ones may become the object of bullying. They need help in understanding the positive effects.

The following strategies may deserve special emphasis.

• Suggesting that older children assist younger children and that younger ones request assistance from older ones such as, "I think you could help Sarah and Alondra figure out how to share the trike." Children of all ages can be encouraged to give and accept emotional comfort from one another.

• Encouraging older children to assume responsibility for younger ones such as by helping them feel at home in a new classroom.

• Discouraging stereotyping or setting expectations strictly by age. A statement like "He can't do that, he's not old enough" should be challenged.

BULLYING AS A TOPIC OF SPECIAL CONCERN

In a study for the *Journal of the American Medical Association,* Nansel et al. (2001) point out that both children who bully and their victims perceive themselves as not being fully accepted members of their peer group. Bullying often seems to be about inflicting pain on another in order to establish a perceived place of prestige by lowering the social status of the other (Gartrell, 2008). Bullying by girls usually involves verbal aggression, such as taunting, gossip, and exclusion. Bullying by boys more often degenerates into physical aggression. Children who are bullied experience real suffering that can interfere with their social and emotional development, as well as their school performance. Some victims of bullying have even attempted suicide rather than continue to endure such harassment and punishment.

Children and adolescents who bully thrive on controlling or dominating others. They have often been the victims of physical abuse or bullying themselves. Bullies may also be depressed, angry, or upset about events at school or at home. "Bullies are often disliked and avoided by classmates and adults alike and are often inaccurate in perceiving others' intentions and likely behaviors" (Tomlinson, 2009, p. 266).

Children targeted by bullies also tend to fit a particular profile. Bullies often choose children who are passive, easily intimidated, or have few friends. Victims may also be smaller or younger, and have a harder time defending themselves.

Bullying is one of the most serious problems in schools today, with long-term negative results for bullies themselves as well as their victims. Teachers and other adults have an important role in both prevention and intervention in bullying. Merely comforting victims and punishing bullies only strengthens the bully-victim patterns. Instead, prevention includes a unified, schoolwide approach to bullying, with open communication about explicit behaviors that will not be tolerated, family involvement in the topic, and channels for support. As children become knowledgeable about available help, peers can feel stronger in addressing the issue. Creating a caring environment and emphasizing relationships within the school are both preventive components.

Direct adult intervention focuses on helping the child who is being bullied express feelings about being bullied, and learn strategies of meeting the bullying. It also focuses on helping the bully discover that bullying does not help with finding an identity within a group, and encourages onlookers to understand what is happening to both children, and how they can help.

Numerous resources are available for teachers to consider how to create classrooms where children can feel safe and be without fear. Some are:

Beane, A. (2005). *The Bully Free Classroom: Over 100 tips and strategies for teachers K–8*. Minneapolis, MN: Free Spirit Press.

Jackson, C. (2007). The ABCs of bullying. *Teaching Tolerance, Classroom Activities (January)*. Available at www.tolerance .org/teach/activities/activity.jsp?ar=771

The Web site at http://www.bullyingnoway.com.au has information about creating learning environments that are free from bullying.

Books to read with elementary-age children include:

Bateman, T., The Bully Blockers Club.

Carlson, N., Arnie and the New Kid.

McCain, B., Nobody Knew What to Do

Moss, P., Say Something.

Teachers can, and must, help with bullying and the dynamics that lead to it.

- Helping children understand and accept their current limitations ("I think you'll be able to climb that ladder too when you're a bit bigger") and helping older children appreciate their own progress, as in, "Wow, I can remember when that ladder was hard for you too."

- Helping children focus on their peers' needs, feelings, and interests: "Jamie would like to play with you. What do you think you two could enjoy doing together?"

- Encouraging older children to read to younger ones, and all children to contribute their skills to appropriate projects: "Maybe Jamie could hold the dinosaur steady for you while you outline its head."

Children in mixed-age classrooms are likely to become more dependent on one another and less dependent on the teacher, if such strategies are used.

For more information about implementing mixed-age groupings, see Stone and Miyake (2004).

HELPING PRIMARY-AGED CHILDREN WITH MORAL DEVELOPMENT

During the primary years, children are slowly moving to internalize the social constraints of behavior they have been taught by their parents and teachers—the beginnings of conscience formation. Moral development is a complex process that involves both cognitive and social/emotional development. The ultimate goal of moral development is to supply children with both the information and the controls they will need to take over regulating their own decisions and actions. It is likely that they are not truly yet able to reach the level of moral development that allows them to make their own correct moral judgments, because the ability to reason logically and to take the perspectives of others is not reached until age seven or eight.

Progress toward moral development as the ultimate self-control is helped when teachers

- design activities and use informal experience to help children develop perspective-taking abilities. The ability to understand the different viewpoints of others in any situation can be helped through discussion. Good children's literature can be used to promote discussion about moral issues (Koc & Buzzelli, 2004) (see Figure 12-12).

Ms. An Hoc planned a group time in which she told the children a story about two boys who had a disagreement about who could use a computer in a classroom. Tom had a turn the day before, but had a small part of his project yet to finish; Eric had not had a turn and felt he should have a turn today. As the children discuss who, in their opinion, should get the turn, the teacher helps them clarify issues of fairness and justice.

When an argument erupts in the project area, the teacher discovers that the problem is that Anna Maria had accidentally knocked down the structure built by Dennis and DeJuan, when she joined them to help build. The teacher brings the builders together to discuss intentions of helpfulness versus deliberate destructiveness.

These teachers are helping children become able to make independent decisions about correct actions.

- help children make more logical decisions for actions, which is part of the teacher's role in moral development. Teachers can do this by leading group discussions about the actions

Figure 12-12

Children's literature may be used to promote discussion of moral issues.

children choose, the reasons, and the results. Through guided discussion, children may help one another see alternative actions and better choices. Such discussions will help children in their future actions. Meeting times in the child-centered classrooms become opportunities to discuss issues that teachers believe will help children understand social actions of general importance to everyone. They are not allowed to deteriorate into public humiliation sessions.

> Mr. Hammons asked his first-graders to think with him about what to do about the problem of children being disruptive on the school bus. The children thought through the consequences of the present behaviors and decided on what they believed to be the right actions for teachers and bus drivers to take with the children in question.

• support children to find their own answers and solutions in interpersonal situations. Teachers do not provide solutions or ready-made moralizing, but instead ask serious and pertinent questions to help children arrive at a more autonomous morality, not dependent on the adult's presence or prescriptions.

> As he guides the discussion, Mr. Hammons asks, "What do you think the problem is here? What could happen if people continue to behave in this way? What are the important ideas to consider here? Whose rights should we think about? What do you think is the right way to control this—who should do that? Why?"

• use authoritative guidance systems, rather than **authoritarian** or **permissive** styles in limit setting and discipline. The differences in the three styles create corresponding differences in children's ability to govern their own behaviors. Permissive and authoritarian styles are at opposite ends of a spectrum, in that permissive teachers and parents exert few demands on children's behavior, and authoritarians exert too many arbitrary demands for obedience to behavior standards. Permissive teachers do not "hold children accountable to acceptable standards of behavior and ignore unacceptable behavior. . . . [A] lack of clear limits on unacceptable behavior and . . . disproportionate reliance on children to solve all their own social problems . . . leaves the classroom without order and the teacher without authority" (Copple & Bredekamp, 2009, p. 301). Authoritarian teachers, conversely, "place themselves in an adversarial role, spending considerable time threatening children for lack of impulse control and punishing infractions" (Copple & Bredekamp, 2009, p. 301). As different as these two styles are, their effects are similar, in that children fail to develop the feelings of empathy and mental understandings needed to internalize a code of ethical standards for behavior. Both groups remain dependent on adults to guide their behavior.

PRACTICAL IMPLICATIONS

Supporting Moral Development

Teachers do not support students' moral development when they:

- manage behavior themselves, solving problems and ignoring opportunities to help children understand the moral issues involved in their actions.

- talk about moral practices without demonstrating the principles in their own actions.

- expect more sophisticated moral judgment than the children's cognitive level allows.

- use either permissive or authoritarian styles of guidance, setting either no limits or too many harsh and arbitrary limits.

- maintain a narrowed perspective on cognitive learning that leaves moral issues and character education out of the curriculum.

On the other hand, adults who are authoritative in their guidance, respond to children's needs with warmth while establishing clear behavioral boundaries. They teach children how to behave and help them understand the reasons behind the required actions, using a variety of direct teaching strategies such as suggestions, demonstrations, explanations, and consideration of the impact of their behavior on others. Authoritative styles of guidance have been found most effective in developing internal behavior controls in children. Children know what is expected of them and understand how to make their own decisions fit in with the needs and rights of others. Authoritative teachers offer children reasons for why certain behaviors are appropriate, knowing that personal morality must be built upon cognitive foundations. They frequently remind children of reasonable rules for social living, and help children experience the consequences of their decisions. They understand the gradual process of building moral understanding and control and use every opportunity to help children work on questions of justice and social harmony.

Mr. Hammons draws Luisa aside when he sees her hit a friend. He tells her he will not allow her to hurt others, just as he will protect her right not to be hurt. They discuss the situation and alternatives of action. He supports her in later attempts to consider a friend's point of view and reach a fair solution.

- discuss issues of responsibility and morality that affect the larger community beyond the classroom. Primary-age children are ready to consider a larger perspective.

Mr. Hammons has initiated a classroom recycling project. The children have investigated the town's recycling efforts, talking with an environmental group and working with the collection group in their neighborhoods. At the last class meeting, the children talked of ways their efforts would benefit others.

HELPING PRIMARY-AGED CHILDREN WITH EMOTIONAL GROWTH

During the preschool years, children began to learn skills necessary to control and express their emotions in socially acceptable ways. The primary years bring increasing cognitive ability to identify feelings in oneself and in others, recognizing emotions as factors to be reckoned with in relationships and behavior. New situations, such as school and peer relationships, and increasing awareness of the surrounding world as well as family circumstances, may cause stress and anxieties not found in younger children. Teachers of primary-age children can help children with both of these aspects when they

- provide opportunities for children to identify feelings in themselves and others. Young school-age children begin to understand that people can hold more than one emotion at a time, but still do not recognize that people can hold contrasting emotions about the same event, such as being both excited and frightened at the prospect of a new classroom. One way teachers can help children identify feelings is by talking about emotional responses.

Time for individual conversations is important, especially when children are involved in problem solving. Teachers can help children identify feelings by asking questions.

"How did you feel when he said that to you? Did you feel anything else?"

"What do you think she was feeling when that happened?"

- plan group discussions and activities that help children focus on understanding feelings and their influences on people's actions. Reading stories that portray emotional responses stimulates discussion that can further understanding.

> Miss Alfred read her students *A Chair for My Mother* by Vera Williams, the story of a little girl whose hardworking family loses everything they have in a fire. In the discussion that followed, Roberto said, "They were scared when they came home and saw the fire, and they were scared that something had happened to the grandma. They felt happy when they found her, but they were still upset that they had lost all their stuff. That's why it was so important to save for the new chair."

- provide materials and encouragement for children to express their emotions in positive, constructive ways. Primary-age children can be helped to represent their feelings in creative arts, such as drawing, painting, sculpting, or creative movement, and in writing, such as in a journal or story (see Figure 12-13).

> Teachers may make direct suggestions to stimulate such activity: "I wonder if you would feel better about that if you wrote it all down." "Lots of great artists paint out their feelings like that—what about trying to show how you feel?"

- create a low-stress classroom. In her book *Think of Something Quiet: A Guide for Achieving Serenity in Early Childhood Classrooms,* Cherry (1981) describes fundamentals of a low-stress

CULTURAL CONSIDERATIONS

Children's Emotions

EXPRESSING EMOTIONS: Reactions to emotional expression are a product of a family's cultural values. Some cultural environments do not value open expression of emotions in words or actions, and teach their children to suppress emotional expression. There are also cultural opinions about the differences between how the genders express feelings. It is vital that teachers get to know families and their goals for their children before making assumptions that healthy emotional expression is a positive goal for all families.

BEING SEEN AS "DIFFERENT": For a primary-age child, being perceived as culturally different can be a cause of stress. Consider that when making invitations to families to demonstrate their cultural uniqueness. Because each family is in fact culturally unique, it would be appropriate to invite all families, rather than just those that are obviously different by reason of language or racial background.

Figure 12-13

Primary children can be encouraged to use art materials to express their emotions in constructive ways.

Figure 12-14

All children should feel valued as members of their classroom community.

program. These include relationships among children and teacher-child relationships based on respect, trust, and caring; stressing self-awareness and self-expression; classrooms that permit movement; a predictable schedule; reduced visual and auditory stimulation; a balance of quiet and active experiences and comfortable pacing; developmentally appropriate activities for success; a sense of humor; and fantasy and creative movement incorporated into classroom activities. When children feel physically and emotionally at ease in their classrooms, the stress and anxiety often associated with school are diminished. When teachers actively teach strategies to reduce stress, children learn skills to help in their future emotional health. For more ideas to use with children to help reduce stress, see Thomas (2003) and Oehlberg (1996) listed in the references at the end of the chapter.

- promote children's sense of self-worth. As children feel accepted for themselves in classrooms, stress is lowered. All children should feel valued and included as worthwhile members of their classroom communities (see Figure 12-14). Teachers should take care to ensure that each child has positive experiences each day. Their awareness of diversity helps them monitor classroom materials and allow for various racial and ethnic backgrounds, differences in ability, and the particular interests of individual children. Issues of self-esteem have enormous impact on children's overall emotional health.

Brandon has been quite unhappy lately. His teacher presumes his feelings could be related to the family stress with his father's layoff from his job. One of her strategies to help is to make sure that he has opportunities to help one or two peers with math each day; Brandon has superior skills in math, and this seems to contribute to his positive feelings about himself.

- develop partnerships with parents to facilitate continuous home-school communication. When teachers and parents share information, they can often help with emotional stress children may experience in either setting. Teachers can help parents ease children's transitions to classrooms and more advanced academic work, and understand educational practices so that they are less likely to pressure their children for inappropriate academic achievement. Parents can help teachers understand the particular circumstances of children's home lives that may be emotionally upsetting or need individual attention.

    The teacher talks regularly with Brandon's parents, so she understands the home situation. Thus, the parents are aware of his emotional responses exhibited at school, and the teacher makes herself available as a friendly support during the family's difficult time.

- recognize signs of excessive stress and emotional distress in young children. David Elkind refers to the stresses of hurried children whose lives are complicated by family stress, premature advancement in lessons and accomplishments, and heavy expectations for mature behavior (Elkind, 1981). Teachers are often in a position to identify signs of unhealthy stress and emotional unhealth in the children in their classrooms. Sometimes these stresses can be alleviated by home-school collaboration, and sometimes they need attention by other professionals. In either case, as teachers care for all aspects in children's lives, stress is something they must recognize.

- monitor primary-age children's exposure and reactions to frightening and disturbing real and fantasy events, such as media exposure to real-life disasters, movie and television violence, or violent computer games. Although they are now able to distinguish between reality and fantasy, primary-age children can be disturbed or preoccupied by frightening events. Teachers help children by recognizing signs of overstimulation and helping children deal with and express their feelings. Teachers and parents need to share information, so everyone is sensitive to children's needs for protection from potentially overstimulating situations. For example, a popular movie about dinosaurs was marketed as if it were for young children, but turned out to actually be terrifying to them.

The first-grade teachers at Oakwood School realized that a large downtown fire the week before was preoccupying the attention of many of their children. They planned group discussions to try to help the children understand what had happened, held individual conversations with the children who appeared most frightened, and provided a lot of art materials for expression. Later in the week, they planned a lesson on safety techniques in an emergency, so children could feel more confident of their own knowledge.

PRACTICAL IMPLICATIONS

Nurturing Healthy Emotional Development

Teachers do not support healthy emotional development in primary-age children when they:

- omit discussion of feelings from curriculum or informal conversations.

- provide no materials, opportunities, or encouragement for children to express or identify feelings.

- create a classroom environment that produces stress through its restrictions and expectations, and provides no opportunities to relieve stress or teach children skills to reduce their stress.

- have poor communication with parents, so teachers are often unaware of emotionally upsetting factors in the child's environment.

- fail to monitor children's exposure to potentially frightening situations.

SUMMARY

Primary-age children move on in development when adults plan for social/emotional environments that

- help children develop skills for peer group acceptance.

- nurture positive self-esteem.

- encourage moral development.

- allow for emotional development and decrease stress.

Developmentally appropriate social/emotional environments consider a balance between competition and cooperation and may provide mixed-age groupings.

THINK ABOUT IT ACTIVITIES

1. Find out if there are any mixed-age groupings in your local schools and after-school programs. If possible, visit. What activities do you see younger and older children cooperating on? What do you notice about the social interaction of the younger and older children? Talk to the teachers involved about their perceptions of how the system works.

2. Observe children at play on a school playground or after school. How are the games being organized? What references to rules and fairness of play do you hear?

3. In discussions with your classmates, recall the games of your childhood. What were the games and who were the players, the leaders, and the rejected? How does the issue of competition relate to your memories? What competitive practices initiated by the teacher do you recall from your early classrooms?

4. If you have opportunities to observe or work with primary-age children, draw a sociogram based on your observations of children's preferences in play and work partners. What are the peer group skills displayed by the most popular children? by the least popular? Are there specific skills that you see could be directly taught and coached?

5. Tell Kohlberg's famous story (following this paragraph) for evaluating stages of moral development to several six-and seven-year-olds and then to older primary-age children. Do their responses suggest that the younger children are still tied to arbitrary moral judgments based on egocentric perspectives?

A woman was dying from cancer. Only one drug might have saved her, a form of radium that a druggist in the same town had recently discovered. The druggist was charging $2,000, ten times what the drug cost him to make. The sick woman's husband, Heinz, tried to borrow money from everyone he knew, but could raise only about half the cost. He told the druggist his wife was dying and asked him to sell it cheaper or let him pay later. When the druggist said no, the husband got desperate and broke into the man's store to steal the drug for his wife. Should the husband have done that? Why? (Adapted from Kohlberg & Kramer, 1969)

6. Plan a classroom activity to help children grow in their ability to take the emotional and social perspectives of others. Carry out and discuss the activity with your classmates.

QUESTIONS TO ASSESS LEARNING OF CHAPTER OBJECTIVES

1. Discuss several social/emotional issues of the primary years.
2. Identify ways teachers can help children develop social skills for peer group acceptance.
3. Describe practices for enhancing self-esteem.
4. Discuss considerations of children's games with rules, related to competition versus cooperation.
5. Discuss positive aspects of mixed-age groupings for young children.
6. Identify ways teachers can nurture moral development in primary-age children.
7. Describe teachers' contributions to emotional development and stress reduction in primary-age children.

APPLY YOUR KNOWLEDGE QUESTIONS

1. Plan a parent meeting in which the discussion centers on building classroom communities to prevent bullying. What are some of the main points about the social development of primary-age children that you will emphasize?
2. Plan a teaching unit for primary-age children to help them explore their emotions and those of others, as well as positive ways of expressing emotions.

HELPFUL WEB SITES

http://www.stopbullyingnow.com	This Web site has helpful information about bullying.
http://www.bullying.org	This Web site also has helpful information on bullying, including FAQs.
http://www.nccic.org	The National Child Care Information Center, which is run by the U.S. Department of Health and Human Services Administration for Children and Families, has information and helpful links. To access this information, scroll down on the home page and click on Positive Youth Development.

http://www.casel.org	The Collaborative for Academic, Social, and Emotional Learning promotes coordinated, evidence-based social, emotional, and academic learning as an essential part of education.
http://www.niost.org	The Web site for the National Institute on Out-of-School Time has information on positive practices in after-school programs.
http://www.ericdigests.org	Search for an article by Robert Stack titled "Essential Elements of Cooperative Learning in the Classroom," ERIC Document Reproduction Service No. ED370881.

 Please visit the premium Web site for Developmentally Appropriate Practice, *4th edition, to access more chapter web links, additional book chapters, suggestions for further reading and study, interactive quizzes, video exercises, online journal activities, flashcards, and much more! Go to www.cengage.com/login to register your access code.*

GUEST EDITORIAL

by John Holt

John Holt (1923–1985) was a teacher and writer who was a lifelong supporter of school reform. He is best known for his insights about children's learning and the environments that support their learning, as described in How Children Fail (1964, revised 1982) and How Children Learn (1967, revised 1983), from which this excerpt is taken.

Let me sum up what I have been trying to say about the learning style of young children. He wants to make sense out of things, find out how things work, gain competence and control over himself and his environment, do what he can see other people doing. He is open, receptive, and perceptive. He is experimental. He does not merely observe the world around him, but tastes it, touches it, hefts it, bends it, breaks it. To find out how reality works, he works on it. He is not afraid of making mistakes. He does not have to have instant meaning in any new situation.

Except for those physical skills that can't be learned any other way, children rarely learn on the slow, steady schedules that schools make for them. They are more likely to be curious for a while about some interest, and to read, write, talk, and ask questions about it for hours a day and for days on end. Then they may drop that interest and turn to something different, or even seem to have no interests at all. This usually means that they have all the information on the subjects that they can digest, and need to explore the world in a different way, or perhaps simply get a firmer grip on what they already know. Children's need to make sense of the world is as strong as their need for food or sleep.

Realize that children learn independently, not in bunches; that they learn out of interest and curiosity, not to please the adults in power; and that they ought to be in control, deciding for themselves what they want to learn and how they want to learn it. I can hear the anxious voices of a hundred teachers asking me, "How can you tell, how can you be sure what the children are learning, or even that they are learning anything?" The answer is simple. We can't tell. What I am trying to say about education rests on a belief that, though there is much evidence to support it, I cannot prove. [I believe] that man is a learning animal. Birds fly, fish swim; man thinks and learns. Therefore we do not need to "motivate" children into learning, by bribing or bullying. All we need to do is bring as much of the world as we can into the classroom; give children as much help and guidance as they need and ask for; listen respectfully when they feel like talking; and then get out of the way. We can trust them to do the rest (Holt, 1983, pp. 287–293).

Developmentally Appropriate Cognitive/Language/Literacy Environments

INTRODUCTION

In this section, we will examine the nature of the cognitive and language environments most appropriate for various stages. The discussion of cognitive/language environments will include appropriate materials and curriculum ideas, teaching practices and interaction to facilitate optimum cognitive and literacy/language learning, and special issues in the cognitive/language domain. Some topics that are common throughout the stages, such as components of literacy (Chapter 15) and assessment (Chapter 16), will be dealt with at length in only one chapter.

Developmentally Appropriate Cognitive/ Language/Literacy Environments: For Infants

Newborns are born with the ability to cry. During the year that follows, they move through stages that allow them to make increasing varieties of sounds: cooing, babbling, laughing, advanced babbling—complete with inflections, and finally a real word or two. They also become increasingly able to decipher the meanings of the sounds and language used in their environment, as well as facial expressions and body language of others. At the same time that they are learning to make sense of words, they are learning to figure out how the world around them works and how they can act on the world. The learning and cognitive development in infancy are truly amazing, though often unrecognized. This chapter will focus on understanding how to support language and cognitive development in infancy.

LEARNING OBJECTIVES

Upon completion of this chapter, students should be able to

- understand the nature of brain development and learning in infancy.
- discuss an understanding of the infant substages in sensorimotor learning.
- discuss typical patterns of infant language development.
- identify ten principles to guide adults facilitating sensorimotor learning.
- identify ten appropriate practices for adults nurturing literacy and language development.
- identify inappropriate practices in the cognitive/language environment.

BRAIN DEVELOPMENT AND LEARNING

New brain-imaging technologies have allowed neurobiologists and other scientists to confirm what early childhood educators have known for years: the earliest months and years of a child's life are crucial in providing the stimulating environment and experiences that literally help brains grow and develop (Newberger, 1997; Begley, 1997; Shore, 1997). The combination of nature and nurture together determine the brain structure. Briefly stated, the brain at birth produces billions of neurons that produce trillions more synapses, or connections, than the infant will ever need. Almost all the neurons are present at birth, but most are not connected in networks. The connecting process is rapid during the first year, with the sensorimotor areas most active during the 2- to 3-month period, and the frontal lobe becoming active by six to eight months (Bergen, 2004). Stimulation through interaction with the people and objects in the baby's world strengthens these connections; if they are not used, they will wither away. With fewer connections, potential for cognitive capacity in the future is decisively affected. During the early weeks and months, the brain has the greatest capacity for change; therefore, early stimulation sets the stage for how children will learn throughout their lives. Brain studies have found that there are different times when these synapses are forming in different parts of the brain; the peak period for development of the visual cortex, for example, begins at around two to four months and peaks at eight months (Newberger, 1997). Similarly, the window of opportunity for language learning occurs during the first year: "By 12 months, an infant's auditory map is formed. He will be unable to pick out phonemes he has not heard thousands of times for the simple reason that no cluster of neurons has been assigned the job of responding to that sound" (Begley, 1997, p. 31). National attention is now focused on understanding the implications of this scientific research for early care and education. The importance of the earliest periods in infancy for cognitive and language development is attracting important awareness at this time.

Babies demonstrate more clearly than at later stages the complex intertwining of all aspects of development, for only on paper can we separate learning into distinct and separate domains. "Perhaps the most salient finding of the past decade's infancy research is that loving and learning are intrinsic and intertwined for infant flourishing" (Honig, 1991, p. 39). Emotions play a significant role in learning, with learning occurring when children feel safe and confident. Stress can actually cause chemical changes in the brain that can destroy brain cells and cause problems with learning. The early social and emotional experiences provide the environment to nurture the neurons that will provide the cognitive potential for learning. In reality, it is through the same social relationships that introduce infants to the emotions of love and trust and to the behavior of people in their environment that babies learn language as part of the complex system of communication they will use throughout their lives. Infants explore and discover through their physical abilities to manipulate objects and move through space to come into contact with ever more objects, developing their first very practical understanding of the world around them. Before children acquire language, they have learned something about their world. They have rudimentary concepts, waiting for words to name those concepts. When they learn language, there is possibility for even greater understanding of the world, as they can more directly communicate their need for knowledge and for labels to put on things, people, experiences, and eventually concepts. Without learning, there is no need for language; without language, there is no way to organize learning. With understanding, comes the need to communicate. Cognitive and language learning are inseparable, and also inseparable from the rich mix of relationships with others.

One of the most difficult concepts for adults not trained in child development to grasp is the idea that cognitive development is occurring in infancy, even though traditional school-type learning activities are not seen. In recent decades, entrepreneurs who want to capitalize on parents' desire to give their children the best start in education as soon as possible have promoted the concept of "building better and brighter babies." To counter those forces that proclaim the need for "infant stimulation" programs, complete with videos and flashcards, it is important to become familiar with the concepts and substages of sensorimotor learning. Adults who want to provide the most developmentally appropriate cognitive/language environments for infants begin by recognizing innate abilities and unfolding patterns that need appropriate responses and support from adults. "Time spent flipping flashcards—at the age of 1 or 3—is precious time wasted" (Hancock & Wingert, 1997, p. 36). "In the most extensive study yet of what makes a difference, Craig Ramey of the University of Alabama found that it was blocks, beads, peek-a-boo, and other old-fashioned measures that enhance cognitive, motor, and language development" (Begley, 1997, p. 30).

UNDERSTANDING SENSORIMOTOR INTELLIGENCE

According to Piaget (1952), infants are born with no initial ability to "think," but with a selection of reflexive behaviors that allow them to begin acting physically on objects to gain sensory information (assimilating) and adapting to their environment (accommodating). Thus, they begin to actively construct their own intelligence. The name he gave to this first stage of cognition in infants and toddlers is the **sensorimotor period**, because physical development and intellectual growth are so closely intertwined at the beginning. Babies begin to learn about the world through their senses and muscle movements of their bodies. This information is organized mentally for later use. (Students have probably learned more detail on Piaget's theory in basic child development courses. For a good, brief summary of sensorimotor learning, see White, 1988.) The sensorimotor stage extends from birth to about age two and consists of six substages. The first four substages occur in the first year of life.

THE FIRST FOUR SUBSTAGES OF SENSORIMOTOR LEARNING

Substage 1—Babies begin by using simple **reflexes** to take in information and act on the world right after birth. They suck; they grasp; they cry. Much of what happens at first is accidental, caused by random movements. They use their abilities one at a time; a baby will grasp a rattle placed in his fist, but not look at it.

Substage 2—After about a month of this behavior, infants gain a measure of control over their bodies; thus, they are able to combine their behaviors. With repetition and practice comes increased ability, and ability to act more purposefully. For example, they learn to bring their hands to their mouths to suck on them. Babies' discoveries of being attached to their hands (a wonderful event for observant adults to watch) help move them past purely random behaviors to events and behaviors they can control on their own body.

Substage 3—Sometime after four months, babies take a more active interest in the world around them. With increasing manipulative and maneuvering abilities, they discover they can make rather interesting things happen outside themselves, and they want to make them happen repeatedly. In this shift to making results happen, the first primitive understanding of cause and effect emerges, although at first repeating an event is more an accidental occurrence.

Substage 4—As babies enter the fourth substage at around eight months, a new level of understanding is evident. For the first time, they demonstrate intentional behavior. Experience has helped them develop an understanding of cause and effect; thus, they are able to coordinate actions to solve problems in a more sophisticated way. The baby discovers that he or she can get his or her ball out of the corner where it is stuck by poking it with his or her broom handle, or lifts the blanket to find a toy underneath. This is primitive planning: to look ahead to see "What will happen if I do this?"

Imitation also becomes a factor in learning during this fourth substage. This is about as far as the infant goes in the first four **substages** of sensorimotor development; the last two substages are accomplished during toddlerhood. However, one more momentous cognitive occurrence takes place in later infancy: the development of **object permanence** at around eight to ten months of age.

Object permanence refers to the concept that babies gradually come to realize that objects and indeed people still exist even though they are not physically present. The development of object permanence represents infant ability to mentally call back the object they have experienced. This is the first real evidence of memory, of stored mental concepts.

And brain research indicates that parallel events in brain development make these learnings possible. The formation of **synapses** in the motor cortex begins at about two months; this is when the infant loses the reflexes and begins to master purposeful movements. At around eight or nine months, the **hippocampus**—the area of the brain that organizes and files memories— becomes fully functional, allowing object permanence to appear (Begley, 1997). The connection between changing brain biology and the early stages of sensorimotor development are evident. Infants' play follows a pattern that reflects the development of the brain areas. Much early play is related to practicing the sensorimotor system. When the frontal lobe begins to be activated during the last half of the first year, the social nature of play expands.

Language Development

Children acquire much of their language in the first three years of life. The amazing accomplishments of infancy alone are worth noting. Note that language involves both listening and deciphering skills, and sound production. Babies appear to be born with innate capacities to begin with each of these—"brains wired for the task" (Cowley, 1997, p. 16).

Babies are born with a reflex to cry, and can quickly communicate different needs with different sounding cries. Within a month or two, they begin to make cooing, open-vowel sounds. The universally similar babbling of all possible sound combinations for all possible languages begins a month or so later. Yet the development of **neurons** to attend to the particular phonemes, or distinctive sounds, of the language that surrounds the infant means that by six to ten months, they are no longer attending to or producing sounds that are not used by the speakers around them (Cowley, 1997). In late infancy, babies begin to produce two-syllable combinations of sounds they hear around them (Da-Da; Ba-Ba); at around their first birthday, they usually produce a word or two that is attached to real meaning. Language that is produced by the child is called **expressive language,** and it always lags behind language that is understood by the child, or **receptive language.** The first words are understood at around eight or nine months.

Babies react to sound from the beginning, startling when they hear a loud one, quieting when they hear a familiar voice, turning their heads to seek the source of sounds. It seems evident that they have already been attentive to sound when in utero; "babies just four days old can distinguish one language from another. French newborns suck more vigorously when they hear French spoken than when they hear Russian—and Russian babies show the opposite preference" (Cowley, 1997, p. 17). After a few months, they respond with differential attention to the voice of a loved caregiver, beginning to smile even when that person is still out of view. Babies get a lot of pleasure out of listening to their own vocal play and practice. Their listening is evidenced by the inflections of speech they add to their own babblings and by their receptive understanding after eight months or so. "Time for your bottle," says Mary, and Joshua looks expectantly toward the fridge. "Come here," says Grandma, and the baby crawls rapidly toward her.

There is as of yet no exact understanding of how babies learn language. Although the beginning stages of sound production appear to be innately patterned, the controversy over later sound production divides itself between those who believe that language is a product of environmental teaching and reinforcement (B. F. Skinner for one) and those who believe that children learn language because they were born with a capacity to do so, with what has been called a **language acquisition device** programmed into the brain (Chomsky). What is evident is that neither theory seems to completely answer all the evidence. Current brain research studies indicate that infants whose caregivers speak with them frequently recognize far more words later than do infants who have not been exposed to similar vocalizations. Early exposure to language helps the brain build the neural connections that will enable later language learning (Newberger, 1997). Therefore, adults promoting language development will want to consider their roles in responding to infants' sounds and realize that their communication offers language teaching and modeling.

A long-term investigation by Hart and Risley (2003) researched how home experiences influenced children's development. Verbal interactions between parents and children were studied by

VIDEO ACTIVITY

Go to the premium Web site and watch the video clip for Chapter 13 titled "Supporting Infant Language Development." Then consider the following questions:

REFLECTIVE QUESTIONS

1. How does this activity support the development of language and literacy?

2. What do you notice about how the adult responds to the baby's attention and response?

3. What other ideas do you have from this chapter about how the adult is modeling and teaching language?

 Visit the premium Web site to complete these questions online and email them to your professor.

analyzing one-hour tape recordings from about age ten to thirty-six months in forty-two families. The families in the study were divided into families from professional backgrounds, working-class backgrounds, and families on welfare. Although all the children started to speak at about the same time, their vocabulary, as measured by the number of different words used, varied significantly. By age three, the children from the professional families had an average vocabulary of 1,100 words; the average vocabulary for children from working-class backgrounds was 750 words, whereas the vocabulary of children from the welfare backgrounds was just around 500 words. The children heard very different amounts of language: the children from professional backgrounds heard an average of 2,153 words per hour, whereas the other two groups heard 1,251 (working-class) and 618 (welfare) per hour. In addition, the study found that the most positive parenting practices included specific ways of talking.

- Lots of "just talking," using a wide vocabulary
- High rates of verbal approval and few prohibitions
- High information content in the speech
- Giving children choices and asking children about things
- Listening to children and responding to their communication

Positive correlations existed between the verbal abilities and intellectual development, as children were followed up to age nine or ten. Perhaps most strikingly, the researchers later found that low-income parents who were trained in parenting skills could change their methods of communication, resulting in children's attainments equal to the national average. These researchers concluded that the quality of parenting and communication is the key factor that determines cognitive abilities and accounts for achievement—certainly a finding that should have implications for caregivers and families.

JOURNAL REFLECTION

Curriculum for Infants

What do you think when you hear discussion of curriculum for infants? Are your images those of flashcards and videos, or of playful interaction and play? Are you able to reconcile the ideas of intentional learning for infants with developmentally appropriate practice?

Visit the premium Web site to complete this journal activity online and email it to your professor.

It is important here to consider Vygotsky's sociocultural theory of cognition, which recognizes that, in addition to the biologically grounded human abilities, social experience and communication shape the way of thinking and interpreting the world available to the individual. For Vygotsky (1978), the acquisition of language is the most significant milestone in children's cognitive development. Vygotsky's focus on collaboration with mature partners as a source of cognitive growth emphasizes the crucial role of the adult in giving infants "tools of the mind." Here we will look at ways that interaction with adults can optimally support infant cognitive and language development.

Principles of Cognitive Development

As infants actively construct their knowledge of the world around them and learn to communicate, caregivers should consider their own developmentally appropriate behaviors. These ten principles provide useful guidelines.

Principle 1—Relationships Come First. Caregivers promote social/emotional security and attachment relationships as a prerequisite to the comfort needed for infants to put energy into

Figure 13-1

Loving relationships and learning are intertwined.

actively exploring the environment. Securely attached infants will trust enough to move away for independent exploration. They use the caregiver as a secure base from which to move out, their "refueling station" (Honig, 1991), when infants need affirming from adults. From exploration comes understanding, but relationships come first. "The security of attachments early in infancy predicts competence and autonomous explorations later on" (Honig, 1991, p. 18).

The emphasis on relationships in quality infant centers has an absolute connection with the optimum environments for cognitive and language development (see Figure 13-1). Trained staff members, working in conditions with small adult-child ratios, have the time and ability to form these important relationships.

Watch eight-month-old Melinda playing on the carpet. She glances over at Kim, the teacher for infants, and when she catches her eye, she sends a wide grin. Minutes later she has crawled to the far corner of the room and is busily engaged in trying to fit two containers together, without another glance at Kim.

Putting attachment first prevents caregivers from inappropriate emphasis on cognitive "teaching." A baby propped up in her swing for long periods to (supposedly) watch *Sesame Street* is missing out on the important human contact that is a prerequisite for interest in the world and all that it contains, including alphabet letters and big birds.

Principle 2—Learning Comes through Interaction. Caregivers recognize that the basis for cognitive development is interaction with objects and people. Babies play an active role in creating their own understanding of the world. Sometimes they need to play with toys and other simple objects or have sensory materials to explore. At other times conversation or simple games with adults introduce new ideas and extend language and practice at reciprocal interaction for infants, as well as strengthening the relationship. Adults observe babies carefully to know when babies are ready and responsive to adult interaction and when it is time for solitary exploration (see Figure 13-2). In either case, they recognize that infants absorb their learning through interaction.

Vygotsky gave us insights on how adults help children develop through recognizing the zone of proximal development or ZPD (Vygotsky, 1978). He defined the ZPD as "the distance between the actual developmental level as determined by independent problem-solving and the level of potential development as determined through problem-solving under adult guidance or in collaboration with more capable peers" (p. 86). By giving children experiences within their ZPD, adults challenge

Figure 13-2

There are times for solitary exploration.

children but help them reach new levels with sensitive adult guidance. Vygotsky viewed education in the form of interaction as leading development, allowing children to actively construct new cognitive abilities (Berk & Winsler, 1995).

Melinda is finished with the nesting toys. Kim hears her begin to whine and interprets it as a signal that the baby is ready for some one-on-one interaction. Soon the two are enjoying a game of "Where's the Baby?" with Kim putting a scarf on Melinda's head and waiting for Melinda to pull it away, chortling. This is a suspenseful experience for Melinda, who seems to have a new awareness of her role in cause and effect and of turn-taking communication. This is not a game that Melinda would have thought of initiating yet, but Kim knew that she would be able to meet the new challenge.

Principle 3—Learning Is Sensorimotor. Caregivers recognize physical play and exploration as an indivisible part of cognitive development. They do not feel pressure to stop the play and teach the babies something, because they realize infants who are exploring are actively constructing their own intelligence and understanding. Caregivers become familiar enough with Piaget's stages that they can enjoy perceiving the cognitive component that is the invisible element behind the physical activity they see.

As Kim and Melinda play the hiding game, Kim is very aware that just a few weeks ago this would have been beyond Melinda's cognitive capacity. But now that she is developing object permanence, it is great fun for something to be hidden and then found.

Principle 4—Learning Is Playful. Important learning takes place in infancy in the context of joyful, spontaneous play. Babies find pleasure as they maneuver their bodies, manipulate objects, and use all their senses. Adults find pleasure as they watch infants absorbed in their learning. Most importantly, there is mutual pleasure as babies and adults come together for brief learning partnerships. Adults introduce babies to games (involving language, imitation, and turn taking) that have been played for time beyond memory, games such as patty-cake, peek-a-boo, hide-the-doggy, and where's-the-baby. These games have in fact profound meaning for infants who are working on serious cognitive concepts such as object permanence, and physical abilities such as **midline hand coordination**. The greatest value of these games, however, comes in the joyous mix of play, interaction, language, and participation. This is not forced learning, but learning at its best, with caregivers being sensitive to individual children's tolerance for active play (see Figure 13-3).

Kim is not acutely conscious of her role as teacher as she plays with Melinda, but loses herself in the pleasure of the moment, laughing as Melinda squeals again in anticipation. She is teaching, but the mutual pleasure is the main thing.

Figure 13-3

Learning is playful and joyful.

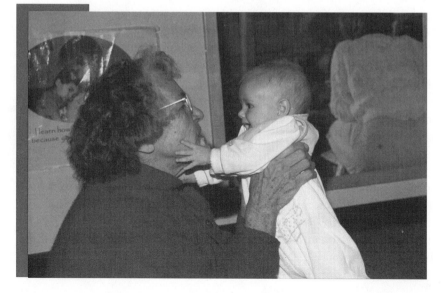

Figure 13-4

Infants need time and space to move and explore, over and over again.

Principle 5—Learning Involves Repetition. Caregivers support the need for infants to practice and repeat physical actions and abilities. "Children cannot push themselves on until they have done very thoroughly what it is they need to do" (Gonzalez-Mena & Eyer, 2006, p. 80). A lot of time and space to move and explore repeatedly is provided to babies as necessary for physical, and thus cognitive, growth (see Figure 13-4).

When four-month-old Daniel wakes up from his morning nap, Kim puts him on the exercise mat on the floor under a cradle gym with interesting things to reach for. He seems more confident in his reaching skills now. There is none of the hesitation that was evident not long ago as he struggled to coordinate his eye and hand movements. Repetition makes his moves less tentative each time.

This is very different from the forced repetition of adult-directed learning assignments for babies, as when adults try to show the infant how to fit the correct shape into the hole on the container over and over again until they believe the lesson has been learned. Adult-directed repetition quickly exhausts and frustrates infants, as indicated by the fretful baby who rubs her eyes and keeps looking away from the "lesson."

Principle 6—Learning Follows a Sequence. Caregivers recognize that physical development moves through predictable sequences of events, so they are aware of which forthcoming behaviors to watch for and support with appropriate positioning, space, or materials. Similarly, they are aware of the pattern of cognitive stages. This does not mean that caregivers push babies on to the next stage; rather, they are able to be more sensitive to cues babies offer that they are moving on, and respond accordingly. Because they accept the idea that babies will do what they can when they are ready, they do not put babies into positions that they could not assume themselves. Trying to hold a position for which muscles are not yet ready is uncomfortable and exhausting.

Daniel has been rolling from his stomach to his back for about a week now. Sometimes when Kim lays him on the mat, she puts him on his back, so he can work with the muscles he'll use for his next turning, from his back to his side.

Principle 7—Learning Is Unique to the Learner. Caregivers learn the individual timetable and learning style of each infant in their care; thus, they are able to provide the best possible learning experiences for each child. Honig (1991) calls this "matchmaking"—individualizing the learning situation for each baby. Such individualizing is only possible when adults observe and get to know the temperament, characteristic style of behavior, pace, and interest of each infant, as well as where he or she is in the predictable sequence.

Daniel is a very active baby, reacting with apparent frustration when he is unable to inch forward on his stomach as he frantically tries to do. Kim recognizes this frustration, and soon moves him over to the reaching area where he seems more comfortable with his mastery. Alicia is about Daniel's age, but seems content to lie on her back, busy with a soft toy to handle. She rarely moves her body in the same frantic ways Daniel does, although she allows Kim to change her position from time to time. Seth, six months now, is contented playing in a lying position, whereas Francisco protests loudly until he's propped into a sitting position. Each baby needs a different approach and response from the adult.

Principle 8—Infants Take the Lead. Caregivers recognize that the motivation and choices for learning originate from the babies. No one has to teach a baby to want to explore, assuming the baby's normal physical capabilities and nervous system are functioning. (The only infants for whom it is appropriate to discuss "infant stimulation" are those who have special needs, with physical disabilities and limitations that do not allow them to initiate exploration.) This does not mean, however, that adult caregivers have no role to play. Sometimes this responsibility includes watching to see babies' cues for when to become involved or when involvement might be interference. Other times, adult responsibilities include planning to provide activities and materials that challenge and reinforce developing skills, providing a balance between what is already accomplished and a new situation, and considering novel experiences to offer. In other words, adults recognize that the responsibility for learning and moving on is the infant's, although it is the adult's task to provide appropriate choices and opportunities.

Caregivers follow the lead of infants, rather than intruding on their exploration and play interests. They recognize their roles as supporters, offering attention and encouragement as babies proceed with their self-imposed tasks.

Kim perceives Daniel's frustration with being unable to creep forward, so the next time he is on his belly, she lies on the floor beside him, making admiring comments as he tries again. She places a favorite stuffed animal just out of reach in front of him and reacts with verbal pleasure and physical excitement when he inches toward it.

Principle 9—Caregivers Provide the World. If infants are to learn by means of their own free exploration of the world around them, adults are primarily responsible for providing a safe and interesting world to discover. Caregivers realize that an environment rich in sensory experiences and safe, interesting objects to manipulate invites exploration with eyes, fingers, and mouth. The specifics in the world are not left to chance, but are provided by caregivers who have thought carefully about what will be appropriate. *The Creative Curriculum for Infants, Toddlers, and Twos* (Dodge, Rudick, & Berke, 2006) suggests eight activity areas to introduce infants to: playing with toys, including homemade toys; sensorimotor art experiences; imitating and pretending; stories and books; tasting and preparing food; sand and water explorations; music and movement; and outdoor experiences. Appropriate materials in each area allow infants to begin exploratory play.

Kim carefully inspects the room each day to make sure there are no items that are potentially dangerous as her babies become increasingly mobile. She is eager to watch Daniel's reaction this morning. The day before she filled a small clear plastic plumber's tube with beads and colored water and glued corks securely in each end. Just big enough to grasp securely, she thinks it might make attractive responses if Daniel can give it a push as he maneuvers. She opens the window slightly so the breeze can sway the pastel streamers that hang down near the mat for Alicia to enjoy. It will be a good morning to take the older infants out in the big wagon. There will be new things to explore today, as well as some of the old favorites.

Principle 10—Learning Demands Communication. As infants make discoveries or get stuck in their exploring, they want to share the experience with their beloved adults. At first much of this sharing is nonverbal on the infant's part: smiles, bouncing pleasure, pointing, holding toys out to caregivers, frustrated howls. Helpful play partners verbalize what the baby is doing and discovering. As babies learn more about the world around them, they rely on alert caregivers to supply the labels and language so they can communicate more verbally. Thus, we see the inseparable union between the learning process and language (see Figure 13-5).

"Daniel, you're working hard. You want to go, don't you? Pretty soon, I'll bet."

"Yay, Melinda, you got those two cups apart. Problem solved!" The babies respond bright-eyed to the sound of encouragement, although the exact meaning may still be beyond them.

These ten principles of cognitive development will guide adults to provide for the most appropriate cognitive environments and responses.

Materials Appropriate at Various Stages

One of the important roles for adults wanting to nurture cognitive development is to provide developmentally appropriate materials.

Early Infancy: Materials for Visual Reaching. In the first month or so, it won't be necessary to worry too much about enriching the environment. Much of the time will be spent sleeping, and infants' adjusting nervous systems do not need bombardment from too many stimuli. As they have longer wakeful periods during the next couple of months, they are interested in looking about them. Caregivers provide interesting things to look at. First and foremost will be the face of the caregiver, by far the most fascinating item a baby can have access to. A loving grown-up has been called the ideal first plaything for a baby. Look at the characteristics that come with that grown-up as plaything.

It moves (no switches, buttons, batteries, or windup keys required).

It talks, makes music, plays back baby's first coos and calls.

It's cuddly (provides security and hours of pleasure).

It's highly educational.

Figure 13-5

Learning demands communication.

Figure 13-6

Strategically placed unbreakable mirrors are intriguing to infants.

It's entertaining; encourages curiosities.

It's composed of resilient, flexible, nontoxic, 100 percent natural materials.

It's a unique toy, crafted to meet an individual child's needs.

It's available only through private distribution.

(From Oppenheim, 1984, quoted in Weiser, 1991)

In addition to infants' human companions, mobiles placed within the baby's visual capability, a distance of 8–24 inches, become useful in the second and third months. Mobiles need to be chosen or created that are interesting from the baby's viewpoint—looking up. Some commercially produced mobiles are still primarily designed to be attractive to adults, not infants. Interesting mobiles can be devised from things like paper plates with colorful designs facing down, or colored tennis balls. Infants like patterns, circles, and distinct contrast, like black against white.

Strategically placed, unbreakable mirrors may be intriguing at this time, and will continue to be through infancy (see Figure 13-6).

An occasional change of scenery, by changing the baby's location or position, may be another stimulus to interest in the surrounding world.

Toward the end of this period, as babies discover their hands, they become ready to physically reach and grasp, so fragile mobiles should be replaced with cradle gyms, as reaching devices are called. (Recall from our discussion in Chapter 5 that babies ready for play are on the floor, so the cradle gym is suspended in a play area.) Sturdy arrangements using dowels or broomsticks can be created, so that a changing array of objects can be suspended with semi-rigid materials, such as plastic wire or pieces of thick cord (to avoid the frustration of having the object escape the infant's first tentative grasp) within range for visually directed reaching. Reaching devices are used when infants are on their backs or in an infant seat.

During the times of play on the abdomen, babies are positioned on brightly patterned soft surfaces with a variety of textures, and small toys are placed within view.

Materials for Infants Who Use a Palmar Grasp. As babies roll, play on their bellies, and sit to explore, they need an assortment of objects on the floor. Up until about eight months, infants use a **palmar** grasp, using the thumb and fingers as if the fingers were in a mitten. For this scooping grasp, babies need large, soft items that are easily attained (see Figure 13-7).

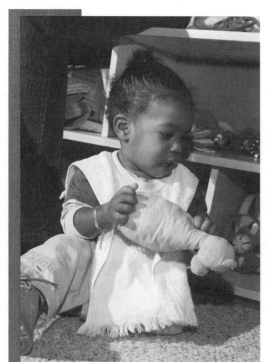

Figure 13-7

Stuffed animals are perfect for infants using a palmar grasp.

Examples of this include stuffed animals, hand puppets, foam blocks, large rings, teething toys, bead necklaces, soft balls, and objects about 4–5 inches in diameter. Because they are also in the sensorimotor stage, where babies try to repeat interesting sensory events, toys that make sounds are fascinating, such as squeeze toys, sound toys with bells or chimes, and large rattles. Note that any play objects that make noise should be constructed so that the baby can see and learn where the noise comes from (Copple & Bredekamp, 2009). Safe household items such as wooden spoons, plastic bowls, and measuring cups are appropriate materials.

Materials for Infants Who Use a Pincer Grasp. After about eight months or so, babies are able to manage more complicated grasping using a **pincer** grasp, which allows them to use thumb and forefinger together. They are also able, soon after, to bring both hands together to hold things in the midline. This improved manipulative ability allows the exploration of things that fit into one another or move in some way. Examples of this type of material include nesting toys (bought or made); stacking rings; toys with parts that move, such as knobs, dials, doors, and push buttons; the sturdy board books that are also present as part of the language environment; and hinged objects, which may include household discards like cigar boxes or boxes for wooden matches (see Figure 13-8).

Added to this increased physical dexterity is the cognitive stage of investigating simple cause and effect; caregivers realize this is the time for toys for which the infant becomes the active agent. Some of the simpler busy boxes that allow for gross hand movement are intriguing. Although they can't manage them themselves, infants love jack-in-the-boxes at this stage. Balls continue to have great exploring possibilities, never behaving quite the same way when the infant pushes or drops them. Ordinary kitchen items like pots and pans are interesting, with the banging possibilities. Many throwaways have a lot of exploring possibilities: empty detergent bottles, in which air squeezes out the opening; diaper wipe containers with their hinged tops, as well as space for filling; a selection of sizes of plastic containers with lids; old purses that can be stuffed with safe noisemakers. (Walk around your house to see if you can think of more.) Puzzles with two or three pieces grasped by knobs interest older infants.

Examples of "loose parts" that are easy to accumulate from household discards include:

- plastic tubing
- plastic hair curlers
- canning jar rings
- juice can lids
- small brushes
- funnels
- clothes pegs
- large wooden spoons, knobs, or dowels
- large washers and plumbing connections
- airline food containers
- margarine tubs
- empty match boxes or cigar boxes
- plastic vegetable baskets or vegetable netting
- plastic tops from spray cans, etc.
- plastic panty hose containers
- different sizes of cans

Keep going—what else can you find in your own home throwaways? Attention is always paid to health and safety issues, including sharpness, choking, toxic materials.

Figure 13-8

"Loose parts" offer infants unlimited opportunities for exploration. Adapted from *Prime Times* by Greenman, Stonehouse, Schweikart, (2008).

Materials for Mobile Infants. Interesting to the older infant are simple, small dolls and realistic-looking cars and trucks. Push and pull toys, such as lawn mowers, shopping carts, and baby carriages are appropriate, as well as varieties of outdoor equipment, such as wide ramps and slides, tunnels, or swings. (See Gonzalez-Mena & Eyer, 2006; White, 1988; Bronson, 1995; Greenman & Stonehouse, 1996; and Dodge et al., 2006, for lists of suggested appropriate materials.)

Part of creating the environment for exploration requires positioning items where they will encourage movement toward them by newly mobile infants.

Again it should be said that all these objects will be thoroughly mouthed and handled, so size (nothing smaller than about 2 inches to prevent accidental choking) is important, as are sturdy quality and safe materials.

When these objects are combined with abundant floor space for free movement, with rails or low furniture when babies are ready to stand and move about, the cognitive environment is almost complete. The only thing missing is the adult, available to indicate supportive interest and appreciation of infants' self-directed exploration and movement.

Appropriate Adult Roles to Nurture Cognitive Growth

Although infants set their own goals, do their own exploring, and create their own understanding of the world, adults have several roles in nurturing cognitive growth.

Caregivers create the physical environment for exploration (see Figure 13-9). Safe areas large enough for movement, with abundant interesting materials and strategically placed and available adults are part of the physical environment. Attention is given each day to ensuring safety, as well as providing materials that are in good condition.

Caregivers create the social/emotional environment for exploration. The evident interest and support of infants, the interaction to sustain interest, and the praise for their accomplishments—all of this adult interaction strengthens infants' desire to continue in their efforts and to succeed. Adults stay available for social interaction even while infants are playing by themselves.

Figure 13-9

Independent movement in a safe environment is essential for learning by exploration.

Caregivers create the cognitive match. As caregivers learn physical and cognitive development stages of infancy, they are able to know where each infant is and what are appropriate materials and activities for each infant. The cognitive environment is not left to chance or instinct. Caregivers observe and record regularly, so that they can assess where each infant is in the developmental continuum of learning. Creating the cognitive match requires infant caregivers to be constant observers and recorders who are able to find out where the baby is at a given time on the developmental ladder. This is responsive curriculum planning (Lally & Mangione, 2006).

Effective caregivers observe throughout the day, making brief notes as babies explore on their own. They use their observations to set long- and short-term goals and objectives, to be able to plan appropriate experiences to support growth toward those goals. They carefully plan materials and experiences that they believe will interest each baby—activities that they are ready for. Planning for sensorimotor events is part of the caregiver's responsibility in creating the cognitive match.

See the sample planning sheet in Figure 13-10 to see how a caregiver has planned materials and strategies for individual children. Planning in the infant classroom is done on an individual basis, with adaptation and change expected to meet momentary interests. Planning allows for the occurrence of cognitive experiences that are suited to the infant's level. Because the brief exploratory episodes fit into the baby's day among the baby-run rhythm of other curriculum encounters of feeding, diapering, cuddling, and so on, the caregiver plans ahead so that she can be prepared for the spontaneous games or play; that is, materials or activities are preplanned, but not scheduled. The caregiver has thought of what the next learning game will be, for when the

Name	Gross Motor	Reach and Grasp	Language/ Cognitive	Social/ Emotional
Brianna (4 months)	Time on back under cradle gym	Change objects on cradle gym (chore girl, circle of beads	Nursery rhyme songs	Tummy tickles
Trenarie (6 months)	Prop to sit with support	Give objects to hold in both hands	Name body parts when dressing	Sit to play in front of mirror
Danielle (6 months)	Encourage rolling over by placing favorite lamb just out of reach	New shaker bottles	Picture book of objects	Pat-a-cake
Jehan (9 months)	Playing catch with me (on all fours)	Stacking two big blocks	Hiding objects	Encouraging him to show affection

Figure 13-10

Caregivers plan for individual babies according to specific goals and observed development.

Language Is Acquired	
By Inborn Mechanism?	**By Environmental Teaching?**
All children acquire language about the same time, in the same ways.	Children always acquire the language heard in the environment.
Deaf babies cry, laugh, coo, babble.	Deaf babies imitate sign language formed by parents' hands.
Children invent original structures, words, and expressions they could not possibly have heard.	Sounds and words that are reinforced are more dominant in children's speech.
Adults rarely "teach" language or grammar.	Hearing infants born to nonhearing/ speaking parents learn to speak by exposure to other language sources.
Neither explanation accounts for all language development.	

Figure 13-11

The mechanisms of language development are not completely understood, but interaction with others is definitely important.

opportunity arises. This is not the "10:30 a.m.: language lesson" kind of planning! (For ideas of games and activities appropriate for each stage of infancy, see Cryer & Harms, 1987; Silberg & D'Argo, 2001; Kinney & Ahrens, 2001; Hollyfield & Hast, 2001; and Dodge et al., 2006).

You will have noticed the overlapping of adult's cognitive and language roles. Let's look more closely at language practices.

Nurturing Language Development

Infants require language partners, for both brain development and growth in their knowledge of the communication process. They need to discover that speech sounds have value and meaning as a method of communicating between persons. Many linguists believe that children probably learn language by processes that include imitation and reinforcement, but also include an increasing sensitization to interpreting the meaning of a partner in communication (Bruner, 1977) (see Figure 13-11). This understanding has real implications for adults who will be involved in helping infants "fine-tune" their language learning.

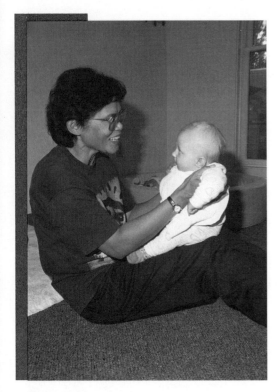

Figure 13-12

Language is taught as conversation.

Infant language is nurtured by adults paying attention to the ten ideas that follow.

1. Adults speak directly (face-to-face) with babies from the beginning, regularly, during every caregiving encounter, throughout every day. From the very beginning, long before adults think babies understand, they speak as though they believe babies can understand. Their speech is in a natural tone, clearly enunciated and "following ordinary polite rules for adult dialogue" (Bruner, 1978, p. 284). There is no "baby talk," meaning adult words being mispronounced—"weally"—or turned into diminutive forms, such as "fishy-wishy." This attention to correct communication pays off; studies show that the vocabulary of toddlers of talkative mothers is dramatically higher than children who heard less talk around them in their early months (Hart & Risley, 2003).

> "You're having a really good time with that ball, aren't you," Angela says to five-month-old Paolo.

> "It's almost time for your bath. I'm going to put your pink fish in," says Enrico to his three-month-old daughter.

2. Recognizing that language is taught as conversation, adults demonstrate turn-taking skills of communication. After they speak, they pause and look to infants for a response, which will be nonverbal or verbal. They look infants in the eyes and direct words to them physically (see Figure 13-12).

> Angela's silence and physical indicators of expectation show Paolo that it's his turn to talk. "Woo-wa-ooo," he replies.

> "You really like bath time now, don't you?" Enrico says, smiling at Maria.

3. Adults reinforce infants' first cooing and babbling sounds. Sometimes they respond to them with words as if the infant were really speaking; other times they repeat back what they heard. In either case, they respond and continue the dialogue, adding nonverbal methods of communication such as gestures and intonation for additional clues. In these ways, infants come to discover that language communication is valued and effective.

> "Ma-ma-ma-ma," says six-month-old Jennifer. Her caregiver smiles at her and moves her face toward her. "Ma-ma-ma-ma," she repeats.

> Jennifer grins with delight. "Ga-ga-ga-guh-ooo." Her air of expectancy indicates she knows it's the adult's turn.

> "Aah-ma-bababa." This time the caregiver says, "Yes, I know you like that ring. You can really chew on it."

4. Caregivers tie their monologues into objects and actions that are present in the environment. This kind of descriptive commentary provides the names for things that babies will learn first, as part of their daily life. Forming the habit of commenting about what they are doing will both encourage adults to talk before the baby can talk back, and also strengthen adult awareness of respectfully involving children in the actions that concern them. As infants explore and handle objects, sometimes adults provide commentary on their learning activity as well. Relating words directly to concrete objects and experiences is a helpful language-teaching technique. One researcher theorizes that this is why only live language encounters, not television, produce

vocabulary and complexity of speech effects in infants: "Language has to be used in relation to ongoing events or it's just noise" (Huttenlocher, cited in Begley, 1997, p. 31).

> "I'm going to put your socks on now. First one sock on this foot, there, now the other sock on your other foot. There we are, two clean socks. Two feet, two socks. Are you ready for your shoes now? Here comes shoe number one."

> "Look at you. You've got a cup in both hands. Bang, bang, bang. They make a good noise, don't they?"

5. With infants who have begun to babble, adults occasionally simplify speech, frequently using one-word labels, repeating them, and linking them by physical indication to the object referred to. Adults also isolate and stress key words to make it easier for infants to understand. These modifications of speech help infants focus on the single words. These are a number of features of **parentese**, the modifications to speech patterns made by adults all over the world speaking to babies. Other factors include using a higher pitch to capture the child's attention; speaking more slowly, with careful, exaggerated enunciation; shortening statements; and repeating and expanding on the child's speech (Baron, cited in Cowley, 1997).

> "Bottle, Emma, bottle. Here's your bottle," spoken while holding out the bottle for Emma to see.

> "Isn't that a big, big dog!"

6. Adults sing and recite rhymes to infants. This singing and reciting is not just for entertainment value. "One of the first and most important conclusions is that the mother tongue is most rapidly mastered when situated in playful activity" (Bruner, 1991, p. 79). With songs and rhymes, the playful quality of the speech patterns involves the babies in a different kind of listening and responding. When action and gesture are tied in with the words, infant understanding is enhanced. Engaging infant attention directly in language and physical activity helps them focus on the language. Adults can make up songs too, using the babies' names for recognition (see Figure 13-13).

> ### CULTURAL CONSIDERATIONS
>
> #### Communicating with Infants
>
> There are cultural attitudes that influence how comfortable parents are in talking with babies who do not speak in reply. Many adults would express that they feel foolish talking to one who doesn't understand or respond. There are also gender-role differences in ways fathers and mothers relate to babies and play with them. Consider how you would respond if you noticed that some of the parents of infants in your care were mostly silent in their interactions with their babies. What responses from you might be helpful, and what might not be helpful?

> "Where's my Sarah, where's my Sarah, there she is, there she is. Going to come and get her, going to come and get her. Big, big kiss; big, big kiss." Seven-month-old Sarah grins happily; this song her mother made up is becoming familiar. "This little piggie went to market," begins the familiar rhyme and toe touching.

7. **Literacy** begins at birth. Reading books with infants should be a regular activity from the beginning. This simply cannot be emphasized enough. The activity leads partly to the positive associations of books and reading with pleasure, as does being held closely while listening to the soft rhythms of a loved adult's voice. As childcare centers attempt to replicate the conditions found in homes in which children find success in early literacy, rich early experiences with books need to be part of the environment in infant rooms. A wide variety of books, including nursery rhymes, song picture books, repetitive-sound pattern books, variously shaped books, chunky board books, and vinyl, cloth, and texture books can be available, with these latter books accessible for infants to explore (see Figure 13-14) (Birckmayer, Kennedy, & Stonehouse, 2008).

Figure 13-13

Adults sing to infants, another way of engaging their attention to language.

Figure 13-14

Infants need early opportunities to look at and handle books.

In addition to the good beginning for literacy, language acquisition is nurtured by hearing the words; watching the adult point to large, clear pictures; and going back through the same book and hearing the same words, making the same visual connections. Story time probably won't last long for infants and will be a one-to-one experience, rather than the small group that might be possible with older toddlers. But research has shown that reading to infants stimulates all areas of development. See a list of great infant books for babies in Figure 13-15.

This page can be a handout for teachers to give to families in an effort to involve them also in the literacy process from the beginning. Teachersmay have a supply of these board books in plastic Ziploc bags, available for families to use at home.

> Kim has selected several new books for her infant room. They include *Pat the Bunny,* which she likes for its short sentences and things for babies to touch; a collection of Mother Goose rhymes, which gives her a large selection of "mini-stories" just long enough for the babies; and several well-illustrated alphabet books, which she uses to talk about the large single objects on each page. She has a selection of heavy board books the babies can manipulate by themselves, and she points out the objects on each page. She has also made books, with large pictures from magazines laminated on cardboard, fastened together by rings.

8. Adults who want to encourage words in older infants give them experiences and objects to label. Language is learned in particular contexts. Caregivers create patterns of repeated activity that can be labeled the same way each time. As caregivers respond to infant clues for communication—the pointed finger to indicate an object they want—they supply the words asked by for the infant.

> There are bright pictures of familiar objects around the room to talk about. "Let's go look at the bunny. Oh, here's the bunny. Do you see the bunny?" And finally, "Where's the bunny?"

> "Time for Daddy to go," says Kim. "Let's go to the window and wave bye-bye. Bye-bye," she gestures and encourages the infant to wave also.

Figure 13-15

Great books to use with babies.

Good books for infants are:

- sturdy board or vinyl, and easily cleaned after mouthing;
- illustrated with large, colorful pictures, one per page;
- relevant to infant's life experiences;
- respectful representations of diverse cultural groups;
- filled with familiar words and phrases, rich language, rhyming words, and repetition.

Look for books by:

Sandra Boynton:	Barnyard Dance
	Moo, Baa, LaLaLa
	The Going-To-Bed Book
	One, Two Three!
Mem Fox:	Time for Bed
Tana Hoban:	Who Are They?
	Black on White
	Red, Blue, Yellow Shoe
	Construction Zone Board Book
	What Is That?
Dr. Seuss:	Hand, Hand, Fingers, Thumb
	Mr. Brown Can Moo, Can You?
Nancy Shaw:	Sheep in a Jeep
Helen Oxenbury:	Family
	Friends
	All Fall Down
	Clap Hands
Margaret W. Brown:	Goodnight Moon
Rosemary Wells:	Goodnight Max
	Max's Birthday
Joy Cowley:	Mrs. Wishy-Washy
Eric Carle:	1-2-3 to the Zoo
	The Very Hungry Caterpillar
	I Can Do It
Karen Katz:	Counting Kisses
	Where Is Baby's Mommy?
	Daddy and Me
Marion Bauer:	Toes, Ears, Nose
Dorothy Kunhardt:	Pat the Bunny
R. Intrater:	Baby Faces Board Books: Eat! Splash! Smile! See also Spanish books
I. Opia:	My Very First Mother Goose Note: Do use Mother Goose—it is worth it to find a well-illustrated book, as you will use it for years. Each rhyme is a mini-story, complete with rhyme and rhythm.

Books in Spanish for babies:

Thierry Courtin:	Bebes Dinamicos. (Dynamic Babies)
	Bebes Juguetones (Playful Babies)
Lucy Cousins:	A Maisy le gusta jugar (Maisy Driving)
	A Maisy le gusta conducir (Maisy playing), and other Maisy books
	El tren de Maisy
	El coche de bomberos de Maisy
Susanne Rotraut:	Buenas noches (Good Night) and Buenos dias! (Good Morning)
Roberto Intrater:	Sonrie! (Smile!)

9. Caregivers recognize that many infants are exposed to the sounds of different languages in the home and the center or even more than one language in the home. Many infants who come to the center having heard only another language at home are very young English learners. Babies with hearing impairments may have begun learning signs. As well, many hearing infants are being taught sign language, so that they can communicate with their families before they develop speech (Briant, 2004). Caregivers need to respect the choices parents make regarding the language relationship they will have with their child, and support parents in continuing to use their home language, even while they can value the ease with which infants can learn more than one language. It is critical for socialization and identity formation that children retain their fluency in their home language, and centers need to endeavor to employ staff so that children are able to hear their home language in the center (Chang, 1993). Caregivers working with infants who have already begun to understand one language will have to adapt and emphasize nonverbal clues if they speak in a second language to the infant. Supporting home language and developing bilingual ability for infants is supporting the cultural choices their parents make (Gonzalez-Mena, 2008).

> "Ball," says Kim to Francisco as she holds out the ball to him. She has heard his parents call it "pelota," but they have agreed for her to use English words when he is in the center, to help develop both English and his parents' native Spanish, which they speak to him at home.

PRACTICAL IMPLICATIONS

- **Unsupportive Cognitive/Language Environments**. The cognitive and language development of infants is not helped by the following behaviors, which are unfortunately too common.

- **Restricting the Physical Movements of Infants.** This restriction might include confining them much of the time to equipment such as cribs, infant seats, swings, or playpens, where babies cannot take the initiative in exploring. It might be by removing them frequently from interesting areas or activities. Restricting movement prevents the natural emergence of locomotor abilities, frustrates infants, and turns them into passive observers, rather than active learners.

- **Restricting the Sensory Exploration of Infants**. This happens when adults do not recognize the necessity for infants to handle and mouth the objects they are in contact with, and infants are continually thwarted when they try to do so (Ooh, nasty! No! Don't touch that! Don't put that in your mouth!). It also happens when adults do not recognize the cognitive activity behind physical exploration, and provide limited or unchanged selections of inappropriate toys and materials. Infants must touch and manipulate objects to take in the sensory information that will lay the base for cognitive concepts. Infants explore less and less when objects do not catch their interest or ability.

- **Super Stimulation and Teaching Beyond Infant Ability**. The programs that have developed around the country to attempt to include precocious advanced learning involve practices and interaction contrary to the active, self-directed learning style advocated by developmentally appropriate practice for infants. Most of these programs also concentrate almost exclusively on the cognitive aspect, failing to recognize that all aspects of development are interrelated, important, and necessary.

- **Absence of Play Partners.** Adults who do not play active roles interacting with infants who are busy at play miss opportunities to reinforce and sustain learning experiences and to introduce new ideas or games to the play. Programs that have high ratios of babies to caregivers do not support adult time for becoming play partners.

- **Noisy Environments.** Noise hinders the ability of infants to tune in to the speech they need to hear for language development. Too many people in one space create noise: another argument for small adult-child ratios. But other noise comes when adults fill the room with too much adult-to-adult speech, which does not involve the infant in the dialogue, or when adults constantly play music or television to create chronic noise clutter.

- **Silent Environments**. Silence hinders language development, as well as the important developmental task of forming attachment. When adults go about caregiving tasks routinely, without personal interaction, so many learning opportunities are lost. Caregivers must speak frequently, comfortably, warmly, and reciprocally with infants.

10. Adults who endeavor to figure out what the infant is interested in are more likely to provide meaningful language. What this probably means is that effective language partners will not always be talking, but will frequently be silently observing the infant. In addition, caregivers create helpful language environments when they limit environmental noise, such as constant music or television playing.

SUMMARY

Brain development in infancy is rapid, needing sensory stimulation for optimum conditions, with critical periods for learning new skills. Developmentally appropriate cognitive/language environments allow infants to proceed at their own rate of development by allowing freedom for sensorimotor exploration. Adults observe babies to learn their stages of physical and cognitive development, so they can provide the most appropriate materials and activities to match the child's abilities. They encourage and support infants who are actively involved in learning. When appropriate, they talk with babies as they play and initiate simple games. Language is used in the context of daily life and routines. Infant communication is imitated and responded to. Learning and language both grow out of the context of joyful, responsive relationships.

THINK ABOUT IT ACTIVITIES

1. Make a collection of interesting, durable, and safe household throwaways that would encourage infant exploration. Bring them to class. As you show your collection in small groups, differentiate the items most suitable for infants who grasp with the palmar grasp and those more suitable for babies who can manipulate objects more completely.

2. Go to the library and check out for books that would be suitable for reading one-to-one with infants. Explain your choices.

3. Create a mobile designed from the baby's viewpoint.

4. Observe for a half hour in an infant room. Record examples you see of: reinforcing babbling, talking about activity and objects surrounding the infants, and simplifying speech to emphasize and label words.

QUESTIONS TO ASSESS LEARNING OF CHAPTER OBJECTIVES

1. Explain what is meant by sensorimotor learning. Describe behaviors infants use to explore during the four substages of infancy. Identify the term *object permanence*. Identify the term *zone of proximal development (ZPD)*.

2. Describe the normal sequence of language development during infancy.

3. Discuss ten principles of learning that influence adult behavior in the cognitive environment.

4. Discuss ten things adults do to support infant language development.

5. Identify six practices that are unsupportive of infant cognitive/language/literacy development.

APPLY YOUR KNOWLEDGE QUESTIONS

1. Write a newsletter that contains your professional, informed response to the request of three parents in the infant room to play French-language tapes while the babies are sleeping to facilitate their learning of a second language.

2. You are interviewing a potential caregiver for the infant room. Formulate three questions that might help you assess her understanding of the importance of cognitive stimulation and how adults support infant learning.

HELPFUL WEB SITES

http://www.zerotothree.org	The Web site for the Zero to Three organization has much valuable information. Click on Professional Journal to find a list of twenty classic articles related to infant learning.
http://www.iahop.org	The Web site for the Institute for the Achievement of Human Potential states that its mission is to introduce parents to the field of child brain development. Consider whether the information offered here is compatible with the ideas about best practices discussed in this chapter.
http://www.pitc.org	The Program for Infant/Toddler Care Web site promotes responsive care for infants and toddlers with many resources.

Please visit the premium Web site for Developmentally Appropriate Practice, *4th edition, to access more chapter web links, additional book chapters, suggestions for further reading and study, interactive quizzes, video exercises, online journal activities, flashcards, and much more!*
Go to www.cengage.com/login to register your access code.

Developmentally Appropriate Cognitive/Language/Literacy Environments: For Toddlers

It has been said that the peak of curiosity occurs in toddlerhood. Just watch the tireless exploration of children between ages one and three years, and you will be convinced that toddlers are indeed driven to learn and are actively coming to terms with the way the world operates. Around the middle of toddlerhood, an explosion of language allows toddlers to interact more verbally, thereby giving us clearer insights into their perceptions and learning.

After adults become aware of this absorbent mind, many are tempted to begin to "teach" toddlers. Indeed, it seems rather rare to find many two-year-olds who have not been taught the "Alphabet Song," blissfully unaware that these nonsense syllables (ellemenopea) have the profound meaning that adults assume they are teaching. If such direct instruction is not in line with what we know of toddler development, what then is the adult's role in providing a cognitive/language environment that will nurture optimum toddler learning? That is the question we will explore in this chapter.

LEARNING OBJECTIVES

After completing this chapter, students should be able to

- discuss an understanding of toddler cognitive development.
- describe typical patterns of toddler language development.
- list three roles identified by Burton White for toddler education.
- discuss behaviors of an adult acting as consultant.
- discuss principles for teaching toddlers.
- list appropriate materials for toddler interest centers.
- describe principles for teaching language and literacy.
- recognize/identify inappropriate cognitive/language practices.

UNDERSTANDING TODDLER COGNITIVE DEVELOPMENT

You will recall from Chapter 13 that infants and young toddlers are defined by Piaget as being in the stage of sensorimotor intelligence, meaning that they use senses and manipulative abilities to gain a practical understanding of the world around them. The first four substages of the sensorimotor period occur in infancy, and the last two substages describe the cognitive abilities of children from age one to about two. We will consider these last two substages here, and then look in detail in Chapter 15 at the preoperational stage into which toddlers are moving.

Substage 5 of Sensorimotor Development

From about twelve to eighteen months of age, toddlers are in the fifth substage of sensorimotor development. Now much more adept at getting around and using their hands, the possibilities for exploration are increased greatly. But there is a new twist to this exploration: No longer content to just repeat actions that have been interesting or pleasurable, toddlers use their increasing repertoire of physical skills to make new things happen. This is scientific research in its purest form: with no predetermined hypothesis of what will happen as the result of certain actions, toddlers systematically try to see what will happen "if."

Insights into typical Substage 5 exploration in toddlers might go something like this: "If I drop the ball, what will happen?" After enjoying that discovery, a new question occurs: "If I climb up to the chair and drop it from there, what will happen? Oh, my—interesting. Now let me see, what else could I drop? Hmm—here's something (a tomato left on the counter to ripen). Not very interesting—no noise, just a splat. Oh, looks to me as if that bowl of sugar might make an interesting effect when it falls." Not only achieving a very satisfying crash and a lot of action, that experiment produces an interesting response from Mom.

Most long-suffering and bewildered adults do not realize that there is truly no malice aforethought here; the trial-and-error attempts to produce a novel effect produce absolutely unlooked-for consequences. Because the toddler has not looked ahead and known what would happen, he can't be accused of deliberately making a mess of breaking the sugar bowl. He was simply caught up in the "here-and-now" desire to create a new event. And all this experimentation is not just for the sake of entertainment. With each new strategy, toddlers learn more about the relationship between their actions and the results.

Incidentally, in just the same style of conducting research on what new event can be created, toddlers investigate the changing properties of human responses. "If Mom got all upset when I dropped the sugar bowl, wonder what she'll look and sound like when I touch this, or drop that, or climb up here?" "If Stephen screamed when I grabbed his toy, wonder if I can make that happen again, or even louder?" Some of the toddler "aggression" discussed in Chapter 10 may have begun as an innocent accident, such as stumbling over another child as the first toddler was moving to something she wanted. Many adults have observed that the toddler who caused the first child to scream gets a very interested look on her face and goes back, the second time quite deliberately, to see what else can be produced. Many adults find it a little more difficult to see this as innocent exploration in the name of trial-and-error research, but this is most likely a product of Substage 5 sensorimotor cognitive development.

This ability to go beyond merely repeating or using old methods of exploring that have worked before indicates a new understanding of the distinction between the toddler himself and the world about him. Being able consciously to vary earlier familiar ways of acting shows the increasing flexibility of learning that toddlers are capable of in the first half of their second year. They are not yet able to mentally imagine actions and probable consequences; however, they are limited to making physical discoveries in their physical environment.

(There are obvious safety implications for caregivers here; because toddlers cannot look ahead to consequences and are so powerfully motivated to explore everything in their environment, they must be protected from the results of limitless curiosity.)

Substage 6 of Sensorimotor Development

At around eighteen months, toddlers show evidence of increasing mental activity—true thinking at last. Toddlers show us that they can remember various actions and situations by their **deferred imitation** (Piaget's term) of behaviors they have seen at another time or place (Piaget, 1951).

Piaget described the scene his daughter witnessed as another toddler had a strong, screaming and kicking temper outburst. Never having seen such a scene before, she reproduced it exactly in her own behavior in a similar situation a day or so later. The memory of one's own or another's actions allows toddlers to find solutions mentally, rather than only by physical trial and error. This representation allows toddlers to take all they have learned from past experiences in different situations, to test the possibilities mentally, and to choose the most appropriate response. Adults say they can literally see the "wheels going around"; toddlers pause and appraise the problem before acting with some certainty. In earlier stages, they would have simply rushed in to try a variety of methods of solving the problem physically. For example, in playing with a shape-sorting toy, a toddler in the sixth substage would most likely look at each hole the cube could go in and decide mentally where it will fit. A younger toddler would have to actually try each different hole to try to physically figure out the answer by trial and error.

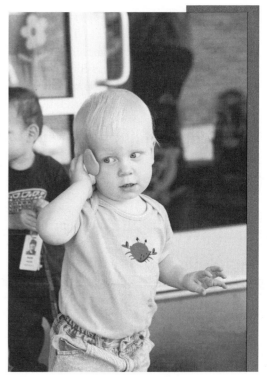

Figure 14-1

Being able to use an object to represent a phone shows new evidence of true thought in toddlers.

Other behaviors that seem to evidence this new ability for representational thought include the ability to think about the relation between objects that are not physically present. A toddler was seen to lift an elbow-shaped noodle to his ear and say "Hello." He was able to associate the similar shapes of the tiny macaroni and the telephone receiver, which was not actually in the room (see Figure 14-1). This ability to make the symbolic connections, as well as to remember earlier scenes, allows toddlers to begin pretend play, another evidence of representational thought. Bobby takes a block and pushes it along the floor, making car sounds. His thinking transforms the block into a car. The emerging use of language is also tied to representational thought, as the word stands for the object, person, or event. "Ba," says Julia, looking for the ball she likes to play with. The ball is in her mind and symbolized by her word.

Having actually achieved representational ability and true thought, the end of sensorimotor development shows us how much has been achieved in infancy and toddlerhood. However, this is thinking at its most primitive level, and it will take several more years of interaction and refinement before the child's thinking even remotely resembles that of an older child or adult. This statement has serious implications for caregivers interested in developmentally appropriate guidance and learning activities for toddlers.

At around age two, toddlers move into the next phase of cognitive development, called by Piaget the **preoperational period**. The entire preoperational period actually extends from ages two through seven and is discussed extensively in Chapter 15. Understanding the functioning of the toddler's mind allows adults to plan appropriately challenging and interesting experiences within the toddler's zone of proximal development (ZPD).

Toddler brain development continues with expanded synapse connections—about twice as dense and as active as the adult brain. The structures of the brain that are sensitive to language production and comprehension become active during this period, which explains the language development that we expect during toddlerhood (Bergen & Coscia, 2000).

Language Development

Near the beginning of toddlerhood, the first real words in a child's expressive vocabulary appear. These are usually naming words that are in some way related to toddlers' actions and experiences; again we see the intertwining of cognitive (sensorimotor) development and language.

For example, Rosa's first word was "ca-ca" for "cracker"; Benjamin's was "woo-woo" for "blanket." These examples show that first words may either approximate adult pronunciation or be an unconventional sound combination the toddler chooses to apply.

Single words, or **holophrases**, continue to be used for six months or so, with toddlers conveying quite a bit of meaning with one word, depending on inflection, context, and a lot of adult interpretation to fill in the rest. So "woo-woo?" means Benjamin is looking for his blanket; "woo-woo!" indicates he wants it now!

Expressive vocabulary increases dramatically between eighteen and twenty-four months; "around the age of 18 months, children's abilities explode. Most start acquiring new words at the phenomenal rate of one every two hours" (Cowley, 1997, p. 20). During this time, a commonly used phrase is "Whatzat?" meaning "What's that?" It is as if, toward the end of the sensorimotor stage, toddlers are hungry to apply labels to the categories of experience and information now stored in memory (that cognitive/language connection again!).

When toddlers begin to combine words as they get close to two years, it is in two- and three-word combinations, leaving out the less important words in a message, thus called **telegraphic** messages. An older Rosa says "Cracker allgone"; an older Benjamin says "Where woo-woo?"

The second year is a critical period for language development, and success depends on available adult language partners, as well as on the earlier brain development from the language stimulation of infancy. Shortly, we will examine recommended practices to nurture toddler language development.

DEVELOPMENTALLY APPROPRIATE COGNITIVE ENVIRONMENTS

Having briefly reviewed the cognitive abilities and learning interests of toddlers, we are now ready to consider the adult's role in providing the most suitable environment for nurturing optimum development.

Burton White on Toddler Education

Some of the most extensive research on optimum development of infants and toddlers has been done by Dr. Burton White in the Harvard Preschool Project, The Brookline Early Education Project, and the New Parents as Teachers programs (see White, 1988, 1995). His findings merit serious consideration for caregivers wanting to provide the most appropriate experiences for toddlers. His research finds that there are few obvious differences before age eight months, yet "relatively few families, perhaps no more than 10 percent, manage to get their children through the 8- to 36-month age period as well educated and developed as they can and should be" (White, 1995, p. 114). White goes on to say that groups of children who underachieve in elementary grades never look particularly weak at one year of age, but begin to lag behind sometime toward the end of the second year. Optimum cognitive development in toddlerhood is related to language development, the development of curiosity, social development, and the roots of intelligence; what he refers to as learning-to-learn, "laying the substructure of sensorimotor exploration upon which higher levels of intelligence are built" (White, 1995, p. 123). The abilities related to intellectual competence that White pinpoints as crucial to develop in toddlerhood include the following:

- Good language development
- The ability to notice small details or discrepancies
- The ability to anticipate consequences
- The ability to deal with abstractions
- The ability to put oneself in the place of another person

- The ability to make interesting associations
- The ability to plan and carry out complicated activities
- The ability to use resources effectively
- The ability to maintain concentration on a task while simultaneously keeping track of what is going on around one in a fairly busy situation (dual focusing) (White, 1995, p. 185)

White finds specific differences in rearing conditions to be responsible for later variations in children's abilities to flourish in cognitive settings. He makes specific recommendations for helpful practices for adults interested in nurturing these specific abilities. They include three roles for adult caregivers: designer of the child's world (see Chapter 6), consultant (specifics to be discussed in the next section), and authority (see Chapter 10).

CULTURAL CONSIDERATIONS

"Early" Academic Learning

There is a uniquely American question, as Piaget once remarked, and that is: how can we speed up cognitive development? In current times, the urge to be competitive about children's achievements and education is definitely a cultural emphasis. As toddlers become capable speakers, parents and teachers as well often feel they should push early academic learning and teaching methods. This is clearly incompatible with what is actually going on in the independent, self-directed learning style of toddlers. So how does a toddler teacher respond when pressed for curriculum that is "real teaching"? What would you do, given the societal press for more, earlier?

The Adult as Consultant. In Burton White's research, he discovered that the real differences between caregivers who produced children with the intellectual, language, and social competencies listed earlier and those who did not, were measurable in terms of availability as a resource person, or consultant. Having created a safe, interesting environment with plenty of intriguing things to manipulate, the adults left it to the natural curiosity of toddlers to propel themselves into a variety of explorations. Effective adults were found to be tolerant of messes, accidents, and natural curiosity. The adults remained "on call," available for brief interaction when toddler exploration leads them into situations in which they experience excitement with discoveries, frustration, puzzlement, or pain (see Figure 14-2).

Characteristics of Effective Consultants. When toddlers come to adults in excitement and puzzlement, effective adults are available to *respond to them as soon as possible*. They do not keep the children waiting or fail to recognize the teaching opportunity. Even if they have to say, "You will have to wait a minute while I finish helping Sally," they give toddlers the sense that they care about their discoveries or concerns.

The important learning for toddlers in this is that their excitement and curiosity are valued, and that others can be used as resources in situations they cannot handle for themselves.

Figure 14-2

Effective consultants respond to toddler interest.

Having responded, effective caregivers pause to see what it is that interests the toddlers. They identify the subject, then *provide whatever is appropriate to the situation*. Adults need to exercise judgment here. When providing assistance to children who cannot completely handle the task themselves—in effect, *scaffolding*—adults "allow the child to move forward and continue to build new competencies" (Berk & Winsler, 1995, p. 26). The manner in which adults give assistance is important for promoting children's learning and mastery. The degree of directiveness or explicit assistance influences children's learning and participation in discovering solutions. This means that toddlers will not learn that adult help is the fastest way to accomplish something or get attention. Adults find ways of helping toddlers succeed by providing suggestions, demonstration, or realistic understanding of task limitations, with the least possible interference.

In cases where toddlers ask for assistance, they are learning something about completing tasks for satisfaction and discovering that they can do things for themselves with only slight assistance.

JOURNAL REFLECTION

Exploration in Learning

Consider the attention spans and activity level of toddlers, and their inability to be a member of a group. What typical classroom activities and teaching styles would be incompatible with those developmental aspects? Reflect on what you have experienced regarding the importance of exploration and experimentation in learning.

 Visit the premium Web site to complete this journal activity online and email it to your professor.

As adults interact with toddlers, they *express an idea related to the child's interest or discovery.* To a child holding out a play dough ball, an adult might say, "You made a ball, didn't you? Can you pat the ball and make it flat?" or "You've got a little ball. A little ball in a little hand. Now I'm holding it in my big hand." The adult has referred to the topic that interested the child, and connected it with something else the child is familiar with and can understand concretely.

The toddler's intellectual world is broadened by such brief cognitive connections. The brief interaction also allows adults to *provide a few words related to the topic,* whether it is answering a question or interpreting the child's discovery. They use language at or slightly above toddlers' own levels. "A ball. You rolled it round and round."

The toddler gets a language lesson, because the adult is providing language that makes sense with its relevance to the situation.

The *interaction is brief* (White estimated that no more than 10 percent of adult time was spent deliberately interacting with toddlers in a home setting), and the toddlers break away when ready, sometimes stimulated by adults' suggestions, sometimes ready to repeat the exciting accomplishment. Effective adults, says White, do not bore toddlers. Most encounters such as these might last twenty or thirty seconds—truly teaching "on the fly."

In this description of effective adults as consultants, it is obvious what is missing. There is no push to teach lessons adults have decided toddlers are ready for. Nor is there a good deal of restriction to make toddlers available for formal instruction. The toddlers are directing the pace and style of learning.

Figure 14-3

Interesting things in the environment allow for toddler exploration.

Principles of Teaching Toddlers

From the previous description of characteristics of consultants, we can formulate six principles for toddler teaching.

Principle 1—Environment Is Everything. Perhaps this is a slight overstatement, but it is important to realize just how important the decisions are that teachers make regarding the materials arranged in the classroom. "How children behave in their environment depends to some extent on how the space is organized and the messages the room arrangement conveys. When there is a clear path from one interest area to another, the message is "Come see what else there is to do" (Copple & Bredekamp, 2009, p. 97). The physical arrangement of play spaces allows adults to be available to toddlers, while allowing the children freedom to work on their own and allowing for active movement. Emphasizing the importance of environment helps teachers move from assuming the dominant role in teaching to focusing on toddlers as dominant in directing their learning. (see Figure 14-3).

Principle 2—Curriculum Is Materials. The choice of interesting, novel, and challenging materials is a key to extending the toddlers' sensorimotor investigations. Teachers have a major role in selecting items that are not so simple as to cause toddlers to lose interest quickly nor so difficult as to frustrate attempts to use. In many cases, the solution is to use materials that are so open-ended that toddlers may use them in a variety of ways, depending on their interest and ability levels (see Figure 14-4).

TODDLERS AND TELEVISION

Both White and Brazelton question the value of television viewing experiences for toddlers (Brazelton, 1974; White, 1995). Although toddlers can and do learn from television—notice the words and tunes picked up from commercials or the ability to "sing out the letters with tunes culled from *Sesame Street*" (Brazelton, 1974, p. 160)—learning is richer and much more individualized and meaningful in an interpersonal setting. Although White acknowledges that toddlers may pick up some vocabulary from children's shows like *Sesame Street*, words that are not tied in to concrete action or meaning are just words. "If he never sees a single television program he still can learn language through you in an absolutely magnificent manner" (White, 1995, p. 180).

The American Academy of Pediatrics has actually made a statement titled "Television and How It Affects Children" (2002), available at the Web site listed at the end of the chapter. In this statement, the academy says that it does not recommend any television or videos at all for children ages two or younger, stating that, until more research is done on the effects of television, they have concerns that too much television can negatively affect early brain development. (For older children, the academy recommends no more than one or two hours of educational, nonviolent television viewing per day.)

The reliance in many childcare centers on television as a curriculum event decreases the amount of active exploration time and time with other children and adults available for toddlers. Surely the most discouraging sight is to see toddlers being scolded for not sitting quietly through a television presentation; this seems the height of developmental inappropriateness.

Principle 3—Toddlers Initiate. For teachers who feel that teaching means telling things, working with toddlers requires a major adjustment in style. Rather than setting aside time during the day for "lesson times" when play is stopped and the teacher takes over, teachers observe toddlers and remain available to respond briefly during the times when toddlers indicate a readiness for conversation, assistance, or ideas from adults. By responding to toddlers' initiatives, teachers reinforce toddlers in their "learning-to-learn" strategies, by far the most important lesson to be taught.

When teachers observe toddlers engaging in aimless wandering behavior (different from the very purposeful wandering of toddlers intent on exploration), they may offer or suggest new interests to the children, then allow the toddlers to initiate their activity. For example, a toddler may be encouraged to notice the wood shavings and animals in the sensory table today.

Principle 4—Adults Observe. When some adults hear that they are meant to allow children to become the active initiators in learning through play, they interpret this to mean that their only role is to set up the environment and supervise for safety. This interpretation loses sight of the important role of observing: observing initially to learn the toddler's level of ability and interest, before making first decisions about materials; observing later to see how the child uses the materials and what kinds of responsive interaction will support and extend the toddler's initiative; using those observations to make next decisions about materials that may extend and reinforce the current learning; and continuing to observe at each step of the learning cycle.

Caregivers position themselves strategically near play areas for maximal observation. They observe while interacting, assisting, comforting, and tidying.

Figure 14-4

Play dough is an example of an open-ended material for toddlers to explore.

Figure 14-5

Scaffolding means adjusting the amount of adult assistance necessary for the child to succeed.

Principle 5—Adults Scaffold. "Scaffolding" is a term not originally used by Vygotsky, but introduced by Wood, Middleton, Bruner, and Ross to describe the specific process whereby adults support children to take a next step in their play and learning as discussed in Vygotsky's theory (Berk & Winsler, 1995). Effective scaffolding has these components:

- Joint problem solving, in which children are engaged in collaborative problem-solving activities and interaction with others while jointly trying to reach a goal (see Figure 14-5).

- Intersubjectivity, in which a shared understanding is reached by those who begin a task with different understandings. As adults share insights that are within a child's ZPD, children are drawn into more mature approaches to the situation.

- Warm and responsive emotional tones of interaction, when adults genuinely "tune in" to the child's activity and interests.

- Keeping the child in the ZPD, by structuring the environment and tasks so that demands are at appropriately challenging levels and constantly adjusting the amount of adult intervention to the child's "momentary competence" (Berk & Winsler, 1995, p. 29).

- Promoting self-regulation by allowing children to regulate the activity as much as possible, with adults relinquishing control and assistance as soon as children are able to work independently (Berk & Winsler, 1995).

In scaffolding, adults have to look to see what the child has achieved, and then consider several of the possibilities of learning that might build on this. An example of scaffolding might be when the toddler holds a plastic bottle filled with colored marbles out to the teacher. The teacher might say, "Shake the bottle," to help her discover the sound produced by this action; the teacher might take the bottle and pretend to drink, to encourage pretend play; or the teacher might roll the bottle on the floor toward the toddler, to help her notice how a bottle moves when rolled. The result is more sophisticated behavior than the child could have performed all on her own; the adult has provided a learning situation that then moves the child forward in development.

Principle 6—Adults Play as Partners. In the small scenarios when toddlers approach adults, adults interact with them as partners, not as dominant leaders. Partners use the skills of observation and scaffolding to help toddlers see additional play possibilities, and they wholeheartedly convey the impression of support and respect for the serious learning embedded in the play. They do this by positive attention and approval of active discovery. They convey partnership by pausing, turn taking, and seeing things from the toddler's perspective. Partners pause long enough to follow the other's lead; think of it as a dance, where the best partner doesn't try to throw in several complicated new steps that might trip the other up (see Figure 14-6).

PLANNING

Does all this emphasis on toddler initiative in exploratory learning and downplaying of direct teacher lessons mean that toddler teachers do not write lesson plans? Not at all. Effective toddler teachers definitely plan so as not to leave to chance the supply of varied, interesting, and appropriate materials. They recognize, however, that they are simply planning a variety of choices and experiences from which toddlers may choose an assortment of learning possibilities. Thus, they are not planning absolute blueprints for their own teaching actions, but instead they are creating a framework of learning choices and possibilities. Toddlers will choose which activities and materials attract them at a particular time and will initiate their activities from the materials

WHAT would you DO when...

"I've got a question about some of my toddlers' parents who insist that we should really be learning something. By that, they mean having sit-and-learn lessons. How do I convince them that this is inappropriate?" How would you respond, if you were this toddler teacher?

Actually you agree; both parents and caregivers believe that toddlers should be learning something. The difference is in your understandings of how this learning actually happens. When an adult believes that toddlers learn only through direct instruction from adults, it is often very difficult to see the learning that is actually occurring. Your best strategy may be in making that learning become more obvious to parents.

Try using a camera to capture the active involvement of toddlers with their materials. Display these with appropriate notations on your parent bulletin board, or mount them in a photograph album, with explanatory notes, and send it home on a rotating basis. Display documentation panels that can describe sequences of learning experiences in narrative and with pictures. Use a tape recorder to capture some language interchanges or singing times. Make a display of favorite books shared recently.

Offer articles and books that explain toddler learning styles and responsive teaching: parents who are readers often take information better from reading than from a personal source. Make available the NAEYC statements on developmentally appropriate and inappropriate practices in centers serving toddlers. Emphasize development of the whole child. Record development and share changes with parents in informal conversations.

Perhaps most importantly, invite parents to come and observe for periods during the day. Share your plans for the week based on your own observation and objectives. Call their attention to the real involvement of toddlers busy at self-chosen exploration. Play your usual role as consultant, then make an opportunity later to discuss this role of the teacher with the parents. Have them watch the self-help skills developing during the period before, during, and after lunch.

Have a morning in the toddler room videotaped, and plan a parent get-together to discuss what they see. Sometimes the support of other parents helps others look at new ideas.

Remember that imposing your views on parents will not change their opinions, but allowing them to have real opportunities to experience the learning that is happening may help them see the developmentally appropriate orientation you come from. Allow time for dialogue and don't force agreement. Gonzalez-Mena (2001–2008) refers to this issue in her fine book on multicultural issues in childcare, saying "the purpose of a dialogue is to understand—not to get your points across. You have to step out of a win-lose mindset" (p. 114).

Figure 14-6
Adults plan activities to stimulate toddler curiosity.

planned for by the caregiver. No child's play is interrupted to urge them to participate in activities planned by the teacher; toddler play is valued in its own right.

Planning, as discussed earlier, is based on observed developmental levels. Because teachers are familiar with physical, cognitive, and language landmarks, they are aware of where individuals in the group are in the developmental sequence. They can then plan experiences that support the level achieved and help children move on to the next level.

Planning takes into account the particular learning style of toddlers, with the pattern of brief interaction with materials, moving on to other activities, and then returning to repeat the experience. Although teachers plan appropriate materials and activities for the brief times when a small group of toddlers may come together to enjoy stories or songs, they recognize that the majority of learning time will be spent by toddlers in solitary exploration and self-determined tasks. Planning also takes into account the need for toddlers to have some novelty to stimulate their curiosity, as well as the familiarity of known objects and activities (see Figure 14-6).

Planning is also based on observed interests. As teachers discover topics that are important to toddlers, they sustain that interest by extending their explorations with additional related learning experiences. If this sounds very much like the kinds of emergent curriculum discussed in more detail in Chapter 3, that is because this is appropriate when modified for toddlers also. Many of the problems that occur in toddler classrooms are probably the result of teachers' thinking that toddlers are too young for any real learning and thus require no real planning. Often in such a classroom, toddlers are simply left free to play with the collections of toys that adorn the shelves of most classrooms, unchanged for months on end. Although nothing is wrong with the typical collection of puzzles, shape sorters, balls, trucks, and hollow blocks— indeed, these are among most lists of appropriate materials—reliance on these items alone without planning to provide for variety, increasing levels of challenge, and toddlers' desire to create new effects leads to increased wandering behavior, shortened attention spans, increased friction among toddlers, and increased reliance on adults to entertain them.

LeeKeenan and Edwards (1992) describe a project approach in planning curriculum for toddlers to allow toddlers to make connections between different experiences. For example, one of their projects worked with water, with toddlers using water in many activities over a period of time, from washing babies to painting with water in spray bottles. They found that the connecting experiences allowed toddlers to comprehend the basic and related concepts and use the vocabulary more extensively in their everyday play.

A sample planning sheet for a toddler classroom might look like the one shown in Figure 14-7. Note that the teacher has planned for specific children's interest as well as for experiences that anyone in the group might enjoy. Note also that the plan is in the form of notations for teachers

Figure 14-7

Sample planning for toddlers.

Talking about:	Things we do and use at home
Sensory table:	Cedar shavings, plastic scoops and hand rakes
Paint:	Using objects: pot scrubber, sponges
Water table:	Soapsuds and plastic dishes to wash
Manipulatives:	Tongs to put cotton balls in plastic jars
Puzzles:	Fisher-Price house with knobs (shows interior)
Blocks:	Foam blocks and small family figures
Dramatic play:	Babies and baby bottles, box of scarves
Special:	Butter crackers to sprinkle with sesame seeds
Consider:	Put train out for Ian?
	See if Jessica is still interested in climbing?
Stories:	*My Daddy and Me; Our Garden*
Songs:	"This Is the Way We Sweep the Floor"

to follow as they prepare for the day. They will be prepared to initiate these adult-planned activities at opportune times, rather than having set times in which the activities must be done.

Caregivers need to be ready to forego the planned activities for the day, depending on children's interest and receptivity. Teachers follow toddlers' leads in determining when and how to implement their planned activities.

Materials and Activities for Sensorimotor Learning

As noted in the "Planning" section, materials are emphasized that lend themselves to the kinds of sensorimotor exploration toddlers do, including testing out all the characteristics of objects and finding new ways to use familiar items. This means the majority of materials need to be open-ended, that is, open to use in a variety of ways and able to be used in increasingly complex play.

The suggestions provided in the following sections are by no means exhaustive. As you read, note other similar items you have seen used. Any good book on toddler education activities will add suggestions. (At the end of the chapter, see Catlin, 1996; Dodge, Rudick, & Berke, 2006; Herr & Swim, 1999; Kohl, 2002; Miller, 1999, 2002; Schiller, 2003; White, 1988, 1995.)

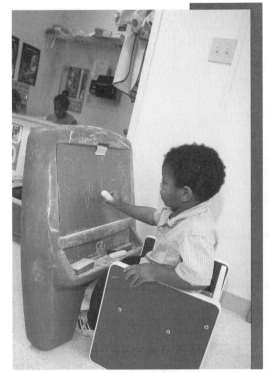

Figure 14-8

Chalkboards provide appropriate toddler art experiences. Note the adaptation of the chair for the child with special needs.

Creative Corner. Toddlers will enjoy using

- fat crayons, including the chunky ones homemade in muffin tins. Tape the paper to the table, or tie the crayons with yarn to the easel. Toddlers are less interested in having their own product than in making a scribble.

- finger paint, which may be homemade from a variety of recipes (see Kohl, 2002), and used on trays, table tops, mirrors, windows, meat trays, or anything else that will help contain the mess.

- jumbo chalk and chalk boards (see Figure 14-8).

- water-based felt tip markers.

- play dough (yes, it will be tasted), with tools such as tongue depressors or potato mashers.

- paint and varieties of brushes with thick, short handles and other applicators, such as empty deodorant bottles with rollers, squeeze bottles, or sponges held with clothespins.

- tissue paper and magazines for tearing.

- occasional opportunities for gluing, as long as teachers are willing to allow children to experiment with the stickiness. Small brushes or cotton swabs and containers help.

- any kind of paper at all for use with these materials. Get castoffs from parents. Use large sheets of paper to accommodate toddlers' large arm motions.

Minimize the mess, by use of an old shower curtain or plastic drop cloth on the floor, as well as smocks or old shirts to cover toddlers.

Table Toy Area. Many commercial items are appropriate for toddler fingers. A selection should include the following items:

large Legos	shape-sorting boxes
puzzles with single-piece pictures, some with knobs	stacking or nesting toys
bristle blocks	self-help boards to practice fastening and unfastening
cubes for stacking	busy boxes (See White's [1995] recommendations.)
plastic snap beads	small table toys
large beads for stringing	

Figure 14-9

Recyclables and homemade toys provide necessary variety.

Recyclable materials provide necessary variety (see Figure 14-9). Manipulative toys can be made from:

an assortment of plastic containers and jars	milk jugs
lids and tops, as from aerosol cans, especially screw tops	popsicle sticks
	large nuts and bolts
canisters	belts and buckles
clothespins	hinges, castors
boxes and lids	sponges
egg cartons, margarine containers, and things to put in them	wheels or other safe, large parts from broken toys

Items from the natural world also make for interesting exploration. Care must be taken to choose items that hold up to manipulation, and are large enough not to present choking hazards. Suggestions include the following items:

large, smooth rocks	large shells
pinecones and large seed pods, always being aware of toxicity	pieces of bark and sections of tree branches

Used in any kind of combination, there are a lot of possibilities for manipulation here.

Sensory Exploration. Toddlers need regular access to materials for sensory exploration and accessories to use with sensory materials. When teachers do not have access to commercially available water/sand tables, they can improvise with dishpans or baby bathtubs. Mess is minimized when children are given interesting accessories to suggest play that is more constructive than throwing. Having a small broom, mop, and dustpan nearby will also help. Materials for the tubs include:

- sand, both indoors and outdoors, with accessories such as spoons, shovels, containers both big and small, funnels, strainers, shape molds, and small dump trucks. Occasionally, water can be added to the sand.

- water, both indoors and outdoors, sometimes varied indoors with the addition of color or bubbles, ice chips, and accessories such as boats, containers, egg-beaters, sponges, colanders, hoses or tubing, watering cans, basters, squeeze bottles, straws, and baby dolls or dishes to wash (see Figure 14-10).

Figure 14-10

Water with things to wash and pour from provides endless fascination for toddlers.

- dry rice, cornmeal, oats, dried beans and macaroni mixtures, styrofoam bits, wood shavings, sawdust, cedar shavings, large stones, Easter grass, leaves and nuts, potato flakes, birdseed, coffee sand (coffee grounds mixed with sand). All these things do need supervision so stones or beans (even those large enough to be considered safe from choking hazards) don't get into noses or ears, but the variety is worth it.

- boxes or trays of other sensory manipulatives, such as sandpaper, fabrics of all kinds, ribbons, elastic, sticky papers, balls of yarn or masking tape; natural materials, such as seeds, nuts, seed pods, bark, sea shells, sometimes arranged as games to match or compare.

Construction Area. Toddlers are likely not yet ready for many experiences with the traditional wooden unit blocks of the preschool classroom. Instead, they enjoy constructing with items such as these (see Figure 14-11):

sturdy cardboard blocks	giant Legos
foam and fabric blocks	boxes of various sizes
teacher-made blocks from boxes or milk cartons covered with contact paper	large cardboard or plastic tubes
	additions of props such as animals, people figures, or cars

Two-year-olds may begin using unit blocks to line up and carry around.

Figure 14-11

Sturdy cardboard blocks are easy for toddlers to use for construction.

Imitating and Pretend Play. For nurturing the first pretend kinds of play, toddlers need a clearly recognized house area that includes:

- a table and two small chairs, stove, stroller, and bed. Toddlers will be playing simple repetitions of home-based scenes, so they need a simply furnished area, easily recognizable.

- a few pots, pans, dishes, and big spoons. The real thing, rather than toys, appeals to toddlers.

- a small mop and broom.

- dolls and baby blankets (leave out the doll clothes for a while; toddlers will remove them and then want you to put them back on— repeatedly). Make sure you have both boy and girl dolls and dolls that represent ethnic diversity.

- realistic-looking materials from home life, such as empty food containers.

Book Area. In trying to encourage toddler interest in books, teachers will want to provide books the toddlers can handle themselves, as well as books for reading to toddlers. The area should include:

- board books (rather than cloth or plastic books, which are less easily cleaned and more difficult for toddlers to handle).

- homemade picture books, with stiff cardboard pages, useful to place in a loose-leaf notebook.

- photo album books, using either familiar photos or large magazine pictures for naming objects.

- flannel board books with large figures for toddler use.

- simple picture books (see Figure 14-12).

Again, watching the toddlers use all these materials will probably give teachers more ideas. A developmentally appropriate cognitive environment for toddlers provides for the needs and interests of individual children as well as the broad abilities of the group.

Figure 14-12

Toddlers enjoy reading to themselves.

Rosa added a firefighter's hat to the dress-up clothes, a new picture book featuring firefighters, and two new small fire trucks to the block area after Michelle repeatedly used her new word *fire* when the sirens raced by.

Realizing that DeJuan preferred not to put his hands in the shaving cream available to smear on the art table, she added some fresh paper to the easel, where two fat crayons were tied.

Noticing that Sarah had mastered the puzzles with one-piece shapes, she found some three-piece puzzles in the storage closet.

Cognitive development, then, is encouraged by the thoughtful preparation of an environment that encourages exploration and movement, using carefully selected open-ended materials and sturdy toys. Adults remain available, observing toddlers' levels of understanding, and responding promptly to toddler approaches to share discoveries or ask for help. They use these brief encounters to support curiosity and learning, to add related ideas, and to add language. Let's now consider the adult's role in providing an optimum language environment for toddlers.

Principles of Teaching Language to Toddlers

Someone once said that adults in our culture teach two important things to toddlers: how to talk and how to eliminate in appropriate places. The difference between the two is that adults are frequently frustrated in teaching the latter and have more success with the first because of the differences in methods of instruction! With toilet teaching, adults usually decide on a time for instruction, teach quite directly what to do and how to do it, and clearly let toddlers know when they have succeeded or failed according to adult standards. With language, however, most adults allow children to choose their time to begin speaking, teach quite indirectly (mostly by modeling), and are nearly always extremely positive with toddlers about any effort to speak at all. Although this does bear thinking about (primarily for considering new tactics with toilet instruction), adults who want to provide the optimum language environment for toddlers will become more conscious of behaviors that research has found particularly helpful.

Figure 14-13

Language teachers encourage speech.

Principle 1—Language Teachers Respond to Toddler Communication. If toddlers are to move on in language development, they need to perceive that their efforts at speech are important. If adults do not attend to speech, toddlers quickly learn that language is not valued or necessary (see Figure 14-13). Even when adults are unable to understand toddlers' first words, they use context and nonverbal cues to attempt to understand and respond appropriately. Even when adults are tiring of the persistent "Whatzat?" they respond patiently, knowing their key role in helping toddlers sort out labels for objects.

"Wuh," says Rodney, holding out his cup. "More juice, Rodney? You want more juice?"

"Muk wal." "Hmm," says a toddler teacher. "I don't understand. Show me."

"Whatzat?" "That's a mirror. Mirror."

Principle 2—Language Teachers Model Speech. Knowing that toddlers depend on adult speech for their example of vocabulary, as well as for extracting their own understanding of grammar usage, adults speak frequently, clearly, and distinctly to toddlers, enunciating more distinctly than in ordinary adult speech, and emphasizing key words. Sometimes they repeat the child's word with correct, emphasized pronunciation. This is done as a form of positive reinforcement, instead of a negative correction. They model not only the mechanics of speech, but also the logistics of conversation, making it clear when they are speaking to a particular child and waiting for response before speaking further.

"Mok," says Jeffrey. "Yes, here's your milk," says his mother.

"Randy, here's your jacket."

"Snack time, Michelle."

Principle 3—Language Teachers Simplify Utterances. Adults simplify much of their speech so it is only slightly more complex than the child's current level. For example, if a child is speaking in two-word sentences, adults use three or four words. Long, complex sentences are used less frequently, but not avoided altogether. Some complexity appears to build children's grammatical structures. A study showed that mothers who used complex sentences (those with dependent clauses, such as "when. . ." or "because. . .") 40 percent of the time had toddlers who did so 35 percent of the time; mothers who used such sentences in only 10 percent of their utterances had children who did so only 5 percent of the time (Begley, 1997). Another common simplification that many adults make—substituting proper nouns for pronouns, such as "Does Bobby want some juice?"—may not be helpful to toddlers trying to sort out pronouns (Cowley, 1997).

"Time for jackets."

"Do you want more juice, Jennifer?"

Principle 4—Language Teachers Expand on Toddler Efforts. One strategy known to be effective with toddler language is to expand on their original utterances, adding vocabulary and ideas. Expansions fill in children's missing words or offer more specific words, and extend ideas that children begin. Such expansions are important for both cognitive and language development.

"Ju," says Michelle, holding out her cup. "More juice. You want more juice," expands her caregiver.

"Want dat," says Sarah. "You want your bunny?" says Mom.

"Daddy car," says Peter. "Yes, Daddy went in the car. He went to work."

Principle 5—Language Teachers Link Words with Actions and Experiences. Toddlers learn vocabulary in a particular context. When gestures, pointing, and other nonverbal cues help children understand the meaning of words, their learning is assisted. But language teachers do not use gestures instead of words and are explicit in their word choice: "Take the ball" instead of "Take this." When caregivers describe their actions and the activities of toddlers, the concrete context helps toddlers recognize meaning. Caregivers provide an abundance of objects, pictures, and experience in toddler environments to offer interesting things to stimulate communication.

"Shoes, Jennifer, please get your shoes," as the caregiver points to the shoes.

"You're playing in the soap bubbles, aren't you," as the caregiver puts her own hand into the soapy water.

"Where's the duck, Jacob? Show me the picture of the duck," as they look at some bright pictures taped to the wall.

Principle 6—Language Teachers Correct Indirectly. There is much for toddlers to absorb about grammar and word usage. In the process, they typically make mistakes by **overgeneralization**; for example, having deduced that plurals are formed by adding an "s," and past tenses by adding "ed," toddlers apply those rules in all cases, including irregular English words, producing such phrases as "my feets" (or foots), or "Daddy goed" or "wented." Actually such constructions show

Figure 14-14
Puppets and other toys, such as telephones, encourage communication.

clearly the toddler's amazing understanding of a number of grammar rules! Adults are most helpful when they repeat the idea back, correctly phrased, rather than directly pointing out the mistake. Toddlers quickly self-correct, without feeling failure. Brazelton (1974) lists too much direct emphasis on correct speech as one possible reason for language delay.

"Yes, Daddy went to the office."

"You *do* have new shoes on your feet, don't you?"

Principle 7—Language Teachers Encourage Speech. After toddlers have the ability to link sound and word, adults encourage toddlers to attempt speech. They do this by not immediately responding to a perceived need before the toddler has had a chance to verbalize it. They also encourage speech by asking questions the toddler can answer with a word or two. They do not frustrate toddlers, however, by demanding a word before they give an object to a child if the child is unable to speak.

Sometimes they encourage speech with the materials in the environment, such as toy and/or real telephones, puppets, and pictures and objects that intrigue (see Figure 14-14).

"Tell me what you want, Michelle."

"Do you want one cracker or two?"

"Hello? There's somebody who wants to talk to you, Danielle," holding out the telephone.

"Turtle," says Jennifer, when Bobby points to the picture in the book.

Principle 9—Language Teachers Sing, Recite, and Play Games. The reason traditional nursery songs, rhymes, and games have lasted is their appropriateness for language experiences of toddlers. The rhythm, rhyme, repetition, and linking of action and meaning help toddlers acquire understanding and vocabulary.

"Head and shoulders, knees and toes," sings LaToya, moving her hands so the toddlers can imitate her.

As Anthony recites "Humpty Dumpty sat on the wall," Sarah and DeJuan wait with anticipation to "fall off the wall" along with the words.

Principle 10—Language Teachers Read Books, Lots of Books. The important association of word and picture helps toddlers increase their vocabulary. Although most toddlers are not ready to sustain interest in actual stories until well into the second year, picture book sessions are important labeling sessions. In addition to vocabulary, the positive connection between books and pleasurable experiences is reinforced by book time with adults. Literacy is an important consideration in toddler classrooms. Careful book selection will help sustain toddler attention. Rhyme, rhythm, repetition, and familiar sequences, as well as bold illustrations provide the main interest. Cozy areas with low bookshelves will encourage interaction with books. Early literacy experiences with toddlers lay important foundations. See Figure 14-15 for a list of toddler favorites.

▶‖ VIDEO ACTIVITY

Go to the premium Web site and watch the video clip for Chapter 14 titled "Supporting Toddler Language Development." Then consider the following questions:

REFLECTIVE QUESTIONS

1. What do you notice in this scenario about the adult's distinct roles and strategies in supporting toddler language development?

2. Consider ideas from this chapter about how adults function to expand toddler utterances, and to model listening and speaking.

3. How does the adult illustrate good speech?

4. Do you see any areas that could be improved upon?

 Visit the premium Web site to complete these questions online and email them to your professor.

Figure 14-15

Favorite books for toddlers.

FAVORITE BOOKS FOR TODDLERS

Peek-a-Boo! Janet & Allan Ahlberg
Maggie's Moon, Martha Alexander
Hush Little Baby, Aliki
Ten, Nine, Eight, Molly Bang
Airplanes, Byron Barton
Goodnight Moon, Margaret Wise Brown
Miffy at the Zoo, Dick Bruna
The Baby, John Burningham
Dear Zoo, Rod Campbell
1, 2, 3 to the Zoo, Eric Carle
Jesse Bear, What Will You Wear? Nancy Carlstrom
Ten Black Dots, Donald Crews
Tomie De Paola's Mother Goose, Tomie De Paola
Do Bears Have Mothers Too? Aileen Fisher
Mother Goose, Gyo Fujikawa
Little Bo-Peep, Paul Galdone
Trucks, Gail Gibbons
Spot's First Walk, Eric Hill
A Children's Zoo, Tana Hoban
My Feet Do, Jean Holzenthaler & George Ancona
When I'm Sleepy, Jane Howard
Titch, Pat Hutchins
I Hear, Rachel Isadora
Animal Mothers, Atsushi Komori

Carrot Seed, Ruth Krauss
Kitten Can, Bruce McMillan
Ten Bears in My Bed, Stanley Mack
Is Anyone Home? Ron Maris
Brown Bear, Brown Bear, What Do You See?
    Bill Martin
Farm Counting Book, Jane Miller
Friends, Helen Oxenbury
*Mary Wore a Red Dress and Henry Wore His Green
    Sneakers,* Merle Peek
Circus Numbers, Rodney Peppe
Colors, John Reiss
Big Wheels, Anne Rockwell
Animals on the Farm, Feodor
    Rojankovsky
Three Ducks Went Wandering, Ron Roy
Gobble, Growl, Grunt, Peter Spier
Who's Counting? Nancy Tafuri
Pumpkin, Pumpkin, Jeanne Titherington
How Do I Put It On? Shigeo Watanabe
Max's Bath, Rosemary Wells
A Good Day, A Good Night, Cindy Wheeler
Animal Homes, Brian Wildsmith
The Chicken Book, Garth Williams
Hush Little Baby, Jeanette Winter

Look for other books by these authors.

Group Time for Toddlers?

As caregivers hear the importance of books and songs for toddlers, it might be tempting to consider planning group times to introduce these activities to toddlers. For most of toddlerhood, children are unlikely to be able to sustain interest long enough for an organized group time to be very meaningful. The sheer logistics of trying to encourage a number of independent toddlers to occupy the same space and to sustain the quiet listening skills demanded by an organized group time are daunting. Generally, formal group times for toddlers are extremely frustrating for everyone involved.

A far better method is to form small, less formal groups by sitting on the floor with interested toddlers and beginning a singing session or looking at a picture book with those who are nearby (see Figure 14-16). As the activity appears interesting, toddlers will wander over to join in. Just as they casually come, caregivers should be willing for them to casually leave when something else attracts them. For book-sharing time, the adults in a room may find it advantageous to form small groups distant from one another. Often adults read to toddlers sharing some space on their laps, rather than grouped in a distant semicircle as in a preschool group time. Sometimes it is helpful to read to a few toddlers seated in chairs at a table; this arrangement encourages staying a bit longer. The brief pleasure of sharing a song or singing game like "Ring around the Roses," is a pleasant introduction to extended group participation appropriate for later on.

With toddlers, it is more important that they have pleasurable experiences with books and language games than that they stay, sit still, and learn group time skills.

After many such experiences, the very oldest toddler—those well into their third year—may be ready for short, more structured group experiences. Teachers may create half-circles, with a space clearly marked for each child, by a carpet square, for example. They will plan very short reading and music experiences, coaching children daily with group skills, such as sitting quietly, listening when others talk, and so on.

Figure 14-16

Informal group times may involve looking at a book with nearby toddlers.

PRACTICAL IMPLICATIONS

Unsupportive Cognitive/Language Environments

In order to find the best developmental match for toddler learning style, toddler caregivers avoid the following extremes.

1. *Creating an environment without challenges or responses:* When caregivers decide that toddlers are "too young for any real learning," there is a danger of offering an environment that bores and stifles curiosity. Looking very much like an infant room minus the cribs and high chairs, such a room usually offers space and toys on shelves—not nearly enough to interest curious toddlers. Then adults see their task as supervising toddlers in an uninteresting room and stepping in to referee the squabbles that are frequently the result of too little interest or novelty to otherwise occupy interest.

2. *Creating an environment that imposes structured adult-decided learning experiences:* When caregivers decide that toddlers are "not babies anymore," this frequently translates into imposing rote learning experiences and dribbling down ideas from the preschool. The plans often include flashcard sessions or producing some product to take home "so we can show our parents we're really teaching them something," which usually means adults have to do most of the "work" themselves—producing a ditto sheet of farm animals for toddlers to color or gluing together the precut parts of an Easter bunny.

   Rote learning experiences do not match the active, self-initiated learning style of the toddler. Although toddlers can sometimes parrot back the words taught by the flashcards (red, yellow, up, out, or whatever concept is pictured on the card and repeated by the adult), their true understanding is certainly questionable. Toddlers don't learn just by being told things, but by their own active exploration. Moreover, to coerce toddlers into such experiences usually requires trying to get them to sit and attend by persistent adult direction, often resulting in powerful toddler resistance. The question remains whether anything is gained by such cognitive practices.

3. *Creating an environment that emphasizes sitting to learn:* Toddlers are creatures on the move. Their drive to explore and use their whole bodies, along with an average attention span of two minutes, means that toddlers learn to go and learn as they go. When toddlers are asked to sit and do, it is contrary to their nature. They much prefer to stand and move, even for stories and songs. Because they will be asked to sit to eat, this should be the only time of the day that this is required.

SUMMARY

The natural sensorimotor learning style of toddlers demands responsive adult behaviors. These include preparing interesting environments; observing as a basis for planning and interaction; playing as partners; and using brief, child-initiated encounters for adding language and ideas. Individual, rather than group, learning experiences are emphasized. Adults who are careful to model, expand, correct indirectly, and simplify their speech patterns support toddler language development. Books and songs are important language experiences. Talk is part of the whole environment.

THINK ABOUT IT ACTIVITIES

1. Visit a toddler classroom. Notice the kinds of planning done by the teachers. What about planned group times? Does this suggest developmental appropriateness to you?

2. Observe the teachers. What behaviors do you see that suggest the characteristics of White's description of a consultant?

3. List the materials that are available for toddlers to use in their play. Note those that were suggested by the materials list in this chapter and those that are additional ideas.

4. Select one toddler and watch him or her at play. Record activity for a ten-minute period. What behaviors do you notice? What strategies does the toddler use to explore materials?

5. Note several examples of language interchanges between adults and toddlers. Which of the principles of language teaching discussed in this chapter do these interchanges illustrate?

6. What materials do you see in the room that would encourage language exchanges?

QUESTIONS TO ASSESS LEARNING OF CHAPTER OBJECTIVES

1. Describe the characteristics of the last substages of sensorimotor development.

2. Discuss typical language development patterns of toddlerhood.

3. Describe the behaviors of a consultant, as defined by Burton White.

4. Identify several principles of teaching toddlers for cognitive development.

5. Think of as many materials as you can that are appropriate for toddler learning.

6. Discuss several techniques for nurturing toddler language development.

7. Identify several inappropriate practices relating to toddler cognitive/language development.

APPLY YOUR KNOWLEDGE QUESTIONS

1. Plan two appropriate language experiences for toddlers that could be carried out with individuals or small groups.

2. Having observed two toddlers for a number of days, plan appropriate learning experiences that match their developmental and interest levels.

HELPFUL WEB SITES

http://www.aap.org   The Web site of the American Academy of Pediatrics has much information. For the position statement on Television and How It Affects Children, click on Health Topics, and then look in the Topics bar on the right for Television.

http://parenting.ivillage.com

At this Web site, you can find much information about toddler learning and language. Search for an article on free play and toddler learning.

http://www.kidsource.com

This Web site has many articles about children's education and health. Search for toddler learning and language.

 Please visit the premium Web site for Developmentally Appropriate Practice, *4th edition, to access more chapter web links, additional book chapters, suggestions for further reading and study, interactive quizzes, video exercises, online journal activities, flashcards, and much more! Go to www.cengage.com/login to register your access code.*

Developmentally Appropriate Cognitive/ Language/Literacy Environments: For Preschoolers

In her article "Why Not Academic Preschool?" Polly Greenberg responds to the following inquiry from a preschool director:

> *I have looked into NAEYC's accreditation system to see whether I want to discuss getting into it with our board and staff. I see the obvious advantages. . . . Of course we seek educational excellence. We want to be the best.*

> *This is where I balk at accreditation. We believe that three- and four-year-olds can learn, and expect them to. Our parents are educated and would never put up with an inferior program where children just play. (Greenberg, 1990, p. 70)*

> *This statement summarizes the wide separation between programs advocating developmentally appropriate practices for preschool children and those stressing more formal academic learning. The first implication of the director's statement is that learning is quite narrowly cognitive, overlooking the complex learnings for preschoolers already discussed in the physical, social, and emotional domains, as well as the importance of achieving positive self-esteem and attitudes toward life experiences and learning. The second implication is that play is something rather trivial and time wasting, indeed "inferior." The crux of the matter is differences in opinion about what young children should be learning and how they should be taught. In this consideration of developmentally appropriate cognitive/language environments for preschoolers, play takes a central position as offering the most appropriate curriculum and medium for learning. This chapter will examine central issues regarding play and the teacher's role in providing optimum play experiences.*

LEARNING OBJECTIVES

After completing this chapter, students should be able to

- discuss characteristics of preoperational thinking.
- identify and describe teacher behaviors in supporting play.
- discuss what is meant by early literacy and reasons for its appropriateness in the preschool language and literacy environment.
- describe eight components of the appropriate language environment.
- discuss issues related to dual-language children.
- discuss topics related to literacy development, including large-group time, practices such as show-and-tell and calendar, and small-group time.
- identify several developmentally inappropriate teacher practices.

PREOPERATIONAL THINKING

Piaget described the thinking and cognitive functioning of children ages two to seven or so as the preoperational stage, meaning it is a time before children are able to make truly logical connections in their thinking. During this stage, "children are incapable of formulating or understanding true concepts, concepts that are reliable and stable, not in constant risk of contradiction" (Van Hoorn, Nourot, & Scales, 1998, p. 222). This is because, according to Piaget, young children reason from particular to particular rather than by understanding how particular cases relate to the whole set of possible cases (Piaget, 1969).

In actuality, Piaget defined two distinct substages within the preoperational period: one from about age two to four, when children begin to apply familiar action patterns to something outside themselves, and the next from age four to seven, when cognition becomes more sophisticated, enabling children to understand contingencies and relationships somewhat. Nevertheless, in both phases, preschoolers' preoperational thought is limited in particular ways that have implications for those wanting to understand how these children best learn.

Centration

Centration, or **unidimensional thought**, is the tendency of preoperational thinkers to focus attention on one aspect of any situation while ignoring all other aspects. Thus their concepts are limited by one outstanding appearance or perception, to the exclusion of true understanding based on considering the total picture; that is, they confuse some aspect of appearance with reality. In Piaget's classic experiment regarding **conservation**, preschoolers were unable to understand that the amount of water did not change when poured from a short, broad beaker into a taller, thinner one where the water line appeared higher, even when they had watched the pouring from the first container to the second.

The ability to decenter is needed to be able to focus on details, while still keeping the whole in mind. This, after all, is the skill required in learning to read, to perceive the individual letters as part of a word. Math operations require an understanding of transformations, which is difficult for preoperational minds. Thus, the mental characteristic of centration suggests that beginning reading and math academic work in the preschool years, as some educators do, does not match the child's developmental abilities.

Egocentrism

Egocentrism is part of the inability to center on more than one aspect of a situation at a time, according to Piaget. Thus, egocentrism causes preschoolers to interpret every event in reference to themselves and makes it impossible for them to understand others' points of view or feelings. Egocentrism causes preschoolers to engage in conversations in which they leave out vital bits of information, becoming impatient with those who do not visualize what they have in mind. Egocentrism also leads preschoolers to believe in **animism**, assuming all objects have the same lifelike characteristics they have experienced. Egocentrism is very developmentally appropriate for preschoolers. It is only through multitudes of experiences and encounters with persons and objects that preschoolers slowly become able to decenter, that is, to gain a wider understanding of their world.

Irreversibility

Irreversibility is another limitation of preoperational thinking. Preschoolers are unable to reverse their thinking to reconstruct mentally the actions that got them to the final point. This inability again contributes to centration; they can focus only on the end or beginning state, without understanding what happened in between. That child who says there is more liquid in a glass that is tall and thin than in one that is short and fat, even after she saw the contents poured from one glass to the other, is demonstrating the concept of irreversibility.

Concreteness

Concreteness is another characteristic of preoperational thought. Young children are able to understand real objects, situations, and happenings they have actually experienced firsthand, but have difficulty with abstract ideas, things beyond their personal knowledge, things they hear described in words only. This characteristic also ties them to the literal interpretation of words and phrases. Much of academic learning deals with abstractions; the numeral 5 is an abstraction until the child has had enough firsthand experiences with 5 to turn the concept into reality.

Transductive Reasoning

Reasoning in preschoolers appears faulty when compared with the reasoning of older children. This is due to the tendency to reason from particular to particular, as in "The neighbor's dog barks and jumps up on me, so all dogs bark and jump up on me." They also assume cause and effect between events closely linked in time or make connections between things that are actually quite superficial—"I got sick because I went to my grandma's house."

Symbolic Thought

Symbolic thought, or the ability to mentally represent objects, events, and actions, increases extraordinarily through the preschool period. This ability is readily seen in the increased language use that allows preschoolers to think ahead, solving problems and anticipating consequences, without having to tie these activities to action. Thus their activities become more purposeful and goal oriented. Symbolic thought is also evident in the increase in complex make-believe play. (See Figure 15-1.)

Understanding the abilities and limitations of preoperational thought has serious implications for matching learning style and ability for those planning curricula for preschoolers. Because of their facility with language (and their desire to please adults), preschoolers can be taught to repeat many of the conceptual words that some adults feel they should be taught. Many four-year-olds can count rapidly to ten or twenty, but get bogged down when asked to count while pointing to objects or to get ten napkins. And why is this? In Piaget's view, children are active in constructing their own understanding of the world about them. They can't just gain knowledge by being given information by rote learning methods or imitating others, but they bring what they already know to each new learning situation to try to make sense of new information. They take in information (assimilation) and they organize the information so it makes sense in relation to what they already understand (accommodation). As they manipulate, experience, do, interact, observe, play, and problem solve, they move to true understanding of basic concepts. "Knowing requires spontaneous action, which takes the form of play: the self-initiated recreation of one's experiences in order to understand (assimilate) them" (Jones & Reynolds, 1992, p. 4). After enough meaningful, active experiences, young children achieve for themselves a sense of "ten-ness," or whatever concept it is that adults are hurrying to teach them. And they really understand it, because they have constructed their own real knowledge of it, rather than learning by rote someone else's abstraction.

Figure 15-1

Symbolic thought is evident in complex make-believe play.

Constructivism

This **constructivist** theory lies close to the heart of developmentally appropriate practice. Constructivist theory refers to those ideas of Piaget, Vygotsky and his sociocultural constructivist theory, and the cognitive researchers who followed: that intelligence and understanding are actively created, or constructed, by the individual through interaction with elements of the environment, including objects, people, and experiences. Thus, constructivist perspectives force educators to call into question the traditional teaching-by-telling methods. Adults can tell and preschoolers can repeat back, but the learning remains superficial, not a part of the child's constructed cognitive reality.

If constructing intelligence is viewed metaphorically as building a tower of blocks, the solid base is the sensorimotor information taken in during infancy and toddlerhood and continuing during the preschool years. The next part of the structure is comprised of the blocks added during the preoperational years, as children work/play through to understandings of how that information relates together. After these basic concepts are formed, the building can proceed to learning academic skills that need the foundation of conceptual understanding. The tower stands solidly. If, however, in the rush to move children on to intellectual tasks that are meaningful and measurable for adults, the preoperational blocks are added quickly and casually or left out altogether, the tower will likely topple due to lack of the necessary underpinnings.

Understanding the characteristics of preoperational minds in defining developmentally appropriate practice leads to finding a medium for children to be able to actively construct their intelligence. That medium is play.

Through play, children actively re-create their experiences and understandings of the world, forming and linking their own concepts.

It is in this stage (the preschool years) that the child first becomes a competent representer of experience rather than simply a doer of it. Human society and thought are built on the achievement of *representation,* which makes possible both looking back and looking ahead, rather than simply living in the moment, and communication removed in both place and time, rather than simply face-to-face. The exploration of the toddler is direct encounter, not representation. But the dramatic play of four- and five-year-olds is an increasingly sophisticated representation of both real and imagined experiences. (Jones & Reynolds, 1992, p. 4)

The goal of developmentally appropriate preschool classrooms is to allow children opportunities to both construct and represent their growing understandings orally and through action by having experiences, materials, and support for their active cognitive learning through play.

TEACHERS' ROLES IN PROVIDING FOR PLAY

Although a criterion for play is that it is spontaneous and freely chosen, teachers still have specific roles in supporting, extending, and enriching play. In our world of early learning standards, teachers have the responsibility of integrating play activities within a framework of specific guidelines for content and skill acquisition. This requires a high degree of intentionality.

For children to benefit fully from play, teachers must take their own roles seriously. Early childhood educators cannot wander about the classroom operating on the vague assumption that children learn through play while, at the same time, lamenting the challenges to play coming from parents and administrators. Instead, teachers must recognize play as one of the key teaching and learning contexts in the early childhood classroom, must acquire skills themselves in research-based effective teaching strategies such as scaffolding language use during play, and must incorporate play along with more directive teaching throughout the preschool day. (Bredekamp, 2004, p. 171)

The underlying structure created by teacher decisions provides the optimum play-learning environment for particular children at a particular time. Many of the teacher roles are played behind the scenes, setting a stage for the beginning point of play and resetting it as the play unfolds and develops. Some of the roles involve more direct interaction, although even then the traditional image of the teacher as teller and dispenser of information is replaced by the teacher as facilitator, scaffolder, and guide. The roles we will consider include creator of the environment, observer-and-recorder, planner, scaffolder, model, questioner, and responder.

Creator of the Environment

In Chapter 7, we considered the decisions teachers make when physically arranging the classroom space. Here we will consider briefly the rationale for using learning centers as the primary focus of learning activity in the preschool classroom and the creation of a positive atmosphere for play.

A developmentally appropriate classroom for preschoolers recognizes that some time periods in the day need to be spent in play in learning centers. Thus, the environment is arranged into separate areas where children can choose their materials, activities, and playmates (see Figure 15-2).

The interest area approach supports active play because it provides for

- *Choices:* Enough separate play spaces are available in the room so that each child has a choice of several play options.

- *Free movement:* The need to be active is recognized by the variety of options and styles of play provided. Children decide when they will move on to another activity.

- *Range of developmental differences:* With the variety of materials provided in each center, children with different interest and attention spans can be accommodated within a learning center arrangement.

- *Facilitating play:* Because children take the dominant role in play in learning centers, teachers are free from primary instructional duties with a large group. They are then able to move about among children at play, effectively reinforcing the learning they observe or extending and stimulating discoveries on an individual basis.

These points so far show little difference from the reasons for creating active areas for exploration in toddler classrooms. Because preschoolers are now ready for more peer interaction as well as true symbolic and sociodramatic play, however, their interest centers make possible additional and more complex learnings, such as

Figure 15-2

There are enough choices in the room for each child to have several options.

Figure 15-3

There is room in the house corner for several children to play, and room in the block corner for several builders.

- *Cooperative learning:* Most interest areas provide space for several preschoolers to play together at the same time, fostering language, interaction, and social skills (see Figure 15-3). Careful environmental arrangements create opportunities for project work and increasing understandings through interactions with others whose experience and learning may be more advanced. Teachers provide for scaffolding opportunities when more-experienced children and less-experienced children play together.

- *Initiative:* Children are the active agents in an interest area arrangement. They are encouraged to plan and initiate their own activities, not merely to passively follow adult instructions. When materials are organized in predictable places, children can follow through on dynamic and developing ideas.

The core centers (those always available for play) in a classroom for preschoolers most likely include creative-arts/construction, blocks, house and pretend play, gross motor, math/manipulatives, science, language arts (reading and writing), computers, and music. Depending on space and available adults, other centers may be occasionally available, such as woodworking, cooking, and sand, water, or other sensory exploration.

Materials include blocks, books, writing materials, math-related games and manipulatives, dramatic play props, equipment for physical movement, art and modeling materials, sand and water, and tools for science investigations. (Copple & Bredekamp, 2009, p. 154)

With all these materials, the goal is to have children explore, discover, represent, and elaborate on their understandings of the world.

The decisions teachers make about physical placement of centers; about the kinds, amounts, and developmental span of materials provided; and about a schedule that offers blocks of time for play are all important in creating a rich environment that helps children get started and stay focused on play. Teachers stay alert to children's needs, abilities, and play interests, and make responsive changes in the environment. Because there are children with disabilities or various special needs in the classroom, teachers continually modify the space and materials to meet the needs of all children. Such modifications in physical arrangements and materials make it possible for all children to play and explore together, no matter what their special need. For specific modifications and strategies, see Grisham-Brown, Hemmeter, and Pretti-Frontczak (2005); Klein, Cook, and Richardson-Gibbs (2000); and Schwartz and Sandall (2002).

Figure 15-4

When teachers create an environment that makes choices clear, play is enriched.

An important role of the teacher in regard to the environment is to bring order to the surroundings to make the play possibilities clear to children (see Figure 15-4). As children play, they mess up the teacher's order, transforming it to their own conceptions. The teacher accepts this "messing up" as a right and inevitable part of play, and then re-creates the predictable order so children can again see play choices.

Factors that teachers consider in designing an environment for play include

- enough materials.
- range of different kinds of materials, of various levels and complexity.
- enough novelty and variety in materials to stimulate curiosity and interest.
- the ease of selecting and returning materials, as well as ease to keep clean.
- enough space for activity and carrying out ideas.
- ease of supervision and interaction with adults.

Perhaps the key ingredient of an environment that supports play is adult attitude. When adults convey their respect for the importance of play, they encourage children's meaningful activity; children are extremely susceptible to adult opinion and attitude.

> [An] answer . . . about what produced prolonged concentration and rich elaboration in play rather took us aback. It was the presence of an adult. I do not mean an adult "over the shoulder" of the child, trying to direct his activity, but one in the neighborhood who gave some assurance that the environment would be stable and continuous, but would also give the child reassurance and information as, if, and when the child needed it. (Bruner, 1991, p. 80)

Observer-and-Recorder

For teachers to understand how best to support children's play, they must become astute observers of children. Teachers have likely learned the general developmental characteristics of the age group with which they work. However, the individual level of development and the particular needs, interests, learning style, and preferences of each child within the group can be learned only by teachers' careful observation.

When a child is in your care, you must function as if you know who she or he is at any given moment. The danger is that you can delude yourself into thinking that in fact you do have

PRACTICAL IMPLICATIONS

Respecting Play

Adult respect for play is shown by

- showing obvious pleasure and interest in observing children at play.
- displaying relaxed playfulness in their interaction with children.
- accepting children's invitations to play occasionally and following their lead.
- protecting play from interruption, including interruption by the teacher and schedule.
- enriching their play by providing appropriate materials.
- encouraging children to talk about their play.
- recording examples of their play for later discussion and reflection.
- taking pictures of children at play to preserve special moments.
- showcasing and interpreting their play to parents and others.

Unsupportive practices related to children's play include

- supervising play indifferently.
- coming close only when intervention is necessary.
- providing only limited time for play and interrupting casually when there is something adults want to do or teach. ("Put those blocks away now, it's time for our lesson.")
- offering a cluttered, unattractive environment, with toys and materials that are in disrepair or unchanged over time.
- busying themselves with housekeeping tasks or preparing materials for teacher lessons during children's playtime.
- speaking of play in ways that belittle its importance and try to impress parents with the "real" learning offered instead. ("We don't spend much time 'just' playing; we have set lesson plans and follow XYZ curriculum.")

that knowledge. You can reduce this danger by regularly observing and recording behavior, whether or not it fits your preconceptions. (Clemens, 1983, p. 100)

Observing children at play allows teachers to practice taking the child's perspective and to ask themselves key questions. What is happening for the child in the play; what is the child's agenda? Does the child have the skills and materials needed to accomplish the intent? And finally, how can the teacher support and extend this play, to help meet both the child's and teacher's goals?

Observing is the only way to make appropriate decisions for curriculum and materials, based on what is noted about each child's special interests and developmental progress, and on the goals on which teachers are focused. Therefore, as discussed in Chapter 3, observing is a cyclical activity; teachers observe children's play initially to assess individual needs, strengths, and interests. They then provide materials and activities they feel will challenge and support children's play and learning. The observations of subsequent play help teachers assess the effectiveness of their plans, continue to plan next steps for curriculum, and so on.

Observing is possible because of the learning center approach to classroom learning. Teachers are free to take specific times to observe and record information because children are initiating their own learning. Teachers who realize the crucial importance of observing for planning individually appropriate experiences make observation a priority, not just something they "never have time for."

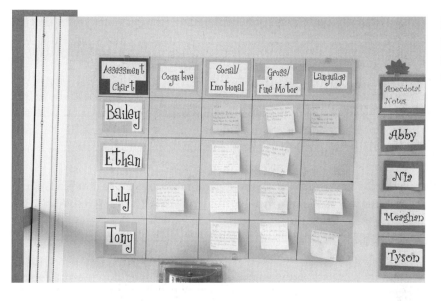

Figure 15-5

Teachers find methods to be sure observations are made in all domains for all children, regularly.

Teachers need to develop skills for observing and recording information in usable forms. The key questions for teachers in focusing observations are:

1. What do I want to find out?

2. When and where should I observe to get the information I need?

3. How do I record what I observe?

4. How do I organize the information I collect? (Jablon, Dombro, & Dichtelmiller, 2007)

5. They work on

   • strategies to support observing, such as designating times, keeping pencil and paper handy, and using checklists to be sure no child or aspect of development is being overlooked (see Figure 15-5).

   • setting particular goals and defining tasks for observation, such as making notes on three children each playtime or observing different ways the children explore the water-and-bubbles activity. They know this will help keep them focused on observing.

   • planning in advance for which aspects of developmental progress will be done on a particular day, such as observing language development on Antonio, Michelle, and Rose on Monday, and the skipping skills of all the boys during outdoor playtime.

   • planning particular times of each day that will be used for observation, including writing lesson plans.

   • recording objective, nonjudgmental facts, concentrating on describing what happened and what was said and communicated nonverbally, without using words that express subjective opinion. This practice gives enough description and fact that teachers can return to written documentation over time, without losing the incident in their memory.

Teachers can learn about children by

• observing over time.

• watching children in varied situations, such as different social settings, different times of day.

• watching them with family members.

• asking questions that help children describe their thinking.

• noticing them play and work with materials and other children.

• talking with children about what they are doing or making.

• listening as they talk with others.

• studying children's work.

• observing while participating in the action.

• reflecting on the action afterward and making notes.

(Ideas adapted from Jablon, Dombro, & Dichtelmiller, 2007)

- finding methods for recording that work well, including making brief notes on: a sheet of mailing labels that can be peeled off and placed in an individual child's section in a notebook: index cards attached to a file folder; daily logs; grids, tallies, and rating scales. See more ideas for making and organizing notes in Chapter 3.

- including relevant information, such as date, time, and place of observation, and other children involved. This allows teachers to organize the records in notebooks or file boxes and to provide information over the years as children change and develop. (See Chapter 16 for a discussion of developing portfolios.) Observing without meaningful recording is less valuable.

- using their observations to make tentative assessments and formulate goals and plans for individual children. Teachers will read back through previous observations to search for growth and patterns and to ensure that the whole child is being noticed.

Carefully recorded observations are valuable for reasons beyond planning appropriate curriculum and assessing children's play. As teachers focus on observing the whole child, not just those aspects that are most disturbing, they see strengths and learn to appreciate children more. The question moves beyond the management question of "What can I do about him?" to more child-centered questions such as "What interests him? What issues is he dealing with? What does he know? What might he learn next?" (Jones & Reynolds, 1992, p. 74). Observed patterns of behavior may help children who need more specialized assessments and assistance. Observations are also valuable for sharing information with parents and other staff members. Observations should form the basis of decisions that parents and teachers share about appropriate next steps for the children. Ongoing observation is a much more accurate method of assessing children's developmental levels than any test. (See the discussion on assessment and testing in Chapter 16.) Observing children's progress and achievement helps evaluate the program's effectiveness and assists teachers in setting professional goals for themselves.

In general, observing and recording seems to be one of the most neglected teacher roles. When teachers take on dominant and central roles in the classroom, they naturally have insufficient free time for such activities. After teachers learn to adopt roles that are more supportive of children's self-initiated play, time for observing and recording becomes available (see Figure 15-6). Through these observations, teachers learn how to interact more appropriately to support productive play. Challenge yourself to think more about observing as you explore the books *The Art of Awareness: How Observation Can Transform Your Teaching* (Curtis & Carter, 2000) and *The Power of Observation* (Jablon, Dombro, & Dichtelmiller, 2007).

Figure 15-6

Teachers learn to observe while children are busy at their play.

Planner

In Chapter 3, we explored teacher responsibilities in planning curriculum for developmentally appropriate learning experiences. The spontaneous play of preschoolers and teacher planning do go together, although the concepts may sound contradictory. In this context, the planning comes from teacher observations in the context of their classroom environments and their involvement and facilitation of children's play. In their efforts to support children's next steps, teachers plan materials and experiences designed to start where children are and to take them in the direction of next learnings and interests. Teacher planning is not, however, based on narrowly defined objectives of "what children will learn," but rather on understandings of broad goals for preschool children, knowing children will find their own curriculum within the contexts offered.

How do we make the curriculum of play more specific in its answers to the question "What can and should young children learn?" Catherine Landreth, in a classic book about preschool learning and teaching, outlines seventeen different sequences of learning in from-to progressions, along with materials, activities of interest, and learning checklists for each area of learning (Landreth, 1972) (see Figure 15-7).

The list makes it obvious that teachers are helping children move from simple levels of understanding and acting to more complex levels, and from general ways of acting on the world to more specific ones. As discussed in Chapters 2 and 3, the early learning standards enunciated by individual states give specific objectives and benchmarks for learning to guide teacher planning. The Developmental Continuum that is part of the goals and objectives developed in the Creative Curriculum (Dodge, Colker, & Heroman, 2002) offers guidelines for specific progressions in the various developmental domains, noting specific forerunner behaviors, as well as three levels of behaviors that indicate growth and learning in fifty specific areas. The Head Start Performance Standards provide broad guidelines for curriculum decisions, emphasizing literacy and numeracy, communication, gross and fine motor skills, as well as social and emotional foundations. High/Scope offers ten categories of key experiences that include concepts based on Piaget's summary of thinking about the cognitive characteristics and learning potential of preschoolers. The concepts emphasized in the key experiences include use of sensory and manipulative materials for representation, use of language, initiation and social relations, opportunities for classification and seriation, opportunities to explore number concepts and spatial relationships, and understanding of time. See more about this in the discussion of the High/Scope approach in Chapter 4. All these guidelines for curriculum goals help teachers make their planning decisions.

From-To Progressions in Seventeen Related Areas of Early Learning

- From sensing to sorting to symbolizing
- From spontaneous to controlled, coordinated, self-directed, and imitative movement
- From babbling to language
- From decoding graphic symbols to reading
- From scribbling to writing
- From experiencing to processing information
- From magic to natural phenomena
- From birds and berries to organism and to systems
- From lines, daubs, and smears to pictures
- From making things to using simple tools and developing handicraft skills
- From bouncing to dancing
- From lalling to singing
- From hearing music to listening to it
- From awareness of others to getting along with them
- From being taken care of to taking care of himself
- From home and center to community
- From "me" to "who am I?"

Figure 15-7

Seventeen sequences of preschool learning. Adapted from *Preschool Teaching and Learning*, Catherine Landreth (1972).

WHAT would you DO when ...

"My director insists that the children in my classroom have some artwork to take home each day, and that it be related to the theme we've been studying. A lot of the children frequently aren't interested in doing the art, and I usually end up having to virtually force them, doing most of it myself." What would you do in this situation?

This may be one of the most common issues facing teachers in preschool classrooms. The director and parents most likely want measurable proof that something has been accomplished each day, implying that "just play" isn't productive enough. Frequently, art that is specifically related to a theme is more of a crafted product made to match teacher specifications or models than a creative experience in which children select materials and create whatever they want. The lack of opportunity to initiate is one of several reasons this practice needs to be considered developmentally inappropriate for preschoolers. The frustration involved in working to someone else's standards, the infringement on spontaneous choice, and the intrusion of teacher plans into children's tasks are also negatives. The school's message to parents, who can usually figure out that these products are made with teacher instruction, is that teacher-dominated learning is the most valuable experience they can offer children.

Adults need to realize that creativity comes in many forms, more than just using art materials and making pictures. In all areas of the classroom, children are able to express themselves and their original thinking whether in their pretend play, the way they use math manipulative materials, their building-block creations, or the way they work with play dough, sand, or water.

This is such a large issue that it deserves some thorough discussion among staff. The real crux of the matter seems to be how to show parents that children are truly learning through play that is creative and expressive in personal ways. As staff direct their creative energies to helping parents understand and appreciate the value of play and all kinds of creativity, they can leave children free to create their own work. Newsletters, accounts of daily activities, pictures, display panels, anecdotes, parent visits and observation, workshops and reading for parents—there are many ways to get across to parents that real learning is happening without mass-producing unwillingly made art products.

What children need to learn is the knowledge of the world that surrounds them in particular geographical and cultural contexts living with particular families who have particular ideas about what is important for their children. In addition, the state standards provide a specific framework for making curriculum decisions. Such broad and individual understandings help teachers plan appropriate classroom experiences for preschoolers.

Teachers' ways of thinking about curriculum influence the kind of planning they do. A useful construct is found in Scoy's (1995) curriculum model, providing for the Four E's: Experience, Extension, Expression, and Evaluation. Such planning considers the need for hands-on, active learning in real experiences; for activities that allow children to revisit and reconstruct understandings; for opportunities for children to communicate their learnings as they can; and for teachers to consider the progress made and the next steps for which to plan.

The most important caution for teachers planning for preschoolers is not to become so caught up in their own plans and ideas that they are unable to let go in favor of the children's responses. Good planning should allow for well-thought-out starting points for children's play; good teaching means modifying or even discarding plans as teachers continue to observe children's play. Good planning requires teachers to stand back and ask what they have found out as they have watched children's interactions with materials and activities. This thoughtful consideration inevitably leads to the next plans. "Through this process the curriculum keeps emerging and the teacher, together with the children, keeps learning" (Jones & Reynolds, 1992, p. 105).

Scaffolder

As teachers understand the complexity of children's play and participation in the classroom, they become aware that children have a variety of skills and levels of ability in their play. Life experiences, communication abilities, social ease, cultural diversity, disabilities or limitations, and

Figure 15-8
There is no reason for an adult to intervene in this productive play scene.

intellectual competence make for wide variations. The adults' understanding of "scaffolding" behaviors that may facilitate play and learning is important in helping them find ways and times of intervening in play that allow children to reach new levels of competency as players. Because adult intervention can sometimes be disruptive to play, valuable learning opportunities can be lost if adults do not learn to play appropriately with children and to participate in ways that extend, rather than control or interrupt, play (see Figure 15-8).

What are some of the reasons for adults to participate in children's play? One reason is to increase children's involvement with peers or with play materials. Adults can help children increase their social skills and play abilities by the support of their presence and by demonstrating and guiding children to new levels of play (Smilansky, 1968).

Another time to enter play is when the play shows evidence of beginning to break down. Teachers may play a subtle role of introducing new ideas or materials, helping the children clarify or organize their thinking, or changing the mood.

Another reason is to guide play to more complex levels, resulting in greater social and cognitive development. When teachers observe that play seems to be "stuck" on simple, repetitive levels, adult comments or questions may enrich the play. As teachers closely observe the play, they find the appropriate "teachable moments" that might develop thinking and communication.

Still another reason for adults to play with children is to accept their invitations, at least some of the time. Playing with children is yet another way of enhancing adult-child relationships and making personal contact. Teachers often learn about children as they reveal themselves through play. "Deciding whether or not to participate in children's play requires thought about children's need for challenge, their skills in sustaining play, and one's own preferred teaching style" (Jones & Reynolds, 1992, p. 35).

Just as there are reasons to enter play, so too there are times when teacher intervention can be harmful. When children are playing in organized, thoughtful, and cooperative ways with peers, there is likely no need for teachers to become involved—even if they see a golden opportunity to teach cognitive concepts. When it becomes evident that children are depending too heavily on adult presence to sustain their play, as when play breaks down whenever the adult leaves, the adult may be playing too dominant a role. Sometimes children make it very clear when adults are becoming an unwelcome presence. Elizabeth Jones tells the story of a teacher who was "overfacilitating" a grocery store play episode, interrupting frequently with questions

To be an excellent teacher means:

- being intentional.
- creating a caring community of learners.
- teaching to enhance development and learning.
- planning curriculum to achieve important goals.
- assessing children's development and learning.
- establishing reciprocal relationships with families.

like "Where do you get all the food you sell in your store?" and "Are you going to charge more for your eggs or for your milk?" Finally, the weary shopkeeper asked, "Could you please go help somebody else play?" Teachers must guard against this kind of intrusive and unnecessary involvement in play.

Being an effective facilitator or scaffolder depends on teachers becoming sensitive to times when their intervention in play will extend and support the play and other times when their participation will be disruptive. The strategies they use will depend on their sensitivity to the play situation and their assessment of how much support is needed at a particular time. Common strategies include modeling play techniques, questioning, and responding to children's comments and interests.

Model

The teacher as model takes the role of a player. Although children's play is self-initiated, teachers sometimes enter into the play. Their purpose is to support the play by subtly introducing ideas and information. This information is not given by telling, but by showing, **modeling**, and conversing. Teachers are most likely to play the role of model with younger preschoolers or those less experienced in play. When children are short on ideas, teachers may enrich their thinking.

Teacher:	(entering the housekeeping area) Good morning, I was passing by and wondered if you were home so I could visit? (Katie and Rachel have been silently manipulating dishes up to this point.)
Katie:	Yes, you can. Sit there.
Teacher:	Thank you. Is it almost lunch time?
Rachel:	(bringing over a dish and handing it to teacher): Yes, here's your lunch.
Teacher:	Oh, it looks great, what have you cooked for me? (pretending to eat)
Katie:	It's pizza.
Rachel:	With mushrooms.
Teacher:	Mmm. Are you going to eat too? (Both girls sit down.)
Teacher:	(after a minute or two) Would your little girl like some pizza too? (pointing to the baby doll)

As the lunch scene unfolds, the teacher takes his leave, promising to come again. When he leaves, the children are busy feeding a couple of babies and chatting together. Teachers not only may model role behavior *for* children, they may model *with* young players.

The same teacher later notices Pia observing the play in the housekeeping area. He approaches and asks if she'll accompany him as he delivers a package to the household.

Teacher:	Let's knock on the door and tell them the delivery man has a package for them.
Pia:	Okay. (He hands her the package.)
Teacher:	Here we are. Knock loud and tell them their package is here.
Pia:	(knocks and says) Your package is here. (The children take the package from her.)
Pia:	I've got another one. I'll go get it.

By involving themselves, teachers can help children understand the roles and possible strategies for play. They can also help sustain play by responding to the children's ideas.

> *Katie:* Hey, Tom, come and see us all dressed up.
>
> *Teacher:* Wow, you look as if you're going someplace special.
>
> *Rachel:* We are, we're going to New York.
>
> *Teacher:* Hmm, that's a long way. Who's going to look after your house while you're gone?
>
> *Katie:* (looking around) Hey Pia, want to look after our house? We're going to New York.
>
> *Rachel:* Yeah, and when we come back we'll bring you presents.
>
> *Pia:* (happily) Okay, I'll clean it up while you're gone.

The adult as model also enters the play to model problem solving as a way to sustain play: Rachel and Katie begin to argue over who will drive the train to New York.

> *Teacher:* (pulling a chair over to their area) I hope this train for New York is going to leave soon. Nobody's even taken my ticket yet. And I've got a round-trip ticket, because I'm coming back later. What this train needs is a ticket taker. (Rachel and Katie look at each other.)
>
> *Katie:* You can be the ticket taker.
>
> *Rachel:* Okay, and then you can be when we come back.

This role of teacher as model is quite different from that of an intrusive adult who tells children what to do, or redirects children to other activity when they squabble This is not an adult who takes over and directs the play or becomes so involved that children become an audience to the adult's sophisticated performance. This adult only introduces ideas or questions that children can develop from their own experience.

The teacher as model also enters play as an interested and supportive adult, not one following his own agenda. The model role is played briefly, as teachers move in and out of the play. Always as adults move in, they pick up on the play script the children have already developed, moving into a role that builds on what children are already doing. And when the adult leaves the play, advance work has already prepared the children to continue the suggested roles.

Wolfgang (1977) formulated a Teacher Behavior Continuum that moves from the most teacher interaction behaviors to the least, depending on children's abilities to sustain their productive play (see Figure 15-9). As teachers perceive that children need their assistance and responses less and less, they become less actively involved in the play.

Questioner

As teachers move back and forth on the continuum of teacher behaviors, finding the best strategies to help children reach new levels of competence, they frequently adopt the role of questioner. By this, we don't mean that the teacher is tester, throwing out pop quiz–type questions as a

Figure 15-9

A continuum of adult behaviors in play. Adapted from Wolfgang (1977).

	Open Teacher Behavior						Structured Teacher Behavior

Show interest in play. Unobtrusive observation, e.g., sitting near dramatic play area.	Offer occasional non-directive suggestions or supplying of props, e.g., "What's the family going to do after dinner?" or "Maybe the baby's getting tired."	Model play behavior by enacting roles **with** children, e.g., (briefly) "Let's get ready for our trip. Here's a suitcase for you, too."	Model play behavior **for** children, demonstrating particular pretend behaviors, e.g., "I'm going to drink some juice. Mmm. that's good. I'll pour you some and you can drink, too."

dominant form of interaction—"What color is that piece? How many blocks do you have there? Which one is the biggest? What is this shape called?" Such convergent, or closed, questions, designed to test children's concepts and learning, require specific answers, which are either correct or incorrect. They are basically low-level questions, demanding simple recall of facts, not extending or challenging further cognitive development. One study found that more than 50 percent of adult verbal interactions with young children comprised adult questions such as these or questions that offered alternatives—"Do you want apple or orange juice?" As teachers learn to ask better questions, such questions can scaffold to more mature cognitive understandings for children. As teachers pose questions, they also increase their understanding of children's thinking processes and construction of knowledge (see Figure 15-10).

Learning to ask good questions that really cause children to analyze experiences, synthesize and communicate their understandings, and evaluate and deepen understandings is an important skill. Good questions are generally open-ended and divergent, able to be answered with any number of responses. Often such questions are referred to as "wh" questions, including "what, who, when, where, why, and how" question forms . Good questions are those that adults are genuinely interested in and do not already know the answers to, as they do to all those "pop-quiz" questions. Good questions cause children to question too, instead of just focusing on giving the teacher the correct answer. Good questions also have the potential to lead to more challenging questions.

Good questions help a child focus on his actions, reconsidering the ideas and inherent learning about causes.

"Well, how *did* you make those pieces stick on top of each other?"

"What did you do to make that loud sound?"

Figure 15-10

Teachers who ask good questions may challenge children to think more deeply.

Good questions may help a child verbalize what he has been noticing with his senses or activity.

"How does that stone feel to you?"

"What does that taste like?"

Good questions may cause children to consider alternatives.

"What is another way you could make a sound with your body?"

"How can you both play with the tricycle at the same time?"

Good questions may cause children to mentally reconstruct previous experiences and learnings.

"What did we add to the play dough that we made yesterday?"

"What were some of the seeds we planted in our garden?"

Good questions may offer challenges to further exploration or extension of the activity.

"Hmm. I wonder what would happen if you added more water to that mixture?"

"What else could help you reach that high?"

Good questions may require children to distance themselves in time and space from their present actions, making mental representations and connections between experiences and learnings.

"What else have you seen that flies like that?"

"When will you be able to visit your grandma again?"

Good questions may encourage children to put "objects, events, and actions into all kinds of relationships" (Kamii, 1982, p. 28).

"How are those two flowers alike? How are they different?"

"When were you able to use hot water? When else?"

Good questions may create discrepancies for children between what they see and what they already know. Resolving the discrepancy causes children to reconstruct their understandings of the world.

"Why does this very little stone sink and this big piece of cork float?"

"Why aren't those flowers both the same size, since they're growing in the same pot?"

Good questions may also be used to respond to children's own questions. Before teachers determine what kind of answer to give children or whether an answer is, in fact, needed, they may ask questions themselves.

Child:	"What is this?" holding up an odd-shaped magnet.
Teacher:	"What do you think it could be?"
Child:	"I think it's one of those sticky things."
Teacher:	"Do you know what that's called, when things stick to it?"
Child:	"No."
Teacher:	"It's called a magnet. What can you find that sticks to it?"

When teachers respond to children's questions with the information that is actually needed, they support children's cognitive growth appropriately, helping them move on within their zone

▶❚❚ VIDEO ACTIVITY

Go to the premium Web site and watch the video clip for Chapter 15 titled "Scaffolding Language and Thinking." Then consider the following questions:

REFLECTIVE QUESTIONS

1. What kind of questions is this adult using?

2. What kinds of thinking and responses from the child do these questions elicit?

3. Can you formulate at least three other kinds of questions that would lead to the thinking suggested in this chapter under the section Teacher as Questioner?

Visit the premium Web site to complete these questions online and email them to your professor.

of proximal development (ZPD). Their own questions help teachers determine where children are in their understandings, so they can support them most appropriately. Teachers use questions to understand children's mistakes or levels in thinking.

"How did you figure that out?"

"Why do you think that?"

Such questions often help adults understand best how to structure the next learning experience to scaffold children's cognitive growth. Good questions require that teachers listen to, and reflect on, the answers in order to be effective.

Responder

As teachers move and observe children at their play, they see opportunities to reinforce and enrich children's learning experiences. In the role of responder, they individualize their perception of what would help children build on their learning. Sometimes a response is an appreciative comment that acknowledges or puts into specific words what children have been doing and discovering (see Figure 15-11).

"The colors you used in your painting are very bright. It makes me feel like I'm wide-awake!"

"Hmm. I see some very smooth clay. Looks like you pressed very firmly when you rolled it out."

Sometimes a response is support in the form of information, hints, assistance, and encouragement as a child struggles with a difficult challenge.

"That is a hard puzzle. I think you can do it. Take another look at the picture you're making. He's got one foot—where's the other?"

"I'll show you something that might help. If you use this hand to hold the paper tightly, it might work better."

Figure 15-11

A response may be an appreciative comment about a child's efforts.

Sometimes a response is a suggestion or addition of more materials that could extend the play or add challenges.

"I wonder if you might like to find a friend who could help you work on balancing the scales."

Sometimes a response is some direct instruction or demonstration of skills that would help a child succeed at a task.

"Let me show you a good way to hold that stapler."

Sometimes a response is simply being available with focused interest to help children sustain their own activity and interest because they perceive that the adult values their involvement (see Figure 15-12).

> The teacher sits near a group of children working at the water table. From time to time, she comments on the activity. Mostly she watches and listens attentively. Her body language indicates attentive appreciation.

All such strategies may come under the heading of *scaffolding*, the term that means supporting children to move to more sophisticated behavior than they would be capable of without adult additions and assistance. Notice that all possible responses are focused on follow-up to what children are presently doing. This is true responsiveness, not adults assuming the dominant role. Responses are open-ended and tentative, so that children may easily decide to disregard them in favor of their own initiative. Recall the different teacher strategies in Wolfgang's continuum.

"Would this be helpful for your grocery store?"— said while offering a new prop.

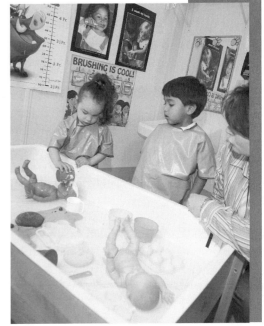

Figure 15-12

The adult is available, with focused interest, to help children sustain their activity.

LANGUAGE/LITERACY ENVIRONMENTS

Learning to understand the world and other people, and to represent that learning, involves language. Language is an inseparable part of the play and learning of the preschool classroom. By the age of three, children have accomplished amazing feats in language. They probably have a spoken (expressive) vocabulary of nine hundred to one thousand words and an understood (receptive) vocabulary of several hundred more. Adding about fifty words a month, most children's vocabulary reaches eight thousand to fourteen thousand words by age six. Sentence length increases, as does increasingly complex sentence structure. They are speaking in sentences that follow the grammar rules of their language, and they have mastered complexities, such as plurals and past tenses, with occasional tendencies to overgeneralize their understandings of grammar rules into such constructions as "feets" and "wented." They have generally learned to control the rhythm and **fluency** of their speech, with occasional nonfluency. They can usually pronounce words clearly enough that a stranger can understand about 75 percent of their utterances, and they are good at understanding much of what is said to them. What is evident, however, in listening to any group of three-, four-, and five-year-old children, is the wide variation in children's language development. Linguistic, cultural and social backgrounds, family communication patterns, and individual experiences all affect children's abilities to express themselves in language. Considering that they

PRACTICAL IMPLICATIONS

Ineffective Teaching Practices for Preschool

Developmentally appropriate and effective preschool teachers avoid:

- relying heavily on teaching as telling, and on questioning children just to see if they remember what they have been taught.
- directly correcting children's errors or misunderstandings.
- controlling all decisions about planning and learning.
- using static lesson plans or prepackaged curricula.
- substituting secondhand learning experiences, such as pictures, videos, or lectures, for firsthand experiences.

first produced sounds with meaning to them only roughly two years earlier, this is a remarkable accomplishment. With bilingual children, the feat is even more astounding, as they attempt to mentally separate two separate dictionaries. How did they achieve so much in such a short time? The answer is without specific lessons or drills in language tutoring, but with opportunities to speak and hear others speak; with no pressure, but a lot of time to experiment and experience.

Today, speaking and listening are considered related to language and literacy development, along with reading and writing. In past decades, these skills were thought to develop in sequence. Now, thanks to theorists, researchers, and practitioners who speak in terms of language and early literacy, the belief is that learning the various aspects of oral and written language is a continual process that takes place at the same time and from birth.

The philosophy of emergent literacy does not rely on the skill work sheet and direct-instruction approach that is indeed removed from the developmentally appropriate active-learning style of the preschool. Individual components of literacy need to be considered as preschool teachers plan experiences that lay foundations for literacy.

In this section, we will define early literacy and describe practices in the preschool environment that facilitate developing all language and literacy skills.

Early Literacy

Early literacy describes laying the foundations for literacy learning in preschool (see Figure 15-13). The set of ideas about how children learn to read, write, and understand written language is based on theory, research, and practice (Baker, Fernandez-Fein, Scher, & Williams, 1998; Campbell, 1998; National Early Literacy Panel, 2004). The basic idea is that children are motivated to find ways to represent their experiences both through play and action and through communication. Children need tools for thinking and communicating. Children learn that communication meets their needs, brings pleasure and friendship, and helps them understand their culture. As they are exposed to the literacy of adults at home and in the classroom, they discover that oral and written language are related and that print is another form of communication. Reading and writing are then viewed as part of a larger system for accomplishing their goals. In the same ways that children play to construct their own concepts about the world, so their active engagement with print helps them construct an understanding of how written language works. This awareness and motivation, along with adults providing meaningful literacy materials, activities, and support, combine to develop what is called early literacy (Dickinson & Tabors, 2001; Morrow, 2001). There is no beginning point at which children are asked to study language arts in the classroom

Figure 15-13

The foundations for literacy are developing in the preschool years.

and no separate time when literacy is specifically taught. Instead, the children use language continually, experience how print-language functions, and gradually move themselves into print-media experiences. A continuity exists between all language experiences, from birth through the primary years, not a discontinuity of "now it's time to learn to read."

The changed expectations about what children should know and be able to do before entering kindergarten have increased pressures on literacy learning in the preschool. The entire Good Start/Grow Smart Initiative, with all the early learning standards developed by the states, as well as the Head Start Performance Standards, include specifics on literacy skills and knowledge. This is no excuse for incorporating inappropriate academic methods into preschool classrooms, however. Instead, preschool teachers need a thorough understanding of the components of literacy and the appropriate activities and experiences that will allow them to support children in gradually acquiring literacy knowledge. The early literacy approach recognizes the need to offer children abundant experiences to help them develop the various components of literacy. Some of the traditional ways preschool and elementary children have been introduced to reading and writing are conspicuously absent. No clear-cut division exists between reading and writing lessons, with reading being mastered before writing is approached; no learning the isolated skills, such as letter-sound drills or printing a row of "h" that might later lead to understanding the "whole" of how to read or write; no work sheets; no alphabet letter of the week being drilled; no required practice of name writing; and no rote counting to one hundred. Teachers use enjoyable texts of children's literature to introduce children to meaningful print and then continue to use print as it functions in many ways in daily life. Reading and writing are important parts of daily activity, and equally as important are the other play materials and experiences that bring children into dialogue and interaction with others. Oral language proficiency is seen as related to growth in interest in reading and writing, but is not a prerequisite; written and oral communication continue to develop in an interrelated manner. Parents and teachers have a key role in encouraging spoken communication and in fostering pleasurable adult-child interaction related to print; they model literacy and its functions. It has long been recognized that children who come from homes in which communication and literacy are valued and demonstrated move more easily into school reading and writing. The early literacy approach brings practices of literate families into the school, recognizing the developmental appropriateness of encouraging children's active participation in literacy activities. Literacy develops as a social and cultural process (Gaffney, Ostrosky, & Hemmeter, 2008). It is important to distinguish between academic content and academic methods in curriculum.

HEAD START MANDATES FOR LEARNING

Congress has mandated that Head Start implement standards of learning in early literacy, language, and numeracy skills in order to:

- develop phonemic, print, and numeracy awareness.
- understand and use language to communicate for various purposes.
- understand and use increasingly complex and varied vocabulary.
- develop and demonstrate an appreciation of books.
- progress toward acquisition of English language (in the case of non-English-background children).
- know that the letters of the alphabet are a special category of visual graphics that can be individually used.
- recognize that words are units of print.
- identify at least ten letters of the alphabet.
- associate sounds with written words.

Successful readers and writers:

- have phonological awareness (can hear and distinguish individual sounds and can rhyme).
- understand the alphabetic principle and have letter-name knowledge.
- have good vocabularies, showing the ability to use words to express themselves.
- have good fluency.
- can comprehend what they read.
- have the interest and motivation to read for a variety of purposes.

Adapted from Jacobs, G., & Crowley, K. (2007). *Play, projects and preschool standards: Nurturing children's sense of wonder.* Thousand Oaks, CA: Corwin Press.

Components of Literacy. Seven components of literacy are generally recognized as important foundations: acquiring vocabulary and language, acquiring **phonological awareness**, having a

Figure 15-14

All the good classroom talk helps children expand their vocabularies.

knowledge of print, having a knowledge of letters and words, comprehending meaning, having an awareness of books and other texts, and seeing literacy as a source of enjoyment (Heroman & Jones, 2004).

Vocabulary and Language. Written language requires rich vocabulary and an understanding of the rules of speech. As children learn to read, they use their listening and speaking vocabularies to make sense of printed words. Most vocabulary is learned through everyday experiences and conversations. Researchers find that the majority of reading problems can be prevented by increasing children's oral language skills (see Figure 15-14).

Phonological Awareness. Phonological awareness includes a continuum of skills in hearing and understanding the different patterns of spoken language. Children begin with listening to the sounds in the environment. This is followed by learning the skills of rhyming (recognizing the sounds in the ending of words) and alliteration (hearing similar initial sounds). A later skill is learning to hear the separate syllables in words. The most complex skill in the continuum of phonological awareness is being able to focus on the phoneme, the smallest unit of sound. Phonological awareness is promoted with the classroom use of songs, stories, rhythm, rhymes, and nonsense language games (Yopp & Yopp, 2009).

Knowledge of Print. Knowledge of print describes all the ideas related to how print is organized and used. This includes understanding the functions of print, including all the purposeful ways in which print can be used. It also includes understanding the various forms of print and the distinct appearance of specific letters and words. Children also have to learn that there are conventions of print, rules that govern the appearance of writing to convey meaning to others. Exposure to print in the environment is the way that children learn about print.

Knowledge of Letters and Words. Children who learn to read have to understand that letters are symbols representing a sound in the language, that symbols are grouped together to form words, and that words have meaning. Far more than learning to recite the ABCs or recognizing letters, this understanding allows children to match spoken to written words. The concept that written letters correspond to spoken words is called the alphabetic principle. Children develop this as they learn to recognize and then print their names, as they look at alphabet books, and as they explore the sensory attributes of magnetic or foam alphabet letters (see Figure 15-15).

Comprehension of Meaning. Comprehension involves understanding the meaning of both spoken and written language. Children's background knowledge helps them understand the meaning of

(a)

Figure 15-15 (a & b)

These boys are both exploring letters.

(b)

the language. The more firsthand experiences that children have, the more they increase their understanding of the world. Later, as they encounter the words in print, they have the memory of sensory information to enhance their understanding. Dramatic play and story retelling are other ways that children increase their comprehension of language. Teacher questions help children connect new information to ideas they already understand (see Figure 15-16).

Awareness of Books and Other Texts. Because children have books in their environments and are read aloud to, they discover the many purposes of written language. They develop knowledge about books and the mechanics of their use, and discover that there are conventions to the story structure— "Once Upon a Time."

Seeing Literacy as a Source of Pleasure. Children who have had abundant pleasurable experiences with books are highly motivated to learn to read for themselves. When activities involving books include fun, play, and positive relationships with adults, children develop positive attitudes toward reading and writing. When adults enjoy reading to children, their pleasure is communicated to children.

It should be clear that these components of literacy are a part of all the activities and interactions that occur throughout the day in good preschool classrooms. Now let us consider specific aspects of any developmentally appropriate literacy environment for preschool children: conversation, acceptance, experience, and children's literature.

Conversation. Adults recognize the importance of direct conversation in giving children experience with oral communication and thought (Jalongo, 2008; Kalmar, 2008). The learning center approach to instruction encourages conversations among children at play. Teachers are

Figure 15-16

Dramatic play helps children increase their comprehension of language.

also free to have individual conversations with children. Teachers recognize that conversations give children unpressured opportunities to formulate and communicate their thoughts, to learn how to listen, and to learn how to respond to others. In their conversation, teachers ask questions that encourage children to think and use additional language and that pick up on topics of interest to children (Burman, 2008). Adults foster communication by listening attentively. They use every opportunity—mealtimes, transitions, playtimes—for personal conversation. Materials in the classroom encourage conversation; there is always something new and interesting to discuss, as well as telephones and tape recorders. Adults value and encourage conversations among children, recognizing that more skillful speakers can scaffold the less-experienced speakers. As discussed in Chapter 7, space is arranged to encourage conversation and social interaction during play and work times.

Working with English-Language-Learning Children

Teachers take particular opportunities to talk to quiet or bilingual children who may need more encouragement to communicate, making it a priority to engage English-language learners in meaningful ways. They recognize that children who speak and understand oral language well have some basic knowledge that will lead naturally to print media. Silence is not valued in appropriate preschool settings (see Figure 15-17).

Teachers who are working with English-language learners need to understand the importance of the strong base in their first language. When English is a second language, children need to be able to express themselves in their primary language first. Teachers gather books and tapes/CDs in each child's language, and involve family members and others who speak the home language in the program. As teachers help children acquire proficiency in English, they encourage their families and others who speak in the child's first language to support their conversational skills. Teachers need to recognize that in the stages of learning a second language, the first stage is a quiet stage, when children will not speak. Activities that allow participation without having to speak, such as table toys, blocks, and puzzles, are helpful. Their home language should be encouraged at school with other children and adults. Ultimately, they will learn to speak in both the

Figure 15-17

Teachers take particular opportunities to talk to quiet or bilingual children who may need more encouragement to communicate.

Figure 15-18

Teachers encourage English-speaking children to play with English-language learners, as well as encouraging play with children who speak the child's home language.

primary language and English. Teachers may need to reassure parents who are anxious that their children learn English that using their home language well first is a priority.

As children learn, teachers keep language simple, and combine nonverbal communication with speech. Cues such as gestures, pointing, and pictures help children learn what the words mean. Adults allow plenty of time for young English-language learners to respond, and do not force talking until children feel comfortable and willing. They also encourage English-speaking children to help and play with English-language learners, as well as encouraging play with children who speak the child's second language (Espiritu, Meier, Villazana-Price, & Wong, 2002) (see Figure 15-18).

Adults recognize that overt correction or judgment of oral or written communication may discourage children from making further attempts. Controlling, directive language usually hinders language development. One difference that research has found in the speech of parents to their speech-delayed children is their approval and disapproval of their children's speech. While accepting of children's current level of speech, adults themselves are careful to speak with the best model of grammar and pronunciation they can, knowing children will speak as do their best models. Adults do not allow children's efforts to be mocked or belittled. They accept the added challenge of children who come to school with a primary language or dialect that is not standard English. They realize that linguistic ability in another language is a positive factor in cognitive development, rather than perceiving the child as less capable, less intelligent, or even educationally delayed. Recognizing that the child's language is part of who he or she is, adults try to have children hear words that are familiar. They display a few words in each child's language and incorporate the home language in daily classroom activities, such as in counting or songs. They use predictable books that allow English-language learners to join in repeating key phrases.

Teachers use questions and interest to understand and clarify what children are attempting to communicate. They accept young children's "invented spelling" and explain to troubled parents its place as a stage in early literacy. They have faith in children's desire to acquire the skills and abilities used by important adults, and so assume children will eventually correct themselves when exposed to good models.

Experience. Teachers recognize that firsthand experiences provide the fuel for children's continued representation through play and communication. They arrange visits in the classroom and in the community that extend children's horizons and vocabulary, and then offer materials and time for children to re-create their experience. Teachers recognize that learning through experience broadens children's comprehension of the connections between spoken and written words.

Inappropriate Cognitive and Language Development Practices

Teachers who support appropriate cognitive and language development in preschoolers are careful to avoid the following practices:

- talking mostly by teachers, demanding children's quiet attention.

- large-group times that consist mostly of repeating teachers' words, identifying objects from flashcards, or rote lessons on letter naming and sound matching.

- work sheets and other teacher-dictated activities that suggest pushed-down curriculum of learning isolated skills for reading and writing.

- reading and writing skills taught in isolation from the active-play context.

- lack of respect for new English-language learners and their process of language development.

Children who have had an opportunity to visit a skyscraper under construction come back to the classroom with words like *architect, blueprints, beams, derrick, foreman.* With paper and art materials, with clay, with blocks, with dramatic-play props, with books, with tape recorders, and with writing materials, they will be able to communicate orally or with constructive, dramatic, or creative play about their experience. They may record the news of the event, with their own pictures or print, or watch as the teacher writes about it for the parent bulletin board. When teachers keep families informed of learning experiences, families can continue the conversations with their children at home, increasing the language-learning opportunities.

Children's Literature. Reading good children's books, to both individuals and groups in the preschool classroom, plays a major part in the instructional part of the day. Research shows that the single most important activity for building the components of literacy essential for reading success appears to be reading aloud to children (NAEYC, 1998).

Teachers recognize that children must learn why people read; pleasurable experiences with books offer real evidence. They share books of all kinds: storybooks, including traditional stories; concept books; wordless books; books that invite participation; books carefully selected to mirror children's experiences; and books that convey acceptance of diversity in race, culture, socioeconomic circumstances, age, sex, and ability. Sometimes they read from big books that allow the children to see the print as the teacher reads and occasionally points out words. Children also have to learn *how* to read; and by watching the teacher, they discover that it is the print, not the pictures, that is read. Then they have to learn how to follow the print placed on the page and how pages turn (see Figure 15-19).

Teachers read favorites again and again, and make the books previously read to the group available for personal reading and retelling in the library area. Repeated readings appear to

Figure 15-19

Oral and print communication proceed together; these preschoolers are enjoying "reading" out loud to each other.

Figure 15-20

Favorite books for preschoolers.

FAVORITE BOOKS FOR PRESCHOOLERS

Look for these and others by the same author. The reference book A to Zoo: Subject Access to Children's Picture Books by Carolyn Lima will be helpful in finding more ideas, as will a listing for Caldecott award books.

Why Mosquitoes Buzz in People's Ears: A West African Folktale, Verna Aareema
Who Sank the Boat? Pamela Allen
Bear Shadow, Frank Asch
Cleversticks, Bernard Ashley
Annie and the Wild Animals, Jan Brett
Mr. Gumpy's Outing, John Burningham
Mister Seahorse, Eric Carle
Shortcut, Donald Crews
Busy Beaver, Lydia Dabcovich
The Cloud Book, Tomie De Paola
May I Bring a Friend? Beatrice De Regneirs
Are You My Mother? P.D. Eastman
Gilberto and the Wind, Marie Hall Ets
Olivia, Ian Falconer
Bark George, Jules Feiffer
In the Tall, Tall Grass, Denise Fleming
Shoes from Grandpa, Mem Fox
Dandelion, Don Freeman
Three Blind Mice, Paul Galdone
Miss Tizzy, Libba Moore Gray
Chrysanthemum, Kevin Henkes
In the Rian with Baby Duck, Amy Hest
Bread and Jam for Frances, Russell Hoban
A House Is a House for Me, Mary Ann Hoberman
Amazing Grace, Mary Hoffman
Aunt Flossie's Hats (and Crab Cakes Later.), Elizabeth Howard
The Doorbell Rang, Pat Hutchins
Whistle for Willie, Ezra Jack Keats
Anansi and the Moss-Covered Rock, Eric Kimmel
Leo the Late Bloomer, Robert Kraus
Frog and Toad Are Friends, Arnold Lobel
George and Martha, James Marshall
Blueberries for Sal, Robert McCloskey
Pigs Aplenty, Pigs Galore, David McPhail
If You Give a Mouse a Cookie, Laura Numeroff
Benny Bakes a Cake, Eve Rice
Where the Wild Things Are, Maurice Sendak
It Looked Like Spilt Milk, Robert Shaw
Caps for Sale, Esther Slobodkina
Who's Counting? Nancy Tafuri
Owl Moon, Jane Yolen

reinforce the language of the text. Teachers may offer parents lists of good children's books, such as that shown in Figure 15-20, to encourage parents to join with the classroom efforts to involve children with books.

Attention and care is given to the selection and display of books in the library area. There are abundant books, frequently replenished from the library. Children and families are encouraged to read together at home by having family book-lending systems. The library area in the classroom is comfortable and inviting, with cozy areas to sit in and protection from noise and interruption. Interesting books are also displayed throughout the classroom, added to materials in other interest centers; books of art treasures are in the art area; books about building are in the construction area; and books showing natural wonders are in the science area.

Book Extenders. Teachers know that as preschoolers engage in literature experiences, they continue to see the relevance of print to their lives. Teachers provide materials and activities that allow children to continue processing the books they have heard read, playing out and retelling the story. The book area may include flannel board characters to act out stories, puppets, and taped stories to listen to while looking at the book. Teachers may add props for playing out stories that were read. They may add specific materials to the art area that suggest making a visual representation of the story. Food experiences or cooking might follow particular books. Some teachers and children have enjoyed following all the works of a particular author. Vivian Paley's *The Girl with the Brown Crayon* (1999) is one example of such an exploration.

Print-Rich Environment. To learn the meaning and structures of written language, young children need to see print used daily in meaningful ways around them. This is different from the decorative frieze of alphabet letters high on the walls of many classrooms that is usually just visual clutter. Teachers print and let children know what they're printing. They post print around the room in various ways. Children's names are printed on their cubbies; on their places at table, nap, and group; on the helpers' and attendance charts; and on their art and stories where children are also encouraged to write their own names (see Figure 15-21). Labels are on the learning centers and on the boxes of materials for children to find. There are printed charts that give children recipes, directions, rules, and schedules, and keep track of progress on projects. Teachers and children discuss topics of interest and write down their conversations, including lists of favorite songs and books or records of experiences, news, and events. Sheets are available where children can sign up for turns at activities or for the agenda at meeting time. Signs are posted that read: "This area is closed today" or "Trike area." There are shopping lists, lesson plans, and reminders. A child sees parents and teachers communicate by notes, notices, notebooks, newsletters, and bulletin boards. Teachers help make the print explicit to children: "This says it will be Antonio's turn next." "This says we need to put in one cup of water." "This note from your mom says your grandma will pick you up today. That word there—it says grandma." It is important that children see print in functional, useful ways, so that they understand it is a real resource for their everyday lives. Print is used for information (daily schedules); for pleasure and recreation (posted poems and songs); for recording (weather graphs); for creation (child-dictated or -created books); for communication with others in the school setting (mailbox system); and for creating strong ties between home and school (calendars and newsletters).

Part of the print-rich environment will include books as part of every learning center, not placed only in the library area. There may be counting books in the math center; information picture and reference books in science; cookbooks, newspapers, magazines, and telephone books in the home-living area, including some in children's home languages other than English (and relevant books for other dramatic-play options); alphabet books in the writing center; and so on.

The print-rich environment reinforces for children the concept that functional, meaningful activities involve reading and writing.

Figure 15-21

Teachers post printed lists, experiences, and jobs on wall charts.

Writing Center. A writing center should be one of the learning center choices in a preschool classroom. Teachers recognize that children learn to write by writing, just as they learn to talk by talking (Love, Burns, & Buell, 2007). This center should include materials that lend themselves to exploring writing. Materials may include chalk and chalkboards, lined and unlined paper, stationery and envelopes, markers, crayons, pencils, pens, scissors, pads, notebooks of various kinds, index cards, typewriters, computers, hole punchers, staplers, and other materials for making books. An alphabet chart and other posters may give children something to model from; magnetic letters may be used for tracing. Children may be encouraged to keep their own "journals"—notebooks for their own use of drawing, scribbling, or first writing. Message areas with boxes labeled for each person in the classroom may encourage written communication.

As with books, writing materials may be added to centers other than the writing center. Materials to create signs and labels are appropriate in blocks, appointment pads for the doctor's office or hair salon in dramatic play, menus and order pads for a restaurant, and lists and notebooks for the grocery store or office. And of course the markers, crayons, paint materials, and colored pencils in the art area all stimulate an interest in drawing and writing. Teachers discover that children find their own creative use for writing materials when they are available.

Many teachers who entered early childhood education in past decades, when having preschool children form or use letters met disapproval, definitely have to stop and reconsider when they see a writing center recommended. But when examined in the context of active play to construct hypotheses and concepts as discussed earlier in this chapter, learning to write by writing makes sense. As children identify the areas in which they want help and instruction, teachers can help them move on. Formal instruction comes only from following children's leads.

CULTURAL CONSIDERATIONS

Helping English-Language Learners

America has always been a nation of immigrants. In the last century, immigrant families were often very quick to try to assimilate the language and customs of their new country, feeling that the sooner their children appeared "American," the sooner they would be accepted and succeed in this new life. More recent immigrants are equally anxious that their children not lose the language and culture of their families and native countries. This means a delicate balance of keeping the old while also learning the new.

Often their conflicts about this issue can be helped when teachers indicate their interest in incorporating a family's language and culture respectfully into the classroom (Kirmani, 2007). It is also important that families understand that their child's first language gives them a good foundation for later learning of English. Families should be encouraged to continue to read to and speak with their child in their home language, trusting that English will come from experiences, interaction, and instruction at school.

MATHEMATICS IN PRESCHOOL AND KINDERGARTEN

The NAEYC and the National Council of Teachers of Mathematics (NCTM) provide specific guidelines in helping teachers of young children be intentional in their approach to helping develop mathematical concepts and ideas. In their joint position statement *Early Childhood Mathematics: Promoting Good Beginnings* (2002), the following ten points are noted as recommendations for teachers to

1. enhance children's natural interest in mathematics and their dispositions to use it to make sense of their physical and social worlds.

2. build on children's experience and knowledge, their individual approaches to learning, and their informal knowledge.

3. base mathematics curriculum and teaching practices on knowledge of young children's cognitive, linguistic, physical, and social-emotional development.

4. use curriculum and teaching practices that strengthen children's problem-solving and reasoning processes, as well as representing, communicating, and connecting mathematical ideas.

5. ensure that curriculum is coherent and compatible with known relationships and sequences of important mathematical ideas.

6. provide for children's deep and sustained interaction with key mathematical ideas.

7. integrate mathematics with other activities and other activities with mathematics.

8. provide ample time, materials, and teacher support for children to engage in play, a context in which they explore and manipulate mathematical ideas with keen interest.

9. actively introduce mathematical concepts, methods, and language through a range of appropriate experiences and teaching strategies.

10. support children's learning by thoughtfully and continually assessing all children's mathematical knowledge, skills, and strategies.

From *Early Childhood Mathematics: Promoting Good Beginnings* (2002). Available online at www.naeyc.org/positionstatements.

In a more recent publication, the NCTM (2006) has created content standards in five areas for children from prekindergarten through the eighth grade. These include the knowledge of

- number and operations, which encompasses counting, a sense of number, comparisons, order, numerals, adding, subtracting, dividing, and multiplying.

- geometry and spatial sense, including recognition of shapes, understanding of space relationships, and visualization.

- measurement, including behaviors and process of measurement, understanding measurement attributes, and comparing and ordering objects.

- patterns, or algebra, involving recognizing, creating, and extending patterns.

- data analysis, which involves sorting and classifying, representation of data, and describing data. (See Figure 15-22.)

Most state early learning standards use these guidelines to create their own objectives for preschool learning.

What this translates into in classroom activities and experiences involves things that preschool teachers have always done:

- using counting songs and rhymes at group time.

- displaying birthday charts and other class-made charts and graphs.

- creating a numerically rich environment, with numerals in every area of the classroom.

- reading number and pattern books.

- modeling counting strategies.

- encouraging all children to use the block area.

- providing shape toys and opportunities to clean up by placing shapes on a shelf.

- playing pattern games.

These and many other ideas for teachers to plan appropriate math experiences can be found in *Mathematics: The Creative Curriculum® Approach* (2007).

Large-Group Time

The natural vehicle for extended communication in the preschool classroom is large-group time. Not only is large-group time an essential opportunity to learn the skills and joys of group membership and sharing experiences, it is also the occasion for teachers to introduce concepts and information. Bruner found that one such large-group experience each day greatly enriched the individual play of children later that day (Bruner, 1991). Communication, both oral and written, lies at the heart of group time. "Large-group time gives children opportunities to practice skills such as talking to a group, listening to their classmates, responding appropriately with questions or comments, working cooperatively, and using and processing new information" (Copple & Bredekamp, 2009, p. 39).

Oral participation and understanding are fostered by songs and chants; children's attention is gained more pleasantly through singing "Where is Galen?" than by an impatient demand for his presence. Finger plays, action songs, and poetry are part of the rhythmic mix. Language games

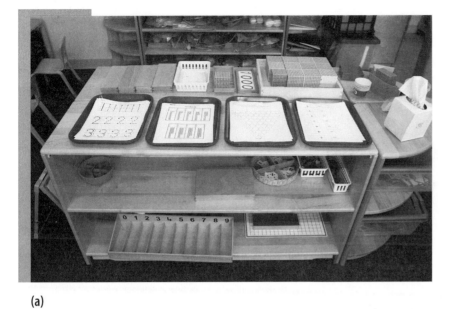

(a)

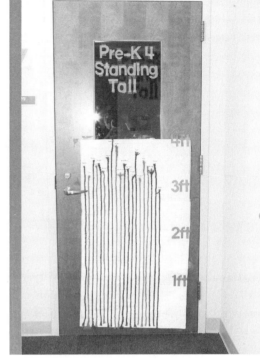

(b)

(c)

(d)

Figure 15-22 (a-d)

Appropriate preschool math experiences include measurement and data analysis, geometry and shape awareness, and number knowledge.

Figure 15-23

Listening skills are fostered during large-group time.

also foster phonological awareness, new words and ideas, and confidence in speaking in a group and in the risk taking that is needed in an early language environment. Listening skills are fostered as the teacher presents books and other enjoyable experiences (see Figure 15-23). Teachers concentrate on developing verbal and nonverbal methods of delivery that engage children's interest and participation. New information and discussion of group projects can be shared during large-group times, sometimes also called class meetings.

Large-group times may range from seven to twenty minutes, depending on the experience of the preschoolers, and may go even longer as children participate more. Teachers are alert to the children's cues, and end group time after they start to lose interest. Large-group times are planned carefully to balance quiet listening with active participation. Having ritual songs and activities, such as a beginning song or a tradition of counting the children present, helps children recognize cues for listening behavior. A sample time plan for a group of threes and fours appears in Figure 15-24.

Some practices that have traditionally been incorporated into large-group times should be evaluated for their developmental appropriateness. These include show-and-tell and calendar time.

Show-and-Tell. Sitting through many show-and-tell sessions in preschool classrooms makes observers wonder how teachers think either speaking or listening skills are being developed. Called by one author Bring-and-Brag sessions (Gartrell, 1994), the items displayed frequently attest to the power of television advertising; what comments are being made by the shower are usually drowned out by a chorus of "My dad is going to get me one too" or "I've got one of those too." The ability to listen to others is often pushed far beyond the typical preschool attention span while waiting for one's turn. The session usually deteriorates into frequent teacher requests for quiet while someone else talks. Although providing structured opportunities for preschoolers to talk and listen to one another is appropriate, this long-honored method may be less so.

To avoid some developmental difficulties, try

- giving each child a special day to tell about something that is important to them. Some teachers send home a show-and-tell calendar, with no more than three names per day, so that families understand the structure and have time to discuss ideas and prepare for the appointed day.

- giving specific guidelines, such as suggesting that children describe a family experience.

- asking children to display or talk about something they worked on in school that day, such as is part of High/Scope's plan-do-review approach.

Activity	Purpose	Principle
Action song: Head and Shoulders, Knees and Toes	Familiar starting activity energizes and captures attention	Familiar cues help focus attention and remind of behavior pattern.
Rhyme: Sing, Talk, Whisper, Shout	Quietening activity encourages auditory discrimination	Change the pace from active to quiet before listening activity.
Book: *Ten, Nine, Eight*, by Molly Bang	Related to theme of families Encourage discussion of who puts children to bed at night and bedtime rituals	Book ties in with focus for learning this week. Portrays nurturing African American father: and inclusion of nonsexist materials, diversity of culture.
Record: Lullabies from around the world	Creative movement to soft, quiet music	Value of sharing ideas and experiences with group. Discrimination of quiet music for relaxing and movement.

Figure 15-24

Sample plan for a preschool group time.

- having parents help children fill a "mystery bag" with an object (not a toy) from home and design three clues for their classmates at large-group time, inspiring thinking and conversation as all try to guess the object.

- asking children to share a picture or item from a family vacation or holiday celebration.

Calendar Time. The guessing game that characterizes most preschool calendar sessions goes something like this: "What day is it today?" "Thursday." "No, it's not Thursday. Yesterday was Monday, so today is . . . " "Sunday." "No, it's not Sunday. We don't come to school on Sunday." And so on, until some lucky guess or extraordinary rote memory puts the day on the board. Cognitive researchers have told us that young children's sense of time is vague. In addition, they learn things only in a meaningful context; even though they may be able to sing "There are seven days in a week" and name them all in the song, this rote learning does not translate into real knowledge of calendar time. Learning days of the week and months of the year may be one of those things that seems to have meaning for adults, but usually has little for children. See Figure 15-25.

There are, however, some concepts about time that preschoolers can come to understand in the course of their daily activities, such as before, later, next, and after (Beneke, Ostrosky, & Katz, 2008). Because these are worthy understandings needed for both literacy and math learning, it is appropriate for teachers to consider how to use ideas about time in developmentally appropriate ways.

The most appropriate discussions of calendar time are embedded into the context of meaningful experience. For example, after a child knows his birthday comes in October, that month and whether it is coming soon takes on new significance. As children anticipate a trip to the zoo, counting and marking off the days until then acquires significance. Knowing that three more days remain until their parents come for a picnic gives some meaning to looking at a calendar.

Other appropriate alternatives to the calendar itself could be picture representations; classroom journals with photographs of classroom events, projects, or field trips; documentation displays that illustrate the evolution of learning experiences (the first day we did . . ., and then the second, etc.); or linear representations, such as making a paper chain to represent the number of days till a particular event (Beneke, Ostrosky, & Katz, 2008). Preschool calendar experiences are more appropriate in this way than would be a guessing game about days or months. Just because commercial producers have created materials that seem attractive and cute (leprechaun faces to cover each day marked off in March) does not make calendar recitation experiences meaningful or appropriate for preschoolers.

Figure 15-25

Learning the calendar often has little meaning for children.

Small-Group Time

Small-group times allow teachers to individualize their planning to meet specific needs and goals for three to six particular children. A small-group setting allows teachers to give children more focused attention, providing support matching each child's individual level. A teacher could design a small-group activity to help reinforce a concept for children who were assessed as needing more time with that idea. For example, after making a chart comparing the color of children's eyes during the large-group time yesterday, the teacher noticed that several of the children in the group still had trouble identifying the difference between colors. So today, she asked those children to join her in a game of Candyland, feeling the game would provide another related learning activity.

A teacher might also plan a small-group time for children who had a particular interest in a topic. The lively conversation about the visit several children had made to the dinosaur exhibit at the local museum prompted the planning of an activity with classifying a collection of plastic dinosaurs. Later, if more children show interest, the teacher may repeat this small-group time with a different group, or make the figures available during free-choice time.

Sometimes, if there are two teachers in a room, teachers will plan small-group times for activities that would permit more participation. For example, a cooking activity done in a small group would prevent having to wait too long for a turn to mix or measure (see Figure 15-26). A language activity would allow children to be able to hear and concentrate more on the words of others. Small groups allow for more direct teacher interaction and observation. Small groups may be appropriate to plan when children are finding challenges with large-group time, as a beginning introduction to group participation, then gradually shifting to the large-group times. When there are two teachers, dividing the group allows them to guide children carefully through the mechanics of sitting and listening that will be needed when they move to large group later.

As with large-group time, successful teachers plan their specific goals and objectives in advance, prepare all needed materials, and consider the teaching strategies that will best suit the activity. Effective preschool teachers use small-group times to teach and then reinforce new topics, to assess children's progress, to respond to children's interests, and to demonstrate new skills. Both small- and large-group times have their place in the preschool schedule.

SUMMARY

Play is the absolute stuff from which cognitive development in preschool children occurs, allowing them to actively create and represent their developing understandings of the world. This is a much more complex form of play than was possible for toddlers. Preschoolers who play in carefully planned and arranged learning centers using a variety of open-ended materials that

Figure 15-26
Small-group experiences like cooking allow for more participation.

match their learning abilities and interests are able to construct an understanding of the world around them. In such an environment, adults carefully observe, plan for the children's active involvement with materials, playmates, and adults in extended projects, prepare the environment, model play, design questions to stimulate children's more mature thinking and understanding, and respond in ways designed to deepen and extend the learning experience. The appropriate emphasis is on children as active learners, with adults available as supportive resources. Skillful teachers make complex and rich play possible and help children keep getting better at becoming adept players.

The developmentally appropriate language environment for preschoolers works from an understanding of early literacy and its component skills, emphasizing all forms of communication for children to represent their experiences and concepts to others. The use of language and language materials is completely integrated with active play and an interest center–based learning environment. Teachers provide materials and experiences to encourage early literacy in oral and written communication. Children are encouraged to develop oral language and listening skills through conversations with playmates and adults. Teachers present attitudes of acceptance and confidence in children's desires to figure out communication skills. They use experiences, children's literature, book extensions, and a print-rich environment to help children discover a need for reading and writing. They offer materials that help children practice writing skills and understanding. They plan for appropriate mathematics learning through intentional materials and experiences. They work knowledgeably with children who are dual-language learners. They plan large- and small-group times that involve children in all aspects of communication.

THINK ABOUT IT ACTIVITIES

1. Visit a preschool classroom. What learning centers do you see? How are they set up and used? How do the teachers function during center time? How do your observations match the content of this chapter?

2. Write down examples of teachers having created a print-rich environment. What additions, if any, could be made?

3. Talk with two preschool teachers about how they plan for their classroom. What provision is there for including children's interests and specific goals for children?

4. Talk with two parents of preschool children about what they feel their children should be learning during the preschool years and the style of classroom they would look for. How do their thoughts and/or questions conflict or agree with the ideas about developmentally appropriate practice in this chapter?

QUESTIONS TO ASSESS LEARNING OF CHAPTER OBJECTIVES

1. What is meant by preoperational thinking? Describe several characteristics of preoperational thought and how they relate to preschoolers' learning style.

2. Identify several teacher roles in providing for play and describe ways teachers fill each role.

3. Discuss what is meant by the term early literacy and why emphasis on its various components is appropriate for preschool language environments.

4. What are several necessary components of a preschool language environment? Describe as many specifics as you can.

5. Describe ways of effectively supporting children who are dual-language learners.

6. Identify effective practices for both large- and small-group times.

7. Identify teacher practices that are not part of appropriate cognitive/language environments.

APPLY YOUR KNOWLEDGE QUESTIONS

1. Obtain the early learning guidelines for your state and compare those recommendations for literacy with the ideas discussed in this chapter. Devise a plan for meeting the requirements by using developmentally appropriate strategies.

2. Several of your parents are eager for you to start teaching their preschoolers to read. Explain the components of literacy to them and describe what learning to read looks like in your developmentally appropriate preschool classroom.

HELPFUL WEB SITES

http://www.acei.org	The Web site for the Association for Childhood Education International has the latest position statements of the organization regarding guidelines for early childhood education. Click on ACEI and NCATE Standards to find "Global Guidelines for Early Childhood Education and Care in the Twenty-first Century" (2002), and an individual checklist for self-assessment on the standards. You can also download a copy of the ACEI brochure "Play's Role in Brain Development."
http://www.naeyc.org	The Web site for the National Association for the Education of Young Children has all the position statements on developmentally appropriate practice and early childhood curriculum and assessment, as well as the statements on appropriate teaching of mathematics and literacy. Click on Resources, and then on Position Statements.
http://www.famlit.org	The Web site for the National Center for Family Literacy has much information on literacy. Click on Programs and Initiatives, and then on Family Partnership in Reading to find the report of the National Literacy Panel (2004).
http://www.biculturalfamily.org	The Web site for the Bilingual Family Network has articles and resources to support those who want to support bilingual education and related issues.

http://www.nctm.org

The Web site for the National Council of Teachers of Mathematics offers a free download of the most recent position statement, *Curriculum Focal Points for Prekindergarten Through Grade 8 Mathematics.* Click on Standards/Focal Points.

 Please visit the premium Web site for Developmentally Appropriate Practice, *4th edition, to access more chapter web links, suggestions for further research and study, additional book chapters, interactive quizzes, video exercises, online journal activities, flashcards, and much more! Go to www.cengage.com/login to register your access code.*

Developmentally Appropriate Cognitive/Language/Literacy Environments: For Primary-Age Children

Six-year-old Aaron says, "See my story? That says, 'We went to the farm.' (We wnt to th frm.)"

Seven-year-old B.J. says, "I hate school. All we do is boring stuff." The math papers he brings home show signs of a lot of corrections.

Eight-year-old LaKeisha says, "I can read almost this whole book. Except some of the hard words. It's my favorite; it's about dogs."

Children in the early school years seem so very different from the preschoolers they recently were. Their leaner, stronger bodies and increased muscular strength allow them to participate energetically in physical activity and games. Their confidence away from adults allows them to enter the world of friends and children's fun. They pour into and out of their school buildings with varying degrees of enthusiasm and excitement, eager to succeed in the world of the grown-ups or fearful of the new and unfamiliar expectations. There are serious new cognitive standards and goals. Most of us are familiar with the story of the first-grader who came home in tears at the end of the first day because she hadn't learned to read yet. In their inner cognitive world, however, these primary-age children are still closely linked to the preschool years in ability and style of thinking and learning. Preoperational thinking and learning dictates clear implications for decisions in primary cognitive/language environments. Learning and language are always closed linked, and in the early primary years, the emphasis in both children's and adults' minds is on learning to use the skills of written language. In this discussion of appropriate cognitive/language/literacy environments for children in their first years of elementary school, we will focus on the curricula and teaching methods that support optimum development, regardless of the high-stakes testing that dominates the scene.

LEARNING OBJECTIVES

After completing this chapter, students should be able to

- understand current issues in education.
- identify the implications of preoperational and concrete operational thought for primary cognitive/language environments.
- describe components of implementing integrated curricula in primary classrooms.
- discuss reading in developmentally appropriate practice.
- describe aspects of a developmentally appropriate writing program.
- identify developmentally appropriate aspects of a primary math curriculum.
- understand the difference between standardized testing and broader assessment, and describe the role of assessment in a developmentally appropriate primary classroom.

CURRENT ISSUES INVOLVING SCHOOLS

During the primary years, the emphasis in the community places inordinate attention on acquiring cognitive skills. Stressing the cognitive and minimizing attention to other aspects of children's development may be a root cause of some children's failures in school experiences. Ignoring the interrelationships among all the domains of development and failing to develop the kind of integrated curricula that offer the chance to make meaningful connections when presented with new information are all aspects of inappropriate practices. Even though this chapter will focus on cognitive/language aspects of best practice, the discussion connects with the earlier discussion of all areas of development.

In recent years, the educational systems in our country have received close scrutiny and criticism. The Carnegie Task Force (1996) raised concern that by the fourth grade, the performance of most children in the United States is below national standards and "certainly below the achievement levels of children in competing countries" (Carnegie Task Force, 1996, p. vii). The report goes on to summarize the major reasons why schools are failing to educate children to expected levels:

> They fail because of the low expectations they hold out for many students; the heavy reliance that schools place on outmoded or ineffective curricula and teaching methods; poorly prepared or insufficiently supported teachers; weak home/school linkages; the lack of adequate accountability systems; and ineffective use of resources by schools and school systems. (Carnegie Task Force, 1996, p. ix)

The most recent result of this national concern regarding primary and other education was the passage of the No Child Left Behind Act, signed into law by President George W. Bush in January 2002. The law has now become a focal point of educational policy nationally, particularly targeting improving conditions for disadvantaged students. This latest educational reform has four major emphases:

- Stronger accountability for results
- More freedom for states and communities
- Encouraging proven educational methods based on scientific research
- More choices for parents

One of the provisions of the bill is that the progress of every public school student in the areas of reading and math will be tested at the end of Grades 3 through 8, with assessment in science added in 2007–2008. Two new reading programs are created in this legislation:

- Reading First has grants to help states and districts set up "scientific, research-based" reading programs for children in Grades K to 3, with priority to high-poverty areas.
- Early Reading First is a smaller reading program designed to help states better prepare children of ages three to five, from disadvantaged areas.

Reading assessments using tests written in English are required for any student who has attended school in the United States for three or more consecutive years, although states may use their discretion for an additional two years. Annually, states must assess English proficiency for all LEP (Limited English Proficient) students. The mandatory testing in reading and mathematics "has led to roughly one-third less instructional time spent on learning in other disciplines" (Center on Educational Policy, 2008, cited in Copple & Bredekamp, 2009, p. 258).

The law tightens the definition of adequate yearly progress to include annual statewide measurable objectives for improved achievement for all students, as well as specific groups: economically disadvantaged, students from major racial and ethnic groups, students with disabilities, and LEP students. States are required to provide detailed report cards on schools and districts, pointing out which schools are succeeding and why. Schools that receive Title I funding that fail to meet their targets for two years in succession will receive technical assistance and are required

Figure 16-1

Children are at the center of the controversies about testing and NCLB.

Michael Prince/Corbis

to offer students options of transferring to better-performing schools, entering after-school programs, or getting tutoring.

The act also authorizes giving State Academic Achievement Awards to schools that meet their achievement goals, with a designation as a Distinguished School and financial awards to teachers in those schools. More information on the act can be found at http://www.nclb.org.

With such visible high stakes for schools, teachers, districts, and states attached to the reliance on regular testing, the dialogue in the education community about the results for appropriate learning for children has been intense (see Figure 16-1). The National Education Association has been strong in calling for evaluation of children and schools on more than just test scores. See their positions at http://www.nea.org; more information is available at the end of the chapter. This discussion will no doubt continue while teachers and students struggle to find a way to reconcile developmentally appropriate practices with legislated demands.

PREOPERATIONAL AND CONCRETE OPERATIONAL THINKING AND DEVELOPMENTALLY APPROPRIATE PRACTICE

In Chapter 15, we considered the various characteristics of the stage of preoperational thinking as defined by Piaget, seen in children from about ages two through seven or so. To review, these characteristics include centration, or focusing on one perception at a time; egocentrism in thought; irreversibility; and concrete thinking. All these characteristics limit children's abilities to learn about abstractions and through methods related to abstractions, such as learning through someone else's words or through being asked to find mental solutions to problems. Because of this remaining preoperational thought during the early school years, primary-age children are linked with the preschool period, and thus unsuited for the learning tasks and methods of many typical elementary school classrooms.

In Piaget's theory, around age seven gradual changes in the way children process information and solve problems lead to changes in thinking and reasoning. Vygotsky and some of the sociocultural theorists who followed him emphasized that at about age seven, changes are made by adults in the expectations, demands, and social structure that influence children's thinking. Recent neuroscientific information suggests that this time is when the synapses of the brain go through "pruning," allowing the brain to function more efficiently (Chugani, 1996).

Figure 16-2

Primary children need physical objects to help them make mental connections.

Although these different theoretical perspectives exist on the reason for the change, any observer of primary-age children can agree that there are real changes in the thinking and problem-solving abilities of these children.

Slowly during the primary years, children move into the stage of *concrete operational thought*. Increasingly they become able to understand the ideas of others, to consider several aspects of a situation, and to reverse their thinking. At this time, they acquire mental ability to think about and solve problems in their heads, no longer needing only physical contact and manipulation of objects to be able to learn. They are still limited in their ability to think about purely symbolic or abstract ideas and need real things to think about. "When presented with a new concept, primary grade children need physical actions or direct experiences to help them grasp the idea, much as adults need vivid examples and illustrations to grasp unfamiliar concepts (Tomlinson, 2009, p. 272). Needing physical actions to help make mental connections, children benefit from active, firsthand experiences and manipulating real objects, things that are relevant, interesting, and meaningful to the children themselves. It is also developmentally appropriate for teachers to recognize that some thinking skills—notably mathematical skills—related to time and distance are beyond children who are developing only concrete operational thinking (see Figure 16-2). Some kinds of learning and lessons are delayed until after the primary years, for easier learning and less risk of failure.

Moving out of the egocentric thought of the preoperational period is dependent on interaction, conversation, and communication with other children and adults. Developmentally appropriate practice demands, therefore, that children be given opportunities to work in small groups on common activities that provide the basis for communication and interaction. Children's abilities to reason are strengthened by such opportunities for group work and conversation.

Teachers realize that one of their key roles is to facilitate discussion among children by making comments and soliciting children's opinions and ideas. Learning how to stimulate children's thinking through communication is a vital component in the cognitive/language environment.

Every child is on an individual timetable of moving between the preoperational and concrete operational stages. Only teachers who are familiar with characteristics

JOURNAL REFLECTION

Legislating Performance Standards

Consider the idea of individual timetables for children, thinking of examples from your experience. Then consider whether the legislation that demands certain performance standards of all children at the grade level is appropriate. How has this created conflict for children, families, and teachers?

Visit the premium Web site to complete this journal activity online and email it to your professor.

of thinking in the two stages and aware of likely responses of children within each stage will be able to match the most appropriate learning experiences and materials for each child. The legislation that demands performance at a defined level by all children of the same age in the same grade is incompatible with the concept of individual timetables. It takes teachers who know how to unite absolute standards with individual needs and styles to help children move successfully through these first learning experiences.

Other Aspects of Readiness for School Learning Tasks

By about age six, **binocular vision**—the ability of the eyes to work together—is usually well established. This ability is necessary for reading and work at close focus. However, children continue with farsightedness in their vision until about age nine, requiring larger print.

Fine motor development continues to undergo refinement in the primary years, enabling children to have more control and precision in drawing and writing, without the neurological fatigue of the preschool years. Girls continue to be ahead of boys in fine motor development at this time.

Social skills vary in any group of young children. The average primary classroom has one adult for every twenty-five to thirty children; many children may have come from preschool arrangements in which the ratios were about half of that, or from home or care arrangements in which it was even less. This makes a lot more children with whom to learn to cooperate and share, to take turns and wait to listen; for many children, becoming comfortable in a social setting offers the first challenge to be resolved before being able to concentrate on tasks of formal cognitive learning. Primary-age children become more prone to social comparison; these comparisons become part of their self-concept and may affect their motivation in learning activities. Schools that rely heavily on competition and comparison may increase this tendency.

Emotional comfort and security affect children's readiness to learn. Many of the factors mentioned previously create physical and emotional stress that may manifest itself in a variety of ways, including toilet accidents; the physical symptoms such as stomachaches and nausea, collectively known medically as **school phobia**; inability to pay attention; and general distress and unhappiness. The cognitive environment must recognize all these aspects of the whole child when considering "readiness to learn." (See Figure 16-3.)

Figure 16-3

Inability to pay attention may be related to emotional readiness to learn.

Adriane Moll/Corbis

Cognitive/Language/Literacy Goals of Primary Education

Most children, unless weighed down with the burdens of abuse, debilitating illness, or disability, arrive at school eager to learn and confident they will succeed. The number who fail, are held back, need special assistance, lose confidence in their abilities to learn, and eventually drop out, is far too high in a country that prides itself on and needs an educated citizenry. This fact alone suggests that our goals are not being met. What are the basic goals for primary-age children?

1. Ensure that children have successful early experiences in learning. Lifelong patterns are being set, and children's self-esteem and feelings of confidence as learners are critical. When schools rely on competition and comparison among children, children's confidence as learners is put at risk.

   Children will not have successful early experiences if the fundamental nature of their abilities to think and learn is not recognized, and if they are not engaged in active experiences, using concrete objects to investigate, with curriculum content that is relevant and meaningful to them, and integrated across the disciplines. "The purpose of integrating content is not only to make school more enjoyable and interesting, which promotes enthusiasm and a love of learning; it is also to support children's ability to connect new learning to prior knowledge, which has the effect of expanding children's memory and reasoning capacity" (Tomlinson, 2009, p. 259).

2. Ensure that children play active roles in their learning. To feel that they are competent learners, children must perceive their importance as decision makers, initiators, and active participants in primary classrooms. As children perceive their ability to direct their own learning, motivation increases (see Figure 16-4).

3. Ensure that children develop dispositions toward learning (Katz, 1988). **Dispositions** are different learning from skills and knowledge, and as such, cannot be tested for with end-of-grade tests. They are "habits of mind, tendencies to respond to situations in certain ways" (Katz, 1988, p. 29). An example of a disposition is curiosity; it is not a skill or a piece of knowledge. Children must acquire the disposition or inclination to use the skills they acquire. There is a big difference between having the skills and having the disposition to be a reader. Much evidence suggests that too much emphasis on developing narrow skills in children through drill and rote learning may threaten children's dispositions to use those skills: "I hate reading," when what is hated is the school's method of teaching reading.

4. Ensure that children have appropriate learning opportunities to develop basic competencies of literacy and numeracy. Continuing to develop competence in communication as well as the basic skills required for further instruction in the knowledge deemed essential

Figure 16-4

Children's self-esteem as learners grows as they play active roles in their classrooms.

Simon Jarratt/Corbis

Deborah Jaffe/Corbis

Figure 16-5

Children recognize that mastery of literacy and math skills is considered important in our culture.

by culture and communities are part of primary learning. These are skills recognized as most important by our culture, and children recognize that mastery of these tasks is success (see Figure 16-5).

5. Ensure that children have opportunities to continue developing their individual and personal interests. Educators recognize that children's motivation for learning is an intense desire to make sense out of their own unique world. These interests extend beyond the purely cognitive and broaden the narrowly defined subjects of curriculum. Gardner has proposed a theory of **multiple intelligences**, each following its particular developmental path (Gardner, 1983, 1991). Gardner's theory is that people naturally have specific areas of strength and weakness, in fact "different ways of knowing," and learners should be allowed to experience a concept in a variety of ways, demonstrating their learning through using their strength, rather than the traditional curriculum focus areas of language and logico-mathematics that are used for most instruction and assessment. Schools need to consider their roles in optimizing the development of various kinds of intelligence, which may include

- linguistic
- musical
- logico-mathematical
- spatial
- bodily-kinesthetic
- interpersonal
- intrapersonal
- naturalistic, and
- existential (Gardner, 1983, 1991; Campbell, Campbell, & Dickinson, 2003)

How best to meet these goals will be explored as we discuss basic components of what is considered developmentally appropriate practice for the cognitive/language tasks in primary-age classrooms.

Components of Developmentally Appropriate Cognitive/Language Environments

The school environment is charged with helping children learn the basic knowledge and skills demanded of our high-tech society. There is much to be considered in evaluating the developmental appropriateness of classrooms and learning experiences.

JOURNAL REFLECTION

Your Strengths in Elementary School

What do you remember that you were good at or interested in during your elementary school years? Did school offer you a chance to show these strengths? How did that affect your self-esteem?

Visit the premium Web site to complete this journal activity online and email it to your professor.

Integrated Curriculum. The traditional separation of subject areas in the curriculum, with segments of time allotted for each, implies that children construct their understandings of the world in a separated, linear fashion. In fact, this is not so; children learn by making connections between ideas and experiences, between learning skills needed to be used in a meaningful context that is of interest to them. Isolated facts about related subjects seem irrelevant, important only to the teacher, not likely to catch children's interest and extend their confidence or dispositions toward learning.

Integrated curriculum, instead, helps children build meaningful connections when presented with new information, exactly what recent brain research tells us is best for learning. The mind organizes pieces of related information into complex webs, called schemata. **Integrated curriculum** takes advantage of this process by having all the subjects organized around a central idea, enabling children to construct webs of interconnected information. Integrated curriculum allows children to use knowledge and skills from one area to explore other subject areas, as in using reading and writing skills in social studies exploration or using math concepts in music study. Integrated curriculum also allows children to use the multiple intelligences described by Gardner. Integrated curriculum also allows teachers to negotiate the tricky balance between standards and developmentally appropriate practice (Park, Neuharth-Pritchett, & Reguero de Atiles, 2003).

How do primary teachers integrate curriculum? Several practices are relevant here.

Projects. The learning is organized around large projects, or themes, that relate to learning goals, rather than on particular subjects. This is quite different from, say, what a teacher in a traditional primary classroom might do regarding the subject of Valentine's Day. Here the children might read a story about it, discuss the story, learn a Valentine's song, write and illustrate stories or poems about what Valentine's Day means to them, and paste their math work on red valentines. The next week they do something quite different. Although the focus is on a topic of interest and combines several school subjects, this approach falls short of what is meant by project or theme study that truly integrates curriculum in primary classrooms.

Theme study in a project forms the core of developmentally appropriate learning activities in primary classrooms. The project defines the center of attention, incorporates many subject areas within it, and develops over a long period of time. Through holistic study of a topic, children learn the basic subjects through activities based on the theme, thus coming to see how and why the skills are meaningful. (Some subjects, for example math, cannot always be fully included in theme work, because the theme studies do not always offer enough exposure to the concepts. Whatever fits naturally into the theme is included; what does not is dealt with separately.) But a large amount of time each day and week is devoted to activities related to the project. Project activities may take up a large part of the curriculum and be pursued several times a week. The theme may be integrated into learning centers or form the basis for most classroom curriculum activities.

Real project work involves in-depth work over time. Many classrooms spend months or even the full academic year pursuing their interests (see Ostrow's account [1995] of an entire year spent with her second- and third-graders on the "island" constructed by the children in the classroom and the integrated learning). Other criteria for project work and theme study include:

- topics of great interest to the children—in fact, a topic negotiated between teachers and children.
- topics related to the surrounding community.
- topics broad enough to be divided into smaller subtopics that also interest the children.
- relationships of subtopics to the wider context made clear.
- topics that lend themselves to extensive investigation of real situations, materials, and resources, to comparing and contrasting ideas.
- topics that encourage rich cross-disciplinary work (Diffily & Sassman, 2002).

For example, an appropriate theme for primary-age children living in rural Maine or Oregon might be "The Forest." A selection of subtopics might be the growth cycles of trees, kinds of trees and their uses, harvesting lumber, history of lumbering, forest animal families, habitats, and ecological issues. Each of these subtopics offers a wide scope for study. Children studying kinds of trees and their uses might draw different kinds of trees, make charts that indicate the wood products of each, use carpentry and measuring skills to make some things from wood, and write letters to wood product companies as part of their research. Children's interests and questions will be a

Image Source/Corbis

Figure 16-6

Children involved in project work are incorporating traditional subjects like reading and writing in their work.

force in determining the direction the theme study takes; in fact, children are highly involved in discussing and planning ways to explore the topic.

Eleanor Duckworth refers to the learning process for children as the "having of wonderful ideas." She says:

> There are two aspects to providing occasions for wonderful ideas. One is being willing to accept children's ideas. The other is providing a setting that suggests wonderful ideas to children—different ideas to different children—as they are caught up in intellectual problems that are real to them. (Duckworth, 2006, p. 7)

Although the topic and not the academic subject is emphasized, there are still ample opportunities for incorporating the traditional subjects in the children's learning. Children involved in project work use reading, writing, spelling, math, technology, and creative arts to explore and record their thinking and observations about content usually involving science, social studies, and health (Trepanier-Street, 2000) (see Figure 16-6). As particular skills are needed for the activities of the study, they are taught. In this way, children understand the purposes of reading, writing, and math skills. Yet the theme study is undertaken because the content is important to know; it is not just a

. . . thin excuse for teaching children to perfect their recognition of words, spelling, punctuation, and so forth. These skills are indeed learned but not through drill. They are learned because they are identified as necessary tools for achieving another purpose. (Gamberg, Kwak, Hutchings, & Altheim, 1988)

In-depth study organized around themes is usually called the project approach (Katz & Chard, 2000; Chard, 1998a, 1998b; Helm & Katz, 2001; Helm & Beneke, 2003). As children participate in projects to gain a "deeper and fuller sense of events and phenomena in their own environment and experience" (Katz & Chard, 2000, p. 17), they get extensive and varied practice in analyzing and questioning. By so doing, they develop confidence in their own intellectual powers and strengthen their disposition to go on learning. The project work complements and enhances what children learn from spontaneous, thoughtful activity as well as from systematic instruction. Wonderful ideas are built on other wonderful ideas that improve learners' understanding of the world around them and strengthen their dispositions to go on learning.

Joint Planning. Integrated curriculum involves joint planning by teachers and children. Children are involved in identifying topics that are interesting to them, but this does not mean that the classroom curriculum is solely dictated by children's whims. Project work is a focused study, guided intentionally by teachers. Children and teachers collaboratively select projects, plan activities, and decide what materials are needed.

Teachers are very likely to make initial decisions about the overall topics, because they know the characteristics of themes that will prove successful for in-depth study, as well as the state guidelines for curriculum. Teachers also do preliminary research on resources of print, materials, people, and places within the community that would support project research. They also plan ideas and classroom activities to introduce the topics.

The children may be involved in a process of brainstorming—free-flowing discussions to identify what children already know or have experienced about a topic. Brainstorming questions that they do not know may also guide teachers and children in selecting the topics they want to study with more depth (see Figure 16-7). With such curriculum development, subjects are not being covered, but are being uncovered, as Duckworth (2006) says.

Children are encouraged to make their own decisions and choices about the work to be undertaken: what it will be, how it will be undertaken and with whom, and how will their learning be represented and shared with others? Thus, through the theme study/project approach,

Figure 16-7

Brainstorming sessions help teachers select appropriate topics for extended project study.

primary-age children learn not only about the theme itself, but also how to be active participants in their learning, how to plan and organize their study. The disposition to engage in thought about active learning is being established.

> They are not passively following someone else's instructions. Instead, they are required to consider alternatives and make their own decisions based on reasons they can explain and justify. They are learning to become independent and critical thinkers. (Gamberg et al., 1988, p. 30)

Collaborating in Small Groups. In an integrated curriculum, teachers create situations in which children collaborate in small groups to work on individual projects. Group work is valuable both socially (see Chapter 12) and cognitively (Kumar, R. 2009). Research indicates that peer interaction can foster cognitive development by allowing children to attain new skills and recognize ideas through discussion. Collaborative efforts increase the amount of time children work on a task, because peer presence prevents children from giving up on difficult tasks and makes work more enjoyable. Working together facilitates acquiring knowledge and skills, because different members bring different skills and interests to the activity. Verbal interaction among the children makes a rich basis for extending ideas and supporting efforts. As they learn to express their learning to others, children truly process their understandings. Children benefit from the feedback they give to and receive from group members.

Sometimes children select their work partners; sometimes teachers suggest groups to children for social reasons or to complement learning styles. By working together on projects, children exert powerful influences on one another's work habits; when certain behaviors of an individual are a problem for the group, it is the group's responsibility to find appropriate ways of changing those behaviors. Children learn that they can be useful and contributing members of a work group, and that they have a responsibility to that group in pulling their own weight (see Figure 16-8).

Obviously not all experiences in the primary classroom are group activities, although most of the project work in studying themes is accomplished in groups. An

---

▶❚❚ VIDEO ACTIVITY

Go to the premium Web site and watch the video clip for Chapter 16 titled "Learning in the Primary Years." Then consider the following questions:

REFLECTIVE QUESTIONS

1. What are the advantages to peer support for learning in the primary years?

2. Consider some strategies mentioned in this chapter that support peer interaction for scaffolding.

3. How do the responses of these two boys indicate the advantages of peer learning?

 Visit the premium Web site to complete these questions online and email them to your professor.

Figure 16-8

Children learn to fulfill responsibilities to the group for project completion.

example of a solitary activity may be writing in a journal, although children are free to consult with one another about spelling and ideas. In addition, teachers will work with individuals or small groups on particular skill development.

Teachers as Facilitators. When using an integrated curriculum, teachers function as facilitators in addition to being instructors. In effect, the teacher is often removed from center stage, and the group members take up many of the functions of the teacher. However, teachers are not less involved in or less accountable for children's learning. What does the teacher do in planning and carrying out an integrated curriculum?

The teacher does the advance preparation, choosing theme topics and gathering resource materials for classroom activities. Projects are often initiated and developed in response to teachers' suggestions, questions, or materials (Trepanier-Street, 2000). It is important that the teacher be curious, enthusiastic, and open to learning new ideas and following children's lines of questioning. Because the individual interests of children help guide the direction of projects, teachers will probably find that the same theme undertaken in different years with different groups will take quite different directions. Teachers will not necessarily know initially all the information that the children will gain from the projects undertaken, but model the role of interested and active learner themselves. When the teacher is learning along with the children, the importance and seriousness of their work is emphasized.

Teachers prepare the environment for project work, adding interesting and relevant materials to interest centers for choice times, displaying other resource materials, and displaying records of finished project work. Preparation continues as the project progresses, as various possibilities, needs, and interests emerge. Preparation may include planning for relevant field trips, classroom visitors, and follow-up activities. Teachers ensure that there is a rich variety of materials and activities that will stimulate and extend children's interests. They schedule time so children have extended, concentrated periods to become involved in their project work.

Teachers prepare children to work in groups. They may help them select working partners and remind children of their responsibilities to others in group functioning. Students do not automatically know how to work with others in a constructive fashion and need participation in direct conversation about this subject. Teachers may help children define their roles within the group, so everyone has a part to play for which he or she is suitably skilled.

Teachers act as resource persons. Being a resource person means being available to teach skills as the need arises in the activity. Literacy or math skills needed for the project to progress are embedded in a meaningful context. The teachers' job is not to tell children everything, but to help them locate information and figure out how they can find their answers. As they oversee the children's busy activity, they see where support is needed at any time.

Teachers help themselves and the children keep track of the children's works in progress. They may make charts of the brainstorming and plans, listing the steps of the group project so that children can keep progressing in an organized way. They make observations and notes on children's interests, abilities, and difficulties to guide them in meeting individual needs for assistance and to discover what the children are ready to learn. They keep samples of children's work to assess progress and plan the next steps in curricula and instruction. See a helpful collection of data collection tools and techniques for documenting children's literacy development in Owocki and Goodman (2002).

They question to help children clarify their thinking and be able to express their learning verbally and in writing. A question may be the impetus for children to take another step in their work. They give feedback, guidance, and encouragement, and they provide opportunities for children to summarize and display their learning to peers and parents.

They hold individual conferences with children to assess their progress in learning and thinking and to help children learn to evaluate the quality of their own work. Teachers schedule reading, writing, or math conferences with individuals during the times when children are busy at their own work. Usually such conferences are held on a weekly basis to help both teacher and child plan the next learning events.

As facilitators, teachers also provide direct instruction as they see that children need skills and are ready to acquire them (see Figure 16-9). Such instruction is usually offered individually or in small groups and uses the child's chosen reading, writing, or math interest as a basis for the instruction, instead of lessons from standard texts. Teachers who use integrated curricula find themselves in the midst of busy, active groups of children, rather than standing at the front of a classroom teaching lessons determined by a textbook, where everyone is on the same page at the same time.

Figure 16-9

Teachers teach individually when they see that children need help with particular concepts.

Obviously it is difficult for teachers to individualize their instruction and interactions when the class size is too large. Then, for expediency, they often have to resort to whole-group instruction. It is in the best interests of using the developmentally appropriate practices discussed here for teachers, families, and communities to support the smallest class sizes possible. Advocating for smaller class sizes is one way for teachers to work toward more appropriate practices.

Language and Literacy. Brian Cutting, a noted New Zealand educator, points out that children learn to talk successfully, naturally, and with apparent ease well before they go to school. There are several contributing factors to this.

- No one expects children to fail at the task.

- Children are responsible for much of their learning, instead of being given daily lessons from a learning-to-talk manual that is broken down into successive steps.

- Children practice for a long time, amid an environment that is patient, tolerant of "mistakes," and delighting in their early attempts.

- There are no tests in talking.

PRACTICAL IMPLICATIONS

Stressing Skill Acquisition over Active Learning

In classrooms that stress imparting measurable content and skill acquisition rather than meaningful content gained through an active process of learning, these less appropriate practices will be found:

- Primary emphasis is on reading and math, with specific lessons taught each day, and children progressing through workbooks and basal readers.

- Curriculum is divided into separate subjects—such as social studies, science, health—and are taught only as time is available after the reading and math skill lessons.

- Little time is left for "enrichment" activities such as projects and learning centers. Often the creative arts are omitted altogether, as there is no time.

- Emphasis is on teacher instruction and pencil-and-paper practice of skills at desks.

- Student conversation is discouraged as disruptive to teacher lessons and quiet seat work.

If we really wanted to make learning to talk a non-success story, the easiest way would be to design tests that would set a standard, which all children would be expected to reach. We all know that such procedures would be futile for children learning to talk. So why do we use similar procedures for children learning to read and write? (Cutting, 1991, p. 65)

The development of language and literacy in the primary classroom is seen as a continuum of earlier experiences. The goal of the language and literacy program in the primary years is for children to continue to develop their ability to communicate orally and through reading and writing. Basic tenets of the language and literacy approach are that spoken and written language interact and influence each other, and that all phases of language development are experience-based. Children learn about reading and writing through observing these skills being used and through using them. Writing and reading are taught simultaneously and are experienced as an integrated part of the total curriculum, not just at assigned times. Oral language skills of listening and speaking are integrated into every aspect of the classroom day. The physical environment is arranged to enhance interpersonal communication.

The results of Cambourne's (1988) study of young children who were successful in learning literacy skills are referred to as "Cambourne's conditions" for learning. These conditions for language classrooms include the following:

- *Immersion:* Children are immersed in text and spoken language, and have abundant opportunities to practice language in the classroom.

- *Demonstrations:* Children are given opportunities to see meaningful and functional demonstrations of how speaking, listening, reading, and writing are done.

- *Engagement:* Children learn from demonstrations only when they are personally meaningful and in a nonjudgmental environment.

- *Expectation:* Adults demonstrate high expectation that children will succeed in developing as readers and writers.

- *Responsibility:* Children are given responsibility for choosing the literacy activities that will enhance their development as learners.

- *Approximation:* Children are free to take risks without fear of correction and insistence on accuracy.

- *Use:* Following the understanding that children learn by doing, children have a lot of time and opportunities to engage in activities and support literacy.

- *Response:* In a classroom where literacy is being supported, children receive feedback from their peers and teacher, so that children are comfortable in expressing how and what they have learned.

So what do the 3Rs look like in a classroom using developmentally appropriate practices? For purposes of clarity only, reading and writing in primary classrooms will be discussed separately; in practice, however, they are integrated. Certainly there is more formal instruction than was seen in the preschool classroom. The International Reading Association (IRA) has a position statement on "Using Multiple Methods of Beginning Reading Instruction" (1999), found at their Web site listed at the end of the chapter. The NAEYC position statement on developmentally appropriate practices in reading and writing points out that no one method is superior for all children, but that some kind of systematic code instruction along with meaningful connecting reading helps children progress. The statement also recommends time for independent practice and integrated reading and writing in classroom instruction (NAEYC & IRA, 1998). One expert says that the most essential elements of successful reading programs are

- teachers who love coming to work and are literacy learners themselves.

- teachers who put high-stakes testing in perspective and reading for meaning at the forefront.

- teachers who make curriculum relevant to children's lives (Routman, 2003).

WHAT would you DO when...

"I've been trying to move away from basal readers and workbooks in my first-grade classroom, but the problem is that the parents get all upset when the work they see is mostly drawings with a few letters and difficult-to-decipher words on it. How am I going to be able to change if their reaction is so negative?" What would you do if you were this teacher?

The parents of children in your classroom undoubtedly attended schools in which the emphasis was on skill acquisition using methods of formal teacher instruction of various subjects, with text-books and workbooks for each. Understandably, they are confused when the system seems so very different for them; this does not look like the education they experienced. Remember that parents can be either your most outspoken opponents or your staunchest supporters. Which of those they turn out to be depends on how well they understand the benefits of offering their children developmentally appropriate curricula and methods. Teachers and administrators who want to get parent support must commit themselves to educating parents and offering them information that helps them understand that the activities are purposeful, designed to meet overall learning goals in the primary years that go beyond mere skill acquisition. As parents come to understand the goals of learning to become independent thinkers, writers, and readers; of learning abilities to work cooperatively and autonomously; and, most importantly, of developing self-confidence and pleasure in their abilities to learn, they will see direct benefits to their children.

How to educate parents? In as many different ways as you can, because parents also have their own individual styles of learning. Give parents articles and excerpts from books that explain the concepts of whole language. See if you can find a teacher who has successfully used these techniques for a time, who can talk about the results that have occurred. Welcome parents into your classroom as observers and/or volunteers, so they can see excited children busily at work. Video-tape, photograph, make audiotapes, and use these materials at parent discussions. Give children rotating turns to take home a "Writer's Briefcase" filled with paper and notebooks, crayons, markers, stencils, envelopes, clipboard, scissors, pencil sharpeners, stickers, and gummed labels. Include an article for parents that explains the reading/writing process and a letter describing the process used in your classroom so parents can get a better understanding of what is happening in the classroom. Let parents who are becoming believers share examples and incidents involving their children's response to learning in developmentally appropriate ways. Make collections (portfolios) of children's work that indicate progress and learning of different skills over time and share these with parents during progress conferences. Keep doing what you're doing and remain aware of ways to inform and excite parents as well as their children. Children need to feel that their parents have confidence in their teachers and classrooms.

After you have read this next section, you might be interested in reading Meier's (1997) account of his experiences teaching in a first-grade classroom, in which he used most of these ideas in creating integrated curriculum, developing reading, writing, and math skills while children were exploring theme topics.

Reading. Teachers say that the most important things in a reading program are exposure, immersion, and purpose. Children are given an understanding that the purposes of reading instruction are to enjoy reading as an activity and to develop strategies to construct meaning in a text.

To foster enjoyment of reading, teachers

- provide time each day for children to look through books, read and be read to, using a carefully selected variety of high-quality children's literature, poetry, and nonfiction books (see Figure 16-10).

> Today in Mr. Bryant's first grade, he reads a book about trains as part of their theme study. Before lunch, he reads a chapter of Charlotte's Web, their ongoing book. There is a half-hour library period in the classroom each morning when children read their own selections.

- provide adults, older children, or "reading buddies" to read to children.

> The fourth-graders come in to the first grade three times a week to read with individual first-graders.

Deborah Jaffe/Corbis

Figure 16-10

Every day, teachers read to children, as well as provide opportunities for individual reading.

- help children write and/or illustrate their own books of stories, riddles, and classroom experiences.

   Each child writes his or her own page for a class book about trains. Each page is illustrated. When the book is finished, it will be available in the library area for personal reading.

- provide activities related to stories, such as dramatic-play props, flannel boards, puppets, and creative art materials (Diller, 2003).

   During the train project, the dramatic-play center might have engineer hats, train tickets, maps, and railway signs. The art center may have a selection of sticks, straws, and so on that have been used to make three-dimensional representations of trains on tracks.

- use the school library and attractively set up the library area of the classroom for children to choose their own books regularly.

- provide books that have meaning related to classroom themes and projects, so children can experience the function of reading to gain information.

- provide materials at a variety of ability levels—wordless picture books, familiar books, books with illustrations that closely match the text, songs and poems that rhyme and have a definite rhythm, books that have portions of the text repeated frequently—in the classroom so each child can experience success at his or her own level.

To help children develop strategies to construct meaning in reading, teachers

- read predictable stories to children regularly, encouraging children to join in with the reading whenever they can (shared reading).

- use "big books" with text large enough to be seen and followed.

- help children learn to read the pictures, using the illustrations to get visual clues that may help children anticipate the words (Teachout & Bright, 2007).

- help children use their own knowledge of language to predict the language of the author, to use their knowledge of the context to get clues about meaning.

   The teacher in a K–1 class reads again the classroom big book *Brown Bear, Brown Bear* to her group. Then children happily join in as she hesitates and points to the next illustration: ". . . an ORANGE FISH looking at me."

- have children draw, write, and dictate their own stories, for their own reading.

   For their writing/drawing experience after the book, the teacher suggests they create their own book about some of the animals in *Brown Bear, Brown Bear*. Anthony is writing a story called "Purple Horse."

- write and post charts, lists, and experience stories so children are familiar with the text.

   After their trip to the zoo, the teacher writes down the words of each child to describe their favorite animal. After each child's words are printed on the chart paper, she reads it aloud to them, and they join in: "And Anthony said . . ."

- encourage children to focus attention on what the text means.

   When Jose is puzzled by a word, the teacher asks him to look at the picture and see if that gives him an idea. To Erica she says: "What do you suppose that little girl feels when her mother goes to work?"

- encourage children reading together to help one another with meaning.

    She suggests that Ricky might like to read the story with Jose, to help him figure out some of the hard words.

- help children who have already been introduced to reading in a natural literature context to develop the skills and subskills needed to accomplish the larger goals of reading.

    "Look at that word carefully, Jose. It starts with an . . .? That's right, an "h." That sounds like . . .?"

- develop an awareness of phonics through interaction with meaningful text, such as pointing out sounds in a song or poem.

    "Hop, Hop, Hop" recites the teacher, emphasizing the beginning sounds as she points to the printed words of the poem.

- hold reading conferences to discuss reading and have children read to one another (see Figure 16-11). By analyzing children's miscues, teachers can help each child individually.

- use reading purposefully to help children acquire the information or the pleasure they want. The issue for teachers of beginning readers is not deciding between phonics, or meaning, or whole word; rather it is how to help children develop a repertoire of strategies to use to develop their reading abilities. These include making sense, knowing what the letters tell, recognizing high-frequency words, understanding word structure, and understanding how our language works.

Figure 16-11

Teachers have children read to one another.

Writing. As with reading, children in primary classrooms that use a developmentally appropriate approach need purposes for writing, and plenty of time to practice it and learn the skills. Again the assumption is that this aspect of language is learned developmentally by making approximations of what children see others doing in writing, and that continual practice will gradually help them reach the correct form and usage over time. (Remember the analogy of how infants learn to produce oral speech, at first sounding quite unlike adult speech, and gradually coming to resemble the speech they hear around them.)

Children in primary classrooms need to see adults writing regularly to realize this as an important means of communication. They need to write a great deal, every day to get better at doing it (see Figure 16-12). In primary classrooms, the process of writing is more important than the finished products, which may indicate varying degrees of understanding of the way grammar, spelling, and punctuation work. What is important is the child's decision about what to write and how to express it. The traditional methods of drill and repetition to teach skills of handwriting and spelling are not the goal of writing in the primary classroom. Instead, the goal is to create a disposition to enjoy expressing thoughts in writing.

This is often one difficult area for adults who do not understand the concept of beginning with the whole and working down to the individual skills, seeing the incorrect spelling and grammar as something that should be corrected at the beginning, so that children do not develop bad habits. "How will he learn to spell correctly if she lets him spell like that?" "I can't believe she lets him bring home a paper with so many mistakes." Parents need to be introduced to concepts of

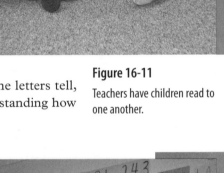

Figure 16-12

There is time to write every day.

PRACTICAL IMPLICATIONS

Reading Instruction Practices

Teachers who use developmentally appropriate methods in early reading instruction avoid:

- teaching reading as a distinct subject, with time in reading groups and workbook practice taking up much of the instructional day.

- emphasizing skills and subskills, taught as ends in themselves, with no context of meaning other than being necessary to pass standardized tests.

- following a rigid sequence of prerequisites, beginning with a focus on letters and sounds of words, rather than looking at language as a whole in books or meaningful text.

- using a single approach for all children, regardless of what children can already do.

- focusing on basal readers, used in the reading groups (and everyone knows which children are reading the lowest-level book).

- omitting reading or listening to children's literature regularly.

- spending most of the time listening to other children read or being corrected in their reading, answering artificial workbook questions, or doing boring workbook pages.

- expecting children to be quiet during much of the day.

developing reading and writing through gradual literacy and language practice, so that they can be supportive and appropriate in their responses to children's work.

Beginning writing skills are nurtured by

- opportunities to observe adults and older children writing frequently, so that they can see that writing has purpose, and that there are conventional forms to learn in writing letters and words.

    Miss Edwards uses chart paper on a large easel at morning meeting time to print the daily news. She talks about what she is doing. "I'll put a capital letter here because I'm starting a new sentence."

- opportunities to learn firsthand that writing is one of the vital ways people communicate with one another.

    "I'm writing a note to your mother, Quiana, to thank her for the cookies she sent us for snack."

- functional print in the classroom that encourages both reading and writing.

    A sign on the Art center says: "Needed: 4 people to wash brushes and tidy the shelves today. Sign up here."

    A sign in the meeting area says: "Write your name here if you have news to tell today."

- individual mailboxes in the room encourage children to communicate with one another in writing.

    Miss Edwards adds stationery and envelopes to the materials in the writing center.

- adults taking children's dictation to describe their creations or experiences.

    "That's an interesting picture you made, Seth. Would you like to tell me the story about it, and I can write the words down, or help you."

- time to draw and/or write every day, including time to discuss ideas with peers and teacher, time to plan how to proceed in the writing, time to work with writing implements and to figure out how words are spelled, and time to share their writing by reading it out loud to a partner or group. Such "writing workshops" help develop skills (McCarry & Greenwood, 2009).

> Every morning after the meeting and story, Miss Edwards's class has writing time. The children each have a writing folder and a notebook where they keep their ongoing writing projects. They sit together at tables and frequently discuss their writing with one another. "How do you spell dinosaur? I'm writing a story about a dinosaur that gets lost." "I'm going to put a friendly dinosaur in my story; I don't like scary dinosaurs." "I'll read you my story when I'm done. You won't be scared."

- experiences and events that encourage and necessitate writing: notes about project plans and progress; project reports; questions for field trips and classroom visitors; thank-you letters and letters to gain information; games, riddles, and jokes; signs, posters, and fliers; messages for friends' mailboxes; lists of favorite things; stories; and journal entries. Topics and reasons for writing emerge primarily from children's own experiences and ideas (Stonier & Dickerson, 2009), rather than from teacher assignments, such as "story starters" that narrow the topic and reason to write.

> Jennifer used her writing time to write a letter to the zoo with a question about what they feed the zebra. DeMario adds a joke to the book of jokes he's writing. LaQuisha and Annie work together on a list of the books they like the best.

- an atmosphere of acceptance of all attempts to express themselves, without undue correction of scribbling, letter formations, **invented spelling**, grammar, word spacing, or punctuation (see Figure 16-13 for stages of invented spelling). When any corrections are made, they are made orally and only incidentally as opportunities present themselves.

> When Briana shows her dinosaur story to the teacher, "dinosaur" is spelled "DNSR." Her teacher comments on the dinosaur's adventure only, while enunciating the word *dinosaur* very precisely, and tells Briana she enjoyed her story. Later she notices that Briana has added an "E"—"DNSER."

- resources children can use independently to assist their writing, such as computers, picture dictionaries, and word lists, and materials to help create finished books to establish authorship (see Figure 16-14).

- encouragement to keep their own personal style of expressing themselves, rather than fitting into some prescribed mold of approved writing. Children are expected to choose their own topics and make decisions about length, organization, and style.

> Kim's writing demonstrates her concern for small creatures; her story today is about a lost puppy. Wally has a scientific curiosity and writes extensively about his observations. Jill's sense of humor comes through in her writing, which she almost always finishes with the words "HA HA."

- portfolios of children's written work maintained over time, for teachers to use as assessment of children's understanding and abilities and to share with parents during progress

Stages of Invented Spelling

1. String of letters: ("This says Dear Mommy")	HTPx
2. Beginning sounds only: ("My Cat")	MC
3. Beginning and ending sounds: ("My Cat")	MI CT
4. Beginning, middle and ending sounds: ("Dear Mommy")	der mome

Figure 16-13

Stages of invented spelling.

Figure 16-14

These primary students are using computers to write and illustrate simple stories.

PRACTICAL IMPLICATIONS

Unsupportive Practices for Beginning Writers

Teachers of beginning writers should avoid:

- emphasizing quality of penmanship as "writing" lessons.

- teaching writing as grammar rather than a form of expressing ideas.

- emphasizing correction of errors in children's work so that the work "looks like a battlefield full of casualties" (Gamberg et al., 1988, p. 201).

- using writing as a punishment or drill practice (a page of M's; a page of "I will not talk out loud").

- using workbook pages extensively.

---

conferences. (See further discussion on portfolios later in this chapter.)

- regular writing conferences between teacher and child to discuss finished work and work in progress. Such individual attention helps teachers work with developing the skills individual children need, as well as supporting and learning unique styles and interests.

Math Skills. As primary-age children slowly leave the stage of preoperational thought and move to understanding concrete operations, they are assisted in this development by opportunities to explore and discover logical-mathematical relationships by acting on concrete objects. Young children need opportunities to use number concepts and skills to explore, discover, and solve meaningful problems. The emphasis in developmentally appropriate primary classrooms is on "developing the thinking that underlies children's ability to read and write mathematical symbols" (Kamii & Kamii, 1990, p. 138). In addition to needing concrete materials to handle, children need time to make the mental connections that help them discover relationships. Young children think better when they physically act upon objects.

An important goal of primary mathematics curricula is to help children develop confidence in their ability to think things through.

> To assess children's confidence in math, a visitor can walk around the classroom while children are completing a worksheet and stop to ask individual children, "How did you get this answer?" (pointing to a correct answer). Many children immediately reach for their erasers, indicating their lack of confidence in their own ideas. (Kamii & Rosenblum, 1990, p. 149)

The components of math described by the national standards include number concepts, patterns and relationships, geometry and spatial sense, measurement, and data collection, organization, and representation (NCTM, 2000). The curriculum standards developed by the National Council for Teachers of Mathematics identify the nature of mathematical thinking and focus on children learning mathematics as problem solving, as reasoning, as communication, and as mathematical connections. Rather than figuring out what the teacher wants them to know or do, these goals focus on children using mathematics to investigate, to think for themselves, to clarify their thinking, and to see the relationship between mathematical ideas. Developmentally appropriate math curricula reflect the idea that children learn from their own experiences, and allow children to make sense of those experiences in their own way (NAEYC & NCTM, 2002). Teachers trying to support the development of mathematical ideas create an environment where children are actively engaged in thinking about mathematics, in which they can come to new insights through the provision of additional experiences that allow them to consider again, from another perspective.

Developmentally appropriate practice for primary-age children related to math includes:

- opportunities to develop number concepts by action in contexts that are real-life and personally

---

JOURNAL REFLECTION

Confidence in Math

Reflect on the above finding about children immediately erasing when questioned about how they got their answer. How do you think this lack of confidence about math develops, and what can teachers do about it?

Visit the premium Web site to complete this journal activity online and email it to your professor.

meaningful to children, such as planning materials needed for a group activity, playing games with peers, and cooking (see Figure 16-15).

> Rosa's group is making cookies to share with the whole class today. "Three cups of flour," she says. "That's only two. You need to add one more."
>
> "You rolled five," says the teacher. "Count out five spaces."
>
> "This is Juanita's sixth birthday. We'll need six stars to paste on her crown, six candles for the cake, and six balloons for decoration."

Figure 16-15

Primary children need opportunities to develop number concepts in real activities, such as cooking.

- daily life experiences in the classroom for children to use mathematical concepts, such as taking attendance, preparing for snack, setting the table, distributing materials, and enforcing the number of children allowed in each center.

> "See if there's a chair for everyone at the table please, Yolanda."
>
> "How many children are absent today, Jodi?"
>
> "Are there more girls or boys in your project group?"

- opportunities to solve practical problems, investigate, and make decisions by themselves.

> "We have six cupcakes left, and there are ten children. How can you divide them so that everyone gets a fair share?"
>
> "He thinks you have more of the blocks than he does. How can you see if that's true or not?"
>
> "Heather said 3 + 5 = 9. Do you think that's right? How can you check?"

- many objects to classify, seriate, create patterns with, count, add and subtract, weigh, and measure. Some objects include traditional math manipulatives such as Cuisenaire rods, dominoes, cards, lotto and bingo cards, board games, table cubes, geoboards, and parquetry blocks. Teachers use their own creativity, community resources, and theme ideas to collect objects for classroom manipulation. Examples include nuts, seeds, pebbles, sea shells, keys, bolts and screws, poker chips, miniature toys, bottle caps, buttons, play money, golf tees, and stamps. Math-related tools are available for use as well: various kinds of balances and scales, rulers and measuring tapes, scales, stopwatches, kitchen timers, and egg timers.

- mini-theme projects that use math skills—such as building, cooking, measuring—and provide a context for math. Such a mini-theme could be setting up a restaurant business, with math activities ranging from planning, buying and cooking the food, selling the food, and calculating the price and the profit or loss. A detailed and fascinating account of such a venture (Chili Enterprise Ltd.) and its integration of math into the theme studies in a primary classroom can be found in Gamberg et al. (1988).

- opportunities to work together on solving math problems in noncompetitive activities that encourage discussions of the reasoning that led to the answers, enabling children to clarify their thinking. Math study groups allow small groups of children to study particular concepts and practice specific skills, and add additional learning opportunities to fundamental teacher-led instruction (Sloane, 2007).

> Tasha, James, and Bradley are figuring out how many cookies they will have to make for each child to get two. Tasha's method is to draw two cookies beside everyone's name and add up all the cookies. Bradley lines up thirty poker chips on the table and takes two away every time he mentions a child's name. James listens silently. At the end, Tasha has a number and Bradley has two piles of poker chips. Tasha explains why her idea worked. James and Bradley both agree.

PRACTICAL IMPLICATIONS

Teaching Math Skills

Unsupportive practices related to teaching children math skills include:

- using a math program that focuses on the math textbook, accompanying workbooks, practice sheets, and board work.

- teaching math only as a set of facts and skills to memorize, rather than as concepts to be understood.

- scheduling a separate time for math instruction each day, unrelated to any other curriculum subject or classroom activity.

- using teacher correction as children's only method of learning whether their answers are correct or not.

- testing number facts, frequently making correct answers the focus and goal, rather than attempting to understand children's methods or thinking.

- providing little time for hands-on activities or materials (only those who finish their workbook assignments in time have the opportunity to play math games).

- using competition as a primary method of motivating children to learn math facts (for example, Row 4 against Row 2).

- mini-lessons for individuals and/or small groups, as teachers assess growth in math understanding and discover areas children are ready to proceed in math learning.

  > The teacher sits down with Tasha, James, and Bradley to show them how to form a column of 2s for addition.

- classroom investigation activities, such as taking surveys (What pet do you have at home? What is your favorite topping for pizza?), doing measurement assignments (See how many cups of sand fill the bucket), and filling in calendar graphs (How many sunny days, cloudy days, or rainy days did we have this month?) to help children become deeply involved in meaningful math.

- much time devoted to playing math games as a vehicle for the repetition needed for children to learn number recognition and value.

  > Cynthia and Robin are playing War, each turning over a card and the one with the higher card claiming it, until all the cards are gone; the winner is the one with the most cards. Stephen and B.J. are ready for Double War, where each turns over two cards, and the winner is the one with the highest two-card total (Kamii & Kamii, 1990).

- Linking books with learning math can help children read to understand how math is a natural part of their physical and social worlds and to use the natural context of stories to discuss and reason about mathematical ideas (Whitin & Whitin, 2005). For a good list of books to tie together literacy and numeracy skills, see Figure 16-16.

The entire issues of *Young Children* in January 2003 and May 2009 are devoted to articles about teaching and learning about math, from infancy through the elementary grades. There is an excellent article on integrating math standards in project work. (See Worsley, Beneke, & Helm, 2003.)

Assessment versus Standardized Testing

When tax dollars in large quantities are spent on education, the issue of accountability naturally arises. Indeed, the legislation in the No Child Left Behind Act (2001) mandates regular high-stakes testing for children from third grade on. High-stakes tests are

- directly linked to decisions regarding promotion or retention.
- connected to changes in the curriculum.
- used for evaluating or rewarding teachers or administrators.
- associated with the allocation of resources to school districts. (See Figure 16-17.)

The report cards mandated to be shared with parents and the community make the results of these tests highly visible. Nevertheless, many educators express concern about relying on testing to assess children's progress in learning. "Attempts to make schools accountable through

Figure 16-16

Good books to link literature and mathematics.

BOOKS THAT LINK LITERATURE AND MATHEMATICS

Counting and Grouping in Sets
One Is a Snail, Ten Is a Crab, April Pulley Sayre
Let's Count, Tana Hoban
The Father Who Had 10 Children, Benedick Guettier
What Comes in 2's, 3's, and 4's? Suzanne Aker
One of Three, Angela Johnson
One Hundred Is a Family, Pam Munoz Ryan
Anno's Magic Seeds, Mitsumasa Anno
Ten, Nine, Eight, Molly Bang
Each Orange Had Eight Slices, Paul Giganti
My Little Sister Ate One Hare, Bill Grossman

Adding Money
26 Letters and 99 Cents, Tana Hoban
The Great Pet Sale, Mick Inkpen
Coin Counting Book, Rozanne Lanczak Williams
If You Made a Million, David M. Schwartz

Comparisons and Patterns
Colors Everywhere, Tana Hoban
More, Fewer, Less, Tana Hoban
Pattern Bugs, Trudy Harris
Spots: Counting Creatures from Sky to Sea, Carolyn Lesser & Laura Regan
Is It Larger? Is It Smaller? Tana Hoban
The Midnight Farm, Reeve Lindbergh

Doubling and Halving
Two of Everything, Lily Toy Hong
Two Greedy Bears, Mirra Ginsburg, et al.
One Less Fish, Kim M. Toft & Allan Sheather

Arrangements for 100
100th Day Worries, Margery Cuyler
Centipede's 100 Shoes, Tony Ross
One Hundred Hungry Ants, Elinor J. Pinczes

Measurement
The Line Up Book, Marisabina Russo
How Big Is a Foot? Rolf Myller
Inch by Inch, Leo Lionni

Shapes
Round and Round and Round, Tana Hoban
Round Is a Mooncake, Roseanne Thong
The Greedy Triangle, Marilyn Burns

Addition
Ten Red Apples, Pat Hutchins
Count on Your Fingers African Style, Claudia Zaslavsky
12 Ways to Get to 11, Eve Merriam
Two Ways to Count to Ten, Ruby Dee

achievement testing have resulted in 'doing more of what has not been working and doing it earlier in children's lives'" (Katz, cited in Kamii, 1990, p. 163). When widespread testing comes into prominence, the result is a "narrowing of the curriculum, a concentration on those skills most amenable to testing, a constraint on the creativity and flexibility of teachers, and a demeaning of teachers' professional judgment" (Meisels, 2000). The common phrase is that teachers find themselves "teaching to the test" (or indeed teaching the test), with the specter of tests

Figure 16-17

High-stakes testing has become a part of life for children.

looming over the lives of children throughout the year. The inappropriate expectations and stress of artificial test situations take a toll on the healthy development of young children, and result in too many children thinking of themselves as failures.

Achievement tests are designed to make half of the children tested come out below the average (Kamii, 1990); children developing more slowly than others, for whatever reason, are labeled and designated in a lower percentile, and everyone knows what they got on the test! Achievement tests work by comparing a group of children of the same grade level at one point in time; although to evaluate a child's progress in learning, the comparison needs to be made between his knowledge at one point in time and his knowledge at a later point in time. Although quality schools readily accept the principle of accountability in establishing the value of the program in maximizing children's potentials, they reject the narrow focus of achievement tests and standardized tests (Wesson, 2001). In response to the testing approach mandated by the No Child Left Behind Act, the National Education Association (NEA) has put forth a statement advocating for "Testing Plus," suggesting alternatives to testing as the sole means of accountability. Teachers believe that children should be protected against high-stakes decisions based on the results of a single test. They argue for multiple opportunities for children to take tests, tests aligned to the state standards, and additions of classroom assessment practices, such as portfolios, projects, and performance assessments. Teachers who are advocates of developmentally appropriate practice need to continue these efforts to press and educate about the dangers and ineffectiveness of achievement tests (Kohn, 2001). The topic of assessment will continue to be an important discussion for early childhood educators in our current social and political climate. The entire issue of January 2004 *Young Children* focuses on various aspects of the debate, including the most current NAEYC and NAECS/SDE position statement (2003).

Observation-based assessment is, however, essential to providing curriculum and instruction that is both age appropriate and individually appropriate; assessment is, in fact, completely integrated with curriculum and instruction. Although achievement tests usually work to the detriment of the child—often resulting in tracking, exclusion, or labeling on the basis of limited factors—assessment results in benefits to the child, such as necessary adjustments to curriculum or more individualized instruction. Assessment demonstrates children's overall strengths and progress, instead of focusing on their wrong answers and what they do not know. Assessment supports, rather than threatens, children's feelings of self-esteem. Children are encouraged and taught skills to participate in self-assessment, rather than being the passive recipients of an outsider's narrow method of evaluating them (Brown, 2008).

CULTURAL CONSIDERATIONS

High-Stakes Testing

Many of the provisions of the No Child Left Behind legislation were designed to remove differences between minority students and others. Yet one of the most discussed provisions of the legislation includes "high-stakes testing." The debate about whether these tests are useful tools to improve education is complex. Nevertheless, most researchers and practitioners believe that high-stakes testing will have the greatest consequences on minority students, English-language learners, and students with disabilities, and will result in these students being disproportionately retained in grades and denied high school diplomas. Critics have argued that schools do not expose these students to the knowledge and skills that are necessary to pass the tests. They point out that simply instituting such tests does not address the concern about how to improve learning. Furthermore, research has shown that "holding children back" increases dropout rates. As a result, high-stakes testing will likely create an increasingly large class of students who are at increased risk of dropping out by virtue of having been retained in a grade one or more times. Moreover, such initiatives have the potential to make otherwise well-qualified students who are English-language learners ineligible for graduation and eventual attendance in the only institutions of higher learning that they can afford: state colleges and universities.

Another potential difficulty for immigrant students is the limitation of many immigrant parents to communicate in the language of the school, or understand its culture and demands. Consequently, many parents have limited knowledge of, and impact on, their children's educational development. Lacking the support and guidance they need from their parents, many students rely heavily on advice from their peers. Although their peers may share their challenges, they generally lack the maturity and understanding to provide wise guidance. Can you think about some possible strategies that would help diverse students (and their families) navigate these complex issues related to high-stakes testing?

The purpose of assessment is:

1. to provide teachers with information needed to plan and adapt curriculum to meet each child's developmental and learning needs;

2. to help teachers and families monitor children's progress;

3. to evaluate and improve program effectiveness; and

4. to screen and diagnose children with disabilities or special learning and developmental needs (Copple & Bredekamp, 2009, p. 321).

We need to evaluate in order to know what level of development a child has reached in various aspects of learning, what attempts the child has made to learn, and what areas the child has mastered. Evaluation helps us see what experiences the child needs in order to make progress and in what areas the most effort should be put. Basically, evaluation helps provide us with a plan for teaching. (Gamberg et al., 1988, p. 216)

Unfortunately, as administrators pressure teachers to make sure that classrooms and schools are meeting their annual achievement goals, too many teachers are succumbing to considering testing more important than their classroom-based assessment. But assessment is an essential component of a teacher's role, because it is teachers who will use the assessment information. This does not mean that teachers function alone in the assessment process. Assessment involves joint effort and communication between teachers and children, between parents and teachers, and between the larger school and community. Each member has information and insights to offer the others. The DAP position statement mandates that decisions that will have a major

Deborah Jaffe/Corbis

Figure 16-18

Assessment should involve the real activities of the classroom, such as reading a report.

impact on children, such as school entry, instructional grouping, or retention in a grade, should be based on multiple sources of information, including information from observations by teachers and specialists and from parents, in addition to formal and informal assessments.

The Guidelines for Appropriate Assessment for Planning Instruction and Communicating with Parents developed by the NAEYC (Bredekamp & Rosegrant, 1992 and 1995) state that assessment "involves regular and periodic observation of the child in a wide variety of circumstances that are representative of the child's behavior in the program over time" (Bredekamp & Rosegrant, 1995, p. 17). The guidelines further state that the procedures used should reflect the ongoing life of the classroom and typical activities of the children—real reading and writing, and math—rather than artificial, contrived situations (skills testing) that are remote from the usual learning process in the classroom (see Figure 16-18).

In creating assessment plans, teachers must decide on answers to these questions:

- What is considered typical development for the age level?
- What should children know or be able to do when leaving the program or grade level?
- What will be assessed on each of the developmental domains or content areas?
- What methods will be used to assess and document progress?

Note that in culturally diverse settings, identifying progress, or even developmental problems, may be a more complicated process because what one culture perceives as a problem, another culture may not. Therefore, accurate assessments require the participation of parents who can "place this information within the context of the child's developmental history and help to correct for cultural biases of the testing instrument or the provider" (Chang, 1993, p. 60).

Assessment involves devising methods of regular observation of children and recording that information systematically for future use.

Methods of Regular Observation. Systematic observation for assessment occurs in the classroom during the variety of typical learning activities in the usual circumstances, rather than in any specially set-up situation that detracts from the natural learning environment. Teachers observe children's performance and activity during real learning times in learning centers, during project group work, and through literacy experiences.

They have conversations and individual conferences with children to gain additional insights into their style of, rate of, and interest in learning. Thus, there is minimal intrusion into children's normal routines and developmentally appropriate activities. Teachers do all of this over periods of time, so that they put together a consistent picture or pattern about a particular child, rather than a single observation that may or may not be representative of the child's actual accomplishment or ability. They are careful to observe for information in all the interrelated domains of development, knowing that a single observation may yield insights in several separate areas. They are aware that assessment is not comparative, that is, the assessment of an individual child takes into account diversity of learning in style and rate of learning, recognizing that family and cultural influences need to be considered. Assessment gives a picture of where each child is now, in relation to where he or she used to be.

For example, as the first-grade teacher focuses this morning on Maria, she is busy at the writing center. Several children are working near her, but she does not converse. She appears very intent on her work. She switches the pencil from her right to her left hand and pauses frequently to rest her hand. She leaves the area to find a book in the library. The teacher observes her finding a word, and then continuing to write her story. She displays quiet pleasure when the teacher

SOCIAL PROMOTION AND GRADE RETENTION

Despite a century of research that fails to support grade retention (repeating a grade) or **social promotion** (being passed to next grade with peers, though not meeting grade level expectations) as methods to improve learning or facilitate adjustment and achievement outcomes, both retention and social promotion are being increasingly used in this era of legislated accountability. It is estimated that as many as 15 percent of students are retained each year, with perhaps 30–50 percent having been retained at least once before reaching ninth grade. Statistics are highest among males, poverty-level students, minority students, those with late birthdays, and those with reading difficulties, including English-language learners. Any initial achievement gains that may occur during the next year consistently decline within two to three years. Retention does not appear to have a positive impact on self-esteem or overall school adjustment and is, in fact, associated with a significant increase in behavior problems on behavior rating scales. In fact, of nineteen studies in the 1990s that compared the outcomes for students who were retained, matched with students who were promoted, retention had a negative impact on all areas of achievement (reading, math, and language) and on social-emotional indicators, such as peer relationships, self-esteem, problem behaviors, and attitude.

The difficulty is that both social promotion and retention try to address problems after they occur, rather than trying to prevent or catch difficulties early on. Suggested alternatives focus on striking at the root causes of poor performance.

In a position statement published by the National Association of School Psychologists (2003), an argument is made for "promotion plus," a spectrum of early intervention and follow-up services that include

- encouragement of parental involvement in their children's education.
- adoption of age-appropriate and culturally sensitive instructional strategies.
- emphasis on improving early development and preschool programs.
- effective early reading programs.
- tutoring and mentoring programs.
- systematic assessment strategies that include monitoring of progress.
- school-based mental health programs.
- appropriate educational services to focus on educational disabilities, including collaboration among all professionals.
- student support teams to assess and identify learning and behavioral problems.
- extended-year, extended-day, and summer programs.
- effective behavior management programs (NASP, 2003).

Intervening early and often is the strategy to help students succeed, rather than relying on retention and social promotion (Johnson & Rudolph, 2001).

comes over to ask her to read her what she is writing. Maria reads: A MTHER luks FTIR hir BBE (A mother looks after her baby). As the teacher makes notes in Maria's file later, she notes the following:

- Comfortable near other children and with adults, although does not initiate conversation. Perhaps the language is still a barrier or her style and background? (Maria's parents speak Spanish with her at home although she has become quite fluent in English.)
- Concentration good, and finds resources independently.
- Still having difficulty with pencil grip and possibly handedness.
- Has progressed with her invented spelling to using some internal vowels.
- Confident and interested in her reading/writing.
- Interest in babies. (Maria's mother has several younger children at home.)

The implications for the teacher for planning future work with Maria include pencil skills, working with her bilingually, dend planning a pairing with an outgoing child. A plan is evolving, as her progress and interests are noted.

Teachers have time for regular observation because of playing roles other than directing all the learning experiences in the classroom. As children are actively involved with reading, writing, math, theme work, or interest center times, teachers circulate among them, asking questions, encouraging efforts, and always observing. Assessment is so essential to developmentally appropriate practice that it must be built into the routine each day. Teachers find their own methods for ensuring a focus that involves each child in the classroom. They may select several children to observe during the day or during a particular activity. They devise quick methods of note taking, such as keeping a roll of gummed labels in a pocket for making brief notes on through the day, then dating them and sticking them in children's folders at the end of the day. If more than one adult is teaching in the classroom, teachers may divide observation tasks or confer with colleagues about their separate observations.

Recording Information Systematically. Teachers use a variety of tools for compiling assessment data on children. These may include videotapes and audiotapes; checklists for literacy and numeration skills, social skills, work habits, or other developmental aspects; anecdotal notes; and student portfolios. Meisels (1993) refers to a Work Sampling System. The three complementary components are developmental checklists, portfolios, and summary reports, offering a record of both learning and instruction.

Portfolios. Portfolios may contain collections of representative work of children that illustrate their progress and achievements, such as

- periodic, dated samples or photographs of drawing and artwork.
- samples of writing, including ideas and plans.
- tape recordings of their reading that can be analyzed for mistakes and self-corrections.
- lists of books and stories read.
- certain core items or examples of repeated work collected from each child several times a year (Shores & Grace, 2005).

Children are encouraged to add their own selections of work that they feel show their progress to the portfolios. Teachers may keep working portfolios, later condensing them to show representative progress, and perhaps creating exit portfolios to move on with students.

Portfolios present primary resources for consideration by parents, teachers, and children. In portfolios, the work itself is presented as tangible evidence of progress for parents and children, rather than having to rely on teachers' reactions to the work, as might be presented in anecdotal reports or checklists. Teachers, parents, and children learn how to look at work as part of a developmental continuum, which is evidence of children's use of skills in a meaningful context.

Another method of recording may be to keep tapes of children talking with the teacher about specific questions that will help evaluate their progress in thinking logically, or their understanding of, and attitude toward, their reading.

Teachers often devise their own questionnaires or descriptive checklists related to the continuum of specific competencies identified as goals for children. For

---

PRACTICAL IMPLICATIONS

Unsupportive Practices for Primary-Age Students

Confidence and success as a learner and feelings of security within the school setting are undermined by unsupportive practices such as:

- evaluating young children by testing and ranking them against only a standardized group norm that assumes all children will achieve the same academic skills at the same chronological age and grade level.

- testing all subjects regularly in the classroom and emphasizing test scores as indications of success or failure.

- reporting progress to parents using letter or numerical grades, comparing primary-age children to others in the same class or to national averages.

- promoting (passing) or retaining (failing) children who have not reached the minimum numbers on tests measuring reading and math skills, with the attendant effects on self-esteem.

- using social promotion for children who are not making adequate progress, without adaptation of other teaching strategies or interventions.

As should be painfully obvious, most of this list has now been mandated by federal legislation. Supporters of developmentally appropriate practice within school systems clearly have their work cut out for them.

example, a teacher questionnaire to document literacy competencies might include these components: knows directional conventions—left-right, top-bottom; understands consistency principle (same word is spelled the same way); knows twelve or more letter sounds. Teachers may decide on a series of books of different levels to use for observing specific reading competencies. A social-skills descriptive checklist might ask questions in areas such as evidence of the child's ability to work cooperatively with others, evidence of tolerance toward others' mistakes, and constructive help of others.

Periodically, teachers review their folders and documentation of children's progress to summarize progress and interests to date. This forms the basis for understanding where the child is before making plans for future instruction. It is also useful to do this before parent conferences or year-end reviews, or when making written reports to parents. Regular opportunities for sharing information between teachers and parents about children's overall progress are a part of the assessment process. This communication, sometimes oral and sometimes written, focuses on descriptive, narrative accounts, using specifics from teacher observation. Because this kind of reporting focuses on children's overall strengths and progress from the last reporting period, it is supportive of parents' relationships with, and confidence in, their children. There is no absolute standard of grades or percentiles that indicates readiness to move on, so children's progress is continuous through sequential curricula.

SUMMARY

Current legislation has created challenges within schools for teachers and children. Primary-age children are supported in developmentally appropriate classrooms that recognize their active and experiential methods of learning. Appropriate practices that facilitate the development of reading, writing, and mathematical skills include integrating the curriculum so that skills can be learned in a meaningful context; using a project/theme approach so that children can become autonomous learners; using carefully researched language methods to help children progress in literacy skills; using a well-articulated, coherent mathematics curriculum; and individualization of teacher instruction to promote early success. The prevalence of testing to measure achievement for children and schools may narrow academic approaches in primary classrooms. Ongoing teacher assessment using observation as well as work sampling, however, is an essential component of determining the direction of curricula and instruction.

THINK ABOUT IT ACTIVITIES

1. With a group of classmates, brainstorm a list of potential project topics for primary-age children in your community. Refer to the criteria in the section on themes to select your most appropriate choice. Create a list of suitable subtopics that might interest children.

2. Do some preliminary research on the resources you would make available for this project study—children's literature and nonfiction books, pictures and posters, field trips, visitors, other classroom materials, and possible activities. Share this with your classmates.

3. Make a collection of creative math manipulatives that could be used in primary classrooms. (Include at least ten to twenty in each of several categories.)

4. Read more about reading and language activities that develop language and literacy skills in primary classrooms. (See the list of references and suggested readings at the end of the chapter.)

5. Where possible, identify primary classrooms in your community that are using developmentally appropriate practices such as projects for integrated curricula, literature-based reading instruction, and daily writing for expression. Talk with the teachers and/or visit their classrooms to see them at work. Identify practices that are different from traditional primary classrooms.

QUESTIONS TO ASSESS LEARNING OF CHAPTER OBJECTIVES

1. Discuss the practices for developmentally appropriate classrooms related to understanding characteristics of preoperational and concrete thought.

2. Identify goals of the cognitive/language primary environment.

3. Identify the components of an integrated curriculum.

4. Discuss currently approved language practices for development of language and literacy skills in reading and writing.

5. Describe practices of a developmentally appropriate math curriculum.

6. Contrast the effects of achievement testing and assessment and describe the importance of assessment in planning developmentally appropriate cognitive/language primary environments.

APPLY YOUR KNOWLEDGE QUESTIONS

1. Write a document to give to parents in a first-grade classroom to describe and explain the approach you will take in reading and writing instruction. Anticipate several questions and concerns of the parents related to their children's later success on end-of-grade tests and respond to these.

2. Your principal is concerned that your second-graders are spending too much time on theme study and not enough time getting ready for the tests mandated by the No Child Left Behind Act for the end of next year. Prepare a document that indicates clearly how you are integrating skill development with the theme project work you are doing.

HELPFUL WEB SITES

http://www.nea.org	The Web site of the National Education Association has several articles and statements regarding its position on the No Child Left Behind Act. Search for Testing Plus to see their ideas of evaluation on more than just test scores.
http://www.reading.org	The Web site for the International Reading Organization has much information, including several position statements, such as "Using Multiple Methods of Beginning Reading Instruction" (1998).
http://www.nclb.org	Read the No Child Behind Left Act at this Web site.
http://www.rif.org	The Web site for Reading Is Fundamental has much information for teachers and parents about helpful literacy practices.

Please visit the premium Web site for Developmentally Appropriate Practice, *4th edition, to access more chapter web links, additional book chapters, suggestions for further reading and study, interactive quizzes, video exercises, online journal activities, flashcards, and much more!*
Go to www.cengage.com/login to register your access code.

GLOSSARY

A

Absorbent mind: Phrase used by Montessori to describe young children's active, natural learning style in their early years.

Academic: Related to learning skills for literacy and mathematics. In early childhood education, this term often refers to methods of learning that use rote memorization.

Accommodation: Piaget's term for changes in cognition to include new information.

Accreditation: Process of recognition in early childhood programs that provide excellent learning environments for young children, based on principles of developmentally appropriate practice.

Active listening: Technique of providing reflective feedback to speaker, including paraphrasing and accepting the words and feelings underlying the communication.

Advanced babbling: Two-syllable combinations of consonants and vowels, of sounds heard around them, produced in late infancy.

Aesthetic: Related to art, beauty, and creativity.

Agility: Being able to move nimbly and quickly.

Animism: Tendency to attribute life to objects that are not alive.

Antibias: Practices and attitudes to prevent development of prejudice and bias.

Assessment: Method of evaluation, usually used in evaluating level of development and learning.

Assimilation: Piaget's term for incorporating new information into an existing cognitive structure.

Associative group play: Play where children interact with each other sporadically in similar activities, with loose association.

Atelier: Term used for area in Reggio Emilia schools where children work creatively on long-term projects.

Atelierista: Person trained in aesthetics who supports children in creative work.

Attachment: Reciprocal, lasting ties between infants and caregivers, contributing to mutual pleasure.

Authoritarian: Term for adult interaction style that emphasizes control and obedience.

Authoritative: Term for adult interaction style that emphasizes respect, warmth, and nurturance for children with high expectations and standards for behavior.

Autonomy: Sense of independence and ability to be self-reliant, of being a separate individual.

B

Babbling: Production of all possible vowel and sound combinations for all languages.

Backtracking: Term used to indicate process of analyzing and interpreting activity after it has occurred to evaluate learning tasks and skills involved.

Behavioral theory: Learning theory that emphasizes role of environment and predictable responses in causing behaviors.

Benchmarks: Standards for evaluating learning.

Bilingualism: Ability to speak two languages.

Binocular vision: Ability to use both eyes at once.

423

C

Centration: From Piaget's theory, tendency of preoperational children to focus on one aspect of a situation and neglect others.

Child-initiated: Activities where children take the lead in making choices, plans, and decisions.

Chronological: Related to time, age.

Coercion: Force, compulsion.

Cognitive: Related to the process of knowing, thinking, learning.

Competence: Belief that one is able to achieve tasks and goals.

Concrete: Things or events that can be perceived by the senses; actual.

Concreteness: Mental characteristic of understanding real objects, situations, and happenings experienced firsthand, but having difficulty with abstract ideas.

Conscience: Internal standards of behavior that control personal conduct.

Conservation: Piaget's term for awareness that two objects that are equal according to a certain measure remain equal even where there is a perceptual change.

Constructive play: The second level of play, involving the use of objects or materials to make something, according to Piaget and Smilansky.

Constructivism: Theory of creating one's own understanding of the world through interaction with materials, experiences, and people.

Constructivist: Related to the theory that individuals create their own understanding of the world through interaction with materials, experiences, and people.

Continuum: A continuous whole whose parts cannot be separated.

Conventional level: Second level in Kohlberg's theory of moral reasoning, in which the child internalizes the standards of adults.

Cooing: Production of open vowel sounds.

Cooperative play: Two or more children act and communicate to maintain play that is focused on common goal or play theme.

Coordination: State of harmonious functions, as of muscles.

Core conflict: Term used by Erikson to describe psychosocial issue to be resolved in each stage of development, for healthy personality development.

Culture: A group's total way of life, including customs, beliefs, values—learned behavior passed on from parents to children.

Curriculum: Methods and content to be taught.

D

Decentering: Piaget's term for thinking simultaneously about several aspects of a situation.

Decontextualization: Understanding things apart from the present context or environment.

Deferred imitation: Piaget's term for reproducing an observed behavior, after a period of time.

Democratic discipline: Discipline in which children participate to solve problems and make decisions.

Developmental delays: Conditions where children's development in one or many domains may lag behind statistical norms.

Developmental principles: Basic, accepted ideas of development derived from research and theory.

Dexterity: Skill in using one's hands or body.

Didactic: Used for teaching. In Montessori's philosophy, refers to materials that teach because their properties are inherently self-correcting.

Disabilities: Conditions that may include physical, mental, or emotional limitations on full function.

Discipline: Methods of molding children's character and teaching them self-control and acceptable behavior.

Disequilibrium: In Piaget's theory, referring to when children take in information that conflicts with prior knowledge and are confused.

Dispositions: Attitudes.

Distraction: Effective strategy when guiding infants or toddlers, of diverting attention to another activity or material.

Divergent: Thinking that produces a variety of possibilities.

Documentation: Note taking and illustration to portray learning.

Domains: Various aspects of development, as physical, cognitive, language, social, and emotional. They are interrelated, although they may be discussed separately.

Dramatic play: Pretend play, where participants take on imaginary roles.

E

Early learning standards: Standards developed by most states to outline required learning for children before kindergarten.

Egocentric thinking: Thought that focuses only on individual's perceptions and experiences.

Egocentrism: Piaget's term for inability to consider another person's viewpoint.

Emergent curriculum: Learning activities that develop from following the interests and interactions of the classroom participants.

Empathy: Ability to recognize and understand another's perspective and feelings.

Equilibrium: From Piaget's ideas, when children reach a new level of understanding by adjusting current ideas to new ideas.

Eurythmy: A movement art that usually accompanies spoken texts or music and includes elements of role play. Unique to Waldorf education.

Experiential: Learning related to experience.

Expressive language: Language that can be produced by the child.

F

Facilitator: One who supports and encourages learning.

Fluency: Ability to write or speak smoothly, with ease.

Foundational: The base on which something rests, the basis of that which follows.

Functional play: The first level of play, involving repeated physical movements, according to Piaget and Smilansky. Also called practice play.

G

Gender identity: Awareness developed in early childhood that individual is male or female.

Gender-specific: The specific characteristics associated with a particular gender.

Genetic: Regulated by inheritance of DNA, for specific characteristics.

Guidance: Leading, explaining, suggesting appropriate behavior. Helping children develop self-control.

H

Heredity: Innate influences on development, conveyed by genes inherited from biological parents.

High-stakes testing: Testing whose outcomes are critical for decision making.

Hippocampus: Part of the brain.

Holophrase: Single words of toddlers that convey much meaning, depending on inflection, context, and adult interpretation.

I

Identification: Process of imitating or adopting ideas of admired individual.

IFSP (Individualized Family Service Plan): A plan required when serving children ages birth through three with special needs according to PL 99-457, to identify and organize effective resources to support the child's development.

Indirect guidance: Behind-the-scenes adult attention to factors in the environment that influence children's behavior, such as arrangements of space, time, and materials.

Initiative: Readiness or ability to take initial steps or actions, independent of others' directions.

Initiative versus guilt: Erikson's third core conflict in psychosocial development, in which children balance the urge to pursue their goals with moral ideas that may prevent them from carrying out ideas.

Integrated curriculum: Curriculum where learning takes place through activity, rather than separating into distinct academic subjects.

Interdependence: Mutual dependence.

Interest centers: Also called activity centers or learning centers. Separate areas in classroom dedicated to particular activity.

Internalize: Process by which children accept societal standards as their own, as a source of self-discipline.

Interrelationships: Having a close, mutual connection with each other.

Intrinsically motivated: Where urge to perform comes from within one's own ideas.

Invented spelling: Early attempts at writing, using sound representation.

Irreversibility: Piaget's term for the preoperational children's inability to mentally retrace their thinking, to understand that operations can go in two or more directions.

J

Jargon: Specialized communication associated with particular profession or body of knowledge.

K

Key experiences: Term from High/Scope curriculum, referring to a set of ten concepts based on Piaget's ideas of the cognitive characteristics and learning potential of preschoolers. These include time, number, seriation, classificiation, music, movement, initiative and social relations, language and literacy, and creative representation.

Kindergarten: Educational program, either full-day or part-day, for children beginning at age five.

L

Language acquisition device (LAD): Chomsky's theory that a language acquisition device is an inborn mechanism programmed into the brain, allowing children to infer linguistic rules from the language they hear.

Large motor: Activities that use the large muscles of the legs and arms.

Literacy: Ability to read and write.

Logical consequences: Consequences directly related to the behavior, used to help a child learn what to do instead, or repair what has been done.

Logical-mathematical knowledge: One of Piaget's kinds of knowledge, the knowledge that develops as children discover relationships among objects, people, and ideas.

Longitudinal studies: Study designed to assess changes in a sample over time.

Loose parts: Also may be called open-ended materials, meaning items that can be used in any number of ways by children in their play. Often recycled materials.

M

Maturation: Unfolding of genetically influenced, sometimes age-related, sequence of physical changes, related to muscle and nervous system readiness.

Midline hand coordination: Ability to bring hands together to coordinate activities.

Mixed-age grouping: Grouping of at least two or more chronological ages.

Mobility: Ability to move all or part of the body.

Modeling: Demonstration of skills and behaviors.

Moral realism: In Piaget's theory, stage of moral development of young primary-age children, who regard rules as unchangeable, absolute, and imposed by an external authority.

Multiple intelligences: According to the theory of Howard Gardner, individuals may be particularly strong in one or two of the eight intelligences, meaning ways of interacting and expressing themselves.

N

Natural consequences: Consequences that happen without any intervention.

Negativism: Resisting or opposing others.

Neurobiological: Related to nervous system and control of the body.

Neuron: Nerve cell.

Norms: Typical for most people in a group.

Numeracy: Understanding of arithmetic principles.

O

Objectives: Goals, aims.

Object permanence: Piaget's term for the understanding that a person or object still exists when out of sight.

Onlooker: Stage of play where a child watches other children but does not engage with them.

Open-ended materials: Materials that can be used in many ways, with no one restricted way to use them.

Outlets: Activities and materials that allow children to express their emotions.

Overgeneralization: Mistaken application of understood rules of grammar to irregular forms of language.

P–Q

Palmar: Grasp in which infant scoops objects, holding the thumbs and fingers as if in a mitten.

Parallel play: Child plays in presence of others, often with same materials and activity, but there is no verbal contact or recognition of the other child.

Parentese: Strategies used by adults to emphasize their speech in speaking with infants.

Pedagogy: Related to study and teaching of children.

Pedogogista: Individual in Reggio Emilia preschools who helps coordinate teacher efforts in planning projects.

Peers: Those who are age-mates or equals.

Performance-based: Method of evaluation and assessment that relies on observing children during daily activities, rather than artificial testing situations.

Permissive: Style of adult interaction that emphasizes warmth and affection with little instruction on appropriate behavior or expectations for behavior.

Phonemes: Discernible phonetic difference between sounds.

Phonics: Emphasizes decoding of words with separate sounds.

Phonological awareness: Hearing and understanding the different sounds and patterns of spoken language.

Physical knowledge: From Piaget, one of the necessary kinds of knowledge, obtained from activities that allow children to observe and draw conclusions about the physical properties of objects.

Pictograph: Series of pictures and drawings that convey messages.

Pincer: Grasp where infants can use thumb and forefinger together.

Plan-do-review: Technique used in High/Scope curriculum, where children make choices with teacher assistance, carry out the activity, and report on the activity.

Pluralist: One who can be comfortable in many settings, with different ideas.

Polarities: Showing two contrary qualities.

Portfolio: Collection of materials that illustrate children's abilities, learning, and thinking.

Preconventional level: From Kohlberg's theory, referring to the time in which moral reasoning is influenced by a concern for obedience and punishment and for satisfying personal needs.

Prekindergarten: Generally considered to be four-year-olds in a preschool program.

Preoperational period: From Piaget's theory, the second stage of cognitive development, in which children are not yet able to use logic.

Preschoolers: Children ages three through five years.

Primary caregiver: One who has major responsibility and time spent with an infant or a small group of infants.

Prime time: Time when caregiver and child are focused on interaction with one another.

Private space: A space in the classroom where a child can go to be alone.

Private speech: Talking out loud to oneself, without intention of communicating with others.

Process-oriented: Where the process of activity or learning is emphasized.

Product-oriented: Where the end result of the activity or learning is emphasized.

Professional standards: Standards for practice articulated by professional organizations.

Progettazione: A word used in the Reggio Emilia system, indicating the theorizing and hypothesizing that is part of building a long-term project.

Props: Materials used by children in their pretend play.

Prosocial: Actions and attitudes that support, assist, or benefit others.

R

Racial/cultural identity: Understanding of one's racial or ethnic identity.

Ratio: Used in early childhood education and childcare to mean the number of children that are cared for by one adult.

Readiness tests: Tests used to assess whether children are likely to succeed in an educational environment, primarily applied to kindergarten.

Reasoning: Ability to think, using cause and effect.

Receptive language: Language that is understood by the child.

Redirection: Guidance strategy where an adult suggests a more appropriate activity to a child.

Reflexes: Automatic, involuntary, innate responses to stimulation.

Reinforcing: Rewarding behavior with a positive response.

Renewal time: Term used by Cherry to suggest occasions when a child needs to withdraw from the group situation to regain emotional control.

Representational play: Play where a child is able to use words, actions, or materials to convey symbols of objects or events.

Representational thought: Piaget's term for the ability to store mental images or symbols.

Resistance: Active opposition of another's words or actions, such as in toddlerhood.

Retaliation: To repay an action or injury with an act of the same kind.

Retention: Holding back, as referring to children repeating a grade.

Rote: Learning by memorization, without thought of the meaning.

S

Scaffolding: The process of linking what a child knows or can do with new information or skills the child is ready to acquire. Another individual is likely instrumental in this process.

Schema: Piaget's term for organized patterns of behavior used in different situations.

School phobia: Fear of going to school that may be linked with physical symptoms.

Screening: Method of testing to identify those with particular difficulties or delays.

Self-concept: Sense of self. Descriptive mental picture of one's abilities and traits.

Self-demand schedule: Schedule set by infants, according to their physical needs.

Self-esteem: Judgment made by an individual about his or her self-worth.

Self-help skills: Abilities to care for oneself, such as in dressing, hygiene, toilet practices, and so on.

Self-regulation: Ability to control one's own actions.

Sense of autonomy: Positive result of core conflict of toddler, according to Erikson.

Sense of industry: Positive result of core conflict of schoolager, according to Erikson.

Sense of initiative: Positive result of core conflict of preschooler, according to Erikson.

Sense of trust: Positive result of core conflict of infant, according to Erikson.

Sensitive periods: Term from Montessori, where she identified periods of learning in which children are particularly sensitive to particular stimuli.

Sensorimotor: In Piaget's theory, the first stage in cognitive development during which infants learn through sensory and motor activity.

Sensorimotor period: Piaget's term for cognitive development in the first two years of life, when infants use their senses and manipulative abilities to learn.

Separation anxiety: Distress shown by an infant when a familiar caregiver leaves.

Sequence: Order of events.

Sex-role behavior: Behavior associated with particular gender identification.

Sexual identity: Awareness of being male or female.

Social comparison: Comparing oneself with peers, as to ability, knowledge, and so on.

Social Promotion: Promoting children to the next grade along with their peers, rather than on basis of learning accomplishment.

Socialized: Having been taught to regulate behavior according to society to get along with others.

Social knowledge: Piaget's third kind of knowledge, acquired directly from others.

Sociodramatic play: Cooperative play that includes a storyline that is shared among players.

Solitary play: A child plays alone with no social interaction.

Stranger anxiety: Wariness of strange people and places, shown by many infants during the second half of the first year.

Substages: The six divisions showing change and development within the sensorimotor stage in Piaget's theory.

Substitution: Offering another object or activity in exchange for one that is desired.

Symbiotic: Close association in which there are advantages for both participants.

Symbolic: Having the ability to understand and represent knowledge, often abstract, in concrete forms, such as letters or numbers.

Symbolic play: Play where objects are used to convey meaning.

Symbolic thought: From Piaget's terminology, the ability to use mental representations, such as words or images, to which a child has attached meaning.

Synapses: Connections between nerve cells.

T

Tactile: That which can be perceived by touch.

Teacher-initiated: Refers to activities and ideas that result from teacher action.

Telegraphic speech: Early form of sentence, consisting only of essential words.

Temperament: Characteristic disposition or style of approaching and reacting to situations.

Theme planning: Organization of activities and materials around a particular concept.

Time blocks: Periods of time within a schedule that may be lengthened or shortened.

Transductive: Tendency to reason from particular to particular, creating faulty reasoning in young children.

Transitional classes: Classes for children who are not deemed ready for tasks of kindergarten or other grade levels.

Transitions: Period of time between the ending of one segment of a schedule and the beginning of another.

U–Z

Unidimensional: See centration.

Universality: Characteristic of something being true in all cases.

Zone of proximal development (ZPD): Vygotsky's term for the difference between what a child can do alone and with help.

LIST OF USEFUL FIGURES AND BOXES

ACEI. (2002). ACEI position statement. *Global guidelines for early childhood education and care in the 21st century.* Also available online at http://acei.org

Ainsworth, M. D. S. (1992). Attachment: Retrospect and prospect. In C. M. Parks & J. Stevenson Hinde (Eds.), *The place of attachment in human behavior* (pp. 3–30). New York: Basic Books.

Ainsworth, M. D., et al. (1978). *Patterns of attachment*. Hillsdale, NJ: Lawrence Erlbaum.

———, et al. (1982). Attachment: Retrospect and prospect. In C. M. Parkes, & J. Stevenson-Hinde (Eds.), *The place of attachment in human behavior* (pp. 3–30). New York: Basic Books.

American Academy of Pediatrics, American Public Health Association, and National Resource for Health and Safety in Child Care. (2002). *Caring for our children: National health and safety performance standards: Guidelines for out-of-home child care* (2nd ed.). Retrieved from http://nrc.uchsc.edu

Anderson, S. (2002). He's watching! The importance of the onlooker stage of play. *Young Children, 57*(6), 58.

Ashton-Warner, S. (1964). *Teacher.* New York: Bantam.

Baker, L., Fernandez-Fein, S., Scher, D., & Williams, H. (1998). Home experiences related to the development of word recognition. In J. L. Metsala, & L. C. Ehri (Eds.), *Word recognition in beginning literacy* (pp. 263–287). Mahwah, NJ: Erlbaum.

Balaban, N. (2006). Easing the separation process for infants, toddlers, and families. *Young Children, 61*(6), 14–18.

Begley, S. (1997, Spring/Summer). How to build a baby's brain. *Newsweek, Special Edition*, pp. 28–32.

Belsky, J. (1988). Infant day care and socioemotional development: The United States. *Journal of Child Psychology and Psychiatry, 29*(4), 397–406.

Belsky, J. (2001). Developmental risks (still) associated with early child care. *Journal of Child Psychology and Psychiatry, 42*(7), 845–859.

Belsky, J., Vandell, D., Burchinal, M., Clarke-Stewart, A., McCartney, K., & Owen, M., et al. (2007). Are there long-term effects of early child care? *Child Development 78*(2), 681–701.

Beneke, S., Ostrosky, M., & Katz, L. (2008). Calendar time for young children: Good intentions gone awry. *Young Children, 63*(3), 12–16.

Bereiter, C., & Engelmann, S. (1966). *Teaching disadvantaged children in the preschool.* Englewood Cliffs, NJ: Prentice-Hall.

Bergen, D. (2004). *Play's role in brain development.* Olney, MD: Association for Childhood Education International.

Bergen, D., & Coscia, J. (2000). *Brain research and childhood education.* Olney, MD: Association for Childhood Education International.

Berk, L., & Winsler, A. (1995). *Scaffolding children's learning: Vygotsky and early childhood education.* Washington, DC: NAEYC.

Bernhardt, J. (2000). A primary caregiving system for infants and toddlers: Best for everyone involved. *Young Children, 55*(2), 74–80.

Berreuta-Clement, J., et al. (1984). *Changed lives: The effects of the Perry preschool program on youths through age 19.* Ypsilanti, MI: High/Scope Press.

Bettelheim, B. (1987, March). The importance of play. *Atlantic Monthly,* 35–46.

Biber, B., Shapiro, E., & Wickens, D. (1971). *Promoting cognitive growth from a developmental-interaction point of view.* Washington, DC: NAEYC.

Birckmayer, J., Kennedy, A., & Stonehouse, A. (2008). *From lullabies to literature: Stories in the lives of infants and toddlers.* Washington, DC: NAEYC.

Bodrova, E., & Leong, D. (2004). Chopsticks and counting chips: Do play and foundational skills need to compete for the teacher's attention in an early childhood classroom? In *Spotlight on young children and play* (pp. 4–11). Washington, DC: NAEYC.

Booth, C. (1997). The fiber project: One teacher's adventure toward emergent curriculum. *Young Children, 52*(5), 79–85.

Bowlby, J. (1988). *A secure base: Parent-child attachment and healthy human development.* New York: Basic Books.

Bowman, B., & Moore, E. (Eds.). (2006). *School readiness and social-emotional development: Perspectives on cultural diversity.* Washington, DC: National Black Child Development Institute.

Brazelton, T. B. (1974). *Toddlers and parents: A declaration of independence.* New York: Delacorte Press/Seymour Lawrence.

Brazelton, T. B., & Greenspan, S. (2000). *The irreducible needs of children: What every child must have to grow, learn, and flourish.* Cambridge, MA: Perseus.

Bredekamp, S. (1993). Reflections on Reggio Emilia. *Young Children, 49*(1), 13–17.

———. (2004). Play and school readiness. In E. Zigler, D. Singer, & S. Bishop-Josef (Eds.), *Children's play: The roots of reading* (pp. 159–174). Washington, DC: Zero to Three.

———. (Ed.). (1987). *Developmentally appropriate practice in early childhood programs serving children from birth through age eight.* Washington, DC: NAEYC.

Bredekamp, S., & Copple, C. (Eds.). (1997). *Developmentally appropriate practice in early childhood programs* (Rev. Ed.). Washington, DC: NAEYC.

Bredekamp, S., & Rosegrant, T. (Eds.). (1992). *Reaching potentials: Appropriate curriculum and assessment for young children* (Vol. 1). Washington, DC: NAEYC.

———. (1995). *Reaching potentials: Transforming early childhood curriculum and assessment* (Vol. 2). Washington, DC: NAEYC.

Briant, M. (2004). *Baby sign language basics: Early communication for hearing babies and toddlers.* Carlsbad, CA: Hay House.

Briggs, D. C. (1975). *Your child's self-esteem.* Garden City, NY: Doubleday.

Bronson, M. B. (1995). *The right stuff for children birth to 8: Selecting play materials to support development.* Washington, DC: NAEYC.

Brown, W. (2008). Young children assess their learning: The power of the quick check strategy. *Young Children, 63*(6), 14–20.

Bruner, J. (1977). Early social interaction and language acquisition. In H. R. Schaffer (Ed.), *Studies in mother-infant interactions* (pp. 271–290). London: Academic Press.

———. (1978, September). Learning the mother tongue. *Human Nature Magazine,* 283–288.

———. (1983). Play, thought, and language. *Peabody Journal of Education, 60*(3), 60–69.

———. (1991). Play, thought, and language. In N. Lauter-Klatell (Ed.), *Readings in child development* (pp. 76–81). Mountain View, CA: Mayfield.

Buell, M., & Sutton, T. (2008). Weaving a web with children at the center: A new approach to emergent curriculum planning for young preschoolers. *Young Children, 63*(4), 100–105.

Burman, L. (2008). *Are you listening? Fostering conversations that help young children learn.* St. Paul, MN: Redleaf Press.

Burts, D. C., Charlesworth, R., & Fleege, P. O. (1991, April). *Achievement of kindergarten children in developmentally appropriate and developmentally inappropriate classrooms.* Paper presented at the meeting of the Society for Research in Child Development, Seattle, WA.

Burts, D. C., et al. (1992). Observed activities and stress behaviors in developmentally appropriate and inappropriate kindergarten classrooms. *Early Childhood Research Quarterly, 7,* 297–318.

Butterfield, P., Martin, C., & Prairie, A. (2004). *Emotional connections: How relationships guide early learning.* Washington, DC: Zero to Three.

Caldwell, B. (2001). Déjà vu all over again: A researcher explains the NICHD Study. *Young Children, 56*(4), 58–59.

Cambourne, B. (1988). *The whole story: Natural learning and the acquisition of literacy in the classroom.* New York: Scholastic Press.

Campbell, C. (Ed.). (1998). *Facilitating preschool literacy.* Newark, DE: International Reading Association.

Campbell, L., Campbell, B., & Dickinson, D. (2003). *Teaching and learning through the multiple intelligences* (3rd ed.). Needham Heights, MA: Allyn & Bacon.

Carlsson-Paige, N., & Levin, D. (1987). *The war play dilemma: Balancing needs and values in the early childhood classroom.* New York: Teachers College Press.

———. (1990). *Who's calling the shots: How to respond effectively to children's fascination with war play and war toys.* Gabriola Island, BC: New Society Publishers.

Carnegie Task Force on Learning in the Primary Grades. (1996). *Years of promise: A comprehensive learning strategy for America's children.* New York: Carnegie Corporation of New York.

Cassady, D., & Lancaster, C. (1993). The grassroots curriculum: A dialogue between children and teachers. *Young Children, 48*(5), 47–51.

Catlin, C. (1996). *More toddlers together: The complete planning guide for a toddler curriculum* (Vol. 2). Beltsville, MD: Gryphon House.

Ceppi, G., & Zeni, M. (Eds.). (1998). *Children, spaces, relations: Metaprojects for an environment for young children.* Washington, DC: Reggio Children.

Chang, H. (1993). *Affirming children's roots: Cultural and linguistic diversity in early care and education.* San Francisco: A California Tomorrow Publication.

Chard, S. (1998a). *The project approach, book 1: Making curriculum come alive.* New York: Scholastic Press.

———. (1998b). *The project approach, book 2: Managing successful projects.* New York: Scholastic Press.

Charlesworth, R. (1998a). Developmentally appropriate practice is for everyone. *Childhood Education, 74*(5), 274–282.

———. (1998b). Response to Sally Lubeck's "Is Developmentally Appropriate Practice for Everyone?" *Childhood Education, 74*(5), 293–298.

Cherry, C. (1981). *Think of something quiet: A guide for achieving serenity in early childhood classrooms.* Belmont, CA: Pitman Learning.

———. (2002). *Please don't sit on the kids: Alternatives to punitive discipline* (Rev. ed.). Grand Rapids, MI: Frank Schaffer.

Chess, S., & Thomas, A. (1977). Temperamental individuality from childhood to adolescence. *Journal of Child Psychology and Psychiatry, 16,* 218–226.

———. (1982). Infant bonding: Mystique and reality. *American Journal of Orthopsychiatry, 52,* 213–221.

Chugani, H. (1996). Neuroimaging of developmental non-linearity and developmental pathologies. In R. Thatcher, G. Lyon, J. Rumsey, & N. Krasnegor (Eds.), *Developmental neuroimaging: Mapping the development of brain and behavior* (pp. 187–193). San Diego: Academic Press.

Clark, K., & Clark, M. (1939). The development of consciousness of self and the emergence of racial identity in Negro preschool schoolchildren. *Journal of Social Psychology, 10,* 591–599.

Clarke-Stewart, K. A. (1989). Infant daycare: Maligned or malignant? Special issue: Children and their development: Knowledge base, research agenda, and social policy application. *American Psychology, 44*(2), 266–273.

Clemens, S. C. (1983). *The sun's not broken, a cloud's just in the way: On child-centered teaching.* Beltsville, MD: Gryphon House.

Clements, D., & Sarama, J. (2003). Young children and technology: What does the research say? *Young Children, 58*(6), 34–40.

Cole, M., Cole, S. R., & Lightfoot, C. (2008). *The development of children* (6th ed.). New York: Freeman.

Copley, J., Jones, C., & Dighe, J. (2007). *Mathematics: The creative curriculum© approach.* Washington, DC: Teaching Strategies.

Copple, C., & Bredekamp, S. (2008). Getting clear about developmentally appropriate practice. *Young Children, 63*(1), 54–55.

———. (Eds.). (2009). *Developmentally appropriate practice in early childhood programs serving children from birth through age 8* (3rd ed.). Washington, DC: NAEYC.

———. (2009). *Developmentally appropriate practice in early childhood programs* (3rd ed.). Washington, DC: NAEYC.

Council for Physical Education and Children. (2001). *Recess in elementary schools.* A Position paper from the National Association for Sport and Physical Education. Retrieved from http://www.aahperd.org/naspe/

Cowley, G. (1997, Spring/Summer). The language explosion. *Newsweek, Special Edition,* pp. 16–22.

Cryer, D., & Harms, T. (1987). *Active learning for infants.* Reading, MA: Addison-Wesley.

Cuffaro, H. (1977). The developmental-interaction approach. In B. Boegehold, H. Cuffaro, W. Hooks, & G. Klopf (Eds.), *Education before five: A handbook of preschool education* (pp. 36–45). New York: Bank Street College of Education.

Curtis, D., & Carter, M. (1996). *Reflecting children's lives: A handbook for planning child-centered curriculum.* St. Paul, MN: Redleaf Press.

———. (2000). *The art of awareness: How observation can transform your teaching.* St. Paul, MN: Redleaf Press.

———. (2003). *Designs for living and learning: Transforming early childhood environments.* St. Paul, MN: Redleaf Press.

———. (2005). Rethinking early childhood environments to enhance learning. *Young Children, 60*(3), 34–38.

———. (2008). *Learning together with young children: A curriculum framework for reflective teachers.* St. Paul, MN: Redleaf Press.

Cutting, B. (1991, May). Tests, independence and whole language. *Teaching K–8*, 64–66.

Davis, S. (2004). *Schools where everyone belongs: Practical strategies for reducing bullying.* New York: Stop Bullying Now.

DeBord, K., Hestenes, L., Moore, R., Cosco, N., & McGinnis, J. (2002). Paying attention to the outdoor environment is as important as preparing the indoor environment. *Young Children, 57*(3), 32–35.

Delpit, L. (1988). The silenced dialogue: Power and pedagogy in educating other people's children. *Harvard Educational Review, 58*, 280–298.

———. (2006). *Other people's children: Cultural conflict in the classroom.* New York: The New Press.

Denham, S. (2006). Social-emotional competence as support for school readiness: What is it and how do we assess it? *Early Education and Development 17*(1), 57–89.

Derman-Sparks, L. (1989). *Anti-bias curriculum: Tools for empowering young children.* Washington, DC: NAEYC.

Derman-Sparks, L., & Phillips, C. (1997). *Teaching/learning anti-racism: A developmental approach.* New York: Teachers College Press.

DeVault, L. (2003). The tide is high, but we *can* hold on: One kindergarten teacher's thoughts on the rising tide of academic expectations. *Young Children, 58*(6), 90–93.

Dewey, J. (1916). *Democracy and education.* New York: Macmillan.

Dickinson, D., & Tabors, P. (2001). *Building literacy with language: Young children learning at home and school.* Baltimore: Paul H. Brookes.

Diffily, D., & Sassman, C. (2002). *Project-based learning with young children.* Portsmouth, NH: Heinemann.

Diller, D. (2003). *Literacy work stations: Making centers work.* Portland, ME: Stenhouse.

Dodge, D., Colker, L., & Heroman, C. (2002). *Creative curriculum for preschool* (4th ed.). Washington, DC: Teaching Strategies.

Dodge, D., Rudick, S., & Berke, K. (2006). *The creative curriculum® for infants, toddlers, and twos* (2nd ed.). Washington, DC: Teaching Strategies.

Duckworth, E. (2006). *"The having of wonderful ideas" and other essays on teaching and learning* (3rd ed.). New York: Teachers College Press.

Durland, M., et al. (1992, November). A comparison of the frequencies of observed stress behaviors in children in developmentally appropriate and inappropriate preschool classrooms. Unpublished information included in paper at NAEYC.

Early Childhood Education Assessment Consortium, Council of Chief State School Officers. (2005). *The words we use: A glossary of terms for early childhood education standards and assessment.* Retrieved from http://www.ccsso.org/proects/SCASS/projects/early_childhood_education_assessment_consortium/publications_and_products/2840.cfm

Edwards, C. (1997). Partner, nurturer, and guide: The roles of the Reggio teacher in action. In C. Edwards, L. Gandini, & G. Forman (Eds.), *The hundred languages of children: The Reggio Emilia approach to early childhood education* (2nd ed., pp. 151–170). Norwood, NJ: Ablex.

Edwards, C., & Raikes, H. (2002). Extending the dance: Relationship-based approaches to infant/toddler care and education. *Young Children, 57*(4), 10–17.

Elkind, D. (1981). *The hurried child: Growing up too fast too soon.* Reading, MA: Addison-Wesley.

———. (1987a). The child yesterday, today, and tomorrow. *Young Children, 42*(4), 6–11.

———. (1987b). Superbaby syndrome can lead to elementary school burnout. *Young Children, 42*(3), 14.

———. (1988). *Miseducation: Preschoolers at risk.* New York: Knopf.

———. (1989, October). Developmentally appropriate practice: Philosophical and practical implications. *Phi Delta Kappan*, 113–117.

Epstein, A. (1993). *Training for quality: Improving early childhood programs through systematic inservice training.* Ypsilanti, MI: High/Scope Educational Research Foundation.

———. (2003). How planning and reflection develop young children's thinking skills. *Young Children, 58*(5), 28–36.

Erikson, E. (1963). *Childhood and society.* New York: Norton.

———. (1968). *Identity: Youth and crisis.* New York: Norton.

Espiritu, E., Meier, D., Villazana-Price, N., & Wong, M. (2002). A collaborative project on language and literacy learning. *Young Children, 57*(5), 71–78.

Evans, B. (2001). *You can't come to my birthday party: Conflict resolution with young children.* Ypsilanti, MI: High/Scope Press.

Fisher, R. (1994). *Getting ready to negotiate—the getting to yes workbook.* New York: Penguin.

Flynn, L., & Kieff, J. (2002). Including everyone in outdoor play. *Young Children, 57*(3), 20–27.

Fox, L., & Lentini, R. (2006). "You got it!" Teaching social and emotional skills. *Young Children, 61*(6), 36–42.

Fraiberg, S. (1959). *The magic years.* New York: Scribner's.

———. (1977). *Every child's birthright: In defense of mothering.* New York: Basic Books.

Fraser, S., & Gestwicki, C. (2002). *Authentic childhood: Exploring Reggio Emilia in the classroom.* Clifton Park, NY: Thomson Delmar Learning.

Fromberg, D. (2002). *Play and meaning in early childhood education.* Boston: Allyn & Bacon.

Gaffney, J., Ostrosky, M., & Hemmeter, M. L. (2008). Books as natural support for young children's literacy learning. *Young Children, 63*(4), 87–93.

Gamberg, R., Kwak, W., Hutchings, M., & Altheim, J. (1988). *Learning and loving it: Theme studies in the classroom.* Portsmouth, NH: Heinemann.

Gandini, L. (1997). Educational and caring spaces. In C. Edwards, L. Gandini, & G. Forman (Eds). *The hundred languages of children: The Reggio Emilia approach to early childhood education* (2nd ed., pp. 161–178). Norwood, NJ: Ablex.

Gardner, H. (1983). *Frames of mind: The theory of multiple intelligences.* New York: Basic Books.

———. (1991). *The unschooled mind: How children think and how schools should teach.* New York: Basic Books.

———. (2000). *Intelligence reframed: Multiple intelligences for the twenty-first century.* New York: Basic Books.

Gartrell, D. (1994). *A guidance approach to discipline.* Clifton Park, NY: Thomson Delmar Learning.

———. (2008). Understand bullying. *Young Children, 63*(3), 54–57.

Gerber, M. (Ed.). (1991). *Resources for infant educaters.* Los Angeles: RIE.

Gestwicki, C. (2010). *Home, school, community relations: A guide to working with families* (7th ed.). Clifton Park, NY: Delmar/Thomson Learning.

Goleman, D. (1995). *Emotional intelligence.* New York: Bantam.

Golinkoff, R., Hirsh-Pasek, K., & Singer, D. (2006). Why play = learning: A challenge for parents and educators. In D. Singer, R. Golinkoff, & K. Hirsh-Pasek (Eds.), *Play = Learning: How play motivates and enhances children's cognitive and social-emotional growth* (pp. 3–14). New York: Oxford University Press.

Gonzalez-Mena, J. (1986). Toddlers: What to expect. *Young Children, 41*(1), 47–51.

———. (2007). *Diversitiy in early care and education: Honoring differences* (5th ed.). New York: McGraw-Hill.

———. (2008a). *Child, family, and community: Family-centered early care and education* (5th ed.). New York: Prentice Hall.

———. (2008b). *Diversity in early care and education.* 5E. Washington, DC: NAEYC.

Gonzalez-Mena, J., & Eyer, D. W. (2006). *Infants, toddlers, and caregivers: A curriculum of respectful, responsive care* (7th ed.). New York: McGraw-Hill.

———. (2008). *Infants, toddlers, and caregivers: A curriculum of respectful, responsive care and education* (8th ed.). New York: McGraw-Hill.

Gordon, T. (2000). *Parent effectiveness training* (Rev. ed.). New York: Three Rivers Press.

Gould, P., & Sullivan, J. (1998). *The inclusive early childhood classroom: Easy ways to adapt learning centers for all children.* Beltsville, MD: Gryphon House.

Greenberg, P. (1987). *Staff growth program for child care centers.* New York: Acropolis Books.

———. (1990). Why not academic preschool? (part 1). *Young Children, 45*(2), 70–79.

———. (1991). *Character development: Encouraging self-esteem and self-discipline in infants, toddlers, and two-year-olds.* Washington, DC: NAEYC.

———. (1992). How to institute some simple democratic practices pertaining to respect, rights, roots, and responsibilities in any classroom (without losing your leadership position). *Young Children, 47*(5), 10–17.

Greenman, J. (2004). Great places to be a baby. *Child Care Information Exchange, 157,* 46–48.

———. (2005a). *Caring spaces, learning places: Children's environments that work* (Rev. ed.). Redmond, WA: Exchange Press.

———. (2005b). Places for children in the twenty-first century: A conceptual framework. *Young Children.* Retrieved May 15, 2009, from http://www.journal.naeyc.org/btj/200505/01

Greenman, J., Stonehouse, A., & Schweikart, G. (2007). *Prime time, 2nd edition: A handbook for excellence in infant and toddler programs.* St. Paul, MN: Redleaf Press.

Greenspan, S., & Greenspan, N. T. (1989). *First feelings.* New York: Viking Penguin.

Grisham-Brown, J., Hemmeter, M., & Pretti-Frontczak, K. (2005). *Blended practices for teaching young children in inclusive settings.* Baltimore: Paul H. Brookes.

Gronlund, G. (2006). *Make early learning standards come alive: Connecting your practice and curriculum to state guidelines.* St. Paul, MN: Redleaf Press.

——— (2008). Standards, standards, everywhere. *Young Children, 63*(4), 10–13.

Gurian, M. (2001). *Boys and girls learn differently: A guide for teachers and parents.* San Francisco: Jossey-Bass.

Gurian, M., & Ballew, A. (2003). *The boys and girls learn differently action guide for teachers.* San Francisco: Jossey-Bass.

Hall, K. (2008). The importance of including culturally authentic literature. *Young Children, 63*(1), 80–86.

Hampshire Play Policy Forum. (2002). *Hampshire Play Policy Position Statement.* Retrieved from http://www.hants.gov.uk/childcare/playpolicy.html

Hancock, L., & Wingert, P. (1997, Spring/Summer). The new preschool. *Newsweek, Special Edition,* pp. 36–37.

Harlow, H. (1958). The nature of love. *American Psychologist, 13,* 673–685.

Harms, T., & Clifford, R. (1998). *Early childhood environment rating scale* (Revised ed.). New York: Teachers College Press.

Harris, T., & Fuqua, J. D. (1996). To build a house: Designing curriculum for primary-grade children. *Young Children, 51*(6), 77–84.

Hart, B., & Risley, T. (2003). *Meaningful differences in everyday parenting and intellectual development in young American children.* Baltimore: Paul H. Brookes.

Hart, C. H. (1991, November). *Behavior of first and second grade children who attended developmentally appropriate and developmentally inappropriate classrooms.* Paper presented at the annual meeting of the NAEYC, Denver, CO.

Hart, C., Burts, D., & Charlesworth, R. (1997). Integrated developmentally appropriate curriculum: From theory and research to practice. In C. Hart, D. Burts, & R. Charlesworth (Eds.), *Integrated curriculum and developmentally appropriate practice: birth to age eight* (pp. 1–28). Albany: State University of New York Press.

Heburn, S. (1995). *Cost, quality and child outcomes in child care centers.* Technical Paper. Denver: University of Colorado.

Heidemann, S., & Hewitt, D. (2010). *Play: The pathway from theory to practice* (2nd ed.). St Paul, MN: Redleaf Press.

Heller, C. (1993). Equal pay. *Teaching Tolerance, 23,* 24–28.

Helm, J. H. (2008). Got standards? Don't give up on engaged learning. *Young Children, 63*(4), 14–20.

Helm, J., & Beneke, S. (Eds.). (2003). *The power of projects: Meeting contemporary challenges in early childhood classrooms—strategies and solutions.* New York: Teachers College Press.

Helm, J., & Katz, L. (2001). *Young investigators: The project approach in the early years.* New York: Teachers College Press.

Hemmeter, M. L., Ostrosky, M., Artman, K., & Kinder, K. (2008). Moving right along: Planning transitions to prevent challenging behavior. *Young Children, 63*(3), 18–25.

Hendricks, J. (2003). *Next steps towards teaching the Reggio way: Accepting the challenge to change.* New York: Prentice-Hall.

Hendricks, J. (Ed.). (1997). *First steps toward teaching the Reggio way.* Columbus, OH: Merrill.

Heroman, C., & Jones, C. (2004). *Literacy: The creative curriculum approach.* Washington, DC: Teaching Strategies.

Herr, J., & Swim, T. (1999). *Creative resources for infants and toddlers* (2nd ed.). Clifton Park, NY: Thomson Delmar Learning.

High/Scope Foundation. (2005). *The High/Scope Perry preschool study through age 40: Summary, conclusions, and frequently asked questions.* Retrieved April 10, 2005, from http://www.highscope.org

Hildebrand, V., & Hearron, P. (2008). *Guiding young children* (8th ed.). New York: Prentice Hall.

Hitz, M., Somers, M., & Jenlink, C. (2007). The looping classroom: Benefits for children, families, and teachers. *Young Children, 62*(2), 80–84.

Hoffman, L. (1989). Effects of maternal employment in the two-parent family: A review of the research. *American Psychology, 44*(2), 283–292.

Hohmann, M., & Weikart, D. (2002). *Educating young children: Active learning practices for preschool and child care programs* (2nd ed.). Ypsilanti, MI: High/Scope Press.

Hollyfield, A., & Hast, F. (2001). *More infant and toddler experiences.* St. Paul, MN: Redleaf Press.

Holt, J. (1983). *How children learn* (Rev. ed.). New York: Delacorte Press.

Honig, A. S. (1991). Recent infancy research. In B. Weissbourd, & J. Musick (Eds.), *Infants: Their social environments* (pp. 16–25). Washington, DC: NAEYC.

———. (1993). Mental health for babies: What do theory and research teach us? *Young Children, 48*(3), 69–76.

Hurless, B., & Gittings, S. (2008). Weaving the tapestry: A first grade teacher integrates teaching and learning. *Young Children, 63*(2), 40–46.

International Reading Association. (1999). *Using multiple methods of beginning reading instruction.* Retrieved April 15, 2005, from http://www.reading.org

Isenberg, J., & Jalongo, M. (2000). *Creative expression and play in early childhood* (3rd ed.). Upper Saddle River, NJ: Merrill Prentice-Hall.

Isenberg, J., & Jalongo, M. R. (2000). *Creative expression and play in the early childhood curriculum* (3rd ed.). New York: Macmillan.

Isenberg, J., & Quisenberry, N. (1988). Play: A necessity for all children. *Childhood Education, 64*(3), 138–145.

Jablon, J., Dombro, A., & Dichtelmiller, M. (2007). *The power of observation* (2nd ed.). Washington, DC: Teaching Strategies.

Jacobs, G., & Crowley, K. (2007). *Play, projects and preschool standards: Nurturing children's sense of wonder.* Thousand Oaks, CA: Corwin Press.

Jalongo, M. (2008). *Learning to listen, listening to learn: Building essential skills in young children.* Washington, DC: NAEYC.

Jarrett, O. (2002). *Recess in elementary school: What does the research say?* Champaign, IL: ERIC Clearinghouse on Elementary and Early Childhood Education. (ERIC Documentation Reproduction Service No. ED466331)

Jipson, J. (1991, April). Developmentally appropriate practice: Culture, curriculum, connections. *Early Education and Development, 2*(2), 120–136.

Johnson, D., & Rudolph, A. (2001). Critical issue: Beyond social promotion and retention: Five strategies to help students succeed. Retrieved April 15, 2005, from http://www.ncrel.org

Johnson, J., Christie, J., & Wardle, F. (2005). *Play, development, and early education.* Boston: Pearson.

Jones, E., & Nimmo, J. (1994). *Emergent curriculum.* Washington, DC: NAEYC.

Jones, E., & Reynolds, G. (1992). *The play's the thing: Teachers' roles in children's play.* New York: Teachers College Press.

Jones, N. (2008). Grouping children to promote social and emotional development. *Young Children, 63*(3), 34–39.

Kagan, S. (1990). Children's play: The journey from theory to practice. In E. Klugman & S. Smilansky (Eds.), *Children's play and learning: Perspectives and policy implications* (pp. 43–61). New York: Teachers College Press.

Kalmar, K. (2008). Let's give children something to talk about! Oral language and preschool literacy. *Young Children, 63*(1), 88–92.

Kamii, C. (1982). *Number in preschool and kindergarten: Educational implications of Piaget's theory.* Washington, DC: NAEYC.

———. (Ed.). (1990). *Achievement testing in the early grades: The games grownups play.* Washington, DC: NAEYC.

Kamii, C., & Kamii, M. (1990). *Negative effects of achievement testing in mathematics.* Washington, DC: NAEYC.

Kamii, C., & Rosenblum, V. (1990). *An approach to assessment in mathematics.* Washington, DC: NAEYC.

Karen, R. (1998). *Becoming attached: First relationships and how they shape our capacity to love.* New York: Oxford University Press.

Katz, L. (1984). The professional early childhood teacher. *Young Children, 39*(5), 3–10.

Katz, L. (1987). *What should young children be learning?* Urbana, IL: ERIC Clearing House of Elementary and Early Childhood Education.

Katz, L. (1988, Summer). What should young children be doing? *American Educator, 28–33*, 44–45.

———. (1994). Images from the world: Study seminar on the experience of the municipal infant-toddler centers and preprimary schools of Reggio Emilia, Italy. In L. Katz, & B. Cesarone (Eds.), *Reflections on the Reggio Emilia approach* (pp. 3–19). Urbana, IL: ERIC Clearing House on Elementary and Early Childhood Education.

———. (1997). The challenges of the Reggio Emilia approach. In J. Hendricks (Ed.), *First steps toward teaching the Reggio way* (pp. 96–110). Columbus, OH: Merrill.

Katz, L., & Chard, S. (2000). *Engaging children's minds: The project approach* (2nd ed.). Norwood, NJ: Ablex.

Kennedy, D. (1996). After Reggio Emilia: May the conversation begin! *Young Children, 51*(5), 24–27.

Kessler, S. (1991). Early childhood education as development: Critique of the metaphor. *Early Education and Development, 2*(2), 137–152.

Kinnell, G. (2002). *No biting: Policy and practice for toddler programs.* St. Paul, MN: Redleaf Press.

Kinney, M. L., & Ahrens, P. (2001). *Beginning with babies.* St. Paul, MN: Redleaf Press.

Kirmani, M. (2007). Empowering culturally and linguistically diverse children and families. *Young Children, 62*(6), 94–98.

Klein, M. D., Cook, R., & Richardson-Gibbs, A. M. (2000). *Strategies for including children with special needs in early childhood settings.* Clifton Park, NY: Thomson Delmar Learning.

Koc, K., & Buzzelli, C. (2004). The moral of the story is . . . Using children's literature in moral education. *Young Children, 59*(1), 92–97.

Kohl, M. (2002). *First art: Art experiences for toddlers and twos.* Beltsville, MD: Gryphon House.

Kohlberg, L. (1976). Moral stages and moralization: The cognitive-developmental approach. In J. Lickona (Ed.), *Moral development behavior: Theory, research, and social issues* (pp. 93–120). New York: Holt, Rinehart & Winston.

Kohlberg, L., & Kramer, R. (1969). Continuities and discontinuities in childhood and adult moral development. *Human Development, 12*, 93–120.

Kohn, A. (2001). Fighting the tests: Turning frustration into action. *Young Children, 56*(2), 19–24.

Kostelnik, M., Phipps-Wiren, A., Soderman, A., Stein, L., & Gregory, K. (2006). *Guiding children's social development* (5th ed.). Clifton Park, NY: Thomson Delmar Learning.

Kostelnik, M., Soderman, A., & Whiren, A. (2003). *Developmentally appropriate curriculum: Best practices in early childhood education.* New York: Prentice Hall.

Kumar, R. (2009). Why is collaboration good for my child? Engaging families in understanding the benefits of cooperative learning. *Young Children, 64*(3), 91–95.

Lakin, M. (1996). The meaning of play: Perspectives from Pacific Oaks College. In A. Phillips (Ed.), *Topics in early childhood education: Playing for keeps. Inter-Institutional Early Childhood Consortium* (pp. 37–59). St. Paul, MN: Redleaf Press.

Lally, R., & Mangione, P. (2006). The uniqueness of infancy demands a responsive approach to care. *Young Children, 61*(4), 14–20.

Lamm, S., Grouix, J., Hansen, C., Patton, M., & Slaton, A. (2006). Creating environments for peaceful problem solving. *Young Children, 61*(6), 22–28.

Landreth, C. (1972). *Preschool learning and teaching.* New York: Harper & Row.

Leavitt, R. L. (1994). *Power and emotion in infant-toddler day care.* Albany: State University of New York Press.

LeeKeenan, D., & Edwards, C. (1992). Using the project approach with toddlers. *Young Children, 47*(4), 31–35.

LeFevre, D. (2007). *The spirit of play: Cooperative games for all ages, sizes, and abilities* (Rev. ed.). Forres, UK: Findhorn Press.

Levin, D. (2004). Beyond banning war and superhero play: Meeting children's needs in violent times. In *Spotlight on young children and play* (pp. 46–49). Washington, DC: NAEYC.

Levine, D. (1998). *Remote control childhood? Combating the hazards of media culture.* Washington, DC: NAEYC.

———. (2003). *Teaching young children in violent times: Building a peaceable classroom* (2nd ed.). Washington, DC: NAEYC.

Louv, R. (2008). *Last child in the woods: Saving our children from nature deficit disorder* (Updated ed.). Chapel Hill, NC: Algonquin.

Love, A., Burns, M. S., & Buell, M. (2007). Writing: Empowering literacy. *Young Children, 62*(1), 12–19.

Lubeck, S., Lubeck, S. (1998a). Is DAP for everyone? A response. *Childhood Education, 74*(5), 299–301 [A and b added to text].

———. (1998b). Is developmentally appropriate practice for everyone? *Childhood Education, 74*(5), 283–292.

Luvmour, J., & Luvmour, S. (2007). *Everyone wins: Cooperative games and activities.* Gabriola Island, BC: New Society.

Mahler, M. (1979). *Separation-individuation* (Vol. 2). London: Jason Aronson.

Mallory, B., & New, R. (Eds.). (1994). *Diversity and developmentally appropriate practices: Challenges for early childhood education.* New York: Teachers College Press.

Marshall, H. (2003). Research in review—opportunity deferred or opportunity taken? An updated look at delaying kindergarten entry. *Young Children, 58*(5), 84–93.

McCarry, B., & Greenwood, S. (2009). Practice what you teach: Writers' lunch club in first grade. *Young Children, 64*(1), 37–41.

Mecca, M. E. (1995/1996). Classrooms where children learn to care. *Childhood Education, 72*(2), 72–74.

Meier, D. (1997). *Learning in small moments: Life in an urban classroom.* New York: Teachers College Press.

Meisels, S. (1993). Remaking classroom assessment with the work sampling system. *Young Children, 48*(5), 32–40.

———. (2000, December). *Using assessments to enhance teaching and improve learning.* Presented at the Head Start Child Development Institute. Retrieved April 15, 2005, from http://www.hsnrc.org

Meisels, S., & Atkins-Burnett, S. (2000). The elements of early childhood assessment. In J. Shonkoff, & S. Meisels (Eds.), *The handbook of early childhood intervention* (2nd ed., pp. 231–257). New York: Cambridge University Press.

Miller, K. (1999). *Simple steps: Developmental activities for infants, toddlers, and two-year-olds.* Beltsville, MD: Gryphon House.

———. (2002). *Things to do with toddlers and twos* (Rev. ed.). Chelsea, MA: Telshare.

Monighan-Nourot, P. (1990). The legacy of play in American early childhood education. In E. Klugman, & S. Smilansky (Eds.), *Children's play and learning: Perspectives and policy implications* (pp. 4–17). New York: Teachers College Press.

———. (2003). Playing with play in four dimensions. In J. Isenberg, & M. Jalongo (Eds.), *Major trends and issues in early childhood education: Challenges, controversies, and insights* (2nd ed., pp. 123–148). New York: Teachers College Press.

Montessori, M. (1995). *The absorbent mind* (Reprint ed.). New York: Owl Books.

Morrow, L. (2001). *Literacy development in the early years: Helping children read and write. Needham Heights,* MA: Allyn & Bacon.

Moyer, J. (2001). The child-centered kindergarten—a position paper. Association for Childhood Education International. *Childhood Education, 77*(3), 161–166.

NAECS/SDE (2000–2001). *Still unacceptable trends in kindergarten entry and placement.* Position paper. Washington, DC: Author.

NAESP. (1990). *Early childhood education and the elementary school principal: Standards for quality programs for young children.* Alexandria, VA: Author.

NAEYC & IRA. (1998). Learning to read and write: Developmentally appropriate practices for young children. *Young Children, 53*(4), 30–46.

NAEYC & NAECS/SDE. (2002). *Joint position statement. Early learning standards: Creating the conditions for success.* Retrieved July 23, 2008, from http://www.naeyc.org/about/positions

————. (2003a). Early childhood curriculum, assessment, and program evaluation: Building an effective, accountable system in programs for children birth through age 8. Retrieved from http://www.naeyc.org

————. (2003b). *Early childhood curriculum, assessment, and program evaluation.* Retrieved April 15, 2005, from http://www.naeyc.org

NAEYC & NCTM. (2002a). *Early childhood mathematics: Promoting good beginnings.* Retrieved February 6, 2009, from http://www.naeyc.org/positionstatements

————. (2002b). *Early childhood mathematics: Promoting good beginnings.* A joint position statement of the NAEYC and the NCTM. Retrieved April 15, 2005, from http://www.naeyc.org

NAEYC. (1990). NAEYC position statement on media violence in children's lives. *Young Children, 45*(5), 18–21. Also available online at http://www.naeyc.org. Click on Resources, and then on Position Statements.

————. (1995a). Cost, quality, and child outcomes in child care centers: Key findings and recommendations. *Young Children, 50*(4), 40–44.

————. (1995b). Mr. Hoagie and his happy, hardworking second-graders: An interview. *Young Children, 50*(6), 40–44.

————. (1996a). Biters: Why they do it and what to do about it. Washington, DC: Author.

————. (1996b). Position statement: Responding to linguistic and cultural diversity—recommendations for effective early childhood education. *Young Children, 51*(2), 4–12.

————. (1998). *Learning to read and write: Developmentally appropriate practices for young children.* A position statement of the International Reading Association and the National Association for the Education of Young Children. Retrieved April 10, 2005, from http://www.naeyc.org

————. (2002). *Early childhood mathematics: Promoting good beginnings.* A joint position statement of the National Association for the Education of Young Children and the National Council of Teachers of Mathematics. Retrieved from http://www.naeyc.org

Nansel, T., Overpeck, M., Pilla, R., Ruan, W., Simons-Morton, B., & Scheidt, P. (2001). Bullying behaviors among U.S. youth: Prevalence and association with psychosocial adjustment. *Journal of the American Medical Association, 285*(16), 2094–2100.

NASBE. (1988). *Right from the start.* Alexandria, VA: Author.

————. (1991). *Caring communities: Supporting young children and families. The Report of the National Task Force on School Readiness.* Alexandria, VA: Author.

NASP. (2003). *Position statement on student grade retention and social promotion.* Retrieved April 15, 2005, from http://www.nasponline.org

National Early Literacy Panel. (2004). *A synthesis of research on language and literacy.* Retrieved April 10, 2005, from http://www.famlit.org

NCTM. (2000). *Principles and standards for school mathematics.* Reston, VA: Author.

————. (2006). *Curriculum focal points for prekindergarten through grade 8 mathematics: A quest for coherence.* Retrieved February 6, 2009, from http://www.nctm.org/standards/focal points

New, R. (1993). Cultural variations on developmentally appropriate practice: Challenges to theory and practice. In C. Edwards, L. Gandini, & G. Forman (Eds.), *The hundred languages of children: The Reggio Emilia approach to early childhood education* (pp. 215–232). Norwood, NJ: Ablex.

Newberger, J. (1997). New brain development research—a wonderful window of opportunity to build public support for early childhood education. *Young Children, 52*(4), 4–9.

NICHD Early Child Care Research Network. (1997). The effects of infant child care on infant-mother attachment security: Results of the NIHCD study of early child care. *Child Development, 68*(5), 860–879.

Oehlberg, B. (1996). *Making it better: Activities for children living in a stressful world.* St. Paul, MN: Redleaf Press.

Olweus, D. (1993). *Bullying at school: What we know and what we can do.* Cambridge, MA: Blackwell.

Orlick, T. (2006). *Cooperative games and sports: Joyful activities for everyone* (2nd ed.). Champaign IL: Human Kinetics.

Ostrow, J. (1995). *A room with a different view.* York, ME: Stenhouse.

Owocki, G., & Goodman, Y. (2002). *Kidwatching: Documenting children's literacy development*. Portsmouth, NH: Heinemann.

Paley, V. G. (1984). *Boys and girls: Superheroes in the doll corner*. Chicago: University of Chicago Press.

———. (1986). *Mollie is three*. Chicago: University of Chicago Press.

———. (1992). *You can't say you can't play*. Cambridge, MA: Harvard University Press.

———. (1999). *The girl with the brown crayon*. Cambridge, MA: Harvard University Press.

———. (2004). *A child's work: The importance of fantasy play*. Chicago: University of Chicago Press.

Papalia, D., Olds, S., & Feldman, R. (2005). *A child's world: Infancy through adolescence* (10th ed.). New York: McGraw-Hill.

———. (2006). *A child's world: Infancy through adolescence* (10th ed.). New York: McGraw-Hill.

Park, B., Neuharth-Pritchett, S., & Reguero de Atiles, J. (2003). Using integrated curriculum to connect standards and developmentally appropriate practice. *Dimensions of Early Childhood, 31*(3), 13–17.

Parten, M. (1932). Social participation among preschool children. *Journal of Abnormal and Social Psychology, 27*, 243–269.

Pelo, A. (1996). Our school's not fair: A story about emergent curriculum. In D. Curtis, & M. Carter (Ed.), *Reflecting children's lives: A handbook for planning child-centered curriculum* (pp. 100–107). St. Paul, MN: Redleaf Press.

Petersen, S., & Wittmer, D. (2008). Relationship-based infant care: Responsive, on demand, and predictable. *Young Children, 63*(3), 40–42.

Peth-Pierce, R. (2000). *A good beginning: Sending America's children to school with the social and emotional competence they need to succeed*. Bethesda, MD: NIMH.

Phillips, D. (1987, November). Infants and child care: The new controversy. *Child Care Information Exchange, 58*, 19–22.

Piaget, J. ([1923]1926). *The language and thought of the child*. New York: Harcourt, Brace and World.

———. (1951). *Play, dreams and imitation in childhood*. New York: Norton.

———. (1952). *The origins of intelligence in children*. New York: International Universities Press.

———. (1962). *Play, dreams, and imitation in childhood*. New York: Norton.

———. (1963). *The origins of intelligence in children*. New York: Norton.

———. (1965). *The moral judgment of the child*. New York: The Free Press.

———. (1969). *The language and thought of the child*. New York: World Publishing.

Plummer, D., Wright, J., & Serrurier, J. (2008). *Social skills games for children*. London: Jessica Kingsley.

Pratt, C. (1948). *I learn from children*. New York: HarperCollins.

Prescott, E. (1994, November). The physical environment—a powerful regulator of experience. *Child Care Information Exchange, 100*, 9–15.

Ramming, P., Kyger, C., & Thompson, S. (2006). A new bit on toddler biting: The influence of food, oral motor development, and sensory activities. *Young Children, 61*(2), 17–23.

Reynolds, E. (2006). *Guiding young children: A child-centered approach* (4th ed.). New York: McGraw-Hill.

Reynolds, G., & Jones, E. (1996). *Master players*. New York: Teachers College Press.

Rightmyer, E. (2003). Democratic discipline: Children creating solutions. *Young Children, 58*(4), 38–45.

Roberts, L., & Hill, H. (2003). Using children's literature to debunk gender stereotypes. *Young Children, 58*(2): 39–42.

Roskos, K., & Christie, J. (Eds.). (2001). *Play and literacy in early childhood: Research from multiple perspectives*. Mahwah, NJ: Erlbaum.

Routman, R. (2003). *Reading essentials: The specifics you need to teach reading*. Portsmouth, NH: Heinemann.

Sandall, S. (2004). Play modifications for children with disabilities. In *Spotlight on young children and play* (pp. 44–45). Washington, DC: NAEYC.

Sandall, S., Hemmeter, M., Smith, B., & McLean, M. (Eds.). (2005). *DEC recommended practices in early intervention/early childhood special education: A comprehensive guide*. Longmont, CA: Sopris West.

Sandall, S., McLean, M., & Smith, B. (2000). *DEC recommended practices in early intervention/early childhood special education*. Longmont, CA: Sopris West.

Schickedanz, J., Schickedanz, D., Forsyth, P., & Forsyth, G. A. (2000). *Understanding children and adolescents* (4th ed.). Boston: Pearson, Allyn, and Bacon.

Schiller, P. (2003). *The complete resource book for toddlers and twos*. Beltsville, MD: Gryphon House.

Schiller, P., & Willis, C. (2008). Using brain-based teaching strategies to create supportive early childhood environments that address learning standards. *Young Children, 63*(4), 52–55.

Schwartz, I., & Sandall, S. (2002). *Building blocks for teaching preschoolers with special needs*. Baltimore: Paul H. Brookes.

Schweinhart, L. J. (1988, May). How important is child-initiated activity? *Principal*, 6–10.

Schweinhart, L., & Weikart, D. P. (1993, Summer). Changed lives, significant benefits: The High/Scope Perry Preschool Project to date. *High/Scope Resource, 12*(3), 1, 10–14.

———. (1997, Spring/Summer). Child-initiated learning in preschool—Prevention that works. *High/Scope Resource, 16*(20), 1, 9–11.

Schweinhart, L., Montie, J., Xiang, Z., Barnett, W., Belfield, C., & Nores, M. (2005). *Lifetime effects: The High/Scope Perry Preschool Study through age 40.* Ypsilanti, MI: High/Scope Press.

Schweinhart, L., Weikart, D., & Larner, M. (1986). Consequences of three preschool curriculum models through age 15. *Early Childhood Research Quarterly, 1*, 15–45.

Scoy, I. (1995). Trading the three R's for the four E's: Transforming curriculum. *Childhood Education, 72*(1), 19–23.

Scully, P., Barbour, N., & Seefeldt, C. (2003). *Developmental continuity across preschool and primary grades.* Wheaton, MD: ACEI.

Seefeldt, C. (2005). *How to work with standards in the early childhood classroom.* New York: Teachers College Press.

Seitz, H. (2008). The power of documentation in the early childhood classroom. *Young Children, 63*(2), 88–93.

Shapiro, E., & Mitchell, A. (1992). Principles of the Bank Street approach. In A. Mitchell & J. David (Eds.), *Explorations with young children: A curriculum guide from the Bank Street College of Education* (pp. 12–23). Beltsville, MD: Gryphon House.

Shell, E. R. (1989, December). Now, which kind of preschool? *Psychology Today*, 52–53, 56–57.

Shore, R. (1997). *Rethinking the brain: New insights into early development.* New York: Families and Work Institute.

Shores, E., & Grace, C. (2005). *The portfolio book: A step-by-step guide for teachers.* Upper Saddle River, NJ: Pearson.

Silberg, J., & D'Argo, L. (2001). *Games to play with babies* (3rd ed.). Beltsville, MD: Gryphon House.

Skinner, B. F. (1938). *The behavior of organisms: An experimental analysis.* New York: Appleton–Century–Crofts.

Slaby, R., Roedell, W. C., Arezzo, D., & Hendrix, K. (1995). *Early violence prevention: Tools for teachers of young children.* Washington, DC: NAEYC.

Sloane, M. (2007). First grade study groups deepen math learning. *Young Children, 62*(4), 83–88.

Smilansky, S. (1968). *The effects of sociodramatic play on disadvantaged preschool children.* New York: Wiley.

———. (1990). Sociodramatic play: Its relevance to behavior and achievement in school. In E. Klugman & S. Smilansky (Eds.), *Children's play and learning: Perspectives and policy implications* (pp. 18–42). New York: Teachers College Press.

Smilansky, S., & Shefatya, L. (1990). *Facilitating play: A medium for promoting cognitive, socioemotional and academic development in young children.* Gaithersburg, MD: Psychosocial and Educational Publications.

Stacey, S. (2009). *Emergent curriculum in early childhood settings: From theory to practice.* St. Paul, MN: Redleaf Press.

Steiner, R. (1970). *Education as an art.* London: Rudolf Steiner Press.

Stone, S. (1995). Wanted: Advocates for play in the primary grades. *Young Children, 50*(6), 45–54.

Stone, S., & Miyake, Y. (2004). *Creating the multi-age classroom.* New York: Goodyear Books.

Stonehouse, A. W. (1986). Discipline. In R. Lurie, & R. Neugebauer (Eds.), *Caring for infants and toddlers: What works, what doesn't* (Vol. 2, pp. 40–58). Redmond, WA: Child Care Information Exchange.

Stonier, F., & Dickerson, D. (2009). When children have something to say, writers are born. *Young Children, 64*(1), 32–36.

Stuber, G. (2007). Centering your classroom: Setting the stage for engaged learners. *Young Children, 62*(4), 58–59.

Taylor, A. S. (2003). What to do with Lee? Academic redshirting of one kindergarten-age boy. *Young Children, 58*(5), 94–95.

Teachout, C., & Bright, A. (2007). Reading the pictures: A missing piece of the literacy puzzle. *Young Children, 62*(4), 106–107.

The ten best schools in the world, and what we can learn from them. (1991, December 2, 1991). *Newsweek.*

Thomas, P. (2003). *The power of relaxation: Using tai chi and visualization to reduce children's stress.* St. Paul, MN: Redleaf Press.

Tomlinson, H. (2009a). Developmentally appropriate practice in the kindergarten year—ages 5–6. In C. Copple, & S. Bredekamp (Eds.), *Developmentally appropriate practice in early childhood programs serving children from birth through age 8* (3rd ed., pp. 187–216). Washington, DC: NAEYC.

———. (2009b). Developmentally appropriate practice in the primary grades—ages 6–8: An overview. In C. Copple & S. Bredekamp (Eds.). *Developmentally appropriate practice in early childhood programs serving children from birth through age 8* (3rd ed., pp. 257–288). Washington: NAEYC.

Trawick-Smith, J. (1994). *Interactions in the classroom: Facilitating play in the early years.* New York: Macmillan College.

———. (2006). *Early childhood development: A multicultural perspective* (4th ed.). Upper Saddle River, NJ: Pearson Education, Inc.

Trepanier-Street, M. (2000). Multiple forms of representation in long-term projects: The garden project. *Childhood Education, 77*(1), 18–25.

Van Hoorn, J., Nourot, P., & Scales, B. (1998). *Play at the center of the curriculum* (2nd ed.). New York: Prentice-Hall.

Vance, E., & Weaver, P. (2002). *Class meetings: Young children solving problems.* Washington, DC: NAEYC.

Verma, A. K. (1992, November). *Achievement of kindergarten, first, and second grade children from developmentally appropriate and inappropriate kindergarten classrooms. Unpublished master's thesis. Included in paper presented at NAEYC, November 1992.* Baton Rouge: Louisiana State University.

Vygotsky, L. ([1930–1935] 1978). *Mind in society: The development of higher mental processes.* Cambridge, MA: Harvard University Press.

Walsh, D. J. (1989). Changes in kindergarten: Why here? Why now? *Early Childhood Research Quarterly, 4,* 377–391.

———. (1991, April). Extending the discourse on developmental appropriateness: A developmental perspective. *Early Education and Development, 2*(2), 109–119.

Ward, C. (1996). Adult intervention: Appropriate strategies for enriching the quality of children's play. *Young Children, 51*(3), 20–25.

Washington, T., & Baker, F. (1996). Curriculum is just one big spider web: A dialogue about changing our Head Start classroom. In D. Curtis, & M. Carter (Ed.), *Reflecting children's lives: A handbook for planning child-centered curriculum* (pp. 151–157). St. Paul, MN: Redleaf Press.

Wasserman, S. (2000a). *Serious players in the primary classroom: Empowering children through active learning experiences* (2nd ed.). New York: Teachers College Press.

Waxman, S. (1976). *What is a girl? What is a boy?* Los Angeles: Peace Press.

Weems-Moon, N. (1991). *An ethnographic study of kindergarten students' literacy skills and stress-related behaviors before and after teacher demonstrations in bookreading strategies.* Unpublished doctoral dissertation, Louisiana State University, Baton Rouge. Included in paper presented at NAEYC, November 1992.

Weiser, M. G. (1991). *Infant toddler care and education* (2nd ed.). New York: Macmillan.

Wellhousen, K. (1996). Girls can be bull riders, too! Supporting children's understanding of gender roles through children's literature. *Young Children, 51*(5), 79–83.

Wesson, K. (2001). The "Volvo effect"—Questioning standardized tests. *Young Children, 56*(2), 16–18.

White, B. (1988). *Educating the infant and toddler.* Lexington, MA: Lexington Books.

———. (1995). *The new first three years of life* (Rev. ed.). New York: Simon & Schuster.

Whitin, P., & Whitin, D. (2005). Pairing books for children's mathematical learning. *Young Children, 60*(2), 42–48.

Wien, C. (1995). *Developmentally appropriate practice in "real life": Stories of teacher practical knowledge.* New York: Teachers College Press.

Wiltz, N., & Fein, G. (1996). Evolution of a narrative curriculum: The contributions of Vivian Gussin Paley. *Young Children, 51*(3), 61–68.

Wolfgang, C. (1977). *Helping aggressive and passive preschoolers through play.* Columbus, OH: Merrill.

Worsley, M., Beneke, S., & Helm, J. (2003). The pizza project: Planning and integrating math standards in project work. *Young Children, 58*(1), 44–49.

Yopp, H., & Yopp, R. (2009). Phonological awareness is child's play. *Young Children, 64*(1), 12–21.

Zeavin, C. (1997). Toddlers at play: Environments at work. *Young Children, 52*(3), 72–77.

INDEX